Cultures of Militarization

Special Edition of

Canadian Journal of Cultural Studies

Twenty-three – Twenty-four

2010

TOPIA: Canadian Journal of Cultural Studies

Theme Editors: Jody Berland and Blake Fitzpatrick
Editor: Jody Berland (York University).
Book Review Editor: Kate Eichhorn (The New School).
Assistant Editor: Mike R. Hunter (Cape Breton University).
Editorial Assistants: Claire Crighton, Flavia Genovese, Jane Kim, Damon Lazzara, Cait McKinney.
Editorial Interns: Adebe DeRange-Adem, Kyah Lloyd, Chris Malcolm.

Advisory Board: Jenny Burman (McGill University), Lily Cho (University of Western Ontario), Blake Fitzpatrick (Ryerson University), Kate Eichhorn (The New School), Bob Hanke (York University), Alison Hearn (University of Western Ontario), Ilan Kapoor (York University), Shahnaz Khan (Wilfrid Laurier University), Cate Mortimer-Sandilands (York University), Roger Simon (Ontario Institute for Studies in Education), Peter van Wyck (Concordia University).

Editorial board: Charles R. Acland (Concordia University), Ien Ang (University of Western Sydney), Ian Angus (Simon Fraser University), Robert Babe (University of Western Ontario), Bruce Barber (Nova Scotia College of Art and Design), Darin Barney (McGill University), Alison Beale (Simon Fraser University), Nandi Bhatia (University of Western Ontario), Bruce Braun (City University of New York), Marcus Breen (Northeastern University), Penelope Ironstone-Catterall (Wilfrid Laurier University), Beverley Diamond (Memorial University of Newfoundland), Jill Didur (Concordia University), Michael Dorland (Carleton University), Greg Elmer (Ryerson University), L. M. Findlay (University of Saskatchewan), Murray Forman (Northeastern University), Michael Gardiner (University of Western Ontario), Gary Genosko (Lakehead University), Noreen Golfman (Memorial University of Newfoundland), Line Grenier (Université de Montreal), Lawrence Grossberg (University of North Carolina at Chapel Hill), Lisa Henderson (University of Massachusetts), Adriene Jenik (University of California, San Diego), Audrey Kobayashi (Queen's University), Peter Kulchyski (University of Manitoba), Bruno Lessard (Ryerson University), Ian McKay (Queen's University), Katherine McKittrick (Queen's University), Meaghan Morris (Lingnan University, Hong Kong), John O'Brian (University of British Columbia), Liz Philipose (University of California Riverside), Christine Ramsay (University of Regina), the late Sharon Rosenberg (University of Alberta), Kim Sawchuk (Concordia University), Bart Simon (Concordia University), Jennifer Daryl Slack (Michigan Technological University), Jonathan Sterne (McGill University), Will Straw (McGill University), Imre Szeman (University of Alberta), Charlotte Townsend Gault (University of British Columbia), Andrew Wernick (Trent University), Anne Whitelaw (University of Alberta), Handel Kashope Wright (University of British Columbia).

Cover: Krista Hansen, Eleven-seventeen.
Cover Images: Stills captured from video posted on WikiLeaks, contributor unknown.
       http://www.wikileaks.org/wiki/Collateral_Murder,_5_Apr_2010

TOPIA is published in Canada by Wilfrid Laurier University Press and Cape Breton University Press.

Publication Mail Agreement Number 40064165
Canada Post: Send address changes to: WLU Press, 75 University Ave West, Waterloo, ON N2L 3C5

Articles appearing in this journal are abstracted and indexed in Contemporary Culture Index, International Bibliography of the Social Sciences, Historical Abstracts, America: History and Life, Canadian Reference Centre (EBSCO), Academic Search Premier, Ulrich's Periodicals Directory, Canadian Business and Current Affairs Database, OCLC, JournalSeek and Gale Licensing. TOPIA is a member of Magazines Canada.

TOPIA is printed on recycled paper approved by the Forest Stewardship Council (FSC), made of 100 per cent post-consumer fibre, processed chlorine free and produced using biogas energy.

For contact, submission and subscription information, see pages 6 an 468.

Library and Archives Canada Cataloguing in Publication

Cultures of militarization / [edited by Jody Berland and Blake Fitzpatrick].

"Special edition of TOPIA, Canadian Journal of Cultural
Studies, twenty-three - twenty-four, 2010".
Co-published by: Wilfred Laurier University Press.
Includes bibliographical references.
ISBN 978-1-897009-56-7

1. Sociology, Military. 2. Sociology, Military--Canada.
3. Militarism--Social aspects. 4. Militarism--Social aspects--Canada.
I. Berland, Jody II. Fitzpatrick, Blake, 1955-
U21.5.C843 2010   306.2'7   C2010-906369-4

Cultures of Militarization

Canadian Journal of Cultural Studies

Twenty-three – Twenty-four - *2010*

Contents

7   Memorial: Barbara Godard

9   Jody Berland and Blake Fitzpatrick
    Introduction: Cultures of Militarization and the Military-Cultural Complex

Articles

28 A. L. McCready
    Tie a Yellow Ribbon 'Round Public Discourse, National Identity and the War:
    Neoliberal Militarization and the Yellow Ribbon Campaign in Canada

52 Howard Fremeth
    Searching for the Militarization of Canadian Culture:
    The Rise of a Military-Cultural Memory Network

77 Carole R. McKenna
    Canadian and American Cultures of Militarism: Coping Mechanisms in a
    Military-Industrial-Service-Complex

100 Uli Linke
    Fortress Europe: Globalization, Militarization and the Policing of Interior
    Borderlands

121 Markus Kienscherf
    Plugging Cultural Knowledge into the U.S. Military Machine: The Neo-Orientalist
    Logic of Counterinsurgency

144 Neil Balan
    A Corrective for Cultural Studies: Beyond the Militarization Thesis to the New
    Military Intelligence

178 Erin Riley
    Operation Nunalivut: Photo Essay

190 Susan Cahill
Conflict(ing) Narratives: Representations of War in *The Battleground Project* and the Performative Potential of Audience

203 Marc Lafleur
Tracing the Absent-Present of Hiroshima and Nagasaki in America as Sensuous Encounter: Notes on (Nuclear) Ruins

227 Mary Alemany-Galway
Peter Jackson's Use of Hollywood Film Genres in *The Lord of the Rings* trilogy and New Zealand's anti-Nuclear Stance

244 Stuart Allan and Kari Andén-Papadopoulos
"Come on, let us shoot!": WikiLeaks and the Cultures of Militarization

254 Bill Burns
Extraterritorial Prison Plans in the Style of IKEA and the Prison Playlist

260 David A. Clearwater
Living in a Militarized Culture: War, Games and the Experience of U.S. Empire

286 Ian Roderick
Mil-bot Fetishism: The Pataphysics of Military Robots

304 Mary Sterpka King
Preparing the Instantaneous Battlespace: A Cultural Examination of Network-Centric Warfare

330 Gary Genosko
The Terrorist Entrepreneur

345 James R. Compton
Fear and Spectacle on the Planet of Slums

Offerings

363 Christopher Dornan
Unknown Soldiers: On the Comparative Absence of the Military from Canadian Entertainment Film and Television

368 Jim Daems
"i wish war wud fuck off": bill bissett's Critique of the Military-Cultural Complex"

381 Darin Barney
Miserable Priests and Ordinary Cowards: On Being a Professor

Forum

388 Jill Didur and Susan Gingell
Editors: Author Meets Critics Forum

393 Susan Gingell
Suffering the Imposition of the European Bourgeois Family on Aboriginal Peoples in Canada and the Routes to Healing

399 Terry Goldie
Familiarizing Flaherty and Freud: A Response to Julia Emberley's *Defamiliarizing the Aboriginal: Cultural Practices and Decolonization in Canada*

406 Deanna Reder
What's Not in the Room?: A Response to Julia Emberley's *Defamiliarizing the Aboriginal*

415 Jennifer Andrews
Re-reading Photographs through the Lens of *Defamiliarizing the Aboriginal*

423 Julia Emberley
When Author Meets Critic ... The Worlding of Epistemologies

Review Essays

429 Len Findlay
Barbara Godard—Navigating Literary and Cultural Traffic

434 Nic Veroli
Dada's Last Dada and the Communism to Come

Reviews

442 Shaobo Xie
Writing "in Terms of a Different Durée": A Review of *Jameson on Jameson*

447 Julia Aoki
Cities in Motion

449 Angela Joosse
Unfurling the Visual

452 Barbara Fister
The Digital Book—Still Pending

454 Cris Costa
There Is More Than One Way to Rethink Poetics

457 Notes on Contributors

The journal acknowledges with thanks ongoing support from the Faculty of Graduate Studies, the Graduate Program in Communication and Culture, the Social Sciences and Humanities Research Council, Faculty of Environmental Studies, Department of Humanities and Office of the Dean, Faculty of Arts, York University, and CBU Press.

Editorial Address:
Please consult submission guidelines www.yorku.ca/topia
Mail manuscripts and correspondence to:
TOPIA: Canadian Journal of Cultural Studies
240 Vanier College
York University
4700 Keele Street
Toronto, ON
Canada M3J 1P3
Email: topia@yorku.ca
www.yorku.ca/topia

Subscriptions and advertising:
Wilfrid Laurier University Press
75 University Ave West
Waterloo, ON
Canada, N2L 3C5
Email: press@wlu.ca
www.wlupress.wlu.ca

© 2010 TOPIA: Canadian Journal of Cultural Studies
Issue no. 23-24, 2010
ISSN 1206-0143 (Print), ISSN 1916-0194 (Online)
ISBN 978-1-897009-56-7 (CBU Press, Trade book)

Memorial: Barbara Godard

By Elena Basile, Jody Berland and Julie Creet
York University

TOPIA commemorates the life and work of York University Professor Emerita Barbara Godard, a professor of English, French, social and political thought and women's studies. A pillar of the York community and one of Canada's pre-eminent literary scholars, Professor Godard broadly influenced the fields of Canadian and Quebec studies, translation studies, feminist poetics, semiotics and cultural studies. She was book review editor for *TOPIA* from 1998 to 2008 and a member of the journal's advisory board until she died May 16, 2010.

She was a generous supervisor and mentor who trained and influenced a contemporary generation of cultural workers, including academics, writers and artists. The scope of her mentorship was fully recognized in 2002 when she became the recipient of teaching awards from York University's Faculty of Graduate Studies and the Northeastern Association of Graduate Schools. Prof. Godard retired from full-time teaching in 2008, but continued a full intellectual and pedagogical life until her sudden passing.

Prof. Godard was a prolific and influential intellectual. An extraordinarily sharp and encyclopedic thinker, Godard's interests encompassed semiotics, translation, gender, textuality and the body, as well as archives, memorials and the history and changing politics of cultural production. With a keen eye for detail and a unique capacity for breadth of vision, she catalyzed interdisciplinary connections among culture, language, gender, politics, poetics and meaning.

After completing her doctorate at the University of Bordeaux, Godard began teaching at York in 1971 as a visiting assistant professor and was hired into a tenure-track position in 1976. She published eight books, 80 book chapters and 115 articles and catalogue entries. She translated the major writers of Quebec feminism, including Nicole Brossard, Yolande Villemarie and Louky Bersianik. She also served as editor or on the editorial board of no less than 22 journals. She was a founding co-editor of the feminist literary periodical *Tessera*, a contributing editor of *Open Letter* and *The Semiotic Review of Books*, and the book review editor for *TOPIA: Canadian Journal of Cultural Studies*. She also made long-standing contributions to *Resources for Feminist Research*, *Voix et Images* and *ECW* among others.

Prof. Godard was committed to and passionate about her graduate students across the Departments of English, French Studies, Film and Visual Arts, the School of Women's Studies and the Program in Social and Political Thought, supervising more than 35 PhD candidates. She built bridges between people and modes of inquiry because of her genuine enthusiasm for ideas. She worked between and across languages which so often divide. She inspired her colleagues and students through her critical creativity and her unwavering commitment to interrogating and producing the conditions for full civic engagement in the University and in the public sphere. We will miss her greatly.

Jody Berland and Blake Fitzpatrick

Introduction: Cultures of Militarization and the Military-Cultural Complex

This special issue of *TOPIA* addresses the ubiquity of militarization as a presence woven into the fabric of civic culture. Our editorial mandate was to invite a broad discussion of cultures of militarization, but also to open the possibility of holding the terms culture and militarization apart for scholars whose work investigates the processes through which military presence is normalized or critiqued in private, public and national narratives. Reading across this collection of essays, it is evident that the relationship between militarism and civic culture pushes us beyond a static binary of culture and militarism to reveal several dynamically related terms and issues. The collection is not a move to summarize militarism into a finite set of conceptual terms, but rather an attempt to offer evidence of the tangential, broad, insidious and revealed presence of militarization throughout culture. As Catherine Lutz argues, militarization is "simultaneously a discursive process, involving a shift in general societal beliefs and values in ways necessary to legitimate the use of force, the organization of large standing armies and their leaders, and the higher taxes or tributes used to pay for them" (qtd. in Allen and Andén-Papadopoulis, herein). Militarization is not just something that happens in war zones; when our government invests billions of dollars in war planes, prisons and the "digital economy," while starving resources in social justice, education, the environment and culture, we are living the consequences of global militarization. To talk about cultures of militarization is to talk about the terms in which collective identity is militarized and resistive forms of agency allowed and disallowed.

Henry Giroux suggests that in the post-9/11 world, images play a particularly crucial role in the militarization of experience. They animate and reveal the orchestrated drive to mobilize fear and to assert personal safety and security over and above a shared sense of social responsibility and agency and the political culture to which these might contribute (Giroux 2006: 2). A collectivity united or divided in its response to this mobilization and these images raises questions about the role of civic culture in a technologically driven and rationalized social sphere that manipulates representational regimes to support a set of predetermined conclusions. How can we talk about public space or civic culture when public knowledge and participation are relegated to the sidelines of the military-industrial-complex—that ambiguous phrase that, as Daniel Pick contends, begs the question of human agency or responsibility (Pick 1993: 11)? What would it mean to rewrite these relations of power in the critical terms of a military-cultural complex? How does such rewriting alter our attention to the world of images? How much of our everyday action in the world—communicating, connecting, researching, playing, watching, feeling—might be assessed or understood differently in terms of the operations of a military-cultural complex? Finally, how might the concept of a military-cultural complex redraw the temporal and environmental modalities of modern conflict, and remain attentive to forms of public response that have been opened or closed by existing cultures of militarization?

The essays in this double issue take up some of these questions and raise others; they comment upon the intersection of militarization and culture as a matter of representation, as a force that emerges in everyday life, as technological reinvention and simulation, and as the fearful fallout that continues to resonate in the wake of 9/11. While some of the authors comment on lived cultures of militarization, others direct our attention to crisis points in history when militarism and civic culture are set apart or in oppositional relation to each other. Such oppositional relations were recently revealed in Toronto on the occasion of the G20 summit, in which a $1-billion security apparatus turned sections of the city into an armed encampment. During the weekend of June 23-25, 2010, and the days leading up to it, the downtown core was cordoned off by a security fence, citizens were warned to stay away from the area, offices were closed, special legislation was passed to allow police and members of the security apparatus to stop and question anyone who looked suspicious, and police were authorized to prevent people from taking pictures or even walking within five meters of the fence. "What has happened to our city?" was a question often repeated as a public confrontation between protestors, vandals, bystanders, police and a militarized security complex erupted into a violent assertion of police power, a graphic warning of what encroaching militarism looks like. The ensuing collision of civic resistance and security operations was heavily documented by security cameras mounted throughout the downtown core, by media representations and by the counter-representations of engaged and enraged citizens. Notable in the fray was that the police targeted people with cameras. (For participant accounts and visual documents see http://www.yorku.ca/topia/militarization/main_mil.html)

The experience of ubiquitous and contradictory media coverage signals a moment of rupture in which a struggle over public space was joined to a struggle over representation in the streets of Toronto. Images of vandals breaking windows and burning police cars (widely photographed but not halted by police) dominated the commercial news media and helped to justify, both politically and visually, the vast security resources and media technologies dedicated to the management of security, property, crowds, law and disorder. These images were disseminated with impressive speed and persistence, confirming that fear is the security operation's ultimate after affect. Images of hooligans smashing things in vacated streets were juxtaposed with images of police troops in riot gear surrounding peaceful demonstrators: played off one another, they communicated the idea that a demonstration against a gathering of politicians is inherently hazardous for everyone, or, to put it in other words, that in image-based cultures of militarization the political runs the risk of being "increasingly constituted outside of the law" (Giroux 2006: 13-14). Indeed, police showed copies of the leftist Toronto journal *Upping the Anti: A Journal of Theory and Action* along with rocks and chains as evidence of terrorist conspiracy. A critical role for the participants of visual culture during such moments of confrontation is not to become mesmerized by the spectacle of fear but, as James Compton suggests herein, it is to "understand the politics of the performance of fear."

The now infamous G20 event in downtown Toronto is a troubling and timely exemplar of this theme. The location was chosen by Harper's conservative government against the advice of city government and the well-being (psychologically, financially, spatially, legally and sometimes medically) of the city population. Horrified viewers *in situ* and on television watched police in full riot gear "kettle" peaceful demonstrators and others, surrounding and holding hundreds of detainees standing in the rain for more than three hours without food, water, or access to bathrooms. Once imprisoned, none of the detainees had access to telephones, family, legal advice or medical supplies. Between Saturday June 26 and Sunday June 27, approximately a thousand people were detained in small makeshift holding cells in what was previously a film studio. These makeshift cells represent a new cultural-military form with eerie familiarity that is parodied herein by artist Bill Burns with his extraterritorial prison plans in the style of IKEA. Echoing the now familiar prison photographs of Abu Ghraib, Guantánamo and elsewhere, these drawings identify a new counter-insurgent market society centred on repressive surveillance and security measures with a target market that suddenly, in Toronto, became much too close. While we do not know how much of the one billion dollars spent on G20 security was invested in placing a camera in each interim holding cell, it is impossible to avoid pausing on the fact that the Toronto version of the Guantánamo prison, part of a major North American practice run with pricy counter-insurgency technologies, was built in a vacant film studio. There was an alarming arbitrariness in the constitution of this prison population, some of whom were simply pedestrians walking down the street. In the fight for public space a referential chain linked a film studio to the workings of a prison complex filled with small flimsy holding cells, each equipped with cameras to monitor the activity of prisoners who were suddenly not citizens at all.

While we would want to avoid the too easy association that equates media technology with the state as a one-sided and quickly ended discussion about domination and control, it is also impossible to consider images of police lines pounding their batons upon their shields and the brutal take down of unarmed protestors in a haze of tear gas or rubber bullets without recognizing that strong feelings are mobilized among the recipients of such images. These feelings might include fear, shame, anger, disgust and/or even ambivalence. Representations of state sanctioned violence are significant because they create affective encounters with events that act on our senses, selectively addressing the citizenship with a call to sustain or rally against such acts on the basis of images. Although viewers might be emotionally moved or traumatized by shocking imagery, the response is short lived if it functions solely to confirm what we already know or falls back on a set of stock responses. The politics of such moments may lead us to becoming critical witnesses not only of the abuse suffered by others but of our own affective responses to such abuse. As Jane Gaines put it in relation to the production of outrage in films about the Iraq war, the question is thus not only about *what we make* of the images that we view but it is also about what *they make of us*, as viewers implicated in our everyday engagements with the meaning of conflict (Gaines 2007: 35; cf. Fitzpatrick, Sandlos and Simon 2009).

With an entire city caught up in the "counter-insurgency" battle, one did not have to be a scholar to recognize that representation plays a significant role in the management and rationalization of modern conflict. But we do need scholars to unwrap the logics and logistics of this increasingly vital social process. A number of the essays in this special issue of *TOPIA* examine representations through which cultures of militarization are made visible. These essays argue that the relationship between language, image and militarism affects the symbolic and material practices of democracy. As Daniel Pick suggests, "words, ideas, images constitute the discursive support for military conflict; they should be understood not as though they are mere froth without consequences, but as crucial aspects of the destructive reality of violent conflict itself" (Pick 1993: 14). There is, as Judith Butler contends, "no way to separate the material reality of war from those representational regimes through which it operates and which rationalize its own operation" (Butler 2009: 29). Thus, with an ear to the ground of lived encounters, a number of the essays in this collection reveal moments when the forcible frame that works on behalf of the state to control affect and the interpretation of militaristic activity incites resistance and commentary on the part of citizens, just as it did in the streets of Toronto. For example, in Mark Lafleur's essay, a blurted out apology for dropping the atomic bomb during the Second World War marks a moment of resistance and traumatic return as a Vietnam veteran addresses a group of Japanese college students visiting a nuclear museum. Lafleur's essay examines the absent-present figuration of Hiroshima and Nagasaki and juxtaposes the affective and submerged subjectivities in the minds/bodies of nuclear survivors, with their literal invisibility in the official narratives of America's nuclear heartland.

Often allegorical, the work of artists can respond to militarism in ways that depart from official or descriptive modes of communication. Mary Alemany-Galway's essay considers Peter Jackson's film trilogy *The Lord of the Rings* as an allegory for New Zealand's anti-nuclear stance. In her account, Jackson's film is a highly coded moral narrative that equates the world-shattering power of the ring to the threat of nuclear weapons. Allegory is also mobilized for political ends in the work of Canadian poet/artist Bill bissett. Jim Daem's account of his critique of the military-cultural complex considers bissett's inventive use or misuse of spelling, syntax and grammar as a demonstration of resistance to order and control, which are aligned with militarism. bissett's writing draws parallels between broken language and the brutal truth of broken lives that have resulted from the violent legacies of militarization. Susan Cahill questions Canadian conflict narratives in exhibitionary practices in terms of their uncritical relation to liberalism and corporate globalization. Specifically, she critiques *The Battleground Project*, a Canadian Textile Museum exhibition on Canada's current military involvement in Afghanistan, and suggests that the static display of war artifacts and impressions may function affirmatively to enhance passive support for war unless interrogated by criticism and/or dialogic modes of social encounter. In her account, museum representations of war do not just reflect, but produce, politics. Similarly, Howard Fremeth's paper examines filmic depictions of Canadian military history, and shows how the formation of a Canadian military-cultural memory network functions to reproduce military subjects of the past as well as in the present. Focusing on the contentious debate over *The Valour and the Horror* as a formative moment for this military-cultural network, Fremeth conceptualizes a method for showing how the politics of memory networks achieve authority as "obligatory passage points" and as rightful carriers of national memory. The articulation of nationhood and material passage points in northern Canada are depicted in Erin Riley's photo-essay documenting her experience as an artist participating in the Canadian Forces Artist Program (CFAP). Recorded through subtle shades of grey and blinding white, Riley's photographs depict encounters between Canadian Forces, Inuit Rangers, vast open spaces and herself. Here militarization is not confirmed by spectacles of conflict but revealed in the tension of military and civilian encounter and in the contingent evidence of a militarized Canadian North. Finally, Christopher Dornan's essay posits another representational absence: the relative lack of attention paid to militaristic combat in Canadian film. His paper constructs a parallel logic where an absence of representation of branded conflict signifies both the impossibility of an adequate response to war and perhaps an absence of interest on the part of Canadians.

Lack of public interest in combat suggests a culture in which militarization has become normalized and the weight of civic responsibility internalized as private feeling and experience. The modern state, argues the Retort collective, "has come to need weak citizenship" and an undermined sociality that compliantly maintains "an impoverished and hygenized public realm" (Retort 2005: 21). "War, in a word, is modernity incarnate" (79). Paul Virilio addresses the intersection of the modern public and the military by tracing a shift to a world of logistics in which communication systems, modes of production and transportation systems function as vectors redirecting war from the battlefield to the scientific and the military economy. Virilio cites a post-Second World War memo from the Pentagon: "Logistics is the procedure following which a nation's potential is transferred to its armed forces, in times of peace as in times of war" (Virilio 2008: 32). This statement exemplifies what Virilio has termed "pure war." Pure war is not about total war, nor does it spell out the drama and spectacle of doom in a nuclear context or conventional war on the battlefront. Instead, pure war proposes a condition of war as "pure" industrial production removed from the site of military use and carnage. Pure war signifies the active preparation of a war during peacetime, war "which isn't acted out in repetition but in infinite preparation" (29). Virilio theorizes logistics as being central to the development of pure war, resulting in the conflation of civilian and military institutions. Under conditions of pure war, the distinction between the citizen and the military becomes "perverted" so that it becomes increasingly difficult to say where the military begins and where, if ever, it ends (32). Militarization seeps into the social, technological and economic, giving specific form and instruction to civic life. In these terms, the permanence of war, and the technical powers and economic dependencies of the war economy, become increasingly entangled in the "hearts and minds" of citizens, the intimate spaces of discrete communities, lived relationships and identity.

Many of the essays here investigate the intersection of militarism and everyday life and discuss affective entanglements that exist between the political and pedagogic, the public and private spheres. In Carole McKenna's essay, the coping strategies of military wives are characterized as conforming to expectations to support the troops and normalize a military-consumerist lifestyle. However, spray-painted on cliffs nearby an army base are the words: "Iraq made our husbands mean." McKenna's paper reveals breaches in the social contract of militarism when domestic coping with isolation, absence and violence can no longer remain within the demoralized realm of the private but is projected back publicly—but anonymously—onto a community accustomed to compliance. Alison McCready's essay examines the "Yellow Ribbon" campaign as a public pedagogy of empire mobilized to instruct and discipline Canadians to comply with the political, social, economic and cultural transformations of neoliberalism through support for the troops. McCready traces the practice of neoliberalism back to the Washington Consensus and the way it serves to provide an analytical structure within which the practices and discourses of the military can be understood. In his analysis of military discourse after 9/11, Stuart Price elaborates this approach, noting that:

[N]ot only are certain types of data inaccessible, but it also seems that powerful collectives are anxious to disguise the process through which they arrive at decisions. If the ordinary business of government is indeed conducted in a conspiratorial manner, it is not unreasonable to ask questions about the internal life of these institutions. Once we acknowledge that much of the "evidence" we have about the workings of executive authority, is *the publicity generated on its behalf*, it is possible to wonder if the contemporary fascination with language and the symbolic has led, in some cases at least, to the study of ephemeral material specifically designed to burn up critical energy. (Price 2010: 13)

McCready's study actualizes this point, showing that the Yellow Ribbon campaign solicits Canadians to invest their "hearts and minds" into a neoliberal economic strategy of privatization and austerity in which militarism is a key engine of social transformation.

The contradictions and disparities of military neoliberalism are situated in transnational terms in James Compton's paper as he questions what is dominant, residual and emergent about spectacle in relation to global fear. In so doing, Compton develops terms to think through the affective relations of fear, anxiety and inequitable privilege made visible by neoliberal globalization. With the slum world predicted to exceed two billion inhabitants within the next twenty-five years (Davis qtd. in Retort 2006: 162), thinking through the increasingly visible gulf between members of the planets of the mall (mainly Western societies) and the slums (mainly the global south) has become more urgent. In a world that is increasingly connected through information and communication technologies as well as the global flow of capital, the increased visibility of mall and slum creates an opportunity for each to be affected by the other at the level of the everyday. In Markus Kienscherf's essay, the militarization of everyday life takes place on foreign soil where the United States engages in combat with non-state enemies operating among civilian populations. He discusses counterinsurgency (COIN) operations and the production of a population-centred pedagogy that legitimates counterinsurgency efforts in Iraq and Afghanistan. The U.S. counterinsurgency machine is depicted as a teaching machine in which civilian academics controversially prepare and produce militarized knowledge that supports the goals of a far reaching military-industrial-academic complex.

As Neil Balan suggests, the line between military, social and academic spheres should be redrawn in more fluid terms. While the militarization thesis presupposes an encroaching military presence contaminating and overhauling cultural and social affairs, he argues, like Kienscherf, that the interdisciplinary state military reciprocally exchanges and creates intelligence with other domains. One of the startling facts to emerge in the recent release of some 90,000 documents about the war in Afghanistan by WikiLeaks (see Allan and Andén-Papadopoulos, herein) was the realization that there are some 600 "civilian" organizations in the U.S., many duplicating one another, involved with military logistics and the conduct of war. The correspondence between military logistics and a militarized world view extends beyond science to personal subjectivity and social consciousness and the assessment of friend-enemy, citizen and civilian categories. Balan's contribution is to show how counterinsurgency operations function within and through these distinctions to blur civil and military objectives in order to domesticate and pacify local populations through site specific forms of persuasion and rule. As Randy Martin observes of the self-justifying rhetoric of the U.S. revolution in military affairs following the defeat of the other superpower: "Military superiority would signal the capacity to defeat the prospect of any challenge to the way the world was being ordered" (Martin 2006: 460).

Taking the cue from these authors, we understand military counterinsurgency as a kind of knowledge production. The cultural study of target populations is only one sphere in which military organizations seek symbiotic relations with economic management and academic knowledge. Indeed, it is increasingly difficult to determine where academic research ends and military application begins. Recent headlines revived a bitter conflict between Canada's two "telecommunications giants" for contracts with the Department of Defense (DND) worth more than $200 million. The rivalry involves a lucrative Global Defence Network contract for telephone, wireless, data and Internet protocol services (Canadian Press 2010). This news reminds us that an increasing proportion of military contracts are being dispensed to companies that specialize in information processing, telecommunications and surveillance technologies. None of the news stories comment on the military context or use of such services. Unlike the 1960s, when students could demonstrate against military research and recruitment on campus, or the 1970s, when faculty and researchers protested against the collaboration between military leaders and top scientists (Halter 2006: 100), today's arrangements contest the distinction between public, commercial and military research while major corporate players ensure their civilian reputation through user-friendly consumer technologies and generous academic and artistic subsidies. The neoliberal turn toward public-private partnerships to support university research, coupled with the increasing imbrication of corporate and military research and tactics, turns universities into research and development centres for the fabrication of "pure war," to cite Virilio once again, in which "a nation's potential is transferred to its armed forces, in times of peace as in times of war" (Virilio 2008: 32). We hardly need to point out how difficult it is to make this last distinction given the number of fatalities produced by "counter-insurgent" or undeclared wars.

We are getting used to hearing about astronomical military budgets, but perhaps not so used to thinking about them in the context of our own research and communications environments. A quarter of defence contract funds in North

America are now granted to companies specializing in telecommunications. Of course their consumer products also make possible the counter-dissemination of images from militarized zones, from the prisons of Abu Ghraib to the streets of Toronto. But the expansion of military research into areas previously associated with the university or public sphere raises questions about the increasingly interdependent relationships between the military, the universities, corporate capitalism and governments, which support various technologies being researched and developed for militaristic ends. Singer reports that the so-called "black budget," the Pentagon's classified budget for research and acquisition, was around $34 million in 2009, an increase of around 78 per cent since 2001. "A core part of this massive post-9/11 budget," he writes, "has been new technologies, with a particular focus on anything unmanned" (Singer 2009: 61). Satellite communications, artificial intelligence, unmanned flight, smart bombs, robotics, face recognition technologies, implantable identification devices and other body enhancements, biomimetic swarm and flock systems, hybrid computer bird and insect species ready for action in hostile spaces, mobile sensors and other cutting-edge technical research are all being generated and/or funded by academic partnerships with quasi-military agencies, often on the groundwork already prepared by subsidized artistic "experiments." Just as the soldier is gradually being mutated into a seemingly omnipotent unmanned, armed and optically equipped vehicle, as Ian Roderick documents, so the citizen body is gradually being mutated into units of manageable information generated in accordance with military and security objectives with the assistance of publicly funded research. The citizen body is complicit because the experience or threat of violence produces traumatized bodies whose energies "threaten to overspill their fragile vessels" (Bukatman 2003: 181); if they are a source of the threat of violence, the technologies wielded by the social order are also perceived as a source of safety. The hyper-connected citizen falls under the gaze of militarized surveillance and informational systems dedicated to harvesting civic experience and perception for repurposed military knowledge, application and support. As David Clearwater points out with respect to video games, most journalists, academic studies, and academic and institutional use of these informational technologies do not adequately address the military funding sources that makes their development technically and commercially feasible.

Co-author of the seminal article, "Network-Centric Warfare: Its Origin and Future" (1998), Vice Admiral Arthur Cebroski believed that the dot-com Internet revolution, as employed by large companies like Walmart, Cisco and Dell, offered a perfect model for a new style of military operation based on information technology and creating "total information awareness" in military operations (Cebroski 1998, qtd. in Singer 2009: 180). Walmart and the Defense Advanced Research Project Agency (DARPA) created a program in 2002 called Total Information Awareness with an investment of $200 million to create a database for "total" information about American citizens and visitors. Functioning seamlessly with other "Revolutions in Military Affairs" (RMAs), these information technology initiatives were meant to give American business new found advantages, which in turn would offer a new model of fighting and winning wars. "Big Brother is not far behind the Big Greeter," Singer writes, noting that Walmart's "total information awareness" over the marketplace, which had permitted them to eliminate "pesky mom-and-pop stores" across the country, had helped to inspire the Pentagon's "perfect picture of the battlefield" (Singer 2009: 180). Sterpka-King's essay for this collection reminds us that corporate-military mimicry works in both directions; network-centric retailing and network-centric warfare are transforming the "ecosystems" of retail and militaristic environments into automated command and control systems. Walmart's operational architecture of scanners, sensors and a transaction grid tracking ninety million transactions per week to provide "just-in-time" information for inventory, production and distribution purposes provides a prototype for a networked military equipped to efficiently deliver orders "just in time" from above (or, in the case of the G20 summit, from Barrie, Ontario) to fighting units on the battlefield. Just as cash registers are being updated to register purchases on their own, so "brilliant" cameras are being programmed to identify faces on their own, telecommunication-equipped weapons to locate and kill targets on their own, and the monitoring and planning of the battlefield to resemble nothing more than the videogames which, as Clearwater points out, the military itself developed to virtualize and teach their new techniques. As Randy Martin argues:

> The point of systems integration from a military management perspective is to render machines as smart as people and people as reliable as machines on the assumption that the machinic and humanist ideals can be applied in practice to places where people work with technology. As such, the [technological] utopias are as much about labor that doesn't resist being told what to do as it is about frictionless machines. (Martin 2006: 464)

Virilio calls this the "logistics of perception" in reference to optical simulation in battle. As Sterpka-King notes in her contribution, and as others suggest, such images bring war closer to viewers even as they are sanitized of war's brutality. The more such devices see the target, the less the spectators see the war. Sterpka-King makes the point that new perceptual technologies and networked war have enabled a "world view" (or what we might call, following Heidegger (1977), a "world picture") to emerge through data and sensing systems and through an updated conceptual template for thinking of military strategy. Sterpka's contextualization of new "smart" autonomous camera/weapons systems finds a connection with the logic of simulated aggression pursued through videogames co-produced by military agencies, as David Clearwater documents in this issue. This virtual-robotic logic of aggression is problematic not only because it reifies an us-and-them visual narrative—as Kevin Robins and Les Levidow put it: "War converts fear and anxiety into perceptions of external threat" (1995: 106)—or because it imagines (and helps bring into being) robotic soldiers who never die. These games offer a personalized pedagogy of simulated three-dimensional conflict bringing together the player's hand, the camera view, the weapon's target, and the laws of movement to eliminate the symbolic enemy. As Robins and Levidow note of the first Gulf War: "Where the Gulf massacre publicly enacted phantasies, video games privatize them. The processes of anxiety and control are actively structured by the computer-video microworld, with its compulsive task of achieving 'perfect mastery'" (1995: 109ref). The privatization of the military encounter within the videogame echoes the privatization of citizenship in neoliberal culture. While the video game simulates a real-time event, the Gulf episode took such images as its reality. In this context, militarization involves the determination to turn human beings into potential weapons, and weapons into simulated human beings.

Just as the weapon is equipped with optical devices to simulate vision, so the image is itself weaponized. As Mirzeoff writes:

> The video camera on a tank with a real-time satellite link back "home" is the military equivalent of [the steadycam and the close-up] that Western viewers have come to take for granted. It embodies a stabilized and centralized viewpoint on globalization as the drama of the Western subject and its sufferings. Such as ER creates an imaginary Chicago where most of the doctors and nurses in a public hospital are white, treating mostly white patients, the war-cam represented a conflict in which Iraqi death and suffering took place outside of shot. The very familiarity of the Humvee domesticated the images for American viewers and that familiarity reinforced their credibility. The image became a weapon and not just as propaganda but as something hard, flat and opaque designed in itself to do psychic harm. Throughout the war military spokespeople talked about various assaults as "sending a message." (Mirzoeff 2005: 75)

Of course, as Stuart Allan and Kari Andén-Papadopoulos point out in their study of WikiLeaks, control over that message is as fraught as war itself. They describe the struggles of Reuters, the international news agency, to gain access to a classified military video made by a U.S. Apache helicopter camera in 2007 that recorded the zealously enjoyed indiscriminate slaughter of more than a dozen people walking along a street in a Baghdad suburb, including journalists and children. Eventually the video was released by WikiLeaks (April 5, 2010). As one commentator cited by Allan and Andén-Papadopoulos points out, the video graphically displays "how similar the logic of the Apache pilots is to that of the average gamer." The question is not simply whether we have access to images of war, but whether we have the capacity to properly witness them, given the saturation of the visual field with their exact visual and narrative logic and given the efforts of military authorities to re-normalize them through the rhetoric of "split-second situations" and the "fog of war." Such images, the authors argue, while produced and normalized through the very media technologies sanctioned by the military and journalist professions, can momentarily unsettle the assumptions and conventions through which the media characterize the Other and help make war routine.

Many commentators have written about the sanitized view of war afforded by new image technologies; Roderick reminds us that waging war is not a rational-antiseptic enterprise, but is made to appear so by a military-industrial-cultural and entertainment complex intent on dramatizing the conception of a risk-managed war. He notes that the prospect of robotic autonomy and agency has resulted in a fetishistic transfer of risk from the soldier to the heavily invested field—in terms of both research funding and the popular imaginary—of battlefield robots. The war in Iraq and Afghanistan, the continual attack from IEDs and the continued public valuation of the soldier's life have resulted in a need to find a technical solution to legitimizing contemporary military aggression. The military robot (mil-bot), a real-life counterpart to the undead warriors animating video games, fills that need. It promises a managed, risk-free technical solution to the problem of death.

In the post-9/11 era, it is impossible to talk about the militarization of culture without acknowledging deep contradictions within the security complex and ongoing tensions between instances of militarism, security, secrecy and spectacle. Spectacle and secrecy form a seemingly contradictory unity of manipulated knowledge production through which public feelings, opinions and fears are actualized. The discourse of war has long been an excuse for covert operations that might otherwise be subject to public scrutiny. An Internet event like WikiLeaks would not achieve front page status without the deep vault of secrets through which the military sustains its power. While secrecy has a long history in military conduct, its spread to multiple levels of government can be seen as further evidence of the militarization of politics. [1] To uncover such secrets, Trevor Paglen, a cultural geographer and artist, maps classified military and intelligence activities. He notes that "every year the United States spends more than $50 billion to fund a secret world of airplanes and unacknowledged spacecraft, 'black' military units and covert prisons, a secret geography that military and intelligence insiders call the 'black world'." (Paglen 2009: 4). These sites are named the "black world" because, like the Pentagon budget Singer refers to above as the "black budget," they do not officially exist or are classified information. Perhaps cultural criticism has a particular role to play here in locating the informational, geographic and affective sites where the line that separates the visible world from the "black world" can be intercepted and breached in the name of public knowledge, interest and freedom of information.

The growing affiliation between spectacle and secrecy leads to sociopathic oscillations in public belief and growing uncertainty about what can be marshaled as evidence. One of the eerie pathologies of the 9/11 era is that the most galvanizing images of the epoch turn out to be the images that we were not suppose to see.

Retort comments that "the fall of the Towers became the image that *had not to be shown*" (Retort 2006: 28). Richard Drew, the veteran Associated Press photographer who took the photograph of the well known but rarely published "falling man" describes it as "the most famous picture nobody's ever seen" (Friend 2006: 136). One must also consider the atrocity images of shackled bodies and covered heads of contemporary prison photographs from Abu Ghraib, Guantánomo and elsewhere. These are also photographs we were not supposed to see. Although it would be difficult to imagine a more public image of contemporary war, the Abu Ghraib prison photographs depict the visual rhetoric of private photography, amateur framings of dehumanizing events not intended for public consumption. Reacting to statements by right wing political commentators and leaders such as Bill O'Reilly and Donald Rumsfeld, who stated that that the publication of the Abu Ghraib photos was un-American because it would create a negative image of the United States, Butler comments:

> Of course, neither considered that the American public might have a right to know about the activities of its military, or that the public's right to judge the war on the basis of full evidence is part of the democratic tradition of participation and deliberation. So what was really being said? It seems to me that those who sought to limit the power of the image in this instance also sought to limit the power of affect, of outrage, knowing full well that it could and would turn public opinion against the war in Iraq, as indeed it did. (2009: 40)

Such photographs combine the paradox of widespread image dissemination with tacit and official image prohibition, and link the affective registers of seeing to shame. As Mark Reinhardt contends, the viewing of these photographs completes the degradation begun in the prison as "the faces of the tortured stare out at us in a moment not only of fear and pain but also of shame, as we by looking, prolong the shaming" (Reinhardt 2006: 16).

We are not supposed to see the nameless falling men and shackled prisoners, but we are supposed to see that most emblematic figure to appear throughout the discourse of the post-9/11 era, the terrorist. As both named perpetrator and generalized figure of fear, the terrorist may be said to function as another "rhetorical umbrella" under which public agendas of aggression and violence are supported (Giroux 2006: 7). In Gary Genosko's essay, the figural construction of al-Qaeda brings with it a new term, the "terrorist entrepreneur," first applied to Khalid Sheik Mohammed (KSM), the mastermind deemed to be behind the 9/11 attack. Extracted from *The 9/11 Commission Report: Final Report of the National Commission on Terrorist Attacks Upon the United States* (Kean 2004), KSM blends characteristics of East and West, *oikos* and economy, radical Islamic faith and a religious foundation of asceticism with entrepreneurial rationality and autonomy. The terrorist entrepreneur violates characteristics of the capitalist entrepreneur introduced by Max Weber by modelling a more fluid figure that asserts Islamic social codes while managing and exploiting the allegedly abhorrent financial flows and money transfers of global capitalism. Uli Linke describes how the figure of the terrorist and the black racialized Other in post-9/11 Europe invigorate a montage of fear that conflates one into the other and entrenches the inherent inequalities and contradictions of the modern European state under the umbrella of the "war on terror." Linke argues that fortress Europe is a contradictory securitized space in which the fluidity of participation in neoliberal global order, based on mobility, flexibility and deterritorialization, is contradicted by an exclusionary geography of whiteness, which is stabilized and enforced by border regimes, anti-immigration legislation and militaristic discourses of national security. The bordered regime works to entrench spatial divisions between a fortified Europe and a threatening exterior, and between lives that are visible and those that are not. Such distinctions recall Compton's description of a planet of malls and slums made visible to each other through new imaging technologies. However, in the relation of belonging and exclusion outlined by Linke, gazes are blocked in a relation of non-mutuality through which social contact is nullified. Evoking the non-existent "black sites" of invisible and unmapped prisons referenced by Paglen, Linke demonstrates that border militarization has resulted in a Europe-wide network of detention camps for refugees, immigrants and non-European asylum-seekers that are typically hidden from view in remote locations, filling up with lives that are detained, put on hold and made to disappear.

Such acts of fortification and demonstrations of "homeland security" reinforce an insight offered by the Retort collective concerning the 9/11 attack. Knowing that they lacked the ability to take over the entire social fabric, what the perpetrators did was expand upon an already weakened sociality by mounting an attack that was designed to "hold us indoors." Inside our homes we were held quite literally by an image of capitalism exploding in upon itself (Retort 2006: 29). But we were and are also held inside the contracting borders of a wounded and demoralized geo-sociality closing in on itself, erecting militarized border controls to assuage its fear. Citing the concept of enclosure as an effective amalgam of capitalist modernity's overall logic, Retort notes that what unites the enemies of neoliberalism is their resistance to attacks on the commons, which provides, for all their differences, a degree of common ground (194-95).

Like Retort, many of the authors in this collection provide a socio-economic context for militarization by reference to neoliberal capitalism. Marazzi claims that:

> The war on terror being waged by the United States represents the *continuation of the New Economy by other means....* [...] What was needed, therefore, were new conceptual instruments, *representations and paradigms*

capable of accounting for the working logic of the world system and its internal contradictions" (Marazzi 2008: 152)

As many of these articles demonstrate, the symbolic and material leakage across cultural domains, identities, institutions or territories can actualize, rather than escape, new types of command; tilted towards power, the flow of instruments and representations can be made functional for contemporary modes of governance. One objective of this collection is to tease apart the relationship between militarism and culture so as to resist the complete incorporation of military matters into everyday life. Militarism, while pervasive, is often culturally invisible until such time as it is mobilized to direct change to predetermined ends. We remain committed to the project of cultural critique as a means to challenge the premise that militarism must be everywhere.

Notes

1. When the "sponsorship scandal" erupted in Canadian politics, for instance, Chuck Guité, the senior bureaucrat responsible for administering the federal program to promote unity, "argued that it was an important part of the federal government's unity strategy. If some funds had disappeared, well, that was a small price to pay for the continued existence of Canada. As he put it, 'We were basically at war trying to save the country [...] When you're at war, you drop the book and the rules and you don't give your plan to the opposition'." (LeBlanc 2004)

References

Bukatman, Scott. 2003. *Matters of Gravity: Special Effects and Supermen in the 20th Century*. Durham, NC: Duke University Press.

Butler, Judith. 2009. *Frames of War: When is Life Grievable?* London and New York: Verso.

Canadian Press. 2010. Telus Asks Feds to Referee Bell Fight: Petitions the Federal Cabinet Regarding Dispute over a $213 Million Military Telecom Contract. 4 August 2010. http://www.thestar.com/business/companies/mobile/article/844119--telus-asks-feds-to-referee-bell-fight.

Fitzpatrick, Blake, Karyn Sandlos and Roger I. Simon. 2009. *War at a Distance: Visual Culture and the Framing of Public Conversations about Canadian Forces in Afghanistan*. On-line as of July 2010 at http://www.gallerytpw.ca/.

Friend, David. 2006. *Watching the World Change: The Stories Behind the Image of 9/11*. New York: Picador.

Gaines, Jane. 2007. The Production of Outrage: The Iraq War and the Radical Documentary Tradition. *Framework: The Journal of Cinema and Media*, 48(2): 36-55.

Gilbert, Jeremy. 2009. Deleuzian Politics? A Survey and Some Suggestions. *New Formations* 68:10-33.

Giroux, Henry. 2006. *Beyond the Spectacle of Terrorism: Global Uncertainty and the Challenge of the New Media*. Boulder and London: Paradigm Publishers.

Halter, Ed. 2006. *From Sun Tzu to Xbox: War and Video Games*. New York: Thunder's Mouth Press.

Heidegger, Martin. 1977. *Age of the World Picture. The Question Concerning Technology and Other Essays.* New York: Harper Torchbooks.

Kean, Thomas H. 2004. *The 9/11 Commission Report: Final Report of the National Commission on Terrorist Attacks Upon the United States.* Authorized Edition. New York: W. W. Norton.

LeBlanc, Daniel. 2004. Guite: When You're at War, You Drop ... the rules, *Globe and Mail*, 3 April, A1.

Marazzi, Christian. 2008. *Capital and Language: From the New Economy to the War Economy.* Trans. Gregory Conti. New York: Semiotexte.

Martin, Randy. 2006. Derivatives Wars. *Cultural Studies* 20(4-5): 459-76.

Mirzoeff, Nicholas. 2005. *Watching Babylon: The War in Iraq and Global Visual Culture.* New York: Routledge.

Paglen, Trevor. 2009. *Blank Spots on the Map: The Dark Geography of the Pentagon's Secret World.* New York: Dutton.

Pick, Daniel. 1993. *War Machine: The Rationalization of Slaughter in the Modern Age.* New Haven, CT: Yale University Press.

Price, Stuart. 2010. *Brute Reality: Power, Discourse and the Mediation of War.* London: Pluto Press.

Reinhardt, Mark. 2006. Picturing Violence: Aesthetic and the Anxiety of Critique. In *Beautiful Suffering: Photography and the Traffic in Pain*, edited by Mark Reinhardt, Holly Edwards and Erina Duganne. Chicago: University of Chicago Press.

Retort (Iain Boal, T. J. Clark, Joseph Matthews and Michael Watts). 2006. *Afflicted Powers: Capital and Spectacle in a New Age of War.* London: Verso.

Robins, Kevin and Les Levidow. 1995. Soldier, Cyborg, Citizen. In *Resisting the Virtual Life*, edited by James Brook and Iain A. Boal. San Francisco: City Lights.

Singer, P. W. 2009. *Wired for War: The Robotics Revolution and Conflict in the 21st Century.* New York: Penguin.

Virilio, Paul. 2008. *Pure War.* Los Angeles: Semiotext(e).

WikiLeaks. 2010. http://www.WikiLeaks.org/wiki/Collateral_Murder,_5_Apr_2010.

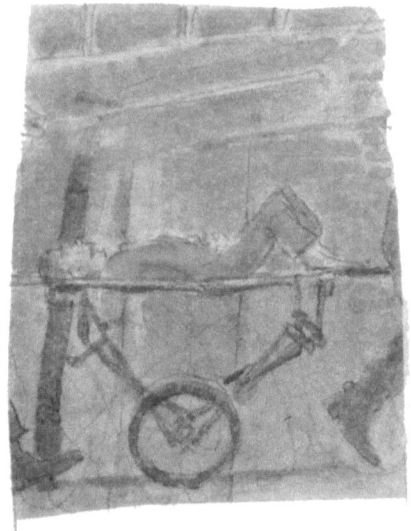 

Bill Burns, GTMO. Courtesy of the artist.

Repatriation, tribute to Sapper Brian Collier, Highway 401 (Highway of Heroes), July 23, 2010. Photo by Blake Fitzpatrick.

G20 Summit, "Police Line," Toronto, June 27, 2010. Photo by Bob Hanke.

Above: G20 Summit, "Citizens Exercise Charter Rights and Freedoms."
Toronto, June 27, 2010. Photo by Bob Hanke.

Opposite: G20 Summit, "Informed Citizen," Toronto, June 27, 2010. Photo by Bob Hanke.

G20 Summit, "Riot Police Guarding U.S. Embassy," Toronto, June 27, 2010. Photo by Bob Hanke.

A. L. McCready

Tie a Yellow Ribbon 'Round Public Discourse, National Identity and the War: Neoliberal Militarization and the Yellow Ribbon Campaign in Canada

ABSTRACT

The yellow ribbons that have become so ubiquitous in Canada as the emblem of the national "Support Our Troops" campaign are highly charged semiotic tools in a battle for control of public discourse, marking the growing militarization of Canadian society in an age of empire. I read the Yellow Ribbon here as neoliberal cultural pedagogy, an everyday means by which individuals learn and teach specific cultural values and tropes, both explicitly and implicitly. As a symbol and a commodity, and perhaps more importantly as an everyday social and cultural practice, the Yellow Ribbon offers a glimpse into the dense cultural and political forces involved in the re-scripting of Canadian national mythologies, according to a logic of militarized neoliberalism.

RÉSUMÉ

Nouer un ruban jaune autour du discours public, de l'identité nationale et de la guerre : la militarisation néolibérale et la Campagne du Ruban jaune au Canada

Les rubans jaunes, devenus omniprésents au Canada en tant qu'emblème de la campagne du soutien aux troupes, sont des outils à forte charge sémiotique dans une bataille pour le contrôle du discours public, qui marque la militarisation grandissante de la société canadienne dans un âge d'empire. Je considère ici le Ruban jaune comme une pédagogie culturelle néolibérale, un moyen quotidien par lequel les individus apprennent et enseignent des valeurs et des tropes culturels spécifiques, à la fois explicitement et implicitement. En tant que symbole et en tant que marchandise, et peut-être plus important, en tant que pratique sociale et culturelle quotidienne, le Ruban jaune offre un aperçu des forces culturelles et politiques denses impliquées dans la réécriture des mythologies nationales canadiennes, en fonction d'une logique de néolibéralisme militarisé.

¤

The yellow ribbons that have become ubiquitous in Canada as the emblem of the national "Support Our Troops" campaign are highly charged semiotic tools in a battle for control of public discourse, marking the growing militarization of Canadian society in an age of empire. I read the yellow ribbon here as neoliberal cultural pedagogy, an everyday means by which individuals learn and teach specific cultural values, both explicitly and implicitly. As a symbol and a commodity—and perhaps more importantly as an everyday practice—the yellow ribbon offers a glimpse into the dense political forces involved in re-scripting Canadian national mythologies according to a logic of militarized neoliberalism. In a global context marked by the triumph of the market over social values, the career of the yellow ribbon in Canada facilitates a shift away from "peacekeeping" as a dominant legitimating narrative, a shift supposedly necessary due to the harsh realities of our so-called post-9/11 world. Rather than suggesting Canada's bygone predilection for peacekeeping was an untroubled manifestation of the national character, however, I examine the discursive and political ramifications of the decline of a peacekeeping narrative as an ideal and as an organizing logic, and the growth of other modes of understanding military engagement—a shift that, I argue, has occurred largely in the absence of broad public support and democratic debate.

The yellow ribbon has a symbolic history quite specific to the United States, and I am interested in how the iconography and language associated with this symbol came to profoundly influence the cultural politics of Canada's participation in the War on Terror. Indeed, the yellow ribbon has been instrumentally cultural in shifting Canada's role in the world toward a much more overt, less ambiguous participation in empire.

First, this paper sketches the global political context in which nation-states have increasingly tended toward militarization. I then examine the cultural history of the yellow ribbon as a symbol within the specific historical contexts in the United States. After elaborating on the turn toward militarization in Canada, I discuss the crucial role played by the yellow ribbon—and the broader "Support Our Troops" campaign—in consolidating support for and silencing opposition to recent wars. The sign's very ambiguity, I argue, has rendered it a potent force for the occlusion of public debate and, to borrow Sunera Thobani's fitting appellation, the "exaltation" of certain kinds of national subjects (2007). We are witnessing a "yellow ribbon coup" with potentially perilous cultural and political ramifications.

Neoliberalism and Militarization

The yellow ribbon may be understood as a uniquely North American, populist response to the recalibration of national politics in neoliberal times. Neoliberalism refers, on a political level, to the set of policies associated with the so-called "Washington Consensus": at the proverbial end of history, nation-states should reject a logic of social welfare and autonomous economic development in favour of free-market policy oriented toward the liberalization of trade regulations and tariffs, the deregulation of industry, privatization and deep cuts to social programs, and tax cuts to private and corporate interests. This agenda—for which the Free Trade agreements between the United States and Canada serve as an example and template—has been part and parcel of the rise of corporate-led globalization wherein new transportation and communication technologies are mobilized to amplify business and financial power. Today, these transnational flows of money and private power police the behaviour of nation-states and their populations to an unprecedented degree. These factors and others have led to a reconfiguration of politics, as described by Zygmunt Bauman. "[O]f necessity," he writes, "the legislative and executive sovereignty of the modern state was perched on the 'tripod' of military, economic, and cultural sovereignties" (2000: 61). Bauman argues that with each leg of that tripod arguably compromised, the proliferation of "weak states" is not incongruous with but a reflection of the interests of newly liberated transnational capitalists (68). These weak states are ideally able to act as "local police precincts" in maintaining the order requisite for business, while lacking the ability to engage in strong autonomous resistance (68). At the same time, under this "new imperialism," as David Harvey terms it, the dictates of capitalist accumulation demand the evisceration of the welfare state and the strengthening and consolidation of the "warfare" or "security" state (Harvey 2003). Such intensified security protocols see the reallocation of state spending from social programs to prisons, militaries and related policing and surveillance—a building up of a particular kind of state bureaucracy, which contradicts the espoused neoliberal antipathy to "big government." This tendency, which Ismael Hossein-zadeh calls "redistributive militarism," consists of "a combination of drastic increases in military spending coupled with equally drastic tax cuts for the wealthy. As this combination creates large budget deficits, it then forces cuts in non-military public spending (along with borrowing) to fill the gaps thus created" (Hossein-zadeh 2007a, 2007b). Hossein-zadeh documents this process by demonstrating a dramatic correlation between post-9/11 militarization and increasing income inequality in the United States as public funds are redirected to semi-private military industries.

As this neoliberal restructuring destabilizes societies around the world, counter-movements rise in resistance (Enloe 2000). This resistance is met with the concomitant rise in militarization that accompanies the advance of privatization, the erosion of the commons and the increasing gulf between rich and poor.

And, as Henry Giroux notes, neoliberalism is also a profound *cultural* politics: in North America, the hyper-militaristic spectacle characteristic of the post-9/11 corporate media environment fuels the cynicism, fear and isolation characteristic of a neoliberal culture (2006). In the absence of a meaningful public sphere, this cultural politics anticipates the security state, rendering dominant conceptions of the public reducible to sites of (classed and racialized) contamination and threat.

In this sense, dispossession, repression and war are literally the business of empire. As Hardt and Negri and others argue, militarization takes on the guise of "international policing," bringing "rogue" governments and regimes into line with the global neoliberal order (2000). The American-led "War on Terror," as Randy Martin points out, is less about the cold-war struggle between opposed ideologies, and more about the United States' need to mitigate risks to global accumulation and open up new spaces for capitalist expansion (Martin 2007). This strain of what Naomi Klein has called "disaster capitalism" creates global spaces of policing and repression in order to extract resources and create cheap sources of labour and opportunities for "reconstruction" (Klein 2007).

This business of international policing frames Canada's revamped role in empire. Canada's capacity for "global leadership" in just this area has been and will continue to be called upon as one of its expanded roles in the new global order (cf. Engler 2009). To a greater extent than most civilians are aware, Canada's armed forces have become deeply integrated with the American military establishment. The two armies share training facilities on both sides of the border and participate in joint training missions outside of North America. In addition, Canadian troops are routinely placed within American regiments on "exchange," sometimes during active-duty combat situations in which Canada is not officially a belligerent, such as Iraq. Indeed, rising stars hoping to advance professionally in the Canadian military often seek the expanded opportunities offered by placement under American command, as the careers of current Chief of Defence Staff General Walter Natynczyk and former Chief of Defence Staff General Rick Hillier attest. This integration has become a central feature of North America's military topography, and is expected to increase in the future; the "Fortress North America" protocols demonstrate the push to create a hermetic security barrier around Canada and the United States in order to defend the two nations' ostensibly mutual interests (Staples 2007).

By the early 2000s Canada had allocated the vast majority of its fighting capacity away from the United Nations (UN) to the North Atlantic Treaty Organization (NATO) and United-States-led global "policing" projects. Chief among these are the naval patrol of the Persian Gulf and participation in the ground war in Afghanistan. Stephen Harper's Conservative government has characterized the Afghanistan operation both as a *war* in the sense of heroism and combat strategy, and as a policing or enforcing mission—an explanation that elides the sort of global neoliberal consensus that is being policed and enforced. In addition, Canada routinely sends Royal Canadian Mounted Police and other law enforcement officers to "at-risk" countries to train local police forces (Engler 2009). Given the complicity of Canada's law enforcement agencies in creating and perpetuating conditions of violence and fundamental human insecurity within Canada's borders—forms of violence that replicate and further patterns of imperial violence against indigenous and racialized bodies—we can discern resonances with older modes of domination in Canada's new role overseas. Sherene Razack, for instance, has written about the crusading impulse of racialized international policing that characterized Canada's "peacekeeping" engagement in Somalia (2004). Indeed, as David Theo Goldberg makes clear, the organizing logic of the contemporary security state is an inherently racial one: historic injustices and local forms of oppression persist and intensify (2007). Under the banner of legal equality and economic indifference, however, the racialized aspects of global violence disappear from public discourse, making way for the preoccupation with white injury that comes to dominate the "colour-blind" neoliberal society (219). Legacies of colonialism thus repeat themselves in the garb of economic necessity and market neutrality.

While there is debate as to the exact degree of autonomy Canada enjoys to set its own foreign and military policy in this new age of empire, it is nonetheless a rapidly militarizing country.[1] Canada's myth of peacekeeping, with its implied—but rarely elaborated—moral authority, positions Canada as a singularly experienced, useful and righteous international policing agent. The nation's increasing militarization and increasingly pivotal role in the new imperialism is negotiated through this mobilization of historic notions of Canada as a colonial icon of "peace, order and good government." The yellow ribbon is a key part of this process and a telling example of the kind of cultural work militarization now entails.

As critics like Cynthia Enloe (1990, 2000), Sandra Whitworth (1994, 2004), Sherene Razack (2004, 2007) and Sunera Thobani (2007) note, militarization is a deeply gendered process that makes use of systemic and cultural racism, sexism, xenophobia and homophobia in historically and contextually specific ways. At the present moment in Canada—as in many historical moments—the curtailing of democratic debate in the interest of "national security" and identification with "our boys in the field" is both a key condition and a key effect of militarization. As Enloe observes:

> the more militarization transforms an individual or society, the more that individual or society comes to imagine military needs and militaristic presumptions to be not only valuable, but also normal. Militarization, that is, involves cultural as well as institutional, ideological and economic transformations. (1990: 4)

We can understand this cultural work of militarization as a pedagogical project in the broad sense that scholars of critical pedagogy have established. The complicated and dynamic ways social values are learned, reproduced, contested and changed exceeds classroom-based learning and involves multiple, overlapping sites of social teaching, from homes and communities to corporate and independent media to the workplace and institutions such as the military (cf. Giroux 2007). This understanding shows that every approach to social transformation contains a crucial pedagogical element. We must attend to the ways militarism is taught and learned through both institutionalized and everyday cultural spaces, and to what militarization teaches people about identity, belonging, hope, fear, privilege and entitlement. The recent surge in Canadian governmental spending for military marketing and recruiting represents a militarist onslaught against public discourse and opinion. But as Giroux makes clear, the militarization of culture does not take place solely through propaganda. Militarism represents the rise of a ubiquitous cultural politics that aims to encourage social institutions and relationships to replicate, accede to, or recognize the ultimate importance of the military in everyday life. For instance, popular broadcast programming in Canada—like the hit TV series *The Border* and the radio-serial *Afghanada*—rehearse a carefully cultivated ambivalence about Canada's participation in the War on Terror while normalizing militarization as an integral aspect of Canadian culture. Similarly, the recent shift in the symbolic politics around Remembrance Day ceremonies, the commemoration of the battle of Vimy Ridge, and the "Highway of Heroes" phenomenon (wherein citizens line the highways along which the repatriated bodies of Canadian soldiers travel on their way to autopsy) have moved the rituals and cultures of militarism from the barracks to the level of everyday life. But, importantly, these and other militarized practices both mobilize and rely on civilians to invest their hearts and minds in these cultural productions and martial ceremonies. Militarization, then, is not merely something that happens *to* culture but something made up of both concerted cultural interventions by powerful forces (like the state, the military or big media) and subtle everyday practices.

It is in this context that the yellow ribbon has emerged as a near ubiquitous symbol. The ribbon appears mostly on car bumpers, but also increasingly as an official symbol displayed on government and private buildings, hanging from flag-poles, emblazoned on T-shirts, and printed under the ice at hockey games. We can understand yellow ribbons as a pedagogy of empire, a means by which the Canadian imaginary is disciplined to understand and acquiesce to the political, social, economic and cultural transformations of militarized neoliberalism. The yellow ribbon works as a dense and ambiguous symbol or cultural touchstone, as a genuine everyday cultural practice, and as a commodity with its own acquired social and material history. Its very ambiguity (does it imply support for the troops or support for the war? What does "support" mean in this context anyway?) is not accidental, but works to delimit, enforce and militarize the borders of public debate around questions of national policy and, by extension, national "character." At the same time, the ribbon affirms and "exalts" certain preferred national subjects: the masculinized, normative and morally unimpeachable young men (and to a lesser extent, women) whose sacrifice is not only the salvation of the national character, but retrospectively becomes its foundation and guarantor.

A slim but consistent majority of Canadians have opposed the War in Afghanistan from its beginning, evidencing a deep tension in the national imaginary—although a tension not reflected in the dominant, one-sided media coverage of the war (cf. Ipsos Reid 2009). In this context, the yellow ribbon teaches citizens that to be Canadian is to support Canadian soldiers (who are, in this formulation, hastily and homogeneously assumed to *want* to be in Afghanistan themselves) and that to question or disagree with the government is to disrespect soldiers. The assumptions bound up in the yellow ribbon circumvent the fact that the debate about Canada's role in the War on Terror has never truly occurred. It binds the national imaginary to the contradictory sense that Canada's role in the world has changed, and yet remains the same: peacekeeping is a noble but failed project eclipsed by a world riven with terror—and therefore Canada, as the great peacekeeper, must engage in waging dubious foreign wars of aggression in the interest of peace and (somehow) democracy. Canada's engagements in the world ostensibly flow directly from a national ethos that Daniel Coleman has dubbed "white civility": a racial fiction of well-scrubbed and industrious fair-mindedness stretching back into the nation's colonial patrimony (2006). Within this imaginary, the troops "over there" are seen to be acting in ways entirely consonant with the national character "over here," both demonstrating and establishing "peace, order and good government" with a courteous but firm civility. The yellow ribbon speaks to these aspirations. As much as it normalizes imperial policing missions in Afghanistan and around the world, it also helps to police public discourse in Canada, ensuring that the tangled web of normative assumptions it propounds from the back of every other car on Canadian highways continues to go unquestioned.

The Cultural History of Yellow Ribbons

Although the yellow ribbon clearly brings to mind the first American-led war in the Persian Gulf, the symbol has a longer (if, in places, somewhat misty) history in the United States, stretching back to 19th-century American artist Frederick Remington. A chronicler of the post-Civil War American West, Remington produced extremely popular depictions of an heroic U.S. cavalry "winning" the West while sporting yellow stripes on their pant-legs and sometimes matching yellow neckerchiefs. Remington's images follow expected racial and colonial patterns of representation: this cavalry's infamous and unspeakable genocidal brutality toward Indigenous peoples and nations is largely invisible. Remington, an armchair cowboy and journalist, lived in New York and is said to have spent only limited time in the West himself, suggesting that the authenticity of his depictions lies more in their representation of how 19th-century Americans imagined the West than in their verisimilitude (Dippie 1994: 3).

She Wore a Yellow Ribbon, a 1949 John Ford film, re-imagines this scene of attempted genocidal conquest for the highly militarized post-Second World War American audience, drawing heavily on both Remington's artwork and the virile, adventuresome notion of masculinity to which he pays homage (Dippie 2006: 39-43). The film was a remarkable cinematic achievement for its day, self-consciously and meticulously re-staging Remington's images for the screen with breathtaking landscape shots filmed in the Arizona dessert. In one of his most popular and iconic roles, John Wayne stars as Captain Nathan Brittles, a beloved cavalry officer facing mandatory retirement at the end of long military service. The female lead, the niece of Brittles's outpost's commander, is wooed by both an incompetent, rich officer from New York and a young roughneck officer who—in true Amercian spirit—has climbed the ranks to become Brittles's second-in-command. She places an ostentatious yellow ribbon in her hair to demonstrate her loyalty to one of her suitors, but doesn't disclose which one. The presence of this well-to-do young lady—ostensibly on a tour of the Arizona country—drives much of the plot, requiring Brittles to lead strategic military manouevers in order to safely deliver her from stereotypically hostile Indians. In the end, Brittles saves the day by disobeying orders and leading a bloodless early morning raid on an Indian encampment to scatter their horses before a looming battle can take place. The cavalry is portrayed as lenient and tolerant, accomplishing its objective without bloodshed and allowing the Cheyennes and Arapahos their lives after Brittles directs his troops to "make 'em walk to the reservation, [it] hurts their pride." A letter commending Brittles's service and offering him a reassignment comes through just in time for him to ride off into the sunset, leaving the fate of the outpost in the now-capable hands of his young protégé who, of course, the female protagonist has chosen as her mate. Love triumphs, the patriarchal nuclear family (that Brittles himself has sacrificed for the army and his nation) is restored, and the spirit of American individualism saves the day, paving the way for westward expansion. This film offers us an early glimpse into the dense and profound cultural work done by the yellow ribbon to bind together the emotive aspirations and meanings of militarized nationhood into one ambiguous symbol.

The film includes a now authoritative version of the traditional folk song "'Round her Neck She Wore A Yellow Ribbon," which is said to date from the Civil War period:

    'Round her neck she wore a yellow ribbon
    She wore it in the springtime and the merry month of May
    When you ask her why she wore it
    She wore it for her lover who was far, far away.

Significantly, the film's version substitutes in the final line,

> She wore it for her lover in the U.S. Cavalry, Cavalry, Cavalry
> She wore it for her lover in the U.S. Cavalry.

The yellow ribbon's apparent origin in this historical moment, and its associations with both the colonial, civilizing mission and with women's waiting, reveal its importance to the ideological work of the imperial project. Virtuous women, willing to be tempted but forever faithful, are stock caricatures of the imperial military adventure, as are renegade bad-boy soldiers who turn out to be ultimately honourable, ineffectual pencil-pushing bureaucrats who get in the way of real men's work, and irrational, racialized belligerents in need of the stern hand of paternal authority. The imperial masculinity of the brave, adventuresome soldier has its classic counterpart in the association of women with the domestic-space-cum-nation that requires defending. Indeed, as Andrea Smith underlines, the attempt to secure the loyalty of settler women to the patriarchal imperial project was among the primary concerns of early colonial culture, and was a major factor in the sexual violence settler men enacted against Indigenous women (2005: 18-30). The icon of the yellow ribbon thus brings together the attempted genocide of Native American Indigenous people, the patriotic nationalism of the colonial settler state, the submission of women to militarized masculinity and patriarchal order, and the American myth of the pioneering, individual spirit's triumph over emasculating bureaucracy and alternative forms of collectivity.

The yellow ribbon next appeared in a popular song recorded in 1973 by the pop group Tony Orlando and Dawn. "Tie A Yellow Ribbon Round the Ole Oak Tree" was the tale of a woman waiting for a man's return from prison and of this man's anxiety about her loyalty; it thus shared the trope of women waiting with the earlier song and film. The song became associated with the return of soldiers from Vietnam, an association that Orlando himself helped to solidify when he performed it to honour returning Vietnam veterans as part of Bob Hope's pre-game show at the 1973 Cottonbowl, an event that elicited a standing ovation from more than 70,000 fans and permanently linked the song and its title symbol to American military adventures overseas and the "war at home."[3] The yellow ribbon emerged as a popular cultural practice during the Iranian hostage incidents of 1979-1981, when Penne Laingen, wife of hostage American diplomat Bruce Laingen, used the ribbon to signify support for American hostages. Penne Laingen was instrumental in disseminating the ribbon through hostage-supporting activist groups such as No Greater Love and the Family Liaison Action Group (FLAG), which received broad and sympathetic media coverage that encouraged other Americans to take up the symbol in support of these families (Heilbronn 1994: 9).

Douglas Kellner documents how, in its next phase, the yellow ribbon came to signify support for American soldiers in the first Gulf War (1992). The Iraqi detainment of Americans and other foreign nationals in the early days of the war was popularly likened in the United States to previous international hostage incidents; initially, the ribbons were linked to detainees rather than to soldiers. The high percentage of reservists "called up" from their everyday lives to serve was another point of sympathy with the American people. American troops were sent to the desert to wait on political orders (chiefly, for President Bush to win approval from Congress) and also to wait out the aerial bombardment before the start of the ground war. The slogan "until they all come home," popular in the early days of the war, facilitated the shift in the yellow ribbon's signification from hostages to soldiers, who were now understood to be "held hostage" by effeminate political bureaucracy and even by the "hostile" and "savage" landscape itself, as dust storms forestalled the action in the desert (Heilbronn 1994: 9; Kellner 1992: 5-16). Kellner scrupulously details how the first Gulf War marked a new level of media and propaganda saturation, and he indicts the media (then-new twenty-four-hour television news and public relations corporations in particular) for their role in creating public support for the war and severely limiting public discourse.[4] Today, corporate control and "embedded" journalism has become so commonplace that the traditional myth of a critical, independent media as the fourth estate of a healthy democracy has lost almost all credibility; that is to say, both the independence of the media and the health of democracy itself are widely acknowledged to be in peril. Responding to the fact that media reports on American casualties had led to social unrest during the Vietnam War, major American news agencies followed the policy of President George Bush's (Sr.) administration and became prominent war-boosters well in advance of public opinion. It was during this time that the yellow ribbon gained widespread popularity and became immediately identifiable as a patriotic emblem espousing a "support our troops" mantra.[5]

The yellow ribbon, then, works as a public force for revising history, one that moves from a celebrated narrative of colonial adventurism through to the epic patriotic sacrifice of undervalued soldiers during the Vietnam War. The ribbon thus constructs a present in the throes of moral decay, in which forgotten values— and the patriarchal and racially organized order in which they make sense—must be salvaged through militarized leadership and order.

As Eric Hobsbawnm argues, traditions are invented to convey both the time and timelessness of the established order to which they belong:

> "Invented tradition" is taken to mean a set of practices, normally governed by overtly or tacitly accepted rules and of a ritual or symbolic nature, which seek to inculcate certain values and norms of behaviour by repetition, which automatically implies continuity with the past. In fact, where possible, they normally attempt to establish continuity with a suitable historic past.... However, insofar as there is such reference to an historic past, the peculiarity of "invented" traditions is that the continuity with it is largely fictitious. In short, they are responses to novel situations which take the

form of reference to old situations, or which establish their own past by quasi-obligatory repetition. (1983: 3)

Further, Hobsbawm shows that while the specific content of "tradition" might be vague, the practices were well defined and nearly compulsory. The crucial element, he writes, "seems to have been the invention of emotionally and symbolically charged signs of club membership rather than the statutes and objects of the club." Traditions work by fabricating a sense of social cohesion and by forming a collective identity (10-11). According to these criteria, the yellow ribbon can be understood as an invented tradition, one that, via the "suitable historic past" of colonial frontierism (from John Wayne to Vietnam), responds to the novel situation of neoliberal militarization in the present. In terms of its effect on public discourse and identity in Canada, "supporting our troops" through the use of the yellow ribbon has become a common cultural practice, encouraging Canadians to increasingly identify national belonging and virtue with soldiers and forms of militarized engagement. Here, the symbol's ambiguity is devastatingly effective. The yellow ribbon ceases to have any real "message" but instead binds together the often contradictory narratives and affective impulses of militarism and national idealism. The proliferation of demonstrably "war-happy" media coverage, the militarization of everyday cultural practices through the idiom of loyalty to "hard-working" soldiers, and the neoliberal militarization of public and civic life—social phenomena that Kellner observed and documented in the U.S. during the first Gulf War—presently constitute identifiable forces of social transformation in Canada, and with similarly alarming results.

Canada's Yellow Ribbon

The Canadian "nation of peacekeepers" narrative is based on the peacekeeping model of international intervention usually understood to have emerged under Lester B. Pearson during the Suez canal crisis of the 1950s. It wasn't until the end of the Cold War that peacekeeping became a dominant style of military intervention, with the 1990s as its hallmark decade. Sandra Whitworth calls our attention to the contradictions and costs inherent to imagining and executing peacekeeping as a military act (2004). Despite the carefully managed image of the peacekeeper as "warrior-prince-of-peace," soldiers serving as peacekeepers under the UN have raped, assaulted and murdered local women and children in numerous cases for, as Whitworth writes, "part of what goes into the making of a soldier is a celebration and reinforcement of some of the most aggressive, and most insecure, elements of masculinity: those that promote violence, misogyny, homophobia and racism" (15). Whitworth points out the vital function of the notion of "moral purity" and the "benign and altruistic" image associated with peacekeeping in Canada's national mythology. In order to imagine the self and the nation as good and moral, it is necessary to imagine the places that require peacekeeping as "disordered, chaotic, tribal, primitive, pre-capitalist, violent and exclusionary" (Whitworth 2004: 19; cf. Razack 2004). I argue that it is precisely through mobilizing the myth of a nation of peacekeepers that the new breed of Canadian militarism is advanced.

Recent critical projects take Canada's peacekeeping to task, critiquing what Himmani Bannerji has called "the dark side of the nation" (2000). There is growing agreement in particular social justice and academic circles that the altruistic, "morally pure" image associated with peacekeeping plays a vital role in furnishing Canada with a sense of national innocence.[7] This cult of innocence, always in danger of slipping solipsistically into culture of national superiority, is central to the way in which Canada reproduces itself as a modern, colonial settler state and institutionally manages internal difference. In Eva Mackey's elegant turn of phrase, Canada all too easily "appropriates the identity of marginalization and victimization to create national innocence, locating the oppressors safely outside the body politic of the nation" (1999: 12).

An example of this dynamic, as it pertains to contemporary militarization, is the government's official response to the question "why are we in Afghanistan?"[8] First, of course, it is interesting that the Department of National Defence *has* a prominent Web page specifically addressing this question, signalling the level of unease around the justification for the war. The Canadian government's official, three-part response, briefly, is that (a) "the Afghan government asked for our help" (b) "what's good for Afghanistan is good for us all" (c) "it's a tough job and we have the right people to do it." Leaving aside the purposeful obfuscation of the conditions under which the Afghan government came to ask for "our help," the dubious legitimacy of any government installed via "regime change," and the blatant absurdity that being subjected to an eight-year bombing campaign is "good" for Afghanistan, it is the third item that is especially telling. The DND website is unequivocal that:

> Afghanistan is not a peacekeeping mission. There are no ceasefire arrangements to enforce or negotiated peace settlements to respect.... As well as military personnel, the Canadian effort in Afghanistan includes diplomats, development workers, police officers and experts in human rights, good governance, the rule of law, and the institutions of a healthy democracy.

Here, peacekeeping is loosely invoked as a failed practice insufficient for the current theatre of combat. At the same time, however, it is precisely Canada's history of peacekeeping that enables the nation to take on a leadership role in an imperial war of aggression, retribution and resource control. The redeployment of the peacekeeping image thus becomes pernicious, enabling military and political goals that are antithetical to what UN peacekeeping, in its most earnest, idealistic moments, might have stood for.

As Sherene Razack cogently argues, military ventures that participate in promoting the "nation of peacekeepers" mythology against a barbarized Other are always about the making of self (2004). This process is fundamental in Canada, a nation that has yet to come to terms with its originary moments of colonial violence. In other words, peacekeeping as a legitimating myth allows Canada a national identity that defines itself against the supposed barbarism of those it targets with "benevolent interventions," thus enabling the nation to avoid facing the ongoing colonial barbarism at its core. Unable to recognize the genocidal policies and practices on which the nation was erected, Canada requires other modes of understanding itself in the world. It is for this reason that Canada is such an important player—both materially and ideologically—in the spread of neoliberal imperium. By erasing its history of colonialism and violence, Canada is able to claim enlightened interventionism and the moral high ground from which international policing becomes not merely a national specialty but an unquestionable moral responsibility.

The political left, however, is not alone in its criticism of the Canadian nation-state's legitimating myths, which the liberal, "civil" imagination holds dear. In the present political moment, the attacks on Canada's self-congratulatory claims to multiculturalism and peacekeeping come most forcefully from those on the right, who see these claims as effeminate relics of a bygone age, both inappropriate for a new world of Terror and responsible for the laxity in national and international policing that allowed that Terror in the first place. Those of us critical of both multiculturalism and peacekeeping from feminist, anti-racist and anti-capitalist positions, then, must redirect our pedagogical and political strategies toward articulating an alternative project to militarized nationalism. Policies currently being put in place—which will shape coming generations— reflect a neoliberal economic agenda and promote militarization as an engine of social transformation. This social transformation is intended by its architects to facilitate Canada's "coming into its own" on the world stage, its assumption of full national manhood. Of course, this version of national maturity is based on a junior partnership in American empire, and Canada can only aspire to "hold the bully's coat," as Linda McQuaig (2007) puts it. It is the function of the Canadian yellow ribbon campaign and other aspects of "Support Our Troops" culture to supercede a desperately needed national conversation on these matters by conflating support for the "brave men and women who serve this country" with a deliberate re-scripting of national social ideals.

Though Canada did not enter into the War in Afghanistan under the direction of Conservative Prime Minister Stephen Harper, his two consecutive minority governments have used it as a pretext to wed their extreme neoliberal agenda for social restructuring to increased military spending and an increasingly militaristic notion of national belonging. Harper, a self-proclaimed Christian fundamentalist, is the former head of the National Citizen's Coalition, a "libertarian-conservative" think-tank and lobby group that protects the identities of its contributing members while funding various secretly far-right political and election campaigns (cf. MacDonald 2006; Mackey 2005).

As Harper's Conservatives ride roughshod over established governmental policies and practices, numerous constituencies have come to recognize that this government is a different beast than even previous Conservative administrations (Healy 2008). With an activist agenda and a zealous fervor—and despite a minority mandate—Harper's administration has successfully managed to cut corporate taxes and social programs (a difference in degree rather than a substantial departure from previous laissez-faire Liberal governments), and has successfully intervened directly in various, ostensibly independent levels of government in order to discipline what they see as lax or liberal elements, to quell dissent and to consolidate power. Recently, this culminated in the use of the 2010 Olympic Games in Vancouver as an opportunity to foster nationalist sentiment and distract attention from the scandal of Afghan detainee torture, as well as a fairly explicit expansion and test of the military's security and surveillance capabilities.

The centrepiece of Harper's self-styled "New Government" agenda is the unprecedented twenty-year, $492-billion *Canada First Defence Strategy: A Modern Military for the Twenty-First Century* (CFDS), first introduced in the 2008 budget.[9] The report mobilized the image of brave Canadian soldiers dutifully accepting their orders despite being woefully undersupplied, and promised to reverse the decline of the Canadian armed forces. This became a key pedagogical moment for the government to link military spending to neoliberal austerity and a purposefully abstract notion of "Canadian values."

The CFDS is, in fact, a key component of the Conservative plan for Canada's economic future. Harper's Conservatives promote the vast expansion of military spending, increased funding for military research, and the development of military infrastructure across the country, insisting that the bolstering of the Canadian military-industrial complex will lead to the economic salvation of the nation. The Strategy marshalls into effect a "renewed relationship" between the Canadian Forces, the defence industry and research and development organizations, which entails "streamlined" protocols for the procurement of defence contracts, greater industry consultation, and a revised "industrial benefits" policy aimed at "encouraging industry to make long-term investments in Canada" (CFDS 2008: 20). The plan claims that Canadians will benefit from this transfer of wealth from the public coffers to the military and its private partners via the creation of "high-tech, high-value sustainable jobs in all regions—directly through the development of military capabilities and indirectly through technological spinoffs and commercial applications" that will "put Canadians to work protecting Canadians" (20). Indeed, the plan even foresees the deep involvement of Canadian institutions like universities in this corporate-led, publicly subsidized militarization of the

Canadian economy, as other, more autonomous sources of research funding are cut or left to atrophy (12). Prioritizing the North Atlantic Treaty Organization and the North American Aerospace Defense Command (formerly known as NORAD), the CFDS outlines the Harper government's vision of Canada's future as a bit-player and bagman in a neoliberal American empire, a future in which the effort to bolster a military-industrial complex by courting American arms manufacturing subsidiaries takes priority over supporting domestic industries (3).

Interestingly, the Strategy bears a striking resemblance to the measures Jack Granatstein advocates in his book *Whose War Is It: How Canada Can Survive In the Post-9/11 World* (2007). An extremely influential public intellectual of the right known for his works *Who Killed The Canadian Military* (2004) and *Who Killed Canadian History* (1999), Granatstein sits on various advisory boards to government and played a formative role shaping the direction of the Canadian War Museum. His work argues against ideals of multiculturalism and peacekeeping in favour of "national interests," including the "return" to a narrow national narrative that privileges the accomplishments of "our" British and European forefathers, glorifies colonialism and celebrates the Western, industrialized nation-state as the pinnacle of enlightenment and progress. Granatstein imagines a dystopian what-if scenario calculated to induce panic and militaristic fervour, in which the Canadian military is over-committed abroad, a major natural disaster hits the West Coast and, simultaneously, a terrorist attack is perpetrated on Canadian soil. Enumerating current military capabilities and equipment, he argues that Canada would be ill-prepared to meet this nightmare constellation of challenges and lobbies for long-term, reliable funding for a modern military. The CFDS forsees—and plans for—just such an eventuality, even using the same rhetoric and examples. This tactic ensures the smooth continuation of the War on Terror and at the same time justified the use of the military as security for the contentious 2010 Olympic Games, which saw the theft and corporate development of unceded Indigenous lands and the channelling of public funds away from low-income housing and social infrastructure (Shaw 2008). Indeed, if the surveillance of Vancouver anti-poverty activists and Indigenous youth is any indication, some of the targets of the "new military" have already been identified as Canadian activists, Indigenous people and any others who oppose the reckless pursuit of individualistic corporate profit at the expense of the common good.

The very title of the Canada First plan recalls the cultural tradition of the popular post-Confederation "Canada First" club and social movement. Encompassing weekly Toronto paper *The Nation*, a club called the National Club and a political party called the National Association, the Canada First movement gained widespread public influence in its day, espousing a nationalist platform that promoted white-Anglo-Saxon-Protestant-only immigration, male suffrage, and a preferential national industry program (Coleman 2006: 20). A lobby group for the interests of the newly formed country's elite, the Canada First Movement espoused a homogenous, pan-British ethnicity as the true or natural Canadian identity, and, infamously, fomented settler unrest in Upper Canada during the Riel rebellion by mobilizing racist militias and lynch parties to meet Riel's representatives as they travelled East to negotiate following the execution of Thomas Scott (Reid 2008: 88-90; cf. Bumsted 2001). In addition, the phrase "Canada First" has subsequently resurfaced in Canadian white supremacist and anti-immigration circles.[10] It is difficult to believe that advisors in the Harper government were oblivious to the history of this movement and the exclusive history associated with the term.

Given the historical tradition that it invokes, it should not be surprising that the CFDS marks a cultural as well as a policy shift away from the mythology of peacekeeping to a far-right vision of a military thoroughly integrated into the social fabric and economy of the country and fit to defend unspecified "Canadian national interests" from a world teeming with external and internal threats. What *is* surprising is that Harper's minority government was able to pass this almost $500-billion plan with so little public attention. It speaks to the way militarization broadly transforms social life at both economic and cultural levels. The importation and local reinvention of the yellow ribbon campaign to "support our troops" has been key to this process in Canada, and it is to this cultural pedagogy that I now turn.

Tying Yellow Ribbons

Although yellow ribbons had begun to trickle across the Canadian border in small numbers during the first Gulf War (1990-1991)[11] it only gained mass appeal during Canada's mission in Afghanistan as part of the War on Terror. While yellow ribbons proliferated on car bumpers soon after Canada joined the War effort in 2002, public debate about the ribbons themselves arose around their use on public property. At the time, the anti-war movement was quick to point out their primary function: to conflate support and sympathy for individual soldiers with support for the mission, and to foreclose debate on whether our troops should be there at all. Longtime members of anti-war circles also acknowledged that challenging even an unpopular military engagement is most effective before troops are deployed. As after soldiers are perceived to be in harm's way, the parameters of public discourse shift from the politics or necessity of the engagement to discussions of soldiers, their families and their sacrifices. The yellow ribbon's function was and is to expedite this shift and, by extension, to imply that the time for "politics" was over, and that it was now time to rally around the flag.

Proponents of the ribbon's use on public vehicles and property argued strenuously that the idea of supporting the troops was apolitical and ought to be inoffensive, because everyone agrees about our duty to support the troops regardless of opinions about the war (Patrick and Kari 2007). Contrarily, those who opposed the ribbons' use on government buildings and vehicles challenged the idea that supporting soldiers waging a contentious war was a neutral or apolitical position, and resented the military incursion into daily life presented by the ribbons. Resulting debates tended to be dominated by the loudest and most affectively successful voices, rather than by the most cogent arguments. After much debate about when to remove the bumper-stickers, Toronto Mayor David Miller arrived at the position that it was not the role of city councilors to debate federal policy. An estimated $3,000 from the city budget had been spent outfitting the city's fleet of vehicles (ibid).

In terms of the material lives of the ribbons themselves, there are two different trajectories by which the bumper stickers (and related paraphernalia) enter circulation. It is impossible to estimate how many have been produced, as there is no single, centralized dispatch. On one hand, anyone can "unofficially" order a batch of ribbons from their local print shop, and many regiments, legion branches, churches and other community groups order them, often for use as fundraisers and sometimes with their own logo, regimental number, maple leaf, cross insignia, camouflage, desert theme or other particularity included in the design. Indeed, the "yellow ribbon" template is the same one that is used for a variety of ribbon campaigns. In one respect, then, the yellow ribbon as a *commodity* has an economic or material life in a small but growing "support our troops" industry that emblematizes the way state mythology and free enterprise can partner in a pedagogical project.

On the other hand, the ribbons' "official" trajectory is the "support our troops" campaign, sponsored by the Department of National Defence (DND) and orchestrated through the semi-privatized Canadian Forces Personnel Service Agency (CFPSA). The "support our troops" campaign is one of the CFPSA's prerogatives, and their military-oriented CANEX discount department stores carry all manner of "support our troops" merchandise, including branded water bottles, T-shirts, hats and other items of clothing. As the name suggests, the CFPSA supports Canadian Forces personnel in a variety of capacities; for example, the agency oversees the operation of privatized on-base services such as barber shops, tailors and fast-food chains, including the Tim Hortons coffee stall on location at Kandahar airfield. Where once those services would have been provided "in house," offering fairly reliable employment opportunities for military spouses prone to frequent relocation, even this militarized reproductive labour is made precarious by its contracting out to third parties. Profits generated from these "public-private partnerships" are ostensibly funnelled back into services that benefit military personnel themselves.[12]

The grey area surrounding the CFPSA and the military chain of command subtly encapsulates a contradictory tendency of militarization under neoliberalism. The state's monopoly on violence is considerably shaken by the global rise of private-security contractors—like Blackwater—that behave as mercenary armies, home-grown militias that arise in suspicion of the state and the systematic privatization of non-combat military roles and services. The contest between state-based and de-territorialized powers marks a different kind of collaboration between capital and the state, in which the normal, supposedly iron-clad rules of free trade, elsewhere held sacred, exist in quite functional, militarized states of exception and compromise. At the same time, in free trade agreements such as the North American Free Trade Agreement and the General Agreement on Tariffs and Trade, military exemptions are virtually the only area protected from the sweeping liberalization of domestic industry for international competition. All this is to say that militarization creates a relatively unique space of contestation, in that it commands a patriarchal affective response that allows for all sorts of deviations from the rule. For this reason, the military in Canada and militaries generally are a kind of laboratory or testing ground for new strategies and technologies of power, social organization and control.

The lack of clarity around the CFPSA's official status muddies the waters as to where, exactly, the impetus behind the "support our troops" campaign originates. Ultimately, the CFPSA answers to the Vice-Chief of Defence Staff, whose office created the CFPSA as an "administrative construct" to help administer "Non-Public Property" and funds—that is, it established the CFPSA to save costs through privatization (CFPSA 2006). Is the CFPSA thus a civilian company owned by the DND? A para-military organization? A military-corporate service agency? In the United States, contracts for the "America Supports You" military support campaign were given primarily to public relations giant Susan Davis International, for a final sum not yet tallied, but expected to be around $5-million annually (Farsetta 2008). The information about Canada's campaign is, as yet, publicly unavailable.[13]

On one hand, it matters a great deal whether private corporations were contracted to manufacture public acquiescence to a controversial military intervention, as it would testify to the growing and un-checked power of public relations firms, the great mercenaries in the battle for our hearts and minds, to intervene in public debate and policy-making. In another sense, however, whether the architects of Canada's public relations strategy on the War on Terror turn out to be military personnel schooled in "psychological operations" against citizens or free agents from a profit-hungry private firm, this is of secondary importance to the function of the ribbons as resources for individuals to create shared narratives.

Despite the media's failure to present balanced coverage of the war and the Harper government's intensive public relations, the general population in Canada seems to conceptually distinguish between the War in Afghanistan and those fighting it. Major pollster Ipsos Reid found that while between 44 per cent and 48 per cent of Canadians overall support the mission in Afghanistan, there are significant regional differences: "Albertans (62 per cent) are most likely to support the mission, followed by those in Ontario (52 per cent) and British Columbia (50 per cent). A minority of residents in Saskatchewan and Manitoba (46 per cent), Atlantic Canada (39 per cent) and Quebec (38 per cent) support the current mission" (2009). However, when asked whether they were proud of the troops, Albertans continued to rank first (93 per cent), followed by Atlantic Canadians (86 per cent), BC and Ontario (82 per cent), Quebec (76 per cent), and finally those in Saskatchewan and Manitoba (64 per cent). According to the most recent figures, 66 per cent of Canadians indicated they oppose extending the mission again, and 53 per cent continue to oppose the mission altogether (ibid.).

It will likely surprise no one that Alberta leads the way in support for both soldiers and the war, but what I find most interesting about these results is that Atlantic Canada, densely saturated with military bases and over-represented in military recruiting, supports soldiers while strongly opposing the war itself. These findings lend credence to my suspicion that yellow ribbons are *least* "politicized" when used by military members and their friends and family. Or, rather, in these instances the ribbons are most severed from a larger political agenda, and do what their proponents claim they do: demonstrate care for soldiers. Whether this ability to maintain conceptual distinction between soldiers and the wars they fight is a good thing, or in the public interest, is another matter of debate, but not one this paper has space to engage.

Conclusions

The yellow ribbon's career outside of the primary instances I have discussed here are telling. For instance, during a 1993 uprising at the Southern Ohio Correctional Facility in Lucasville, Ohio, where prisoners rebelled against inhumane (and highly racialized) conditions, yellow ribbons were used by the local community as a gesture of concern for prison guards held hostage (Hielbronn 1994: 174). They were also used in 1992 to show support for Los Angeles police Chief Daryl Gates who defended the beating of Rodney King "comment[ing] that he hoped the victim had 'learned something' from the beating and that the fifty-six blows would convince him to 'turn his life around'" (Mariscal 1991: 114). These two instances explicitly link the yellow ribbon with a defence of whiteness and an imperial, racially ordered world view.

Despite this telling ideological trajectory, the everyday use of the yellow ribbon is more often than not driven by heartfelt care and concern for soldiers (and their families) who are imagined to be "just like us" and "just doing their jobs." I argue that they provide a powerful pedagogical resource for people to make sense of and find their place within the political, social and economic turmoil and decay caused by neoliberal globalization. By mobilizing hyper-masculinized and patriotic affect, yellow ribbons as performative and declarative acts offer a sense of collective identity and purpose in a changing and obscure world and help map community, politics and nation in a time of crisis.

This new slant on an old nation-building project necessitates the re-production of narratives of colonial belonging and legitimacy through the constantly evolving cultural work of what Goldberg has aptly termed "historical amnesia" (2007). Canada is a nation founded on colonial violence, dispossession and loyalty to Empire, and this legacy is both obscured and perpetuated by the constant reinvention of myths that link militarism, sovereignty and racially coded civility. The yellow ribbons can be best understood as acts of a certain kind of cultural agency, but they are far from neutral. The yellow ribbon has become a key tool by which the Harper government has advanced its own form of neoliberal, redistributive militarization, as its own particularly ideologically driven answer to the contemporary question of Canada's changing role in the world.

The forms of social life and social subjects to which neoliberal policies give rise, stripped of a meaningful democratic possibility, are easily mobilized by the fear and the promises espoused by far-right and neoconservative agendas. It would be intellectually and politically irresponsible to ignore the resonance between the social transformation that yellow ribbon politics inculcates, and far-right and avowedly fascist regimes that have historically quelled dissent by demanding and instituting public displays of loyalty, such as the signing of oaths and the wearing of colours by civilian and targeted minority populations.[14] While everyday users of yellow ribbons and the governments that promote them would insist they are icons of free expression and respect for "the democracy our boys fought and are fighting for," they work to transform and constrain public space and discourse. The ability to move freely as a private citizen is undermined by this kind of imperative to a declarative politics, and part of the work the yellow ribbon does is to act as the thin edge of that wedge. The political and ideological neutrality that proponents insist the yellow ribbon possesses is key to the operation of its power and central to the difficulty public intellectuals and interest groups have faced in challenging it. While the symbol creates a politically expedient ambiguity between support for soldiers and support for the war, the yellow ribbon's deeper success is its sheer ubiquity and its pedagogical work as an invented tradition that normalizes the narrowing and militarization of acceptable forms of subjectivity, collective identity and belonging.

Notes

1. While the sovereignty of transnational capital and its power is threatening the viability of all forms of biological and social life on this planet with increasing blatancy, it is not as yet completely unfettered; my thinking here tends to follow those like David Harvey and Leo Pannitch, who remain unwilling to cede the ground of the nation-state in the context of this question, as it remains the prevailing institutional form structuring the

contemporary contest for democracy. Moreover, this approach is useful to my research, which brings to the fore the material consequences of the ways in which national discourses are contested and the affective power they wield.

2. See http://www.tonyorlando.com

3. In his retrospective on the first Gulf War, Douglas Kellner documents the crucial role played by public relations corporations, which were revealed after the fact to have been instrumental in influencing public opinion in support of governmental objectives. Kellner adds an important caveat and so must I: Lazarsfeld's "hypodermic needle" or "magic bullet" model of communications has been discredited to the extent that it hardly requires riposte any longer, serving today mainly as an accusation against cultural critics who still find structural power relations worth talking about. Of course, individuals create diverse meanings from texts and are not mere dupes blown hither and thither by the winds of corporate media. In the case of the present case, the affective power orchestrated by media and government spectacle is such that we must wonder, however, whether people's individual reading capacities are particularly relevant in the absence of a political and social context in which those diverse reading and meaning-making practices can be said to matter. After all, the War on Terror was launched in spite of the largest global demonstrations of opposition in history. So long as resistance is everywhere in people's interpretations of media texts, and yet nowhere finds recourse to any sort of organizational impulse, this sort of resistance is likely to enable the perpetuation, rather than interruption, of "things as they are."

4. While this research is still very much in progress, it is worth noting that the yellow ribbon bears the hallmarks of a public relations strategy designed to muddy the waters around the justification for the first Gulf War, complete with an invented All-American tradition. As former director of the CIA, George Bush Sr. would certainly have been versed in and have ready access to such tactics. Whether the yellow ribbon emerged primarily as a grass-roots cultural practice, or as a deliberate "Astroturf" strategy to create the appearance of public support for the war is an important question, but not one on which my analysis here hinges. If it were originally an Astroturf tactic, it would be further evidence of cynical corporate and governmental collusion, but, sadly, such evidence proving the world is round is hardly necessary.

5. There is a particularly wide gulf between critical academic understanding and public debate. In the course of my research, I have found that people who work for the military come in nearly as many political persuasions as the general population, but tend not to like it when political theorists don't know anything about their experience of military life, particularly the centrality of specific technologies and kinds of equipment to the work they do. The academics and politicians who tend to know a lot about the details of military equipment and specific regiments tend to be on the right. As critical academics and public intellectuals our tendency to pay greater attention to discourse and analysis at the expense of knowing, say, how many ships the navy has—a problem that is not without class overtones—does not serve the public conversation well, either in rigour or in credibility. (There are thirty-three, but not all of them count.)

6. See http://afghanistan.gc.ca/canada

7. To put this $500-billion price tag in perspective, the national child-care program that was held out as the Liberal party's "carrot" during the 2006 elections, that was so controversial with the political right and took fire for being a communist plot (despite being a user-pay model, based on some provincial systems now in effect, and despite remaining "in waiting" more than thirty years), was budgeted at a mere $12-billion over five years.

8. For instance, Paul Fromm, one of Canada's most infamous white supremacists, runs a Web site called the "Canada First Immigration Reform Committee."

9. Under the leadership of then-Prime Minister Brian Mulroney, Canada contributed four naval ships, a squadron of CF-18 Hornets, and other medical and support personnel to the United States-led "Allied" effort in the first Gulf War. Though the CF-18 bombing missions marked the first time since the Korean War that Canada had been actively engaged in offensive combat, that war was shorter. Canadian troops played a more supportive and relatively more removed role and did not sustain any casualties.

10. See http://cfpsa.ca.

11. I am pursuing this line of inquiry, but so far have run up against "national security concerns."

12. As happened following September 11, 2001, in California and across the U.S., as Muslim men were forced to register with the U.S. government, and also at various points in Canadian history, most notably the internment of Japanese-Canadians during the Second World War.

References

Canadian Forces Personnel Service Agency. 2006. *Strategic Plan 2006-2009*. http://www.cfpsa.com/en/corporate/newscentre/conference/documents/CFPSAStrategicPlan_e.pdf.

Department of National Defence. 2008. *The Canada First Defence Strategy*. 16 June. http://www.forces.gc.ca/site/pri/first-premier/June18_0910_CFDS_english_low-res.pdf.

Bannerji, Himani. 2000. *The Dark Side of the Nation: Essays on Multiculturalism, Nationalism, and Gender*. Toronto: Canadian Scholars' Press.

Bauman, Zygmunt. 2000. *Globalization: The Human Cconsequences*. New York and Chichester: Columbia University Press.

Bumsted, J. M. 2001. *Louis Riel v. Canada: The Making of a Rebel*. Winnipeg: Great Plains Publications.

Coleman, Daniel. 2006. *White Civility: The Literary Project of English Canada*. Toronto: University of Toronto Press.

Dippie, Brian W. 1994. *Remington and Russell: The Sid Richardson Collection Revised Edition*. Austin, TX: University of Texas Press.

———. 2006. One West, One Myth: Transborder Continuity in Western Art. *One West, Two Myths II: Essays on Comparison*, edited by C. L. Highham and Robert Thacker. Calgary, AB: University of Calgary Press.

Engler, Yves. 2009. *The Black Book of Canadian Foreign Policy*. Vancouver, BC: Red Pub.

Enloe, Cynthia. 1990. *Bananas, Beaches and Bases: Making Feminist Sense of International Politics*. Berkeley, CA: University of California Press.

———. 2000. *Maneuvers: The International Politics of Militarizing Women's Lives*. Berkeley, CA: University of California Press.

Farsetta, Diane. 2008. America Scams You: Allison Barber's Many "No-no's." PR Watch.org, 18 December. http://www.prwatch.org/node/8076.

Giroux, Henry. 2004. War on Terror: The Militarising of Public Space and Culture in the United States. *Third Text* 18(4): 211-21.

———. 2006. *Beyond the Spectacle of Terrorism: Global Uncertainty and the Challenge of the New Media*. Boulder, CO: Paradigm.

———. 2007. *The University in Chains: Confronting the Military-Industrial-Academic Complex*. Boulder, CO: Paradigm.

Goldberg, David Theo. 2007. Raceless States. *Race, Racialization and Antiracisim in Canada and Beyond*, edited by Genevieve Fuji Johnson and Randy Enomoto. Toronto: University of Toronto Press.

Granatstein, J. 2004. *Who Killed the Canadian Military?* Toronto: Harper Flamingo Canada.

———. 2007. *Whose War is it?: How Canada Can Survive in the Post-9/11 World*. Toronto: HarperCollins.

Hardt, Michael and Antonio Negri. 2000. *Empire*. New York: Harvard University Press.

Harvey, David. 2005. *The New Imperialism*. Oxford and New York: Oxford University Press.

Healy, Teresa, ed. 2008. *The Harper Record*. Ottawa: Canadian Centre for Policy Alternatives.

Heilbronn, Lisa M. 1994. Yellow Ribbons and Remembrance: Mythic Symbols of the Gulf War. *Sociological Inquiry* 64(4): 151-78.

Hobsbawm, Eric and Terrance Ranger. 1983. *The Invention of Tradition*. Cambridge and New York: Cambridge University Press.

Hossein-zadeh, Ismael. 2007a. Income Redistribution in Disguise Escalating Military Spending. *Counterpunch*, 16 April. http://www.counterpunch.org/hossein04162007.html.

———. 2007b. *The Political Economy of U.S. Militarism*. New York: Palgrave Macmillan.

Ipsos Reid. 2009. Support for Mission in Afghanistan Holds Steady (48%) But Come 2011 Majority (52%) Says It's Time for Canada to Pull Out. 16 July. http://www.ipsos-na.com/news-polls/pressrelease.aspx?id=4458.

Kellner, Douglas. 1992. *The Persian Gulf TV War*. Boulder, CO: Westview Press.

———. N.d. *The Persian Gulf TV War Revisited*. http://www.gseis.ucla.edu/faculty/kellner/essays/gulftvwarrevisited.pdf.

Klein, Naomi. 2008. *The Shock Doctrine: The Rise of Disaster Capitalism*. Toronto: Vintage Canada.

MacDonald, Marci. 2006. Harper and the Theocons. *The Walrus*, October.

Mackey, Eva. 1999. *The House of Difference: Cultural Politics and National Identity in Canada*. London and New York: Routledge.

Mackey, Lloyd. 2005. *The Pilgrimage of Stephen Harper*. Toronto: ECW Press.

Mariscal, George. 1991. In the Wake of the Gulf War: Untying the Yellow Ribbon. *Cultural Critique* 19:97-117.

Martin, Randy. 2007. *An Empire of Indifference: American War and the Financial Logic of Risk Management*. Durham, NC: Duke University Press.

McQuaig, Linda. 2007. *Holding the Bully's Coat: Canada and the U.S. Empire*. Toronto: Doubleday Canada.

Patrick, Kelly and Shannon Kari. 2007. Troop Decal Removal "A Slap in the Face." *The National Post*, 20 June.

Razack, Sherene. 2004. *Dark Threats and White Knights: The Somalia Affair, Peacekeeping, and the New Imperialism*. Toronto and Buffalo: University of Toronto Press.

———. 2007. *Casting Out: The Eviction of Muslims from Western Law and Politics.* Toronto: University of Toronto Press.

Reid, Jennifer. 2008. *Louis Riel and the Making of Modern Canada: Mythic Discourse and the Post-Colonial State.* Albuquerque: University of New Mexico Press.

Shaw, Christopher A. 2008. *Five Ring Circus: Myths and Realities of the Olympic Games.* Gabriola Island, BC: New Society.

Smith, Andrea. 2005. *Conquest: Sexual Violence and American Indian Genocide.* Cambridge, MA: South End Press.

Staples, Stephen. 2007. Fortress North America: The Drive towards Military and Security Integration and Its Impact on Canadian Democratic Sovereignty. In *Whose Canada?*, edited by Ricardo Grinspun and Yasmine Shamsie. Montreal and Kingston: McGill-Queens University Press.

Thobani, Sunera. 2007. *Exalted Subjects: Studies in the Making of Race and Nation in Canada.* Toronto and Buffalo: University of Toronto Press.

Whitworth, Sandra. 1994. *Feminism and International Relations: Towards a Political Economy of Gender in Interstate and Non-Governmental Institutions.* Basingstoke, U.K.: Macmillan.

———. 2004. *Men, Militarism, and UN Peacekeeping: A Gendered Analysis.* Boulder, CO: Lynne Rienner.

Howard Fremeth

Searching for the Militarization of Canadian Culture: The Rise of a Military-Cultural Memory Network

ABSTRACT

During the past twenty years, there has been a shift in Canadian culture from representations that highlight a peacekeeping view of the military and its past to a hardened and more pervasive image. This paper explores the militarization of culture by outlining a theory and method to study the emergence of a military-cultural memory network. Specifically, I reassess the debate over *The Valour and the Horror* as a formative event in this network. I propose that the Dominion Institute has since emerged as an intermediary connecting various interested groups who use popular media forms to canonize and archive military history.

RÉSUMÉ

Chercher à militariser la culture canadienne : l'ascension d'un réseau mémoriel militaro-culturel

Au cours des vingt dernières années, il s'est opéré un glissement dans la culture canadienne, depuis les représentations soulignant une conception des militaires au service du maintien de la paix à une image plus dure et plus prégnante. Cet article explore la militarisation de la culture en soulignant une théorie et une méthode pour étudier l'émergence d'un réseau mémoriel militaro-culturel. Je réévalue en particulier le débat suscité par la série documentaire télévisée, The Valour and the Horror, en tant qu'évènement constitutif de ce réseau. Je suggère en particulier que l'Institut du Dominion est apparu depuis comme un intermédiaire mettant en relation divers groupes d'intérêt qui utilisent les médias populaires pour canoniser et archiver l'histoire militaire.

Canadians are known as a tolerant and peaceful people. We pride ourselves on our multiculturalism and humanitarian outlook.... Nevertheless, although not warlike or militaristic people, Canadians have earned a reputation as brave and capable soldiers. (MacKenzie 2006: 7)

These words, by Major-General (Retired) Lewis MacKenzie in the preface to *The Canadian Way of War* (2006), encapsulate a paradox that pervades the collective memory of Canadian military history and the cultural forms that sustain this memory. On one hand, cultural memory and collective memory emphasize the view of Canadians as, to borrow C.P. Stacey's (1955) words, an "unmilitary community" who value their long history of peacekeeping and humanitarianism. This narrative serves as an important component in a larger interpretation of Canadian history as a series of compromises between different people (e.g., the Quebec Act of 1775) and non-violent political moments (e.g., Confederation). On the other hand, cultural memory and collective memory emphasize the view that Canada has a rich military tradition that is as impressive as the celebrated histories of other nations. Based on the belief that military history has not penetrated public consciousness due to neglect or even organized forgetting, this narrative highlights historic battles that have forged the nation (e.g., "The Plains of Abraham") and combat missions that have given Canadians a reputation as fierce combatants (e.g., Passchendaele).[1]

At the root of these opposing narratives is not only a concern about the past, but also aspirations for the present and future. As Zygmunt Bauman (1982) suggests, "[r]emembered history is the logic which the actors inject into their strivings and which they employ to invest credibility into their hopes. In its after-life, history reincarnates as Utopia which guides, and is guided by, the struggles of the present" (1). In the case of Canada's collective memory of its military past, the attempt to emphasize one narrative over another is tied to a larger worldview about the contemporary role of the Canadian Forces. The politics of memory complements the politics of peace and militarism. A survey of Canadian culture over the past twenty years points to an interesting trend regarding the balance between these conflicting representations of the military's history and contemporary status. Although the softer view of the military through a non-violent and peacemaker lens was dominant during the 1990s, this narrative has waned since the turn of the 21st century with the (re)emergence of a hardened account that highlights events of military glory, heroism and reminders that the Canadian Forces is in the business of war. (See Appendix A for a timeline of military texts in Canadian culture since 1992.)

First, with respect to cultural memory, Ottawa serves as a convenient location to track this cultural trend. The only major monument to be constructed in the

1990s was the National Peacekeeping Monument that was unveiled as part of the Canada 125 celebrations in 1992. Sponsored by the Department of National Defence (DND) and the National Capital Commission (NCC), this $2.8 million monument, entitled *Reconciliation*, was designed to commemorate the 90,000 Canadians who served in UN peacekeeping missions and, as Prime Minister Mulroney proudly boasted at the unveiling, "the victory of a Canadian ideal: the creation of multi-national *peacekeeping* forces under the UN banner" (qtd. in *Ottawa Citizen* 1992: B1). According to Paul Gough (2002), this monument was part of an attempt by the state to not only join, but also to "control the rhetoric of peace" that dominated public discourse at that time (221). However, the turn of the century brought a renaissance for the hardened view of Canadian military history with the construction of several memorials dedicated to warfare and military sacrifice.

As part of a governmental decision in 1998 to give the NCC greater funding and responsibility to turn the National Capital Region into a world-class capital city, Ottawa's Confederation Square served as the primary site for this renaissance. In 2000, the National War Monument underwent renovations to extend its space and reinforce its public significance with the addition of the Tomb of the Unknown Soldier; in 2001, the National Aboriginal Veterans Monument was installed at the front of Confederation Park; in 2003, the Korean War Monument was erected beside the Mackenzie King bridge; finally, in 2006, the Valiants Memorial, which includes a number of statues of historical military heroes, was placed beside the National War Memorial.[2] These monuments were pieces in a larger memorial construction boom that took place in Ottawa, throughout the country and around the world. Not only did these projects renovate dilapidated sites and finish incomplete designs, they also expressed the concern that some events from the past urgently needed to be inscribed onto cultural memory forms in order to penetrate Canada's collective memory.

Second, with respect to public opinion about the Canadian Forces, the 1990s represented what General Rick Hillier labelled a "decade of darkness" (qtd. in Blanchfeild, *Ottawa Citizen* 2007: A1). This decade witnessed several controversies, such as the Somalia Affair, the failed attempt to stop the Rwandan genocide and the barbaric initiation rituals of the Canadian Airborne Regiment, as well as a defence policy, by Minister of Foreign Affairs Lloyd Axworthy, that positioned the military as a "soft power." The effect of these years of "darkness" on the morale of soldiers surfaced during an investigation by parliament's Standing Committee on National Defence and Veterans Affairs (SCONDVA) into the quality of life in the Canadian Forces. Although its primary focus was on issues of compensation, healthcare, housing and transition to civilian life, the report revealed an underlying emotional concern: "the feeling among military personnel that they had somehow been forgotten by the nation they had sworn to serve" (SCONDVA 1998: 4). However, by the turn of the 21st century, this sense of abandonment began to wane as the military took a more prominent public role by helping with disaster relief missions during the 1997 Red River flood and Eastern Canada's 1998 ice storm. The sight of military personnel in urban areas was credited for a shift in public opinion. In 1999, a Pollara poll found that 85 per cent of Canadians had a favourable impression of the military and that 70 per cent agreed that the military needed better equipment to do its job (Ward, *The Canadian Press* 1999). Soon after, the military was propelled even further into the forefront of public consciousness with the beginning of the Afghanistan mission in 2001, which accelerated in 2006 when Canada took a lead role in Kandahar province.

Over the course of this mission, the military has made considerable steps to rebrand itself as an important national institution that not only contributes to humanitarian relief efforts, but also fight wars. Although most of the attention on the new recruitment campaign highlights the thrill of war and the brash public persona of General Hillier, a less discussed but equally important rebranding strategy is Operation Connection.[3] Launched on February 6, 2006, this campaign mobilizes

Fig. 1
An example of Operation Connection with a military display at Dundas Square in Toronto on June 17, 2009. Photograph by Howard Fremeth.

local regiments to play an active part in as many urban and rural community events as possible: concerts, hockey games, charity dinners, fairs and even for no special reason just as long as they are seen in public spaces. The first major event was the 2006 Canadian National Exhibition that marked, according to the *Toronto Star*, the "biggest display of tanks and troops in recent memory" (Campion-Smith and Gombu 2006: A6). Drawing on Michael Billig's (1995) concept of banal nationalism, this campaign can be viewed as a shift from the intermittent displays of militarism to the attempt to make military symbols an endemic condition of the everyday life experience of Canadians. It is not military symbols in general that have pervaded public space; rather, it is the presentation of a more aggressive symbolic culture that provides the public with reminders or "continual flagging" that the military is no longer primarily engaged in peacemaking and humanitarian missions, but also committed to fighting wars and, borrowing from General Hillier's language, in the profession of killing people.[4] What was once only seen on special occasions—veterans selling poppies before Remembrance Day and soldiers in urban spaces aiding in disaster relief—is now an everyday feature of Canadian culture—veterans speaking to classrooms throughout the school year and armed military vehicles parading in public squares (Fig. 1).

Considering this transition over the past twenty years from a softer view of the military and its history to the ascension of a hardened account, a scholar is left with many areas to explore. Although one interesting site examines questions of discourse and the convergence of the narratives of peacekeeping with the war on terror (Jefferess 2009), it is also important to consider the political economy that contextualizes this shift in cultural production and circulation. One approach for answering this question is to focus on why this shift occurs. A scholar can chart the emergence of representations of the military and its history alongside key political events such as the changing role of the military in domestic relief missions and the escalation of violent activities abroad. From this perspective, the cultural transition is explained by the change in policy from the Canadian Forces as a soft power into a hard power. Despite providing the rationale for this cultural shift, the question remains as to how these forms (memorials, texts, films, etc.) have emerged as legitimate components of Canada's public culture.

Simply suggesting that this cultural shift is part of some embedded military-cultural complex that seeks to provide public support for the changing role of the military does not appreciate the complexity that underscores the process of cultural production. The objective of this paper is to propose a theory and method to study how this cultural shift occurred. Specifically, I turn to Michel Callon's approach to Actor-Network Theory (ANT) and Pierre Bourdieu's concept of symbolic power to analyze the political economy of the memorialization of Canadian military history. These scholars provide ways to think about this political economic framework in terms of a military-cultural memory network with groups and individuals (actors) working together to create and circulate cultural forms. Ironically, the beginning of this network is located during a period of turmoil and uncertainty regarding the memorialization of military history: the controversy surrounding Brian and Terence McKenna's *The Valour and the Horror* (1992).[5]

Although this event has garnered much scholarly attention as an example of postmodern politics (Carr 2005; 2007) and the problems associated with docudramas as history (Sloniowski 2002), it was not as divisive as these scholars presume. Not only did it provide a rare opportunity for those interested and engaged in the cultural production of representations about military history to interact with one another, the discussion around the series as a docudrama alludes to the potential of this narrative form and other uses of popular culture as unifying tools for a prospective military-cultural memory network. Furthermore, this period of contestation raises the need for an actor to facilitate the cooperation between these opposing groups and individuals. I conclude by examining how the Dominion Institute has emerged as such an actor who has adeptly positioned itself as an intermediary within the military-cultural memory network.

The Militarization of Culture and the Transmission of Cultural Memory

Since the emergence of a hardened account of military history was paralleled by a rise in banal as well as explicit forms of militarism within Canadian culture, a study of this cultural shift should be grounded in the scholarly literature on both the military-cultural complex and memory studies. Both bodies of literature can be divided into two approaches to the study of the politics of culture. First: a general approach that explores how the content of cultural forms either promotes or reflects certain ideological messages and values. This work provides cultural readings and discourse analyses of a variety of militaristic texts. Second is a more specific approach that is interested in the process by which culture becomes militarized and the process by which memory is inscribed into material forms to be passed down for future generations. This work provides a useful framework for a study of the political economy of the memorialization of Canadian military history because it shows an awareness of two important themes: 1) the complex web of actors that cooperate and compete for hegemony in discourse and interpretative patterns; 2) the political process that unfolds within these networks whereby an actor emerges as a legitimate and rightful carrier of culture.

The literature on the militarization of culture comes out of a larger project investigating the military-industrial complex, which has its roots in the sociological studies of the role of elites within American society (Mills 1956; Lasswell 1941).[6] This scholarship presents a confused understanding of the military-cultural complex and the process by which culture becomes militarized. On one hand, the complex refers to a psychological illness of modern democratic, capitalist societies that are entirely structured around the military objectives of expansionism and organized violence (Aufderheide 1990; Marvin and Ingle 1996; Sturken 1997). Culture is a space for the sublimation of a militaristic social psychology as well as a tool that entrenches the values and social structure of a militarized society. Here the focus is on how certain cultural forms (films, books, ceremonies and video games) reveal underlying militaristic values. For example, these studies examine how Vietnam War films provided therapeutic relief for veterans as well as for American society in general. Although these works offer interesting interpretations of the logic and rhetoric of militarized texts, this approach neglects any extensive concern over the complex process by which rituals or cultural forms emerge. Instead, as suggested in the language of many of these studies, with words such as "symptom" and "reveal," the militarization of culture is an inevitable outcome of a militaristic society.

The other approach takes a more specific view of the context and political process that underlies the militarization of culture (Andersen 2006; Lenoir and Lowood 2003; Robin 2001). In this approach, the term military-cultural complex is not used to refer to a general state of being that reveals itself within a particular society's culture; rather, it refers to the intricate and complex ways in which those who benefit from militarism engage in the process of cultural production. The complex is not located in the "social mind," but in the elaborate web of associations that connect the military, the state and cultural agencies. For example, Tim Lenoir and Henry Lowood (2003) introduce the term "military-entertainment complex" in their account of the development of war game simulation technology. They investigate how changes to the Department of Defence's research and development policy led to the spin-off of many technologies for the video game industry. The military-entertainment complex is rooted in a shift of the military-industrial complex following the end of the Cold War so that "research not only served national defense but also that it ultimately benefited the commercial sector" (453). Therefore, it is necessary to view the militarization of culture not as a permanent social order emanating from the highest echelons of power, but as an amorphous set of mutually beneficial relations between a variety of actors that appear and disappear depending on the context.

In *The Invention and Decline of Israeliness* (2001), Baruch Kimmerling uses the term "military-cultural complex" to describe both a feature of Israel's "social mind" as well as a series of deeply entrenched institutional arrangements. Similar to the general approach, he states that "[d]econstructing texts concerned with contemporary Israeli culture and cultural orientations provides a point of departure for understanding the impact of long-term Arab-Jewish conflict on Jewish mainstream Israeli society and culture" (Kimmerling 2001: 208). Nonetheless, the complex also refers to the intricate and elaborate ways in which Israeli institutions help to inculcate and sustain these cultural codes. In particular, he states that the school system has always been mobilized for the purpose of nation building and perpetuating the view of Israelis as "New Jews" who work, settle and guard the land (211). As a result of this dual analysis, Kimmerling demonstrates the extent to which Israeli culture is affected by militaristic cultural codes, yet he is still able to point to specific sites in which these codes become a part of culture. He accomplishes this task by positioning the militarization of culture alongside the process of inculcating collective memory in citizens.

Almost every scholarly work examining a topic in the area of collective memory begins by referencing Maurice Halbwachs's contribution to the field.[7] Generally, he is credited for challenging the Freudian and Bergsonian understanding of memory as interiorized within the individual by offering a view of memory as constructed by society and through social interaction (Coser 1992). However, Halbwachs's work is limited because of its focus on oral communication as the primary conduit linking the past to the present. It was only in the 1980s that a new wave of scholars, led by Jan Assmann (1992) and Pierre Nora (1984), began to consider the transmission of collective memory through material forms. Whereas Nora uses the term *lieux de memoire* to differentiate from the traditional *millieux de memoire* that Halbwachs studied, Assmann offers the term cultural memory to differentiate from Halbwachs's interest in communicative memory. Aleida Assmann (2008), Jan's wife and colleague, extends this work even further by noting that cultural memory can be categorized into two spheres: the canon and the archive. Whereas the canon refers to the way in which a limited number of memories are actively circulated at any given point in time, the archive suggests that some symbols and cultural forms may remain dormant, but still need to be stored. The question remains as to how something becomes a part of either the canon or the archive. Aleida Assmann can only respond by acknowledging a larger political process: "the selection for what criteria is to be remembered and circulated in the active cultural memory and what is to be merely stored are neither clear nor are they uncontested" (104).

Understanding the politics of transmission is at the core of many studies into collective memory (Appadurai 1981; Meyer 2008; Schudson 1992; Winter and Sivan 1999). The underlying assumption of this work is described in Erik Meyer's (2008) suggestion to treat memory like any other political domain. This domain comprises "forces and counter-forces competing for hegemony of discourse and interpretative patterns" (176). Arjun Appadurai (1981) studies this hegemonic process by considering the past as a scarce cultural product or resource. In his study of a dispute over the ownership of the Sri Partasarati Szami Temple in Madras City that involved the state government and a number of rival Hindu sects, he observes how competing groups claim to be the legitimate owners of cultural memory forms. Whereas Appadurai is interested in the rhetoric employed by competing groups, Michael Schudson (1992), in his study of the Watergate scandal in American memory, combines cultural analysis with political economy. Schudson posits that memories do not die out because better interpretations of the past emerge, but because proponents of memories die out and new generations grow up with new accounts: "the preservation of a memory of Watergate has in many respects been motivated by people deeply moved or hurt by Watergate who feel a commitment to one or another version of it that they want to see others accept" (56). These people with a vested interest in Watergate are organized into a memory industry with memory professionals (historians, politicians and educators).

In their analysis of the collective memory of war, James Winter and Emmanuel Sivan (1999) consider both the networks involved in memorialization and the politics of legitimation that actors undergo to become part of a network. Contrary to a propaganda model approach, the persistence of memory cannot simply be accredited to the will of the state. Rather, the collective remembrance of military history must be viewed as "the outcome of agency, as the product of individuals and groups who come together, not at the behest of the state or any of its subsidiary organizations, but because they have to speak out" (9). Not only is the memory of war a scarce resource, but also a non-renewable one that vanishes once the people directly affected by the events pass away. Therefore, cultural products and practices are created as a way to extend the "shelf life" of particular memories. However, these aids are only effective if they are actively used or participated in by the public. This active participation must be viewed as an outcome of what Roger Bastide labels "networks of complimentarity." Included in these networks are the state, elites, veterans, historians, businessmen, artists and descendants of those who have been affected by war. Although each may have their own motivations, no one group, or "voice" as the metaphor of the choir suggests, is more important than another. Instead, they argue that what makes a group more prominent is not how close their voice is to the microphone (their access to the public), but their moral authority as judged by others within the choir.[8]

Conceptualizing a Method and Theory for Tracking a Military-Cultural Memory Network

The literature that considers the political process involved in the transmission of collective memory as well as the web of actors engaged in the militarization of culture reflects two sociological theories: Bruno Latour's performative view of the social and Pierre Bourdieu's concept of the political economy of symbolic power. Contrary to what he labels the ostensive view of the social, Latour (1986) calls for a performative view that does not assume a stable social order. Under this framework, power lies in the ability to forge associations through "an intense activity of enrolling, convincing and enlisting" (273). Likewise, some of the scholars examined above do not assume that culture emerges either as a result of a widespread social need or the will of a powerful few. Instead, cultural production must be studied as a complex and contested process that involves networks of competing and cooperating individuals, groups, associations, institutions, government departments, professions and other interested parties. Moreover, participation within these networks requires communication with other nodes and to the public that a particular actor is a legitimate and rightful carrier of culture. From this perspective, the formation of cultural networks is grounded in what Pierre Bourdieu (1987) labels the political economy of symbolic power. Actors do not gain legitimacy based upon economic or political capital, but they must convert this prestige, status and wealth into cultural and symbolic capital. Both Bourdieu and Latour consider political action in terms of translations. Whereas Bourdieu considers the ways that actors translate forms of power into cultural capital to assert dominance within a social field, Latour's ANT examines the ways in which actors translate forms of power to forge alliances with other actors in order to construct a network and steer it towards a certain direction. A study of how power operates within the process of the memorialization of Canadian military history must therefore consider these two types of translations.

Michel Callon's approach to ANT in his study of the scallop industry of St. Brieuc Bay provides a useful framework to consider the network involved in the creation and circulation of cultural memory about Canadian military history. ANT assumes that there is no universal structural basis for society and social ties. Instead, as Latour (2005) argues, there only exists "translations between mediators that may generate traceable associations" (108). Translations refer to the way in which actors are able to connect to other actors to form a network of associations—power lies in the ability to cause translations. Callon's 1986 study provides a detailed analysis for tracking the four ways in which this process of translation operates: 1) problematization, 2) incentives, 3) enrolment and 4) mobilization.[9] These terms explain how one actor, referred to as the *primum movens* (first actor), becomes an obligatory passage point by 1) establishing a problem to be solved, 2) embedding procedures to make a solution mutually beneficial, 3) stabilizing the roles and relationships of other actors and 4) ensuring that the leaders of various actors are able to represent their constituencies in a manner that is congruent with the logic of the network.

The starting point for tracking the "complex web of interrelations" of a military-cultural memory network is to consider what problem such a network attempts to solve. In the 1990s, both the military and the status of Canada's collective memory about military history were mired by the perception of a lack of awareness. On one hand, SCONDVA's Quality of Life Report (1998) blamed public apathy about the military on a national media that dwelled on negative stories and failed to recognize the sacrifices of military personnel. On the other hand, in 1995, the CBC's live broadcast of the fiftieth anniversary marking VE Day provided a rare outpouring of public sentiment regarding Canada's military history (Cook 2006: 235). The media, which was previously criticized for being indifferent to military history, rallied behind this outpouring of collective memory. It was during this ceremony that Peter Mansbridge remarked, "there is no shortage of Canadian history. Our history is NOT dull. But we are dull-witted when it comes to learning about it" (qtd. in Miller 1997: 9). Therefore, the problem facing both public opinion of the military and memory of its history was a crisis over media representations: If the public saw a more accurate and appealing picture of the Canadian Forces and its past, then they would forget the negative stories from Somalia and the myth of the military as exclusively a peacekeeping force. Ironically, media is then viewed as a problem and a solution. It is issues of media production and circulation that structures the incentives, enrolment and mobilization of the military-cultural memory network. As well, it is this engagement with media that allows such a network to intervene in Canada's collective memory.

One prominent critique of ANT is that it ignores structural inequalities and power struggles.[10] In Callon's study of the scallop industry, there is little explanation regarding the context in which actors emerge—especially the lead scientists who are positioned as the obligatory passage points. Although ANT describes how an actor can enrol and mobilize other parts of the network, it neglects the political process by which such an actor must first garner legitimacy and authority. It is this blindspot that makes Bourdieu's concept of symbolic power a necessary theoretical feature for charting the political economy of the memorialization of Canadian military history. Bourdieu perceives the social world as a sports field (*champ*) in which different symbols offered by players compete for their place within society's limited system of signs. Once positioned upon this field, players not only draw upon their economic and political capital, but they must translate these forms of power into cultural and symbolic capital in order to "legitimate [their] vision of the social world and of its divisions" (Bourdieu 1987: 13). With respect to the politics of memory networks, as Winter and Sivan (1999) suggest, actors must first achieve some level of moral authority as rightful carriers of memory. Therefore, any study of Canada's military-cultural memory network must not only track the translations that mark the formation of the complex web of interrelations, but also acknowledge how actors translate various forms of capital to garner power as legitimate nodes within the network. Bourdieu's theory suggests that it is inadequate for Callon to claim that the *primum movens* is the natural obligatory passage point. Instead, I propose that the obligatory passage point must continually communicate a level of legitimacy and moral authority to those within and outside of the network to maintain this powerful position.

The Valour and the Horror and the Emergence of a Military-Cultural Memory Network

Although the rapidly diminishing scallop population in St. Brieuc Bay was a natural phenomenon, Callon insists that it only became a problem to be solved after the public proclamations by a group of researchers at an academic conference. A problem does not naturally arise even though it might always be present; rather, it only comes to the fore through some public deliberation and discussion.

In a study on Canada's military-cultural memory network, the challenge for a scholar is to avoid any interjections by conceptualizing what he or she thinks is the problem. Instead, it is necessary to indentify a public event in which actors deliberate on a particular problem and suggest solutions. The public controversy surrounding Brian and Terence McKenna's *The Valour and the Horror* (1992) and the Senate's hearings on this made-for-television docudrama provide a site and body of evidence to explore the problematization of the memorialization of military history.

Previous studies on *The Valour and the Horror* have focused on the problems of this series as a form of history and the rhetoric employed by those engaged in the public debate over the series. In her analysis of its rhetorical techniques, Jeannette Sloniowski (2002) concludes that the series' divisiveness was an outcome of the unproblematic way in which the filmmakers adopted the conventions of popular history without equipping audiences with any historical and media literacy: "the McKennas have taken the past and used it for the ideological needs of the present" (172). Examining the public debate surrounding the series, Graham Carr (2005) argues that the way in which military historians employed the language of empiricism and objectivity allowed them to win this "drama of legitimation" (345). Although both scholars are correct for framing the debate over the series and the interpretations by various segments of the audience as divisive and highly contested, this does not provide a complete picture. Upon closer inspection, the sentiments about the series reveal some level of agreement over the power of the docudrama form, and popular media in general, as a tool for memorialization. My objective is not to offer a critical textual reading, but to identify how some key actors (historians, veterans and filmmakers), who will eventually play a vital role in a military-cultural memory network, will assess the use of docudramas for public history.

Considering the scholarship on docudrama as a form of communication, it is easy to appreciate the contentious reaction that followed the airing of *The Valour and the Horror* by the CBC in January of 1992.[11] According to Derek Paget (1998), the docudrama form is a source of confusion and consternation because "it openly proclaims both a documentary and a dramatic provenance" (1). As a result of this blurring of genres, audiences have difficulty judging this form on both terms—in this particular case, as history and entertainment—and often react with suspicion. Nonetheless, as Paget insists by drawing a metaphor to the trouble with identifying a rainbow, this reaction is due to a problem of perception and is not necessarily an accurate description of a person's final judgement. Therefore, regardless of the many points of criticism levelled by some at *The Valour and the Horror*, the evidence shows a general agreement that docudramas should be a key element for the memorialization of military history.

First, as Carr adeptly argues, the reaction by professional historians was especially harsh. They were quick to point out many factual errors such as the depiction of Canadian pilots using the American instead of the British terminology to locate enemy planes. However, the most significant complaint was that the McKennas did not thoroughly contextualize the past. According to historian Terry Copp, the result was a caricaturization of the past that was "devoid of its complexities and nuances" (qtd. in Sub-committee 1993: 26). The historians preferred Ken Burns's approach in the PBS documentary *The Civil War* (1990). Since this television series did not incorporate re-enactments but the narration of letters and diaries alongside historical images, they considered the documentary form to be more representative of the historical method. Despite this emphasis on delegitimizing the docudrama as a medium for history education, the question remains whether their ultimate problem rested with how the past was represented or with what was represented. In the introduction to the edited book *The Valour and the Horror Revisited* (1994), the historians David Bercuson and S. F. Wise detail the many errors and problems with the series and conclude by calling on the filmmakers to choose other events to represent: "the McKennas could have told a wide audience about Canada in the Second World War that *is* new and that would have changed Canadians' conceptions of their own history" (10). Underlying this severe criticism of the series was a sense, among some professional historians of the power of docudrama to popularize military history and reach a much larger audience than any scholarly book or article.

Second, according to Tim Cook (2006), the reaction to the production and broadcast of *The Valour and the Horror* by publicly funded cultural institutions resulted in the emergence of what he labels "militarized grey power." "Those veterans interested in how their history would be portrayed became more willing to intervene against revisionist history they found distasteful" (230). The veterans who testified and sent letters to the Sub-committee on Veterans Affairs expressed a concern that the McKennas were using historical hindsight to judge the past and ignoring the context of the Second World War as a total war—especially in the episode that questioned the morality of the Allied night bombing raids. According to one veteran, Walter Thomspson, the accusations against Bomber Command were equivalent to criticizing a victim "for reaching for and using a club rather than a rapier" (qtd. in Sub-committee 1993: 12). Leading the charge of this attack against the McKennas was Cliff Chadderton, the Chairman of the National Council of Veterans Associations and CEO of the War Amps, who tried to censure the series from being rebroadcasted and distributed to schools through the NFB catalogue. Despite this animosity towards the filmmakers and the publicly funded cultural institutions, it is necessary to note that Chadderton was not against the docudrama as a form of public history. On the contrary, he called on the filmmakers to release a newly edited series that would take into account the many objections raised by the veterans (*War Amps*, January 26, 1993).

Underlying the campaign by veterans against *The Valour and the Horror* was a respect for the ability of the filmmakers to popularize the past and make it aesthetically pleasing for the public and, in particular, for youth who had trouble relating to military history.

Finally, and not surprisingly, the McKenna brothers reacted to the controversy by vehemently defending their series. Throughout the media debates and Senate hearings, they never veered from the position that the series was generally factually correct and a legitimate historical account: "For every historian attacking *The Valour and the Horror*, there is a serious historian supporting the series" (McKenna and McKenna 1992: 87). That said, they lamented the way in which opponents judged their series as scholarship. The McKennas were frustrated by the inability of some opponents to follow the nuances of the subtle transitions between documentary and dramatic techniques. In fact, they insisted that they never received "a single letter from any viewer who was confused about what was drama and what was documentary in the series" (76). Nonetheless, within this public debate, they did express some contrition toward the veterans. Not only did Brian McKenna admit that he would have fought alongside the veterans if he were alive at the time, he also claimed that his initial inspiration came from his desire to learn more about an ancestor who fought in the military. He acknowledged that the Senate's inquiry was just as much about allowing veterans to express the pain associated with their traumatic experience as it was about scrutinizing the series (McKenna 1992: A11). Moreover, as Carr (2007) notes in his examination of the generational tropes mobilized during the public debate, the McKennas, the historians and the veterans shared the belief that they each had a responsibility to transmit the memory of war to future generations of Canadians.

The challenge of transmitting collective memory was something that all believed to be urgent, even as they disagreed over who had the moral authority to do so. Considering that 20 per cent (4-4.7 million viewers) of the English-language television audience watched each episode, which is especially striking when considering the low viewership ratings for Canadian television drama, clearly *The Valour and the Horror* struck a nerve with veterans and historians re-garding the docudrama's ability to attract audiences and its power as a tool for public history—a problematic, yet necessary tool.[12] The controversy over the series highlighted the need for this contentious tool, yet also the necessity for greater communication and cooperation among those interested in the memorialization of Canadian military history.

The Dominion Institute as the Obligatory Passage Point

Callon argues that the key element in the problematization of a network is the realization by each actor that he or she is fettered in some way. A network can only emerge after actors understand that "they cannot attain what they want by themselves" (1986: 206). With this in mind, the controversy over *The Valour and the Horror* informed those actors interested in the transmission of collective memory that the production of cultural memory forms about military history, especially popular texts such as docudramas, is a contentious public issue that must consider the actions of other significant stakeholders: 1) leading military historians must be consulted or else they might mobilize their expertise against a project; 2) prominent veterans' associations, who hold the moral authority over the traumatic experience of veterans, need to offer assent; and 3) as emphasized in the conclusion of the Sub-committee's report, Canadian filmmakers, who receive funding from the state, must be accountable for receiving public money. Nonetheless, a problem with Callon's conception of the emergence of a network is his uncomplicated view of how the various stages of translation fit together.

In Callon's study, the actor that facilitates the interaction between nodes of the network, which he labels the obligatory passage point, is the first to identify a problem and set up a framework for its solution. However, as Carr (2005) and Sloniowski (2002) observe, the debate over *The Valour and the Horror* left the many parties involved with a sense of animosity and mistrust of each other. Certainly, this period of problematization cannot be compared to the rational and deliberative setting of an academic conference. In the case of the memorialization of Canadian military history, it took several years before an actor arose to help in the process of connecting the many competing actors. A key event leading to this process of consolidation was the 1995 Quebec referendum. According to Lyle Dick (2009), the anxiety over national unity led to the loosening of federal purse strings to fund cultural forms that promote pan-Canadianism. While he points to federally funded programs such as the new Canadian War Museum and the CBC's *Canada: A People's History*, other scholars (West 2006; Rukszto 2008) examine the Historica's *Heritage Minutes* as examples of nationalistic uses of popular culture. However, there is one group, which emerged during the same period, that has garnered very little scholarly attention yet has become an important actor in the circulation and use of innovative forms for public history: the Dominion Institute.[13]

Unlike the other examples of groups and institutions that are producers and hosts of cultural memory, this actor (Dominion Institute) views itself as a facilitator for cultural production, an advocate for better history education and an intermediary for those engaged in the production, distribution and instruction of cultural memory forms. Moreover, the Institute positions military history as the focal point for its public history campaign. A study of the Dominion Institute as the obligatory passage point for Canada's military-cultural memory network should consider the two stages of translation: 1) how it translated various forms of capital to become a legitimate node with moral authority over the collective memory of military history; 2) how it uses this symbolic capital and other forms of power to engage other actors in the production and circulation of cultural memory forms about military history.

In the span of less than fifteen years, the Dominion Institute has transformed from the ambitious idea of three recent Trinity College graduates into a national institution that garners media attention, receives significant public and private grants, operates several public history projects and consults on issues of education and citizenship. Recently, this institution was credited for helping develop the updated citizenship study guide for new immigrants, *Discover Canada: The Rights and Responsibilities of Citizenship* (2009), which offers a more robust historical section and an emphasis on military history. The question needs to be asked: How were three recently graduated Trinity College students (Eric Penz, Michael Chong and Rudyard Griffiths) able to translate their idea of forming a registered charity to promote public history into a significant national authority over citizenship and history?

Although it is important to note the speed at which these founders, who were then in their mid-twenties, were able to receive funding in the form of a $125,000 grant from the Donner Foundation, it is necessary to consider Bourdieu's view of political economy and study how this financial capital was translated into symbolic power (Grey 2002: R3). It is interesting that the Dominion Institute's first step was not a public history project, but the sponsorship of an Angus Reid Group survey of Canadian youth's knowledge of their nation's history. This survey is repeated annually and released just in time for Canada Day. A study of how this survey has entered public discourse will help assess the emergence of the Dominion Institute as a prominent actor in a military-cultural memory network. Specifically, it is necessary to study how other actors consider this tactic.

First, why is it that a large number of historians from all social and political perspectives cite the findings despite criticizing the simplistic and traditional approach to history education as memorizing key names and dates? Clearly, the Dominion Institute has been able to communicate a message about the state of history education and collective memory that has a struck a chord for many historians. Second, as Carr (2007) notes, the debate over *The Valour and the Horror* witnessed a politics of performance regarding generational tropes and who has the moral authority to transmit memory to future generations. With this in mind, news reports of the surveys are accompanied by Rudyard Griffiths' statements about the various problems youth have associating with history and military history in particular. Therefore, two questions need to be asked: How have spokespersons for the Dominion Institute communicated their authority as actors who understand youth, and how do veterans' groups consider this claim by the Dominion Institute? Finally, echoing the suggestion first offered in the 1975 Symons Report on Canadian studies, the Dominion Institute issued a policy report along with the first survey that called for a more innovative approach to national history education and the acknowledgment of the problem of a provincially run system. The question here is how have cultural industries related to this message that Canada lacks a national education content provider? Along with its polls about politics, history and the military, the Dominion Institute also releases surveys pointing to the lack of cultural literacy.

According to Desmond Morton (2002), "[i]n the Prime Minster's office and among business leaders, the Dominion Institute's message has been received, studied, and filed for action" (55). I propose a study that will assess whether this same message has been received and accepted by veterans, historians and cultural producers. It is only after an analysis of how the Dominion Institute has gained moral authority that it becomes possible to track how this group translates symbolic power to act as a critical intermediary within the military-cultural memory network. There are a number of potential sites and projects to study this second element of translation; however, three stand out as propitious ways to observe how this group works with filmmakers, historians and veterans to archive and canonize military history: Paul Gross's film *Passchendaele* (2008), the Memory Project and the promotion of scholarly work through publications and lecture series.

In terms of canonization, Paul Gross's epic dramatic re-enactment of the infamous First World War battle attempted to represent Canada's military history in a manner that is usually only achieved by Hollywood studios.[14] Although the long term effect of this film is unclear, its opening at the Toronto International Film Festival and release in time for the nintieth anniversary of the end of the First World War brought military history to the fore of public consciousness for at least a short period. Coinciding with the film's release was a poll sponsored by the Dominion Institute that highlighted the public's lack of knowledge about military history, but also the public sentiment that this history was as interesting as Hollywood accounts of U.S. history and just as worthy of the cinema. In addition to helping the film garner media attention, the Dominion Institute produced an educational guide to accompany the film's distribution to Canadian schools and even opened up access to financing this expensive endeavour. As for the challenge of archiving military history, the Memory Project, which began in 2000, records the experiences of veterans and makes this content available online. Veterans Affairs Canada has had a similar program (Heroes Remember); what makes the Memory Project unique is that it alsoworks with veterans' associations to connect and train a network of veterans who visit classrooms throughout the school year. Finally, the Dominion Institute's work with historians and other prominent scholars attempts to both canonize and archive national history, including Canada's military past. Not only did it co-sponsor, with John Ralston Saul, the 2000 launch of the LaFontaine-Baldwin Symposium into Canada's civic culture, it has spearheaded the publication of essays and short-story collections that compile the work of historians, novelists and public intellectuals, in plain language and without scholarly jargon, to discuss important contemporary and historical topics. These examples point to potential sites for studying how the Dominion Institute has found areas of mutual interest to enlist actors within a network and enrol them into a larger project that engages popular media forms for a nationalistic public history. Military history serves as a focal point for this program.

In sum, the memorialization of Canadian military history has come a long way since the contentious period of the public debate over *The Valour and the Horror*. The 1990s were not only a difficult time for the collective memory of war, but also for the status of the military in general. The vast array of cultural forms about the military that have emerged since the end of the 1990s points to a shift in the public representations of the Canadian Forces and the memorialization of its past. To credit this shift to the emergence of the Dominion Institute would be misleading—this period also witnessed the rise of a more active communication strategy by the military and DND. Nonetheless, a careful study of the Dominion Institute's engagement in public history reveals a less contentious and more organized political economic framework that underscores the process of cultural memory production and circulation. What is clear is that this framework is organized around the logic of a network. How far this network reaches remains to be explored.

Notes

1. See Jack Granatstein, *Who Killed Canadian History* (1998).

2. Known as "the Chrétien Plan," the initial plan to redesign the capital region called for the demolition of buildings along Metcalfe Street to make way for a grand promenade leading up to the Parliament buildings. However, this plan was soon revised to focus much of the construction along the area known as Confederation Boulevard. Instead of the linear boulevard envisioned by Prime Minister Chrétien, which would have mimicked the Champs-Élysées and Pennsylvania Avenue, this design connected a number of streets to form a corridor around major government, cultural and diplomatic buildings in both Ottawa and Gatineau.

3. With the motto "Fight Fear. Fight Distress. Fight Chaos. Fight with the Canadian Forces," this new recruitment advertisement campaign showcased aggressive weaponry and borrowed cinematic techniques from American war films, video games and geopolitical thrillers to show the seductive allure of modern warfare. The use of handheld cameras with low-angle shots and desaturated colours are reminiscent of films such as Steven Spielberg's *Saving Private Ryan*. As well, the use of music that emulates heartbeats and transitions between the military and politicians evokes American television political thrillers such as *24* and *NCIS*. Finally, borrowing from popular first-person shooter video games such as *Call of Duty*, some of the commercials include first-person camera shots with large guns positioned in the foreground to position the viewer as a combatant.

4. In a press conference following the London subway bombings in July of 2005, General Hillier set an early tone for the course of his tenure as "Canada's top soldier" with his famous remark that terrorists were "detestable murderers and scumbags." However, his task was not just about informing Canadians about their enemy. In addition, as he stated in this same media briefing, his task was to rebrand the military as a force who unabashedly uses violence to protect Canadians at home and abroad: "We're not the public service of

Canada, we're not just another department. We are the Canadian Forces, and our job is to be able to kill people" (qtd. in Leblanc, *The Globe and Mail* 2005: A1).

5. *The Valour and the Horror* is a three-part television docudrama about Canada's role in the Second World War that was produced by the NFB and Galafilms. Aired by the CBC in January of 1992, the initial response was extremely positive with an estimated 4-4.7 million English-speaking viewers and nearly 400,000 French-speaking viewers watching each episode of the series. Within weeks, however, veterans' associations publicly attacked the series and, after it was rebroadcast in March, it became a public controversy.

6. Although most scholars credit C. Wright Mills's *Power Elite* (1956) for being the first major work to identify the structural links between military leaders, politicians and the corporate elite, Harold Laswell makes a similar claim in his article "The Garrison State" (1941). In this article, he predicts a post-Second World War situation that is marked by the blurring of lines of separation between militarism, democracy and capitalism.

7. Collective memory is also referred to as group, social, national or public memory.

8. Artists have creative reasons; businesspeople have economic interests; veterans and those directly connected to the events of war want to deal with traumatic experiences; the state has an economic interest in promoting tourism and cultural activity as well as supporting its efforts as the principal carrier of the brunt of warfare and organized violence; and the interests of elites are related to those of every other group.

9. Callon uses the French words *problematisation, interessement, enrolement,* and *mobilization*.

10. See Sokal and Bricmont (1998) and Winner (1993).

11. For the moral and ethical problems of docudramas, see Lipkin (1999).

12. The Task Force on Broadcasting Policy found that 98 per cent of viewing time of dramatic television shows by Canadians was spent watching foreign content (Caplan and Sauvageau 1986: 95).

13. In September of 2009, the Dominion Institute merged with Historica to form Historica Dominion Institute.

14. *Passchendaele*, in itself, is an interesting example of the use of networks considering the variety of funding sources that supported the film. To make the $20 million film, Paul Gross and Alliance Films went beyond traditional sources of cultural funding such as Telefilm by assembling a wide range of actors: the Government of Alberta, the Royal Canadian Legion, Canwest Global, Astral Media's Harold Greenberg Fund and The Movie Network. It is also interesting to note that the expensive battle scenes were filmed at CFB Suffield in southern Alberta and used Canadian Forces personnel as extras.

Appendix A

A Timeline of Military Texts in Canadian Culture Since 1992

1992

- The Canadian branch of the International Institute for Peace through Tourism convinced Canada 125 and the National Capital Commission (NCC) to organize the planting of peace parks across four hundred cities and towns.

- The unveiling of the National Peacekeeping Monument in Ottawa across from the National Gallery of Canada.

- The CBC aired the controversial three-part television series *The Valour and the Horror*, which raised moral questions regarding Canada's participation in the Second World War.

1995

- The live broadcast of the fiftieth anniversary ceremony marking the end of the Second World War in which CBC newscaster Peter Mansbridge remarked: "there is no shortage of Canadian history. Our history is NOT dull. But we are dull-witted when it comes to learning about it" (qtd. in Miller 1997: 9).

1997

- CBC aired the two-hour movie *Peacekeepers* about the attempt by a Canadian platoon to solve a web of disputes taking place in a Croatian village.

1998

- The Standing Committee on National Defence and Veterans Affairs released its report on the quality of life within the Canadian Forces, which called on the Department of National Defence (DND) to better communicate the contributions of Canadian soldiers to the public.

- The Diefenbunker Museum was opened to the public to exhibit this former nuclear fallout shelter and to serve as Canada's Cold War Museum.

- The CBC aired two documentaries, *Dying to Tell the Story* and *The Unseen Scars*, which focused on the trauma experienced by soldiers and civilians who worked on UN missions.

2000

- The Tomb of the Unknown Soldier was moved from France to the newly renovated steps of the National War Memorial in Ottawa.

2001

- The National Aboriginal Veterans Monument was installed at the western entrance to Confederation Park in Ottawa.

- The completion of the $30 million restoration of the Vimy Ridge monument in France.

- The Dominion Institute launched the Memory Project to record the experiences of war veterans and share these stories with Canadian youth.

- The establishment of the National Military Cemetery at Ottawa's Beachwood Cemetery.
- The Canadian Forces launched a new recruiting campaign, entitled "Strong. Proud. Today's Canadian Forces," which promoted the military as a place for youth to gain work experience.
- The Bank of Canada issued its new series of bank notes that included a $10 bill depicting a female peacemaker and a Remembrance Day ceremony.

2003

- The Korean War Monument was erected beside the MacKenzie King Brudge on the northern side of Confederation Park in Ottawa.
- The Juno Beach Centre was unveiled in Normandy, France to provide an interpretive history of the famous Canadian assault.

2005

- The opening of the new $140 million building at the Lebreton Flats in Ottawa to house the Canadian War Museum.
- General Rick Hillier was appointed Chief of the Defence Staff and began a public campaign to communicate through the media in order to pressure politicians to provide more funding for the military and advocate for Canada to be more aggressive in the global fight against terrorism.

2006

- Conceived by Hamilton Southam, The Valiants Memorial, which includes a number of statues of historical military heroes, was installed beside the National War Memorial.
- The reorganization and integration of the Military Museums in Calgary.
- The CBC launched the radio drama *Afghanada*, which follows a platoon of Canadian soldiers, 3-1 Bravo section, operating in Kandahar Province and led by a female officer, Sergeant Pat Kinsella.
- Canadian Forces introduced a new recruiting advertising campaign, entitled "Fight Fear. Fight Distress. Fight Chaos. Fight with the Canadian Forces," which showcased aggressive weaponry and

borrowed cinematic techniques from American war films and geopolitical thrillers.

2007

- The CBC aired Brian McKenna's *The Great War* starring Justin Trudeau and a cast of descendants from Second World War soldiers.
- Discovery Channel Canada aired the reality television show *Jetstream*, about Canadian Air Force pilots learning to fly CF-18 Hornets.
- Ontario's Ministry of Transportation renamed the stretch of Highway 401 (from Canadian Forces Base Trenton to the Centre of Forensic Science in Toronto) "Highway of Heroes" in response to a grassroots online petition campaign.

2008

- The release of Paul Gross's $20 million feature film *Passchendaele*, which drew funding and support from a wide range of private and government sources (the Government of Alberta, Telefilm, Alliance Films, the Dominion Institute, Canwest Global, Astral Media's Harold Greenberg Fund and The Movie Network).
- Bill C-287 was unanimously passed by Parliament to mark August 9 as National Peacekeepers' Day.

2009

- The unveiling of the Chinatown Memorial Monument in Vancouver to honour the military contribution of Chinese Canadians.
- The completion of the Battle of Hong Kong Monument located along Sussex Drive in Ottawa.
- Discovery Channel Canada aired the reality television show *Combat School* which follows a group of Canadian Forces soldiers from basic training to combat missions in Afghanistan.
- Citizenship, Immigration and Multiculturalism Minister Jason Kenney introduced the new study guide for Canadian citizenship, *Discover Canada: The Rights and Responsibilities of Citizenship*, which put an increased emphasis on military history.

2010

- The NCC announced the construction of the Canadian Navy Monument to celebrate the Navy's 100th anniversary.

References

Andersen, Robin. 2006. *A Century of Media, A Century of War*. New York: Peter Lange.

Appadurai, Arjun. 1981. The Past as a Scarce Resource. *Man* 16(2): 201-19.

Assmann, Aleida. 2008. Canon and Archive. In *Cultural Memory Studies: An International and Interdisciplinary Handbook*, edited by Astrid Erll and Ansgar Nunning, 97-107. New York: Walter de Gruyter.

Assmann, Jan. 1992. *Das kulturelle Gedächtnis*. Munich: C. H. Beck.

Aufderheide, Patricia. 1981. Good Soldiers. In *Seeing Through Movies*, edited by Mark Miller, 81-111. New York: Pantheon.

Bauman, Zygmunt. 1982. *Memories of Class: The Pre-history and After-life of Class*. London: Routledge and Kegan Paul.

Bercuson, David and S. F. Wise. 1994. Introduction. In *The Valour and the Horror Revisited*, edited by David Bercuson and S. F. Wise, 3-12. Montreal: McGill-Queen's University Press.

Billig, M. 1995. *Banal Nationalism*. London: Sage.

Blanchfield, Mike. 2007. Top General Calls Liberal Rule "Decade of Darkness." *Ottawa Citizen*, 17 February, A1.

Bourdieu, Pierre. 1987. What Makes a Social Class? On the Theoretical and Practical Existence of Groups. *Berkeley Journal of Sociology* 32:1-18.

Burns, Ken, dir. 1990. *The Civil War* (film). PBS, prod.

Callon, Michel. 1986. Some Elements of a Sociology of Translation: Domestication of the Scallops and the Fishermen of St. Brieuc Bay. In *Power, Action and Belief: A New Sociology of Knowledge?*, edited by John Law, 196-223. London: Routledge.

Campion-Smith, Bruce and Phinjo Gombu. Looking for a Few Good Soldiers, *Toronto Star*, 25 August, A6.

Caplan, Gerald and Florian Sauvageau. 1986. Report of the Task Force on Broadcasting Policy. Ottawa: Supply and Services Canada.

Carr, Graham. 2005. Rules of Engagement: Public History and the Drama of Legitimation. *The Canadian Historical Review* 86(2): 317-54.

———. 2007. War, History, and the Education of (Canadian) Memory. In *Memory, History, Nation: Contested Pasts*, edited by Katherine Hodgkin and Susannah Radstone, 57-78. New Brunswick, NJ: Routledge.

Cook, Tim. 2006. *Clio's Warriors: Canadian Historians and the Writing of the World Wars*. Vancouver: UBC Press.

Coser, Lewis, ed. 1992. Introduction: Maurcie Halbwachs, 1877-1945. *On Collective Memory*, 1-36. Chicago: Chicago University Press.

Dick, Lyle. 2009. Public History in Canada: An Introduction. *The Public Historian* 31(1): 7-14.

Gough, Paul. 2002. "Invicta Pax'"Monuments, Memorials and Peace: An Analysis of the Canadian Peacekeeping Monument, Ottawa. *International Journal of Heritage Studies* 8 (3): 201-23.

Granatstein, Jack. 1998. *Who Killed Canadian History?* Toronto: Harper Collins.

Grey, Charlotte. 2002. And the Rest Is History. *The Globe and Mail*, 23 April, R3.

Jefferess, David. 1999. Responsibility, Nostalgia, and the Mythology of Canada as a Peacekeeper. *University of Toronto Quarterly* 78(2): 709-27.

Kimmerling, Baruch. 2001. *The Invention and Decline of Israeliness: State, Society, and the Military*. Berkeley, CA: University of California Press.

Lasswell, Harold. 1941. The Garrison State. *The American Journal of Sociology* 46(4): 455-68.

Latour, Bruno. 1986. The Powers of Association. In *Power, Action and Belief: A New Sociology of Knowledge?*, edited by John Law, 264-80. London: Routledge and Kegan Paul.

———. 2005. *Reassembling the Social: An Introduction to Actor-Network-Theory*. Oxford: Oxford University Press.

Leblanc, Daniel. 2005. JTF2 to Hunt al-Qaeda. *The Globe and Mail*, 15 July, A1.

Lenoir, Timothy and Henry Lowood. 2003. Theaters of War: The Military-Entertainment Complex. In *Collection, Laboratory, Theater*, edited by Jan Lazardzig, Helmar Schramm, Ludger Schwarte, 426-56. Berlin: Walter de Gruyter.

Lipkin, Steve. 1999. Defining Docudrama: *In the Name of the Father, Schindler's List*, and *JFK*. In *Why Docudrama? Fact-Fiction on Film and TV*, edited by Alan Rosenthal, 370-83. Carbondale, IL: Southern Illinois University Press.

Marvin, Carolyn and David Ingle. 1996. Blood Sacrifice and Nation: Revisiting Civil Religion. *Journal of the American Academy of Religion* 64(4): 767-80.

MacKenzie, Lewis. 2006. Foreword. In *The Canadian Way of War: Serving the National Interest*, edited by Bernard Horn, 7-9. Toronto: Dundurn Press.

McKenna, Brian and Terence McKenna, dirs. 1992. *The Valour and the Horror* (film). Toronto: CBC, National Film Board of Canada (NFB) and Galafilm Inc., prods.

McKenna, Brian and Terence McKenna. 1994. Response to the CBC Ombudsman Report. In *The Valour and the Horror Revisited*, edited by David Bercuson and S. F. Wise, 73-88. Montreal: McGill-Queen's University Press.

McKenna, Brian. 1992. Horrors of Unveiling Some Truths about Canada's War Role. *Ottawa Citizen*, 11 November, A11.

Miller, J. R. 1997. The Invisible Historian. *Journal of the Canadian Historical Association* 8(1): 3-18.

Mills, Charles Wright. 1956. *The Power Elite*. New York: Oxford University Press.

Morton, Desmond. 2002. Teaching and Learning History in Canada. In *Knowing, Teaching, and Learning History: National and International Perspectives*, edited by Peter Stearns, Peter Seixas and Sam Wineburg, 51-62. New York: NYU Press.

Nora, Pierre. 1984. *Les Lieux de Mémoire: Volume 1*. Paris: Gallimard.

Ottawa Citizen. 1992. Saluting the Peacekeepers, *Ottawa Citizen*, 9 October, B1.

Paget, Derek. 1998. *No Other Way To Tell It: Dramadoc/Docudrama on Television*. Manchester: Manchester University Press.

Robin, Ron. 2001. *The Making of the Cold War Enemy: Culture and Politics in the Military-Intellectual Complex*. Princeton: Princeton University Press.

Rukszto, Katarzyna. 2008. History as Edutainment: *Heritage Minutes* and the Uses of Educational Television. In *Programming Reality: Perspectives on English-Canadian Television*, edited by Zoë Druick and Aspa Kotsopoulos, 171-86. Waterloo, ON: Wilfrid Laurier University Press.

Schudson, Michael. 1992. *Watergate in American Memory: Why We Remember, Forget, and Reconstruct the Past.* New York: Basic Books.

SCONDVA. 1998. *Moving Forward: A Strategic Plan for Quality of Life Improvements in the Canadian Forces.* Ottawa: Department of National Defence and Veterans Affairs.

Sloniowski, Jeannette. 2002. Popularizing History: *The Valour and the Horror*. In *Slippery Pastimes: Reading the Popular in Canadian Culture*, edited by Jon Nicks and Jeannette Sloniowski, 159-74. Waterloo, ON: Wilfrid Laurier University Press.

Sokal, Alan and Jean Bricmont. 1998. *Fashionable Nonsense: Postmodern Intellectuals' Abuse of Science.* New York: Picador.

Stacey, Charles Perry. 1955. *Six Years of War: The Army in Canada, Britain, and the Pacific.* Ottawa: Queen's Printer.

Sturken, Marita. 1997. *Tangled Memories; The Vietnam War, the AIDS Epidemic, and the Politics of Remembering.* Berkeley, CA: University of California Press.

Sub-committee on Veterans Affairs. 1993. *The Valour and the Horror: Report of the Standing Senate Committee on Social Affairs, Science and Technology.* Ottawa: The Senate of Canada.

War Amps. 1993. Chadderton Feels Disclaimer Unhelpful. *War Amps*, 26 January.

Ward, John. 1999. Poll Suggests High Approval for Canadian Forces, *Canadian Press*, 7 December.

West, Emily. 2006. Collective Memory on the Airwaves: The Negotiation of Unity and Diversity in Troubled Canadian Nationalism. In *Canadian Cultural Poesis: Essays on Canadian Culture*, edited by Gary Sherbert, Annie Gérin and Sheila Perry, 67-83. Waterloo, ON: Wilfrid Laurier University Press.

Winner, Langdon. 1993. Upon Opening the Black Box and Finding It Empty: Social Constructivism and the Philosophy of Technology. *Science, Technology, and Human Values* 18(3): 362-78.

Winter, James and Emmanuel Sivan, eds. 1999. Setting the Framework. In *War and Remembrance in the Twentieth Century*, 6-39. Cambridge: Cambridge University Press.

Carole R. McKenna

Canadian and American Cultures of Militarism: Coping Mechanisms in a Military-Industrial-Service-Complex

ABSTRACT

This paper compares and contrasts the Canadian and American culture of militarism working with the Thomas theorem of belief and consequence. Thomas argued that a belief does not have to be real, but consequences result from a perception of what is real. In a political climate characterized by a culture of high-level military and service influence, the perception of what is real is generated and conveyed to specific populations. In this paper, the population is predominantly American and Canadian military wives. Socialization, networking, specific information and organizational dominance strengthen a culture for military families who are involved in war deployment. The culture draws strength from a belief system that promotes certain realities. As the military-industrial-service-complex becomes more pervasive in the lives of Canadians and Americans, their coping mechanisms develop to accommodate the cultural norm. The leading force in the effort to remove autonomy from soldiers and wives and keep them within a pseudo-reality becomes evident from the coping mechanisms they develop.

RÉSUMÉ

La culture militariste canadienne et américaine : mécanismes d'adaptation dans un complexe militaire, industriel et de services

Cet article compare et oppose la culture militaire canadienne et américaine en se basant sur le théorème de Thomas de la croyance et des conséquences. Thomas avançait qu'une croyance n'a pas besoin d'être réelle, mais que les conséquences résultent d'une perception de ce qui est réel. Dans un climat politique caractérisé par une culture de haut niveau militaire et d'influence des services, la perception de ce qui est réel est générée et véhiculée à l'intention de populations spécifiques. Dans cet article, la population est majoritairement composée de veuves de militaires américains et canadiens. La socialisation, les réseaux, l'information spécifique et la prédominance de l'organisationnel renforcent une culture particulière des familles des militaires impliquées dans le déploiement de la guerre. Cette culture tire sa force d'un système de croyances qui valorise certaines réalités. Au moment où le complexe militaire, industriel et de services imprègne davantage les vies des Canadiens et des Américains, ses mécanismes d'adaptation se développent pour épouser la norme culturelle. La force qui guide cet effort d'enlever leur autonomie aux soldats et à leurs épouses et de les maintenir dans une pseudo-réalité apparaît clairement dans les mécanismes d'adaptation qu'ils développent.

¤

I decided to explore the culture of militarism, military wives and soldiers in 1996, well before the September 11, 2001, World Trade Center attacks and the subsequent 2003 Iraq invasion. I never thought, even once, that my journey and the War on Terror would continue into 2010 without an end in sight—or that my children would be involved. At different times during the last decade, three of my sons and my daughter-in-law all served in the U.S. Army. Together, since 2003, they have served six tours in Iraq.

My oldest son just received his most recent orders for another deployment; this time to Afghanistan. It will be his third tour. "Tour" is the official description. This paper touches on the great care that must be taken when creating descriptions that militarize people. The words must deflect attention away from the deaths and suffering, loneliness and distance while they create a vision of heroes, angels, enemies, righteousness, lesser pain and approved violence. Propaganda tools create and keep a culture where coping mechanisms are strategically constructed and tactically enforced. Soldiers and wives are taught to distance themselves from each other before war deployment, which makes the distance real.

The culture of militarism is complex. This paper is not intended to create a reductive set of assumptions about war, volunteerism, capitalism, god or country, but rather to offer some insight into the construction of a rich culture within military communities that help the soldiers and wives survive a world quite different from civilian life. The organization of this paper explains how the women survive the culture of militarism and war and touches only briefly on resistance. This does not mean that the women do not resist or that they follow the whims of militarization. Some may see anti-anxiety or anti-depressants as a form of resistance. Others may perceive religious beliefs and consumerism as means of resistance. This paper suggests that comparing and contrasting the resistance practised by military wives and coping mechanisms they use is negligible and, while resistance may seem hopeless, coping mechanisms seem to make their lives sustainable, at least for some.

I arranged this paper predominately with findings from American soldiers and wives and afterward incorporated parallels with the military-industrial-service-complex and the Canadian Forces. For instance, American military families have access to their own shopping facilities provided to members only—so do the families in the Canadian Forces. The websites for each are strikingly similar and share a service culture of buying, pampering and occupying time. Currently, Canadians do not have as many citizens committed to the wars in Iraq and Afghanistan; nevertheless, Americans and Canadians feel the consequences of war in similar ways that are not necessarily given significance with numbers.

Military wives create various coping mechanisms to adjust to war deployment. War deployments, stop loss policies,[1] field training, schools and extensions mean that the army wives left back home will be "single moms" most of the time. American wives refer to themselves as single moms, as do some of their family, neighbours and friends. It is another reminder of the lengthy, frequent deployments and the ways they cope with the war. They also refer to themselves as "wives," hence the use in this paper. The word "spouse" is the official word but with husband-spouses being negligible in the army, soldiers' wives becomes a more accurate qualifier. This project examines the culture of militarism and specifically how soldiers and wives are socialized to cope with war deployment.

Currently, a very small number of American citizens carry the full weight of military duty and war on their shoulders (Musheno and Ross 2008). The coping mechanisms that the military institution offer these citizens often reflect the impact of war violence and separation, but do little or nothing to end the cause of the problems. Since war is not a natural activity, the people engaged in the violence must be trained to kill people who are designated as their enemies and to justify the brutality (Zinn 2007). It is a culture of war. Soldiers and wives are socialized to live a military life and then they are expected to use the coping mechanisms that are supposed to ease their adjustment to war violence, frequent separations and disparate lifestyles. Their problems are socially constructed, as are the culture and coping mechanisms they are offered to deal with them.

These socially created entities militarize and blur the distinction between the military and civilian life in the everyday lives of people (Enloe 2000, 2007). Symbols, discourse and rhetoric define what enemies are and who the enemies are, and they subsequently demonstrate the need for war and who will fight and kill those enemies (Altheide 2002). In a concerted effort, the decision makers, speechwriters and the president must convince the citizenry that their decision to wage war, with all its consequences, is legitimate (Ivie 2003). People in the upper echelons declare war, but the military, paramilitary and mercenaries carry out the carnage. The soldiers are legally bound to serve God and country and have few choices after they sign their contracts. The wives are expected to support their soldiers and care for their families in a culture of militarism. The military-industrial-service-complex provides the coping mechanisms that are supposed to help them manage their anxious feelings created by war and frequent separation. The culture of militarism can be viewed from many lenses. Soldiers and wives are not one-dimensional, but after interviewing, observing and participating with a group of American army wives, I was able to categorize three themes that may help to explain the coping mechanisms they use and how they come to use them. The coping mechanisms are categorized as follows:

> "Positive Asymmetry" (Cerulo 2006) relates to a culture of militarization and a militarized identity (Enloe 2000).
>
> "Militarization of Fun and Busy Lives" illustrates a culture of strategic fun and necessarily busy lives.
>
> "Wives Teaching Wives" demonstrates a culture where the interaction and bonding between the wives, private contractors, the military community and religious affiliations work together.

Positive Asymmetry

Positive asymmetry is a theory that explains how skewed versions of excellence dominate American culture (Cerulo 2006). The phenomenon results from categories of ideas and cultural knowledge that are stored and necessarily directs social action and shapes social structure accordingly. The cultural goal is that positive viewpoints and behaviours will stabilize and solidify groups within the community. In the military community, the dominant frame of positive ideas derives from the military-industrial-service-complex of private industries who work in unison with the government and with military wives. Within military culture, soldiers and wives are socialized to understand their everyday lives within supposedly well-working, functional dominant social arrangements.

In the military community, being "positive" is a core strategy. War injustice must be justified with selected facts, partial facts, belief, deception, illusion, counselling, fun, support and, if necessary, medication. A healthy, functioning army must have a positive attitude toward their mission. Symbolic language such as being positive and having fun defines what is "real" to the wives. Often, "real" is defined by the (American) Family Readiness Groups (FRG), (Canadian) Military Family Resource Centers (2010 a), numerous private contractors and word-of-mouth. The positive reality is significant because the military and private contractors promote how, when and where the reality occurs. How the public receives information and what the public believes determine how human agents construct the definition of the situation (Thomas 1971). A positive attitude is often the only acceptable attitude that wives let others see, regardless of the crisis.

The media play an enormous role in conveying information and forming opinions. They often use rhetoric and symbols that are difficult to understand or explain while they reroute and reconstruct political accounts that are more palatable. For instance, some examples of denial and ambiguous accountability surface in documents that validated U.S. torture of detainees during the early part of the Iraq War, again in 2007 and in subsequent reports. The International Committee of the Red Cross (ICRC) reported, however, that detainees held in Iraq, Afghanistan and at secret CIA prisons were subjected to humiliation, abuse, forced nudity, stress positions and waterboarding (Leopold 2009).

Further research suggests that Canada has aided the United States with regard to detainees in Guantanamo and Abu Ghraib and that Canadian/American issues on torture mirror each other (McKenna and Salm 2006). A Canada Amnesty International plea for humane treatment in war prisons suggests that torture parallels Canadian affiliates in the United States chapters, but the Canadian government is silent (Amnesty International 2010). In 2007, however, U.S. President George W. Bush declared that "...this government does not torture people" (TPM 2009). As evidence surfaced to support the claim that the U.S. does indeed torture, the cable news downplayed the legal implications of detainee interrogation techniques and torture. In 2009, when denials and concealment were not enough to end public outrage, former Vice President Dick Cheney declared that torture, "paid off" and he had, "[n]o regrets" because it was the "right thing to do" (FTN 2009).

In public relations, the specialists, communications and media experts manipulate the public to favour the goals and policies of the organizations they represent (U.S. Dept. of Labor 2006) and, frequently, political news about policy and war is replaced by sex scandals or hype. The presentation and understanding of information that is conveyed to the general public, soldiers and military wives form their coping mechanisms and play a huge part in positive asymmetry. As the following excerpt from one army wife suggests, replacing factual news with entertainment is not conducive to informed decision making:

> I think recently the story of Anna Nicole Smith ... [FOX News] spent I don't know how many hours on it. Sometimes I just wonder. I would rather see my husband. I'd rather see them following my husband around as many hours as they followed that story. In his normal, everyday, not so exciting life to show people what it's like, not even a patrolling soldier just an average soldier who stays on the post supporting them and what they do. I don't think people as a whole in this country, I don't think they have a clue [about] the men and women in the military, who they are, how they live. (McKenna 2009)

Keeping within positive asymmetry, FOX News (2007) boasts of "fair and balanced" reporting, but instead, the correspondents render an "us (good)" versus "them (bad)" construction of war political rhetoric. The construction of political rhetoric develops within a strategy that includes, but is not limited to, discourse, personality, drama, talent and facade (Edelman 1988). For instance, while the media constructed Saddam Hussein and Iraq as terrorists, or "them (bad)," President Bush and the United States were portrayed as victims of the 9/11 attacks, or "us (good)." In order to promote policies, ideas, doctrines and causes skewed to favour "us," the rhetoric is constructed and conveyed in complex symbolic language, which is often accompanied by unclear behaviours and activities (McKenna 2007).

This work-in-progress documents interviews with American army wives. The Canadian interviews are forthcoming. Drawing from interviews with army wives, several said that FOX is the only news they watch on television, if they watch the news at all. The wives believe that FOX is the only news station that conveys accurate and positive information about their husbands in Iraq and Afghanistan and about war overall. For the most part, some wives trust FOX and the military news they learn at the FRG meetings. One wife, for example, stated that:

> Compared to CNN [FOX] seemed to be, um, less bias. Um, and *FOX and Friends* is actually a show in the morning when there's three people on the panel and they bring you the news and then they have a field reporter.... And they don't always agree and I like that because I'm of the understanding that you can't have an opinion on something unless you hear both sides of it, and then you can make your own choice. And so I enjoy that because it's not one person telling me how I'm supposed to perceive something. (McKenna 2009)

FOX News is the preferred media among the wives, but they prefer to receive war news from the military community. Formal and informal networking of communication among military families, chain of command, community and privatized resources culminate in a command-sponsored organization, the Family Readiness Group (FRG). Two mission goals of the FRG are to provide "accurate" information to the wives and to be the supporting link between the command and its members. Additionally, it advocates privatized and community resources and aids families in problem solving "at the lowest level."[2] The lowest level is the military wife who is expected to maintain a positive attitude about war violence and deployment.

Some of the FRG employees come from private companies, but most are wives who volunteer. Canadians parallel American volunteerism—so much so that the Canadian Forces developed a "Volunteer" handbook that reveals a purpose and philosophy accompanied by thirteen full "Sections" on just about everything one needs to know about volunteering (National Defence and the Canadian Forces 2010). Volunteering wives have been helping each other and soldiers throughout army history (Alt and Stone 1991). Two decades ago, the free and extensive labour was recognized as exploitative and, in 1988, a directive from the U.S. Department of Defense made involuntary volunteering illegal (Enloe 2000). Obscured pressure on officers' wives came from the notion that they would damage their husbands' evaluations if they did not volunteer, and so it continues.

At this point, my research on Canadian mission information is limited to several military support websites and on a massive online group called the Canadian Forces Personnel and Family Support Service (MFSP). It can be downloaded in French and English and contains information for soldiers and their families. One category boasts: "Peace of mind is only a phone call away" (MFSP 2010). Comparable to the American FRG support for military families, the MFSP information and counselling choices range from face-to-face dialogue to collect-calls to fax and toll-free numbers. The website suggests that there is no shortage of support for Canadian military families, including the dining environment at the messes:

> Steeped in a rich military heritage and tradition, messes have been used by the Canadian Forces (CF) throughout Canada's history to foster morale and promote military values including camaraderie and unit cohesiveness. Messes give members a strong sense of commitment to the ideas, objectives and the basic responsibility expected of them within the CF and set the standard for military service within Canada. (CFPFSA 2010)

Military hierarchical arrangements and positive asymmetry influence how the American FRG functions and the soldiers' ranks determine which wife works in what function. Volunteer key-callers use a telephone-tree to convey battalion news. In stride with positive asymmetry, the FRG manual calls the telephone-tree the "chain-of-concern." Key-callers recite a script when an incident occurs or they relay specific information that they receive from the FRG leader.[3] The communication loop is complete when the key-caller accounts her action back to the FRG leader. It is a formal procedure, but other than incidents in which they relay information that soldiers have suffered injuries or death, the phone calls are usually friendly and light. The script for incidents that do not require a briefing transpires in the following format:

> Hi, this is [name] from [unit]. There is a report of an incident. This [date and time] in Baghdad a [Soldier's Company/Troop/Battery; ex. Alpha Company or Charlie Troop] was injured. His injuries were non-life threatening. The family has already been notified by the soldier of his condition. I am calling to keep you updated on the current situation within our Company and/or Battalion. If you have any questions or concerns please call the Rear Detachment Command.

Standard Casualty Query Responses follows:

1. If contacted regarding a report of casualties and have no knowledge of any incident use the following statement:

> I do not know; I have not received any report of an incident. Notifications go directly to the next of kin.

2. If contacted regarding a report of casualties and have knowledge of an incident but official notifications have not been completed, use the following statement:

> There was a report of an incident; I do not know any of the details. The Rear Detachment is gathering the facts. Notifications go directly to the next of kin.

3. If contacted regarding a report of casualties and have knowledge of an incident and official notifications have been completed, use the following statement:

> On [date] [number of Soldiers] Soldiers from [unit] were WIA/KIA when [brief description of incident]. Official notification to family members is complete. (McKenna 2009)

As the FRG script suggests, dialogue, characters, theatre, art and appearance direct the feelings of the wives and develop their militarized identity. This particular symbolic framework promotes or demotes soldier/wife war narratives, soldier/wife war policies, soldier/wife war ideas, soldier/wife war doctrines and explanations for soldier/wife war behaviour. The FRG presentations culminate into what is right and good about war theatrics and what is happening in the Iraqi and Afghan theaters that is bad; or more in tune with military wives' discourse-interchange of positive and negative. The FRG is the hub of war information and the coordinators and actors want the wives to trust them. Trust is important at the FRG meetings and deep into their everyday lives, where they learn from each other and the military community. They learn who to trust and how to make it as an army wife. They learn that a "positive" attitude will help them make it as an army wife. All the actors must be disciplined and positive. They must feel the emotions and then turn lemons into lemonade; turn a frown upside down; look for the silver lining; be positive; not be "so" negative. The culture of militarism secures the positive attitudes that keep them up to the standards of the military community while it curbs their anxiety and depression, and in some cases distances them from anti-anxiety medication.

> And I just get tired of all the negativity because I know so much there's going on that's amazing. And I know that there's Iraqi lives that are forever changed because we're there and because we're doing cool things and I know that there's Iraqi guys who just will hug our soldiers and cry with them and say, "Thank you for all you're doing. You're blessing us and you're doing so much for us." And ya know you never hear that and I just get, oh, it just makes me mad. (McKenna 2009)

The wives mentally distance themselves from negativism by treating it as an obscure concept. Their thoughts and memories gravitate toward an asymmetrical quality continuum where they can remain positive (Cerulo 2006: 9). Unlike the quality continuum where goodness prevails, some wives must live in denial. For this reason, many of the wives do not watch the news, but they understand a terrorist threat and that the United States had to do something:

> I don't watch the news and I'm not very political and I don't know every aspect of what's going on but the basic [idea] is that somebody came into our country, terrorists came in and they took ya know people's lives and our leader decided that that wasn't ok. That we had to fight back.... (McKenna 2009)

Even though anti-anxiety medication is always available, many wives cope through positive asymmetry, mind block or denial. These coping mechanisms keep the following wife away from drugs:

> My dealing with it is denial (chuckles) I'm just, ya know, if I don't think about it, it's not gonna happen. There [are] other ladies who [say] they can't stop thinking about it and they need to get on some type of medication just so they can sleep at night. (McKenna 2009)

Another wife tries not to think about the war, but rather thinks about the future when her husband will be home:

> You always know it could happen, but you try not to think about it because when your husband's home, your life is just wonderful and you try not to face the reality that it could happen. Although, you know it could always happen again. (McKenna 2009)

The fear of violence and death may be temporarily suppressed or avoided, but the reality is always around them and they need to be in touch with each other. It is not unusual for some of the wives to wait all night for their husbands to come online so they can keep connected:

> Well, in the beginning of the deployment, the baby was three months old and [son] was in school so pretty much, it was real hard at first. I just wanted to sleep all the time. I would stay up all night waiting for him to get online or call. And then put my son on the bus and then sleep until the kids woke up and then do whatever I do during the day. Clean, check the computer all the time cause I never wanted to miss him getting on. And then I started working so I try to keep busy. Keeping busy makes the days go by faster. (McKenna 2009)

Teaching people what is necessary to have fun would depend on the marketing strategies and tools that are required to tactically implement specific fun or ways to keep busy while maintaining positive attitudes. Positive attitudes, fun and work may evolve into an environment of fragile cheerfulness, but the economy thrives. Provisional happiness and the tools for having fun develop in the military-industrial-service-complex where profiteering and capitalism seem normal to American and Canadian wives and soldiers.

Wives Teaching Wives

Canadian and American wives learn the culture of militarism from each other and the social institution that envelops them. The war has an enormous influence on their lives, and yet the wives and soldiers have almost no control over it or the information they receive. Canadian wives who seek support from the CFPSA are invited to speaker and discourse sessions and tours that explain some aspects of war:

> "There's a lot more that you're getting here than what we can put into a binder," training leader Major Suzanne Bailey said to the group. "We learn so much. Not just from the presenters but from everyone in the room."

> For Brenda Davidson, a staff member at the Edmonton MFRC, the learning didn't stop when the training sessions ended. A trip to the Canadian War Museum on the group's Sunday off was an especially eye-opening experience for her.

> "We walked around and told stories—the guys who'd been to Afghanistan, the people who'd stayed home," she said. "It really helped us understand what each other had been through." (CFPSA 2010a)

Information control directs their decisions and without it, they are unable to make informed decisions, yet many American wives think that silence is synonymous with support:

> ...if you don't believe in the war that's fine. That's your belief and you have the right to do it but just don't let people know about ... (exhales deeply) because your husband's over there and you need to support him. That's the job of the military wife is to support your husband and his career. Um, and that'd be like if your talking against it and going out protesting against it, you're not supporting him at all. Just wait 'til they come home and then do what ever you want (chuckles). I think it would be hard come to think about it. I mean, not every body's gonna, I mean I don't agree with everything about the war. I think fifteen months is a long time. I don't know if the surge was the greatest idea but I can't control this. [Husband] can't control them. We just deal with it. (McKenna 2009)

Less informed decisions result in discourse and beliefs that war is part of a divine, political, or corporate plan that requires no explanation or understanding. They frequently define their situation in terms of employment and believe that the soldiers are doing the jobs they were trained to do. Their coping mechanisms reflect some resistance to war violence and deployments, but mostly demonstrate positive asymmetry and denial. Coping with the war violence in that frame brings about a diminished quality of human rights to enemies. The enemies are socially constructed entities that they, "just deal with...." Many wives and soldiers do not allow themselves to question how, why or when a human being is labelled an "enemy," and propaganda direct their coping mechanisms. Militarized coping mechanisms are strategically incorporated into their lives and tactically implemented within the military-industrial-service-complex. The FRG is very important in the militarizing process.

The FRG plays an expansive role in preparing, supporting and assisting units and families of an expeditionary army, and volunteering military wives are the primary workers who maintain and manage the FRGs (McKenna 2009). In order to comprehend the extent to which intertwining ambitions between the wives and the institution dominate, one must understand their socialization process and the FRG. The FRG, among other responsibilities, is expected to convey accurate information and build soldier/family cohesion and morale while preparing them for war separation and reunion. This is not an easy task given the nature of war violence.

Wives and soldiers believe that the army solves their money problems and, because they are part of the membership, there is a feeling that they are all in it together. Wives help other wives because they feel it is their responsibility and because they empathize and care:

> I don't think I cried when he left because I had gotten it out earlier and also I was an FRG leader at the time and I felt like I needed to be there and I needed to be strong for the other wives because there were lots of them who were having a hard time. (McKenna 2009)

The camaraderie between the wives leads to enormous time in volunteer work and the FRG leaders encourage the wives to work together, help each other and volunteer their time as the following excerpt suggests:

> How do you get the most valuable asset in a military community? How do you make a military community a wonderful place to live? Ask a military spouse to volunteer ... that's how! There are so many valuable organizations on a military installation that rely in part, or totality, on volunteers. All of these organizations have one thing in common—to improve the quality of life for Soldiers and their families. (Army Spouse Battle Book 2008: 8)

In the military and part of the "American experience," it is normal that soldiers earn wages and their wives work for free. Militarization means that volunteerism is down to a science:

(American) Philosophy on Volunteerism
Volunteerism and the Army

Volunteering is a defining part of the American experience. From the Minutemen at Lexington to today's all volunteer force, the Army relies on the fundamental connection between volunteerism and citizenship. The strength of the Army lies in its Soldiers, and the strength of Army communities lies in the talents and contributions of its volunteers. Volunteerism stabilizes our Army communities by contributing to community cohesion, increasing self-reliance, and enhancing the well-being of our Soldiers and their families. The Army relies on volunteers to contribute to the well-being of Soldiers, families, and civilians.

- recruiting volunteers
- retaining happy volunteers in your group
- letting them know they are appreciated
- awards. (Army Spouses Battle Book 2008)

(Canadian) Purpose of Volunteerism
Defence Department and Volunteering in Schools Overseas

1.1 Purpose
1.1.1 Welcome to the growing ranks of school volunteers. Through our school leaders, we hope to encourage increased participation and partnership in our local school community. For the children to reach their full educational, physical, emotional and social potential requires the commitment and involvement of all the members of the community: students, teachers, parents, guardians, community organizations and school administrators.

1.1.2 We recognize the importance of community involvement and volunteerism and many staff members contribute endless hours of volunteer time. The purpose of volunteers is not to replace the work of the teacher, but rather to assist the administration and staff in improving the quality of the school environment.

1.1.3 Volunteers do make a difference! Volunteer participation will be an opportunity for you to share with others in the enrichment of education for our students. You will discover the rewards of helping students achieve their personal best and at the same time gain useful experience yourself. We hope as well that the experience of volunteering in our schools will offer you a greater awareness of the variety of challenges and opportunities confronting our education system.

How is it that with tremendous global wealth and enormous wealth inequality, the Canadian and American governments do not ban volunteerism and redistribute the wealth more fairly? The Thomas theorem suggests that it is a matter of defining the situation as real. If that is the case, we can redefine the situation of war culture and redistribute the wealth to gain wholesome societies in a culture of peace rather than militarism; but volunteering is also a business.

Volunteerism has become a culture within the framework of the military-industrial-service-complex. As the following vignette suggests, corporate citizenship includes The Corporate Council on Volunteering:

> Corporate Citizenship
> The Corporate Council on Volunteering
>
> The Corporate Council on Volunteering is a unique and exciting initiative, which started in 2005 when Volunteer Canada has joined forces with corporate volunteerism champions from across the country to build a Canadian-born Corporate Volunteer movement and through a partnership with The Home Depot Canada, the Corporate Council on Volunteering was formed. During its first year, the Council comprised of senior executives from 12 national corporations. In only five years, the group has expanded to 22 executives, representing a wide range of industry and sectors. As the largest corporate volunteerism initiative in the country, the Council calls on businesses of all sizes to encourage employees to volunteer time in a collaborative effort in the communities where they work and live. (Corporate Citizenship 2010)

The social construction of human value or economic wage determines who earns a fair wage, an insufficient wage or no wage at all. It becomes normal that soldiers in war earn wages for work in the most appalling conditions and their wives work for no wage at all while corporations like Halliburton and Blackwater profit immensely.

The FRG Handbook reveals 247 instances of volunteerism (Operation Ready 2007a, 2007b, 2007c). The handbook explains how volunteerism makes a difference, and then the instructions teach wives how to train other wives to recognize their responsibilities, rights, records, discipline and code of ethics and to acknowledge the importance of volunteers. Volunteerism is normal. The *Army Spouse's Battle Book* (2008) orients army wives and teaches them the rules and expectations of spouses. Training books use phrases such as "pity party" that diminish the emotional significance of deployment. The wives interact with each other and use idioms and acronyms that they learned in the military teaching process. An instructional source called Family Team Building offers courses that teach wives to volunteer and how to teach other wives how to behave.

The culture of volunteerism and free labour, which is omnipresent for wives during war deployment, is remarkably different from the culture of huge corporate profit-making linked to government contracts and global corporations that do everything from family support to mercenary killings. This form of government contracting is explained with an economic system known as mono-causal capitalism where economics determine reality, capitalists exploit workers and corporate profits mount expediently (Marx and Engels 1998). The huge profits are hardly going to the soldiers or their families, yet the Iraq war is estimated to cost three trillion American dollars or more (Stiglits and Bilmes 2008). The Canadian National Defence and Armed Forces paid more than $6-million to Blackwater to train its troops and the training continued after the American State Department cancelled their contract with Blackwater because of accusations of abuse and reckless killing of civilians in Iraq and Afghanistan (Blackwell 2010). While profits go to private companies such as KBR, Inc. (formerly Kellogg Brown and Root), Halliburton and Blackwater (recently renamed Xe), their employees and soldiers endure war violence and family separation. The wives of soldiers are expected to volunteer and support their husbands' battalions with money raised through fundraisers.

The Canadian and American Morale, Welfare, Recreation (MWR) groups offer services similar to a myriad of other organizations, private contractors and groups that tender aid and advice to the soldiers and families. MWR employees know about army community services including but not exclusive to child and youth services, education, clubs and restaurants, deployment information, education, lodging, recreation, sports and fitness. One wife explains how fundraising becomes a normalized process:

> There was fund raising. Oh yeah we had a bake sale every week or what else did we do? I mean we raised money for a ball. We had a ball in like November. And, we raised money for that and actually half of that was paid for by [Morale, Welfare, Recreation] MWR so we only had to raise half the funds so that was partially paid for. But, um, if we want a community bowling we had to raise funds for that. [It took a lot of time to fund raise] but it was fun because everybody else had their kids and so we'd all bring [sic] and our kids would all play and be goofy and.... Yah, it was really great and we had fun and we raised funds and we ya know sat and talked and joked.... (McKenna 2009)

The military institution and private contractors necessarily create meaning with the symbolic language they use to explain war and "casualties" to the wives; hence, they will understand, cope with the situations and support their soldier husbands. For this reason, American and Canadian fundraisers surface as taken-for-granted means to acquire money for their objectives. Raising money for the military community is a positive way to have fun while supporting each other and their soldiers. The fundraisers are commonplace and they usually allocate the monies toward family entertainment and packages for their husbands in Iraq.

Symbolic language such as fundraising and volunteering provides an economic normalcy that strategically supports and justifies the Canadian/American socio-economic systems even if it means taking part in war violence. Incomplete information about the war is not only welcomed, it is all that many of the wives will allow into their already over-burdened everyday lives. They are encouraged to keep busy during war deployment and live with a positive attitude regardless of their feelings about violence, incidences or separation. Rather than organizing activism and formulating ways that will change the socially constructed entity of war, they are expected to accept and live with it.

Militarization of Fun and Busy Lives

"OH GOD I LOVE SHOPPING"! (American Army Wife)

American and Canadian families live in, among other things, a culture of consumption, shopping, materialism and entertainment. The belief in the benefits of consumption is central to globalization and the military-industrial-service-complex: the culture of militarism. One example is revealed in the Army and Air Force Exchange Service, "We Go Where You Go" (AAFES 2010), and in the Canadian Forces Personnel and Family Support Services, "Serving Those Who Serve" (CANEX 2010a). The home web page for AAFES is stunning, like a carnival with active advertisements. A cruise ship floats across the screen followed by graduation specials, zero per cent interest, no down payment on ZT Data Systems, watch sales, discounts of closeout deals, weekly sweepstakes and Armed Forces weekly specials. The CANEX home web page is much more reserved; nothing floats across the screen promoting shopping. An index on the CANEX page, however, lists flyers, promotions, Club XTra, downloads and "Harley for Heroes," which was a raffle that raised $80,000 for the Military Families Fund (CANEX 2010b). Using these online marketing strategies and others that are everywhere every day, it is little wonder that shopping is a normalized way to acquire things and pass time—a coping mechanism during deployments.

Some coping mechanisms army wives use are drawn from a socio-economic system based on buying products and services. Military support groups encourage entertainment and shopping within a budget because they partially fill the void created by war deployments while sustaining the economy. Solutions from one American source of spousal support are revealed in the Spouse Project Army War College.

The purpose of the U.S. Army War College is primarily to research and educate military personnel but it also sponsors the Spouse Project Army War College. I did not locate a comparable Canadian spouse project.

Canadian Forces College educates officers as follows:

> The aim of the Joint Command and Staff Programme (JCSP) is to prepare selected senior officers of the Defence Team for command and staff appointments in the contemporary operating environment across

the continuum of operations in national and international settings. (CFC 2010)

American Company-level[4] spouses, who were "serving" along with the spouses of the U.S. Army War College Class of 2006, jointly compiled a "solution" book which is titled, *The Company Commander's Spouse Battle Book* (TCCSBB 2006). The 342-page Adobe Web-manual is easily downloaded with a click of a computer mouse. Socials, coffees, teas, fundraisers, volunteering, support groups, no less than fifty different coping mechanisms and at least ninety-one different types of parties ranging from "self-induced pity-party" to a "BYOT" (Bring Your Own Topping) party help to socialize the wives. Suggestion 48, which is on the "When My Spouse is Deployed, I can…" list, reminds them about positive attitudes; "My ATTITUDE DETERMINES AT WHAT ALTITUDE I FLY" (91).

The Army Family Readiness Group Leader's Handbook (Operation Ready 2007) consists of 152 pages of guidance, rules, expectations and support systems with a primary focus on volunteerism for the soldiers' wives. "Fun" is a consistent theme surfacing forty-six times within the document. Examples of chapter titles are "Keep the Fun Times Coming," "Choosing Fun Events" and "Some Fun things to Do." The document argues that fun FRG events are critical to the strength and permanence of the FRG, and the leadership is responsible for the fun and for maintaining a successful FRG (19). In order to control the attitude of military wives and divert their attention from extended deployments and war, the handbook offers fun as a key component to their lives while their soldier husbands are in war, home on R&R, or redeployed.[5] Fun is militarized. "Dining In" is a mandatory party where spouses are not allowed and soldiers must attend wearing their dress uniforms: "Yes [they must attend the mandatory parties]. So, it's mandatory fun (chuckle). It's part of their workday thing" (McKenna 2009).

The manual teaches the wives how to have fun along with information on volunteer work and other activities to fill their days. Many volunteer, but child rearing, cleaning and outside employment prioritize their lives while shopping, dining out with friends and pampering help them to cope with war violence and separation.

Physical and psychological pampering have become conventional means to keep the wives busy while they try to maintain healthy, less-stressful ways of life. Whole body massages, pedicures, manicures, spinning, tanning and dieting are part of their deployment lifestyles, and the future of how they will look to their husbands upon redeployment.[6] One wife whose husband left for Iraq after the interviews had her breasts augmented and shopped at Victoria's Secret the night before her surgery.

Weight Watchers conducts meetings near Coldweather and it is filled with military wives who informally "network" while they attend the meetings and lose weight together. One wife was confident that her husband would love her with the extra pounds that she gained, but other wives discussed how they would lose the weight before the soldiers came home.

> In fact, that's all we talk about, how much junk food we could eat (laughs) and how many points, but it's nice. It's nice because it's a couple familiar faces and it's something, too, that you find, well, my husband's gone. This is the time to work on the weight, which does create a new thing for you to do. Oh heck! I gotta go. I don't want my husband to recognize me when he gets home. So I told my husband tonight I gained a little bit more weight and I joined Weight Watchers and I kinda left it at that 'cause I want to surprise him when he comes home so....

The wives meet at Weight Watchers and at the gym to "work out," and to socialize and lose weight together. A good workout is relaxing and time consuming and it is also a positive way to handle the war and separation. Separation is difficult, but under the violence and death from an unpopular war and then extensions to fifteen months, the pressure on relationships mounts. The women are encouraged to shop as a remedy for unhappiness and it is often viewed as therapy. "Shop therapy" is a coping mechanism but when the effectiveness wanes, pampering seems a logical move to keep sane:

> [Relationship problems] are like popping up. It's just too long, Carole (claps her hands). It's crazy and seriously I am, I know I am a strong woman. I'm a very strong woman. Oh my God! I couldn't do this if I didn't love him. Ya know but it's taking a toll on me and I'm just, and I only have one child, ya know and (sniffles) I can't, the other day, it just, it just... [it is very hard]. Um, but I'm getting a pedicure tomorrow and a whole body massage next week (laughs).... For a while I used shop therapy, ya know, shopping and spending money. You know, especially after we heard that they got extended. You get all this extra money per month, so like that's what the money's for, and if it makes me happy I'll do that. It worked for a little bit and then, uh, I went home ... to be with my parents for a month and make the time go by fast. A little fast and that month was really good, and I got a lot of help so, but then I came back and it was even harder, um, and then I [exercise]. Sport [*sic*] really helped me through this mess. At the Y[MCA] I do step and release and now I run again in the summer. That helps me. Shopping doesn't do it any more. So now I need things like pampering myself like massages, looking pretty and ya know things like this. So I got my teeth whitened, (chuckles) all these things like that. (McKenna 2009)

Keeping busy occupies time, but it is not empty work. The women protect themselves from preoccupation with war and violence by keeping busy, but gruesome reminders arise and cannot be avoided. For instance, one wife copes by

Fig. 1

spray-painting her feelings on the cliffs near family housing on an army post. She printed the words "Iraq made our husbands mean:" (See fig. 1)

> I probably should have mentioned that and I didn't. Somebody had written on the cliffs about a year ago, "Iraq made our husbands mean." It was spray paint, and it was on the cliffs and it very clearly said, "Iraq made our husbands mean." Well, apparently, ya know, somebody was obviously very upset. They had quite an ability to get up there and write the way they did. Well, a lot [of] solders and spouses alike [*sic*] you could not help from seeing this [message painted in] very bold letters on the cliffs. Nobody needs to see that [so I] called housing. It's been almost a year now. It's still there. And it's been addressed so many times. I understand you can't power wash it because they're concerned about eroding the cliffs and I said, ya know what? Fine just go get some spray paint and paint it the same color as the cliffs and that'll cover it. It has not been addressed yet (McKenna 2009).

One wife hand-painted her feelings on the cliffs and made public what another wife felt was a private matter. She said that no one addressed it. No one got rid of the painting. Why? What makes soldiers mean? Iraq? Can a country that has been invaded, bombed, destroyed and occupied by a foreign military do that? War changes the participants whether they are warriors, victims, civilians or wives. As

Howard Zinn (2007) so poignantly argued, war is not natural behaviour. People have to be trained to kill systematically and the violence has to be reinforced. Some grow better at it than others. While some soldiers recover or adjust, others commit suicide, some become mean, self-medicate or stay confused, and some welcome a return to the camaraderie and war to which they have grown accustomed. The wives resist, cope or maybe surrender. What did the hand-painted statement submit to the military community?

Canadian and American soldiers and wives have more in common since the 1980s because it was then the Canadians determined that their military retention and quality was lacking, and turned to the needs of wives and family (Weinstein 1997). A decade earlier the Americans focused on the family when an all volunteer military replaced the draft. Business models provide a military-industrial-service-complex that attracts and retains young people. The marketing strategies make the military lifestyle a shopping and gaming fantasy. Additionally, as long as Americans desperately seek employment, higher education and healthcare, resistance to the culture of militarism will be ineffective. So the soldiers' wives resist, cope and acclimate to war violence. It is within this business model and a culture of militarism that the Canadian and American military wives and soldiers live their everyday lives.

Conclusion

This study revealed a culture of militarization by comparing and contrasting some Canadian and American military strategies that define situations and offer coping mechanisms to normalize and make sustainable a military lifestyle, especially during war deployment. The comparisons were limited to document examination and online access to numerous Canadian military family support groups, information sites, education and marketing techniques. Each document defined each situation persuasively to form a reality that the soldiers and wives are led to believe. The Thomas theorem argues that how a situation is defined determines how it is believed. Whether or not the beliefs are real, the corollaries of those beliefs are the consequences of the actions that are drawn from them. How we define the situation in Iraq and Afghanistan as friend or terrorist has more to do with what we believe is reality than with a particular truth. In this study, American army wives offered some interesting views of their realities and how they coped with war deployment.

The interviews and participant observation focused on Americans. This work-in-progress will be expanded to Canadian interviews and participant observations at a later time. The emerging American themes that I cite were drawn from interviews validated by participant observation and document analysis. The women disclosed various coping mechanisms that help them survive war violence, deployment and redeployment. They are encouraged to think positively in a process that Karen

Cerulo (2006) coined "positive asymmetry." The wives learn that negative thinking is not acceptable. They must think positively about their free labour, the war and deployments, among other things.

Although profit drives a capitalistic society, volunteerism is curiously ubiquitous in the military and, indeed, in American and Canadian culture (Weinstein 1997). The FRG, for instance, sustains itself with altruism and the unpaid labour of the military community. Volunteers, mostly wives, centre their activities on trust and support for the soldiers. Volunteerism should be counterproductive in capitalism, but instead, it is institutionally pervasive (McKenna 2009). Awards and dinners are strategically designed to keep volunteer services alive (Operation Ready 2007b). Part of the strategy is to validate the value of giving while others capitalize on it. Progressive strategies in the form of non-government organizations rely on the free labour of women to institutionalize their plight rather than empowering these women through their volunteerism (Lind 2003).

The FRG is the hub of war information and the coordinators want the wives to believe and trust them. The FRG bombards them with ways to seek counselling from the Military Family Life Consultants (MFLC), who are counsellors hired by the DOD and, "…can help [soldier] and [his/her] family problem solve with issues resulting from deployment, reunions, reintegration and other times of change" (Army Reserve Family Program 2009). Counselling and/or pharmaceuticals are supposed to aid the soldiers and wives in living with war deployment and redeployment. It is supposed to help them understand posttraumatic stress disorder (Operation Ready 2007c). These methods are supposed to help the wives who, among other problems, are clinically depressed or suicidal. If positive asymmetry, keeping busy, having fun, shopping and pampering do not sooth their psyches, then they are given counselling sessions and psycho-pharmaceuticals and other drugs because it is their behaviour and mind-sets that are the focus for cure. What surfaces from my findings is that the focus should not be on soldiers and wives, but rather on the power structure of a profit-driven economy that promotes global exploitation and war violence.

It is easy to understand how the complex culture of militarism cannot be reduced to a simple, one-dimensional entity. This does not mean that women do not resist or that all follow the whims of militarization. Some do resist, divorce and take different avenues in life, but the coping mechanisms discussed in this paper made the everyday lives of women married to soldiers sustainable, at least for some.

Notes

1. Stop loss, for Americans, means a mandatory extension of an expired separation date from military service, whereas Canadian stop loss rules are to prevent taxpayers from realizing deductible losses without any real intention to dispose of the property in question. In the Canadian context, it has nothing to do with military service. http://www.cabusinessadvisor.com/Tax/TaxTraps/StopLoss.htm. Accessed 2010 May 11.

2. From information handout distributed to spouses from the rear detachment command team at the April 2007 extension briefings.

3. An incident refers to war violence—more specifically, when soldiers are injured or killed.

4. A Company (Battalion or Troop) is usually commanded by a Captain.

5. Redeployment means that a soldier is coming home.

6. Spinning is high-intensity cycling on a stationary exercise bicycle. The wives usually engage in spinning at gyms or in settings with other women. The wives who "tan" often go to tanning salons. Weight Watchers supports the wives in their weight loss endeavour while they socialize with others with similar goals.

References

AAFES. 2010. Army and Air Force Exchange Service. http://www.aafes.com/default_s.aspx

Alt, Betty Sowers and Bonnie Domrose Stone. 1991. *Campfollowing: A History of the Military Wife*. New York: Praeger.

Altheide, David L. 1996. *Qualitative Media Analysis*. CA: Sage.

———. 2002. *Creating Fear: News and the Construction of Crisis*. Edison, NJ: Aldine Transaction.

Amnesty International. 2010. http://www.amnesty.ca/blog2.php?blog=hr_canada. Accessed 11 May.

Army Reserve Family Programs. 2009. The Program. http://www.arfp.org/skins/ARFP/display.aspx?ModuleID=8cde2e88-3052-448c-893d-d0b4b14b31c4&Action=display_page&ObjectID=dc78097f-fbcc-49ee-b536-2935dad0f91e. Accessed 19 July 2009.

Army Spouse Battle Book. 2008. http://www.delawarenationalguard.com/family/battlebook.pdf. Accessed 01 June 2008.

Blackwell, Tom. 2010. Blackwater Trained Canadian troops. *National Post*. http://www.nationalpost.com/scripts/story.html?id=2954144. Accessed 11 May 2010.

CFC. 2010. Canadian Forces College. http://www.cfc.forces.gc.ca/210-eng.html.

CANEX. 2010a. Canadian Forces Exchange System. http://www.cfpsa.com/en/CANEX/flyers_e.asp.

CANEX. 2010b. http://www.cfpsa.com/en/CANEX/HH1_e.asp.

CFPFSS. 2010a. Canadian Forces Personnel and Family Support Services. http://www.cfpsa.com/en/. Accessed 12 May 2010.

———. 2010b. http://www.cfpsa.com/en/psp/dmfs/mh%20speakers%20bureau_e.asp.

Cerulo, Karen. 2006. *Never Saw It Coming: Cultural Challenges to Envisioning the Worst*. Chicago, IL: University of Chicago Press.

Corporate Citizenship. 2010. The Corporate Council on Volunteering. http://volunteer.ca/en/corporatecitizenship. Accessed 12 May 2010.

Edelman, Murray. 1988. *Constructing Political Spectacle*. Chicago, IL: University of Chicago Press.

Enloe, Cynthia. 2000. *Maneuvers: The International Politics of Militarizing Women's Lives*. Berkeley, CA: University of California Press.

———. 2007. *Globalization and Militarism: Feminists Make the Link*. Lanham, MD: Rowman and Littlefield.

FTN *Face the Nation*. 2009. http://www.youtube.com/watch?v=SfYov5o5_2s. Accessed 08 June 2009.

FOX News. 2007. *Employment Opportunities with Fox News*. http://www.foxnews.com/story/0,2933,27906,00.html. Accessed 24 Nov 2007.

Ivie, Robert L. 2003. Evil Enemy versus Agonistic Other: Rhetorical Constructions of Terrorism. *The Review of Education, Pedagogy, and Cultural Studies*. 25:181-200.

Leopold, Jason. 2009. Comey Emails Illustrate Concerns over Torture Policies. *Truthout*. http://www.truthout.org/060809J. Accessed 08 June 2009.

Lind, Amy. 2003. Making Feminist Sense of Neoliberalism: The Institutionalization of Women's Struggles for Survival in Ecuador and Bolivia. In *Through the Eyes of Women: Gender Social Networks, Family, and Structural Change in Latin America and the Caribbean*, edited by Cecilia Menjivar. Willowdale, ON: DeSitter Publications.

Marx, Karl and Frederick Engels. 1998. *Manifesto of the Communist Party*. New York: International Publishers.

McKenna, Carole R. and Joao Salm. 2006. State Sanctioned Torture and Its Effect on Canadian and American Relations. *Journal of the Institute of Justice and International Studies* 6:215-32.

———. 2007. Political Speeches. In *Encyclopedia of Activism and Social Justice*. Thousand Oaks, CA: Sage.

———. 2009. *Militarism: Power Arrangements between Soldiers, Wives, and the Military-Industrial-Service-Complex*. Saarbrücken, Germany: VDM Verlag.

Military Family Resource Centers. 2010a. http://www.cfpsa.com/en/psp/dmfs/mfrccontact/canada_e.asp. Accessed 11 May 2010.

———. 2010b. http://www.cfpsa.com/en/psp/dmfs/mfrccontact/usa_e.asp. Accessed 11 May 2010.

MFSP Military Families Strength behind the Uniform. 2010. http://www.cfpsa.com/en/psp/MIL/. Accessed 12 May 2010.

Musheno, Michael and Susan Ross. 2008. *Deployed: How Reservists Bear the Burden of Iraq*. MI: University of Michigan Press.

National Defence and the Canadian Forces. 2010. Volunteer Handbook. http://www.cmp-cpm.forces.gc.ca/dem-epcg/pd/osa-pra/vh-mb-eng.asp. Accessed 11 May 2010.

Operation Ready. 2007a. http://www.mwrarmyhawaii.com/acs/acs_documents/Soldier_%20Family_Deployment_Survival_Handbook.pdf. Accessed 04 September 2009.

———. 2007b. http://www.per.hqusareur.army.mil/frsa/pdfs/Readiness_Handbook.pdf. Accessed 08 September 2009.

———. 2007c. http://www.per.hqusareur.army.mil/frsa/rsc_goodids.htm. Accessed 04 September 2009.

Stiglitz, Joseph and Linda Bilmes. 2008. *The Three Trillion Dollar War: The Cost of the Iraq and Afghanistan Conflicts Have Grown to Staggering Proportions*. New York: W. W. Norton.

TCCSBB. 2006 *The Company Commander's Spouse Battle Book*. Spouse Project Army War College. http://www.delawarenationalguard.com/family/battlebook.pdf. Accessed 02 Mar 2008.

TPM. 2009. Oval Office Speech. http://www.youtube.com/watch?v=g6LtL9lCTRA&feature=related. Accessed 08 June 2009.

Thomas, William I. 1971. On the Definition of the Situation. In *Sociology: The Classic Statements*, edited by Marcello Truzzi, 275-77. New York: Random House.

U.S. Department of Labor. 2006. Public Relations Specialists. *Nature of the Work*. http://www.bls.gov/oco/ocos086.htm#nature. Accessed 04 November 2007.

Weinstein, Laurie Lee. 1997. *Wives and Warriors: Women and the Military in the United States and Canada*. Santa Barbara, CA: Greenwood Press.

Zinn, Howard. 2007. *A Power Governments Cannot Suppress*. San Francisco: City Lights.

Uli Linke

Fortress Europe: Globalization, Militarization and the Policing of Interior Borderlands

ABSTRACT

The intensification of militarized violence, racist terror and destructive dehumanization across the globe makes it imperative to examine the corresponding formations of securocratic regimes in the centres of power. With a focus on a united Europe, my essay interrogates the ubiquitous penetration of militarization into everyday life-worlds. My research suggests that in these interior borderlands, emergent cultures of militarization are normalized by recourse to racialization, criminalization and securitization, which in turn gives rise to new intimacies of violence, dehumanization and othering within expanding networks of fortification in a self-proclaimed white society.

RÉSUMÉ

Forteresse Europe : Mondialisation, militarisation et police des frontières intérieures

L'intensification de la violence militarisée, de la terreur raciste et de la déshumanisation destructrice à travers le monde fait qu'il est impératif d'examiner les formations correspondantes de régimes sécuritocratiques dans les centres de pouvoir. En basant mon essai sur une Europe unie, j'interroge la pénétration omniprésente de la militarisation dans tous les mondes du quotidien. Ma recherche suggère que dans ces frontières intérieures, des cultures de la militarisation en émergence sont normées par un recours à la racialisation, la criminalisation et la sécurisation, ce qui, en retour, produit de nouvelles intimités de violence, de déshumanisation et d'altérisation, à l'intérieur de réseaux en expansion de fortification dans une société blanche autoproclamée.

¤

Rendsburg-Hohn military base, Germany, April 2007 - A public controversy ensues after print media publicize the electronic dissemination of a [You Tube] video clip that shows how a German drill sergeant conjures racist scenarios for soldiers in basic training. The video captures a sequenced instructional exercise. The initial segment records how a recruit learns to load and shoot a machine gun while being told to imagine that he is part of a security detachment at an airport where terrorists have suddenly taken control of a plane. The trainer orders the recruit to fire two short bursts and then concludes, "Good, the terrorists are dead." The recruit is subsequently prompted to imagine himself in the Bronx, in New York, where he is suddenly confronted by three African-American men who emerge from a black van and taunt him by insulting his mother. The recruit is now ordered to open fire on these imaginary black male civilians. He is instructed to release each round of bullets by shouting "mother fucker." This exercise is repeated multiple times, until the trainer is satisfied by the speed with which the soldier-in-training fires his automatic weapon at these conjured phantom enemies, a phantasmatic threat of black masculinity on another continent, in a different nation. (Bundeswehr Ausbildung 2007)

My essay opens with this ethnographic instance of military training because it renders visible the hidden imaginaries of border militarism in contemporary Europe. The videotaped scenario reveals that the recruit is taught how to handle an automatic weapon while learning its application as a killing tool at the same time. The soldier's training begins by staging a social context for the legitimate use of the gun: an airport, as a site of translocal transit and global mobility, is identified as a security risk and imagined as a probable setting for a terrorist attack. As the recruit is ordered to fire his weapon, the use of the gun is given a political function; when the conjured attackers are killed, national space is protected. In the German training session, this staged threat to the national order is subsequently globalized. Situated beyond the confines of established political borders, the source of danger is displaced to a different nation and equated with the contested masculinity of the black Other. The implausibility of the scenario (a German soldier patrolling the streets of New York City) is deflected, even rendered credible, by recourse to a gendered and racialist plot.

As urban global space is transposed into a borderless killing field, black men are imagined as legitimate military targets whose words are judged to be as dangerous as a terrorist event. In acquiring the techniques of warfare through a synchronized coordination of body, mind and weapon, the soldier learns to equate acts of urban military terror against non-white Others with matters of security and with the mandates of European border protection. The soldier's use of deadly force is authorized not only to secure corporate property (the airplane) or to protect national space (terrorism) but in defence of the white female/maternal figure (by an appeal to filial honour). The videotape reveals how a racist imagination is implanted and normalized for soldiers by basic military training exercises. While these machinations and practices are extracted from a single video clip, German historian Jay Lockenour has observed that given standard military training procedures founded on chain of command, obedience, discipline and perpetual practice, it is difficult to "imagine that this is an isolated incident" (Lockenour 2007: n.p.). Lockenour continues:

> The racism inherent in the scenario is so blatant. [The use of] lethal force in response to insults ... is bound to violate the rules of engagement any democratic military would establish for its soldiers.... The scenario is not only racist, it imagines the recruit committing a "war crime." (n.p.)

But why are black males—in this case "Afro-American" men (in the drill sergeant's words)—depicted as potential threats in the German military imagination? The black signifier seems to override political concerns for national sovereignty, citizenship, NATO membership, European Union security and defence treaties. Rooted in colonial fabrications of indigenous and native life-worlds far away from European space, black subjects have been imagined as Europe's antithetical counters throughout the 20th century and into the present (Linke 1999; Mazón and Steingröver 2005; Pred 2000; Scheck 2006). "The idea of Europe," as Goldberg notes, "excludes those historically categorized as non-European, as being not white" (2006: 347). How are such machinations of a white Europe sustained in this 21st-century era of globalization? Why is the social construction of the otherness of "the black Other" so central for this sense of Europeanness, even in contemporary Europe?

Cultural assumptions about non-white criminality and violence continue to resonate in the present despite recent shifts in political regimes. During the past two decades, beginning in late 1980s, the political landscape of Europe has undergone dramatic change. The powerful matrix of global capitalism has deeply affected European nation forms, social ideologies and political systems, as shown by German unification, the collapse of the Soviet regime, the war in the former Yugoslavia and the subsequent formation of the European Union, including the ongoing Europeanization of post-socialist states. In this context, the historical fixity of borders, bodies and spaces has been untethered. The end of the cold war in the 1990s has furnished new possibilities for envisioning society, promoting major realignments of border regimes and fundamental transpositions in the topographic fabric of Europe's political imagination. In addition, the emergent entanglements of state and corporate interests not only changed the political contours of Europe but also altered the social conditions under which ethno-racial imaginaries are brought to public visibility.

Under the conditions of European reformation and globalization in the 1990s, the cultural production of identities, bodies and lifestyles has increasingly shifted to the marketplace and the terrain of advertising, fashion and media. Culture industries manufacture national distinction by means of commodity desire and consumption. The seductive promise of unlimited possibilities made by neoliberal economies is simultaneously and paradoxically defended as a state-protected privilege and a con-cession of citizenship reserved for European nationals. The political spaces of capitalism are closely guarded. Cultural imaginaries of gender, sexuality and race are called upon to authorize participation in the dream-worlds of prosperity. The formation of the European security state after 9/11 has intensified this process by giving rise to fortified border regimes, ethnic profiling and militarized racism. From this perspective, the focus on citizenship in Europe considered according to the master narratives of cold-war national history requires a critical reassessment. The impact of globalization, founded on a cohesive network of political, military and corporate interests, includes fundamental shifts the parameters, discourses and possibilities for negotiating matters of national belonging in Europe.

How have Europeans "fashioned their distinctions" and "conjured up their 'whiteness'" (Cooper and Stoler 1997: 16) in attempts to reconstitute themselves as global citizens in a multi-ethnic, post-imperial Europe? In a post-national Europe, the realities of ethnic diversity and cultural pluralism have unravelled the idea of citizens as a homogenous or undifferentiated group. As Europe strives to achieve political and economic unity in the 21st century, we see a concurrent push toward inequality, exclusion and marginalization. The legacies of colonialism and nationalism continue to imprint the privilege of whiteness onto the new map of Europe, and sustain the political fortification of Europe as a hegemonic white space. Within the post-9/11 European Union, the promotion of this ethno-political project can be documented in "the state-specific forms of attack against asylum, asylum seekers, and foreigners, and the ways in which fundamental rights are being legally altered and police powers built [or expanded] in specific states" (Glick-Schiller 2005: 527). In addition to these state-sponsored security measures against unwanted immigration, the whitening of European space is also attested to by the proliferation of hate crimes and the intensification of racial violence in Europe's interior "borderlands," those everyday zones of contact that Gloria Anzaldúa envisioned as "open wound[s]," "where the Third World grates against the first and bleeds" (qtd. in Fine et al. 2007: 76). In these quotidian border zones, the European intimacies of contact with different cultures and peoples are increasingly patterned by the use of terror against those whose visual appearances and lifestyles are rejected as non-European.

This essay explores the formative possibilities of citizenship and exclusion in the era of European globalization. My aim is to rethink the technologies of othering in Europe's interior borderlands, where the lives of black subjects are increasingly patterned by state surveillance, police brutality and street violence. What spectres of the imperial legacy remain embedded in these spaces of whiteness that govern, wound and sometimes destroy the lives of black subjects in Europe's postcolonial and post-national interior? What politics of representation are at work in the carceral zones of whiteness, where black subjects are forced to inhabit the semiotic prison-house of spectacle and/or the criminally grotesque? My aim is to scrutinize Europe's disavowed blackness by examining how practices of othering and the "militarising of public space" (Giroux 2004) are mutually implicated in expanding networks of fortification in a self-proclaimed white society. With a focus on the European Union from the 1990s to the present, I explore how cultural regimes of representation, racial violence and border militarism operate to produce ever more stringent forms of exclusion, subordination and fear.[1]

Globalization, National Borders and the Place of Race

Despite the enormous interest in the impact of European racial thinking on the colonial histories of genocide, slavery and anti-black violence, relatively little is known about how the self-imagined whiteness of Europe has been propagated *in* Europe. The imperial centre has produced its own histories of violence, exclusion and terror to produce "the peculiar synonymity of the terms European and white" (Gilroy 2004: xii). The making of a white Europe has also affected black people within the frontiers of European space. If whiteness is a measure of national belonging in Europe, such a racial closure of citizenship inhibits a black subject's durable ability to shape a life or to envision a future. Under fascism in the 1930s and 1940s, the phantasma of race became integral to a regime of genocide that equated "whiteness" with the prerequisite condition for the right to life. Those meant to be excluded from participation in the national order were de-Europeanized and un-whitened. The fabricated fear of blackness runs through German anti-semitism. As Sander Gilman (1982) documents, Jews were "negrified" by Nazi racial science: the phantasmatic figure of the "Jew" was not only Orientalized, but regarded as black and African by ancestry. The colour coding of citizen-bodies, as an index of racial status, was embedded in an order of power that Mbembe has termed "necropolitics:" racialization "made possible the murderous functions of the state" (2003: 11). How have these machinations been transformed in contemporary Europe, in the era of global capitalism and the "war on terror?"

The promise of national distinction by racial exclusivity contradicts conventional understandings of globalization. A globalized world marked by "reform" and "openness" is said to unsettle old identities and unlock new imaginaries (Appadurai 2001: 3). From such a perspective, the European racial state is regarded as a matter of the past. Racism in Europe is presumed to belong to colonial history, an era that ended with fascism in 1945. This historical past, with its carceral spaces of race, sex and gender, is opposed to the present, which is conceived as a world without frontiers, "a world of flows" (Appadurai 1996) and "liquid" social forms (Bauman 2000). Accordingly, processes of globalization have been analyzed by recourse to metaphors of fluidity, flexibility and liquidity, rather than ethnic fortification or racial closure. The global order comes into view through the possibilities and signs of motion: mobile populations, permeable borders, transnational flows of capital and the traffic of culture across space and time. The radically altered historical fixity of borders, bodies and identities suggests a progressive weakening of political units and thus the disempowerment of nation states. Such visionary models of the decline of state power and the end of racial thinking have been well expounded.

With a focus on the geopolitics of globalization, Michael Hardt and Antonio Negri deployed the term "empire" to describe the delocalized and decentred system of transglobal control: the world empire operates as "a non-place" of power in a universal terrain (2000: 210). The impact of empire on global life is said to be dramatic: as sovereignties, borders and territories are reconstituted and negated, imaginaries based on place attachment are rendered meaningless. In a world without borders, social constructions of difference cannot be spatially derived to signify membership or otherness: the relational determination of centres and peripheries, or interiority and exteriority, has been annulled. Following this logic, the global empire produces a deterritorialized world that lacks interior vantage points or centre-spaces of privilege from which salient Others can be imagined, marginalized and excluded. According to Hardt and Negri, the unbinding of economic space evaporates the logic of gendered, racial and sexual difference. But global transformations are never so simple. The political realities of globalization reveal a different trajectory.

In the new millennium, globalization has not produced a singular or unified world order. The global empire does not operate as a single-space economy, or as "a non-contradictory, uncontested space" in which all strands of social life are perfectly synchronized (Hall 2000a: 32). As Arjun Apadurai has observed, in a global world marked by flows, movements and fluidities, the structural order of things has been destabilized: "objects, persons, images, and discourses—are not coeval, convergent, isomorphic, or spatially consistent. They are in ... relations of disjuncture" (2001: 5). Political forms, cultural identities, social lives and economic interests engage global possibilities along different, sometimes contradictory trajectories. Globalization operates with a flexible fixity on the ground. Capitalist imperatives, sub-jectivities and the manufacture of elusive authenticities may intersect to produce "counterintuitive" results, as John and Jean Comaroff propose in *Ethnicity, Incorporated*: "Cultural identity, in the here-and-now, represents itself ever more as two things at once: the object of choice and self-construction, typically through the act of consumption, *and* the manifest product of biology, genetics, human essence" (2009: 1). Under globalization, ethno-racial logics can be reclaimed for profit. Likewise, the imaginative geography of a "white Europe" or the sense of Europeanness may be reconfigured by recourse to space, by signifiers of gender, nation and race, and by new consumer practices. Under global consumer capitalism, the "whiteness" of Europe has come to be imagined and defended as a lifestyle. Europeanness is reclaimed, enacted and consumed in ontological space by placing emphasis on "conjuring affect, itself ever more a commodity, by aesthetic means" (Comaroff 2009: 16). While culture can perform the work of race, drawing on variable aesthetic and affective repertoires, the emergent volatility of white Europeanness is stabilized by recourse to border regimes, anti-immigrant legislation and, most recently, discourses of national security and militarism.

In light of these developments, my analysis of Europe's Europeanization of race takes account of how the politics of immigration, national belonging and citizenship are governed by neoliberal security issues: racial exclusivity, inserted into the political terrain of the bio-social (gender, family, sexuality) has once again "become a critical affair of state" (Comaroff 2009: 214). In Europe, as in many contemporary imperialist nation states, we observe resurgent forms of border protection, surveillance, and anti-black and anti-Muslim violence which seek to counter the destabilizing effects of globalization. When critically examining these political realities, we need to acknowledge that the "vision of a decentered empire," as Nicholas Mirzoeff observes, "has come to be overtaken by a more familiar model of empire controlled by a concrete nation state" (2005: 145). Militarization, policing and state intervention are deployed in attempts to securitize Europe. Such a politics of space, with its regime of borders, camps and racial terror, is emblematic "of the renewed desire of nation states to restrict global freedom of movement to capital and deny it to people" (146). This is an important observation. The management of white Europeanness and black-Islamicized alterities through the production of racial boundaries, sexual deviancies and gendered hierarchies is not *naturally* propagated. The negation or integration of racialized, sexualized and gendered Others in Europe's presumed white spaces is sustained by state intervention.

Body Count: Blackness in the European Imagination

How is the violent erasure of blacks from Europe revealed in this phantasmatic space of whiteness? My research suggests that "the threat of race" (Goldberg 2009) is encoded in the ways in which the European Union configures and imagines "the people of Europe."[2] My investigation of population statistics and demographic figures published by government offices began with a relatively simple question: how many black people live in Europe today? The answer has been revealingly elusive.

The actual size of the black community in Europe Union space is difficult to assess. Official estimates are conjectures, approximations based solely on *immigrant*, statistics. According to these figures, first provided in 2002 and then released annually, black Europeans constitute a highly visible although surprisingly small minority population (Eurostat 2002; Copers et al. 2004; Schäfer et al. 2005; Schäfer et al. 2007).

> According to research by the European Union ... it is roughly estimated that ... there are about 300,000 Afro-Germans. In France ... people of

African descent constitute about one million. And in the United Kingdom, the Afro-Caribbean population is about ... 880,000. (Lusane 2003: 251)

European Union records suggest that Europe's black population is numerically insignificant and therefore inconsequential. Although the European Commission acknowledged in 2007 that "[I]t is likely that these figures are under-estimates of the extent of migration flows between countries," because they exclude "clandestine migration such as illegal immigrants or human trafficking" (Schäfer et al. 2007: 75), the statistical disappearance of black Europeans, here explained by criminalizing the vanishing subaltern, is much more problematic.

The magnitude of the numerical erasure of black presence is suggested by a comparison with current United Nations documents, which assess the international migrant population in Europe at sixty-four million (United Nations 2006: 29).[3] Corresponding demographic figures reveal that close to one-third of these "immigrants in Europe" are from Africa and the Caribbean. This data would suggest a seven-fold differential in the approximate size of the black community when compared to the minimalist estimate produced by the European Union: three million versus the United Nations estimate of twenty million. But even these numbers are misleading. With an exclusive focus on *immigrants and immigration*, the demographic figures erase or obscure the reality of blackness among Europe's nationals and citizens. Such statistical estimates work by exclusion. State sponsored census counts with racial markers are prohibited by the European Union (Goodey 2007: 583-84). While the 2007 European Union anti-discrimination directive makes prominent mention of race in order to criminalize racism, Goodey has argued that the "data collection practices in England and Wales" are at the forefront of legislation and policy implementation at present; among other member states, the population's ethno-racial composition remains unreported as well as unrecorded (2007: 571, 575). Although the prohibition against racial data collection is anti-discriminatory in intent, designed to expunge the biometric registers of Nazi persecution from bureaucratic memory, European population statistics are configured by an unspoken discourse of race. What are the truth claims embedded in the manufacture and dissemination of this "official" knowledge?

Black presence is presumed to enter Europe from *outside*: from the Caribbean Islands, Africa, the developing world and the global south. In this statistical universe, immigrant bodies are inferentially blackened (or whitened) on the basis of national origin. According to this procedure, colour is erroneously ascribed as an essential geographical trace. As Lusane points out, it is absurd to categorically assume "that an immigrant from South Africa or Jamaica is black," and "to believe that one from the United States or Canada is white" (2003: 251). Such a vision of human bodies branded by space and invariably marked by a geopolitical territory not only belies the histories of globalization, hybridity and mobility, but also recuperates colonial fantasies of white entitlement. Writing race onto the world map is clearly a political project. The symbolic charting of racial zones across the globe relies on the ontological coupling of nature, race and space, and so is crucial for our understanding of contemporary European Union population politics. A white Europe, imagined without blacks, "serves as the subliminal text for the raceless state:" a body politic conceived as benign (female), civilized, Christian and white (Goldberg 2006: 339-40). In Europe's phantasmatic production, blackness is affixed to the peripheries of a global cartographic project that strives to *see* the citizen-subjects of a united Europe as intrinsically white.

It is no coincidence that the statistical yearbooks produced by the European Community diminish the presence of black people in numerical terms and imagine the "people in Europe" as white citizen-subjects. The statistical erasure of blackness is enmeshed with a visual record. Although the statistical yearbooks feature photos of a diverse multitude of young adults of different ethnic backgrounds on their front covers, the bodies of the publications contains less celebratory images of diversity or ethnic pluralism. Europe's population statistics are illustrated with an assortment of photographs of white babies (Copers et al. 2004; Schäfer et al. 2005: 61, 67, 71; Schäfer et al. 2007). A white child implies a white mother and father: the photos idealize the white European family, and white motherhood in particular. The visual images reveal a pattern: each photo depicts a single white infant cradled, held, embraced, kissed or cuddled by a white woman—a young mother, a grandmother, a female medical caregiver. While the accompanying statistical figures and narratives speak about Europe's "declining fertility rate" and "fewer children" (messages repeated as quantifiable truth-claims in the captions), the photos provide a record of women's sensuous, loving devotion to white children. The fearful message of demographic projections (white Europeans as an endangered species) is countered by a suggested solution: the need for more white offspring.

Apocalyptic visions of Europe's anticipated white depopulation are infused with a fabricated fear of blackness. The demographic analysis of the "People in Europe," as published in the European Union statistical yearbook of 2005, concludes with an untitled photo of babies in a hospital setting: in the centre, six cribs with white infants; on the outer edge, positioned on either side, two cribs with black infants; a population graph is superposed on the photo (Schäfer et al. 2005: 79). Interpreted in context, based on the statistical data presented in the preceding text, the visual message is emphatic: one out of four babies born in Europe is black. The unsettling implications of the numerical decline of Europe's white population are enhanced by a visual focus on the multiplication of black children. Europe's statistical imagination conjures and affirms cultural anxieties about the disappearance of a white European future by reference to diminishing birth rates among white mothers and the disproportionate fertility of the black female body.

From this perspective, the statistical diminution of blacks in Europe is no accident. Indeed, it articulates "Europe's repressed, denied, and disavowed blackness" (Gilroy 2004: xii). The preoccupation with immigration and female reproductivity, as Gilroy asserts, implicates the European Union in the explicit construction of a "white fortress" (2000: 247), a "bleached, politically fortified space" (2004: xii). Europe still imagines black population growth as a movement of bodies from elsewhere: from *outside* the borders of Europe.

Border Militarism and the Carceral Spaces of Whiteness

How are Europe's visible minorities governed, monitored and disciplined in the realm of global security? European concerns about security, safety, protection and defence are circulated as part of a global public discourse of fear that encourages proactive military action, legitimates war as surgical intervention and authorizes faraway acts of violence as a means of national border fortification. The securocratic language of the contemporary Western state is "war" talk: it empowers a state's military reach across national borders, diminishes civil society and limits visions of peace. In global media productions after 2008, the figure of the enemy-other has been conflated with the "the terrorist:" he is imagined as a syncretic figure, as Muslim-Arab-Black. But this image of the dangerous militant Other is a phantasm: it typifies salient ethnicities, "drawing together West Indians, Africans, South Asians into a blackening singularity as uninvited immigrant presence" (Goldberg 2009: 179). Militarized media invigorate a montage of fear, masculinity and race, recuperating an anti-black Orientalism that resonates across the Atlantic divide, into Europe and worldwide.

The intensity, sophistication and speed with which political truth-claims can be mobilized to traverse international boundaries has forged a climate of unprecedented state-legitimated terror against phantasmatic Others. Visions of the "axis of evil" or the figure of "the terrorist" are as illusive as they are reactive, fuelling a popular desire for fortified political borders. These ideological fantasies about fortification and border protection are not merely discursive machinations. They are grounded in the operational logic of an expansive capitalist empire that seeks to disguise inherent instabilities and contradictions by a turn to the so-called war on terror. In Europe, the shifting configurations between politics, power and capital have encouraged a rigid nationalism and vigilant patriotism. But, the economic requirements of mobility, flexibility and deterritorialization in the neoliberal global order collide with the European state's political commitment to securitize space. In this volatile terrain, the imperatives of national security not only restructure the space of the bio-social by an appeal to gender and racial hierarchies, but simultaneously alter the essence of the border regime. In contemporary Europe, as Ticktin has observed, "the struggle to define citizenship and the borders of the nation-state is now also a struggle to define the threshold of humanity and of life itself" (2006: 35). The ubiquity of borders and the liquidity of empire are both symptomatic of this current reality of the capitalist security state: in an imperialist nation-form, founded on fear, policing, surveillance and militarism have become companions to "normal" life.

European notions of a securitized *inside* and a threatening *outside* are enforced by a border regime that monitors, protects and sustains cultural notions of relative human worth. In what spaces can we locate the protective, often dehumanizing capacity of borders? Following Balibar, we need to speak of a *regime of borders* "both in the middle of the European space and at its extremities" (2004: 13). Indeed, any modern state recognizes or creates borderlines, "which allow it to clearly distinguish between the national (domestic) and the foreigner" (4). The outer borders of Europe, as mapped out by single states, have an incontestable geospatial dimension, a territorial reference or landmark, a footprint just beyond no-man's land, where "the entrance of asylum seekers and migrants into the European common space" can be regulated and controlled (14). But on the ground, where matters of belonging and exclusion are decided, borderlines also acquire tangible form as legal, political and social contact zones.

European Union territories, like other federated sovereignties, are defined by "open" borders in the interior—the so-called *Schengen* space—where European citizens can traverse national borders without passport or identity checks. Established in 1995, the *Schengen* area now covers the territory of twenty-seven countries or member states of the European Union. It is an area where internal border controls have been abolished by mutual agreement. This inner *open* space, which guarantees the freedom of mobility for nationals, is protected by the simultaneous fortification of exterior borders. After the 2001 World Trade Centre attack, we observe an intensification of closure. This is one snapshot of "fortress" Europe: an imagined political community with an interior borderland that is envisioned as open, liberal and democratic, and an exterior borderline that is policed and protected against enemy-outsiders, including refugees, immigrants, asylum-seekers and non-Europeans. But such a juxtaposition of internal openness (no policing) and exterior closure (border militarism) is misleading. In the process of monitoring, capturing and detaining unwanted populations—the dark-skinned migrants from the global south—external border guarding has become part of a militarized apparatus that extends into the very centre of Europe, into European "securocratic public space" (Feldman 2004). The regime of borders in Europe is not confined to a fixed periphery, but comes into evidence as a decentred, dislocated and ubiquitous process of exclusion and containment.

The preoccupation with fortification and security has given rise to a "Europe-wide network of detention camps for foreigners" (Hintjens 2007: 412). Border militarism is thereby intimately implicated in detention procedures. In June 2008, the European Parliament approved a new set of common rules for expelling undocumented migrants from European Union space (JRS-Europe Article 15.5 and 15.6). Under these directives, unauthorized border-crossers, refugees, asylum seekers and migrants can be held in specialized detention camps for up to eighteen months before being deported (JRS-Europe 2009a). At the time of publication, 235 detention centres have already been built, scattered throughout Europe, usually in remote locations, "almost invisible to the average EU citizen" (Hintjens 2007: 412). Information about the camps is difficult to obtain. Available data reveal that 150 internment centres administer a combined population of 31,139 detainees. This figure excludes thousands of migrants incarcerated in the remaining eighty-five camps as well as those housed in prisons (in Germany) or other secret facilities (JRS-Europe 2009a, 2009b). Hidden from view, with their existence officially erased, these detainees can be counted among the disappeared (Amnesty International 2009). When placed in this context, the regime of borders performs multiple functions: in its defensive mission, it not only excludes, but also detains, puts lives on hold and even makes them disappear.

The regime of borders, which includes the camps, is expansive, amorphous: it reaches into all contact zones between state officials and non-nationals, both outside and inside of European space. A cartographic view of the location of the camps is revealing. The "empire of camps" (Mirzoeff 2005) extends throughout North Africa, southwest Asia, the eastern parts of Eastern Europe and western Asia; it demarcates Europe's southern and eastern security borders and extends into all interior borderlands, with notable concentrations in Germany, Great Britain, Spain, Italy and Poland (Migreurope 2009). An analysis of contemporary border militarism therefore requires a focus on "the contradictory effects of the violent security policies waged" *by Europe* within its interior borderlands and "*in the name of Europe* by the bordering countries, now aggravated by the conjuncture of the global war on terror" (Balibar 2004: 15, emphasis added). The regime of borders operates as an amorphous buffer zone against global mobility and the presumed threat of race, even beyond Europe's sovereign space.

Europe's political borders may be conceived as a militarized apparatus, a vio-lent procedure for exclusion, tracking and containment that is subject to the operations of the neoliberal capitalist state apparatus, where immigrants and refugees can be envisioned either as a valued labour force or as a potential threat to life and safety. As such, border regimes always have a dual disposition:

> [O]n the one hand, a *violent process of exclusion* whose main instrument (not the only one) is the quasi-military enforcement of "security borders," which recreates the figure of the *stranger as political enemy*...; on the other hand, a "*civil process of elaboration of differences*, which clearly involves ... a basic aporia concerning the self-understanding of Europe's 'identity' and 'community'." (14, emphasis added)

According to documentation provided by humanitarian organizations, border militarism in Europe has resulted in nearly 9,000 deaths of undesirable border crossers between 1993 and 2007 (United for Intercultural Action 2007). This figure includes "statistics of the permanent increase of death cases in some sensitive areas of the 'periphery' (such as the Gibraltar Strait, the sea shores of Sicily and the Adriatic, some passages of the Alps and the Carpaths, the English Channel and Tunnel, etc.), which are recorded officially as casualties or tragic accidents" (Balibar 2004: 15). In addition to recording the fatalities of border militarism in Europe's periphery, these statistics include the deaths of migrants in Europe's interior, in the detention camps and in police custody. Refugees, migrants and asylum seekers are imprisoned, tortured and killed, even after they enter the presumed zones of safety in Europe:

> In January 2005, while detained in a police station in Dessau, Germany, Oury Jalloh (from Sierra Leone) was burned alive in a holding cell, found with his hands and feet chained to a bed, his nose broken, and his pants pulled down to his ankles. A month later, his death was declared an accidental suicide, with a notation by the chief of police: "Blacks just happen to burn longer." (Jansen 2008)

This murder is not an isolated case. In Europe's interior, border militarism is violent and often deadly. Detainees, most often young black men, are murdered in state custody, whether in the camp, the holding cell or the police station. The most frequently used methods of killing, based on my review of the recorded cases (United for Intercultural Action 2007), include the following: asphyxiation (hanging, suffocation with an object, strangulation, manual choking); the use of sedatives; water boarding; drowning in police custody (by pushing a water hose down the victim's throat); forcible drug-induced vomiting (as practiced in Germany in violation of European Union laws); being set on fire or dying in a fire (at airport detention centres or in police custody); and the denial of medical treatment. These murders by European state officials are pronounced and recorded as accidents or suicides. Under conditions of extreme dehumanization, when those who die are perceived as subhuman phantoms, the act of killing becomes inconsequential (Mbembe 2003: 24). Following Noam Chomsky (2001), I suggest that we must rethink such practices in terms of a "silent genocide."

Normalizing Militarized Violence in the Interior

As I have shown, the violent tactics of border guarding in Europe are not confined to an external periphery. Border security extends its reach into the very centre of Europe, where predatory state terror unfolds in the detention camp and the police station, in holding cells, in police custody, in airplanes (during deportation procedures), in airports and in prisons. But Europe's border militarism and attendant racial violence is not limited to the carceral spaces of state detention.

It takes effect in all those public places where non-white subjects are policed, monitored and violated by ordinary European citizens: the street, the park, the subway and so on. The extension of this violent apparatus into vernacular social space remains largely unrecorded and, as such, unacknowledged.

The violent capacity of borders is evident beyond fixed geographies. In analyzing the pattern of terror perpetrated within such "imaginative geographies," Stephen Graham describes "the ways in which imperialist societies tend to be constructed through normalizing, binary judgments about both 'foreign' territories and the 'home' spaces which sit at the 'heart of empire'" (2006: 255). In Europe, these logics of "place attachment" serve to demarcate a putative *us* in opposition to those *others* who are rendered hypervisible. The everyday work of state terror requires visible signifiers and abject difference has come to be visually marked. In the public realm, the binary logic of race is implanted into vernacular socialities, used to identify the enemy-Others on sight. Laura Bilsky's analysis of "citizenship as mask" provides a useful conceptual tool (2008). In the European Union, as in other nation-state systems, the legal persona is defined by "citizenship," which secures the "dimensions of political equality." The corresponding metaphor of the mask exposes the artificiality of this postulate. The right to belong, as Bilsky suggests, is defined by specific requirements of "concealment" or "disclosure:" legal subjectivity may be differently encoded in different subjects. But a black person is "not offered the protection of the mask and thus remains exposed, not able to re-present his or her body in public" (Bilsky 2008: 7). Such a radical fixture of personhood by colour suggests that citizenship status is also encoded by extra-legal dimensions. In the European national imaginary, the very mask of citizenship is racialized. Whiteness *is* the mask of national belonging, rendering all European subjects metaphorically equal under the "white" signifier.

What impact does such an optical mask of citizenship have on the lives of blacks in Europe? Perceived as an external otherness, blackness is most often associated with an experience of utter isolation. As May Ayim expresses it, "I could cry, because I realize that basically I'm ... all alone.... Being Black means ... feeling alone" (qtd. in Wiedenroth 1992: 176). This sense of social isolation is further enhanced by a particular optical regime: black subjects are visually incarcerated by white "looking relations" (hooks 1991: 168). In everyday social encounters, blackness attracts visual attention: black bodies are immediately *seen, recognized* and *identified*, catapulted out of the terrain of whiteness and perceived as alien, foreign and other, as suggested by the following pastiche of comments by black Germans:

> "People think I'm a foreigner." "As soon as they see me, they think I can't speak German." "We're not perceived as European." "A lot of people assume that I have a particular relationship to Africa." "I am not viewed as a German." (Qtd. in Baum et al. 1992: 151, 145, 154)

On the ground, in Europe's interior borderlands, blackness is linked to concrete forms of visual marginalization, where ethno-racial identification operates as a form of terror. As suggested by Frantz Fanon (1967), interactions in public space are encoded by the visual capture of the "black" subject by "white" recognition. The hyper-visibility of "black-inscribed skin" is entrapped in "an imposed othering and dehumanization from which there is little escape" (Lusane 2003: 21). In such a racialized terrain, a sense of visual vulnerability becomes a central experience for non-white subjects:

> With our color we are always visible.... Yes, we're walking targets. We can never "submerge" ... I can't ever "just walk around" ... I can't walk relaxed at all.... I am German, and I'm dark ... "coffee-and-cream brown." [...] But no matter how many nuances are defined, it always comes down to the same thing: You are branded (no, marked) as non-white. (Qtd. in Wiedenroth 1992: 174, 176)

By deploying the panoptics of race, border militarism has extended its reach into the social interior of Europe and the everyday spaces of life. In Europe's national interior, violent exclusion proceeds by what Jonathan Inda (with view to the U.S.-Mexican border) has termed "border prophylaxis," through spatial enclosures (camps, detention centres, prisons), surveillance and by "governing through crime" (2006: 116). Racialization is always a subtext. The conflation of blackness and criminality has several important consequences. African immigrants, by extension black Europeans, are forced to inhabit the figure of the illegal alien, the enemy outsider, the welfare sponger, pimp or prostitute, drug dealer and the diseased body. Identified as criminals and/or as threats to society, the body politic and national security, they are treated accordingly (Menschenrechtsverein 2002). Random passport and identity checks, arbitrary arrests, body searches, physical abuse, torture and sexual humiliation are perpetrated by European state officials and police with increasing frequency (Goldberg 2009: 178, 189). In public space, the non-white signifier is continuously monitored. In this panoptic theater of race, the figure of the male-terrorist-criminal is conjured on sight. The imperatives of border security have transformed European public space into a quasi-militarized zone, in which non-white subjects are monitored, policed and apprehended as presumed criminals.

When Europe's "security package" was drafted into law in spring 2009, it enabled pogrom-like actions against visible minorities. "While disproportionate numbers of Afro-Europeans are beings arrested and incarcerated or deported, police brutality against racial minorities—including murder—has skyrocketed" (Lusane 2003: 253).

By criminalizing unauthorized migration across national borders, the law turned all dark-skinned individuals into potential suspects. In Italy, such a criminalization of the non-European Other synergized latent stereotypes against African immigrants and "gypsies." Fabricated accusations of theft, sorcery, child abduction, blood rituals, sexual perversions and rape were turned into believable truth-claims that unleashed the protective power of state militarism in Rome, Milan and Naples:

> Police operations [against Roma and other groups] are carried out with the use of helicopters, police dog units, and armed men in uniform, both during the day and in the dead of night.... Officials have announced the employment of 30,000 more soldiers to work alongside the police on the streets of the major cities (Rome, Milan, Naples, etc.).... The Ministers of the Interior and Defence initiated [this] project in 2008 ... investing a total of two billion Euros a year. The Italian Prime Minister defined the Roma [gypsies], immigrants, and the homeless as "the evil army" and "the enemy" to be combated using these troops. (EveryOne Group 2009)

In these acts of state military terror against minorities, race is clearly a central factor: non-white subjects are criminalized, defined as a security threat, conjured as "the enemy" of the nation and the state. In Italy, under "the spectre of racial targeting," as Angel-Ajani (2002) has observed, such dissimilar peoples as Nigerians, Senegalese, Moroccans, Tunisians, Albanians, Poles, Colombians and Roma are collectively classified as "criminal types" and "deviants," who are apprehended on suspicion of drug trafficking or prostitution and arrested on sight.

In Europe's interior borderlands, we observe a further intensification of everyday violence and street terror against those subjects who are rejected as non-European. Perceived "as a threat to the body politic" (Campt 2005: 83), salient Others are brutalized, even killed by ordinary Europeans. The attacks appear to be opportunistic encounter-killings (on a train, in front of a pub, on a street, in a park, on a streetcar or subway) perpetrated by close-contact violence; the victim is kicked or beaten to death, stabbed, dowsed with alcohol and burned, bashed with a rock, pushed through a glass door or thrown out of a window.[4] Europe's border war has transfigured the space of the street into a zone of terror. The use of soldiers against civilians transforms immigration into a military matter and provides a legitimating context for non-official acts of violence perpetrated by ordinary citizens.

Violent practices that strip black Europeans of their lives, personhood and identities, "in fact making them a non-entity" (El-Tayeb 2005: 28), are legitimated by public discourse. In police reports and news media, the victims of hate crimes are categorically described as "African," "African-born," "black-African," "coloured" and "tribal." Occasionally a victim will be described as "a holder of a German passport, but never as German," or as French, Dutch or British (El Tayeb 2005: 27). The racialized colour-coding of national belonging, which defines blackness and Europeanness as "mutually contradictory categories" (Smith 2006: 430), confirms the otherness of the presumed Other. The Europeanization of Europe, as propagated by police and media, is embedded in a discourse that renders racial violence acceptable. In this terrain of white-on-black violence, fear becomes a central experience. Europe's "violent security policies...install migrants in a condition of permanent insecurity" (Balibar 2004: 15). In the words of one young African man: "I cannot move freely and avoid certain places; I am always afraid" (qtd. in Menschenrechtsverein 2002). Terror, founded on the panoptics of racial classification, becomes an amorphous instrument of control: the militarized securocratic apparatus is ever-present. By policing the perceptual anti-citizen across European Union territory—from the outer perimeter to the camp to the street—border militarism has become commonplace: it has been implanted into the security habitus of the mundane.

Concluding Reflections

In Europe's securocratic world, the politics of race remain entangled with past histories of empire, social engineering and bio-political experimentation. But in the global present, racial violence and border militarism belong to a new order of terror. An examination of Europe as a late-modern political form "reveals how modern government stages itself by dealing directly in the power over life: the power to exclude, to declare exceptions, to strip human existence of civic rights and social value" (Comaroff 2007: 22). The contemporary exclusion of blacks from Europe is a terror formation with a new political purpose. Border security, underwritten by violence and death, is entangled with the militarization of civil society.

Border fortification is a move against the forces of global mobility. Europeanness is contrasted with the enemy-outsider: the anti-citizen, the fleeting figure of the terrorist, the border crosser, the non-sedentary black body. The figure of the enemy-outsider has emerged as a trope for people in motion, including migrants, immigrants, refugees, seekers of asylum and transient border-subjects, who are perceived as potential threats to "homeland" mobile security. Human figures are criminalized as icons of global instability and disorder. In Europe's imaginative geography, such frictions are articulated through the idiom of race; the home world, populated by white citizen-subjects, is to be protected from those dark others, the mass of "immigrants" and/or "illegals." According to this logic, globally mobile populations must be harnessed, contained and controlled.

By recourse to familiar racial tropes, Europeanness "is imagined as an identity against the Other" (Mbembe 2003: 23). Tangible alterities or figures of difference (the veiled Muslim woman, the Arab terrorist, the black immigrant) occupy a strategic place in the determination of Europeanness and the articulation of the corresponding fields of whiteness. As Stuart Hall has observed, the "largely unspoken racial connotations" of national belonging in Europe are encoded by a cultural logic of othering that promotes either assimilation or exclusion (Hall

2000b). Distinction is manufactured along a narrow register that "accords differing groups cultural normativity or deviance" (Ong 1996: 759). In this volatile terrain, the European nation-state is "caught between the need to enforce sameness and the fear of absolute difference, with no middle ground" (Bilsky 2009: 306). Such an identity formation in turn legitimates the fortification of Europe as a gated, exclusive community. But border militarism, as I have shown, entails more than policing. The regime of borders can grant life or deliver death. The militarized security state, to borrow Achille Mbembe's phrasing, has been endowed with the "capacity to define who matters and does not, who is *disposable* and who is not" (2003: 27). Accordingly, state violence and military security are no longer confined to their former roles. From the security perimeter into the urban interior, border militarism deploys racialization to enhance its capacity to exclude. A distinguishing feature of Europe's border regime is its amorphous quality; ordinary life is militarized as the colour of bodies and the acts of racial violence are woven into the fabric of everyday social governance.

Notes

1. My research on this subject derives from multiple sources over a ten-year period: ethnographic research from 1997 through 2005, when I lived and worked in Germany for four years, with subsequent follow-up trips during the summer. Following to my experiences and findings, I began to investigate popular representations of blackness in Europe. Work at the European University in Budapest during the summer of 2003 allowed me to conduct comparative research with nationals from former socialist countries. My data collection from field research was supplemented by print and media materials on black Europeans and the fortification of a "white" Europe after 2005.

2. Building on my extensive work on immigrants and refugees in Germany and Europe in the postwar era through the 1990s, I expanded the scope of my research and assembled an archive of statistical and demographic information produced by the official publication office of the European Communities: included are "Europe in Figures," the Eurostat year books furnished since 2002, special issue publications on the demographic data produced by the European Union and other materials available from the Eurostat and Europa websites. For comparisons, I have consulted United Nations and World Bank sources on European demographic information, which include different sets of data sources such as financial transactions, remittances and emigration information from the migrants' countries of origin.

3. In contrast to European Union statistics, this figure not only includes the narrowly defined bureaucratic category of the "immigrant," but also short-term migrants, reunited family members, spouses, refugees and other foreign residents who are excluded from the EU statistical roster. The United Nations Recommendations on Migration Statistics suggest that the migrant stock be measured in terms of foreign-born and foreign populations (United Nations 2006: 29, table 2).

4. This summary is based on my review of cases reported in the news media, which I have collected as part of my research since 2000 as they appeared in major newspapers (which I acquired as searchable CD ROMs): *Frankfurter Allgemeine Zeitung, Frankurter Rundschau, Taz, Berliner Zeitung, Die Zeit* and *Der Spiegel*. I have supplemented this information with the data collections on racist violence provided by FRA (2009).

References

Amnesty International. 2009. Italy: Discriminatory Draft Law Affecting Migrants and Roma Community. *Appeals for Action*, 26 June: http://www.amnesty.org/en/appeals-for-action/italy-must-not-pass-law-that-discriminates-against-migrants-and-Roma.

Angel-Ajani, Asale. 2002. Diasporic Conditions: Mapping the Discourses of Race and Criminality in Italy. *Transforming Anthropology* 11(1): 36-46.

Appadurai, Arjun. 1996. *Modernity at Large*. Minneapolis, MN: University of Minnesota Press.

———. 2001. Grassroots Globalization and the Research Imagination. In *Globalization*, edited by Arjun Appadurai, 1-20. Durham, NC: Duke University Press.

Balibar, Etienne. 2004. Europe as Borderland. The Alexander von Humboldt Lecture in Human Geography. University of Nijmegen, 10 November. http://www.ru.nl/socgeo/colloquium/Europe%20as%20Borderland.pdf.

Baum, Laura, Katharina Oguntoye and May Opitz. 1992. Three Afro-German Women in Conversation with Dagmar Schultz. In *Showing Our Colors*, edited by May Opitz, Katharina Oguntoye and Dagmar Schultz, 145-64. Amherst, MA: University of Massachusetts Press.

Bauman, Zygmunt. 2000. *Liquid Modernity*. Cambridge, U.K.: Polity Press.

Bilsky, Laura. 2008. Citizenship as Mask. *Constellations* 15(1): 1-39.

———. 2009. Muslim Headscarves in France and Army Uniforms in Israel. *Patterns of Prejudice* 43(3-4): 287-311.

Bundeswehr Ausbildung. 2007. www.youtube.com/watch?v=EgfWemdK0WY.

Campt, Tina M. 2005. Converging Specters of an Other Within. In *Not So Plain as Black and White*, edited by Patricia Mazón and Reinhild Steingröver, 82-106. Rochester, NY: University of Rochester Press.

Chomsky, Noam. 2001. The New War against Terror. Excerpted transcript of a lecture given at the Massachusetts Institute of Technology (MIT) Technology and Culture Forum, 18 October. http://www.chomsky.info/talks/20011018.htm.

Comaroff, John L. and Jean. 2009. *Ethnicity, Inc.* Chicago, IL: University of Chicago Press.

Cooper, Frederick, and Laura A. Stoler, eds. 1997. *Tensions of Empire*. Berkeley, CA: University of California Press.

Copers, M., V. Guillemet, A. Johansson-Augier, G. Kyi and M. Radulescu, eds. 2004. *Eurostat Yearbook 2004: The Statistical Guide to Europe*. Luxembourg: Office for Official Publications of the European Communities.

El-Tayeb, Fatima. 2005. Dangerous Liaisons. In *Not So Plain as Black and White*, edited by Patricia Mazón and Reinhild Steingröver, 27-60. Rochester, NY: University of Rochester Press.

Eurostat. 2002. *European Social Statistics: Migration*. Luxembourg: Office for Official Publications of the European Communities.

EveryOne Group. 2009. Criminalization of the Roma People in Italy. EveryOne Group for International Cooperation on Human Rights Culture. 8 February. http://www.everyonegroup.com/EveryOne/MainPage/Entries/2009/2/8_Criminalization_of_the_Roma_people_in_Italy._Attacks_in_Rome_spark_off_another_witch_hunt.html.

Fanon, Frantz. 1967. *Black Skin, White Masks*. Trans. Charles Lam Markmann. New York: Grove Press.

Feldman, Allen. 2004. Securocratic Wars of Public Safety. *Interventions* 6(3): 330-50.

Fine, Michael, Reva Jaffe-Walter, Pedro Pedraza, Valerie Futch and Brett Stoudt. 2007. Swimming. *Anthropology and Education Quarterly* 38(1): 76-96.

FRA (Fundamental Rights Agency). 2009. Racist Violence. European Union Agency for Fundamental Rights. http://infoportal.fra.europa.eu/InfoPortal/infobaseShowContent.do?btnCat_11.

Gilman, Sander L. 1982. *On Blackness without Blacks*. Boston: G. H. Hall.

Gilroy, Paul. 2000. *Between Camps*. London: Penguin.

———. 2004 Migrancy, Culture, and a New Map of Europe. In *Blackening Europe*, edited by Heike Raphael-Hernandez, xi-xxii. New York: Routledge.

Giroux, Henry A. 2004. War on Terror: The Militarising of Public Space and Culture in the United States. *Third Text* 18(4): 211-21.

Glick-Schiller, Nina. 2005. Racialized Nations, Evangelizing Christianity, Police States, and Imperial Power. *American Ethnologist* 32(4): 526-32.

Goldberg, David Theo. 2006. Racial Europeanization. *Ethnic and Racial Studies* 29(2): 331-64.

———. 2009. *The Threat of Race*. Malden, MA: Blackwell.

Goodey, Jo. 2007. Racist Violence in Europe. *Ethnic and Racial Studies* 30(4): 570-89.

Graham, Stephen. 2006. Cities and the "War on Terror." *International Journal of Urban and Regional Research* 30(2): 255-76.

Hall, Stuart. 2000a. The Local and the Global. In *Culture, Globalization, and the World-System*, edited by Anthony D. King, 19-39. Minneapolis, MN: University of Minneapolis Press.

———. 2000b. A Question of Identity (II). *The Observer*, 15 October. http://www.guardian.co.uk/uk/2000/oct/15/britishidentity.comment1.

Hardt, Michael and Antonio Negri. 2000. *Empire*. Cambridge, MA: Harvard University Press.

Hintjens, Helen M. 2007. Citizenship under Siege in the Brave New Europe. *European Journal of Cultural Studies* 10(3): 409-14.

hooks, bell. 1991. *Black Looks*. Boston: South End Press.

Inda, Jonathan Xavier. 2006. Border Prophylaxis. *Cultural Dynamics* 18(2): 115-32.

Jansen, Frank. 2008. Rassistische Polizei–Landtag prüft Vorwürfe. *tagespiegel.de*, 14 February. http://www.tagesspiegel.de/politik/deutschland/rechtsextremismus/Sachsen-Anhalt;art2647,2476264.

JRS-Europe. 2009a. Detention in Europe. *Detention-in-Europe.org*. http://www.detention-in-europe.org/index.php?option=com_content&task=view&id=92&Itemid=213.

———. 2009b. Mapping Detention in Europe. *Detention-in-Europe.org*. http://www.detention-in-europe.org/index.php?option=com_content&task=view&id=90&Itemid=212.

Linke, Uli. 1999. *German Bodies: Race and Representation after Hitler.* Philadelphia: University of Pennsylvania Press.

Lockenour, Jay. 2007. PressRPT: Rendsburg Bundeswehr Video Scandal. Posted on H-German@H-NET.MSU, 27 April.

Lusane, Clarence. 2003. *Hitler's Black Victims.* New York: Routledge.

Mazón, Patricia and Reinhild Steingröver, eds. 2005. *Not So Plain as Black and White.* Rochester, NY: University of Rochester Press.

Mbembe, Achille. 2003. Necropolitics. *Public Culture* 15(1): 11–40.

Menschenrechtsverein. 2002. Wenn die Polizei Schwarz sieht: der ganz normale Alltag. *Augenauf*, November. http://www.augenauf.ch/bs/archiv/poldiv/021100.htm.

Migreurop. 2009. Carte des camps 2007. http://www.migreurop.org/.

Mirzoeff, Nicholas. 2005. *Watching Babylon.* New York: Routledge.

Ong, Aihwa. 1996. Cultural Citizenship as Subject-Making. *Current Anthropology* 37(5): 737-51 and 758-62.

Pred, Allan. 2000. *Even in Sweden.* Berkeley, CA: University of California Press.

Schäfer, G., S. Cervellin, M. Feith and M. Fritz, eds. 2005. *Europe in Figures: Eurostat Yearbook 2005.* Luxembourg: Office for Official Publications of the European Communities.

Schäfer, G., M. Feith, M. Fritz, A. Johansson-Augier and U. Wieland, eds. 2007. *Europe in Figures: Eurostat Yearbook 2006-07.* Luxembourg: Office for Official Publications of the European Communities.

Scheck, Raphael. 2006. *Hitler's African Victims.* Cambridge, U.K.: Cambridge University Press.

Smith, Michelle. 2006. Blackening Europe—Europeanising Blackness: Theorising the Black Presence in Europe. *Contemporary European History* 15:423-39.

Tictin, Miriam. 2006. Where Ethics and Politics Meet: The Violence of Humanitarianism in France. *American Ethnologist* 33(1): 33-49.

United for Intercultural Action. 2007. List of 8855 Documented Refugee Deaths through Fortress Europe: 1993-2007. *United for Intercultural Action*, 14 March. http://www.unitedagainstracism.org.

United Nations. 2006. *International Migration and Development, Report of the Secretary-General*, report A/60/871: 1-90. http://www.unhcr.org/protect/PROTECTION/44d711a82.pdf.

Wiedenroth, Ellen. 1992. What Makes Me So Different in the Eyes of Others? In *Showing Our Colors*, edited by May Opitz, Katharina Oguntoye and Dagmar Schultz, 165-77. Amherst, MA: University of Massachusetts Press.

Markus Kienscherf

Plugging Cultural Knowledge into the U.S. Military Machine: The Neo-Orientalist Logic of Counterinsurgency

ABSTRACT

In this contribution to "Cultures of Militarization and the Military-Cultural Complex" I wish to analyze the recent trend toward the militarization of culture; or, to be precise, the military deployment of cultural knowledge in efforts to pacify recalcitrant non-Western populations and extend stable governmental structures to spaces at the margins of Western power. I will map how cultural knowledge is currently sought to be plugged into the U.S., or more broadly Western, counterinsurgency machine and show how this weaponization of culture (re-)produces a sovereign distinction between liberal and illiberal spaces and populations.

RÉSUMÉ

Brancher le savoir culturel à la machine militaire américaine : la logique néo-orientaliste de la contre-insurrection

Je souhaite analyser la tendance récente à la militarisation de la culture, ou, plus précisément, le déploiement militaire du savoir culturel dans le but de pacifier des populations non-occidentales récalcitrantes et pour étendre des structures gouvernementales stables dans les espaces situés aux marges du pouvoir occidental. Je dresserai une cartographie de la manière dont on cherche à l'heure actuelle à brancher le savoir culturel à la machine de la contre-insurrection américaine, ou plus largement occidentale, et je montrerai comment ce fait d'armer la culture (re) produit une distinction souveraine entre les espaces et les populations libéraux et non-libéraux.

> Take up the White Man's burden—
> The savage wars of peace—
> Fill full the mouth of Famine
> And bid the sickness cease;
> And when your goal is nearest
> (The end for others sought)
> Watch Sloth and heathen Folly
> Bring all your hope to nought.
>
> (Kipling 1899)

In 1991, acclaimed military historian Martin van Creveld predicted that "In the future, war will not be waged by armies but by groups whom we today call terrorists, guerrillas, bandits, and robbers, but who will undoubtedly hit on more formal titles to describe themselves" (1991: 197). Since the attacks on the World Trade Center and the Pentagon on September 11, 2001, numerous commentators across the political spectrum have asserted that the West is embroiled in a protracted global conflict with violent non-state actors. This conflict has been assigned a spate of different labels. The initial Bush administration response to the 9/11 attacks was to declare a global war on terror. Since then the rhetoric has been toned down a bit. But Pentagon officials and national security pundits still claim that the United States and its allies are engaged in what is now called a "long war," a "global counterinsurgency," or "global contingency operations" (cf. Berger and Borer 2007; Cassidy 2006a, 2006b, 2008; Kilcullen 2005, 2009; Wilson and Kamen 2009). The Los Angeles-based security consultant, Robert J. Bunker, even goes as far as to state that Western nation states are in the midst of a war "over humanity's new forms of social and political organization" (Bunker 2010: 24). Indeed, a number of security experts and academics argue that Western nation states are now faced by a host of different opponents that differ radically from conventional state competitors. These commentators view the rise of new, non-state, war-making entities—exemplified not only by al Qaeda and Iraqi or Afghan insurgents, but also by drug cartels and so-called Third Generation Gangs[1]—as a direct threat to the international state system (Bunker 2005, 2010; Bunker and Begert 2008; Bunker and Sullivan 2010; Kan 2009; Manwaring 2005, 2008; Sullivan 2005; van Creveld 1991, 2008). At the other end of the spectrum, Michael Hardt and Antonio Negri suggest that with the decline in inter-state conflicts "war seems to have seeped back and flooded the entire social field," leading to what they call a global civil war (2004: 7). In a similar vein, critical development scholar Mark Duffield argues that the current global security environment is marked by a biopolitical conflict over human life itself, or in his own words, "a global civil war between 'developed' and 'underdeveloped' species-life" (2008: 146). Despite their political differences, most of these commentators agree that the global security conjuncture cannot be understood in terms of conventional interstate conflict, but ought to be seen as a global insurgency in which traditional distinctions between combatants and non-combatants, war and peace, military and police operations, victory and defeat, are no longer applicable. Western states, most notably the United States, are now pitted against violent non-state actors who are organized along tribal and/or religious lines and who tend to hide and operate amongst civilian populations.

As a consequence, the United States has scrambled to respond to what is now commonly seen as threats to the very stability of the international state system. A vast array of policymakers and military figures, as well as civilian academics from both the United States and allied nations, most notably the United Kingdom, have stressed that these threats call for more "population-centred" military strategies (Cirafici 2008; Gompert et al. 2009; Kilcullen 2005; Long 2006; Nagl 2002; Ucko 2009: 174). Moreover, they argue that fighting enemies who operate among civilian populations requires thorough knowledge, not only about one's opponents but also about all aspects of the society in which they operate. One prominent and widely publicized response was the shift in U.S. military strategy from conventional firepower-centred warfare toward counterinsurgency (COIN) and stability operations. However the overall direction of the U.S. armed forces' move toward counterinsurgency remains highly contested. In fact, initial attempts to establish a U.S. counterinsurgency capability have met with a lot of resistance from within the U.S. military establishment (Ucko 2009).

Starting under the Bush administration this overhaul of strategy was above all spurred by U.S. and allied forces' difficulties in effectively pacifying and stabilizing post-invasion Iraq and Afghanistan. This brought counterinsurgency and stability operations, which had fallen into doctrinal oblivion since the end of the Vietnam War, back onto the top of the Pentagon's agenda in 2004-2005. In 2006, a new *Counterinsurgency Field Manual* was published, the first manual dedicated to counterinsurgency since the 1980s. The strategic realignment gained additional momentum under the Obama administration. In his speech about the new Afghanistan strategy on December 1, 2009, President Obama stressed that the United States are engaged in a protracted unconventional conflict with al Qaeda that "extends well beyond Afghanistan and Pakistan" (2009):

> [U]nlike the great power conflicts and clear lines of division that defined the 20th century, our effort will involve disorderly regions, failed states, diffuse enemies. So as a result, America will have to show our strength in the way that we end wars and prevent conflict—not just how we wage wars. We'll have to be nimble and precise in our use of military power. Where al Qaeda and its allies attempt to establish a foothold—whether in Somalia or Yemen or elsewhere–they must be confronted by growing pressure and strong partnerships. (Obama 2009)

The new long-term commitment to dealing with "disorderly regions, failed states, diffuse enemies" is also enshrined in the 2010 "Quadrennial Defense Review"

(QDR), which will be the chief blueprint for military planning and budgetary allocations for the next couple of years. The QDR asserts that "the changing international environment will continue to put pressure on the modern state system, likely increasing the frequency and severity of the challenges associated with chronically fragile states" (Defense 2010: 32). In this environment the U.S. military can no longer simply rely on its formidable conventional arsenal but must develop the capabilities to mount a series of low intensity operations across the global south:

> The wars we are fighting today and assessments of the future security environment together demand that the United States retain and enhance a whole-of-government capability to succeed in large-scale counterinsurgency (COIN), stability, and counterterrorism (CT) operations in environments ranging from densely populated urban areas and megacities, to remote mountains, deserts, jungles, and littoral regions. [...] Accordingly, the U.S. Armed Forces will continue to require capabilities to create a secure environment in fragile states in support of local authorities and, if necessary, to support civil authorities in providing essential government services, restoring emergency infrastructure, and supplying humanitarian relief. (Defense 2010: 43)

These conflicts are considered to pit U.S. armed forces against opponents who operate among foreign civilian populations whose support is seen as one of the most critical factors for the success of any counterinsurgency campaign. The QDR thus views the development of "foreign language skills and regional and cultural knowledge" as a pivotal component of a genuine counterinsurgency capability (52). Moreover, the current *Counterinsurgency Field Manual* also stresses again and again that "successful conduct of COIN operations depends on thoroughly understanding the society and culture within which they are being conducted" (Army 2007: 40). Cultural anthropologist Montgomery McFate, co-author of the field manual's chapter on intelligence, regular contributor to military publications and chief scientific consultant with the Army's Human Terrain System, makes the case for cultural knowledge even more forcefully:

> Understanding foreign cultures and societies has become a national security priority. The more unconventional the adversary, the more we need to understand their society and underlying cultural dynamics. To defeat non-Western opponents who are transnational in scope, nonhierarchical in structure, clandestine in their approach, and operate outside of the context of nation-states, we need to improve our capacity to understand foreign cultures and societies. (2005b: 47)

In this article I will analyze current efforts to inscribe cultural knowledge into what I will call the U.S. counterinsurgency machine.[2] Drawing on Foucault's concept of governmentality I will first of all argue that counterinsurgency is more than a purely military endeavour, but rather constitutes an ambiguous program of rule geared towards extending governmental relations to spaces and populations at the fringes of Western power. I will then examine the role of socio-cultural knowledge in general, and of the discipline of anthropology in particular, in enabling more discriminate modes of military targeting and more targeted forms of establishing control over foreign populations. Here I will focus on the design and deployment of the so-called Human Terrain System, an attempt at assembling a neo-Orientalist machine, which produces knowledge through the exercise of power. The effective exercise of power is then legitimated by the new forms of knowledge produced. Last but not least, I will discuss how this neo-Orientalist project centres on the constant (re-)production of differences between liberal and illiberal populations, as well as divisions within illiberal populations.

Counterinsurgency as a Governmental Program

By now we are all too familiar with the complex and ambiguous relations between knowledge and the exercise of power. Zygmunt Bauman claims that the social sciences have always tried to position themselves as the "the intelligence branch" of the modern state by helping it manage its population and territory more effectively (2002: 2). In his book on *The Nation State and Violence* Anthony Giddens argues that the production of knowledge through regimes of surveillance, in the sense of both information-gathering and direct supervision, played a major part in the formation of the modern state (1987: 181-92). Perhaps most famously, Michel Foucault has frequently highlighted the interrelations between knowledge and the micro-political operations of power. In recently published lectures Foucault also explicitly addresses the role of knowledge about the state and its population, what he calls statistics or "the science of the state," in the internal pacification of territory and population and hence also in the rise of modern liberal governmentality (2007: 100-101, 272-77). Indeed, the production of knowledge about territories and populations is the *sine qua non* of government. For Foucault, government aims "to structure the possible field of action of others" (2000: 341). The practice of government hinges on structures of knowledge, expertise and representations concerning those to be governed, as well as on technologies, techniques, instruments and tactics by means of which one actually goes about the day-to-day business of governing (Foucault 2007; Larner and Walters 2004; Rose and Miller 1992). In short, government operates within the frame of what Foucault termed "governmentality" (Foucault 2003, 2007). What is more, governmentality constitutes a form of power that is situated in a zone of indistinction between "the problematics of consensus and will on the one hand and conquest and war on the other" (Lemke 2000: 4).

Military theorist Carl von Clausewitz defined war as "an act of force to compel our enemy to do our will" (1976: 83). Yet, in what is now referred to as fourth-generation warfare (4GW) the use of force is just one particular channel for imposing one's will on the enemy. Indeed, according to retired U.S. Colonel Thomas X. Hammes, fourth-generation warfare, which he defines as "an evolved form of insurgency," has shifted the focus of warfare from the industrial-scale destruction of one's opponent's armed forces, to undermining the political will and staying power of enemy decision makers (Hammes 2006: 207-208):

> Fourth-generation warfare (4GW) uses all available networks—political, economic, social, and military—to convince the enemy's political decision makers that their strategic goals are either unachievable or too costly for the perceived benefit. [...] Unlike previous generations of warfare, it does not attempt to win by defeating the enemy's military forces. Instead, via the networks, it directly attacks the minds of enemy decision makers to destroy the enemy's political will. (2)

In fact, in fourth-generation warfare, war is no longer clearly distinguishable from non-violent forms of coercion. Likewise, the traditional dividing line between crime and war or between internal public safety and external national security, has become increasingly fuzzy (Bunker and Begert 2008). Thus, what Anthony Giddens called the internal pacification of society becomes more and more indistinguishable from the defence against external threats (1987). Indeed, this is what Hardt and Negri mean when they suggest that "war seems to have seeped back and flooded the entire social field" (2004: 7).

When Foucault inverted von Clausewitz's famous dictum that war is "a continuation of political intercourse, carried on with other means," in order to ask whether we should not think of the problematic of political power as the "continuation of war by other means," he sought to draw out the war-like force relations that have always persisted even within stable, internally pacified societies (Foucault 2003: 15; von Clausewitz 1976: 99). Indeed, government in the aforementioned Foucauldian sense of acting on somebody else's actions has always entailed relations of both coercion and consent. But now this tension between coercion and consent that is government, according to Foucault, seems to cut across the traditional divide between internal pacification and external defence.[3]

As a specific response to the rise of fourth-generation warfare, counterinsurgency is geared towards extending instruments of internal pacification across the globe. It is perhaps best thought of as a deterritorialized form of homeland security in that it seeks to protect the homeland from threats held to fester in ungoverned spaces of the global south. The current *Counterinsurgency Field Manual* defines insurgency as "an organized, protracted politico-military struggle designed to weaken the control and legitimacy of an established government, occupying power, or other political authority while increasing insurgent control" (Army 2007: 2). Counterinsurgency in turn is defined as "military, paramilitary, political, economic, psychological, and civic actions taken by a government to defeat insurgency" (2). We have to be careful to distinguish between counterinsurgency and stability operations, on one hand, and so-called peace operations, on the other. Political scientist David Ucko argues that counterinsurgency and stability operations share three significant features: 1) they occur in a context of hostile activity or a non-permissive operational environment; 2) the stabilization effort forms part of a wider state-building initiative; and 3) the stabilizing force is deployed in the midst of a civilian population (2009: 9-11). But counterinsurgency campaigns and stability operations differ from peace-operations in that they are not consensual: counterinsurgents tend to support a particular group, most likely a so-called host nation government, whereas peace-builders and peacekeepers at least pretend to be neutral.[4]

What becomes immediately obvious is that counterinsurgency operations are more than purely military efforts. Therefore, counterinsurgency ought to be understood as an assemblage of rule connecting up techniques of power, forms of knowledge and modes of knowledge-production. This complex and contradictory machine is geared toward managing and containing threats said to emanate from spaces and populations that more often than not tend to be located in the postcolonial global south. In short, counterinsurgency constitutes a governmental ensemble aimed at pacifying ungoverned spaces and populations. This pacification effort pivots on providing security to the local population while building the politico-economic infrastructure that would ultimately enable the so-called host-nation to govern itself (Army 2007).

In a 1965 piece about "The Theory and Practice of Insurgency," written in the face of a steadily escalating "small war" in Vietnam, acclaimed war correspondent and Indochina expert Bernard Fall stresses that success in counterinsurgency campaigns depends as much if not more on promoting and expanding governmental structures as on military operations. Fall's famous assertion that, "*When a country is being subverted it is not being outfought; it is being out-administered*," has become widely accepted within the counterinsurgency community (1998: 4). According to the current field manual, "The primary objective of any COIN operation is to foster development of effective governance by a legitimate government" (Army 2007: 37). So what is ultimately at stake in counterinsurgency is government. As Sarah Sewall, director of Harvard's Carr Human Rights Center, states in her "Introduction to the University of Chicago Press Edition" of the *Counterinsurgency Field Manual*,

> U.S. unwillingness to govern other nations is, in this account, a fatal national flaw. The field manual stresses the importance of effectively employing nonmilitary power. It is not a responsibility that can be left to a beleaguered host nation. Counterinsurgents must harness the ordinary administrative functions to the fight, providing personnel, resources, and expertise. (2007: xxxviii)

Moreover, Sewall holds that in the current global conjuncture the main security challenge for the West consists in "buttressing multiple failing state structures to legitimize the interstate system" (xlii). Accordingly, in order to bolster fragile governments against insurgency and protect the stability of the Western controlled international system, the United States and their allies feel compelled to extend stable governmental structures to populations located at the margins of Western power.

The counterinsurgency machine thus targets populations that are deemed unable to govern themselves. In fact, what we see here is the fundamental sovereign distinction, characteristic of liberal governmentality, between "what can be governed through the promotion of liberty and what must be governed in other ways" (Hindess 2004: 28; cf. Dean 2000, 2002, 2004). In this context the term sovereign distinction refers to the persistence of a specific form of sovereign power within governmentality. In the literature on governmentality, sovereignty is often defined as the exercise of central authority over the subjects of a definite territory working through the institutions of law and the executive. Governmentality, on the other hand, deploys a raft of decentred strategies and tactics in order to optimize the immanent socio-economic processes of the population (Butler 2004: 50-100; Dean 2000, 2002; Dean 2010: 28-30; Gordon 1991; Hindess 2004). Liberal governmentality emerged from a critique of an excess of government that was said to stifle the processes of the population. It seeks to delimit the legitimate scope of government through the promotion of individual liberty and autonomy in order to more effectively regulate and promote the vital socio-economic processes of the population (Dean 2000, 2010; Hindess 2004). Yet not everybody is considered to be equally capable of exercising his or her liberty and some are even construed as threats to the very existence of the liberal order. Thus, sovereignty is redeployed within the field of governmentality and assumes the function of an executive decision as to what constitutes a state of exception, or to be more precise, as to whom or what constitutes a threat to the free development of society's vital processes (Agamben 1998, 2005). In short, within the field of liberal governmentality sovereignty asserts itself in the decision as to who or what represents a threat to the liberal order. This clearly reverberates with Judith Butler's remarks about the justification of contemporary war:

> Lives are divided into those representing certain kinds of states and those representing threats to state-centered liberal democracy, so that war can then be righteously waged on behalf of some lives, while the destruction of other lives can be righteously defended. (2009: 53)

In fact, this holds true for any kind of U.S. military intervention. The targets of potential and actual military operations are construed as barbaric threats to the liberal order so that waging war upon them can be justified vis-à-vis domestic and global audiences. However, in stark contrast with past U.S. military practice and its frequently indiscriminate use of firepower, counterinsurgency aims to avoid the destruction of civilian lives. Within the logic of counterinsurgency the lives of foreign civilians are, in Butler's terminology, "grievable," albeit only to the extent that their loss may undermine the primary military objective of winning the support of the population. The field manual, for example, asserts that

> counterinsurgents should calculate carefully the type and amount of force to be applied and who wields it for any operation. An operation that kills five insurgents is counterproductive if collateral damage leads to the recruitment of fifty more insurgents. (Army 2007: 45)

In his article on the persistence of authoritarian features in liberal governmentality, Mitchell Dean lays out five "(fluid) categories of liberal subjects of government grouped according to their capacities for autonomy" (2000: 48): those in what he calls "Group A" are capable of fully "exercising liberal autonomy;" "Group B" consists of "those who need assistance to maintain capacities for autonomy" (e.g., welfare recipients, etc.); those in "Group C" have the potential for acting autonomously but need further training and education; "Group D" includes all those who "are for one reason or another not yet or no longer able to exercise their own autonomy or act in their own best interests" (48). Groups A to C are capable of exercising some degree of autonomy—they are located on a sliding scale of liberality, with those at the bottom needing a greater degree of assistance; whereas Group D includes those subjects who for some reason have lost or not yet gained their ability to exercise autonomy. Populations of fragile, failed or failing states, or ungoverned spaces, seem to belong to Group D in the sense that they have either lost or not yet obtained their ability to act in their own interest. Elevating them to a more liberal subject position would be a purely objective and philanthropic endeavour, if it wasn't for the fact that these populations harbour what is seen as genuine threats to the liberal order. This is where Dean's fifth category is relevant. Group E encompasses all "those who disrupt or simply get in the way of the establishment and maintenance of a liberal legal and political order within national states or internationally" (48). This group includes all the violent non-state actors who are held to wage war on the international state system and who are no longer seen as legitimate adversaries, but as enemies of peace and humanity who "we despise and seek either to transform into a more acceptable life-form or to annihilate" (Prozorov 2006: 84). Yet, Dean's categories and his sliding scale of liberality are better suited to the domestic sphere of liberal democracies than to those spaces and populations that are the targets of counterinsurgency. Counterinsurgency is a governmental technology targeting those spaces and populations that "must be governed in other ways,"—spaces and populations that represent "threats to state-centered liberal democracy" (Butler 2009: 53; Hindess 2004: 28). It is a governmental mechanism aimed at problem cases. Thus, military operations in the global borderlands are centred on a sliding scale of illiberality, in that targeted spaces and populations are *a priori* viewed as illiberal. But they are, nonetheless, supposed to contain elements that can be transformed and perhaps ultimately lifted up to liberal subject positions through a combination of security, development and information operations.

According to the current field manual, pacification efforts rest on differentiating between an active minority supporting the insurgency, an active minority opposing the insurgency, and a neutral or passive majority that can swing either way (Army 2007: 36). The main objective of the so-called population-centred or "hearts-and-minds" variant of counterinsurgency is to convince the passive majority to throw in their lot with the counterinsurgents.[5] This is supposed to be achieved through the provision of security and development backed by a consistent information strategy (Army 2007). But there are further distinctions within the group that actively supports the insurgency. Counterinsurgents also frequently use financial incentives and amnesty programs to induce common foot soldiers to lay down their arms. Moreover, by adopting a divide-and-rule approach, counterinsurgent forces also frequently aim to map and exploit already existing social antagonisms. Thus, counterinsurgents try to sort members of the targeted population into various categories to be ultimately able to differentiate between those elements that pose a genuine threat to the liberal order and those that can and must be lifted up to more liberal subject positions. In short, counterinsurgents seek to make distinctions within the targeted population between those that can be won over through various non-lethal ways and those hardliners that need to be taken out by force.

However, in order to make these distinctions and calibrate the use of firepower accordingly, soldiers and marines are said to require a thorough understanding of a host-nation's culture and society. Apart from acting as soldiers, policemen, relief workers and spin doctors, soldiers and marines are also supposed to act as amateur social scientists, capable of producing knowledge not only about the insurgents but also about all aspects of the society in which they operate:

> Intelligence in COIN is about people. U.S. forces must understand the people of the host nation, the insurgents, and the host-nation government. Commanders and planners require insight into cultures, perceptions, values, beliefs, interests and decision-making processes of individuals and groups. [...] Intelligence and operations feed each other. Effective intelligence drives effective operations. Effective operations produce information, which generates more intelligence. [...] All operations have an intelligence component. All Soldiers and Marines collect information whenever they interact with the populace. (Army 2007: 80)

The ultimate objective of extending stable governmental structures to ungoverned spaces thus calls for thorough knowledge about the different groups comprising the targeted population. In brief, the targeted population has to be made intelligible before it can be rendered governable.

Making the Other Intelligible

> We are opposed around the world by a monolithic and ruthless conspiracy that relies primarily on covert means for expanding its sphere of influence—on infiltration instead of invasion, on subversion instead of elections, on intimidation instead of free choice, on guerrillas by night instead of armies by day. (Kennedy 1961: 336)

These are the words of President John F. Kennedy not long after his inauguration in 1961. Kennedy's obsession over what is now called low-intensity warfare is well known. Political scientist Roger Hilsman, who served as a key aide and foreign policy advisor to Kennedy, wrote that one of the first questions Kennedy put to his aides after his inauguration was, "What are we doing about guerrilla warfare"? (Qtd in Blaufarb 1977: 52). Kennedy's obsession with communist-influenced insurgencies prompted a flurry of activities at all levels of government: seminars and courses on counterinsurgency; major efforts at bureaucratic restructuring; and the frenetic formulation of new policies and doctrine (Blaufarb 1977; McClintock 1992; Shafer 1988). This culminated in the 1962 formulation of the U.S. Overseas Internal Defense Policy, a comprehensive counterinsurgency program that sought to merge security and development into a coherent policy instrument for thwarting the spread of communist subversion (U.S. 1962). During the Cold War, counterinsurgency advocates also envisaged a major role for social scientists in (1) analyzing insurgencies "along predominantly political, economic, and social lines," in order to "uncover the causes of and solutions to social unrest throughout the Third World by employing both military and nonmilitary forms of analysis and prescription;" and in (2) "helping the military craft COIN doctrine to specifically target the underlying causes and overt symptoms of insurgency" (Clemis 2009: 163, 166).

When counterinsurgency doctrine experienced a renaissance at the beginning of the 21st century, a combination of security and development directed at foreign populations remained at the heart of the doctrine (Clemis 2009). However, as insurgencies are no longer viewed as the outcome of a superpower struggle for hegemony in the Third World, but rather as conflicts along ethnic, cultural and religious lines, there emerged a growing need for more contextual forms of analysis about specific cultures, tribes, religious sects, etc., instead of the sweeping Cold War narratives about the modernization process and its discontents (Heuser 2007). When, after two initially successful invasions, the United States saw themselves challenged by a tribal insurgency in both Iraq and Afghanistan, it was clear that the U.S. lacked the most fundamental linguistic and cultural tools for understanding the environment in which they operated. It was in this context that so-called "culture-centric warfare" seemed to offer a solution (Clemis 2009; Kipp et al. 2006; McFate 2004, 2005a, 2005b; McFate and Jackson 2005, 2006; Renzi 2006). Social scientists, most notably anthropologists, were quickly heralded as invaluable tools for designing and implementing military programs aimed at pacifying recalcitrant non-Western populations.

In a 2005 article in *Military Review*, Montgomery McFate bemoaned what she saw as anthropology's "brutal process of self-flagellation" and demanded that the discipline once again shoulder its responsibilities as a "warfighting discipline" (2005a: 28).

> Once called "the handmaiden of colonialism," anthropology has had a long and fruitful relationship with various elements of national power, which ended suddenly following the Vietnam War. The strange story of anthropology's birth as a warfighting discipline, and its sudden plunge into the abyss of postmodernism, is intertwined with the U.S. failure in Vietnam. The curious and conspicuous lack of anthropology in the national-security arena since the Vietnam War has had grave consequences for countering the insurgency in Iraq, particularly because political policy and military operations based on partial and incomplete knowledge are often worse than none at all (24).[6]

From 2005, the U.S. military has actively sought to plug anthropological knowledge into both doctrine and force structure. The 2006 *Counterinsurgency Field Manual*, whose chapter on intelligence was co-authored by McFate, is peppered with terms such as social networks, roles and statuses, social norms, taboo, culture, identity, narratives, myths, beliefs, ideologies, etc.—terms one would hardly suspect to find in a military field manual (Army 2007: 79-135). What is more, the manual even seems to espouse a mild form of cultural relativism. It explicitly seeks to enlighten soldiers and marines that

> American ideas of what is "normal" or "rational" are not universal. To the contrary, members of other societies often have different notions of rationality, appropriate behavior, level of religious devotion, and norms concerning gender. Thus, what may appear abnormal or strange to an external observer may appear as self-evidently normal to a group member. For this reason, counterinsurgents—especially commanders, planners, and small-unit leaders—should strive to avoid imposing their ideals of normalcy on a foreign cultural problem. (Army 2007: 27)

Due to the identified need for specific socio-cultural knowledge in counterinsurgency and the conspicuous lack thereof in the ongoing campaigns in Iraq and Afghanistan, the military establishment decided to launch the so-called Human Terrain System (HTS) in 2005. This program was "specifically designed to address cultural awareness shortcomings at the operational and tactical levels by giving brigade commanders an organic capability to help understand and deal with "human terrain"—the social, ethnographic, cultural, economic and political elements of the people among whom a force is operating" (Kipp et al. 2006: 9). The Human Terrain System seeks to embed five- to nine-person Human Terrain

Teams (HTT) into military units. According to the "Human Terrain Handbook," Human Terrain Teams are:

> composed of individuals with social science and operational backgrounds that are deployed with tactical and operational military units to assist in bringing knowledge about the local population into a coherent analytical framework and build relationships with the local power-brokers. (Finney 2008: 2)

The first HTT was fielded in Afghanistan in 2006. Several other teams were deployed to both Afghanistan and Iraq in 2007 (Ucko 2009). Human Terrain Teams combine social network analysis with the geo-spatial analysis of human and physical geography in order to identify and track elements of the populations so that they can be targeted either by kinetic or non-kinetic means, depending on what we may call their level of illiberality. But plugging cultural knowledge into the military machine is by no means uncontroversial and the military-social science machine does not always operate smoothly.

Anthropologist David Price disclosed that the definitions of the basic social science terms provided in the manual's chapter on intelligence are based on what he calls "pilfered scholarship" (Price 2007, 2009). He contends that the manual "borrowed" terms, phrases and even entire paragraphs from a large number of unacknowledged sources and that the

> effect of such non-attributions is devastating to the manual's academic integrity, and claims of such integrity are at the heart and soul of the Pentagon's claims for the manual—claims that the military hoped to bolster with the republication of the Counterinsurgency Field Manual at a top academic press. (2009: 64)[7]

What is more, a number of anthropologists quickly began to criticize what they saw as "the weaponization of anthropology" (Feldman 2009; González 2007, 2009b, 2009a; González, Gusterson and Price 2009; Sahlins 2009). In 2007 a group of anthropologists set up the Network of Concerned Anthropologists to provide a common platform for collective action against the creeping militarization of their discipline (González, Gusterson, and Price 2009). Moreover, in October 2009, the American Anthropological Association's Commission on the Engagement of Anthropology with the U.S. Security and Intelligence Communities (CEAUSSIC) issued its "Report on the Army's Human Terrain System Proof of Concept Program," which came to the following conclusion:

> It appears clear that the exigencies of military units operating in a battle space while actively at war are fundamentally incompatible with the Code of Ethics of the AAA, but also with any sort of responsible effort of social scientific research. So far, three HTT social scientists have in fact been killed, a stark reminder that battle zones are first and foremost battle zones

and not research spaces. We suggest that anthropology needs to understand its relationship to the military and to such goals as the "cultural preparation of the environment" from a different vantage point of collaboration. (Albro et al. 2009: 54)

On the other hand, some military personnel have not been particularly eager to have social scientists participate in counterinsurgency operations either. One of the most vocal critics of the new fad of culture-centric warfare is retired U.S. Army Lieutenant Colonel Ralph Peters, who in his influential 2000 article, "The Human Terrain of Urban Operations," argues that future conflicts will increasingly be fought among the populations of major cities in the global south (2000). Although Peters agrees on the important role of socio-cultural knowledge in counterinsurgency operations, he suggests that too strong a focus on cultural issues may place undue restrictions on the use of firepower (2007). What is more, Peters goes as far as to state that "it's immoral to throw away the lives of our troops in repeated attempts to validate somebody's doctoral thesis" (2007: 1). Ironically, while some social scientists argue that their engagement with the military can restrict the indiscriminate use of firepower and thereby both improve and humanize unconventional modes of warfare, Peters maintains that the participation of social scientists could severely hamper the ability of the armed forces to do what they do best, namely war-fighting.[8]

Yet, the actual on-the-ground production and deployment of socio-cultural expertise has also proved highly problematic. David Ucko, for instance, dismisses the Human Terrain System as a stopgap measure intended to provide a quick and cheap fix to "the absence of an equivalent capability within the existing force structure" (2009: 165). He recommends that, instead of recruiting civilian consultants, the military should seek to improve the linguistic and cultural abilities of its own specialist civil affairs personnel. Ucko further notes that Human Terrain Teams had to be "placed at the brigade level rather than at the battalion or company level, where they might have had a greater impact," because the military was unable to find enough "qualified civilian volunteers" (166). Last but not least, he states that the members of Human Terrain Teams deployed in Afghanistan and Iraq are often poorly trained, and thus produce knowledge of "varied quality" and that "the managerial practices and protocols governing their use and activity in a war zone were at times undefined" (166).

Despite the contested and contradictory nature of the counterinsurgency-related production and deployment of socio-cultural knowledge, there clearly is an ongoing attempt to strategically articulate structures of knowledge with the exercise of power. The overall strategic role of socio-cultural knowledge within the counterinsurgency machine consists of differentiating between elements of host nation populations so that they can be targeted more effectively. According to proponents of HTS the human terrain maps produced by HTTs are only meant to be used for benign ends, such as tailoring social programs to particular groups and areas, launching customized information campaigns, or providing the host-nation government with demographic data. But as the information is fed into a central database that can also be accessed by Special Forces, the CIA or host-nation security services, the human terrain maps could also be put to more iniquitous uses (González 2009a; Kipp et al. 2006).

In counterinsurgency, socio-cultural knowledge is ultimately deployed to assign members of illiberal populations a number of illiberal subject positions so that both lethal and non-lethal modes of targeting can be adapted accordingly. As Marshall Sahlins puts it:

> The principal role of academics in the service of counterinsurgency is to develop the human intelligence (HUMINT) that will allow a triage between those elements of the population to be attacked (or assassinated) and those it would be better not to—in brief, sophisticated targeting. (2009: vi)

Conclusion: The Neo-Orientalist Logic of Counterinsurgency

Some critics have remarked that the deployment of cultural knowledge in counterinsurgency operations is based on a new form of Orientalism (Feldman 2009; Gregory 2008). Greg Feldman for instance holds that insofar as counterinsurgency "divides occupied peoples into either modern or regressive" and "depicts those living in geopolitically sensitive areas as in need of a U.S. presence to pacify and develop their countries" it ultimately amounts to an Orientalist and hence also neocolonial project (2009: 92). In its classical sense Edward Said's term Orientalism denotes the complex and ambiguous historical relationship between the production of knowledge about the Orient and the imperial project of establishing occidental control over spaces and populations construed as oriental (1979). McFate's demand that anthropology should reclaim its erstwhile role as a "warfighting discipline" ultimately amounts to saying that the discipline of anthropology should once again turn into a machine for the production of Orientalist discourse—something anthropologists have struggled against for many decades (McFate 2005a: 24). When social scientists submit their work to the exigencies of military power and allow themselves to be embedded into the military machine, the knowledge they produce is unlikely to exert a humanizing influence on the use of military force. Rather, the products of their intellectual labour will be shaped, and ultimately compromised, by the requirements of military strategy.[9]

Insofar as it constantly (re-)produces not only the dividing line between "us" and "them" but also seeks to place "them" on a scale of illiberality, knowledge about the Other becomes just one element in a complex machine geared towards establishing governmental control over foreign populations:

> The emphasis on cultural difference—the attempt to hold the Other at a distance while claiming to cross the interpretive divide—produces a diagram in which violence has its origins in "their" space, which the cultural turn endlessly partitions through its obsessive preoccupation with ethno-sectarian division, while the impulse to understand is confined to "our" space, which is constructed as open, unitary, and generous. (Gregory 2008: 11)

The military deployment of cultural knowledge juxtaposes an Orientalist space, which is construed as illiberal, violent and criss-crossed by multiple divisions, with an occidental space that is by default liberal, unitary and peaceful. Firstly, this is indicative of the aforementioned liberal distinction between "what can be governed through the promotion of liberty and what must be governed in other ways" (Hindess 2004: 28). And counterinsurgency in fact targets those who cannot (yet) be governed through the promotion of liberty, who, in line with classical colonial governmentality require outside assistance so that they may some day attain self-government. Secondly, as previously mentioned, the on-the-ground deployment of cultural knowledge is aimed at dividing populations occupying illiberal spaces into different illiberal subject positions in order to make the human terrain intelligible, "targetable" and ultimately governable.

In domestic governmentality social scientists play a major role in differentiating between *liberal* subject positions so that the quantity and quality of assistance and/or penalties can be adapted accordingly. In short, they provide the intelligence that enables a smarter and more targeted form of government. In foreign counterinsurgency operations, on the other hand, social scientists in general, and the Human Terrain Teams in particular, are supposed to distinguish between *illiberal* subject positions so that foreign population can be targeted more effectively—either by social programs, or by information campaigns, or by firepower.

The immediate post-Cold War hopes that we were about to enter a new era of peace, prosperity and democracy promptly turned into despair over the rise of new unconventional threats to the stability of the international state system. It seems as if the dream of liberal world peace has collapsed into the nightmare of permanent global pacification–a new and potentially endless series of what Rudyard Kipling called "the savage wars of peace" (1899).

In the future the United States and its allies will likely mount numerous counterinsurgency and stability operations across the global south. However, not all of these will entail the deployment of large numbers of ground forces. Aimed at containing the spread of instability, they will range from state- and capacity-building efforts, military assistance programs and small-scale Special Forces operations, as is already the case in Yemen and Pakistan, to outright military interventions as in Iraq and Afghanistan. In all likelihood, the national security apparatus will continue to try to draft socio-cultural knowledge into its global stabilization programs, so that the barbarians at the gate can be made intelligible. Ultimately, the military deployment of cultural knowledge does not serve to bridge the divide between "us and them." It merely seeks to know foreign populations as targets of Western military and political intervention, so that some of them can be brought into the fold of liberal humanity and others annihilated in a more targeted and discriminate fashion. In this context, socio-cultural knowledge is deployed as an instrument, or even a weapon, by the occupying force, whose ultimate goal is the establishment of neocolonial forms of control over foreign populations. Even if these forms of rule were as benign as they are professed to be, socio-cultural knowledge would still be trapped in an endless cycle of reproducing and reinforcing a neo-Orientalist logic. Above all, this logic serves as a justification for the continuing political, economic and military interference in the affairs of the post-colonial global south.

Yet, do the illiberal barbarians who are said to be lurking in the global borderlands pose a threat to the international system of liberal states because they are barbarians? Or are they labelled a threat to liberalism and hence barbarians because they resist the West's neocolonial tendency to extend its economic and political influence across the globe?

Notes

1. The term Third Generation Gangs (3 GEN Gangs) was coined by U.S. law enforcement official and security expert, John P. Sullivan, in an attempt to model the evolution of violent street gangs by categorizing gangs according to their level of "politicization, internationalization, and sophistication" (2008: 160-62). Whereas First Generation Gangs are thought to be predominantly turf-focused and only participate in criminal enterprise opportunistically and locally, Second Generation Gangs are seen as "entrepreneurial and drug-centred" with "a tendency for centralized leadership and sophisticated operations for market protection" (162). According to Sullivan, although most existing gangs belong to the first or second generation, Third Generation Gangs are currently in the process of evolving. They include gangs that "have evolved political aims, operate or seek to operate at the global end of the spectrum, and employ their sophistication to acquire power, money and engage in mercenary or political activities" (163). For instance, Sullivan contends that the originally Los Angeles-based gangs, Mara Salvatrucha (MS-13) and Eighteenth Street (Calle 18 or M-18), are currently transforming into Third Generation Gangs. He argues that they have already spread across North and Central America and that they pose significant challenges to politically weak Latin American states, such as Honduras and El Salvador, by undermining their legitimacy and monopoly over the means of violence. (2008: 165-66, 1997, 2000; Bunker and Sullivan 2010).

2. The almost exclusive focus on the U.S. counterinsurgency machine flows from the simple fact that the trajectory of U.S. military strategy has the most influence on what happens in ongoing military campaigns and also strongly affects the strategic concepts of allied nations. For instance, in Afghanistan the mission of the NATO-led International Security Assistance Force, to which Canada contributes almost 3,000 troops, is based on the tenets of current U.S. counterinsurgency doctrine. The three pillars of the ISAF mission, security, reconstruction and development, and governance, are a staple of the litera-

ture on counterinsurgency (Army 2007; ISAF 2010). Of course, the actual contribution particular nations make to the overall counterinsurgency campaign is still informed by their specific military cultures. For example, Canada, which has been a long-standing and celebrated contributor to humanitarian peacekeeping operations, stresses the humanitarian and development efforts of the Canadian Forces in the Afghan province of Kandahar (Canada 2010). However, this still forms part of a wider U.S.-dominated strategy.

3. Mitchell Dean defines the Foucauldian concept of government as follows:

> Any more or less calculated and rational activity, undertaken by a multiplicity of authorities and agencies, employing a variety of techniques and forms of knowledge, that seeks to shape conduct by working through desires, aspirations, interests and beliefs for definite but shifting ends and with diverse set of relatively unpredictable-consequences, effects and outcomes (Dean 2010: 266-7).

This definition is very concise but is still too focused on consensual forms of acting on somebody else's actions. Government does indeed aim to "shape conduct by working through desires, aspirations, interests and beliefs" but we should add that it sometimes also works through and on the body.

4. This is one of the most significant weaknesses of counterinsurgency strategy. Counterinsurgents can hardly succeed in winning the support of the population if the host nation regime is widely seen as corrupt and unrepresentative.

5. The expression "winning the hearts and minds of the people" is commonly traced back to Sir Gerald Templar who acted as British High Commissioner in Malaya during the so-called Malayan Emergency (Long 2006: 23). The British campaign against the Malayan National Liberation Army from 1948 to 1960 is widely hailed as a model for successful counterinsurgency operations (most prominently by Nagl 2002).

6. Indeed, numerous military analysts now suggest that Vietnam marked the failure of 1960s counterinsurgency doctrine. A detailed analysis of the rise and fall of 1960s counterinsurgency doctrine is beyond the scope of this article, but suffice to say that the counterinsurgency literature provides the following interrelated reasons for the failure of the doctrine: 1) an inadequate implementation of an otherwise more-or-less sound doctrine because of (a) a failure on the part of the U.S military to recognize and adapt to the unconventional nature of the conflict (that is to say the U.S. failed to put the doctrine into practice), and (b) a lack of effective inter-agency cooperation on the ground (Nagl 2002; Hammes 2004); 2) the attempt to prop up a completely corrupt and unrepresentative regime; and 3) inherent limitation of the doctrine itself, mainly in terms of its disregard of socio-historical context (Blaufarb 1977; McClintock 1992; Shafer 1988). Arguably, most of these points also apply to current counterinsurgency operations in Afghanistan. For instance, the recent *Rolling Stone* article, which led to the resignation or rather sacking, of ISAF commander, General Stanley McChrystal, exposed severe tensions between the military and civilian agencies, most notably the Department of State (Hastings 2010). Moreover, the leaked cables of U.S. ambassador to Afghanistan, Karl W. Eikenberry, revealed strong concerns about the Afghan central government and NATO's ability to extend stable governmental structures into the Afghan countryside. Eikenberry indicated that Afghan President, Hamid Karzai, may not be "an adequate strategic partner" and that many of the Afghan population regard the central government as unrepresentative and corrupt (Eikenberry 2009).

7. The top academic press Price refers to is the University of Chicago Press, whose 2007 edition of the manual made a number of bestseller lists.

8. For the "humanization" argument see Kilcullen (2007), McFate (2007) and Sewall (2007).

9. The same also applies to journalistic practice. The system of embedding journalists with military units, devised by the Pentagon in conjunction with major news organizations prior to the 2003 invasion of Iraq, was deliberately aimed at removing the critical distance between journalists and soldiers. It led many journalist to identify with the troops they were embedded with and hence also to produce less critical media portrayals of the military, especially during the initial stages of the war (Tumber and Palmer 2004).

References

Agamben, Giorgio. 1998. *Homo Sacer: Sovereign Power and Bare Life*. Trans. Daniel Heller-Roazen. Stanford, CA: Stanford University Press.

———. 2005. *State of Exception*. Trans. Kevin Attell. Chicago: University of Chicago Press.

Albro, Robert, James Peacock, Carolyn Fluehr-Lobban, Kerry Fosher, Laura McNamara, George Marcus, David Price, Laurie Rush, Jean Jackson, Monica Schoch-Spana, and Setha Low. 2009. AAA Commission on the Engagement of Anthropology with the US Security and Intelligence Communities (CEAUSSIC) Final Report on The Army's Human Terrain System Proof of Concept Program. 14 October 2009). http://www.aaanet.org/issues/policy-advocacy/CEAUSSIC-Releases-Final-Report-on-Army-HTS-Program.cfm. Accessed 9 March 2010.

Bauman, Zygmunt. 2002. *Society under Siege*. Cambridge: Polity Press.

Berger, M. T. and D. A. Borer. 2007. The Long War: Insurgency, Counterinsurgency and Collapsing States. *Third World Quarterly* 28(2): 197-215.

Blaufarb, Douglas S. 1977. *The Counterinsurgency Era: U.S. Doctrine and Performance 1950 to the Present* New York: Free Press.

Bunker, Robert J., ed. 2005. Introduction and Overview: Why Response Networks? In *Networks, Terrorism and Global Insurgency*. London, New York: Routledge.

———. 2010. Strategic Threat: Narcos and Narcotics Overview. *Small Wars and Insurgencies* 21(1): 8-29.

Bunker, Robert J. and Matt Begert. 2008. Overview: Defending against Enemies of the State. In *Criminal-States and Criminal-Soldiers*, edited by R. J. Bunker. London, New York: Routledge.

Bunker, Robert J. and John P. Sullivan. 2010. Cartel Evolution Revisited: Third Phase Cartel Potentials and Alternative Futures in Mexico. *Small Wars and Insurgencies* 21(1): 30-54.

Butler, Judith. 2004. *Precarious Life: The Powers of Mourning and Violence*. London: Verso.

———. 2009. *Frames of War: When Is Life Grievable?* London: Verso.

Canada, Government of. (2010). Canada's Priorities. http://www.afghanistan.gc.ca/canada-afghanistan/priorities-priorites/index.aspx. Accessed 2 July 2010.

Cassidy, Robert M. 2006a. *Counterinsurgency and the Global War on Terror. Military Culture and Irregular War*. Westport, CT: Praeger Security International.

———. 2006b. The Long Small War: Indigenous Forces for Counterinsurgency. *Parameters: US Army War College* 36(2): 47-62.

———. 2008. Counterinsurgency and Military Culture: State Regulars versus Non-State Irregulars. *Baltic Security & Defence Review* 10:53-85.

Cirafici, John L. 2008. On "Other War": Lessons from Five Decades of RAND Counterinsurgency Research. *Air Power History* 55(1): 52.

Clemis, Martin G. 2009. Crafting Non-Kinetic Warfare: The Academic-Military Nexus in US Counterinsurgency Doctrine. *Small Wars & Insurgencies* 20(1): 160-84.

Dean, Mitchell. 2000. Liberal Government and Authoritarianism. *Economy & Society* 31(1): 37-61.

———. 2002. Powers of Life and Death Beyond Governmentality. *Cultural Values* 6(1/2): 119-38.

———. 2004. *Nomos* and the Politics of World Order. In *Global Governmentality: Governing International Spaces*, edited by W. Larner and W. Walters. London: Routledge.

———. 2010. *Governmentality: Power and Rule in Modern Society*. London: Sage Publications.

Defense, Department of. 2010. Quadrennial Defense Review Report. (February 2010). http://www.defense.gov/QDR/. Accessed 1 May 2010.

Duffield, Mark. 2008. Global Civil War: The Non-Insured, International Containment and Post-Interventionary Society. *Journal of Refugee Studies* 21(2): 145-65.

Eikenberry, Karl W. 2009. Two Classified Memos to Secretary of State Regarding COIN Strategy and Civilian Concern. http://documents.nytimes.com/eikenberry-s-memos-on-the-strategy-in-afghanistan. Accessed 2 July 2010.

Fall, Bernard. 1998. The Theory and Practice of Insurgency and Counterinsurgency. *Naval War College Review* (Winter 1998). http://www.au.af.mil/au/awc/awcgate/navy/art5-w98.htm. Accessed 8 May 2010.

Feldman, Greg. 2009. Radical or Reactionary? The Old Wine in the *Counterinsurgency Field Manual's* New Flask. In *The Counter-Counterinsurgency Manual or, Notes on Demilitarizing American Society*, edited by The Network of Concerned Anthropologists. Chicago: Prickly Paradigm Press.

Finney, Nathan. 2008. Human Terrain Team Handbook. (September 2008). http://www.scribd.com/doc/8959317/Human-Terrain-Handbook-2008. Accessed 9 February 2010.

Foucault, Michel. 2000. The Subject and Power. In *Power*, edited by J. D. Faubion. New York: The New Press.

———. 2003. *Society Must Be Defended. Lectures at the College de France 1975-1976*. Trans. D. Macey. New York: Picador.

———. 2007 [2004]. *Security, Territory, Population. Lectures at the College de France 1977-1978*. Trans. G. Burchell. Houndmills, Basingstoke: Palgrave Macmillan.

Giddens, Anthony. 1987. *The Nation State and Violence*. Berkeley: University of California Press.

Gompert, David C., Terrence K. Kelly, Brooke Stearns Lawson, Michelle Parker and Kimberly Colloton. 2009. *Reconstruction under Fire: Unifying Civil and Military Counterinsurgency*. Santa Monica, CA: RAND National Defense Research Institute.

González, Roberto J. 2007. Towards Mercenary Anthropology? The New US Army Counterinsurgency Manual *FM 3-24* and the Military-Anthropology Complex. *Anthropology Today* 23(3): 14-19.

———. 2009a. *American Counterinsurgency: Human Science and the Human Terrain*. Chicago: Prickly Paradigm Press.

———. 2009b. Embedded: Information Warfare and the "Human Terrain." In *The Counter-Counterinsurgency Manual or, Notes on Demilitarizing American Society*, edited by The Network of Concerned Anthropologists. Chicago: Prickly Paradigm Press.

González, Roberto J., Hugh Gusterson and David Price. 2009. Introduction. In *The Counter-Counterinsurgency Manual, or Notes on Demilitarizing American Society*. Chicago: Prickly Paradigm Press.

Gordon, Colin. 1991. Governmental Rationality. In *The Foucault Effect. Studies in Governmentality*, edited by G. Burchell, C. Gordon and P. Miller. Chicago: University of Chicago Press.

Gregory, Derek. 2008. "The Rush to the Intimate"—Counterinsurgency and the Cultural Turn. *Radical Philosophy* 150:8-23.

Hammes, Thomas X. 2006. *The Sling and The Stone. On War in the 21st Century*. Minneapolis, MN: Zenith Press.

Hardt, Michael and Antonio Negri. 2004. *Multitude. War and Democracy in the Age of Empire*. London: Penguin.

Hastings, Michael. 2010. The Runaway General. *Rolling Stone* (July 8-22). http://www.rollingstone.com/politics/news/17390/119236. Accessed 2 July 2010.

Heuser, Beatrice. 2007. The Cultural Revolution in Counter-insurgency. *Journal of Strategic Studies* 30(1): 153-71.

Hindess, Barry. 2004. Liberalism—What's in a Name? In *Global Governmentality: Governing International Spaces*, edited by W. Larner and W. Walters. London: Routledge.

ISAF. 2010. Mission. http://www.isaf.nato.int/mission.html. Accessed 2 July 2010.

Kan, Paul R. 2009. *Drugs and Contemporary Warfare*. Washington, DC: Potomac Books.

Kennedy, John F. 1961. Address "The President and the Press" Before the American Newspaper Publishers Association, New York City, 27 April 1961. In *Public Papers of the Presidents of the United States: John F. Kennedy. January 20 to December 31, 1961*. Washington, DC: United States Government Printing Office.

Kilcullen, David J. 2005. Countering Global Insurgency. *Journal of Strategic Studies* 28(4): 597-617.

———. 2007. Ethics, Politics, and Non-State Warfare. *Anthropology Today* 23(3): 20.

———. 2009. *The Accidental Guerrilla: Fighting Small Wars in the Midst of a Big One*. Oxford: Oxford University Press.

Kipling, Rudyard. 1899. "The White Man's Burden." http://en.wikisource.org/wiki/The_White_Man%27s_Burden. Accessed 9 May 2010.

Kipp, Jacob, Lester Grau, Karl Prinslow and Don Smith. 2006. The Human Terrain System: A CORDS for the 21st Century. *Military Review* 86(5): 8-15.

Larner, Wendy and William Walters. 2004. Introduction. In *Global Governmentality: Governing International Spaces*, edited by W. Larner and W. Walters. London: Routledge.

Lemke, T. 2000. Foucault, Governmentality, and Critique. Paper read at Rethinking Marxism, September 21-24, at University of Amherst.

Long, Austin. 2006. *On "Other War": Lessons from Five Decades of RAND Counterinsurgency Research*. Santa Monica, CA: RAND Corporation.

Manwaring, Max G. 2005. The New Global Security Landscape: The Road Ahead. In *Networks, Terrorism and Global Insurgency*, edited by R. J. Bunker. London, New York: Routledge.

———. 2008. Gangs and *Coups D' Streets* in the New World Disorder: Protean Insurgents in Post-modern War. In *Criminal-States and Criminal-Soldiers*, edited by R. J. Bunker. London, New York: Routledge.

McClintock, Michael. 1992. *Instruments of Statecraft. U.S. Guerrilla Warfare, Counter-Insurgency, and Counter-Terrorism, 1940-1990*. New York: Pantheon Books.

McFate, Montgomery. 2004. ONR Conference Makes Case for Study of Cultures. *Office of Naval Research*. http://fellowships.aaas.org/PDFs/2004_1210_ORIGconf.pdf. Accessed 18 November 2008.

———. 2005a. Anthropology and Counterinsurgency: The Strange Story of their Curious Relationship. *Military Review* 85(2): 24-38.

———. 2005b. The Military Utility of Understanding Adversary Culture. *JFQ: Joint Force Quarterly* (38): 42-48.

———. 2007. Building Bridges or Burning Heretics? *Anthropology Today* 23(3): 21.

McFate, Montgomery and Andrea Jackson. 2005. An Organizational Solution for DOD's Cultural Knowledge Needs. *Military Review* 85(4): 18-21.

———. 2006. The Object beyond War: Counterinsurgency and the Four Tools of Political Competition. *Military Review* (Jan./Feb.): 56-69.

Nagl, John A. 2002. *Learning to Eat Soup with a Knife. Counterinsurgency Lessons from Malaya and Vietnam*. Chicago: University of Chicago Press.

Obama, Barack. 2009. Remarks by the President in Address to the Nation on the Way Forward in Afghanistan and Pakistan at Eisenhower Hall Theatre, United States Military Academy at West Point, West Point, New York, 1 December 2009. http://www.whitehouse.gov/the-press-office/remarks-president-address-nation-way-forward-afghanistan-and-pakistan. Accessed 6 May 2010.

Peters, Ralph. 2000. The Human Terrain of Urban Operations. *Parameters: US Army War College* 30(122): 4-12.

———. 2007. Progress and Perial: New Counterinsurgency Manual Cheats on the History Exam. *Armed Forces Journal International* (February 2007). http://www.afji.com/2007/02/2456854/. Accessed 11 May 2010.

Price, David. 2007. Pilfered Scholarship Devastates General Petraeus's *Counterinsurgency Manual*. *Counterpunch* (October 30, 2007). http://www.counterpunch.org/price10302007.html. Accessed 11 March 2010.

———. 2009. Faking Scholarship: Domestic Propaganda and the Republication of the *Counterinsurgency Field Manual*. In *The Counter-Counterinsurgency Manual or, Notes on Demilitarizing American Society*. Chicago: Prickly Paradigm Press.

Prozorov, S. 2006. Liberal Enmity: The Figure of the Foe in the Political Ontology of Liberalism. *Millennium-Journal of International Studies* 35(1): 75-99.

Renzi, Fred. 2006. NETWORKS: Terra Incognita and the Case for Ethnographic Intelligence. *Military Review* 86(5): 16-22.

Rose, Nikolas and Peter Miller. 1992. Political Power Beyond the State—Problematics of Government. *British Journal of Sociology* 43(2): 173-205.

Sahlins, Marshall. 2009. Preface. In *The Counter-Counterinsurgency Manual or, Notes on Demilitarizing American Society*. Chicago: Prickly Paradigm Press.

Said, Edward. 1979. *Orientalism*. New York: Vintage Books.

Sewall, Sarah. 2007. Introduction to University of Chicago Press Edition. In *The U.S. Army / Marines Counterinsurgency Field Manual*. Chicago: University of Chicago Press.

Shafer, D. M. 1988. *Deadly Paradigms. The Failure of U.S. Counterinsurgency Policy*. Princeton: Princeton University Press.

Sullivan, John P. 1997. Third Generation Street Gangs: Turf, Cartels and NetWarriors. *Crime & Justice International* 13 (10). http://www.cjimagazine.com/archives/cji673a.html?issn=10&vol=13&pub=International. Accessed 27 June 2010.

———. 2000. Urban Gangs Evolving as Criminal Netwar Actors. *Small Wars & Insurgencies* 11(1): 82-96.

———. 2005. Terrorism, Crime and Private Armies. In *Networks, Terrorism and Global Insurgency*, edited by R. J. Bunker. London, New York: Routledge.

———, ed. 2008. *Criminal-States and Criminal-Soldiers*. London, New York: Routledge.

Tumber, Howard and Jerry Palmer. 2004. *The Media at War: The Iraq Crisis*. London: Sage.

Ucko, David H. 2009. *The New Counterinsurgency Era: Transforming the U.S. Military for Modern Wars*. Washington, DC: Georgetown University Press.

U.S. Department of the Army. 2007. *The U.S. Army / Marine Corps Counterinsurgency Field Manual*. Chicago: University of Chicago Press.

U.S. Government. 1962. United States Overseas Internal Defense Policy, September 1962. http://drworley.org/NSPcommon/OIDP/OIDP.pdf. Accessed 15 December 2008.

van Creveld, Martin. 1991. *The Transformation of War*. New York: Free Press.

———. 2008. The Fate of the State Revisited. In *Criminal-States and Criminal-Soldiers*, edited by R. J. Bunker. London, New York: Routledge.

von Clausewitz, Carl. 1976. *On War*. Princeton, NJ: Princeton University Press.

Wilson, Scott and Al Kamen. 2009. "Global War On Terror" Is Given New Name. *The Washington Post*, 25 March. http://www.washingtonpost.com/wp-dyn/content/article/2009/03/24/AR2009032402818.html. Accessed 11 May 2010.

Neil Balan

A Corrective for Cultural Studies: Beyond the Militarization Thesis to the New Military Intelligence

ABSTRACT

This paper theorizes a *new military intelligence* and offers a modest corrective to the orthodoxy of the militarization thesis prevalent in cultural studies and the critical human sciences. The biopolitical orientation of population-centric counterinsurgency (COIN) warfare in Afghanistan reveals the multidirectional travel of rationalities and forms of coherence between modern liberal ways of rule and Western-bloc expeditionary ways of war. Through the work of Michel Foucault, and drawing on Michael Dillon and Julian Reid's analysis of the biopoliticization of war (2008), COIN is interrogated as a continuation of biopolitics by other means. Conceptualizing a continuum of "fast" and "slow" military violence to produce islands of security and stability, COIN generates a mix of persuasive material forces that, while not kinetic or combat-oriented, are internal to the battlespace of military warfighting. The aim of this theoretical intervention is to trouble our understanding of military violence and power. Rather than subscribe unconditionally to the idea of a domineering military contaminating domestic civilian environments, the paper establishes a different trajectory: perhaps there is always-already a spirit of counterinsurgency internal to the art of biopolitical governmentality, which in turn conjugates contemporary military ways of war.

RÉSUMÉ

Correctif à l'usage des études culturelles : au-delà de la thèse de la militarisation, vers une nouvelle compréhension du militaire

Cet article théorise une nouvelle compréhension du militaire et propose un modeste correctif à l'orthodoxie de la thèse de la militarisation qui prévaut en études culturelles et au niveau critique des sciences humaines. L'orientation biopolitique de la guerre de contre-insurrection (COIN) au milieu de la population en Afghanistan révèle les trajectoires multidirectionnelles des rationalités, des logiques et des formes de cohérence entre les modes de gouvernement modernes et libéraux et les modes guerriers des corps expéditionnaires du bloc occidental. En nous basant sur les travaux de Michel Foucault et sur l'analyse faite par Michael Dillon et Julian Reid de la bio-politisation de la guerre (2008), nous examinons la guerre de contre-insurrection sous l'angle d'une prolongation de la biopolitique par d'autres moyens. En conceptualisant un continuum de violence militaire « rapide » et « lente » pour produire des îlots de sécurité et de stabilité, la guerre de contre-insurrection génère un mélange de forces matérielles de persuasion et de coercition qui, bien que n'étant pas en mouvement ou orientées vers le combat, sont inhérentes à l'espace de bataille de la guerre militaire. L'objectif de cette intervention théorique est de mettre en question notre compréhension de la violence et du pouvoir militaire. Plutôt que de souscrire inconditionnellement à l'idée d'une domination militaire contaminant les environnements civils domestiques, cet article définit une trajectoire différente : peut-être y a-t-il déjà toujours eu un esprit de contre-insurrection interne à l'art de la gouvernance biopolitique, qui en retour conjugue les manières militaires contemporaines de faire la guerre ?

¤

The blurring of spatial, temporal and ontological categories that defined modern warfare has definite although certainly complex and contingent implications for military forces.
—Deborah Cowen (2008)

Insurgency and counterinsurgency (COIN) are complex subsets of warfare.... Achieving victory still depends on a group's ability to mobilize support for its political interests (often religiously or ethnically based) and to generate enough violence to achieve political consequences.
—U.S. Army General David Petraeus
FM 3-24 Counterinsurgency Field Manual

A COIN campaign is conducted using the same means as any other campaign: through the application of a military force's fighting power [moral, intellectual and physical]. It is set within the continuum of operations and is executed through a combination of tactical level activities and tasks. However, it is a distinct campaign with its own philosophy and set of principles that provide guidance for the application of fighting power and the conduct of activities.
—Chief of Land Staff, Canadian Forces
BG-L-323-0004 Counterinsurgency Operations

The continuum of operations embraces the concept of campaign themes and encompasses both war and operations other than war.
—Joint Doctrine Branch, Canadian Forces Experimentation Centre
CFJP 01 Canadian Military Doctrine

Afghanistan, Critique and Cultural Studies

According to Randy Innes, the Afghan war cannot be relegated to "contemporary history" and must be considered as an unruly "contemporary present" that is unfolding independent of the epistemological constraints and aesthetic assignments imposed by acts of institutional representation (2008: 94, 100). Innes writes, "like war, representation has the potential to have a fatal effect in and on the present" (102). In Canada, keeping up with the cycle of events in Afghanistan is impossible for reasons of geographic, empirical and ontological distance: the reliance—initially, at least—on the messages constructed by social and cultural authorities. Amid the drifting war narratives that populate Canadian cultural and political environments, the problem remains: tracking the production and politics of truth specific to the war, its legitimacy and its orchestrators. Discourses regarding the war hail us and ask us to judge the fuzzy temporal and territorial limits of both this war and war itself. The truths we accept about the war do not simply assign declarations but implicitly teach. The descriptions always come with their own quiet but prescriptive pedagogical supplements.

Where we spend time likely determines the inventory to which we subscribe. We may heed the arguments of John Warnock, who recounts with clinical precision not only the existence but also the ongoing creation of a failing Afghan state (2008). The invasion, premised on retribution, was sour from the start, and thoughts of a foreign-imposed but harmonious future Afghanistan continue to curdle. We may remain suspicious of neoliberal accounts of Afghanistan Year Zero, wonder about the quietude regarding the nine-year Soviet occupation from 1980 to 1989, and maintain some curiosity about the fetishization of recalcitrant Pashtuns who were once categorized as stoic mujahidin warriors but now stand degraded as evil Islamo-fascist Taliban. We encounter curious distinctions about the time and space of warfighting and the transition to reconstruction and development, wondering if and how such distinctions stand. Whether the war was unexpected or actively pursued to prove the mettle of Canadian Forces (CF) troops depends on who frames the narrative. What of the Canadian imagination of "classical" peacekeepers—honest adjudicators providing services and security— and the compromise of this facile and mythologized custodial role (Härting and Kambourelli 2009: 660; cf. Jefferess 2009)? Or what of renewed calls by analysts in the Canadian defence sector, who decry the logistical toll of Afghanistan and argue for a new kind of "peace warrior" deputized to ensure human security on more pressing global (South) frontiers coincident with Canada's 2005 Doctrine to Protect (Bercuson 2010)? Commentators dispute the proper objects of the war amid civilian casualties and remote-controlled precision drone strikes. Debates emerge around the sacrifice of Canadian troops, radiating into discussions regarding the contents of acceptable dissent, and dictating how heroic sensibility can justify not simply scholarships but military branding exercises at Canada's public universities. The unfolding "Afghan detainee scandal" is suffused with non sequiturs and the egregious legacy of Somalia, revealing pervasive state censorship, which served as a major catalyst for the prorogation of Canada's 2010 parliamentary session. The arithmetic of occupation and escalation remain constant considerations, especially after the November 2009 announcement by U.S. President Barack Obama on the latest U.S.-troop surge of 30,000.[1] Additionally, popular recourse to proto-feminist arguments justify the alleged egalitarian mandate of the war as a benevolent intervention on behalf of imperilled women.[2] These arguments occur alongside a recent tour of Canada by Afghan MP Malalai Joya, who demanded the immediate withdrawal of all occupation forces[3] while declaring that the rhetoric of liberation fundamentally undermines any kind of Afghan self-determination. And the inventory grows.

This meshwork of guiding narratives demands our attention, regulating but not resolving our categorical efforts as we consider the war. Of course, our own adherence to and suspicion of these narratives, along with our criticisms, have their own sets of effects. Some of them can be just as fatal. What goes for our public authorities, our neoliberal managers and our political elites goes no less for those working in Canadian cultural studies, regardless of the way we claim an oppositional status, self-identifying as speakers of some really-existing truth. Judgements about the war imply distinctions about the constellations appropriate to cultural studies, sometimes weakly shared but policed nonetheless.

A Corrective to Orthodoxy's Fatal Effects: Displacing the Militarization Thesis

To consider the expeditionary war in Afghanistan is to think about how the method of conduct reflects the very ontological conception of war itself—its objects, its time and space, its basis as a material-cultural phenomenon. As suggested above by Deborah Cowen (2008), the breakdown of traditional boundaries and categories specific to the production of war has significant implications. These collapsing boundaries and compromised jurisdictions have been crucial to critical work in cultural studies (alongside cultural theory and the theoretical humanities) addressing war as a complex process constituted in power and political violence. The migration of war into different domains of life is accepted almost as a truism (i.e., war as matter of semiotic, territorial and material ecology) and is understood as a historical event (i.e., in the contemporary era, we understand that war is everywhere, is the condition, is the exception that is the rule). Yet Cowen goes further, suggesting that the implications have material consequences for the familiar agents of war: state militaries. As such, considering the Afghan war necessitates a consideration of Canadian military affairs and the Canadian Forces.

Clearly, military institutions remain heavily invested in controlling and defining the debate over war's objects, its spaces and its temporality. If we agree that contemporary wars are in fact epochal post-industrial "new wars" comprised of state and non-state actors, exacerbated by the "intensifying interconnectedness" of global capital and knowledge flows, and waged away from the battlefield and "among the people," we may be inclined to argue that war has strayed from narrow military constraints (Kaldor 2006: 4; Smith 2007: 271). This is not inaccurate, but it does not give any reason to assume that war was ever wholly the exclusive domain of military organs, nor that "the military" simply posits or sustains the terms for its own standing. If anything, military discourses on war actually indicate the ongoing epistemological and proprietary struggle over the concept of war itself, and expose its permanent place in cultural life.

In what follows, I address three interrelated areas—the Afghan war, the military and war itself—and offer something of a corrective to work heretofore undertaken in Canadian cultural studies. A corrective is always a diagnosis, and is usually supplemented by the simultaneously self-effacing and self-positing proposition of appointing oneself to move the debate along. Such propositions are often made by neophytes or interlopers not yet part of the flock—or at least this is the nominal logic to which the appointee adheres, attuned perhaps to the prospect of minor transgressions and ready to capitalize on the waves created by internecine conflict within the faculty. Whatever the resulting disagreements, the corrective is a straightforward proposition: create a trajectory in proximity to but outside of what I call the orthodoxy of the militarization thesis, a tendency specific to work in cultural studies. The thesis is a durable black-box and makes its own object—the military encroachment on and insemination into everyday life—a taken-for-granted, depoliticized process. Arguments and analyses foregrounding the domineering process of militarization are thus ideological; that is, they prescribe that one must be against "the military," and are prohibitive and regulatory while disavowing their function as such. The militarization thesis functions as a blockage, canonized as it canalizes, a big Other providing argumentative cover.

Of course, the militarization thesis is an allusion to Clausewitz's continuation thesis—"[war is] not a mere act of policy but a true political instrument, a continuation of political activity by other means"—and to Michel Foucault's inversion of this war-politics dyad in his seminal 1976 lectures, Society Must Be Defended (von Clausewitz 1976: 87; Foucault 2003: 15-16). Both Clausewitz's and Foucault's theses are taken at face-value, but become more complicated in explication than their initial expressions suggest.[4] My deployment of the militarization thesis, however, is a kind of summary shorthand. There are complex variations of the thesis I may obscure, but the thesis revolves around a basic premise: military interests and the rationalization of those interests direct the determination of objectives in other domains, whether political, economic or social. At its most general and abstract, the militarization thesis is an argument regarding the social and cultural power of coercive military logics, and the colonization of ostensibly non-military environments by adversarial military agents, materials and methods. According to the thesis, because a military organ's primary concern is the conduct of war on behalf of state interests, the cultural and social authority of a military tends to animate non-military affairs with a military point of view. The lesson: the military remains the dangerous supplement. At its most extreme, the militarization thesis argues that non-military (civilian) culture becomes military affairs by other means, where civilians are all effectively militarized and subscribe in some way to a general form of militarized subjectivity.

In cultural studies, the militarization thesis is typically deployed as a symptomatic indicator to theorize a set of related concerns: the state of exception and emergency; indefinite detention, the securitization of citizenship and the empire of camps; pre-emptive politics and new constellations of authority; neoliberal globalization, disaster capitalism and new rounds of primitive accumulation; and the contemporary constitution and philosophy of war. While proximate— and quickened by the bracket "post-9/11"—these concerns may not necessarily affiliate in the ways we desire, nor are they necessarily new phenomena. Further, many of the explanations unfold in American-centred ways, with an emphasis on American military, political and cultural orbits. Certainly, these topics are significant concerns for cultural studies, and their entanglement suggests the complicated process of locating the material effects of each; however, while attempting to explain and theorize conditional or epistemological movements, the militarization thesis often blurs different material processes. Making links and drawing connections should not obscure or assume continuities where none exist. Further, in positing a critique of military rationalities, the militarization thesis reinscribes a binary opposition between "military" and "civil," confining military organs and activities to some vacuum as if they exist independent of the very discursive and material processes that produce military organs themselves. Instead of imposing a set of analytic conditions and drawing our criticisms from a reliable standing-reserve, we may do better to think the violence of military conduct in more fluid terms linked always-already to spaces deemed "non-military."[5]

In liberal nation-states like Canada, military agents traditionally exert a monopoly on external acts of political violence alleged to serve the general will of the parent community and the interests of the people. Constituted with legally-endowed, unlimited liability as an instrumental surrogate for the population, a military is a bellicose organization institutionalized to undertake violence in a rationally-defensible form (DND/CF 2004: 26). The representational ethos has become a civil-military contractual responsibility built into the military profession of arms,[6] with this covenant animating a military's "distinct practical purpose" and forming the cultural "bedrock" of committed military effectiveness (DND/CF 2004: 25; English 2004: 10, 31). Yet, an institutionalized state military subordinate to sovereign state control is a relatively recent invention, a state technology enmeshed with the very imagination and formalization of the nation-state itself (Cowen 2008: 11).[7] Perhaps legal, political, economic and imaginary conceptions of the state provide a framework for the most decisive revolution in military affairs

(RMA). Further, maintaining permanent military preparedness for war is not a corollary effect of "the state" but constitutive of the state, its jurisdictions and its domestic bodies politic worthy of protection (Dillon and Reid 2009: 9). Consider here the recent warning issued by a group of retired American military leaders, Military Leaders for Kids (2010). Under a national security policy initiative called "Mission: Readiness," the group decried obesity trends among American youth in a report entitled "Too Fat to Fight." Motivating their advocacy to protect the health of a domestic population was their collective concern that "75 per cent of 17- to 24-year-olds do not meet the basic minimum standards required for military service" (MLS 2010). These champions of public health predicted grave implications for an American military already over-extended and suffering a decline in recruitment. In a field populated by the asymmetric influences of private industrial food corporations and a whole band of pharma-physiological wellness providers, military men return as cultural defenders of the people in a double sense.

Beyond the material conduct of war itself, military organs limit and prioritize the objects and ontology of war. While citizens in liberal states experience war as a complicated constellation and resilient existential "complex," the contents of this complex are shaped by hegemonic military nominations sanctioning what can be seen and said about war (Torgovnick 2005; cf. Elshtain 1987; Hedges 2003). Channelling Derrida, we[8] can say there is an archival capacity here, a simultaneous act of commandment and commencement producing fables and a distinct "sophistry of belief" about war (Derrida 1984: 24). When we talk about a Heideggerian military worldview (or world target, to borrow from Rey Chow, 2006), or when we speak of the logistics of military perception, we are referring to two different but connected things (Virilio 1989). The first: the aesthetic and epistemological concepts produced by militaries themselves on matters of war and its conduct. An example is the military conception of a holistic and continuous battlespace populated with different objects and made intelligible by an array of optics. The second: a militarized view of war generated by military agents to which we subscribe from a militarized subject position. This subjectivity deeply affects how we map the world, how we speak and see, how we conceptualize our lives through the categories of "citizen" and "civilian," and how we make basic but powerful friend-enemy distinctions (Feldman 2006; Hartoonian and Miyoshi 2002; Thorne 2006). Accordingly, the military-industrial complex[9] is not simply an index of build-and-destroy capitalism, or what political economist Seymour Melman (1974) called "the permanent war economy" in the later stages of the Vietnam War. Rather, the military industrial complex establishes an existential set of coordinates that continuously mobilize consciousness.

The corrective does not necessarily stem from my disagreement with the general premise of the thesis. It is imperative to critique the ways military logics endow our cultural lives with meaning. Challenging experts' monopoly on expeditionary war and military conduct is essential, and allows us to consider how we think about the world and life itself though war and military operations. My main problem is less conceptual and more based on the selective judgements and positions advanced by the thesis, which is to say my concerns rest on how the thesis forecloses other ways of considering military affairs and war. When Robert Marzec (2009) writes about the coming "militareality" as a conjugation of biopolitics and the "metamilitarization" of all living environments, the perpetual war-footing he describes reads like the completed arrival of the catastrophe, a *fait accompli*. In "Treatise on Militarism" (2006), Ian Buchanan argues that many military institutions face a self-referential problem on an institutional scale: how to retain the credibility to act; how to remain socially and culturally relevant; how to validate the normalized, state-based monopoly on war; and how to determine the proper pragmatic and symbolic objects of war (Buchanan 2006: 163). This analysis is precise: challenged to stay relevant, militaries reconstitute their own capacities. Yet, while holding out weakly for some sort of multitudinous politics of opposition, Buchanan argues that the result will be military colonization and encroachment into different domains of life, which will in turn supplant any lasting shreds of democratic politics, drive neoliberal globalization and harvest capital to create ever-commodified objects with limited use- but high exchange-value (165-66). While these are two brief examples, both Marzec and Buchanan extol the militarization thesis and lean heavily on the notion of an encroaching military presence contaminating cultural and social affairs. What is more—and following from security scholar Mark Neocleous's excellent observation on the facile distinctions made between war and peace as distinguishable states—the militarization thesis implies the ultimate if mythic origin of an uncontaminated civil sphere (2010). The affairs of military agents somehow remain outside unsullied domestic civilian environments before compromising the monolith of non-military matters.[10] In short, the militarization thesis alerts us to ontological and cultural danger but overdetermines its own historical operation rather than reconciling the coupling of military and civil environments.

How do we account for the dependence on the militarization thesis, and the production of its own fatal scholarly effects? We could begin by suggesting the thesis is symptomatic of two interrelated things: the political economy of academic work and the political relevance of cultural studies as an interpretive approach attuned to the triad of meaning, materialism and power relations. Called to account by neoliberal indexes of research intensity and knowledge-mobilization bibliometrics, cultural studies is under pressure to produce some commensurate form of contribution adequate to the administration of "useful" knowledge friendly to capitalism. There are different and simultaneously unfolding possibilities inherent in cultural studies: maintain something like the good, stoic fundamentalism of indifference to these political economic initiatives and continue to create while knowing such creations will not be heeded; build bunkers in which to take cover in a form of disciplinary survival and bear the brunt of prevailing institutional currents; or revoke the founding tenets of cultural studies—interested in revealing hegemonic formations and social power relations—in favour of analyzing everything under the academic sun from some watered-down theoretical perspective. The first tends toward increasing institutional irrelevance, the second tends toward increased domestication and pacification and the third resembles the dematerialization of cultural studies as a relatively distinct field.

Following from these scenarios, perhaps the reliance on the militarization thesis indicates what Dina Georgis, channelling Stuart Hall, calls "our habits of mind" (Georgis 2008: 109, 124). In addressing a series of questions on feminist responses to war—both in general and to the current round of Western expeditionary wars—Georgis eloquently opens a route to move past stock readings. She suggests that these default settings represent victimized and melancholic feelings of resentment, and indicate psychic attachments to the inefficacy of specific political perspectives (124). According to Georgis, we attend not simply to ideas or beliefs but to the stakes of those positions and to our investments in them. To cling to arguments is also to cathect feelings of inadequacy. Arguments themselves become fetishes marking the uncanny—the return of the repressed failure of our intellectual investments and interventions. Georgis writes: "While it would seem I have argued against a politic of opposition [to war], my concern is only to be wary of turning opposition into a kind of law without reflecting why it has come to mean so much" (124).

Georgis's insights interest me because they help to describe the formalization and embedding of the militarization thesis as the way to speak about military affairs in cultural studies. I remain curious about the imperative to continually make the militarization thesis stick, and of the recurring interest in activating the thesis to explain the materialism of military matters. In his manifesto on intellectual play, Fuyuki Kurosawa (2007) suggested working against embedded theoretical dogma and analytic idols, and allowing for ambiguity in the face of entrenched orthodoxies. This advice should carry over to discussions of military affairs, where an uncoupling from the predictable findings of the militarization thesis may provoke new lines of inquiry. In particular, it might go some distance to explain not an ominous military take-over but an interdisciplinary state military operating with a new aggregate kind of "intelligence" fostered by exchanges with other cultural domains.

Cross-Pollination: A Military Does Not Exist Outside Its Own Cultural Contexts

In subscribing wholly to the militarization thesis, I am concerned we risk two things: dismissively reading military institutions as shifting to a comprehensive "whole of government approach" to military operations; and missing implicit economies of political violence at work in Afghanistan that are perhaps less detectable but in no way benign (DND/CF Joint Doctrine Branch 2009: 5). The latter concern amounts to obscuring the conceptualization of battle and battlespace, and the distinctions made about the conduct of the war. In tracing and explaining the anonymous migration of military worldviews into civil spaces, unidirectional straight lines stand in for what is a more complex exchange between military organs and broader social and cultural jurisdictions. Effacing this complexity is dangerous, especially after nine years of expeditionary war and the resulting meta-mission creep exerting substantial pressure on the Canadian Forces, an organization in the midst of its own RMAs (Sloan 2007). This is especially so for the Canadian Army, running for some time at a high operational tempo. Fixating on the militarization thesis obscures the Canadian Forces' conduct within the war. What is clear is that after being deployed under direct American command and now waging war in southern Afghanistan under the auspices of a NATO International Security Assistance Force (ISAF), the Canadian Forces' way of war is changing as it nears its proposed withdrawal from ISAF in 2011. Specifically, population-centred counterinsurgency (COIN) doctrine has become the messianic way to achieve results in Afghanistan, and is fast becoming a conceptual framework through which military agents are re-conceiving their own capacities as providers of limit-event emergency services. A way of war changes partly as an instrumental response to problems requiring solutions but also because available cultural, discursive and epistemological materials inside and outside of military organs fertilize warfare.

Materials and concepts travel, and boundaries are never rigid borders but interstitial trading zones with multidirectional flows. Following from this, the Canadian Forces is a porous institution into which external ideas infiltrate, ideas that are not of a military pedigree. So too is the Canadian Forces' way of war in Afghanistan, which we can view as a result of the displacement of wider cultural influences; that is, it is in military organs that wider material and cultural practices accrue and become embedded. In an abstract sense, there are homologies or "common rationalities" in circulation, from which military affairs and organs are not exempt (Nadesan 2008: 4). A military is arguably internal to a more general economy of cultural production (cf. Bataille 1991). Therefore, if we plan to make arguments about a current state of indistinction between military and non-military zones of production—"everything is militarized"—and plan to stake out a defence of the civilian sphere free from military contamination, we ought to attend to what comes across the divide both ways. Otherwise, we should find ways to explain both as indistinguishable and commensurate domains without adequate differentiation.

The spectre of "the military" deliberately preying on helpless and uncontaminated cultural objects and ideas obscures and effaces one basic fact: a military is an organization that does not exist outside of its own cultural contexts, regardless of the extraordinary measures it undertakes. To compose another continuation thesis, it is more accurate to state that a military is a continuation of culture by other means, and that perhaps a Canadian military is in many ways a continuation of Canadian culture by other means. Or, going further, the emerging Canadian way of war—vested firmly in COIN doctrine—is an indication of not only the demands of the Afghan war and the need for new military methods but a continuation of Canadian biopolitical enclosures with its neoliberal ways of life. This is the key kernel of the corrective: it is not the militarization of life that demands analysis but, following Dillon and Reid (2009), the biopoliticization of military affairs and ways of war. Just as the Canadian Forces and its American and NATO counterparts are conceptualizing a continuum of operations across different activities, our critique of military agents and ways of war must also look at the multidirectional continuum existing beyond strict military materials.

This much is uncontroversial: a military organization, constituted in its organization of tasks, objectives and forms of conduct, is an expressive relay and indexical register for wider cultural materials and practices. Yet, largely because of Deleuze and Guattari's work on the war machine and on state organs as "apparatuses of capture," the notion of "capture" has been an optic through which to frame accounts of contemporary military affairs in cultural studies and the theoretical humanities. According to Deleuze and Guattari, war and military bodies are not mutually inclusive: war and the war machine—a non-military phylum or space of action—are concepts first, and concepts external to any organized state military (whether mercenary, citizen, welfare-state volunteer or non-status precariat) subsequently assembled and put to use by a sovereign state apparatus (1986). In effect, their martial materialism proposes a significant historic-material event: the militarization of war itself by military organs, with the military "capturing" the martial to pacify and order it for more controlled prosecution. Recurring cycles of discussion inflected by Deleuze-Guattari war studies almost thirty years along continue to endow military organs with an ominous, predatory drive bent on aggressively accumulating any and all.[11] While not wanting to underscore the calculated strategic interests of military operators in foreign or domestic contexts, the logic of capture is overdrawn. I suggest understanding capture not as a determined, forceful act but rather as a kind of cellular or geological process in fidelity to Deleuze and Guattari's wider epistemological and ontological project. This is to say, abstractly, that a military institution "captures" ideas in the way that a membrane accrues an aggregate of different elements, which become nested and produce implicit and explicit effects—thus, a non-linear military history of aggregation.[12] The integration of the "captured" elements furthers the standing of the organization and its relation to other specialized organs. Instead of an intractable drama of an invisible military hand, a process of capture historically contingent, but not incidental, is more appropriate.

By considering multidirectional change instead of unidirectional colonization, reappraising military affairs invites a set of related questions in relation to the Afghan war and our understanding of war more generally. The prescriptive equipment provided by the militarization thesis obscures other answers. For instance, in arguing that the war is illegal and unjust, do we not circumvent other difficult questions? As in, what constitutes the legal fiction of an acceptable expeditionary war (*jus ad bellum*), and are cultural studies scholars willing to go down the road of jurists and grammarians and issue syntactic and ethical qualifications? What should one do with a state military, and how could the constitution of a state military be subjected to reform or repudiation in concrete ways? What of the material realities of military service itself "in theatre," with members acting as instruments for counterinsurgency doctrine? Can one regard but not "support the troops"? What are the material implications of confining our analysis of what military organs do, beyond making assertions about Western barbarism and the militarization of life? And where does the default position of "anti-war" and "anti-military" leave us—does it not shut the ontological door on war altogether, a door forced closed by military experts and by an overreliance on carved-out academic positions? While the expeditionary war in and occupation of Afghanistan demands opposition, perhaps war itself should not be over?

An Answer: Foucault, Populations and the Biopoliticization of Battlespace

Substantiating the corrective begins to address the blockage of the militarization thesis in modest ways. Michel Foucault's work on biopolitics and liberal governmentality provides this substance, though in a way that is not immediately apparent. Harvested for better or worse as the answer to any number of wide-ranging questions, Foucault's interrogation of politics, security and war across his Collège de France lectures in the late 1970s is useful for understanding military affairs, their relation to the civilian, and the way of war known as counterinsurgency. The most interesting aspect of Foucault's work is precisely his own difficulty thinking across proximate and contiguous processes. Dillon and Neal argue that Foucault's establishment and subsequent abandonment of trajectories of investigation—in "Security, Territory, and Population," for example, his initial consideration of security gives way to a more pronounced exploration of biopolitics—indicate lacunae in his thought (Dillon and Neal 2009: 1-2). This is to say there is nothing "complete" about Foucault.

Foucault's work connects productively with the contemporary military zeitgeist. After a plurality of cultural, organizational and technical RMAs, such a zeitgeist resembles the outline given by retired British General Rupert Smith. Smith argues that contemporary conflicts "tend to be timeless, even unending" and that, in a self-referential wrinkle, expeditionary wars are undertaken to preserve the very capacity for military force "rather than risking all to gain the objective" (Smith 2007: 271). The ends of these kinds of wars are increasingly virtual: rather than meeting "hard objectives that decide a political outcome," the emphasis is now on "establishing conditions in which the outcome may be decided" (271). The means-ends relation is not vehicular or linked in any straightforward way. Military means themselves become pure means on their own terms, generating feedback and affecting the shape of conditions and decisions. In this way, military agents rationalize doctrine increasingly as a kind of grand risk theory premised on anticipating risks (Rasmussen 2006; cf. Coker 2008). As "conventional" wars have given way to asymmetric and fluid expeditionary engagements, military organs are working to accommodate a wider range of operations, which in turn allow them to engineer "conditions" by anticipating different types of intervention. In a way, the exceptions have become the new rules. Notably, the Canadian Army's own doctrinal planning initiative for 2021 centres on "adaptive dispersed operations," testifying to an inherently self-correcting capacity to adjust to specific fscircumstances.[13]

A Foucauldian approach to understanding expeditionary wars waged under the sign of counterinsurgency allows us to see not the dissemination of military influence everywhere but rather the increasing biopoliticization of war itself (Dillon and Reid 2009: 36). With population-centred doctrine that aims to protect indigenous communities from the threat of insurgency, the object of the war is not necessarily "killing scumbags" but securing the people's ways of life. This is also the core of Foucault's biopolitical theory of liberal governmentality and authority. In the well-known last part of his 1976 *The History of Sexuality, Vol. 1*, Foucault outlines how the object of emerging liberal governmentality became the productive administration of life itself via a continuum of normalizing apparatuses (Foucault 1990: 138, 144). In the imagination of military doctrine, freeing the people from the orbit of the insurgency ensures that the conduct of daily life is unfettered by the influential demands of local insurgent leaders and power structures. More pragmatically, the delivery of this freedom puts coercive pressure on active and passive popular support for the insurgency by supplanting foreign military presence and military-led initiatives (in conjunction with the nascent governing apparatus of the "host nation") to manage local life. According to the Canadian Forces COIN manual,[14] counterinsurgency is "those military, paramilitary, political, economic, psychological and civic actions taken to defeat the enemy." To qualify further:

> The constant is the fact that insurgency and counterinsurgency are essentially about the battle to win and hold popular support both at home and in the theatre of operations. If the strategic focal point is public

opinion in the local, domestic and international arenas, most initial military tactical efforts will be focused on breaking the link between the insurgent and the people. This is not only a physical link, but the psychological link of moral support. The former will entail physical [combat] activities, whilst the latter will entail influence activities that undermine and attack insurgent ideology, narrative and claims to authority and legitimacy.... Only a comprehensive approach that addresses the root causes of an insurgency and attack the authority and legitimacy of the insurgents will ensure an enduring solution. (DND/CF COIN Operations 2008: 1-3)

In Afghanistan, securing the population is not an "operation other than war." Rather, it is a different means of conducting the war—what RAND Corporation analysts call without question "war by other means" (Gompert and Gordon 2008). In his foreword to David Galula's seminal 1964 Counterinsurgency: Theory and Practice, counterinsurgency expert John Nagl is unequivocal: rather than isolated concentration-camp-like enclosures, COIN demands modulation where continuous presence and the use of "static elements of population control are ultimately more important than clearing the enemy using kinetic raids and sweeps" (Nagl in Galula 2006: ix).[15]

In addition to concepts, Foucault's method of genealogy is instructive for approaching military agents and their specific warfighting activities. Genealogy accounts for cross-fertilizing rationalities—a consideration essential to thinking through counterinsurgency warfare. Approach-ing a state military with genealogy in mind allows "three displacements": "extra-institutional, non-functional, and non-objective," which together provide a point of departure for reappraising the black-box of militarization (Foucault 2007: 119). They do so, first, by refusing interpretations that define military organizations as self-evident or rigid institutions; second, by moving past typical assertions about a state military's function (e.g., to undertake combat and to exert pressure on the opinions of domestic civilian society); and third, by revoking any ready-made object around which military activities cohere. Genealogy acknowledges "the military" as a stable object for analysis while ensuring an open door to consider the assemblage-like coherence of syncretic elements. It allows for an unruly military materialism not at all complete despite a military's—and sometimes our own—best efforts. Thus, a genealogy of a military organ positions the military conduct of war as exclusive but never excluded from elements external to it.

Looking to Foucault may seem initially counterintuitive, due to efforts to position him as a theorist of militarization. His lengthy discussions in *Discipline and Punish* (1977) on the barracks and the camp/cantonment identify military forms of organization as elements moving into the capitalist factory, the regulated city and other modular spaces of social order. For Foucault, a military life premised on hierarchical command power, ongoing examination, visibility and repressive disciplinary violence begins to take root in non-military environments. Yet this analysis was not necessarily an end in itself. Foucault's analysis of military methods was motivated by an increasing interest in the way technologies of power regulate domestic ways of life in liberal societies, which are ostensibly premised on individual freedom and economic liberty. His question: How do the methods of institutions designed to exercise political violence with the sovereign sanction of state power leak into everyday power relations? The migration of military methods into civil environments is less a matter of "hard," predatory militarization and more the drift of ordering processes that make life in liberal societies predictable and productive. Inverting von Clausewitz's continuation thesis[16] in his Society Must Be Defended lectures, Foucault explicated the historical displacement of war as a grid of intelligibility for public authorities intervening to manage increasingly population-centred social antagonisms in domestic civilian environments (Foucault 2003: 239). Foucault's theory of power defines everyday micropolitics and the macro-policies constituted to govern domestic life as a field of battle, social antagonism and irresolvable civil conflict. The condition of *polemos* is not the Hobbesian state of nature but the constituting state of political life, with prescribed ways of life defended and aberrant ways of life deemed dangerous and repressed with violence.

In Foucault's estimation, war has not become conditional in a domestic or geo-political sense at a magical point of origin. His proposition on origins is one of ongoing recurrence. War does not, at some specific moment, come penetrate the civil in a crisis of peace that produces a new permanent state; rather, modern forms of state-sovereign power never solve the problem of antagonism and polemos but rather institutionalize them in anonymous forms, as a kind of constituting power. To borrow tangentially from Wendy Brown, conflict is dressed up in the institutional garb of a democratic paradox, where the promise of democracy as a formal system of government needs a formal thing deemed "anti-democratic" dissent in order to oppose and ultimately integrate, via the guarantee of representation and pacification (Brown 2001: 122). For Foucault, the state of war remains, never fully resolved by the arrival of Leviathan and the promise of peace, and always a problem for social elites and civil authorities. The "general race war" (Foucault 2003: 106) Foucault summarizes—exacerbated by the social imaginary of nation as a bounded political community of insiders and outsiders—this premise: put simply, civil authorities and apparatuses of power undertake colonization, domestication and pacification within the domestic-civil enclosure in order to counter different forms of insurgency.

Continuing his derivations from *History of Sexuality*, Foucault's investigation toward the end of the Society lectures formalizes "biopolitics"—the politics of human populations' biology. Different from "anatamo-politics," which target individual but heterogeneous bodies, the population-centric capacity of biopolitics regulates life at the level of generality to maintain homeostasis (Foucault 2003:

246). In the 1977-1978 lectures Security, Territory, Population, Foucault defines biopower as "the set of mechanisms through which the basic biological features of a human species become the object of a political strategy, of a general strategy of power" (2007: 1). Foucault's development of biopower occurs in direct relation to apparatuses of security and governmentality—the mentality or operational art and intelligence of government. The emergence of biopolitics does not eclipse or render ineffective juridico-legal or disciplinary technologies of power; rather, against this crude kind of progression, the metrics of control augment a spectrum of existing technologies of power (6-7).[17] Not stapled to the State alone, but to state organs, dominant institutions and social and cultural practices—like the emergence of neoliberal capitalism described at length in the Birth of Biopolitics lectures (1978-1979)—biopolitical affairs are in Foucault's paradigm, the crucial avenue for modern and contemporary ways of rule (Nadesan 2008: 8).[18] The biological basis of biopower and biopolitics thus also recalls the question of bios—a way of life and living, connected to Aristotelian notions of the good life—specific to and deemed appropriate and normal in a given society.[19] Bios is not inherently negative but subject to contingent, particular cultural and social contexts, by which some ways of living become prioritized, idealized and secured in order to reproduce the conditions of social life. Above all, Foucault's point is clear: the object of life itself—the life of the individual, the population, the people as a "society to be defended"—becomes a focal point for the art of government, the object mediated by prescriptive and always-pedagogical missives about the routine and the common sense, linking the politics of living with life itself.

According to Foucault's explication, biopower operates through the provision of conditions for securing life itself—"making life live"—and the creation of security and welfare for the population. Foucault emphasizes that biopolitics and governmentality are together concerned with the problems of uncertainty and circulation, and with the distribution of heterogeneity around a normalizing pole. In Foucault's analysis, the question of life is a question of conduct, and the idea of conduct itself is a problem that demands the intervention of public and private authorities. They must determine how to manage the material and spiritual conduct of all, and how to convey all to a central goal—namely, by implanting a particular form of political, economic and social order under the sign of liberalism and, later, neoliberalism. In "Security, Territory, Population," Foucault spends two lectures addressing the historical emergence of the "police state" (2007: 311-45). "Police" in this context does not refer to repressive, law-enforcing state organs, but rather to the early political science and economy of a nascent general welfare state for bodies politic inside political enclosures (i.e., from the market town to the nation-state). This emerging science of police was aimed at securing predictable, institutionalized protection against the fallouts of increasing aleatory and uncertain social, political, economic, industrial and agricultural flows, and ensuring such security within a jurisdiction. In this framework, security becomes the rationalization of governmentality mitigating risks in managing the life of the population. Foucault links biopower not to the city's magistrate or governor, but to the Christian pastorate. A shepherd-figure is charged with safely seizing and securely delivering the flock—a delivery fraught with the threats of a non-linear environment outside of the enclosures of the pastures or barns. For the domesticated flock, what remains is subordination and obedience to this pastoral power in exchange for momentary safe passage (174-75). Submission to this notion of protection and delivery—as a project of conveying the lives of a population toward some goal—is at the operational heart of biopower and biopolitics. Paul Virilio elegantly calls this agreement on the provision of protection an ongoing "semi-colonial" pact made durable, and Charles Tilly equates this capacity to an organized protection racket "with the advantage of legitimacy" (Virilio 1990: 46; 1985: 169).

The Continuum of Counterinsurgency: Biopolitical War in Afghanistan

> Our argument is not that liberalism became biopoliticized, but that it was biopolitical from its very inception.... One of the entailments of all forms of rule is the way in which it also authorizes and executes violence. There is, then, a martial face to liberal peace. The liberal way of rule is contoured by the liberal way of war. (Dillon and Reid 2009: 81)

Following Foucault, and Dillon and Reid's assertion, we can trace an ongoing confluence between ways of war, ways of rule and ways of life, which allows for a better assessment of the war in Afghanistan, and of war itself. Counterinsurgency's centre of gravity is the life of the population,[20] and military agents conducting the war effectively "weaponize" the biopolitical methods specific to Western liberal states outlined by Foucault. While COIN doctrine suggests the solution to an insurgency is ultimately political and appropriate to "the context of the culture at hand," its prescriptions advocate a mixture of biopolitical intervention from fostering life to killing and death (DND/CF COIN 2008: 2-22). Ironically, COIN warfare actually exposes military warfighters to increased risk—short-term risk is an "operational necessity"—as they harvest the political benefits of waging war by other non-combat means and work to close the gap between instructional doctrine and practical action (U.S. Army/Marines Corps 2007: xxvi).

The messianic arrival of democratization and the benefits of democratic accountability in Afghanistan shed light on the general contours of desired political solutions. According to political theorist Adrian Little, the promise of democratic deliverance expresses pious fundamentalism: "with democratic piety, democracy becomes an end in itself, no matter how bastardized the form that emerges from its pursuit or the emptiness of its conceptualization" (Little 2008: 165). The driving justifications for the continuance of the Afghan war offer the promise of a "legitimate" and centralized way of rule beyond the operations of rural tribal structures, urban sectarian divisions and local power relations motorized by coercion and nepotism. Yet, in effect, the promise rests on substituting a more predictable, centralized biopolitical form of governmentality for other organized ways of rule and ways of life. The ways in which the invasion and war have exacerbated corruption, affected swaths of the population involved in the economy of opium production and trade, and enabled criminality, remain unknown.[21] The known fact is clear: enforced global democratic reform in the counterinsurgency era weds itself to biopolitical war (Fenton 2009a).

The renewal of counterinsurgency doctrine and its leakage into wider operational contexts encourages contemporary Canadian Forces doctrine to imagine a continuum of operations for military agents. General Andrew Leslie argues the key to Canadian Forces success in Afghanistan and in future engagements and deployments is the development of the "comprehensive approach to operations" eschewing "silos" and "stovepipes" in favour of a network-centred approach across different domains of war (Leslie et al 2009: 11; CFJP 01 2009: 0226/2-10, 0232/2-14).[22] This comprehensive approach is to be "JIMP-capable": Joint, Interagency, Multinational and Public, ensuring interoperability and continuity with other military, state and civilian agents and agencies(Leslie 2009: 14). In the JIMP paradigm, the "business" of state military agents shifts toward an adaptive meta-level rescue/response role, able to provide edgework and emergency services in limit-event scenarios.[23] This justification often becomes a tautological loop, especially as those providing the service of intervention often see wars as exceptional disaster zones a priori, which demand and justify the very provision of such specialized services. Arguably, flexible military actors are performing varying types of affective and material labour with increasing regularity in the context of post-industrial warfare. Undertaking distant expeditionary wars—under the name of righteousness and for the public's well-being—is one mission meeting this mandate. Of course, according to the JIMP paradigm, state militaries will (and already) share the edgework industry with private contractors and with state and non-state agencies who have varying interests and investments. Given these collaborative players, the state military and reconceptualization of its own activities is not without cause.

The nuance of the Afghan war effort and a campaign based on population-centred activities means Canadian Forces units find themselves fulfilling a multi-headed role to prosecute the war in legal, disciplinary and biopolitical ways. They retain the authority to undertake security operations and deploy lethal force in the interests of occupation and pacification, always under juridico-legal cover as the instrumental moral agent of political violence. They also largely determine and decide "normal" and "secure" behaviour itself in occupied territories under the sign of security, which is to say they undertake a disciplinary function of panoptic-like interdiction and dissuasion to produce these distinctions. Last, they intervene at the level of local life itself which, in the case of the Canadian Forces' concerted efforts, may result in development projects and stabilization teams centred on establishing civil strongholds free from the risk of insurgent influence. The medical analogy of COIN given in the American COIN manual—"stop the bleeding: impatient care and recovery, and outpatient care and movement to self-sufficiency"—is echoed by Dillon and Reid, though in a darker light: "the emergency of emergence requires a form of global triage. Global triage specifies who gets what treatment, where, when and how" (2009: 89-90; US Army/ USMC 2007: 153-54). The Canadian COIN manual goes further, with the medical metaphor of a communicable disease counteracted by a systemic approach involving a wide range of means: changes to behaviour and the environment, such as the reduction of risk factors, quarantine, inoculation and treatment of the clinically infected (CF COIN Operations 2008: 2-21).

"Treatment" includes persuasion, dissuasion, conversion, marginalization and killing (2-21). "Canada's Engagement in Afghanistan" outlines the Canadian federal government's interventionist treatment (GOC 2009). The "targeted set of objectives"—security, basic services, humanitarian assistance, border management, institution building and political reconciliation—are pursued largely under Canadian Forces auspices.[24] The actualization of these objectives depends on how the Canadian Forces synthesizes these priorities via modification efforts to secure the population as a pastorate to protect. Establishing law and order, building police capacity, supporting "democratic processes" and fostering "sustainable peace" are not external to the war effort or to warfighting but, as promises of their own eventual provision, become the means to weaken the insurgency and persuade adversaries to cease opposition (GOC 2009). In Afghanistan, the next invasion by marauding white knights with a bankrupt mandate of assisting imperilled Others gains another dimension if we view the counterinsurgency project as the establishment of a military pastorate working via guns and development to wage a war of establishing a stable and a habitat for the continuance of life (Razack 2004, 2008).

If we attend more closely to Canada's war in Afghanistan, we begin to see the establishment of life-preservation zones alongside aggressive combat. In effect, the Canadian Forces is tasked with the simultaneous creation of both "kill-sacks" and "life-sacks." Grievous bodily harm occurs alongside the preservation of life, with counterinsurgency war exposing indigenous populations to killing and nurture. Dillon and Reid are further instructive:

> The military is as interested now, for example, in life-creating and life adaptive processes as it is in killing because, like the liberal way of rule and war more generally, it locates the nature of the threat in the very becoming-dangerous of the vital signs of life itself. (2009: 125)

In effect, any emergent element registers as dangerous, and anything not in compliance with the way of life proper to Afghan environments designated "secure" demands the attention of military agents (Deleuze and Guattari 1986: 119).[25] Life-supporting zones become fortified strong-holds of a different type. After scaling back remote operating bases and combat outposts, the population-centred approach rests in creating islands of security—archipelagos that mitigate insurgencies and enable "normal" life. The creation of "actively-humane warfare" was the reason that *Prospect Magazine* named the American architect of contemporary COIN warfare—General David Petraeus—the 2008 Intellectual of Year (Crabtree 2009). Seen as a "softer" way of waging what is no less a war, biopolitical battlespace is territorialized through "secure and stay" stabilization teams, Key Village Approaches, or efforts to stimulate local infrastructure and agriculture programs via the much-touted provincial reconstruction team in Kandahar. Recall the initial scenario through which Foucault developed the concept of biopower: grain yields, the management of scarcity, and ecologies of circulation affecting the security and general welfare of a population within the territory of the market town (2007: 31). While the traditional dyad of repressive military action coupled with cultural, institutional and economic violence continues to enforce transformation in Afghanistan and elsewhere, military units are fighting with the restorative offering of enclosures. The anticipated "rings of stability" to be created around Kandahar in the summer 2010 offensive suggest static, concentric spheres of military influence augmented by probing mobile elements. Hard and soft measures create an even wider spectrum of political violence to be deployed in synchronized if asymmetric ratios. The varying speeds of fast-kinetic and slower non-kinetic force—reconstruction, anti-corruption measures and infrastructure development—endow military agents with enough political violence to achieve political consequences (Virilio 1978).[26]

To understand this mix another way, consider the traditional categories of military philosophy and military arts and science. In a strict sense, military philosophy is the invention of concepts that nominally distinguish between material events in order to stabilize them, and to make them susceptible to evaluation. Military science is the correlation of different sets, domains or operations. Military art is the ability to invent sensations and affects at different intensities.[27] Of these military concepts, correlations and sensations, some are direct while others are indirect; some are mobile while others remain almost imperceptible and immobile. Counterinsurgency war does all of these: invent the security of population as the determining conceptual kernel around which to organize efforts; correlate combat and civil environments through which to impose one's will; and ensure a mixture of fast and slow forms of military-backed political violence to generate sensations producing an anticipated, acceptable set of effects never in isolation.[28] War is sending missives and missiles and—depending on the speed, the density and the type of communication—leaving those addressed with little freedom to produce an oppositional decoding.[29] In a sense, war is the undertaking of media-effects (think "shock-and-awe"), with different generated affects mediating the operational environment. As such, the Afghan war is always-already a matter of persuasion and communication at varying speeds. For units on the ground, biopolitical effectiveness augments combat effectiveness and vice versa. Through the elaborate creation of an institutionalized, continuous "teaching and learning" cycle, the Canadian Forces revokes the injunction to training in favour of reinventing itself as a flexible learning institution. The Army Lessons Learned Centre, the Centre of Excellence for Peace Support Training, and the Afghan village simulacrum at the Canadian Manoeuvre Training Centre at CFB Wainwright (with its insurgents and "authentic" civilian populations) are conduits through which to channel learning from deployments. The process of teaching how to wage interoperable war across different environments—the social, the economic, the psychic—speaks to the continuum of ways a military prosecutes counterinsurgency war and conceives war itself. COIN enables and demands the development of different capacities like Civil-Military Cooperation, Psychological Operations, Information Operations, and Operational Mentor and Liaison Teams, which together add to the mixture of approaches and effects.

In this regard, the repeated recourse by military agents to "operational doctrine"— "the organization necessary for the effective employment of military forces"—and the operational art is telling (CFJP01 2009: 1-3; English et al. 2005). The art of operational doctrine is an in-between hinge, translating abstract strategic goals into concrete tactics by conceptualizing objects for engagement. In Afghanistan, this means bringing different measures to bear in waging a biopolitical war. The essential question of the Afghan war is not necessarily combat or confrontation, but a battle of ways of rule and life: how will people be ruled and how will their lives, in a biopolitical fashion, be conducted toward certain wider social goals, if such are possible? In targeting the so-called "hearts and minds" of pan-Afghans, the war foments more than allegiances for or against occupying armies. It actually activates small indigenous wars in local settings where the village or city block is the thing defended. The question is: Who has the credibility to undertake this defence? The war finds non-aligned local elites, self-identifying insurgents and foreign expeditionary forces engaged to occupy different populations. Each of these agents decides who is in and who is out—who finds refuge and who finds exclusion and further vulnerability. So rather than assess the war as a series of battles or engagements, we would be better to see the war's escalation in the post-2009 "surge" as an escalation in biopolitical efforts on all fronts.[30]

Effects-Based Approach to Operations (EBAO) is another concept colouring Canadian Forces operational thinking. EBAO is a framework antici-pating the intended and unintended outcomes activated by different mixtures of political violence. The framework moves away from strict objectives and envisions a non-linear, complexity-based approach, "which facilitates development and sharing of a holistic understanding of the environment" (DND/CF 2007). As a method of "coordinated sets of actions (or inactions)" directed toward "shaping the behaviour of intended targets"—whether adversary, friend or ally—Effects-Based Approach to Operations:

> consists of operations designed to influence the long- or short-term goals of an operation by achieving desired physical or psychological effects. In an effects-based approach, military actions are integrated with other instruments of national power, such as humanitarian aid agency or diplomatic efforts. (Grossman-Vermaas 2007: 67; Leslie et al. 2009: 20; DND/CF 2007)

The emphasis on a system-like ecology aims to manage effects so as to reach a desired if relative "end-state" (Leslie et al. 2009: 14). Whether in generating affects to cause material and psychic dispositions to shift, or in managing the consequences of potential outcomes and virtual threats, EBAO animates the counterinsurgency campaign in Afghanistan. The mix of peace support, counterinsurgency and major combat is the work of an interdisciplinary military using a variety of "influence activities." Rather than closing down points of exchange with other practices not traditionally combat-related, the Canadian Forces is opening up to integrate them. Notably, while granted ethical licence in its attempt to mitigate harm—the U.S. COIN manual was vetted by Harvard University's Carr Center for Human Rights, with the introduction written by director Sarah Sewell—the consequences of COIN's ontologico-ethical orientation remains problematic. In his treatise on the revolution in warfare ethics, Gregory Challans calls EBAO a "pseudo-science" and a logical fallacy that is recursive, reasoning from effect to causes so as to reverse-engineer the sought after end-state (Challans 2007: 109).

In organizing the exposure to life and death, and in deploying fast and slow forms of military violence, biopolitical war espouses an anthropological fetish about "the population" itself. With Canadian Forces operations increasingly attuned to war at the level of the biopolitical, commanders need better ethnographic intelligence in the conduct of their population-centred missions. First initiated under American auspices, mapping the "human terrain" and generating ethno-graphic intelligence are now characteristic of military operations sensitive to the biopolitical (McFate and Jackson 2005; Renzi 2006; Scales 2004). Mapping is a representative act of diagramming in order to manage and control. The will to anthropological information—surveying and knowing rituals, customs, habits and beliefs—is the necessary supplement, opening an avenue to alternative forms of persuasion and offering a way to mitigate the fog of exchange between Western military professionals and indigenous people. For COIN operators, population statistics, social demographics and local knowledge mitigate the friction created by time- and space-sensitive friend-enemy distinctions. Deriving critical information to leverage all elements in the battlespace enables "smart war," based not on precision or surgical bomb strikes but on biopolitical intelligence. According to Canadian Forces Brigadier-General David Fraser: "I underestimated one factor—culture. I was looking at the wrong map—I needed to look at the tribal map and not the geographic map. Wherever we go in the world, we must take into account culture" (qtd. in Spencer and Balasevicius 2009: 40).

Fraser admits to the inability of institutional military operations to detect the problems particular to the ways of life of the people. As the Canadian Forces remains intent on generating and harvesting knowledge about the ordinariness of everyday culture in the southern Pashtun tribal areas, "culture" in this instance remains a formal-procedural hurdle to be solved.

Based on his T. E. Lawrence-like reflections on his role as a mentor for the fledgling Afghan National Army (ANA), CF Lieutenant-Colonel W. D. Eyre writes:

> The Afghan people are brave, hospitable, respectful and cunning—characteristics clearly reflected in their national army.... The ANA has a different way of doing business from what we are accustomed to. Get used to it because it will not change. They have a different sense of time that is not based on achieving success in six-month increments. They have a different sense of subordinate empowerment.... The role of personal networks that sometimes supplants the chain of command is sometimes a source of frustration. The Afghan culture is very much one of personal connections, and in this the role of rumour is important.... The culture of Afghanistan—in which Pashtunwali (code of honour) has a strong influence—is based on personal respect and honour. Keeping your face is incredibly important. (Eyre 2008: 1-3)

The seeming opacity of a pan-Afghan culture is a recurring trope in military circles. The fetishization of this gulf of difference is apparent in the publication of popular and academic manuscripts regarding dense cultural networks, historical chaos and turbulence, and the unyielding recalcitrance of indigenous Afghans in the face of foreign invaders. This nativism invites us to consider Edward Said's four dogma of Orientalism adhered to by Occidental interlopers: systematic differences between the West and the rest; a preference for fixed representations of Oriental Others derived from texts as opposed to direct evidence of experience; a tendency to position Oriental culture as fixed, eternal, reconciled and self-evident; and the need to convert threatening Oriental cultures into controllable entities (qtd. in Jiwani 2008: 19). Eyre's observations border on veneration and his experiences suggest a polychromic and high-context environment, implying the need for Canadian Forces to both mimic and develop a polyvocal orientation itself. Yet, in arguing whether the culture warriors get it right or wrong in their new nativism, or in debating whether they do or do not further the dogma of Orientalism, do we implicitly suggest that there is a more refined way to "do" military intervention at the level of ways of life, or that there is some tolerable future form of intervention? Are we not then holding out for something like an acceptably cosmopolitan military?[31]

Some in the Canadian Forces are calling for the institutionalization of cultural intelligence as an essential domain within the continuum of operations, and for—misconstrued nomenclature notwithstanding—a Canadian Forces Centre for Cultural Studies to meet ethnographic and cultural knowledge needs (Spencer and Balasevicius 2009: 47). While the debate over human terrain has raised significant questions about the militarization of anthropology and the military extraction of knowledge from social and human sciences,[32] the recurring problem of cultural knowledge speaks more readily to the increasing military need to become more cosmopolitan than to the compromise of academic discourses and the military perversion of anthropology.[33] James Der Derian's recent documentary *Human Terrain: War Becomes Academic* (Der Derian et al. 2010) investigates the rise of human terrain mapping and its political fall-out among scholars in support or opposition; however, the film belies the ongoing interface of different arts and science, whether military or otherwise. In the most general sense, war is always a diagnostic method of inquiry, or a forensic activity comprised of academic and anthropological undertakings that create different epistemological economies of how to know friends and enemies (Appadurai 2006: 21). Describing something as recently modified—"becomes," as in "it just, now, became"—obscures this feature. Perhaps it is more precise to describe the intensification of counterinsurgency war's anthropological bent as designed to quantify habits, measure complexity and "informationalize life" in the interests of persuading more pliable local populations (Dillon and Reid 2009: 75). Intelligence, cultural and otherwise, is always important to military operations, and the renewed faith in generating "white situational awareness" that allows military agents to understand the meshwork of local cultures should be no surprise, given the biopolitical shift in warfighting. Rather than rear up and blame our problems on the next round of military Orientalism, a critique of military operations is served by asking how, at the level of ways of life, there remains the acknowledgment of opacity, of not getting it, but of still striving to make difference itself into an equivalence amenable to the grammars of biopolitical war and the promissory arrival of democracy, with its attendant forms of normal conduct. We can question the employment of military agents to guarantee security by pacifying local populations under the sign of enforced reforms while making the biopolitical commons of security the object of the war itself.

Toward a New Military Intelligence

Security for a given population is never simply a provisional measure but is created to persuade and dissuade, and is always part of the communicative constitution of war itself. In Afghanistan, islands of stability under the sign of the military pastorate must perform as such in order to produce a condition appropriate for foreign withdrawal. The biopolitical way of war always makes a coercive injunction: the price of protection demands that one signal "security." Incumbent on the population is the role as a relay indicating its own security, a sign signifying "normal enough" and satisfying the nominal criteria of an expeditionary endstate. Democracy is a slogan camouflaging another state-ment by overextended expeditionary military agents: get us out.

If at one point the philosophy of full-spectrum military operations suggested bringing all possible assets and weapons to bear, biopolitical war invites and encourages the use of comprehensive assets across a continuum of operations constituted in the cultural, social and psychic domains of human life. It is a mistake to locate the material effects of non-combat elements of biopolitical warfare as external to warfighting. The continuum of operations creates a continuum of political violence deployed via the mixture of military mediations in a counterinsurgency war. The integration of biopolitical methods into the war effort indicates, above all else, the hegemony of biopolitical governmentality in Western liberal states. Put another way, what is ongoing in military battlespace is the incorporation of a foundational but "'objective,' systemic, and anonymous" economy of political violence—a kind of constituting violence inherent in systems of civil order (Žižek 2008: 13). This is the quiet violence explained away in biopolitical cultures, which prioritize life itself and animate the conduct and regulation of ways of life in Western domestic enclosures.

At the outset, in claiming that ecologies of power in non-military settings fertilize the fast and slow violence of counterinsurgency war, I challenged the naturalization of the militarization thesis and its entailments, in the hope of disturbing debates and provoking an alternate line of inquiry. If we can move past the militarization thesis and begin to consider the emergence of a new interdisciplinary military intelligence, we may have a framework through which to consider military affairs, counterinsurgency warfare and the constitution of war, and to rethink ways in which Canadian populations are occupied and modulated. In the political enclosure "Canada," can we conceive of constituencies as human terrain monitored for signs and mined for ethnographic intelligence, as objects of an asymmetric population-centred counterinsurgency effort? The history of refined military methods alone does not provide any sole model for contemporary counterinsurgency. We ought to look to hegemonic ways of rule and the cultural affairs of neoliberal societies for the core kernels. In this sense, the expeditionary way of war is an index for the domestic way of life. The mix of fast and slow violence addressed to life within Canada has historically persuaded new and old Canadian hearts and minds in varying intensities. Persuasion has occurred as a confluence of military, missionary and pastoral initiatives, notably directed in systematic ways to indigenous populations in Canada and against other minority populations and publics too vital for the norm. The current low-intensity campaign is a mix of different measures and conversion narratives. As seen during Tim Hortons 2010 Vancouver Olympics advertising campaign, the pan-Canadian breakwater of Tim Hortons coffee posits a mundane participatory but pacifying commercial experience for newly-arrived immigrants. This operates alongside constitutional tactics that emphasize an increasingly narrow and obligations-based conception of citizenship as military-like professional service (Cowen 2008: 230).

In his essay on militareality, Marzec tells us, via von Clausewitz, that what is in the war—the passion or will to wage war, to maintain a "war footing"—must be already a firm foundation or desire in the people (Marzec 2009: 144). I think he is correct, but in a way he does not intend. The foundation is not an appetite for war but the subscription to the pastorate and to a general condition of counterinsurgency within domestic enclosures guaranteeing security from uncertainty and risk, a condition that simultaneously exposes the unruly to insecurity as insurgents requiring triage or permanent containment. What is in the biopolitical war waged in Afghanistan is already in us in Canada as a spirit of counterinsurgency. Ordinary, neoliberal ways of rule serve as prototypes for export, the source and template for biopolitics and biopower translated for military use in foreign environments. It is in these cultural affairs stretching across the distinctions of "military" and "civil" where we can locate the continuum of political violence.

Notes

Many thanks to the peer reviewers, whose criticisms and comments helped me to refine and revise the arguments in the paper. Further, I want to thank Deborah Cowen and Jody Berland for their invaluable insights and ongoing support. Whatever gaps, incoherencies and conjectures emerge are certainly my own.

1. Canadian commentators framed the Obama announcement as an opportunity for the Canadian Forces to scale down its warfighting and security signature and focus on the "good" work of reconstruction and development.

2. Work in cultural studies has decisively revoked these claims by challenging the logic of the rescue narrative, problematizing the reductive notion of imperilled Muslim women as a form of racism and interrogating the constellation of Islam, gender and liberation in the post-9/11 era. See Hunt (2006), Khan (2008), Philipose (2008), Razack (2008).

3. The tour also launched Joya's *A Woman among Warlords* (2009), co-written with Canadian activist Derrick O'Keefe. See Olivia Ward (2009).

4. War is not external to macro- or micro-political concerns but ensconced as a constituting element of politics. The cleavage or gulf between "war" and "politics" is not as clear-cut as some make it out to be, whether in the interests of maintaining war as carefully deployed instrument or in assertions that claim now, at this historical moment, permanent war is the norm, having overtaken civil-political discourse. As Foucault and von Clausewitz were at pains to show—if for different reasons—war was and continues to be a constituting force, regardless of the liberal mechanisms in place to govern its use. For Clausewitz, the danger of rising to extremes and the impossibility of isolating different elements of war testified to this power; for Foucault, it was the function of war as a grid of intelligibility and strategic condition for social power relations.

5. Cynthia Cockburn's (2004) description of a continuum of gendered violence stretching across the spaces of peace and war is useful for conceptualizing this fluidity. For Cockburn—and for feminist war scholar Cynthia Enloe—different patriarchal gradients of gendered political violence, from the symbolic to the grievous, expose women to vulnerability.

6. See Samuel Huntington's and Morris Janowitz's canonical work on the state, the armed forces and civil society.

7. See, among other sources, Foucault (2008: 5-6) on the rise of a "military-diplomatic" apparatus.

8. Of course, the use and implied constitution of this unsatisfactory "we" remains open to scrutiny. "We" refers to any number of small interpretive communities or publics loosely constituted in proximity to this journal.

9. See Nick Turse (2008) and Retort (2005) regarding the permanent war economy, and how cycles of build-and-destroy capitalism wed to American military exceptionalism.

10. From Neocleous:

> What I do want to challenge ... is the major historical assumption being made within it. For these accounts rely on an assumption of a "classical" age in which war and peace were indeed distinguishable; they assume that the destabilization is somehow new—hence the references to wars in "the past," in the "old sense" and in the "classical" age. (Neocleous 2010: 3)

Paul Virilio's work on speed, space and pure war aligns with this assertion. In Virilio's proto-anthropological theory of war, human organizations and political enclosures (i.e., towns and cities) are always-already organizations and formations for war, and the rise of civil society conceals but does not eliminate this imperative. For him, the origin/differentiation question is moot, precisely because, according to his position, human systems are constituted in political violence and built to wage war from the start. That said, Virilio remains an outspoken critic of military logics and advocates against the control exerted by military experts on the question of war (Virilio 1978).

11. Theorists and scholars like Eyal Weizman, Chris Hables Gray and Henry Giroux (among others) have shown the ways in which state military philosophy has "mined" and harvested poststructuralist theory, non-linear and complexity theory and ecological thinking from non-military and academic environments. See also note 31.

12. This is in line with Manuel De Landa's (1993, 1997) work on war, self-organization and materialism.

13. See the Canadian Army's Directorate of Land Concepts and Design on the "future" force employment concept, Land Operations 2021: Adaptive Dispersed Operations (DND/CF fs2007).

14. A 2007 draft version of the Canadian Forces COIN manual was released and subsequently pulled from the public domain. While now allegedly available, the current Canadian Forces manual is difficult to locate. I received an unclassified 2008 copy after a lengthy Access to Information request to CF/DND.

15. A touchstone for contemporary COIN theory, Galula's treatise is a meditation on the failure of French forces to suppress and defeat the national liberation struggle in Algeria.

16. For von Clausewitz, war waged by state military forces remained an appropriate expression and means to the ends of a sovereign state achieving its interests and enabling its policies. Crucially—and often implied otherwise—war is not external or an exception to politics but an extension for achieving political goals. War is one strategy by which

a state can rationalize its ends and achieve its goals. Typically, the end (or the intended strategic result of an engagement) is not necessarily victory but, rather, the sapping of the adversary's will to fight or to resist. Von Clausewitz writes another ontological gem: "War is thus the act of force to compel our enemy to do our will," which is to say that war becomes any number of communicative and persuasive measures to actualize such a result (von Clausewitz 1977: 75).

17. It remains worth stating that Foucault's conception of biopolitics differs somewhat from Agamben's concept of biopower (Agamben 1998: 1). Agamben's distinction between bios and zōe—between political life guaranteed by the cover of the sovereign state, and the basic animal capacity for life—facilitates his theory of bare life, a life that is exposed to exceptional capacity of sovereign power. Seeking to theorize civil wars and insurgencies in the global South, Achille Mbembe has extended Agamben's idea of bare life into a decidedly postcolonial context, by developing the idea of necropolitics, a politics premised on a continuum of exposure to death, which becomes a Bataille-coloured mode of productive expenditure (2003).

18. See Nadesan 2008, chapter 3, and Lemke (2001).

19. In his posthumously published book, *Fearless Speech* (1982), Foucault describes the difference between logos and bios: between ways of speaking and ways of living.

20. Military scholar Jonathan North (2003) points to French Revolutionary General Louis Lazare Hoche as an important figure who formalized and codified COIN doctrine. North points to Hoche's use of already-existing French treatises on small wars and irregular tactics based on French colonial experiences in 1740s North America.

21. On the displacements of criminality in spaces opened up by neoliberalism and of martial insecurity accelerated by foreign interventions, see Comaroff (2006). If there is any known quantity, it is that corruption and coercion are neither external to nor outside the "really-existing" democracy in Western liberal states.

22. It is important to avoid taking the notion of network-centred war and operations in too narrow a technological sense. The dreamlike promise of network-centred warfare resides in generating a real-time, stable, and updated image of war across the spectrum of military battlespace. It is the promise of delivery that keeps the network intact. See Weber's discussion about how a "net works" (2006: 102-103).

23. The Critical States of Security Network based in the Department of Politics, University of Bristol, has produced working papers and a colloquium on the notion of military labour as emergency response and rescue. See The Rise of the Rescue Industry. http://www.bris.ac.uk/politics/cssn/workshop1/. Further, see the departmental working papers by Ryerson Christie, Colleen Bell and Paul Higate at http://www.bris.ac.uk/politics/workingpapers/.

24. While "whole of government" (WOG) includes the Canadian International Development Agency, Department of Foreign Affairs and International Trade, and the Royal Canadian Mounted Police, the Canadian Forces provides a broader umbrella. Rather than cite the "militarization of aid and development," I'm inclined to read the WOG approach and its attendant agencies as invested and engaged in biopolitical warfare.

25. In his book on the political possibilities of constituent power, Antonio Negri describes an insurgency as a constituted movement and continuous mediation (2009). The notion of an emergent presence as the logic of insurgency connects to Dillon and Reid's notion of vital life itself as a threat to order.

26. Virilio's concept of speed—or of a speed—is tied again to the rate and duration of a given act of war.

27. This tripartite categorization of art, science and philosophy come from Deleuze and Guattari (1994). See also Stephen Zagala (2003).

28. Beyond the continuation thesis, one of von Clausewitz's most pressing points is that the different elements of a war never exist in isolation from one another (1977: 78). In an updated compendium of Canadian Forces military doctrine, von Clausewitz is still positioned as an important and essential thinker guiding doctrine (CFJP01 2009: 2-4).

29. An allusion to Stuart Hall's canonical encoding/decoding essay.

30. See Englehardt (2009). See also Lloyd Axworthy's (2009) anthem for incipient biopolitics.

31. As stated clearly in the 2004 publication *Duty with Honour*, the Canadian Forces is intent on harmonizing and closing the culture gap between the military profession of arms and the parent community of Canada and Canadian "liberal" values (26-27, 37-42). Okros, recent "gaps" study (Hall and Dinch 2008) reflects on the "civilianization" of the Canadian Forces through considerations of the trinity of armed forces, government and society. On these matters, Deborah Cowen's analysis and critique of military labour is wholly pertinent to these cosmetic institutional narratives. Specifically, Cowen argues that racial, gender and sexual hierarchies still constitute Canadian Forces culture despite the espousal of liberal, multicultural values. See (2008: 169-94).

32. The creation of the Minerva Research Initiative—an interagency knowledge centre for cultural intelligence and human terrain funded by the U.S. Department of Defense—generated controversy in U.S. academic circles. For a useful overview of human terrain in a CF context, see the collection of news items and commentary on human terrain on Max Forte's blog Zero Anthropology (http://zeroanthropology.net/). For anthropologists' critical responses to human terrain systems, see Network of Concerned Anthropologists (2009) and Roberto Gonzalez (2009).

33. It is more precise to speak of the historical and *ongoing* military-academic interface, from cybernetics and targeting systems to early computer engineering to the military uptake of research from the canon of social sciences, anthropology, fsgeography and area studies.

References

Agamben, Giorgio. 1998. *Homo Sacer: Sovereign Power and Bare Life*, trans. Daniel Heller-Roazen. Palo Alto, CA: Stanford University Press.

Appadurai, Arjun. 2006. Fear of Small Numbers. Durham, NC: Duke University Press.

Axworthy, Lloyd. 2009. Time for a Civilian Surge: More Troops Can't Rebuild Afghanistan's War-Torn Economy or Uproot Rampant Corruption. *The Globe and Mail*, 16 December. http://www.theglobeandmail.com/news/opinions/time-for-a-civilian-surge/article1403150/.

Bataille, Georges. 1991. *The Accursed Share, Vol. I*. Trans. Robert Hurley. Cambridge: Zone/MIT Books.

Bercuson, David. 2010. There's a New "Peace Warrior" In Town, *The Globe and Mail*, 1 March.

Brown, Wendy. 2001. *Politics Out of History*. Princeton, NJ: Princeton University Press.

Buchanan, Ian. 2006. Treatise on Militarism. *Symploke* 14(1-2): 152-68.

Challans, Timothy. 2007. *Awakening Warrior: Revolution in the Ethics of Warfare*. Albany, NY: SUNY Press.

Chow, Rey. 2006. *The Age of the World Target: Self-Referentiality in War, Theory, and Comparative Work.* Durham, NC: Duke University Press.

Cockburn, Cynthia. 2004. Continuum of Violence: A Gender Perspective on War and Peace. In *Sites of Violence: Gender and Conflict Zones*, edited by Wenona Giles and Jennifer Hyndman, 24-44. Los Angeles, CA: University of California Press.

Coker, Christopher. 2008. *Ethics and War in the 21st Century.* London: Routledge.

Comaroff, Jean and John Comaroff, eds. 2006. *Law and Disorder in the Postcolony.* Chicago, IL: University of Chicago Press.

Cowen, Deborah. 2008. *Military Workfare: The Soldier and Social Citizenship in Canada.* Toronto: University of Toronto Press.

Crabtree, James. 2009. An Intellectual Surge. *Prospect Magazine* 154(January). http://www.prospect-magazine.co.uk/printarticle.php?id=10558. Accessed 23 October 2009.

Department of National Defence/Canadian Forces. 2004. Duty with Honour: The Profession of Arms in Canada. Ottawa: Government of Canada.

DND/CF Canadian Army Directorate of Land Concepts and Design (DLCD). 2001. Land Operations 2021: Adaptive Dispersed Operations. http://www.army.forces.gc.ca/DLCD-DCSFT/specialPubs_e.asp. Accessed 23 October 2009.

———. 2008. BG-L-323-0004 Counter-Insurgency Operations. Ottawa: Chief of Land Staff – DND/CF.

———. 2009. Executive Summary. Canada First Defence Strategy. http://www.forces.gc.ca/site/focus/first-premier/defstra/summary-sommaire-eng.asp.

DND/CF Experimentation Centre. 2007. Effects-Based Approach to Future Military Operations (EBAO). http://www.cfd-cdf.forces.gc.ca/sites/page-eng.asp?page=2979.

———. 2009. CFJP 01 Canadian Forces Doctrine. Ottawa: DND/CF.

DND/CF Joint Doctrine Branch, Canadian Forces Experimentation Centre. 2009 CFJP 01 Canadian Military Doctrine. Ottawa: DND/CF.

DND/CF Land Forces Development. 2005. Canada's Soldiers: Military Ethos and Canadian Values in the 21st Century. Ottawa: DND/CF.

De Landa, Manuel. 1993. *War in the Age of Intelligent Machines.* New York: Zone.

———. 1997. *1000 Years of Non-Linear History.* New York: Zone.

Deleuze, Gilles and Felix Guattari. 1986. *Nomadology: The War Machine.* Trans. Brian Massumi. New York: Semiotext(e).

———. 1994. *What Is Philosophy?* New York: Columbia University Press.

Der Derian, James, Michale Udris and David Udris, dirs. 2010. *Human Terrain: War Becomes Academic*, film. Watson Institute/Global Media Project/ Udris Film/Oxyopia Productions.

Derrida, Jacques. 1984. No Apocalypse, Not Now (Full Speed Ahead, Seven Missiles, Seven Missives). *Diacritics* 14(2): 20-32.

Dillon, Michael and Andrew Neal. 2008. *Foucault on Politics, Security, and War.* Basingstoke, U.K.: Palgrave Macmillan.

Dillon, Michael and Julian Reid. 2009. *The Liberal Way of War: Killing to Make Life Live.* London: Routledge.

Elmer, Jon and Anthony Fenton. 2007. Growing Insurgencies, Irregular Warfare, Part 1 and 2. *The Dominion: News from the Grassroots*. http://www.dominionpaper.ca/articles/1089.

Elshtain, Jean Bethke. 1987. *Women and War*. Chicago, IL: University of Chicago Press.

Englehardt, Tom. 2009. The Nine Surges of Obama's War: How to Escalate in Afghanistan. *The Huffington Post*, 10 December. http://www.huffingtonpost.com/tom-engelhardt/the-nine-surges-of-obamas_b_387068.html.

English, Allan. 2004 *Understanding Military Culture: A Canadian Perspective*. Montreal: McGill-Queen's University Press.

English, Allan, Richard Gimblett and Howard Coombs. 2005. *The Operational Art: Canadian Perspectives, Context, and Concepts*. Ottawa/Kingston: Canadian Defence Academy Press.

———. 2007. Networked Operations and Transformation: Context and Canadian Contributions. Montreal: McGill-Queen's University Press.

Eyre, W. D. 2008. 14 Tenets for Mentoring the Afghan Army. *The Bulletin* 15. Kingston, ON: DND/Army Lessons Learned Centre.

Feldman, Allen. 2005. On the Actuarial Gaze. *Cultural Studies* 19(2): 204-26.

Fenton, Anthony. 2009a. Obama and the Counterinsurgency Era. *ZMag*. http://www.zmag.org /znet/viewArticle/20626. Accessed 25 November 2009.

———. 2009b. Canada: "Cheek by Jowl" with U.S. on COIN in Afghanistan. International Press Service. http://www.ipsnews.net/news.asp?idnews=49700. Accessed 15 December 2009.

Foucault, Michel. 1977[1975]. *Discipline and Punish: The Birth of the Prison*. Trans. Allan Sheridan. New York: Vintage.

———. 1990[1976]. *The History of Sexuality, Volume 1: An Introduction*. New York: Vintage.

———.2003[1976]. *Society Must Be Defended: Lectures at the Collège de France, 1975-1976*, edited by F. Ewald and A. Fontana. Trans. D. Macey. New York: Picador.

———.2007[1978]. *Security, Territory, and Population: Lectures at the Collège de France, 1977-1978*, edited by F. Ewald and A. Fontana. Trans. G. Burchell. London: Palgrave MacMillan.

———.2008[1979]. *Birth of Biopolitics: Lectures at the Collège de France, 1977-1978*, edited by F. Ewald and A. Fontana. Trans. G. Burchell. London: Palgrave MacMillan.

———. 1982. *Fearless Speech*. New York: Semiotext(e).

Galula, David. 2006[1964]. *Counterinsurgency Warfare: Theory and Practice*. London: Praeger Security International.

Georgis, Dina. 2008. Moving Past Ressentiment: War and the State of Feminist Freedom. *TOPIA* 20:109-28.

Gompert, David G. and John Gordon IV. 2008. *War by Other Means: Building Complete and Balanced Capabilities for Counterinsurgency*. Santa Monica, CA: RAND Corporation Defense Research Institute.

Gonzalez, Roberto. 2009. *American Counterinsurgency: Human Science and the Human Terrain*. Chicago: Prickly Paradigm Press.

Government of Canada. 2009. Canada's Priorities. Canada's Engagement in Afghanistan. http://www.afghanistan.gc.ca/canada-afghanistan/priorities-priorites/index.aspx?menu_id=15&menu=L.

Grossman-Vermaas, Robert. 2007. Future Perfect: Effects-Based Operations, Complexity, and the Human Environment. *Effects-Based Approaches to Operations: Canadian Perspectives*, edited by A. English and H. Coombs, 64-82. Ottawa: DND/CF.

Hartoonian, Harry and Masao Miyoshi, eds. 2002. *Learning Places: The Afterlives of Area Studies*. Durham, NC: Duke University Press.

Härtung, Heike and Smaro Kamboureli. 2009. Introduction: Discourses of Security, Peacekeeping Narratives, and the Cultural Imagination of Canada. *University of Toronto Quarterly* 78(2): 659-86.

Hedges, Chris. 2003. *War Is a Force That Gives Us Meaning*. New York: Anchor.

Hunt, Krista. 2006. Embedded Feminism and the War on Terror. *(En)Gendering the War on Terror: War Stories and Camouflaged Politics*, edited by K. Hunt and K. Rygiel, 51-96. Hampshire, U.K.: Ashgate.

Huntington, Samuel. 1991[1957]. *The Soldier and the State*. Cambridge, MA: Belknap Press.

Innes, Randy. 2008. Contemporary Presents: The Canadian War Museum's Afghanistan—A Glimpse of War and the Unfinished Business of Representation. *TOPIA* 20:93-108.

Janowitz, Morris. 1960. *The Professional Soldier: A Social and Political Portrait*. New York: Free Press.

Jefferess, Davis. 2009. Responsibility, Nostalgia, and the Mythology of Canada as Peacekeeper. *University of Toronto Quarterly* 78(2): 709-27.

Jiwani, Yasmin. 2008. Sports as a Civilizing Mission: Zinedine Zidane and the Infamous Head-Butt. *TOPIA* 19:11-34.

Kaldor, Mary. 2006. *New and Old Wars: Organized Violence in a Global Era*, 2nd ed. Palo Alto, CA: Stanford University Press.

———. 2007. *Human Security: Reflections on Globalization and Intervention*. Cambridge, MA: Polity Press.

Khan, S. 2008. From Rescue to Recognition: Rethinking the Afghan Conflict. *TOPIA* 19:115-36.

Kurosawa, Fuyuki. 2007. The State of Intellectual Play: A Generational Manifesto for Neoliberal Times. *TOPIA* 18:11-42.

Laxer, James. 2008. *Mission of Folly: Canada and Afghanistan*. Toronto: Between the Lines.

Lemke, Thomas. 2001. The Birth of Bio-Politics: Michel Foucault's Lecture at the Collège de France on Neoliberal Governmentality. *Economy and Society* 30(2): 190–207.

Leslie, Lt. Gen. A., P. Gizewski, Lt. Col. M. Rostek. 2009. Developing a Comprehensive Approach to Canadian Operations. *Canadian Military Journal* 9(1): 11-20.

Little, Adrian. 2008. *Democratic Piety: Complexity, Conflict and Violence*. Edinburgh: Edinburgh University Press.

Marzec, Robert. 2009. Militareality. *Global South* 3(1): 139-49.

Mbembe, Achille. 2003. Necropolitics. *Public Culture* 15(1): 11-40.

McFate, Montgomery and Andrea Jackson. 2005. An Organizational Solution for DoD's Cultural Knowledge Needs. *Military Review* (July-August): 18-21.

Melman, Seymour. 1974. *The Permanent War Economy: American Capitalism in Decline.* New York: Simon and Schuster.

Military Leaders for Kids. 2010. About Us. *Mission: Readiness.* http://www.missionreadiness.org/index.html. Accessed 20 April 2010.

Nadesan, Majia Holmer 2008. *Governmentality, Biopower, and Everyday Life.* London: Routledge.

Negri, Antonio. 1999. *Insurgencies: Constituent Power and the Modern State.* Minneapolis, MN: University of Minnesota Press.

Neocleous, Mark. 2010. War as Peace, Peace as Pacification. *Radical Philosophy* 159:8-17.

Network of Concerned Anthropologists. 2009. *The Counter-Counterinsurgency Manual.* Chicago: Prickly Paradigm Press.

North, Jonathan. 2003. Document of Note: General Hoche and Counterinsurgency. *Journal of Military History* 67:529-40.

Okros, Allan, Sarah Hall and Franklin Pinch. 2008. Between 9/11 and Kandahar: Attitudes of Canadian Forces Officers in Transition. Claxton Paper No. 8. Kingston: School of Policy Studies/Queen's University.

Philipose, Liz. 2008. Slippery Speed Acts: Conference Report: Gender, Race, Islam and the "War on Terror." *TOPIA* 19:153, 166.

Rasmussen, Mikkel. 2006. *The Risk Society at War: Terror, Technology, and Strategy in the Twenty-First Century.* Cambridge: Cambridge University Press.

Razack, Sherene. 2004. *Dark Threats and White Nights: The Somalia Affair, Peacekeeping, and the New Imperialism.* Toronto: University of Toronto Press.

———. 2008. *Casting Out: The Eviction of Muslims from Western Law and Politics.* Toronto: University of Toronto Press.

Renzi, Fred. 2006. Networks: Terra Incognita and the Case for Ethnographic Intelligence. *Military Review* (Sept/Oct). http://www.army.mil/ professionalwriting / volumesvolume4.

Retort Collective. 2005. *Afflicted Power: Capital and Spectacle in a New Age of War.* New York: Verso.

Scales, Robert. 2004. Culture-Centric Warfare. *Proceedings: Magazine of the U.S. Naval Institute* 130(10). http://www.usni.org/magazines/proceedings/archive/month.asp?ID=33.

Sloan, Elinor. 2007. *Military Transformation: Key Aspects and Canadian Approaches.* Ottawa, ON: Canadian Defence and Foreign Affairs Institute.

Smith, Ruppert. 2007. *The Utility of Force: The Art of War in the Modern World.* New York: Alfred A. Knopf.

Spencer, Emily and Tony Balasevicius. 2009. Crucible of Success: Cultural Intelligence and Modern Battlespace. *Canadian Military Journal* 9(3): 40-49.

Thorne, Stephen. 2006. *The Language of War.* London: Routledge.

Tilly, Charles. 1985. War Making and State Making as Organized Crime. In *Bringing the State Back In,* edited by Peter Evans, Dietrich Rueschemeyer and Theda Skocpol, 169-91. Cambridge: Cambridge University Press.

Torgovnick, Marianna. 2005. *The War Complex*. Chicago, IL: University of Chicago Press.

Turse, Nick. 2008. *The Complex: How the Military Invades Our Everyday Lives*. New York: Metropolitan.

U.S. Army and Marine Corps. 2007. *Counterinsurgency Manual FM 3-24*. Chicago: University of Chicago Press.

Virilio, P. 1978[1977]. *Speed and Politics*. Trans. M. Polizzotti. New York: Semiotext(e).

———. 1990[1978]. *Popular Defense and Ecological Struggles*. Trans. M. Polizzotti. New York: Semiotext(e).

Virilio, Paul. 1989. *War and Cinema: The Logistics of Military Perception*. London: Verso.

von Clausewitz, Carl. 1976. *On War*, edited and translated by Michael Howard and Peter Paret. Princeton, NJ: Princeton University Press.

Ward, Olivia. 2009. "Liberation was just a big lie." Outspoken Afghan MP says Canadian Mission is a big waste of time. *The Toronto Star*, 12 November.

Warnock, J. 2008. *Creating a Failed State: The US and Canada in Afghanistan*. Black Point, NS: Fernwood.

Weber, Samuel. 2005. *Targets of Opportunity: On the Militarization of Thinking*. New York: Fordham University Press.

Zagala, Stephen. 2003. Aesthetics: A Place I've Never Seen. In *A Shock of Thought: Expression After Deleuze and Guattari*, edited by Brian Massumi, 21-22. London: Routledge.

Žižek, Slavoj. 2008. *Violence: Big Ideas, Small Books*. New York: Picador..

Erin Riley

Operation Nunalivut: Photo Essay

Disembarking from the darkened belly of the Hercules I am immediately blinded. Squinting. I stare at the sky. Tiny crystalline explosions fill the air. I am told later they are the result of the light refracting off frozen particles in the air.

The Arctic air snaps me to attention. Like a good soldier I collect my bags and walk single file towards the long red trailer that will be my home for the duration of my stay. I notice the sound of the snow as it squeaks under my heavy boots.

As a participating artist in the Canadian Forces Artists Program (CFAP), I am invited to attend Operation Nunalivut, a yearly sovereignty mission held on Ellesmere Island, which sits at 80 degrees north, only a couple of hundred kilometers from the North Pole.

The Defence Department established the CFAP program in 2001, under the directorate of the Department of History and Heritage. Following in the long established tradition of the war artist, which dates back to 1916, the program allows Canadian artists the opportunity to portray Canadian military experience through art while providing artists with a taste of military life.[1]

Operation Nunalivut is operated under the command of Joint Task Force North (JTFN). JTFN is a Canadian Forces command headquartered in Yellowknife, NT. The command is responsible for conducting all routine and contingency operations in Canada's North in support of sovereignty and territorial defence, and is on call to Canadians in times of emergency and civil disaster. JTFN covers a vast region encompassing approximately four million square kilometres, or one-third of Canada's land mass.[2]

JTFN relies on the unique skills and collective knowledge of the members that comprise the Canadian Rangers. The Canadian Rangers, identified by their signature red sweatshirts and ball caps, are part-time reservists comprised mainly of Inuit from remote and often isolated communities. The Canadian Rangers provides a military presence in the North, and they are charged with keeping watchful eye out for any suspicious activities. Their motto is "Vigilans." Translated—"The watchers."

Fort Eureka on Ellesmere Island—79°58'59"N 85°56'59"W—is the second northernmost settlement in the world.

I am an artist and my role is to observe, to photograph, to document, to record.

By training and by choice, I am not a landscape photographer. Yet here I find myself confronted by the sheer vastness of this place. I am immediately struck by such open space, while at the same time experiencing the feeling of total confinement. White. Everywhere a thousand shades of white. The temptation to photograph this landscape is overwhelming.

To photograph this landscape, this vastness, this great space, would be to somehow contain it. To confine it within the edges of the frame. To somehow make it more manageable. To create a sense of ownership over it. To photograph this space is to perform an act of sovereignty.

For the duration of my stay at Fort Eureka I negotiate the tensions between space and place. These photographs are part of my investigation into the dualities of inside/outside, representation/reality, military/civilian.

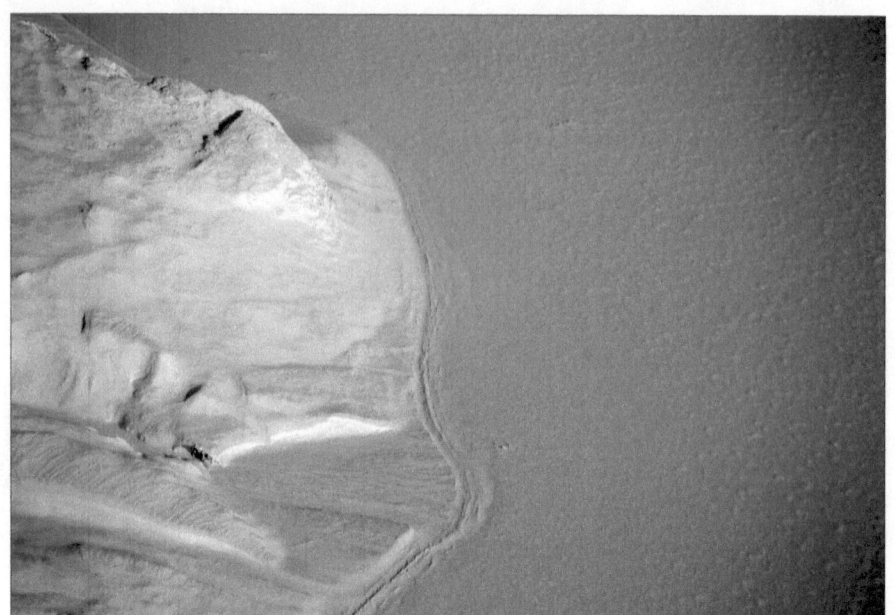

The window of the Twin Otter frames my view. Watching the passing landscape below is a cinematic experience. I push my lens against the window. The landscape below is at once real and a representation.

Sergeants from JTFN are the patrol leaders. In preparation for their sojourn onto the land, they plot their routes on maps, examine satellite imagery, read weather reports and prepare their handheld GPS systems. It's a kind of intelligence gathering. Maps are information—showing boundaries, lines that differentiate between landmass and water, indicate elevation, etc. There is an implied notion that by studying these representations of this land, you can know it. Reading the map, you find names: Johan Peninsula, Thorvald Peninsula, Smith Sound, Stanfield Point, Cadogan Glacier, Aleksandra Fijord. Naming is a strategy to transform space into place; with these names, these places are forever tied to the past, to the explorers and past expeditions that touched this land.

Patrols consisting of eight members each set out from Fort Eureka and traverse the terrain of Ellesmere Island. As the patrols push forward, they leave behind tracks created by their snowmobiles and the komatiks they tow behind them. The

From above, my conflicting sense of isolation and confinement is made visible. The sense of space and place, and the scale of it, are fully laid bare.

tracks trace their movements, leaving evidence of their presence on this otherwise untouched space, creating a new map written on the land itself.

I watch the landscape pass below the window of a Twin Otter aircraft. The 404 Squadron provides air support to re-supply the patrols while on the land and performs aerial surveillance. Looking down from the window of the Twin Otter, the tracks recall the markings on the maps. Real, yet ephemeral. As the next big wind comes up, blowing snow erases the tracks, and evidence of their presence disappears.

The Rangers I meet appear to have a different relationship to the land. In front of the main building, with snowmobiles idling, the patrols gather for one last inspection.

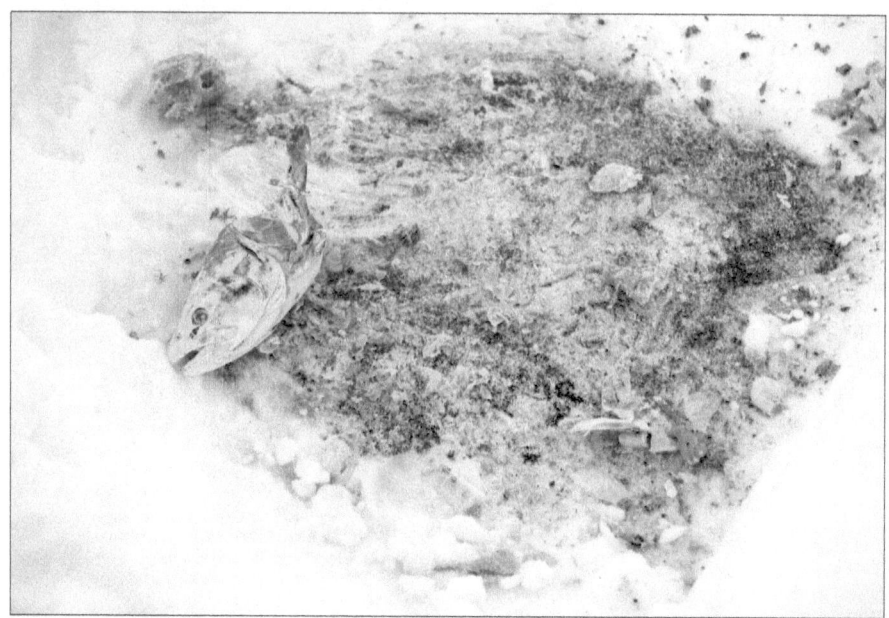

Fragments of a meal.

Rangers are issued standard military gear, as are all members of the Canadian Forces. In the sea of army green you can spot the odd pair of caribou boots and a pair of seal and polar bear mittens. Ernie from Arviat wears a full caribou parka, pants and boots—made from the hides of game he hunted himself that were sewn together by his grandmother.

On the komatiks (traditional Inuit sleds), the Rangers have written not their names but where they are from. What they bring with them to this mission is not individual skill, but collective knowledge gained through generations of living in the Arctic and in their communities.

This space, thousands of miles from where they live, is an extension of where they live. There appears to be no distinction between space and place.

The aim of the yearly patrols is to provide a regular human presence in the Arctic. A way to claim national sovereignty over this land.

At the base, the outdoor urinal is a marker pointing to our human presence and interventions on this landscape.

Canadian Rangers with their specialized knowledge and experience of the land are integrated into these yearly missions, bringing with them their own unique ways of doing things and their own unique perspective on the land. Komatiks are traditional Inuit sleds. Made of wood, they are held together with rope to withstand being towed over the frozen terrain; nails and screws break under the sub-zero arctic temperatures.

If sovereignty is about asserting dominion, power and authority over this vast and barren landscape, then photographs become a way to contain space. These photographs, a series of constructed images, live as independent states. The idea of author and authority come to bear on my role as artist.

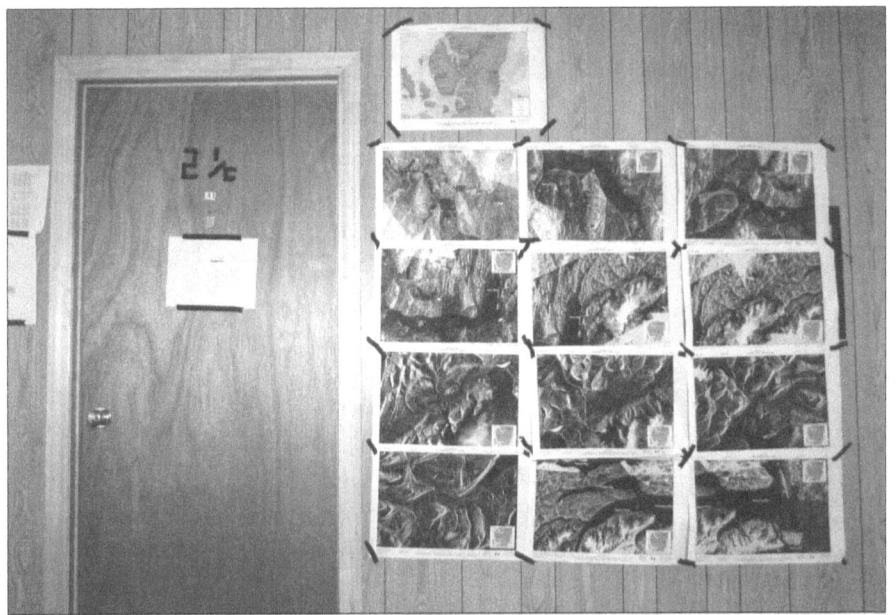

Inside, satellite imagery of the island posted on the wall. Flattened, abstracted, a tool for knowledge and learning, the land is contained in the two-dimensional world of the photograph.

Ernie, a Canadian Ranger from the community of Arviat, wears a caribou parka made from hides of game he hunted himself.

Post-work activities: Military personnel play a virtual war game.

Notes

1. Information compiled from the following sources: http://www.cmp-cpm.forces.gc.ca/dhh-dhp/gal/ap-pa/index-eng.asp; http://www.dnd.ca/site/news-nouvelles/news-nouvelles-eng.asp?cat=03&id=2498.

2. http://news.gc.ca/web/article-eng.do?m=/index&nid=540869; http://www.cfna.dnd.ca/main_en.asp.

Susan Cahill

Conflict(ing) Narratives: Representations of War in *The Battleground Project* and the Performative Potential of Audience

ABSTRACT

In the ongoing debates revolving around Canada's continuing mission in Afghanistan, museum representations engaging with conflict narratives are especially relevant. These exhibitions cannot be treated as apolitical representations, but, rather, need to be contextualized within dialogues of the politics of war. Using my own engagement with *The Battleground Project* (2008) at the Textile Museum of Canada in Toronto as an entry point, I chart the role and function of cultural institutions in legitimating and constituting dominant conflict narratives, and the performative potential of audiences in producing meanings that support, question, resist and subvert such narratives.

RÉSUMÉ

Récits conflictuels : représentations de la guerre dans « The Battleground Project » et potentiel performatif du public

Parallèlement aux débats continus au sujet de la mission que poursuit le Canada en Afghanistan, les représentations muséales abordant le thème des récits des conflits sont particulièrement pertinentes. Ces expositions ne peuvent pas être considérées comme des représentations apolitiques, mais elles doivent plutôt être mises en contexte dans le cadre des dialogues politiques au sujet de la guerre. En me servant de mon propre engagement dans « The Battleground Project » (2008) au Textile Museum du Canada à Toronto comme point de départ, j'esquisse le rôle et la fonction des institutions culturelles dans la légitimation et la constitution de récits dominants au sujet des conflits, ainsi que le rôle performatif du public dans la production de significations qui entérinent, remettent en question, résistent ou subvertissent de tels récits.

Although we are all constantly bombarded by the messages and meanings of culture and the media, we are not merely passive receivers or consumers. We constantly make new meanings out of our cultural world, resist the dominant messages, and discover new modes of social expression. We do not isolate ourselves from the social world of dominant culture but neither do we simply acquiesce to its powers. Rather, from inside the dominant culture we create not only alternative subcultures but, more importantly, new collective networks of expression. (Hardt and Negri 2004: 263)

A recent collection of essays, *Afghanistan and Canada: Is There an Alternative to War?* (Kowaluk and Staples 2009), provides a critical account of Canada's current military involvement in Afghanistan. Featuring the work of academics, activists, economists and political organizations, this anthology provides an historical context for the present situation, challenges the Canadian government's official justifications and expresses a desire to end Canada's combat role in Afghanistan.

A recent news story within the Canadian mainstream media provides another example of the public debate regarding representations of conflict. In September 2009, *The Globe and Mail*, a nationally circulating newspaper, described a plan by the Canadian government for Canadian Forces to build a mock Afghan village in the courtyard of the Canadian embassy in Washington.[1] Although this plan has since been discarded, its proposal demonstrates a recognition of the importance of representation in politics, by both the media and the state. The idea was to simulate a conflict several times during October 2009; the performance was to include the detonation of improvised explosive devices that, if used in the real war, would cause mass damage to the village and injuries to the Afghan civilians who live there. The dramatic re-enactment would finish with Canadian medics rushing in to save the wounded. The purpose of this scenario was to demonstrate the importance of the Canadian war effort in Afghanistan, and its performances were scheduled to coincide with a two-day conference hosted by the embassy focusing on discussions of the war effort in Afghanistan between Canadian, American and Afghan officials. The orchestration of this performance relied heavily on the trope of Canada-as-peacekeeping-nation, and was intended to reproduce and legitimate this identity.

These examples illuminate the extent to which this conflict is not only a physical mission taking place in Central Asia, but also a cultural and political battle occurring in North America. While mainstream broadcast news coverage often uncritically reinforces the Canadian state's policies, many cultural producers have challenged these hegemonic depictions in their own artistic practices. For example, Allyson Mitchell's 2008 short film, *Afghanimation*, uses an Afghan "war rug" as the visual focal point to critique military and media relations in regard to Canadian involvement in Afghanistan, while Tobey C. Anderson's ongoing project *KIA_CA_Afghanistan* uses wall-sized portraits of all Canadians killed on duty in Afghanistan since 2001 to highlight the lack of government or media recognition of the human cost of war (Mirchell 2008; Anderson 2010).

This battle of representation in relation to Canadian conflict narratives and the war in Afghanistan forefronts the importance of cultural representations as political expedients for hegemonic and counter-hegemonic histories. It also demonstrates the blurring of boundaries of representational forms and spaces where discussions of culture, politics and conflict history occur; debates are no longer viewed as operating in disparate and autonomous categories of academia, public debate, mass media, visual art, literature and government policies. Rather, cultural representations in each of these arenas support, question or resist the representations found in others.

Although I have emphasized processes of representation, this is just one level of a topic with multiple layers. In this article I use the space of the museum to elucidate the complexities of cultural representation. Conventionally, museums are examined as apolitical spaces for preserving a state's collective national memories by way of material objects. Often, studies that attempt to move beyond this framework in order to analyze the role of museums within larger historical, economic and political contexts suggest that these cultural institutions reflect rather than produce these contexts. This approach, I suggest, characterizes the production of meaning as unilateral representation. The meanings of the objects—as organized by the curator—are presented to the viewers, who passively absorb these static interpretations. Representation, then, is framed as a top-down process of knowledge creation whereby meanings are communicated directly to museum visitors through the arrangement of objects.

My recognition that meaning cannot be seamlessly transmitted through direct representation occurred when I attended the April 2008 opening of *The Battleground Project* at the Textile Museum of Canada (TMC). As I walked among the objects on display, I felt as if I had a very different understanding of the narrative than that of the curator and other museum visitors. If interpretation is guided solely by representation, how can we account for different understandings of the same cultural object in the same exhibition? Through interacting with and reacting to this example of public history, I realized I needed to rethink my own evaluative criteria to account for conflicting narratives between different viwers' interpretations.

Viewed in this manner, the representation of conflict like that exhibited in *The Battleground Project* at the TMC—is but one element in the process of producing narratives; in this paper, I argue that a more comprehensive analysis of conflict narratives involves acknowledging the performative potential of audiences to produce meanings that support, question, resist and subvert such narratives.

Understanding the potential for a dialogic relationship in the act of viewing means moving from the conventional view of meaning as static representation determined by the objects or curator, to recognizing that meaning is produced through a dynamic process that involves audience subjectivity.

The narrative of this paper is mapped around my own experience with and thoughts about the politics and policies of representation in relation to Canadian conflict history. In the first section I offer a brief description of the arrangement of *The Battleground Project*, which opened in 2008 in Toronto. Combining drawings of Canadian troops in Afghanistan by a Canadian war artist, military patches from around the world, and Afghan "war rugs," this display united cultural objects from a variety of historical periods and geopolitical sites under the umbrella of warfare.

In the second section I use the TMC exhibition as a basis from which to examine the representation of conflict. I interrogate its arrangement and display questions surrounding in order to elucidate the representational politics and policies of museums as dominant cultural institutions. In questioning exhibits in cultural institutions, I am not only examining the organization of the display, but I am also analyzing the broader political demands related to Canadian conflict narratives that are constituted in and legitimated by the exhibits.

In the third section of this article, I suggest a method of understanding the production of meaning that extends beyond representation to account for audience subjectivity. What has conventionally been understood as audience agency, I argue, is more productively framed as audience performativity. Using the work of Irit Rogoff and George Yúdice, I offer a mode of analysis that situates cultural representations within the politics of audience engagement and neoliberal globalization. By suggesting that performance, rather than representation, guides meaning-making, I explore ways in which the theme of conflict exceeds static, dominant narratives, and can be framed in a multitude of interpretations guided by the political subjectivity of viewers within a particular time and space.

I use a reflexive interpretive, or auto-ethnographic, approach, so that my own experience becomes part of my analysis.[2] This makes me part of the study. Building on the recognition of performance as central to the production of meaning, I aim to acknowledge and unite the duality of object and subject, exhibition and audience, in order to recognize that my analysis cannot occur outside of my own lived experience. I begin my discussion of the interrelationship between cultural institutions, representation, performance and conflict at the same place that my thought process started: *The Battleground Project*.

The Battleground Project

The exhibition *The Battleground Project*, curated by TMC co-founder Max Allen, was composed of three smaller displays united by the theme of warfare. These exhibits were "The Kandahar Journals of Richard Johnson," "Patches: Military Uniform Insignia" and "Battleground: War Carpets from Afghanistan," with the third display as the main focal point. Arranged in spatially distinct galleries that spanned two floors of the museum, each of the three exhibits offered museum visitors visual and material examples of the cultural products of conflict.[3]

"The Kandahar Journals of Richard Johnson" was the first display that greeted the museum visitor upon entry into *The Battleground Project*. This selection of drawings depicted Canadian troops and Afghan soldiers and civilians in Kandahar, where Johnson spent two months in 2007 with the Canadian military. The black and white sketches ranged from personalized portraits of Canadian soldiers to pictures of Afghan children playing. Originally created as pictorial reports for the *National Post*, these drawings were intended to document the artist's personal observations about military life in Afghanistan, paying particular attention to the relationship between Canadians and Afghans.[4] Johnson's drawings were hung along the walls of a hallway on the second floor of the museum which led toward a small room that hosted "Patches: Military Uniform Insignia."

The military patches were presented in a series of glass display cases, organized by date, geographic location, military unit and war. These souvenirs of battle represented a wide array of national military forces and war campaigns, forming a large cross-cultural selection. The cultural products in this exhibit were both official patches for military uniforms and off-duty patches that were personally commissioned. This latter collection was framed within the exhibit as "offering an insight into the mindset of the soldiers on the ground."

To reach "Battleground: War Rugs from Afghanistan," museum visitors continued up to the next floor of the TMC. Upon entering this exhibit, viewers faced a wall didactic that asked the questions. "Are these rugs pro-war or anti-war?" and "Whose side are they on?" The display of approximately 120 Afghan textiles occupied this entire floor, along with scattered display cases containing military patches that demonstrated some of the visual material that may have influenced the images that unnamed Afghan rugmakers wove into the rugs. Interweaving scenes of battles, weapons, troops, cities, maps and animals, the Afghan "war rugs" were divided into eleven distinct sections, including such topics as Cities—Real and Imagined, Landmines, Minarets, Western Perspectives and Symbolic Animals. These textiles were framed within the exhibition as anonymous testimonials of war and disaster. They have been produced since 1979, the year Soviet troops first invaded Afghanistan, and continue to be produced today, according to the information included in the exhibition.

Spaces of Representation

The Battleground Project, and specifically its display of Afghan "war rugs," are my entry point into a critical analysis of the politics of representation. My goal is to contribute to our understanding of how visual and material culture and museum exhibitions are imbricated in larger processes of transnational conflict narratives, liberalism and corporate globalization. Museum exhibitions do not just reflect, but actually produce, politics. That is, as Tony Bennett writes, it is necessary to recognize "[visual] cultural practices from the point of view of their intrication with, and within, relations of power" (1992: 361). My critique of the display examines its arrangement in order to situate the exhibition in the politics of negotiating Canadian conflict narratives in the present historical moment.

The Battleground Project presented viewers with transnational and cross-cultural materials in order to acknowledge a variety of histories, experiences and opinions of war. However, when I first walked through this exhibition, I felt slightly unsettled because the arrangement of the three sections, organized according to the identity of the materials, seemed confusing. There was no coherent narrative beyond the objects' association with the broad theme of battle. Each of these sections—drawings, patches and rugs—were made to represent particular points of view, time periods, geopolitical sites and conflicts. Only Johnson's drawings were associated with a specific individual, whereas the patches and rugs were arranged to represent national culture: for example, Russian patch or Afghan "war rug." There is a danger, according to Stratton and Ang, in uncritically using the nation as a privileged site of the particular because it runs the risk of "hypostatizing differences into static, mutually exclusive categories" (1996: 367). The division of this larger exhibit into three distinct components resulted in disconnected, discrete histories of conflict. In particular, I felt that the spatial and theoretical detachment of each of these sections from the others ignored the intersecting narratives involved in the current realities of a Canadian military presence in Afghanistan.

This lack of recognition of the current conflict, disassociating the cultural products on display from Canadian involvement in war, ignores the brutal realities of warfare, as Kirsty Robertson suggests in a 2008 article discussing this exhibition for *Fuse* magazine. Without engaging the current realities, *The Battleground Project* historically, culturally, politically and geographically separated its representation of conflict from the past and present experience of warfare. The display disavowed the political complexities of cross-cultural narratives, creating a museum display about conflict as a general theme autonomous from conflict as a reality. That is, the exhibit presented these cultural objects for visual consumption within the white-walled, track-lit and carefully arranged gallery space, but failed to confront the complicated historical, political and cultural conditions of ongoing warfare.

Additionally, the presentation of the drawings, patches and rugs was further disconnected from the politics of conflict through a lack of acknowledgement of the ways in which cultural objects circulate in relation to corporate globalization. These themes could be an integral component of the debates concerning the war in Afghanistan. Yúdice uses the term "transnational cultural brokering" to describe "the negotiation of culture in relation to national expression in an international arena" (2003: 239). In this process, culture is deployed differently, that is to say, performatively in different locations. It is no longer only the content of cultural productions that establishes their value, but also their utility—economic, social or political—within neoliberal development that determines their circulation in global markets. Increasingly, culture has become a resource for capitalist development and for "sociopolitical and economic amelioration" (9). This culturalization of the economy does not occur organically, but is carefully fostered through agreements on trade and property, laws controlling the movement of mental and manual labour and, I would add to Yúdice's suggestions, transnational policies relating to conflict. In *The Battleground Project*, the objects were represented as visual and material products of war; however, there was a distinct lack of contextualization of the objects' production in relation to conflict and corporate globalization.[5] By displaying the artifacts as art objects representing individual (Johnson's drawings) or cultural (patches and "war rugs") experiences of war, the exhibition did not account for their relationship to global development within neoliberal cultural markets.

This disassociation from the politics of conflict also occurred through the labelling of the Afghan textiles as "war rugs." By highlighting the term "war rugs," I emphasize the danger of categorizing cultural products, because this can subsume objects into a genre within the modernist art canon. This categorization, as Susan Buck-Morss writes, reduces works to artistic style, to the genre of "political art" or "war art," thus covering over the complexities involved in the politics and culture of conflict (2003: 70). "War rugs" was not placed in quotations in the exhibition, nor in any of the literature I have encountered to date. I draw attention to this phrase in order to problematize the label as empty and nondescriptive. Does it refer to their production within war time? Or perhaps to the images of battle that many—but not all—of them depict? Or maybe to the question of whether the rugs are pro-war or anti-war? The term "war rugs" needs to be clarified through cultural, historical and political contextualization in order to have representational value.

The negotiation of the politics of cultural objects needs to occur not only in the way in which cross-cultural objects are presented, but also in their very inclusion within the liberal museum. Museums pose an interesting entry point into issues of cultural representation because the realm of art has conventionally been viewed as autonomous from larger social processes. A critical history of Canadian cultural institutions reveals the politics inherent in their inception throug the mutually constitutive relationship of the formation of the museum as a public institution and the installation of liberalism as the politico-economic logic of Canada;[6] in relation to cultural representation, objects within the museum were considered part of the materiality of the nation, displayed to citizens in order to create a visual national character as well as to civilize and modernize national subjects. Despite this history, a crticial history of Canadian cultural institutions reveals the politics inherent in their inception through the mutually constitutive relationship of the formation of the museum as a public institution. Critical studies have only recently challenged the view of museums as apolitical spaces for preserving a state's collective national memories by way of visual and material objects.

Museums can no longer be thought of as autonomous from social existence, but need to be recognized as sites where culture and politics are discussed and debated. These politics are multidirectional; that is, cultural products and institutions do not simply legitimate and reflect politics, but also constitute them. Exhibitions dealing with topics such as conflict cannot be treated as apolitical representations of cultural objects, but rather must explicitly acknowledge and negotiate the politics of space and display within their representation and arrangement.

The representation of Afghan cultural products in the exhibition at the TMC needs to be framed within the current relationship between Canada and Afghanistan, as well as within the history of museum representations and the unequal exchange of cultural objects in the global marketplace. Part of this critique involves questioning the very identity of the museum as a privileged site, a space that can include or exclude cultural products without ever having to acknowledge any loss to itself as a dominant cultural institution.[7] As art historian Irit Rogoff writes, "This infinitely expansive inclusiveness practiced by so many exhibiting institutions is actually grounded in an unrevised notion of the museum's untroubled ability simply to add *others* without losing a bit of the self" (2002: 66).

The Battleground Project was able to include Afghan material culture without having to account for any loss to itself as a dominant cultural institution. The Afghan "war rugs"—many of them produced since the 2001 invasion of Afghanistan— were not included in order to question, or even to acknowledge, the fact that the Canadian military could be part of the conflict to which the images in the textiles refer; rather, the non-Canadian cultural products were subsumed into a narrative with the project of a hegemonic, Canadian national/ist identity at its centre. The inclusion of Afghan "war rugs" simply contributed to the exhibit's overall theme of warfare, leaving untouched the identity of the museum as site of universal plenitude and the dominant narrative of Canadian conflict history that situates Canada as a peacekeeping and multicultural nation.

Although *The Battleground Project* offered material and visual objects from a variety of geopolitical sites and historical periods, the lack of coherent narrative—beyond the general theme of warfare—disconnected the exhibit from the cultural and political realities of conflict. As outlined, my disagreements with the exhibition concerned its detached and discreet representations of war, which disconnected the different histories, cultures and societies represented within the display. The representation of conflict within the museum failed to acknowledge the lived experiences and unequal power dynamics of past and present events. Finally its rhetoric seemed to uncritically support the Canadian military as a peacekeeping force.

Spaces of Performance

While I felt uncomfortable with the representation of conflict history within *The Battleground Project*, it received positive reviews in the mainstream Canadian press. It was also named one of the best visual arts shows of 2008 by *Now* magazine and the *Toronto Star* praised it as "the year's strongest war-themed exhibition" that "interweaves culture, materials, history and expression with rare and urgently necessary curatorial clarity" (Jager et al. 2008). The variety of reactions to the same display demonstrates how the curator's irepresentation is not simply absorbed by an audience. While I can critique Allen's exhibition for its arrangement and lack of political engagement, this analysis remains in the realm of representation because itdoes not account for the obviously diverse subjectivity of other viewers.

I want to suggest that cannot be simply interpreted as a top down system of knowledge creation. Rather, the role of audience is central to the negotiation of meaning. What has previously been considered audience agency is more productively examined as audience performance. The shift from representation to performance is not a transformation in how meaning is produced; rather, it is a change in how the production of meaning is discussed and recognized. With this shift, I intend to move from the conventional view that meaning within the museum is determined by curation, to a recognition that meaning is a result of dynamic processes that involve constantly changing audiences. This acknowledgement is tied to the notion of performative force developed by Yúdice as a theory of difference, whereby culture is taken up perfomatively within and between different societies (2003).

In order to follow through on this insight, the museum needs to be acknowledged as a site where politics and ideas are created, not simply legitimated. That is, I needed to move my interrogation into an area that accounts for the fact that "meaning is not excavated for, but rather, … *takes place* in the present" (Rogoff 2004: n.p.). While I can critique Allen's presentation of cultural objects relating to the current conflict in Afghanistan, this analysis is only half of my actual engagement with the exhibition. What is my own role in this disagreement?

The concept of performativity within the gallery space recognizes that meaning is made through a convergence of the display, the audience and the arena of critical or interpretive reception In highlighting the importance of the relationship between viewers and exhibitionary spaces over that between viewers and objects, the significance of the location and time takes centre stage because different audiences in different cultural circumstances will produce different knowledges. According to Rogoff:

> when something called "art" becomes an open interconnective field, then the potential to engage within it as a form of cultural participation rather than as a form of either reification, of representation, or of contemplative edification, comes in to being. (2004: n.p.)

Approaching exhibitions such as *The Battleground Project* in this way recognizes that interpretations and narratives are not static, but can be reframed to accommodate multiple interpretations, including the possibility of a dialogue of dissent that counters the Canadian government's foreign policies. The space of the gallery is thus resituated as a politicized site not simply reflecting dominant narratives of conflict, but also potentially constituting and resisting these narratives in relation to cross-cultural dialogues and transnational conflict.

Identifying the role of audience performance enables analysis to account for constantly shifting dialogues between infinite subjectivities and interpretations. The concept of performance is very useful in a consideration of meaning as a constitutive process from which the analyst is not exempt. It denies the autonomy of the subject who critiques as well as that of the object that is critiqued, and shows that critics are not operating at similar levels of critical distance from the images and objects they interpret. Critique becomes criticality, a term suggested by Rogoff that situates my own subjectivity as part of the study (2004). Criticality is a state of embodiment, a way to marry knowledge, experience, perspectives and politics. This promotes movement away from distanced critique to a new state of analysis, where it is not only the politics of the display that are studied, but also our own roles in the performance of culture. This performative interaction is the key to bridging the gap between those who are doing the interpreting (consumer/viewer) and those who are being interpreted (producer). This approach acknowledges that meanings occur within particular spaces and times, shifting critiques away from the notion of immanent meanings of the objects.

To Rogoff's concept of criticality, however, I suggest an additional qualifier that identifies subjectivity and performance not only in relation to the political negotiation of representation, but also as occurring beyond the gallery space. Embodied criticality is a way to study how knowledge production is inextricably linked to political position. This supports audience performance as integral to negotiating museum representations, but recognizes that this performance is based on the political, cultural and historical position of the viewer. Therefore, my own politics and culture need to be acknowledged as inextricably interwoven with my engagement with and critique of *The Battleground Project*.

To account for the ways in which culture and politics affect audiences' interpretation, I return to the importance of Yúdice's notion of performative force. This theory suggests that specific cultural behaviours aquire performative force, in response to the social imperative to perform, which is understood and experienced differently in different societies as opposed to the assumption of one hegemonic or monolithic viewpoint. Yúdice highlights "a different field of force generated by differently arranged relationships among institutions of the state and civil society, the judiciary, the police, schools, and universities, the media, consumer markets, and so on" (2003: 43). The differences afforded by these relationships function not only between different nations, but also among the different cultures and societies within national boundaries.

Viewed in this way, performative force provides a politicized context for the ways viewers negotiate the representation of Canadian conflict history presented in an exhibition such as *The Battleground Project*. This reframing of meaning does not just refer to the narrative of conflict, but can also refer to the category of Canada itself; as representations of cultural products and conflict narratives are questioned within fields of performance, so too must the project of "Canada" be examined as a contingent category. To cite Stratton and Ang once again, it is important to question "the unstable, provisional and often jeopardous status of the national itself" (1996: 381) by recognizing "that there is not one 'culture' in 'society' but that any 'society' consists of a plurality of historically specific 'cultures' structured in relations of dominance and subordination to each other" (377). Audience performativity can support, question, resist or subvert the narrative of Canadian identity and, more specifically, the conflict history presented in *The Battleground Project*. The performative forces that guide such interactions relate to the constant negotiation of dominant and subordinate narratives of conflict history and Canada and must be considered as part of the constitution of politics itself.

In the ongoing debates revolving around Canada's continuing mission in Afghanistan, museum representations engaging with conflict are especially relevant. These representations are neither disconnected from the politics of conflict, nor simply reflective of political opinion; rather a museum's engagement with conflict narratives is central to circulation of ideas about the war in Afghanistan. It is not simply representation that governs the ways conflict narratives operate within museum exhibitions. The shift from representation to performance recognizes the integral role of audiences in making and negotiating meaning. In the same way that the exhibition cannot be exempt from politics, so too must the interpretations by different audiences be inextricably linked with their subjectivities and politics. With this in mind, conflict history is not simply represented in the cultural objects of an exhibition but is interpreted and negotiated by audiences.

The rethinking of the ways in which narratives are produced—actively performed, rather than statically represented—recognizes the contingent and shifting processes occurring in the circulation of conflict narratives. This approach attempts to decentralize power from the curator and cultural institution in order to include the significance of the collective performativity of a constantly changing audience. Acknowledging the performative potential of audience means framing the very production of meaning as a political act. My intention has been to use this exhibit as a case study to demonstrate the importance of acknowledging the political implications of discussing conflict, from which the museum and its audiences must not be exempt.

Notes

1. For more information on this scenario, see the coverage in *The Globe and Mail*, 18 September 2009, http://www.theglobeandmail.com/news/world/canada-to-stage-mock-afghan-attack-in-washington/article1275341/; and *The Globe and Mail*, 22 September 2009, http://www.theglobeandmail.com/news/world/military-abandons-plans-to-erect-mock-afghan-village/article1294035/. At the time of writing, no official reason had been given as to why the plans for this performance were discarded.

2. My auto-ethnographic approach here is based on the methodology as seen in an article on souvenirs, tourism and memory. See, Nigel Morgan and Annette Pritchard, "On souvenirs and metonymy," *Tourist Studies* (2005: 29-53).

3. Most of the visual and material objects represented in the three exhibits of *The Battleground Project* can be found on the TMC's website, http://www.textilemuseum.ca.

4. This statement regarding Johnson's focus on the relationship between Canadians and Afghans was taken from a wall didactic in the exhibition; I could not find this focus stated explicitly in his online journal. More information, drawings and blog postings about Johnson's time in Afghanistan with the Canadian military can be found on the *National Post*'s website: http://network.nationalpost.com/np/blogs/kandaharjournal/default.aspx.

5. For more information about the conditions of production of Afghan "war rugs," see Bonyhady (2003).

6. For more information on the history of the symbiotic relationship of museums and liberalism, see Bennett (1995). For an analysis of the installation of liberalism under the specific conditions of northern North America, see McKay (2000).

7. One could make a counter-argument to my point here, stating that the increased presence of previously excluded histories within the museum space would eventually change the norm within cultural institutions. I can see the benefits of this approach, but I still maintain that an actual restructuring of the politics of display, including acknowledging a loss to the dominant culture, must occur so that inclusions and marginalized histories are more than perfunctory additions to the museumscape. For an investigation of the politics of inclusion within cultural institutions, see Jessup (2002).

References

Anderson, Tobey C. 2010. *KIA_CA_Afghanistan* (painting). Canadian Casualties in the Afghanistan War. Installation at Grimsby Public Art Gallery, Grimsby, ON.

The Battleground Project. Textile Museum of Canada. http://www.textilemuseum.ca.

Bennett, Tony. 1992. Putting Policy into Cultural Studies. In *Cultural Studies*, edited by Lawrence Grossberg, Cary Nelson and Paula A. Treichler, 34-50. New York and London: Routledge.

Bennett, Tony. 1995. *The Birth of the Museum: History, Theory, Politics*. London and New York: Routledge.

Bonyhady, Tim. 2003. Out of Afghanistan. In *The Rugs of War*, exhibition catalogue, edited by Nigel Lendon and Tim Bonyhady, 4-18. Canberra: Australia National University.

Buck-Morss, Susan. 2003. *Thinking Past Terror: Islamism and Critical Theory on the Left*. London: Verso.

Hardt, Michael and Antonio Negri. 2004. *Multitude: War and Democracy in the Age of Empire*. New York: Penguin Press.

Jager, David, Leah Sandals and Fran Schecter. 2008. Year in Review: Top 10 Art Shows, 2008. *Now Magazine* 28 (17)(December): 22-29.

Jessup, Lynda. 2002. Hard Inclusion. In *On Aboriginal Representation in the Gallery Space*, edited by Lynda Jessup and Shannon Bagg, xiii-xxviii. Hull, Quebec: Canadian Museum of Civilization.

Johnson, Richard. N.d. Postings from Afghanistan. *The National Post* online. http://network.nationalpost.com/np/blogs/kandaharjournal/default.aspx.

Kowaluk, Lucia and Steven Staples, eds. 2009. *Afghanistan and Canada: Is There an Alternative to War?* Montreal: Black Rose Books.

McKay, Ian. Dec 2000. The Liberal Order Framework. *Canadian Historical Review* 81 (4): 617-45.

Mitchell, Allyson, dir. 2008. *Afghanimation* (film). Commissioned for Canadian Filmmakers Distribution Centre project *ReGeneration*.

Robertson, Kirsty. 2008. Battlegrounds and Carpet Bombing. *Fuse magazine* 32(1): 6-13.

Rogoff, Irit. 2002. Hit and Run: Museums and Cultural Difference. *Art Journal* 61(3): 3-73.

———. 2003. Smuggling: An Embodied Criticality. European Institute for Progressive Politics. http://www.eipcp.net.

———. 2004. WE: Collectivities, Mutualities, Participations. Kein. http://www.kein.org.

Stratton, Jon and Ien Ang. 1996. On the Impossibility of A Global Cultural Studies: "British" Cultural Studies in an International Frame. *Stuart Hall: Critical Dialogues in Cultural Studies*, edited by David Morley and Kuan-Hsing Chen, 361-91. London and New York: Routledge.

Yúdice, George. 2003. *The Expediency of Culture: Uses of Culture in the Global Era*. Durham and London: Duke University Press.

Marc Lafleur

Tracing the Absent-Present of Hiroshima and Nagasaki in America as Sensuous Encounter: Notes on (Nuclear) Ruins

ABSTRACT

This article considers the politics of ruin in sites of atomic and nuclear heritage in the United States. I argue that nuclear ruin is better understood as a force existing in and across bodies instead of as a material by-product of the nuclear era. Understood in this way, ruin operates simultaneously as both a trace of violence and, perhaps more importantly, of hope. I show this through an examination of the ways in which Hiroshima and Nagasaki fade in and out of the commemorative politics of the atomic era in America. Caught between presence and absence, Hiroshima and Nagasaki appear and disappear in the most unlikely places. Forcibly absented from museums and other places of official memory, Hiroshima and Nagasaki erupt effectively and corporeally on the interstices of and in tension with the national war narrative of the A-bomb in the United States.

RÉSUMÉ

Le présent absent d'Hiroshima et Nagasaki en Amérique comme rencontre sensuelle: À propos de ruines (nucléaires)

Cet article condidère la politique relative à la ruin atomique et nucléaire retrouvée aux sites commémoratifs aux Etats-Unis. Je soutiens que la ruine nucléaire est mieux comprise comme une force qui existe dans et à travers le corps au lieu d'être un sous-produit matériel de l'ère nucléaire. Interorétée de cette façon, la ruine se manifeste simultanément autant comme gestes de violence et, peut-être avec plus d'importance, d'espérance. J'arrive à cette énoncée en examinant les maniéres pat lesquells Hiroshima et Nagasaki se remémorisent et s'évanouissent dans la politique commemorative de l'ère atomique en Amérique. Coincées entre cette presence-absence, Hiroshima et Nagasaki apparaissent et disparaissent dans les lieux les plus improbables. Absentes forcément des muse et autres endriots de souvenirs officiels, Hiroshima et Nagasaki jaillissent sensiblement et corporellement dans les interstices de, et en tension avec, le récit national de la guerre concernant la bombe atomique auz Etats-Unis.

There was recently a time when the threat of ruin literally bore down on the New Mexico nuclear complex in Los Alamos. In 2000, the Cerro Grande wild fire raged on the mountainsides that ring the town, and the evidence of that time still lingers. Today, it is as if the town is surrounded by an undulating belt of black spikes—the trees now seem so ominous that they lend an even greater sense of the uncanny to the already heady uneasiness that blankets the place. One cannot help but think dialectically of those pictures of the charred landscapes of Hiroshima and Nagasaki.

"The fire came right down to those trees over there," Dick pointed out to me five years later. "I was up on the roof with my hose trying to keep it from getting the house. I've never been so scared." I asked him if he felt that the Los Alamos National Laboratory (LANL) was the priority. "Yeah, I blame the lab—all the firefighters were down there protecting it and here I was all by myself.... I mean we're *people* up here—down there it's just buildings and science experiments.... We're people." Dave, a lab employee, told me about having to leave his house with his family to stay in an emergency shelter one night when the fire was getting perilously close. He remembers all kinds of talk about the fire being some sort of cosmic payback for the kind of work that went on there. Telling me, he jerked his arms this way and that to demonstrate the anxious, enforced stasis of the scene, the thwarted desire to *do* something. Dave told me, too, that one of the lab's most prominent nuclear scientists was also there that night with his family; fearing for his house, the scientist was able to get the Secretary of Defense on the phone and ask him to send in the military. Dave couldn't forget the strange congruity of these kinds of speech, which positioned the lab somewhere in between nature and science, between the mythical and the military. It stayed with him, and set him thinking in a way he hadn't before. "Ever since then," he told me, "I sometimes get bogged down in all this.... I mean, I never thought that I would spend my life, you know, doing *this*."

These days, one can drive the road through Los Alamos and see precisely where the fire stopped. Just a few metres up one side of the road, the hillside opens up into a bramble of dead trees buffered by a row of healthy pines. On the other side, one can see the rooftops of the laboratory buildings. While the Cerro Grande fire destroyed dozens of homes and some outbuildings on lab territory, the LANL— the centre of the American nuclear weapons complex—escaped the worst of it. The fire never managed to jump the road into the most vulnerable and populated areas, and the town and the laboratory remained, for the most part, unscathed. But the threat of the ruin still persists in its bodily state. For Dave and for Dick, the fire awakened a sense that the nuclear complex was both something more and something less than it was cracked up to be. It also forced them to reimagine their place within it, with unnerving consequences. Both employees were unable to put to rest their reservations. But they were also unable to *change* anything, and it was this in-between feeling that led to a lingering, overwhelming sense of ruin. It was as if a new reality had been revealed to them in the ashes of the fire, and yet they had never been able to clear away those ashes and to see the potential beneath them.

...

Unlike the museums at Hiroshima and Nagasaki, where the contemplation of nuclear ruins constitutes the basic motivating desire to visit, nuclear museums in the United States—and, in particular, in New Mexico—are marked by a profound and sometimes disconcerting absence of nuclear ruins. The two nuclear-themed museums in New Mexico are largely organized around the display and narration of the stories of Little Boy and Fat Man, the Los-Alamos-built bombs responsible for the devastation of Hiroshima and Nagasaki. Recently, Joseph Masco (2008) has asserted that the production and consumption of spectacular nuclear ruins—the result of a complex web of televised nuclear tests, dramatized movie-of-the-week apocalypses and civil defence strategies such as the building of domestic bomb-shelters—were and remain central to the production of compliant, disciplined American citizens. Given this, what does it mean that the central nuclear ruins of our time, the only ones marked by the large-scale destruction of life and property, seem to be entirely absent from the very places in which it would be appropriate to consider them?

This essay examines the nuclear ruins brought on by the absence of Hiroshima and Nagasaki in American nuclear museums. To be clear, Hiroshima and Nagasaki themselves do not exactly constitute the ruins I speak of, although they certainly qualify as ruins as the term is conventionally understood. Nor do I locate ruins in Nevada's proving grounds[1] or even in the South Pacific atolls of the Marshall Islands. The ruins here are more elusive and not readily apparent. This essay argues that the ruins that nuclear museums embody and encapsulate are nothing less than human life itself. I begin and continually return to the issue of ruin's absence—particularly Hiroshima and Nagasaki—from the spaces of American nuclear contemplation. By locating ruin in absence I do not mean to imply that it simply is not there. Instead, I wish to make a case for a notion of ruin that—while remaining intensely material—both exists in a state of continuous deferral and can only be understood as a cultural form that is deeply corporeal. In other words, I argue that nuclear ruin in America must be understood as a force lodged in the body and comprehensible only in terms of the body's affective rhythms and immanent qualities. To locate ruin in the space of absence is to simultaneously deny and affirm the paradoxes it implies, and this essay draws out this proliferation of productive paradoxes. What does it mean to witness the absence of ruin? What are the implications of this act of witnessing? Given that absences are never complete and always leave traces of presence, how do we experience and narrate these absences?

The complex interplay between presence and absence is not a new concern in philosophy and cultural theory. Jacques Derrida perhaps most notably opened up the relationship between presence and absence and placed it in motion. In applying deconstruction to what he called the "metaphysics of presence"—by which he meant the enduring and seemingly transcendent connection of presence to the production of knowledge, meaning and truth—Derrida sought to highlight the ways in which presence and absence, far from acting as a binary pair, are co-indicative of one another (1976: 143). Proceeding as a series of fragments that track moments of presence-absence and their implications, Derrida's notes accumulate a collective force yet never aspire to a seamless collectivity, thus invoking and mimicking their subject.

The present essay seeks to engage with the essential slipperiness of presence and absence in an ethnographic sense. Particularly, how and when does the absence of Hiroshima and Nagasaki morph into a lingering presence? What is the trace of Hiroshima's and Nagasaki's presence in America, and how is that trace experienced? Rather than confronting a metaphysics of presence as Derrida does, however, this article engages with its flipside, a metaphysics of *absence*, or at least the sovereign aspiration for such a state, an aspiration that, given the qualities of presence and absence, is always being exceeded and undermined. To what can we attribute this desire for absence? And how is this absence-presence experienced and manifested? Nuclear museums are places suffused with an almost unbearable potential. The tensions of their potentials—realized and unrealized, accepted and denied, visible and invisible—create conceptual gaps in the museums' exhibits, which complicate the intended unidirectional leap between the exhibits' signifiers (objects and images) and the meanings they produce. These gaps open up unregulated spaces of thought and experience, between, for example, the technical marvel of the missiles and bombs, and their potential consequences; between deterrence and mutually assured destruction and between security and freedom. These gaps and deferrals, which create a space between presence and absence, and are articulated sensuously as moments of affect, impact, haunting, doubt or unqualifiable intensity, are what I am calling "ruin."

Walter Benjamin called attention to the unlikely but everyday presence of ruins in our midst (1968: 2002). For Benjamin, the once grand 19th-century shopping arcades of Paris existed as instances of "petrified history," evidence of capitalism's obsession with the new and of the short-lived fetish power of its objects, but also of capitalism's ephemerality and fragility (Buck-Morss 1989: 160, 164). Note the sense of elegy and mouldering decay that punctuate Benjamin's description of the arcades:

Many are the institutes of hygiene, where gladiators are wearing orthopedic belts and bandages wind round the white bellies of mannequins. In the windows of the hairdressers, one sees the last women with long hair; they sport richly undulating masses, petrified coiffures. How brittle appears the stonework of the walls beside them and above: crumbling papier-mâché!.... In the arcades one comes across collar studs for which we no longer know the types of collars and shirts. (Benjamin 2002: 872)

For Benjamin, the arcades existed as signs of capitalism's phases—fossils of the 19th century—but also, and more importantly, as signs of capitalism *itself* as a phase of history. For Benjamin, then, the production of ruins in capitalism revealed both the internal machinations of capitalistic enterprise and the ruin embedded within capitalism itself. It was allegory that endowed ruins with force. In stressing that the arcades were to be viewed as allegories and not as symbols, Benjamin sought to temporally reorient them, to prevent them from being swept up in the mythologization of the past to which symbols are susceptible. Allegorically, ruins gesture to the past, but they do so not to heroize, rescue or redeem it. Instead, allegory highlights the transitoriness of the past, a viewpoint steeped in an awareness of death and decomposition. The ruins of the present fold back on themselves, getting tangled along the way with all the discarded fragments and traces of the past, becoming both more and less than the sum of its parts. Confronting us allegorically, rather than symbolically, the ruin accumulates intensity, momentum and memory.

Benjamin's allegorical conceptions of ruin and decay are instructive and politically important because they demonstrate not only that ruin is a by-product of civilization, but that civilization itself is susceptible to ruin. It is in this susceptibility that potential exists. In the ruin's kinship with allegory—which leads not forward or back but resides in the virtual profusion of a moment of impact, stoppage and inhabitation of the space of apparent paradox—it exists and operates as a fragment, a trace, or better yet as what Giorgio Agamben (1999) calls " a remnant."[2] In this way, the ruin haunts, suggests, reminds, disturbs, interferes and interrupts but it does not, cannot, declare. Instead, it exists within the realm of the potential, frozen forever between the possible and the impossible, at the very frontier of the archive and its dissolution.

This suggests the possibility, largely unexplored, that the concept or allegory of ruin need not be tied to or deployed from material remains in order to retain what Benjamin would call its dialectic power. To take this one step further, I am suggesting that the consideration of ruins has been limited by precisely this allegiance to their literal existence and presence as *things* and *places* in states of decay. It is not that this is wrong, but that it is perhaps too exclusive. Moving away from this allegiance requires us to free ruins from the spatially oriented sites through which we have historically understood them. I would like to suggest a supplementary rendering of the ruin, one that not only preserves and allegorically highlights past sites of ruin such as Hiroshima and Nagasaki, but also allows for new sites of ruin to be imagined.

…

Imagine the ruin not as a crumbling structure that, in its decay, hints enigmatically at its past nobility. Try to resist the forceful temptation here to gather up the fragments and traces of the past. Think not of ruins as relics or fossils, or as people, places and things caught in a forever petrified freeze-frame. I am asking you here to consider a different kind of ruin, one that is perhaps more difficult to identify yet no less destructive. Imagine ruin not as a place or a thing but as a force that comes to reside in the body. It is as a force that ruin can be seen to actualize itself, not in the decomposing remains of a bygone era, but in the gleaming, still new, formations of an imperial present. This is to consider the paradoxical possibility of ruins in the moment of their profound absence.[3]

This idea suggests that we consider ruin less as a physical circumstance or outcome of capitalism, and more as the virtual-corporeal quality of biopolitical sovereignty itself.[4] It releases the idea of ruin from the constraints of centre and periphery, or the appearances of violence, peace, poverty or prosperity. In the scenario I am proposing, dream and nightmare, success and failure, ruin and triumph exist alongside of and always immanent to one another. Seeing ruin as a virtual force (a resonating paradox, a dialectical image vibrating with tension) that lodges in bodies epistemologically liberates the deployment or identification of ruins from the plodding persistence of presence. In doing so, it sets in motion a circuit of doubling and folding, where ruin ping-pongs between presence and absence, settling indistinguishably between the two. It is precisely the absence of ruins—in nuclear museums, for example—that signals them as places facilitating intensified destruction and decay. Conversely, it is the ruin that points metonymically to the success of the sovereign enterprise, ruin's absence.

Reading ruin as embedded within the body updates for the biopolitical era Benjamin's sense of ruin as a doubled entity, as both evidence of society's decay and a sign of humanity's possibility for redemption. Power, sovereignty and capitalism can no longer be read or deployed apart from the desiring body as though clumsily imposed on it from the outside. Rather, they must be read together in order to decipher the complex ways in which ruin both acts on and is produced by the body in simultaneously structural and intimate ways. This reading not only allows us to understand ruin as a bodily self-impact of biopolitical sovereignty, it also allows us to understand the flipside of ruin—the possibility of redemption—in a bodily manner. To be caught up in the body's intensities, its in-betweeness, is to recognize that the body contains folds that elude the structuring zeal of ruin, and to position the body as Benjamin intended, as both ruin and redemption, despair and hope.

...

In the autumn of 1976, the National Atomic Museum in Albuquerque, New Mexico, received an envelope from Japan containing a letter and two pieces of paper. The letter, written in careful and precise English script, was from Akira Yasui, a Japanese citizen who had visited the museum more than three years earlier. One of the enclosed pieces of paper was a clipping from the Japanese newspaper *The Asahi Shimbun*. The article describes an air show in Texas in which a B-29 bomber recreated the 1945 dropping of the atomic bomb. The article, says Yasui, had reminded him of his visit to the National Atomic Museum, which had taken place on a trip to Albuquerque "to give a speech about Japan-U.S. Trade relation for the members of the Albuquerque Chamber of Commerce." He writes that at the time of his trip, a visit to the museum was a "MUST" for him in order to see the model of Little Boy, the bomb dropped on Hiroshima.

By way of explanation, he writes that his wife was "at the Hiroshima Station waiting for a street Car in the morning of Aug. 6, 1945." Yasui goes on to explain that while it was imperative for him to visit the museum and to see the museum's exhibit of Little Boy, he never told his wife about it. To this day, he writes, his wife knows nothing about the museum or its display, or of his visit to witness them. He emphasizes in his letter that while his wife continues to suffer enormously as a result of her exposure to the radioactive fallout of the bomb and detests war and violence in all its forms, she harbours no ill will toward Americans. "She hates wars and armed conflicts, not the person who dropped the bomb," he writes, and he describes two "enjoyable" vacations spent in the United States. The other piece of paper enclosed with the letter is one produced by the museum itself. "Recently I found the leaflet and [the] question paper which I didn't fill up and return to you." The "question paper" he refers to is a visitor feedback form, of the sort often found near a museum's exit. He returns the feedback sheet empty "as a mere visitor ... although it's more than three years old."[5]

...

The National Atomic Musum's historian was let go shortly after he showed me where to find the museum's archive—a few dusty boxes stowed in a cubicle corner. His job termination was part of a larger rationalization of the organization of which the museum was just a small part. A museum chartered with the task of interpreting and displaying the nation's atomic and nuclear history did not, it seemed, need a historian. The archive itself contained many of the memos and documents exchanged between military and municipal leaders that led to the museum's establishment, as well as a chronologue of the changing styles of the museum's flyers, visitor maps, displays and handouts. These documents form the archive's foundation, seamlessly fitting together like joints and sockets or posts and beams, securing the past in a continuous narrative that "articulate[s] the unity of an

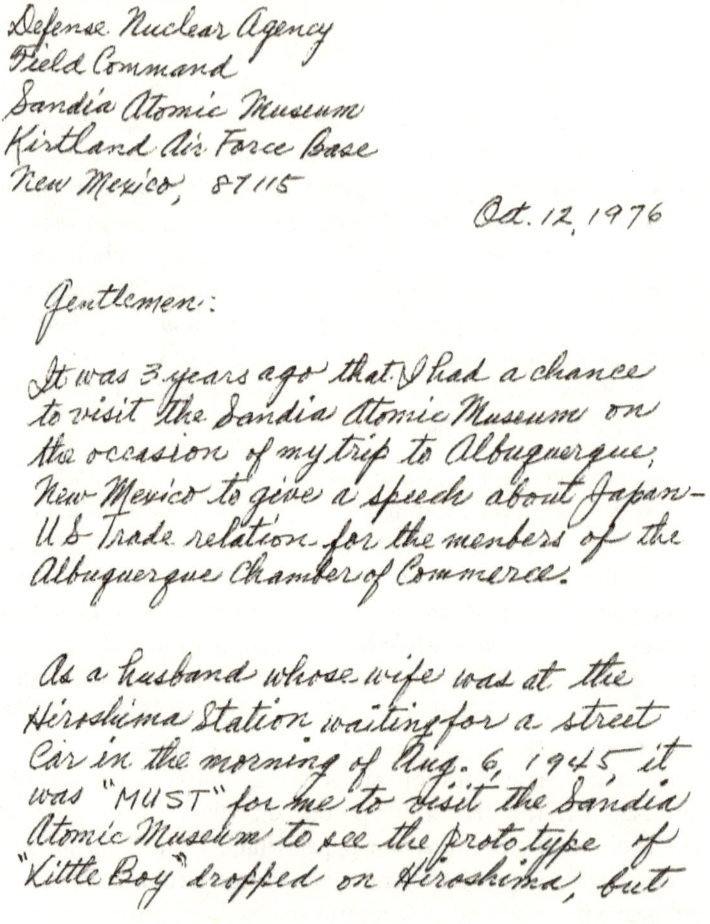

> Defense Nuclear Agency
> Field Command
> Sandia Atomic Museum
> Kirtland Air Force Base
> New Mexico, 87115
>
> Oct. 12, 1976
>
> Gentlemen:
>
> It was 3 years ago that I had a chance to visit the Sandia Atomic Museum on the occasion of my trip to Albuquerque, New Mexico to give a speech about Japan-US Trade relation for the members of the Albuquerque Chamber of Commerce.
>
> As a husband whose wife was at the Hiroshima Station waiting for a street car in the morning of Aug. 6, 1945, it was "MUST" for me to visit the Sandia Atomic Museum to see the prototype of "Little Boy" dropped on Hiroshima, but

Fig. 1 A portion of Akira Yasui's letter

ideal configuration" (Derrida 1994: 3). But because nuclear museums are among the few public faces of the nuclear history and reality of present-day America, they also form another kind of archive. Sitting in the back of the museum, sifting through its modest archive, I became acutely aware that I was sitting in what itself amounted to a larger archive. This collection of documents and artifacts provided a story of the museum's own history, but they also contributed to a larger experience of nuclear history steeped in sovereign power. The orderly narrative of the museum's archive can be ruptured by the museum itself *as* archive. As an archive of nuclear America, the narrative is undermined by the interplay of secrecy, fear and trauma which mark this history. It is this relationship between my exploration of the museum's own archive, where I found the letter by Akira Yasui, and the museum *as* archive that I will explore.

Derrida's psychoanalytic analysis of the archive as, in part, a response to and a hedge against the death drive is perhaps particularly apt here. But it is not the stewardship of the violence of the past—recorded or not, as the case may be—that makes the archive so alive with potential danger. Rather, Derrida insists, it is the way in which the archive speaks with the future, offering to it but *one* highly codified, classified, unified and ultimately conservative story of the past. This "very singular promise of the future" makes the archive central to our understanding of "modernity's pain" (1994: 36, 15).

Clues embedded within the archive itself light the fires of internal combustion. These fires erode the laws by which the archive governs itself and governs memory now and in the future. The clues reveal the archive's centrality to the making of memory and thus to the making of ourselves. In a nod to Nietzsche, Derrida argues that the need to archive is also a *mal d'archive*, which can be translated as sickness of the archive, but also—perhaps more accurately in this case—as a passion or a compulsion to archive (Derrida 1994: 89-90). This urge pushes us to archive right to the limits of the archive itself. The moment "when the archive slips away," when it shifts from a finite to an infinite register, is a moment tense with paradox. The compulsive desire to archive in the place where the archive begins to dissolve is both the moment of the archive's greatest destructive power and the moment of the archive's greatest vulnerability (94). This desire to archive what cannot be trained or disciplined to fit into the archive situates the archive within the space of a lacuna. It is in the liminal space of the hiatus that the archive can be read oppositionally, or that moments of rupture and impact can be identified that interrupt the seemingly continuous circulation of the archival narrative.

Recently, Ann Cvetkovich has articulated a different kind of archive, what she calls an "archive of feelings" (2003). In contrast to mainstream archives, these archives are organized largely around sites of trauma, and oriented toward the kinds of knowledge and memory that would not normally find their way into archives. Composed of ephemera, pamphlets, flyers, scraps of paper with jottings and casual notes, as well as pornography, comics and other kinds of graphic art, such archival collections are largely oriented around expressions of affect, "sentiment and emotion" (269). The "archive of feelings" disturbs the traditional ordering and boundary-forming impulse of the mainstream archive, museum or memorial. Moreover, it institutionalizes as its very purpose "practices of mourning" that preserve the ephemera of memory and the marginal histories of traumatized groups in ways that do not siphon off the pain and wounds left by such histories. By keeping history open, "the successful archive enables the work of mourning" (271).

Cvetkovich argues that "archives of feeling" are not what Derrida is referring to in *Archive Fever*, and this encounter between Cvetkovich and Derrida demands momentary examination. Cvetkovich is right, I believe, to infer that Derrida's

Archive Fever is largely interested in "traditional institutions" rather than in the "material specificities of a more experimental grassroots ... archive" (Cvetkovich 2003: 268). However, she seems to think that the different nature of the archives she is articulating puts them beyond the logic of the archive articulated by Derrida. I am not so sure. My interest here is less in critiquing one or another notion of the archive, and more in how these dual notions of the archive might be productively brought together in a way that illuminates the kinds of archival evidence I have encountered in my own work. For Cvetkovich, the traumatic nature of these archives, and the counter-pressure they exert against the "institutionalizing" ideology of museums, monuments and archives, puts the grassroots archive of feelings beyond "the impossibility of the archive articulated by Derrida toward collections of texts and objects that embody the sentiments and obsessions of archive fever" (Cvetkovich 2003: 271).

Does an archive of feelings move beyond the "impossibility" of the archive cited by Derrida? The answer is more complicated than a "yes" or "no." The archive of feelings is entangled complexly with both the possibility and the impossibility of the archive (i.e., the archive's institutionalizing tendencies and the lines of flight that a deterritorialized archive of feelings embarks upon). Any archive of feelings is, after all, an *archive* and cannot totally escape the ordering tendencies implicit in such an enterprise at the same time as it strains against or unsettles them. To me, it seems as if the archive of feelings exists right at the frontier of the archive, the edge that in Derrida's view flirts with its own possibility. Tacking between possibility and impossibility, the archive of feelings is unable to finally assert either one; to do so would render it an archive in the traditional sense, or preclude it from being one. Neither option is satisfactory, neither is accurate.

What the archive of feelings *does* do is alert us to the possibility that emotions and sentiments, affectively-inspired statements of intensity, do not easily inhabit both archives and "the archive." They strain against the impositions of form and storage; they exist but they do not build. Unable to contribute to the architecture of the archive, no coherent narrative can be erected from them; they inure.

Understood this way—in ceaseless dialogue with the impossibility of the archive, threatening to take it over the edge—archives of feelings and instances of affect in otherwise "traditional" archives are politically radical and potentializing. In Cvetkovich's understanding, archives of feeling establish their own separate strain of traumatic memorial that is an archive without being an archive. In this way, it seems to me, they really have little to say about the power of the archiving impulse at all, nor about the hegemonic power of the archive to define what counts as knowledge. But understanding archives of feeling as part of the archiving impulse, albeit in continuous tension with it, leads to a different interpretation. Archives of feeling hold open the archive, or at least aspects of it, by concomitantly falling short of and exceeding the archive's domains of classification. This accomplishes one of the main goals for Cvetkovich's archive—that of mourning. It places mourning at the centre of power, as an unassimilable and undiminishable question or contemplation.

The archive of feelings, then, helps to articulate ruin from *within* the archive. Here we can switch registers; the archive I refer to can be both specific and general, can refer to an archive but also to *the archive* of knowledge. Archives of feeling, alerting us to ruin, a ruin that doubly encompasses the bodies articulating those feelings and the archives in which they are contained, are what Deleuze and Guattari (1987) might term "minoritarian" impulses. In other words, archives of feeling exist within the disciplinary limits of the archive at the same time that they articulate a counter-disciplinary impulse. Read together, Derrida's and Cvetkovich's archives shed light on the ways in which Akira Yasui's letter resonated in the archive of the National Atomic Museum. This reading of archive and ruin allows us to move forward with a series of paradoxes revolving around the questions of possibility and impossibility, of mourning, witness and testimony that the letter provokes.

Akira Yasui's letter hints not (just) at the grand disaster of nuclear war, but at the quiet disasters of his wife's life and of his life with his wife. He meets the museum's absence of displayed disaster with his own equally powerful statement of absence. Both absences contain their own ruins. I would like to explore what Yasui's letter and the returned, empty feedback form reveal to us about how witnessing and testimony confront the experience of visiting the museum. The letter contains no demands or requests and is not marked by anger or a desire for redress. The letter does not explicitly call the museum to task for its representation of the bomb and its lack of any meaningful consideration of its effects. Nor does it seek to morally resurrect the issue of whether the bomb should have been dropped in the hopes that a penance of guilt or regret may be offered. Instead, with its mixture of the matter-of-fact and the intimate, revelation and refusal, said and unsaid, the Japanese visitor's intervention seeks, "as a mere visitor," only to recognize the absence and to leap into the unknown ethical territory it represents. If the absence of Hiroshima and Nagasaki represents a wound, this is not an attempt to suture or heal it, but is, more courageously, an attempt to both keep the wound open and dwell inside it. That is, Yasui seeks to bear witness.

...

According to Agamben, the only "true" or "complete" witness to atrocity is, paradoxically, he or she who can never bear witness at all. The true witnesses are the dead, for only they have experienced the annihilation of life that the survivors have escaped. A survivor, then, is at best a "pseudo-witness," a proxy for those who fell (Agamben 1999: 34). Yet this represents a problem, for how are the dead—who themselves cannot speak—able to testify? Such is the negation at the heart of witnessing, where it implodes before it even begins. Bearing witness, then, is fundamentally a process of acknowledging the very impossibility of the act, of ever truly bearing witness (39). It is an act of constant deferral, always gesturing toward its inadequacy to take up the very task it embodies. This situates witnessing in the space of an aporia, a paradox from which it cannot emerge.

Yet the task of witnessing is not emergence, Agamben argues, but rather to dwell in the aporic space ever more deeply, for it is only here that the ethical subject materializes and the testimony of the witness is able to articulate its potentiality. Testimony itself is a relationship based on the potential of speech; "between the sayable and unsayable in every language—that is ... between a possibility and an impossibility of speech" (145). It is not that testimony, or the articulation of the witness, simply exists between the possibility and impossibility of speech, but that "their inseparable intimacy is testimony" (Agamben 1999:146). For testimony to be possible, it must maintain a relationship with its own denial, it must embrace its impossibility. The witness and testimony can only exist undivided from their negation: the witness with the dead, testimony with the impossibility of speech. Undivided, they provide the platform from which the subject's testimony enables an ethical intervention that does not seek to classify or to explain, to assign blame or responsibility; rather, it seeks to open up spaces of potentiality provided by the embrace of the moment of deferral. Agamben argues that modern biopolitics seeks to shut down this moment of deferral by cleaving apart the paradoxical pairs—separating human and inhuman, animal and organic life, the witness and the dead—until it has achieved its goal of creating a living body stripped of all subjective attributes save simple survival. Witnessing and its declarative act, testimony, constitute simultaneously the trace of the ruin and the refusal to be reduced to survival, to bare life, to "being subject to desubjectification" (146). Witnessing and testimony constitute subjectivity itself, Agamben writes, and they do so not in a closed, linear process that orients us in history—not as ends, but as remnants that elude structure, classification, foundations and the archive itself (158-59).

As noted above, the physical archive occasionally contains that which is unarchivable, something that strains the mandate of the archive itself by inserting a gap between meaning and structure or between body and system. In its endless deferral to impossibility, witnessing always creates such a gap. It is in this context that I wish to examine Akira Yasui's envelope more closely.

As mentioned, Yasui's envelope contained both a letter to the museum and a museum feedback form. This extraordinary pairing of filled and unfilled sheets of paper is important. The documents' coupling perfectly demonstrates the paradoxical pair that Agamben insists constitutes witnessing and testimony, the intimate embrace of the possibility and the impossibility of speech. But there is something else important here: the kinds of speech these two documents potentialize. Agamben writes that testimony is always, and can only be, a kind of poetics, a speech that eludes the archive. Witnesses are by definition poets, and the poetic word is "always situated in the position of the remnant," as that which perseveres in the face of the impossibility of testimony. The letter constitutes such a poetic testament, a witnessing of subjectivity in the face of desubjectification. The visitor questionnaire, however, represents the possibility of another kind of language. Akira Yasui's refusal to fill in the very form that requests his opinion does not represent the absence of testimony. Instead, it must be read as refusal to participate in the archive, in language that is non-poetic, utilitarian, structured, segmented and enclosed by the questions posed. The visitor feedback sheet, oriented as it is toward the end of "evaluat[ing] our program and insur[ing] that it maintains its high standards," refuses the deferral of the remnant and seeks instead the closed finality of improving the visitor experience.

...

In Alain Resnais's now iconic film about the atomic bombings, *Hiroshima Mon Amour* (1959), the protagonists spar over the possibilities of knowing what happened in Hiroshima. "I saw everything," the French female lead contends. "You saw nothing," her Japanese lover replies. This exchange is repeated throughout the film. The woman claims her knowledge on the basis of what she has seen in pictures and film footage and at the Hiroshima museum. In return, her lover denies that these images can serve as the basis for knowledge about the event. "You saw nothing," he repeats. The film positions the viewer between the desire to know about the event and the impossibility of ever attaining such knowledge. As the two characters struggle with each other over their competing claims to knowledge and its limits, the film positions spectators permanently in the "incommensurable gap between perception and reality" (Maclear 2003: 234). In her article "The Limits of Vision," Kyo Maclear argues that it is Resnais's refusal to close this gap, and his insistence that we remain perpetually at the limit or within the deferral, that forces the viewer to deconstruct the easy one-to-one relationship between vision and knowledge and to interrogate the "what one does and doesn't see in epistemological and ethical terms" (234).

In claiming the archive as the basis for her knowledge of the event, the woman in the film clings to the available representations of the Hiroshima bombing as a means of understanding. However, her absolute claim to knowledge, "I saw everything," also closes the event and, as a misguided means of lamentation, assigns it to the past. Her repeated assertions of comprehension, however, also point ever more excessively to the realization of the gaping hole, a wound of sorts, that the event opens up. It is only in the modest and humble recognition of the event as unknowable that any ethical mourning can begin to replace the desire for comprehension in the face of events of such violent magnitude.

It is this theme of violence embedded in the gaze's appetite to *know*, that Cathy Caruth (1996) identifies as *Hiroshima Mon Amour's* most potent critique. The problem, she observes, is not that the woman simply does not see enough to come to an informed opinion on Hiroshima; it is not a matter of the consumption of information and images. Rather, the repeated refrain "you saw nothing" is meant to indicate that the problem with the woman's sight lies in the way it translates what it sees into an objective picture or understanding of the event. As Caruth contends,

> [T]he man's denial suggests that the act of seeing, in the very establishing of a bodily referent, erases, like an empty grammar, the reality of an event. Within the insistent grammar of sight, the man suggests, the body erases the event of its own death. (Caruth 1996: 29)

Vision's persistent desire to see something, to identify, to regulate, to classify and thereby to know is the antithesis of the open-ended desire to mourn and to lament not just the dead but the consequences for the living as well. For as much as the atomic bomb took hundreds of thousands of lives, its effects did not end there. A consideration for the billions of lives put in peril by the bomb must also be built into this mourning.

The parallel dialectics between *Hiroshima Mon Amour* and Akira Yasui's envelope are important here. The dialogue between the two film characters operates in a similar fashion to the juxtaposition of the letter and the visitor questionnaire—both enact a deferral of knowledge about the event, Hiroshima, in the interest of ethical contemplation and mourning. By prolonging the gap, they resist the temptation to expedite the circulation of the archive—a circulation to which both film and museums traditionally contribute. Perpetual circulation is the natural condition of the archive, and one it aches to return to in the prolonged impact. By extending the moment of impact, and letting it seep and linger, Yasui and the film both enact the poetics of witnessing in Agamben's sense of the term. Both moments explicitly call attention to the impossibility of witnessing in the face of such incomprehensible atrocity and destruction. This is their sole moment of declaration, the declaration that it cannot be done—what Taussig in a separate context calls "the labour of the negative" (1999). Paradoxically, the declaration of impossibility is not a conclusion to but the launch of testimony.

If testimony exists in the gap of knowledge, in the moment of impact where the linear flow of thought stops moving forward and builds up, creating tension and pressure, what exactly is being testified? The testimony of both the film and Akira Yasui's envelope is the testimonial of ruin itself. In the face of its impossibility, or what Maclear (2003), following Drucilla Cornell, calls the "philosophy of limits," witnessing can only testify to the witness's bodily ruin. This is what Yasui articulates in the passage where he writes:

I didn't tell my wife about the museum and my visit there till today. She does not know at all about the museum and "Little Boy." More than thirty years since the explosion of the A bomb on the human heads of Hiroshima—was the continuation of the radioactive influences for her *as well as for me*. She hates war and armed conflicts not the person who dropped the bomb. (Emphasis added)

This excerpt speaks to Yasui's encasement within the ruin that was and continues to be Hiroshima, a ruin that manifests intimately and bodily. It is expressed in his shame at having visited the bomb as a museum attraction—a shame that is the basis of his silence to his wife on the matter even after three years, a shame grounded in his desire to see. "It was," he writes, "a MUST for me to visit ... the museum to see the prototype of 'Little Boy' dropped on Hiroshima...." This contradiction illustrates the ways in which the biopolitical body is compelled toward what Benjamin (1968) described as the contemplation of its own destruction. Yasui's body is the biopolitical body that is caught between the sovereign decision on life and death. The paradox of contemplating one's ruin reveals the twisted logic of contemporary sovereignty, the ways in which it in-builds certain kinds of desire or pleasure. But Yasui also points at the inherent, though hard to trace, incompleteness of sovereign exceptionalism, which seeks to police its frontiers in order to maintain clear boundaries between inside and outside, presence and absence. By meeting absence with a parallel absence, refusing to square off the dialectic with an "appropriate" response, this Japanese museum visitor exceeds or penetrates the circular logic of exceptionalism. Yasui's actions, I believe, attest to the body's complex relation to the event, its existence in a messy state that doubles back and folds in on itself. Such folds create provisional interstices and air pockets that escape and persevere in the totality of biopolitical capture. Ruin inhabits these spaces as a force lodged in and written on the body and thus subject to the body's simultaneously disciplined and insurgent rhythms. The nature of ruin is revealed as an intricately bundled moment of both overcoded, potentially infinite violence and—in the tenacity of testimony—resolute hope.

...

On an early summer afternoon I am in a roomy auditorium, part of an old warehouse in Santa Fe's railyards that has been given over to local cultural, arts and activist groups. Roughly thirty Japanese college students occupy the middle rows, sitting in twos, threes and fours. The Japanese students are taking a class on the subject of "Violence in America" and are in the midst of a three-week American tour organized by their instructor, Sumiko, a former journalist working as a media studies professor at a university just outside of Tokyo. A group of four men ranging in age from their early thirties to their early sixties are on the stage in front of the Japanese students. The men are members of the local chapter of Veterans for Peace, and they are there to tell the students about their experiences in Vietnam and how these experiences have informed their subsequent anti-war activism.

I listen as the third of the four veterans begins his talk. The first two have stuck fairly close to a fairly conventional script. They speak about the disillusionment they experienced in Vietnam and the gap between what they were told they were going to do and what they actually did there. They are, by and large, confident narratives which seem almost rehearsed. And, in a way, they are. In films, television and books, Vietnam—and veterans' agonizing experiences therein—has acquired a commonplace narrative. The disillusioned Vietnam veteran has, in some circles, become the stuff of the American Dream, a hero constructed in the very act of questioning the state. Yet I realize only in retrospect that the first two veterans' narratives are striking in their easy digestibility. For in recounting their experiences of trauma, pain and suffering—which include the loss of limbs and unending horror stories of post-traumatic stress disorder—the two men have discovered and honed a language which normalizes, contains and, ultimately, dispels the very trauma they narrate.

The third veteran, Jeremy, is different. He visibly struggles to find the words to begin his story. His face seems etched with tension and grief, and he tentatively begins to offer up some reflections on his past. He stops, looks up and starts again, this time somewhat differently. Again he halts his narrative. His nervous, fidgety demeanour and the unpolished rawness of his words are beginning to ripple outward. Professor Sumiko, who has been translating, is also beginning to struggle a little to articulate Jeremy's words. Straining to summarize his varied, uncollected reflections on Vietnam, Jeremy is clearly shaken, and his voice wavers as he says to his Japanese audience, "Before I finish, I just want to say sorry. I want to apologize on behalf of my country for what we did to you in 1945, for dropping the atomic bombs. If there is one thing I want you to know ... I just want you to know that not every American agrees with their government."

A silence follows this statement, as Jeremy takes his seat. Sumiko has not translated what the veteran has said, and as the silence persists her class begins to eye her expectantly. As she turns to the class, it becomes clear that she is openly weeping. After a long pause, the professor apologizes profusely for her tears and translates Jeremy's statement.

The Veterans for Peace workshop, located in the same converted warehouse as the auditorium, is lined with shelves that hold dozens and dozens of *papier maché* skulls. The skulls were part of an art and activism project on the Iraq war that the veterans put together to coincide with the celebration of the Mexican Day of the Dead. When I ask Jeremy about what he had said in the auditorium, he didn't seem to want to reflect on it and became increasingly irritated with my desire to explore his motivations and meaning. After a while, he cut me off. "Really, what else could I say?"

I hesitate to explore this moment further, in the fear that I may betray the truth that underlies Jeremy's question. So here I seek not to explain or contextualize the moment but to prolong it and draw it out. I am mindful of a situation that Allen Feldman describes experiencing at a conference on violence he attended in Sweden in 1992. There, a keynote speaker, a folklorist from Croatia,

> delivered a paper punctuated in the white space between her words, by barely concealed emotional disorder approaching public mourning. This did not seem to be the aftershock of her life in a war zone, nor the catharsis of having momentarily exited. Rather, her distress exposed the frustration, risk, and uncertainty of communicating local terror to an audience at an historical and experiential remove. (Feldman 1994: 404-405)

Faced with the impossibility of understanding this narrative suffused with the almost palpable sensoria of terror, the assembled scholars rushed to suture the open wound of the folklorist's body and her experience of violence by reorienting her narrative in ways they could more readily understand and thereby close down. The press of questions that sought to fill the threatening void in the aftermath of her speech channelled the discussion toward questions of media representation of the war in the Balkans. By recasting the discussion in normative ways, the audience was able to enter what had been a space of sensory alterity, with which they could not engage. Feldman calls this inclination "cultural anaesthesia," by which he means "the banishment of disconcerting, discordant and anarchic sensory presences and agents that undermine the normalizing and often silent premises of everyday life" (405). The desire to identify a common and thus normative thread that pushes forward, past or around moments of profound sensory impact—Feldman's cultural anesthesia—does not just characterize extreme moments like the one he describes. It permeates everyday life to such an extent that it becomes the lubricant of the social; a lubricant, incidentally, that not only facilitates everyday violence but constitutes it. Feldman writes that although faced with a "Croatian choking on the experiential inadequacy of conventional representation," the audience sought to steer the conversation right back to the ways in which the media in Bosnia and Croatia were representing the war in the Balkans (405). As the body of the Croatian woman dramatically illustrated the failure of representation to contain and palliate trauma, the cultural tendency was to return to the safety of representation itself. Mindful of this inclination, I seek to prolong and extend trauma in the interest of allowing each body a passage of emergence that avoids the ever-present desire to contextualize and explain.

By asking me "what else could I say?" Jeremy sought to challenge my desire to push past his apology, an apology that came from the body, from an anger, a disillusionment and a disease that preceded and exceeded the articulation of all of these things. From his perspective, "what else could I say" simultaneously meant two things: there was both nothing other than the apology to say, and there was nothing *more* to say.

...

Thus far I have been using the word "ruin" to describe a bodily orientation between the possible and the impossible. Ruin profoundly marks the territories from which Jeremy's apology emanated and from which Sumiko responded. These are moments of ruin as affect, as a force that resides in the body and sometimes emerges with an impact that cannot be anticipated. It also reveals the ways in which ruin operates outside the confines of clear physical conditions or appearances of ruin, the ways in which ruin folds and diffuses into the virtual space of the everyday.

The desire to make sense of such a situation would seek to contextualize Jeremy's apology and Sumiko's affective reaction within multiple legacies of historical trauma and anti-war activism, and by doing so it would cover over the deferrals and gaps that permeate the event. Acknowledging and maintaining the gaps at the heart of the event calls attention to the event's sensations. Rather than threatening the authenticity of the event, these gaps are key to establishing the event's truth. Let me enumerate the moments of deferral—those gaps that defy sense—that characterize the event. Then, I will offer a model by which these deferrals are enhancing and productive moments, indicative of a vitality, rather than moments that do not essentially add up. First, there is the status of Jeremy. A Vietnam veteran not yet born in 1945 when the atomic bombs were dropped on Japan, Jeremy's connection to the event seems absent. Sumiko and her class were also not born when the atomic bombs were used, and neither the professor nor her students were from Hiroshima or Nagasaki. Moreover, the class and their presence in America—as critics, no less—could be taken to indicate the success of postwar Japan, the status of the two countries as allies and friends and the cessation of tensions and animosities stemming from the past conflicts. The only connection to be drawn, in fact, is that Jeremy is American and Sumiko and her students Japanese.

In many ways, the gaps I have termed "deferrals" may be read as rendering the event insignificant. What possible consequence or importance can be attributed to an apology offered under such circumstances? An apology, no less, between parties whose connections to the events of Hiroshima and Nagasaki are distant and disempowered. What effect or relevance does this apology have when no apology has ever been offered by a president of the United States or sought by the government of Japan? To subscribe to such a reading, however, would be to accept an understanding of politics as something that exists on the level of nation-states, rather than between and among people in everyday settings. This reading would also cast history as a contained and segmented enterprise in which the past does not seep into the diverse arenas of the everyday. Such a conception would render apologies and forgiveness, in the case of Hiroshima and Nagasaki, as irrelevant or meaningless at any scale other than that of nation to nation.

...

In a short text, Derrida considers the groundwork and the conditions necessary for forgiveness to take place (2001). His reflections on forgiveness are informative here, for they do not seem to dismiss the conditions of Jeremy's apology but rather to affirm it in all its humility. In fact, it is the structural definition of forgiveness as something sought and granted between states that Derrida seeks to dispel. He notes that in the aftermath of the Holocaust and the Nuremberg trials, Hannah Arendt wrote that forgiveness can only occur where one can properly judge, in order to evaluate the truth and punish the guilty (Derrida 2001: 59). Arendt's assertions form the basis of Derrida's thinking on forgiveness, if only as a platform from which to articulate an alternative set of claims. For forgiveness to be subject to an evaluation of judgment, an architecture of power—in other words, a sovereignty—must be established. However, it is Derrida's "dream" in this text to sever the link between forgiveness and sovereignty, to make forgiveness pure and unconditional (59). A forgiveness that emanates from a sovereign enterprise or entity is always infected with the violence that marks every founding claim to sovereignty. Even nations whose claim to sovereignty is made in the name of the people and the aspiration to justice and freedom are always founded in violence, because the establishment of the sovereign is always prior to "the law or legitimacy it founds" (57).[6]

It for this reason that Derrida insists that forgiveness must have no tie, residual or otherwise, to legal or justice systems. Moreover, it must not be aimed at achieving a reconciliation, a return to a previous state of affairs, what he calls a "normalization." In other words, for forgiveness truly to achieve its mandate, it cannot participate in the politics of the possible—what can be achieved through an apology or via the granting of forgiveness. Rather, it can only ever seek to engage with the horizon of its own impossibility. Impossibility—the unforgivable—marks both the inauguration and the limit of the force or usefulness of forgiveness (Derrida 2001: 30-31). For forgiveness to be oriented toward what is forgivable is to amputate the vitality of forgiveness and render it redundant; the forgivable is, by its very nature, always already cocooned within the realm of forgiveness. Like the category of the witness discussed above, forgiveness must announce itself in relation to the conditions of its own negation. The horizon of impossibility places forgiveness permanently between presence and absence; in doing so, it marks forgiveness as a site of ruin, but one from which potential and hope are simultaneously always in the process of emergence.

The poignant question that animates Judith Butler's recent book, *Precarious Life*—"what is a grievable life?"—is surely also relevant here (2004: 20). Like Derrida, Butler eschews the legal frameworks delineating personhood and consequently marking out the normative contours of the grievable life. For Butler, the primary, radical component of grief is the way in which it serves to connect us indiscriminately to the other; how grief "tear[s] us from ourselves, bind[s] us to others and transport[s] us, undo[es] us, implicate[s] us in lives that are not our own, irreversibly, if not fatally" (Butler 2004: 25). It is the vulnerability of grief that Butler seeks to re-imagine, not as a form of weakness but as the basis on which to build a new kind of community unburdened by the designations and fractures of identity politics.

A new politics, she asserts, lies in keeping open the "unbearability" of grief and making it the basis of a new commonality. In seeking to keep the radically connective tissues of vulnerability and grief closed, violence itself enters into a strange zone of abdication or effacement. In fact, it is (at least) a double effacement. By closing down the material and ethical possibilities that present themselves through a public articulation of grief, or by denying the impossibilities of forgiveness and operationalizing the apology within a purely instrumental, future-oriented framework, the victimized bodies of the past are negated and violence itself disappears from the tools of state power. The denial of grief and the negation of the impossibility of forgiveness, a denial of the dead—which, to be clear, is violence *par excellence*, violence raised to its highest standard—is what I am calling this double effacement of violence, an erasure not only of the material traces of violence but of violence itself. However, as we have seen elsewhere, the dead do not just quietly disappear; they linger, they call out and they haunt.[7]

In pointing to this double abdication of violence, Butler gestures to the largely hidden cultural and political mechanisms at work which deem some lives ungrievable or not worthy of grieving. The ungrievable life is reminiscent here of Agamben's category of *homo sacer*, the life that has the capacity to be killed but not sacrificed, and is thus held "in a zone of indistinction" by dint of its inclusion in the political order by the fact of its exclusion (1999: 9, 73). Butler argues that

> we have to consider how the norm governing who will be a grievable human is circumscribed and produced in these acts of permissible and celebrated public grieving, how they sometimes operate in tandem with a prohibition on the public grieving of other's lives, and how this differential allocation of grief serves the derealizing aims of (military) violence.... In this sense we have to ask about the condition under which a grievable life is excluded and maintained, and through what logic of exclusion, what practice of effacement and denominalization? (Butler 2004: 37-38)

If we can place Jeremy's apology within the logic of forgiveness or "grievability"— and I believe we can—it tells us a lot about the way in which Hiroshima and Nagasaki operate as mobile sites of bodily ruin, even after more than sixty years. Jeremy's apology seeks no redress, no outcome and no finality, and it is not met with any reaction but grief—a grief that itself was met with no urge to contain or mollify. More than this, Jeremy's statement rejects, by its very existence, the role of nation-states to seek or grant such states of absolution. It seeks and finds only the recognition of its own impossibility, and it is there it grounds its ethical truth or authenticity. Actively recognizing the impossibility of its own terms—its marginal, disempowered status, its inability to make up for the past—it issues forth not simply in spite of these limitations but also because of them. Speaking to its own impossibility, it achieves the ethical not by attempting to exorcise ruin but by acknowledging it. Moreover, even though the apology and the grief it is met with act from locations of impossibility—or, perhaps, *because* they do—both utterances radically potentialize new, emergent forms of connection and becoming that, by evading sovereign forms of control, are enormously threatening to state power.

By contrast, museum representations of Hiroshima and Nagasaki in New Mexico operate to mould and tightly constrain the memory of the bombings into a patriotic and highly technocentric narrative. These exhibitionary narratives either ignore the human cost of the bombs altogether and focus on the bombs as extraordinary national technological achievements, or perform a rhetorical and philosophical trick by trading the category of "Japanese lives lost" for the hypothetical, but much more potent, category of "American lives saved." Here, grief is displaced in favour of relief; lives lost are replaced by lives saved. Museum displays of Hiroshima and Nagasaki in New Mexico are emblematic of the violence of effacement Butler discusses. The lives of the Japanese victims are effaced in these exhibits, which act as media through which sovereignty "re-kills" the already-dead victims of the past in order to rejuvenate itself.

Jeremy's apology, which both is and is not a seeking of forgiveness, reveals the ways in which the after-effects of Hiroshima and Nagasaki greatly exceed the normative containers in which they are placed and by which we, almost casually now, understand them. New Mexico's nuclear museums, which attempt to cast America's memory of the atomic bomb through the official lens of scientific achievement, turn the logic of logocentrism on its head; instead of a "metaphysics of presence," we encounter a metaphysics of *absence*. The violent results, however, are the same. A crude but clever machinery of exclusion is installed, whereby absence precludes presence and vice versa. In this scenario, time and history exist independently of the bodies that live them. The absence of any portrayal or discussion of the human and material devastation of Hiroshima and Nagasaki forecloses the need to contemplate or even *know* of these effects. Again and again, the violence of Hiroshima and Nagasaki is re-enacted to suture the tears in the sovereign fabric. The irony is that the sovereign is both unable and unwilling to limit the ruins to the past.

...

The cultural and memorial politics of Hiroshima and Nagasaki in America exceed the national or state frames that sanction official memory, which occurs in places such as museums and exhibitions. In thinking beyond these monopolistic forms, I have tried to track the ways in which Hiroshima and Nagasaki erupt at unexpected times and places, defying the logocentrism of absence and the discrete periodization of historical time, if only momentarily, and coming to reside in the virtual vicissitudes of the body. Here, Hiroshima and Nagasaki lie largely dormant, not interfering with the everyday circulation of culture. Nevertheless, they occasionally emerge with force and impact, catalyzed as affects that slide into anger, sadness, despair, guilt, grief or sorrow—wounds that suddenly appear, erupting and interrupting, breaking through the silence of everyday anaesthesia.[8]

Taking a cue from Walter Benjamin, I have tried to extend the concept of ruin to these corporeal appearances of Hiroshima and Nagasaki. In locating the ruins of Hiroshima and Nagasaki in bodily eruptions of affect, I seek a way to examine the lasting effects of Hiroshima and Nagasaki in American locales where the material destruction and the dead of those cities are largely absent. The corporeal ruins of Hiroshima and Nagasaki catch up with individuals long after and far away from the event itself, washing over bodies that have no apparent connection to the ruins, save for a hazy, accidental relationship of nationality. So, while ruin exists here as a material condition of the history of Japan's atomic bombings, it is not exactly an objective place "out there" that can be identified, mapped and archaeologically excavated. Instead, ruin here is an expression of the condition of bodies caught within the sovereign logic of permanent exception, a place that Agamben describes as a profound "zone of indistinction" (1998: 5). Ruin, as a bodily realization of sovereign indistinction, nullifies another, perhaps lower order of sovereign logic, the binary code of presence and absence by which the state attempts to control the memorial status of Hiroshima and Nagasaki in America. Ruin vacillates between presence and absence, increasingly blurring the differences between the two, making them harder and harder to identify without reference to one another.

But the bodily ruins of Hiroshima and Nagasaki are not simply expressions of the despair of being caught in the continuously renewing violence of sovereignty. The materiality of ruin, its corporeality, makes sure of that. As Massumi has written, the body works as the edge at which virtuality seeps into actuality (2002: 43). The virtual quality of ruin, mediated by the body, ensures that ruin always exceeds or escapes the total enclosure of sovereignty. If ruin were a geographical feature of landscapes, it would, according to Deleuze and Guattari, striate the smooth landscapes that sovereignty seeks. The transition of ruin from virtual to actual, its seepage into the body, is the source of its potential. For Benjamin, ruin was allegorical. It pointed to the disasters of the past while hinting at the potential of a future that learned from those historical mistakes. Ruins were tangible symbols of the simultaneity of past disasters and future becomings. Ruins as affective bodily outbursts are not allegorical in the way that Benjamin's ruins were. Bodies contain, in the very structure of affect, an unassimilable aspect that turns ruin outward and reveals the possibility for something else. This ruin confronts the impossibility of witnessing with the poetics of testimony, and the impossibility of forgiveness with the apology that does not seek forgiveness. Ruin operates here as an awareness of bodies' paradoxical tenacity, and as such it points toward hope, a hope that is not an orientation toward a specific future but an openness, a "capacity" to experience the possibilities embedded in the future.

Notes

1. For a fascinating analysis of these ruins, particularly the environmental legacy of the American nuclear complex, see Kultez (1998).

2. My use of the term virtual, here and throughout this essay, draws on Brian Massumi's description of the virtual as a "realm of potential" or "lived paradox where what are normally opposites coexist, coalesce and connect" (2002: 91).

3. See Dominick LaCapra (1999) for an important discussion of the non-binary distinction between "absence" and "loss" and their respective relationships to the concept of (historical) trauma. Most important for our purposes here is LaCapra's observation that the two terms are too often conflated, with deleterious effects for both the comprehension of past traumas and the ability to work through them. LaCapra's basic distinction sees loss as historically rooted in particular events, whereas absence must be situated "transhistorically" and is ambivalent, unspecific and not amenable to practical solutions or strategies in the way that historical losses might be. The main problem, as LaCapra sees it, of "converting" absence to loss is the possibility of asserting a "misplaced nostalgia or utopian politics in quest of a new totality or fully unified community." Conversely, in carelessly exchanging loss for absence, "one faces the impasse of an endless melancholy, an impossible mourning" (698).

4. For a compelling argument that proceeds along these lines, see Stoler (2008).

5. Based on conversations with staff and volunteers and using past museum publications as a guide, let me say that, although the location of the museum is now different than it was in 1976, the display of Little Boy seems to have changed very little from the time that Akira Yasui visited to the times I visited between 2003 and 2005. Little Boy, along with Fat Man, constitute the museum's premier attractions and they are among the first exhibits encountered as one moves through the weapons exhibit in the back half of the museum. Little Boy is mounted on a squat black metal pedestal and, although significantly smaller than Fat Man, is 3 metres (10 feet) long and .75 metres (2.5 feet) wide. A small black placard with white writing reveals just the barest details of the bomb: its technical specifications, including its explosive "yield"; some details regarding its invention and construction; and, finally, the fact of its use on August 6, 1945.

6. Elsewhere, Derrida has elaborated on the violent underpinnings of sovereign foundations in greater detail. See, for example, "Declarations of Independence" in Derrida (2002).

7. For an extended and fascinating discussion on ghostliness, see Gordon (1997).

8. On anaesthesia, see: Buck Morss (1992); Stewart (2000).

References

Agamben, Giorgio. 1999. *Remnants of Auschwitz: The Witness and the Archive.* Trans. Daniel Heller-Roazen. New York: Zone Books.

Benjamin, Walter. 1968. *Illuminations.* New York: Schocken Books.

———. 2002. *The Arcades Project.* New York: Harvard University Press/Belknap Press.

Buck-Morss, Susan. 1989. *The Dialectics of Seeing: Walter Benjamin and the Arcades Project*. Cambridge, MA: MIT Press.

———. 1992. Aesthetics and Anaesthetics: Walter Benjamin's Artwork Essay Reconsidered. *October* 62(Fall): 3-41.

Butler, Judith. 2004. *Precarious Life: The Powers of Mourning and Violence*. New York: Verso.

Caruth, Cathy. 1996. *Unclaimed Experience: Trauma, Narrative and History*. Baltimore, MD: Johns Hopkins University Press.

Cvetkovich, Ann. 2003. *An Archive of Feelings: Trauma, Sexuality and Lesbian Public Cultures*. Durham, NC: Duke University Press.

Deleuze, Gilles and Félix Guattari. 1987. *A Thousand Plateaus: Capitalism and Schizophrenia*. Trans. Brian Massumi. Minneapolis: University of Minnesota Press.

Derrida, Jacques. 1976. *Of Grammatology*. Baltimore and London: Johns Hopkins University Press.

———. 1994. *Archive Fever: A Freudian Impression*. Chicago and London: University of Chicago Press.

———. 2001. *On Cosmopolitanism and Forgiveness*. New York and London: Routledge.

———. 2002. *Negotiations: Interventions and Interviews*, edited and translated by Elizabeth Rottenburg. Palo Alto, CA: Stanford University Press.

Feldman, Allen. 1994. On Cultural Anesthesia: From Desert Storm to Rodney King. *Cultural Anthropology* 21(2): 404-18.

Gordon, Avery. 1997. *Ghostly Matters: Haunting and the Sociological Imagination*. Minneapolis: University of Minnesota Press.

Kultez, Valerie. 1998. *The Tainted Desert: Environmental and Social Ruin in the American West*. New York: Routledge.

LaCapra, Dominick. 1999. Trauma, Absence, Loss. *Critical Inquiry* 25(Summer): 696-727.

Maclear, Kyo. 2003. The Limits of Vision: *Hiroshima Mon Amour* and the Subversion of Representation. *Witness and Memory: The Discourse of Trauma*, edited by Ana Douglass and Thomas A. Vogler, 233-47. London and New York: Routledge.

Masco, Joseph. 2008. "Survival Is Your Business": Engineering Ruins and Affect in Nuclear America. *Cultural Anthropology* 23(2): 361-98.

Massumi, Brian. 2002. *Parables for the Virtual: Movement, Affect, Sensation*. Durham, NC: Duke University Press.

Resnais, Alain (dir.). 1959. *Hiroshima Mon Amour* (film).

Stewart, Kathleen. 2000. Real American Dreams (Can be Nightmares). *Cultural Studies and Political Theory*, edited by Jodi Dean. Ithaca: Cornell University Press.

Stoler, Ann Laura. 2008. Imperial Debris: Reflections on Ruin and Ruination. *Cultural Anthropology* 23(2): 191-219.

Taussig, Michael. 1999. *Defacement: Public Secrecy and the Labour of the Negative*. Palo Alto, CA: Stanford University Press.

Mary Alemany-Galway

Peter Jackson's Use of Hollywood Film Genres in *The Lord of the Rings* trilogy and New Zealand's anti-Nuclear Stance

ABSTRACT

In his screen adaptation of J. R. R. Tolkien's book, Peter Jackson appeals to the audience's familiarity with a number of film genres, which are themselves related to the literary genres that Tolkien drew upon. In many of his films, Jackson uses the familiar modes of Hollywood genres but gives them some peculiar New Zealand twists. My article explores Jackson's use of multiple genres in the *Lord of the Rings* trilogy and the ways in which his appropriation of these genres evinces particular national concerns, especially those concerning nuclear power. The films fall within the fantasy genre but also feature elements of the war film and the horror film, and it is his use of these genres that I will discuss.

RÉSUMÉ

L'Anneau autour de la Comté : une lecture de l'utilisation par Peter Jackson des genres hollywoodiens dans la trilogie du Seigneur des Anneaux à la lumière de la position antinucléaire de la Nouvelle-Zélande

Dans son adaptation à l'écran du livre de J. R. R. Tolkien, Peter Jackson a recours à la familiarité du public avec un certain nombre de genres filmiques, qui sont eux-mêmes liés aux genres littéraires dont Tolkien s'est inspiré. Dans la plupart de ses films, Jackson utilise les modes familiers des genres hollywoodiens mais en leur donnant un tour néo-zélandais particulier. Mon article explorera l'utilisation que fait Jackson de genres multiples dans la trilogie du Seigneur des Anneaux et la manière par laquelle cette appropriation de ces genres élude certaines préoccupations nationales, en particulier celles concernant le nucléaire. Les films relèvent du genre fantastique, mais présentent également des éléments des films de guerre et des films d'horreur, et c'est de cette utilisation de ces genres que je discuterai.

In his screen adaptation of J. R. R. Tolkien's *The Lord of the Rings* (1954), Peter Jackson appeals to the audience's familiarity with a number of film genres. My article will explore the use of Hollywood genres in the *Lord of the Rings* trilogy (Peter Jackson, 2001-2003), and the ways in which Jackson's appropriation of these genres evinces particular national concerns, especially those concerning nuclear power. As Douglas Kellner points out, both the books and the films invite a plurality of allegorical readings (2006: 18). However, I am interested here only in the possible meanings particular to the New Zealand context in which the films were made. According to Kristin Thompson, Jackson's *Rings* are popular genre films that incorporate conventions from various film genres into their overarching fantasy structure (2007: 57). I am interested here in the ways the films incorporate elements of the war film and the horror film within the fantasy film genre.

As Stephen Crofts points out, the idea of national cinema has historically been informed by the desire to develop a non-Hollywood cinema, particularly an art cinema. In the 1960s, radical political theorists extended the notion of national cinema to include films made in the contexts of postcolonial struggles. Until the 1980s, ideas of national cinema tended to focus only on films produced within a certain territory, while ideas of the nation-state were defined in essentialist terms. However, the effects of the migrations and diasporas resulting from post-Second World War processes of decolonization have informed recent accounts of national cinemas. These accounts seek to resist the homogenizing fictions of nationalism and to recognize these fictions' historical variability and contingency. The cultural hybridity of nation-states has also been noted. Thus U.S. culture, for example, is now seen to play a part in most national cultures (Crofts 1988: 385-86). This interaction is evident in all of Jackson's films, in which he uses Hollywood genres but gives them a peculiar New Zealand twist (Grant 1999).

Some of Jackson's films, for instance, seem to have an anti-U.S. message embedded in them. In *Bad Taste* (1989), an alien power decimates a small New Zealand town in order to send back its inhabitants as raw meat to the mother planet—a good metaphor for the process of exploitation of one society by another, and could be seen as an image of a great world power's relationship with a small marginal country like New Zealand. *Meet the Feebles* (1989) is a scatological version of an American children's television program that has colonized many a young mind. *Forgotten Silver* (1995) is a mockumentary that parodies New Zealanders' need to claim that they are the best in the world. These films point to the complex relationship between a small nation like New Zealand and the world's largest power (Alemany-Galway 2006: 31-43).

Bill Willmott, a New Zealander writing during the Cold War, explains that for him, though the American way of life is attractive, it involves the heaviest exploitation of energy and other resources the world has ever known. It also requires the exploitation of other societies, for without the cheap food and raw materials extracted from the poorer societies, America would not be so affluent (Willmott 1989: 19).

Willmott points out that while imperialist nationalism can often be dangerous, New Zealand's anti-imperialist type of nationalism may offer the only hope of altering the present course of history by preventing the domination of the world by the superpowers. The confrontation with America that followed New Zealand's stand against nuclear weapons entering the country in 1984 brought home to many New Zealanders the possibility that the country might have to face economic and military threats. New Zealand's adoption of a nuclear-free stance has driven the importance of national identity issues home to many there (2). It is interesting to note that Jackson was born on October 31, 1961—the day before the Soviet Union detonated a fifty-megaton hydrogen bomb. At the time, the U.S.S.R. and the U.S. were boasting about who had the biggest arsenal of bombs, and the world was just months away from a missile crisis in Cuba that almost resulted in nuclear war (Pryor 2004: 25).

I argue that New Zealand's anti-nuclear stance influenced Jackson in his approach to adapting *The Lord of the Rings* for the screen. One could view the Ring of Power itself as analogous to nuclear power. Jackson started the first film of the trilogy, *The Fellowship of the Ring* (Peter Jackson, 2001), with Galadriel's voice recounting the history of the Ring and emphasizing how the fate of the world will be determined by the outcome of a battle between good and evil. This, however, is not how Tolkien's book starts. In addition, at the end of the first film, Galadriel tells Frodo that even the smallest can save the world. This statement is not part of her speech in this scene in the book, and it suggests that Jackson associates New Zealand's fate with Frodo's since New Zealand itself is a small country of only four million people. When asked by *Variety* if he would move to Hollywood, Jackson replied, "Why would we leave the Shire to go and live in Mordor?" (Calder 2000: 10). In an interview, Phillipa Boyens, one of the scriptwriters for the films, declares that Tolkien's fantasy asks if we could unmake something that we know should never have come into being. For her this is not just a straight allegory of the atomic bomb (Hardy 2008: 207). I do not claim that the film is a straight allegory of the atomic bomb either, but for at least one of the scriptwriters the link to issues surrounding the use of nuclear power is there. I lived in New Zealand from 1997-2007. Every day I would walk past a fence on which was written "Keep New Zealand Nuclear Free." I found that this was a highly popular sentiment throughout the country. And, as Ian Conrich points out, the New Zealand industry and the national population have embraced the film as distinctly Kiwi (Conrich 2006: 120).

The Lord of the Rings was written before the creation of the atomic bomb, and J. R. R. Tolkien had very complex ideas on the subject of war. The book's depiction of the Ring of Power might prophetically speak to current global dilemmas, but I do not believe that Tolkien was a pacifist like his contemporary Bertrand Russell. Janet Brennan Croft believes that Tolkien greatly desired peace but felt that war was sometimes necessary. According to her, Tolkien was not a pacifist, nor did he appear to agree with pacifists that their philosophy would ensure peace (2004: 138).

Tolkien's Ring, a book written by David Day and illustrated by Alan Lee—one of the chief designers for the films—delves into the historical and mythic influences on Tolkien's concept of the Ring of Power (Day 1994). Day explains that the secret of the Ring dates back to the secret of the smelting and forging of iron, which is believed to have been discovered around 1000 BCE in the region of the Caucasus Mountains. Day suggests that this discovery was the atomic secret of its day, as iron was forged into weapons and tools, allowing those who possessed the secret to conquer and often exterminate those who did not. Before changing the face of the world, the Iron Age engendered a large number of rites, myths and symbols, which have reverberated throughout the spiritual history of humanity. The ring-quest myths of most cultures contain certain constant features: the magician, the smith, the warrior, the sword, the dwarf, the maiden, the treasure and the dragon (Day 1994: 26-27). These mythic elements clearly appear in Tolkien's book. However, he brings something original to the way that he develops the story.

According to Day, Tolkien deemed the allegorical view too narrow for his tale. Nevertheless, he did believe readers were free to apply this tale to their circumstances. Although *The Lord of the Rings* was written during the war years (Tolkien began work on the book in 1937), it was not published until 1954. By this time, the atomic bomb had become a central concern to many. The student anti-war and ban-the-bomb movements of the 1960s, as well as the hippie dropout culture, saw Frodo as the perfect anti-hero. As Day points out, activists did not miss the parallels between the Ring of Power and the atomic bomb in the late 1960s and early 1970s. Day claims one might see in *The Lord of the Rings* the reversal of the traditional ring quest. The Iron Age mentality of "might equals right"—which underlies the traditional quest—ends with the nuclear age, when possession of such power entails mutual destruction (177-82).

The War Movie

Jackson himself has a longstanding interest in war, and some of his earliest films, which he made as a child, were war movies. He once attended a memorial service at Gallipoli, site of the Australia and New Zealand Army Corps (ANZAC) defeat in the First World War. As early as 1988, Jackson planned to make a war movie based on Gallipoli, but dropped the idea after seeing Steven Spielberg's *Saving Private Ryan* (Pryor 2004: 340). Of course, *Lord of the Rings* is in good part a war movie, and battle scenes form a large part of the film. New Zealand itself has taken part in both world wars as a colony of Britain, providing resources and manpower for that country's wars. In "War and National Identity," Jock Phillips states that from the early 1900s on, New Zealand boys were inculcated with a knightly model of manhood that essentially imitated the values of the English public school. *The School Journal*, first started in 1907 for distribution to schools, contained endless homilies on chivalry, loyalty, service and discipline (Phillips 1989: 95). As Tolkien drew upon these stories of knightly valour, these values also underlie Jackson's films and their depictions of male characters who battle on the side of good (Tolkien 1983a:75). As Phillips points out, a pacifist idealism and the idea of a national identity forged through war co-exist in present-day New Zealand. ANZAC parades are still popular even as New Zealand refuses entry to all nuclear-powered or nuclear-armed ships (Phillips 1989: 107).

According to Thomas Schatz, this sort of basic conflict in the values held by a society is central to the formulae of popular genres (1981: 24). The possible disharmony between basic social values is usually not acknowledged in genre films, and *Lord of the Rings* follows this trend by both glorifying war and the ideals of pacifism. This conflict is already present in Tolkien's books, which are influenced by his own experiences as a soldier in the First World War and as a besieged Englishman in the Second World War (Chance 1992: 14). The First World War was so devastating that the cultural products that depicted it in the aftermath were overwhelmingly pacifist in tone. As Thomas Doherty explains, the retrospective films of the interwar years projected the futility of combat and the nobility of pacifism (1993: 87-88).

The construction of the Second World War film had its own peculiarities. Contrary to the usual construction of the American film, the narrative focused not on the lone hero, but, rather, on the regular guys who made up the combat unit. As Jeanine Basinger demonstrates in her book *The World War II Combat Film*, the real champion of the genre is the combat unit, the crew of male characters from different parts of American society who bring complementary skills to the task at hand. These men work and fight together in the service of the nation (Basinger 1986: 51-52).

In the Second World War combat film, there appears a conflict of values that one could associate with the conflict between the ideals of pacifism and the ideals of war. Within the combat unit itself, the ideals of peaceful harmony and communitarian purpose are predominant. Nevertheless, that unit is forged for the sole purpose of effective warfare. The "fellowship of the Ring" resembles the combat unit in that it too is forged from members of different races who come together to fight the power of evil. However, this group differs from the combat unity in that its primary purpose is not to fight, but to destroy the Ring of Power. In his conception of the fellowship, Tolkien comes close to the idea of the United Nations as a peacekeeping institution in his conception. Michael Stanton argues that, for Tolkien, the best hope for eventual peace and order in a world of several intelligent species is mutual respect (2001: 125).

Jackson's films also emphasize the idea of a fellowship of diverse cultures forming to save the world. Jackson claims that the films are a labour of love made by fans of the book. He hopes that those who see the films will "experience something of the complexity, the magic and the fascinating themes found in Tolkien's book." (Sibley 2001: 7) He also states that:

> the Elves, the Dwarves and Hobbits of Middle-Earth all live in their own isolated communities. And, just as in our own world everybody's culture—European, American, South American, African, Australian—represents the evolution of those people through history, so it is in Middle-Earth. Which is why we have taken so much care in building cultural histories for the characters in these films. (19)

This focus on the coming together of different cultures to save the world is central to the book and the films, and it is for this reason that Faramir is such an important character. Faramir is the brother of Boromir, the warrior who wants to use the Ring to save Middle-Earth. Faramir, however, willingly lets Frodo take the Ring to be destroyed. The significance of this action is heightened in the film version of *The Two Towers* (2002), as Faramir first takes Sam and Frodo to Osgilith, and then changes his mind and lets them go. In the book, Faramir makes the decision to let Frodo take the Ring to Mordor in a cave in which they have taken shelter.

Jackson's films are mostly preoccupied with depictions of war, and it could certainly be argued that it is in great part a war film trilogy. Nevertheless, the films were made in the 21st century; although they can be linked to the themes of First and Second World War films, they are also influenced by the attitudes to war displayed by more contemporary American war films. The legacy of the war in Vietnam and its problematic outcome has affected the way Hollywood has depicted wars since the 1970s. Michael Hammond argues that the Vietnam War's inconclusiveness entailed a blurring of boundaries between good and evil in Hollywood war films. For example, Robert Altman's 1970 *MASH*, Michael Cimino's 1978 *The Deer Hunter* and Francis Ford Coppola's 1979 *Apocalypse Now* all use and rework generic conventions common to Second World War combat films. However, they significantly change these conventions in order to acknowledge, at least tacitly, the defeat in Vietnam, using that war as the setting for meditations on futility, duty and sacrifice (Hammond 2002: 62-65).

The Horror Movie

Later films about the Vietnam War depict the guerrilla warfare fought in the jungle as a kind of living nightmare akin to that constructed by horror movies. Oliver Stone's 1986 *Platoon*, for example, draws on the familiar figure of the "monster in the swamp" (66). Of course, *The Lord of the Rings* trilogy also uses many aspects of the horror genre in its construction of the enemies that threaten "the world of men." The orcs and various monsters that make up the armies of Saruman and Sauron borrow obviously from the horror film. Even more interesting are the ruling powers of evil—Saruman and Sauron themselves. Christopher Lee plays Saruman in the trilogy. This is a direct reference to the horror genre, as Lee is famous for appearing in Britain's Hammer Film Productions' horror films (Wells 2000: 67).

In many ways, Saruman and Sauron resemble the "mad scientists" that have appeared in many horror films and have their origin in Mary Shelley's *Frankenstein* (1818). Although they are wizards and magicians rather than scientists, scientists in horror films often closely resemble magicians. As Andrew Tudor points out, horror movie science has much in common with magic. Magical knowledge can be positive, or it can be a corrupting influence on those who hunger for knowledge itself (Tudor: 1989: 87). Although Mary Shelley wrote *Frankenstein* in 1816, the issues raised by the story are even more pertinent today. In the modern age, the monster that threatens or destroys its maker can function as a metaphor for nuclear weapons (Worland 2007: 175).

If Dr. Frankenstein creates a monster in his search for knowledge, the threat created by the scientists who invented atomic power is one of total annihilation. According to Tudor, by the 1950s and 1960s the key concept was radiation, and the key opposition was not between life and death, but between normal and abnormal physical matter. Science itself is thus at fault. By investigating that which we should not—by splitting the atom, the fundamental constituent of matter—science occasions the monstrous attack (Tudor 1989: 88-89). In *The Lord of the Rings*, this idea is suggested by the awakening of Balrog, the fiery monster from the deep that Gandalf fights in the mines of Moria. Balrog lurks in the mines because the dwarves greedily dug too deep and awakened the monster. Jackson emphasizes the importance of this fiery monster by beginning the second film of the trilogy with a reiteration of the battle between Gandalf and Balrog.

Although the dwarves are not really magician-scientists like the wizards, they are associated with technology and manufacturing, and Tolkien himself makes a connection between factories and bombs. For him, "it is after all possible for a rational man ... to arrive at the condemnation ... of progressive things like factories, or the machine guns and bombs that appear to be their most natural and inevitable, dare we say 'inexorable', products" (Tolkien 1983: 150).

According to Tudor, the belief that science is dangerous is as central to the horror film as the belief in the malevolent inclinations of vampires and other supernatural beings. The mad scientist figure encompasses both the misguided obsessive seeking knowledge for its own sake and those traditional villains who want no more than to rule the world. Disorder in these movies can be a direct consequence of an individual scientist's actions or the unanticipated consequence of scientific investigation and discovery (Tudor 1989: 133). Tolkien believed that science and magic were similar processes, as demonstrated by his assertion that:

> magic produces, or pretends to produce, an alteration in the Primary World. It does not matter by whom it is said to be practiced, fay or mortal, it remains distinct from the other two; it is not an art but a technique; its desire is power in this world, domination of things and wills. (Tolkien 1983: 143)

Tudor states that the ultimate power of domination is to destroy life. The atom bomb could annihilate all life on earth through the radioactive poisoning of the atmosphere. In the horror movies of the 1950s and 1960s, the primary cause of scientific disaster was atomic energy, and authorities, scientists and ordinary people were the major resource for defence. However, from the late 1970s on, the threat was posed by the military and the state rather than by science. The destruction that was once a result of scientific over-ambition, or individual misuse of knowledge became part of the activities of the very authorities that were once central to the world's defence. This presumed conspiracy between institutions of science, state, military and industry is a thread running through many modern horror movies even when they do not make overt reference to science (Tudor 1989: 134-52).

Arthur Morgan examines Tolkien's conception of the Ring and its relation to Wagner's opera cycle *Der Rings das Nibelungen* (1848-1874). For Morgan, Tolkien moves a critique of power to the centre of the narrative and defines evil as the will to dominate. Sometime in the year preceding the outbreak of the Second World War, Tolkien adopted Wagner's conception of the Ring as conferring unlimited power and the ability to destroy identity. Hitler's dictatorship was the first dictatorship of an industrial state that employed the mass media to manipulate the minds of others. Of course, there is not a direct correlation between the Ring and modern technology. Rather, for Morgan, Tolkien's book presents a correlation between psychology and materiality. Tolkien's myth recognizes that there is a Sauron in each of us; the Ring is a symbol of any means that we use to impose our wills on the world and its inhabitants (Morgan 1992: 17-26).

I believe that it is for this reason that the Ring is highlighted in the films. Jackson uses a number of devices to bring a malevolent life to this small object. He states that:

> This is just a regular-sized ring and yet you have to convey the power that makes it more than just a piece of metal on somebody's hand. So every time we show the Ring I use a close-up, I get in very tight with the camera so that it seems much bigger. In addition there are sound-effects with which we have created a presence, a sense that the Ring is alive and can almost be heard breathing. (Sibley 2001: 84)

In *The Lord of the Rings: The Mythology of Power*, Jane Chance describes the cultural context in which Tolkien's book achieved popularity. For readers, the book became popular during the Korean and Vietnam wars. Its success in the late 1960s coincided with worldwide student demonstrations. For college students and others, the U.S. government took on the guise of a Dark Lord demanding universal domination in tiny countries of little interest to most Americans. As well, the U.S. demanded the submission of Americans' individual rights and beliefs to the national demand for more combat troops in an alien country (Chance 1992: 5-9).

New Zealand in the 1960s was also affected by the worldwide student rebellions and the ideals of the counterculture. The idea of the USA as a threat to personal life and freedom is plainly pictured in Roger Donaldson's 1977 *Sleeping Dogs*, a film that is usually credited with initiating the contemporary film industry in New Zealand. In this film, the threat of dictatorship is internal, but the dominating New Zealand forces are aided by the USA. New Zealanders could also have associated the U.S. with the Dark Lord due to the nuclear tests that were being carried out in the Pacific by the U.S., France and Britain.

In 1962, people living in and around Auckland witnessed an unnatural glowing in the night sky during one of the tests. Roy Smith quotes one of these observers:

> Beams of light radiated from the northern horizon and intersected with each other through the blackness of the night. I climbed to the open balcony on the first floor of the old house and was arrested with awe as the sky pulsated with brilliant shafts of light. They were red and white. They extended across the night like ribs of a fan. They were spinning, they were intermingling. The sky was diffused with a ghastly brush of red. It was an unnerving spectacle. (2000: 13)

Smith states that the test had been conducted by the U.S. over Johnston Atoll, thousands of miles to the northeast of New Zealand. For New Zealanders, maintaining a belief in a pastoral paradise became difficult within the context of mutual assured destruction on a global scale. The perception that colonial and neocolonial powers were responsible for the threat of a nuclear war was central to the anti-nuclear movement in the Pacific, and became a focus of the campaign to establish a nuclear-free zone across the Pacific (13).

One of the predominant images that one takes from Jackson's films is that of a glowing red sky over the darkness of Mordor. Another predominant image is, of course, Sauron's eye, which flashes red beams of light across the landscape. These images are similar to those described by the New Zealander who observed the nuclear tests in the Pacific. And, like a nuclear blast, the fires of Sauron create a devastated wasteland around them. An earlier New Zealand film, Geoff Murphy's 1985 *The Quiet Earth*, also depicts what could result from a nuclear catastrophe: the earth emptied of any human beings but the two protagonists.

According to Smith, the anti-nuclear issue thrust New Zealand into the international spotlight. There were those within New Zealand who were opposed to the 1984 decision and said that it undermined the "Western" alliance. But, a significant number of New Zealanders actually felt less secure under the nuclear umbrella offered by the U.S. than they did if they distanced themselves from it. For the majority of the population this was an issue that had positive, even heroic, associations (26-27). In this context, it does seem as if one of the smallest nations might indeed save the world or, at least, set an example for other nations to follow in resisting the lure of nuclear weapons so as to make the world a safer place.

New Zealand's anti-nuclear stance can be seen in relation to Boromir's and Faramir's differing attitudes toward the ring. In the second installment of the film trilogy, Sam tells Faramir that Boromir died because he tried to take the Ring from Frodo, stating that "the Ring drove your brother mad." Although Boromir wanted to use the Ring to save Gondor and the world of men, Faramir understands that the Ring must be destroyed. He thus lets Frodo and Sam go, even though this contravenes the laws of his father and therefore his own life will be forfeited. New Zealand seems to take a similar stance when it opposes nuclear power. The atom bomb was used by the U.S. to end the Second World War and "save the world," but many fear that the proliferation of nuclear weapons may well mean the end of the world of men.

Of course, the Ring is not the atom bomb or even nuclear power per se. It symbolizes the destructive power of domination, and this power can take many forms. One of the powers that Sauron wields is the ability to see into the minds of others who use his instruments, and one of the film's predominant images is Sauron's glowing eye above the Dark Tower surveying the land and seeking to enter the minds of others. Jane Chance argues that Sauron's eye resembles Michel Foucault's "Eye of Power." In *Discipline and Punish*, Foucault describes the "panopticon," an 18th-century architectural device designed by Jeremy Bentham consisting of a watchtower in the centre of a circular prison building. Since the doorways of the prisoners' cells look out at the watchtower, the prisoners feel as if they are always being watched, and therefore internalize that feeling (Chance 1992: 147-55). The image of the panopticon has become a tool for many writers to describe the workings of the dominant ideology, in that we internalize the myths and values of our society and become our own prison-wardens. In Tolkien's book, the eye of Sauron enters men's minds and tries to control them. The Ring itself seems to control the minds of men in order to use them. The third film in the trilogy, *The Return of the King* (2003), begins with the story of how Gollum got the Ring by killing the friend who had found it. Right from the beginning, he insists it is "mine, my precious." The power of domination is here expressed as an act of great selfishness that destroys life to possess an object. The scene that follows portrays an opposite act of unselfishness, or charity, as Sam gives Frodo some of their dwindling supply of food but doesn't eat any himself.

Perhaps what is portrayed here is the opposition of two important values in our world—that of capitalism, with its emphasis on individual desire and the power of money, and that of communal caring. If Mordor is the example of what extreme selfishness will bring, then Lórien is a portrayal of its opposite. Jane Chance maintains that Galadriel signals the principle of supernatural, communal harmony. Lórien offers the delight of living things—especially trees—and acceptance (Chance 1992: 49). Of course, it is Frodo's acceptance and toleration of Gollum that allows the happy ending to occur. For even Frodo cannot give up the Ring of Power in the end, and it is Gollum's leap to get it for himself that lands the Ring in the fires that will destroy it.

The conflict between individual freedom or self-interest, and social order or communal caring, underlies many American genres, so perhaps it is not extraordinary to find it in Jackson's films. For instance, this conflict is the basis of the classic Western, in which the lone cowboy is caught between his need for individual freedom and his need to settle down and become part of the community (Schatz 1981: 51). New Zealand society sees itself as very distinct from the rest of the world but it is also very influenced both by British culture and by American culture. In his description of New Zealand cinema, Roger Horrocks explains how both of these imperial centres have affected New Zealand culture, arguing that the influence of American capitalism has become especially strong today:

> There have been many moves to align New Zealand closely with the United States. Indeed, this has been (by implication) the main drive of government policy over the past fifteen years. In terms of popular culture, the current generation of young New Zealanders (both Maori and Pakeha) is the most Americanized ever. (Horrocks 1999: 129-37)

Horrocks goes on to describe New Zealand as full of diversities, disjunctions and incongruities, and one of the incongruities is certainly between the Americanization of its culture and the rural, egalitarian society that is part of its heritage (136). This juxtaposition also occurs in both the *Lord of the Rings* books and films. In the film version of *The Two Towers*, we hear the voice of Sauron speaking to Saruman, claiming that together they will rule the earth. Chance claims that Saruman has used his ingenuity like a capitalist, pursuing profit at any cost. He exploits the labour of slaves, and has turned the once-green valley into a wasteland to gain riches and power (Chance 1992: 64). In the book and the films, this image of industrial hell is juxtaposed with that of the farming community that is the Shire. The fight, in many ways, is to preserve the communal values of this rural haven. At the end, Sam is left to carry on his life in the Shire. Chance claims that this is because society is best maintained by the caretaker and the gardener, who nurture others and continue the work of the family (107).

There are many similarities between the depiction of the Shire and certain popular ideas of New Zealand. Conrich and Woods argues that the formation of national identity is dependent on the acceptance of certain myths. One of these, for New Zealand, is the idea that it is a pastoral paradise, clean and green. The most dominant and persistent New Zealand myth is of an Edenic garden, a natural utopia. This is a fantasy that was devised for the purpose of inventing the country's identity. It helped to bring in immigrants and later to sell New Zealand's food abroad. At the same time, New Zealand is viewed as the premier nation for high living standards, and a popular belief prevails that it offers "a great place to bring up kids," security and equality, and a society of good neighbours. Recently, New Zealand has experienced a boom in tourism. Visitors from heavily industrialized nations appear seduced by images of a pre-urbanized, uninhabited landscape (Conrich and Woods 2000: 8-9).

New Zealand thus seems to hold itself between those two extremes of capitalist greed and communal caring. This was presumably true from the country's naissance, as it was founded as a settler colony, which prospered by disenfranchising the indigenous Maori. Of course, many settler colonies (like Canada and the U.S.) have similar histories, in that they appropriated the native people's land in order to build a better world for themselves. I believe that this conflict of values is central to the films and is one reason why the depiction of Gollum's internal battles is given such a predominant place. Frodo pities him because he knows what the temptation of the Ring is like since he carries it himself. In the second film of the trilogy, we see Gollum debating with his double, his evil side, his twin. The good twin wants to trust Frodo and help him, but the bad twin claims that Gollum can never have friends since he is a murderer. The values of trust, caring and friendship thus battle with those of suspicion, hatred and aggressive selfishness in this small pathetic figure, just as they do in present-day New Zealand or anywhere in the world.

The Fantasy Genre

The choice between these two sets of values is central to the book and to the films, as it is also a choice that Frodo, the central figure, must make. As Chance points out, Frodo is a hero on a mythic quest. In the first volume of the book, he encounters the continuum of life and death. In the second, against an historical backdrop (the history of the rise and fall of nations), he learns that moral understanding transcends accurate vision (Chance 1992: 110). This quest for moral understanding is also at the heart of the fantasy genre and, of course, *The Lord of the Rings* is a primary example of that genre. Tolkien himself states that, "there is indeed no better medium for moral teaching than a good fairy story" (1983: 72). That this is also true for Jackson becomes particularly evident in the last scene of *The Two Towers*. Here, Sam compares his and Frodo's predicament to the stories that really mattered, stories in which the characters kept fighting for the idea that there was some good in this world. Ian Pryor sees this as a courageous moment for Jackson:

> It is difficult to read this scene as anything other than an argument for the worth of fantasy in a complicated world. One of Jackson's only obvious statements of theme to date comes in the form of a defense of storytelling as a force linked to courage and good. (Pryor 2004: 304)

Tolkien claims that, for him, a real taste for fairy stories was "awakened by philology on the threshold of manhood; and quickened to full life by war" (Tolkien 1983b: 135). One wonders why this should be so, and the answer is undoubtedly complex. The influence of Tolkien's studies in philology can be seen in his assertion that "the mind that thought of light, heavy, grey, yellow, still, swift, also conceived of magic that would make heavy things light and able to fly, turn grey lead into yellow gold, and the still rock into swift water" (122). Perhaps, war also awakened in him a taste for fairy stories because it made him want the world to be other than it was. Tolkien believed that magic's ability to produce an alteration in the physical world entailed a capacity for domination. But fantasy, for him, was akin to the elvish craft of enchantment, which seeks not delusion or domination but shared enrichment, and seeks not slaves but partners in making and delight (143).

This way of defining fantasy brings Tolkien close to a utopian ideal of human relationships. Robert Crossley warns that no one should be fooled by Tolkien's political disclaimers into assuming that *The Lord of the Rings* lacks an ideology that is plainly, if somewhat eccentrically, utopian. In many important ways, Middle Earth is related to the Arcadian, green world of William Morris's *News from Nowhere* (1891) (Crossley 1982: 188). Morris clearly writes applied fantasy. Imagination, in his case, is put to the service of social welfare. *News from Nowhere* abolishes the organized misery of a consumer society by encouraging the universal exercise of creative imagination (179). As we have seen, this is the very purpose of fantasy or enchantment for Tolkien.

Crossley argues that had Tolkien kept his hobbits in the Shire and explored the arrangements of their pastoral life, *The Lord of the Rings* would belong to utopian literature. In sending the hobbits out to contend with an external enemy, he moved his narrative out of utopia and into Faerie (180). However, by Crossley's own account, the utopia of *News from Nowhere* has to be fought for. It only becomes fact "at the cost of generations of struggle, suffering, disappointment and bloodshed" (177-78). I believe that it is exactly this cost that Tolkien shows us in *The Lord of the Rings*. Even at the start, the Shire has its own strife and internal divisions, and, as Raymond H. Thompson states, modern fantasy explores currently relevant concepts such as the problems of power, the conflict between individual freedom and social responsibility, and the upheavals of change (Thompson 1982: 223). According to Wolfe, the primary basis of fantasy is that it is the literature of the impossible. Fantasy writers deliberately violate norms and facts essential to our conventional conception of "reality" in order to create an imaginary counter-structure of counter-norms (Wolfe 1982: 1). For this reason, the fantasy genre can suggest utopic worlds. Some fantasy films, such as Frank Capra's 1937 *Lost Horizon*, are also preoccupied with depicting utopias, worlds that seem ideal in contrast with our own reality.

Although the fantasy genre in film has not been written about as much as fantasy literature, Wade Jennings's article on the genre gives us a useful overview of its characteristics. He sees the primary element of fantasy as a central situation that defies rational or even pseudo-scientific explanation (Jennings 1988: 249). It is the very fact that fantasies deny natural laws that opens the door to freedom; characters find that they are free and can therefore choose. According to Jennings, this is the most significant theme to be found in fantasy films, as most films involve a journey that leads to necessary self-discovery, to a rejection of conventional values or previous understandings, and to a climax where the protagonist decides between two worlds (252). In Victor Fleming's 1939 *The Wizard of Oz*, Dorothy chooses to leave Oz and return to Kansas. For her, there is no place like home. In *Lost Horizon*, however, the protagonist chooses to return to the world of fantasy (Jennings 1988: 250-51).

Tolkien's *The Lord of the Rings* is built around a series of choices. Bilbo chooses to give up the Ring to Frodo, who undertakes the task of destroying it. Gandalf and Galadriel refuse to use the power of the Ring. These choices are highlighted in dramatic and intense scenes in the films. Boromir's choice is to use the Ring to save his people and he realizes his mistake too late. Faramir chooses to let the Ring and the hobbits go. As I have shown, the films' narratives highlight the importance of these decisions. The freedom to choose one set of values over another is also central to the debates that Gollum has with himself. And, of course, Frodo has to constantly fight the desire to put on the Ring, and even continues to struggle with himself on the edge of Mount Doom. The fact that the choice to be made is between two different worlds is emphasized at the end of the narrative, when Frodo collapses before entering Mount Doom and Sam tries to comfort him by talking to him about the Shire, and the sound of water and the touch of grass. Frodo replies that there is nothing between him and the wheel of fire, which he can see. Then Sam offers to carry him into Mount Doom so they can finally destroy the Ring of Power.

Jennings describes a particular kind of fantasy film, which he calls the philosophical fantasy. The point of which is to examine basic values—the very meaning of life—from the distance offered by fantasy. Such films may take us far away from ordinary reality, but it is nonetheless our reality that they comment on (257). Due to its examination of basic values, *The Lord of the Rings* can certainly be called a philosophical fantasy. For its characters, the choice is not just between good and evil, but also between a particular *type* of good and evil. As I have explained, the opposing values are those of power and domination over nature and humans versus those of caring and preservation of life. Although the idea of New Zealand as a pastoral paradise is a prevalent one, there are also darker aspects to that reality. As Jonathan Rayner explains, New Zealand's variety of landscapes can suggest an accommodating Edenic diversity or an imprisoning, infernal purgatory. This varied palette is thus useful in dramatic narratives of national, symbolic or spiritual significance. In the films of Vincent Ward, a New Zealand filmmaker, the natural landscape is seen to present the potential for both damnation and redemption (Rayner 2000: 39-40). The landscape of New Zealand is also used in this way in *The Lord of the Rings* trilogy, but it is not only the physical landscapes of New Zealand that Jackson's films portray. *The Lord of the Rings* films evidently address the spiritual and ideological concerns of the country's people.

This use of dramatic narratives to illustrate the lived dilemmas of the present can be seen in many New Zealand films. Perhaps the most nearly related to *The Lord of the Rings* is Vincent Ward's 1988 *The Navigator*. This is another fantasy film that starts at the time of the plague in a village in Medieval England whose inhabitants end up in contemporary New Zealand by climbing down a mineshaft. One of the sights they see in New Zealand is a television carrying footage of nuclear submarines and debates over the country's determination for "nuclear-free" status. Rayner explains that the apocalyptic threat embodied in these images reinforces the villagers' reaction to the appearance of a surfacing submarine as they cross Auckland harbor; "their fear of the Leviathan of the Day of Judgement is indivisible from contemporary global (but in this case poignantly national) fears of an arbitrarily imposed Armageddon," he writes (Rayner 2000: 46).

This pervasive fear has led New Zealand to opt for "nuclear-free" status, and this, in itself, is a choice made in full knowledge of possible repercussions. New Zealand has chosen certain values over others by insisting on its nuclear-free status. As I have demonstrated, it is precisely this kind of moral choice that is constantly being put forward by Jackson's *Lord of the Rings* films.

References

Alemany-Galway, Mary. 2006. Peter Jackson as a Postcolonial Filmmaker: National Cinema and Hollywood Genres. *Post Script* 25(2): 31-43.

Altman, Robert, dir. 1970. *MASH* (film). Aspen Productions, prod.

Basinger, Jeanine. 1986. *The World War II Combat Film: Anatomy of a Genre*. New York: Columbia University Press.

Calder, Peter. 2000. Kiwi Lord of Rings. *Variety* 389(9): 10.

Capra, Frank, dir. 1937. *Lost Horizon* (film). Columbia Pictures Corporation, prod.

Chance, Jane. 1992. *The Lord of the Rings: The Mythology of Power*. New York: Twayne Publishers.

Cimino, Michael, dir. 1978. *The Deer Hunter* (film). EMI Films, prod.

Conrich, Ian. 2006. A Land of Make Believe: Merchandising and Consumption of *The Lord of the Rings*. In *From Hobbits to Hollywood: Essays on Peter Jackson's Lord of the Rings*, edited by Ernest Mathijs and Murray Pomerance, 119-35. Amsterdam: Rodopi.

Conrich, Ian and David Woods, eds. 2000. Introduction. In *New Zealand—A Pastoral Paradise? Studies in New Zealand Culture* no. 6. Clifton, Nottingham: Kakapo Books.

Coppola, Francis Ford, dir. 1979. *Apocalypse Now* (film). Zoetrope Studios, prod.

Croft, Janet Brennan. 2004. *War and the Works of J. R. R. Tolkien*. London: Praeger.

Crofts, Stephen. 1988. Concepts in National Cinema. In *The Oxford Guide to Film Studies*, edited by John Hill and Pamela Church Gibson, 385-94. Oxford: Oxford University Press.

Crossley, Robert. 1982. Pure and Applied Fantasy, or From Faerie to Utopia. In *The Aesthetics of Fantasy in Literature and Art*, edited by Roger C. Schlobin, 176-91. Notre Dame, IN: University of Notre Dame Press.

Day, David. 1994. *Tolkien's Ring*. London: Harper Collins.

Doherty, Thomas. 1993. *Projections of War: Hollywood, American Culture, and World War II*. New York: Columbia University Press.

Donaldson, Roger, dir. 1977. *Sleeping Dogs* (film). Aardvark Films, prod.

Fleming, Victor, dir. 1939. *The Wizard of Oz* (film). Metro-Goldwyn-Mayer, prod.

Grant, Barry Keith. 1999. *A Cultural Assault: The New Zealand Films of Peter Jackson*. Nottingham: Kakapo Books.

Hammond, Michael. 2002. Some Smothering Dreams: The Combat Film in Contemporary Hollywood. In *Genre and Contemporary Hollywood*, edited by Steve Neale, 62-76. London: BFI.

Hardy, Ann. 2008. There and Back Again: *The Lord of the Rings*, Contemporary Religiosity and Cinema. In *Studying the Event Film: The Lord of the Rings*, edited by Harriet Margolis, Sean Cubitt, Barry King and Thierry Jutel, 205-13. Manchester, U.K.: Manchester University Press.

Horrocks, Roger. 1999. New Zealand Cinema. In *Twin Peaks: Australian and New Zealand Feature Films*, edited by Deb Verhoeven, 129-38. Melbourne: Damned Publishing.

Jackson, Peter, dir. 1989. *Bad Taste* (film). WingNut Films, prod.

———. 1989. *Meet the Feebles* (film). WingNut Films, prod.

———. 2001. *The Fellowship of the Ring* (film). New Line Cinema, prod.

———. 2002. *The Two Towers* (film). New Line Cinema, prod.

———. 2003. *The Return of the King* (film). New Line Cinema, prod.

Jackson, Peter and Costa Botes, dirs. 1995. *Forgotten Silver* (film). WingNut Films, prod.

Jennings, Wade. 1988. Fantasy. In *Handbook of American Genres*, edited by Wes D. Gehring, 249-65. New York: Greenwood Press.

Kellner, Douglas. 2006. *The Lord of the Rings* as Allegory: A Multiperspectivist Reading. In *From Hobbits to Hollywood: Essays on Peter Jackson's Lord of the Rings*, edited by Ernest Mathijs and Murray Pomerance, 17-40. Amsterdam: Rodopi.

Morgan, Arthur. 1992. Medieval Victorian and Modern: Tolkien, Wagner, and The Ring. In *A Tribute to J. R. R. Tolkien*, edited by Rosemary Gray, 17-26. Pretoria: University of South Africa.

Murphy, Geoff, dir. 1985. *The Quiet Earth* (film). Cinepro, prod.

Phillips, Jock. 1989. War and National Identity. In *Culture and Identity in New Zealand*, edited by David Novitz and Bill Willmott, 91-109. Wellington: GP Books.

Pryor, Ian. 2004. *Peter Jackson: From Prince of Splatter to Lord of the Rings*. Auckland: Random House.

Rayner Jonathan. 2000. Paradise and Pandemonium: The Landscape of Vincent Ward. In *New Zealand—A Pastoral Paradise? Studies in New Zealand Culture* no. 6, edited by Ian Conrich and David Woods, 39-51. Clifton, Nottingham: Kakapo Books.

Schatz, Thomas. 1981. *Hollywood Genres*. New York: Random House.

Shelley, Mary. 1992[1818]. *Frankenstein or the Modern Prometheus*. New York: Penguin Classics.

Sibley, Brian. 2001. *Lord of the Rings: Official Movie Guide*. London: Harper Collins.

Smith, Roy. 2000. New Zealand and the Nuclear Free Pacific. In *New Zealand—A Pastoral Paradise? Studies in New Zealand Culture* no. 6, edited by Ian Conrich and David Woods, 11-30. Clifton, Nottingham: Kakapo Books.

Stanton, Michael N. 2001. *Hobbits, Elves and Wizards*. New York: Palgrave Macmillan.

Stone, Oliver, dir. 1986. *Platoon* (film). Hemdale Film, prod.

Thompson, Kristin. 2007. *The Frodo Franchise: The Lord of the Rings and Modern Hollywood*. Berkeley, CA: University of California Press.

Thompson, Raymond H. 1982. Modern Fantasy and Medieval Romance: A Comparative Study. In *The Aesthetics of Fantasy in Literature and Art*, edited by Robert C. Schlobin, 211-25. Notre Dame, IN: University of Notre Dame Press.

Tolkien, J. R. R. 1983a. Sir Gawain and the Green Knight. In *The Monsters and the Critics and Other Essays*, edited by Christopher Tolkien, 72-108. London: George Allen and Unwin.

———.1983b. On Fairy-Stories. In *The Monsters and the Critics and Oher Essays*, edited by Christopher Tolkien, 109-61. London: George Allen and Unwin.

Tudor, Andrew. 1989. *Monsters and Mad Scientists: A Cultural History of the Horror Movie*. Oxford: Basil Blackwell.

Ward, Vincent, dir. 1988. *The Navigator: A Mediaeval Odyssey* (film). Arenafilm, prod.

Wells, Paul. 2000. *The Horror Genre*. London: Wallflower Publishers.

Willemen, Paul. 2006. The National Revisited. In *Theorising National Cinema*, edited by Valentina Vitali and Paul Willemen, 29-43. London: BFI.

Willmott Bill. 1989. Introduction: Culture and National Identity. In *Culture and Identity in New Zealand*, edited by David Novitz and Bill Willmott, 1-20. Wellington: GP Books.

Wolfe, Gary K. 1982. The Encounter with Fantasy. In *The Aesthetic of Fantasy in Literature and Art*, edited by Robert C. Schlobin, 1-15. Notre Dame, IN: University of Notre Dame Press.

Worland, Rick. 2007. *The Horror Film: An Introduction*. Oxford: Blackwell.

Stuart Allan and Kari Andén-Papadopoulos

"Come on, let us shoot!": WikiLeaks and the Cultures of Militarization

ABSTRACT

This paper explores the controversy generated by the nonprofit WikiLeaks website's posting of a video documenting the shooting of a group of civilians by U.S. forces situated in a helicopter gunship hovering over a Baghdad neighbourhood. Sparking press attention around the world, the brutal rawness of the black and white footage—compounded by the harrowing exchanges between the air crew recorded on the audio track—proved acutely unsettling to viewers otherwise habituated to routine (effectively sanitized) renderings of the horrors of a warzone. This paper considers the video as an instance where the cultural normalization of militarization was disrupted in ideological terms, thereby threatening to unravel officially-sanctioned relations of communicative power.

RÉSUMÉ

« Allez, laissez-nous tirer ! » WikiLeaks et les cultures de la militarisation

Cet article examine la controverse générée par le site Internet à but non lucratif WikiLeaks, qui a mis en ligne une vidéo montrant la fusillade d'un groupe de civils par les forces armées américaines du haut d'un hélicoptère de combat survolant un quartier de Bagdad. Ayant attiré l'attention de la presse dans le monde entier, la crudité brutale du film en noir et blanc – accentuée par les échanges atroces entre les équipages aériens enregistrés par la bande-son – se sont avérés extrêmement perturbants pour les spectateurs par ailleurs habitués aux comptes rendus routiniers (efficacement aseptisés) des horreurs d'une zone de conflits. Cet article considère cette vidéo comme un cas où la normalisation culturelle de la militarisation a été interrompue en termes idéologiques, menaçant ainsi de dénouer les relations officiellement approuvées du pouvoir des communications.

To contend that journalism is implicated in cultures of militarization is to invite an active reconsideration of certain cultural—indeed, profoundly mythologized—norms underpinning ostensibly mundane, everyday inflections of militarism in media discourses. "We can kill thousands because we have first learned to call them 'enemy'," British historian E. P. Thompson (1980) pointed out when campaigning for nuclear disarmament years ago. "Wars commence in the culture first of all," he added, "and we kill each other in euphemisms and abstractions long before the first missiles have been launched" (51). In a similar vein, Lutz's (2002) analysis of militarization leads her to argue that it is "simultaneously a discursive process, involving a shift in general societal beliefs and values in ways necessary to legitimate the use of force, the organization of large standing armies and their leaders and the higher taxes or tribute used to pay for them." In her view, it is

> intimately connected not only to the obvious increase in the size of armies and resurgence of militant nationalisms and militant fundamentalisms but also to the less visible deformation of human potentials into the hierarchies of race, class, gender, and sexuality, and to the shaping of national histories in ways that glorify and legitimate military action. (2002: 723)

For James Der Derian, Western news reporting's distanced, one-sided representations are indicative of a broader reconceptualization of war as being remote, virtuous and bloodless (or at least with "minimal casualties" on "our" side). "More than a rational calculation of interests takes us to war," he contends. "People go to war because of how they see, perceive, picture, imagine, and speak of others: that is, how they construct the difference of others as well as the sameness of themselves through representations" (Der Derian 2009: 238; cf Andén-Papadopoulos 2009; Matheson and Allan 2009; Stahl 2010).

The cultural politics of representation invites further consideration of the socially contingent normalization of militarization. Of particular interest for our purposes here is an instance where these uneven, contradictory (yet largely tacit) imperatives of normalization are thrown into sharp relief, namely by the nonprofit WikiLeaks website's posting of a video documenting the shooting of a group of civilians by U.S. forces situated in a helicopter gunship hovering over a Baghdad neighbourhood. The site introduces the cockpit footage, titled "Collateral Murder," with a short written statement, the opening paragraph of which asserts:

> WikiLeaks has released a classified US military video depicting the indiscriminate slaying of over a dozen people in the Iraqi suburb of New Baghdad—including two Reuters news staff [on July 12, 2007]. Reuters has been trying to obtain the video through the Freedom of Information Act, without success since the time of the attack. The video, shot from an Apache helicopter gun-site, clearly shows the unprovoked slaying of a

wounded Reuters employee and his rescuers. Two young children involved in the rescue were also seriously wounded. (http://WikiLeaks.org/wiki/Draft:CM)

The statement continues, pointing out that the military had refused to reveal to Reuters how its staff members, photographer Namir Noor-Eldeen and his driver Saeed Chmagh, were killed (two of the twelve people who died in the attack). Evidently, WikiLeaks received the video in question, together with supporting documents, from "a number of military whistleblowers." Due care was taken to verify the authenticity of the information, the statement adds, which included the analysis of a range of source materials and the interviewing of "witnesses and journalists directly involved in the incident." Two versions of the video, composed primarily of the gun-camera tape, were posted on the site—the full-version running at thirty-eight minutes, as well as a seventeen-minute edited version—with both containing subtitles of speech recorded from the helicopter's radio transmissions.

In examining the video and the ensuing controversy its release generated, this paper devotes particular attention to the ways in which officially sanctioned—and, all too typically, journalistically endorsed—relations of communicative power threatened to unravel. There can be little doubt, in our reading at least, that the brutal rawness of the video's black and white footage—compounded by the harrowing exchanges between the air crew recorded on the audio track—will be acutely unsettling to viewers otherwise habituated to routine (effectively sanitized) renderings of the horrors of a warzone. Indeed, we argue that its ideological significance is underscored by its unnerving contravention of the emotional detachment ordinarily prefigured in the military's preferred narratives, and as such signals a telling moment when the cultural norms of militarization were dramatically transgressed.

"A Real-World War Scenario"

"Collateral Murder" swiftly became an Internet sensation when it was posted on the WikiLeaks website on April 5, 2010, attracting news media attention around the globe while, at the same time, igniting heated debate in the blogosphere (the seventeen-minute version having gone viral via YouTube). The footage of U.S. soldiers killing what appears to be a group of innocent citizens—and doing so in a manner that seemed as jocular as it was arbitrary—invited impassioned responses from across the political spectrum. Among the array of voices were those expressing their outrage at what they perceived to be a war crime, some contending that the Geneva Conventions for humanitarian treatment of casualties had been violated. Others debated the nature of "murder" in WikiLeaks's choice of title, calling into question the legal complexities associated with the U.S. military's "rules of engagement." Still others blamed the "fog of war," insisting that the incident was little more than a regrettable example of what can happen in the heat of battle.

While space does not permit a detailed analysis of the video here, several moments proved particularly salient in the ensuing news coverage. After being told by command that they are "free to engage," one of the fliers is heard saying: "Light them all up. Come on, fire!" The gunships open fire on the group, killing several people and wounding others. After releasing one of the multiple rounds of 30 mm canon fire shot during the incident, one crewman shouts: "Ha-ha. I hit 'em." A few seconds later, another voice says: "Oh yeah, look at those dead bastards." The response from the other pilot is "Nice." One survivor, identified in a subtitle as Reuters driver Chmagh, can be seen crawling towards a courtyard to safety. A voice is heard urging the wounded man to pick up a gun—"Come on buddy, all you gotta do is pick up a weapon"—on the pretext that the rules of engagement permit him to be killed as a consequence (no weapons were actually visible, but a camera and tripod may have been confused as such). Minutes later, when a van pulls up in what appears to be an attempt to transport those still alive to a hospital for medical attention, the air crew request permission from ground control to stop the rescue effort. As unarmed Iraqis begin to help a wounded victim into the van, the voices of the air crew grow impatient—"Come on, let us shoot"—before permission is granted to attack. The crews open fire, riddling the van with armour-piercing shells. As the helicopter continues to circle overhead, U.S. ground forces arrive. They soon discover that among the injured in the van are two children. "Well it's their fault for bringing their kids into a battle," one of the pilots says. Soon after, an armoured military vehicle appears to run over one of the corpses (believed to be Chmagh). "I think they just drove over a body," one of the pilots observes with laughter in his voice.

In placing the video into the public domain, WikiLeaks succeeded where Reuters had failed. The latter had actively petitioned the U.S. military to release the video since July 25, 2007, when its editors where shown a version during an off-the-record briefing in Baghdad. Having been denied its own copy, Reuters had proceeded to make a request under the Freedom of Information Act to pry it loose. No progress had been made in securing a copy by the time of the WikiLeaks intervention over two and a half years later. In posting the video (once its encryption had been broken) alongside other military documents, the site provided an evidential basis to challenge the military's version of events—namely its insistence that the helicopter had been engaged in an active fire-fight, and that those killed had been insurgents. For WikiLeaks director Julian Assange, the video provided proof that both claims were untrue:

> Why would anyone be so relaxed with two Apaches if someone was carrying an RPG [rocket-propelled grenade] and that person was an enemy of the United States? [...] The behaviour of the pilots is like a computer

game. When Saeed is crawling, clearly unable to do anything, their response is: come on buddy, we want to kill you, just pick up a weapon.... It appears to be a desire to get a higher score, or a higher number of kills. (Qtd in McGreal 2010).

Pressed for comment about Namir Noor-Eldeen and Saeed Chmagh, Reuter's editor-in-chief David Schlesinger stated that their deaths were "tragic and emblematic of the extreme dangers that exist in covering war zones." The video, he added, "is graphic evidence of the dangers involved in war journalism and the tragedies that can result" (qtd. in Reuters 2010). Several members of Chmagh's family wept as they watched the video, the *New York Times* reported. "I saw the truth," his 19-year-old son Samir is quoted stating. "They saw clearly that they were journalists and that they were holding cameras. It was painful when we saw this movie" (qtd. in Arango and Bumiller 2010).

Judgements regarding precisely what the video revealed varied markedly from one viewer to the next, of course, with much depending upon prior opinions about the relative legitimacy of the U.S.-led invasion, as well as assumptions about what constitutes the appropriate use of lethal force (including distinctions between combatants and non-combatants). For some the video relayed an "unfiltered reality" that was highly disturbing in

Fig. 1 (left) and Fig. 2 (below)
Stills captured from video posted on WikiLeaks. Unknown contr.
http://www.wikileaks.org/wiki/Collateral_Murder,_5_Apr_2010

its own right, but also because it highlighted the extent to which news coverage of the conflict "filters" away such im-agery on the basis of "good taste" censorship. A reading of the reportage covering the video's release provides further insights into the attendant complexities of journalistic mediation in this regard. The actions of the "trigger-happy" pilots were widely deplored, with their "callous and bloodthirsty comments" often singled out for particular criticism. "The radio transmissions show not only the utter callousness of the soldiers, laughing and swearing as they kill," Amy Goodman (2010) pointed out, "but also the strict procedure they follow, ensuring that all of their attacks are clearly authorized by their chain of command." Words such as "chilling," "wrenching" and "grotesque" surface repeatedly in reports, with some dwelling on the extent to which the video resembles "first-person shoot-'em-up" computer games (echoing Assange's observation above). Douglas Haddow (2010), on *The Guardian*'s "comment is free" site, writes:

> One of the most alarming aspects of Collateral Murder is that it demonstrates how similar the logic of the Apache pilots is to that of the average gamer. The video allows us to examine the entire process of how a rationale for attack is reached. We see exactly what the Apache pilots saw, the black-and-white gun-cam footage underscored by their darkly cynical colour-commentary of the ensuing carnage. As the helicopter approaches the men, we hear a pilot say: "See all those people standing down there?" The camera zooms in on the group and we see Saeed with a camera bag slung on his right shoulder. "That's a weapon," a pilot says. "Fucking prick," comes the reply.
>
> And with that, a few unarmed, relaxed civilians hanging around a courtyard are transformed into a contingent of dangerous insurgents that must be destroyed. (Haddow 2010)

Other commentators stressed how the apparent similarity between the video and a war game revealed what they considered to be the moral corruption of soldiers by this hyper-tech rendering of warfare in which civilian deaths become "collateral damage." The pilots' behaviour was debased, they suggested, because "the enemy" had been effectively dehumanized.

"Looking at the War through a Soda Straw"

In the immediate aftermath of "Collateral Murder," pressure was brought to bear on the U.S. military to reopen its investigation of the incident (its initial inquiry concluded that the gun crews had "exercised sound judgment"). "This is evidence of calculated, cold-blooded and horrifying violence," argued Jim Boumelha, President of the International Federation of Journalists. "The United States cannot ignore this atrocity and the killings of unarmed civilians. We insist on a completely new review of these and all the killings of journalists and media staff in the Iraq conflict" (qtd. in IFJ 2010). A similar call was issued from defence experts, such as Lieutenant-Colonel Anthony Shaffer, who told *The Times* of London that the Pentagon would have to publicly account for the killings "or al-Qaeda will continue to use this sort of thing as a recruiting tool" (qtd. in Whittell and Fordham 2010).

Speculation was rife across the mediascape regarding the lasting impact of the video on global perceptions of the U.S. military's conduct. James Fallows, national correspondent for *The Atlantic*, made the point directly:

> I can't pretend to know the full truth or circumstances of this. But at face value it is the most damaging documentation of abuse since the Abu Ghraib prison-torture photos. As you watch, imagine the reaction in the US if the people on the ground had been Americans and the people on the machine guns had been Iraqi, Russian, Chinese, or any other nationality. As with Abu Ghraib, and again assuming this is what it seems to be, the temptation will be to blame the operations-level people who were, in this case, chuckling as they mowed people down. That's not where the real responsibility lies. (Fallows 2010)

This question of responsibility, not surprisingly, focused the efforts of military and Pentagon officials mobilizing to re-appropriate the video footage into their preferred frames of understanding. Appearing on ABC's *This Week*, Defense Secretary Robert Gates admitted that the video made for difficult viewing. Asked whether he thought the events in question would "damage the image of the U.S. in the world," he replied:

> I don't think so [...] They're in a combat situation. The video doesn't show the broader picture of the firing that was going on at American troops. It's obviously a hard thing to see. It's painful to see, especially when you learn after the fact what was going on. But you talked about the fog of war. These people were operating in split-second situations. [...] And, you know, we've investigated it very thoroughly. And it's unfortunate. It's clearly not helpful. But by the same token, I think it should not have any lasting consequences. (qtd. in Stein 2010)

Gates went further in a later interview, insisting that videos such as this one provided an incomplete picture of what was happening on the battlefield. "That is the problem with these videos," he argued. "You are looking at the war through a soda straw and you have no context or perspective" (qtd. in Barnes 2010).

Just a few days later, however, two soldiers from the Army unit responsible for the attack offered an alternative perspective of their own, stating that: "The acts depicted in this video are everyday occurrences of this war." Josh Steiber and Ethan McCord's words appeared in "An Open Letter of Reconciliation and Responsibility to the Iraqi People" (Steiber and McCord 2010), in which they apologize to "all of those who were injured or lost loved ones during the July 2007 Baghdad shootings" depicted in the video, recognizing that "our words can never restore your losses." The letter states that the WikiLeaks footage "only begins to depict the suffering we have created," such is "the nature of how US-led wars are carried out in this region." They continue:

> We acknowledge our part in the deaths and injuries of your loved ones as we tell Americans what we were trained to do and what we carried out in the name of "god and country." The soldier in the video said that your husband shouldn't have brought your children to battle, but we are acknowledging our responsibility for bringing the battle to your neighborhood, and to your family. We did unto you what we would not want done to us.
>
> More and more Americans are taking responsibility for what was done in our name. Though we have acted with cold hearts far too many times, we have not forgotten our actions towards you. Our heavy hearts still hold hope that we can restore inside our country the acknowledgment of your humanity, that we were taught to deny. (Steiber and McCord 2010)

They then proceed to directly address Gates's claim that the reputation of the U.S. would not be damaged by the incident, stating "we stand and say that our reputation's importance pales in comparison to our common humanity." Precisely what this reassertion of humanity meant for McCord was based on the tragic experiences that day. He is shown in the video, striving to help the injured children—twelve-year-old Sahad Salah and his six-year-old sister Duaa—caught up in the strafing (their father, the driver of the van taking the children home from school when they stopped to help, was dead). "When I saw those kids," McCord later recalled, "all I could picture was my kids back home" (qtd. in Press Release 2010).

In retrospect, it is apparent that the controversy generated by WikiLeaks's decision to make the video public was short-lived. It virtually disappeared from the mainstream media following the 24-hour news cycle, with most of the remaining reporting and commentary shifting onto online news sites and blogs—facilitated, of course, by the availability of links to the video in question. The waning of the controversy was attributable by some to the fact that it was released while the U.S. Congress was in recess, thereby making its overt political implications more difficult for journalists to explore. Others contended that the graphic nature of the video made it "too hot to handle" for television news networks, presumably concerned about the risk of upsetting their audiences or, perhaps more to the point, advertisers. Still others maintained that it was all too indicative of the extent to which news from Iraq has dropped off the news agenda, with the video simply deemed to be insufficiently newsworthy to warrant sustained attention.

While recognizing all of these possible factors, a further reading might dwell on the way in which the video challenges the everyday cultures of militarism otherwise so prevalent in Western war reporting from Iraq. The experience of viewing it is acutely jarring, we would suggest, in part because it is made available in the absence of the customary forms of journalistic mediation that usually accompanies such imagery. The performative capacity of war reporting to sustain detachment, to effectively normalize the cultural imperatives of militarism in such familiar repetition that killing becomes almost banal, is taken for granted. In other words, it is customary for news reports to offer a sense of reassurance (a blurring of ontological security with national security) in their reaffirmation of official truth-claims regarding the waging of war by "us" against "them." What makes this video so powerful, then, is its disruption of the ideological purchase of militarism by recasting these codified strictures, namely by representing in horrific detail how "we" are being transformed into a reprehensible Other.

References

Andén-Papadopoulos, K. 2009. Body Horror on the Internet: US Soldiers Recording the War in Iraq and Afghanistan. *Media, Culture and Society* 31(6): 921-38.

Arango, T. and E. Bumiller. 2010. For 2 Grieving Families, Video Reveals Grim Truth. *The New York Times*, 6 April.

Barnes, J. E. 2010. Gates Criticizes Leaks Group for War Video. *The Los Angeles Times*, 13 April.

Der Derian, J. 2009 *Virtuous War*, Second Edition. New York and London: Routledge.

Fallows, J. 2010. In case you missed them.... http://TheAtlantic.com, 6 April.

Goodman, A. 2010. Collateral murder in Iraq. http://www.TruthDig.com, 6 April.

Haddow, D. 2010. Grim truths of WikiLeaks Iraq video. http://Guardian.co.uk, 7 April.

International Federation of Journalists. 2010. IFJ Demands Probe into Iraq Media Deaths After US Army Film Exposes Killing of Unarmed Civilians and Journalists. http://www.ifj.org, 6 April.

Lutz, C. 2002. Making War at Home in the United States: Militarization and the Current Crisis. American Anthropologist 104(3): 723-35.

Matheson, D. and S. Allan. 2009. *Digital War Reporting*. Cambridge: Polity.

McGreal, C. 2010. WikiLeaks Reveals Video Showing US Air Crew Shooting Down Iraqi Civilians. *The Guardian*, 5 April.

Press Release. 2010. Veterans of "WikiLeaks" Incident Announce "Letter of reconciliation" to Iraqis Injured in Attack. info@civsol.org, 15 April.

Reuters. 2010. Leaked Video Shows Reuters Journalists Killed by US Gunships. http://www.independent.co.uk, 6 April.

Stahl, R. 2010. *Militainment, Inc*. New York: Routledge.

Steiber, J. and E. McCord. 2010. An Open Letter of Reconciliation and Responsibility to the Iraqi People. http://www.lettertoiraq.com.

Stein, S. 2010. Gates: WikiLeaks video "painful to see" but won't have lasting impact. HuffingtonPost.com, April 11.

Thompson, E. P. 1980. Protest and survive. In *Protest and Survive*, edited by E. P. Thompson and D. Smith. Harmondsworth: Penguin.

Whittell, G. and A. Fordham. 2010. Leaked Video Footage Shows Iraq Journalists Killed by US Gunships. *The Times*, 7 April.

Bill Burns

Extraterritorial Prison Plans in the Style of IKEA and the Prison Playlist

In fall 2001 U.S. Navy Seabees began refurbishing and constructing the first phase of the detention camps at the U.S. Navy Base in Guantánamo Bay, on the southeast corner of Cuba. The first section of the camps had been previously used to house asylum seekers from Haiti and Cuba in the 1990s. It was called Camp X-Ray. It opened as a prison camp and interrogation centre on January 11, 2002 under the jurisdiction of the U.S. Southern Command.

Camp X-Ray's prison cells were open air. Each cell consisted of a concrete slab foundation, a galvanized steel chain-link fence, and a metal roof. The cells measured eight feet by eight feet by eight feet (2.4 m cube). Because the cells did not have any plumbing, prisoners were given two buckets, one was for water and the other was for waste.

Most of the prisoners were brought to Camp X-Ray on large transport airplanes from Afghanistan. Some came from other parts of the world. When they arrived they were given a kit consisting of two orange boiler suits, a sleeping mat, a blanket, a set of sheets, a wash cloth, two towels (one for washing and one for praying), a bar of soap, shampoo, a modified toothbrush, a tube of toothpaste, two buckets, a flask, a copy of the Koran, and a prayer cap.

On April 29, 2002 Camp X-Ray was closed. All the prisoners were moved to a new facility known as Camp Delta. Camp Delta consists of seven prison camps numbered one through six as well as one that has no number.

Following are: A playlist cataloguing popular songs that were played to the prisoners at high volume for prolonged periods of time; plans for guard towers and prison cells. I have strived to make them as accurate as possible.

PLAYLIST

1. "Shoot to Thrill" by AC/DC
2. "Gold" by Matchbox Twenty
3. "Stayin' Alive" by the Bee Gees
4. "Born in the USA" by Bruce Springsteen
5. "Dirty" by Christina Aguilera
6. "Sesame Street Theme Song" by Joe Raposo
7. "March of the Pigs" by Nine Inch Nails
8. "American Pie" by Don McLean
9. "Die MF Die" by Dope
10. "Bodies" by Drowning Pools
11. "Raspberry Beret" by Prince
12. "White America" by Eminem
13. "All Eyes on Me" by Tupac
14. "Fuck Your God" by Deicide
15. "Enter Sandman" by Metallica
16. "America" by Neil Diamond
17. "We Are the Champions" by Queen
18. "Killing in the Name" by Rage Against the Machine
19. "Click Click Boom" by Saliva
20. "I Love You" by Barney the Purple Dinosaur

CELL

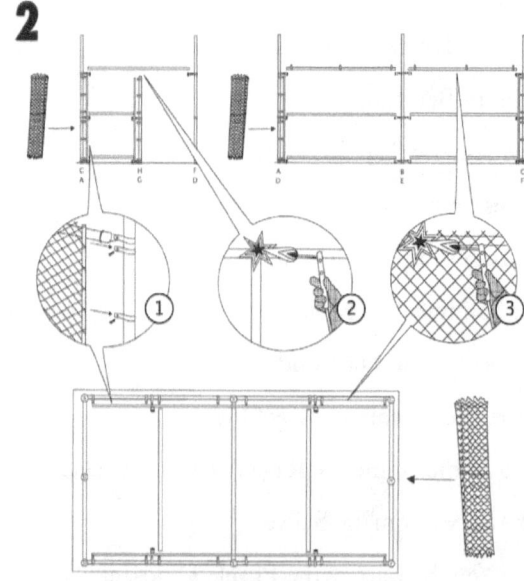
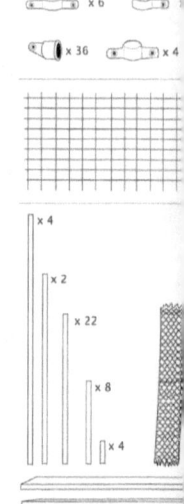
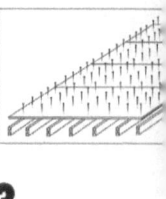
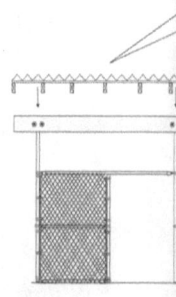

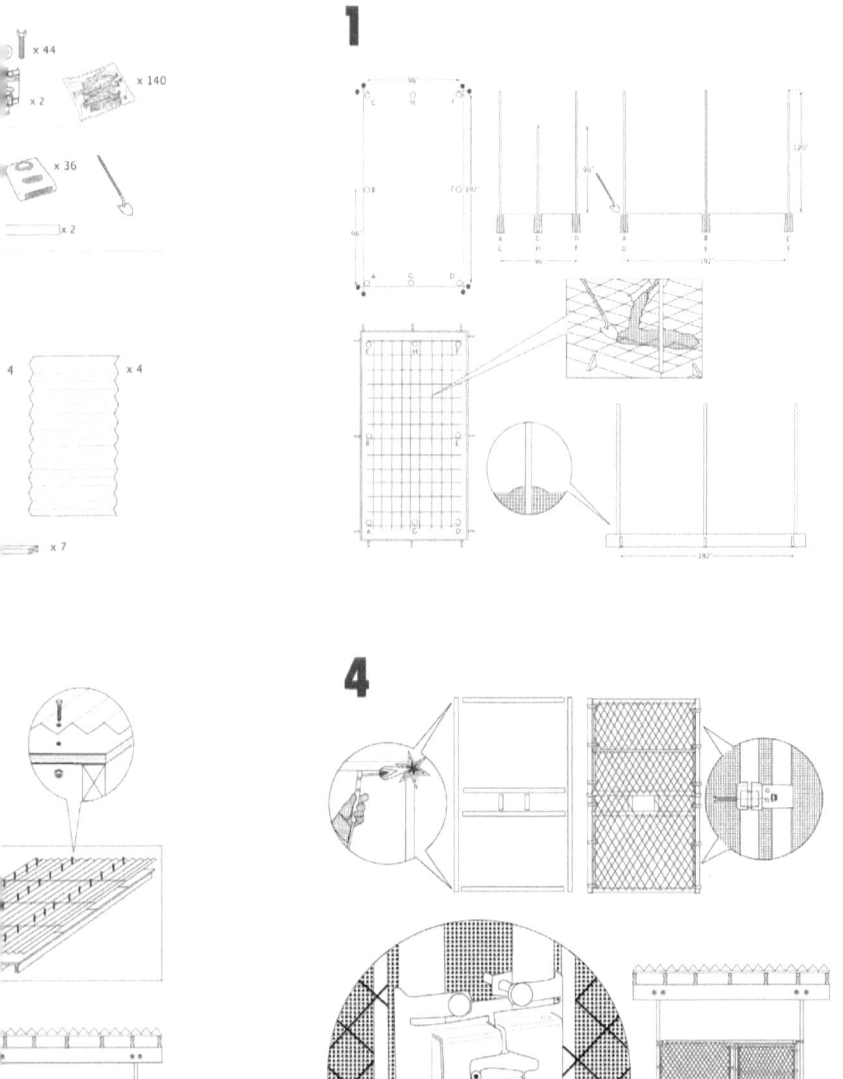

TOWER

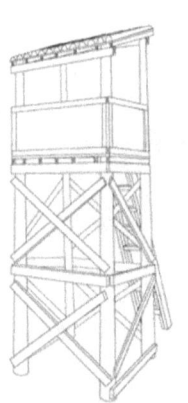

4
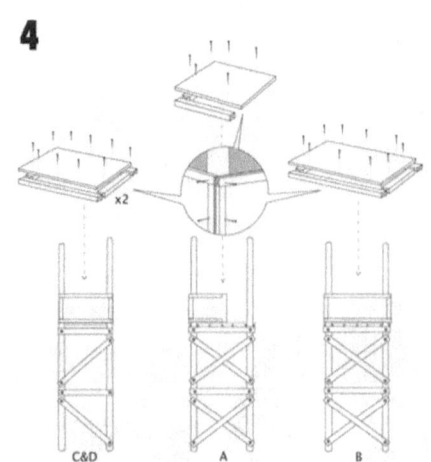

5
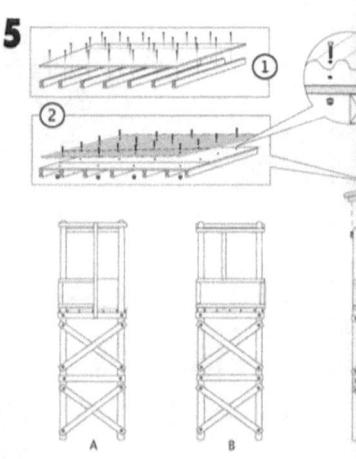

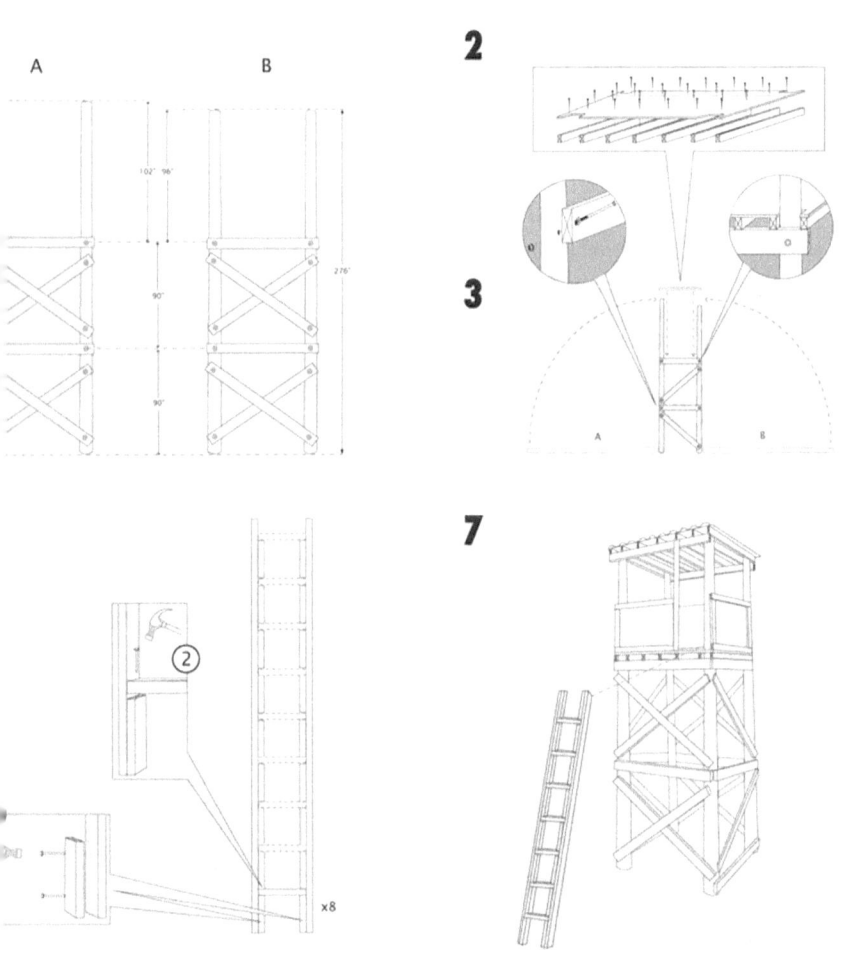

David A. Clearwater

Living in a Militarized Culture: War, Games and the Experience of U.S. Empire

ABSTRACT

Over the past few decades, the image of war and the U.S. military in popular entertainment has waxed and waned along with the (un)popularity of specific conflicts. This essay explores the evolving role of the "hex" board game and the videogame genre of the military-themed shooter in maintaining positive portrayals of the U.S. military and war more generally within U.S. popular culture. In particular, these videogames are considered as both a remediated and interactive version of the Hollywood combat film and as virtual spaces where citizens can experience combat, interact with history, and become immersed in a larger militarized culture.

RÉSUMÉ

Vivre dans une culture militarisée : Guerre, jeux et expérience de l'Empire américain

Au cours des dernières décennies, l'image de la guerre et de l'armée américaine dans les jeux populaires a cru et décliné parallèlement à l'(im)popularité de conflits particuliers. Cet essai explore le rôle évolutif des jeux « Hex » de plateau et des jeux vidéo de thématique militaire (jeux de tir subjectif) dans le maintien de portraits flatteurs de l'armée américaine et plus généralement de la guerre dans la culture populaire américaine. Ces jeux vidéo sont, en particulier, considérés à la fois comme une version palliative et interactive des films de guerre hollywoodiens et comme des espaces virtuels où les citoyens peuvent faire l'expérience du combat, interagir avec l'histoire et s'immerger dans une culture plus largement militarisée.

War, Media and the Generation of Culture

In 1999, Sony Computer Entertainment and Toshiba released the Emotion Engine, the processor for Sony's upcoming PlayStation 2 videogame console. Naming processors and graphics chips was nothing new to the hardware-obsessed videogame industry, but Sony designed much of its pre-release marketing for its highly-anticipated console around the emotion-generating wonders of this new chip. While it was a marketing gimmick more than anything else, the term emotion engine is emblematic of the period; one which saw the videogame industry expand in terms of reach and sales but also through advances in game design and hardware, all of which would open new aesthetic and interactive possibilities for the medium. During this period, fully three-dimensional and real-time environments became the norm, as did the use of narrative, character creation/development, complexly scripted events and highly refined sound and art design. Games of the period could render convincing and increasingly interactive environments, with rich (and often heavily remediated) symbolism that could be experienced individually or as part of a group. It was also a period in which modern combat, especially from the point of view of the individual soldier, came to dominate the industry, particularly in North America. As a result modern warfare (especially from the perspective of the U.S. and at times its allies), has become a prominent subject in an increasingly important form of popular entertainment (Bayer 2003; Dyer-Witheford and de Peuter 2009; Leonard 2004).

There is nothing new about warfare as subject matter for entertainment or art, but the emergence of video and computer games is interesting because the medium itself is largely the result of massive state intervention in a number of industries and sectors in Western society, including electronics, aeronautics and aerospace, weapons development, radio, network and satellite communications, and entertainment (Lenoir 2000). Generally, while Europe, Britain and other regions are important markets and sites of production, the international videogame industry has been dominated by the U.S. and Japan. This is largely because many of the technological developments required for today's mature videogame industry emerged from post-Second World War United States and Japan. Essentially a military protectorate of the U.S., Japan became a crucial industrial and financial engine for the U.S., especially in the latter stages of the Cold War. As the capitalist-democratic half of the world's dual superpowers, the U.S. poured billions into weapons development, electrical engineering and communications where—fulfilling the promises of capitalist ideology—new "civilian" applications were found for the bewildering number of technological breakthroughs being produced by engineering and applied science (Hooks 1990). The military-industrial complex turned out to be the ideal economic engine of Cold War capitalism and helped spawn our contemporary world filled with millions of networked screens and devices. Whether it was described as the "military-industrial-media-complex" (Leslie 1997), MIME-Net (Der Derian 2001), or the "militainment" industry (Anderson 2003), this state-military-industrial nexus has had important effects on international entertainment industries and popular culture more generally; the medium of the videogame is the most recent development but also, in important ways, the logical consequence of everything that came before.

While it should not be surprising that modern warfare came to occupy such a central place within the videogame industry at the end of the 20th century, this happened at a moment in political and cultural history when popular re-presentations of the U.S. military and warfare had been waning for years. The spectre of Vietnam and the spectacular but controversial experience of the Persian Gulf War meant that portrayals of warfare or the military in popular entertainment after the 1960s were often ambivalent, irreverent or even negative. Despite the remasculinization of the 1980s, *Top Gun* or gung-ho-but-second-rate P.O.W. movies still had to compete with *M*A*S*H* (especially in syndicated form) and the cultural legacies of the civil rights and anti-war movements, particularly in popular music. The videogame industry was born in this period and, after the industry's crash in the mid-1980s, expanded greatly in the 1990s as more and more PCs and consoles found their way into homes worldwide. And within this emerging medium and expanding industry, representations of warfare and the U.S. military in particular would come to take very different, and overwhelmingly positive, forms.

The evolution of videogames has taken a trajectory similar to that of other modern representational technologies in that it was produced by perceptual logics that emanated from industrial-military needs. Whether it was cinema (Virilio 1989), computing and artificial intelligence (De Landa 1991), networked computer simulations (Der Derian 2001) or simply the mythological origins of the Internet, modern society swims in a technological and representational ocean created by the military-industrial-entertainment complex,[1] and whose composition is, at least initially, dictated by the logics and fantasies of warfare. Beyond its foundational imprints, the military-industrial-entertainment nexus is also effective and influential in terms of content. The close and mutually beneficial relationship between Hollywood and the U.S. military, for example, has been long and at times deep (Robb 2004; Suid 2002), with the Pentagon's film liaison offices sometimes receiving script approval in exchange for assistance and access to military equipment and personnel. The videogame industry is similarly affected by military-industrial relations and patterns of influence.

Typically, these relationships are most evident in the subgenre of the military-themed shooter and first- and third-person shooter genres more generally. These genres represent individual combat (usually from the perspective of infantry), using first-, third-person or even hybrid perspectives to allow players to adopt the point of view of an individual soldier in historical, contemporary or fantasy-based environments. By 1999, when Sony was bragging about its Emotion Engine, the technology and design of games allowed for player interactions within fully three-dimensional, real-time space. As the genres evolved, they provided increasingly convincing 3D environments. These are discursively controlled and perceptually guided spaces which, in the vast majority of cases, provide a positive view of warfare and perpetuate pro-war and militaristic attitudes.

If the genre of the military-themed shooter offers a glorified and propagandistic perspective on warfare, it butts up against similar and competing discourses in other media. As part of the larger world of media spectacle, the context in which these games exist is, as Kellner points out, a highly "contested terrain" where a "plurality and heterogeneity of contending spectacles" exists (2003). While tiny and often marginalized, there is a tradition of raising questions about the close relationship with the military within the videogame industry. Anti-war attitudes can be seen in the genre of role-playing games where the influence of Japanese anime and manga is strong. On the whole, however, the industry embraces violence as a core game-play mechanic and warfare as a noble undertaking. How much of this is due to the genre of the military-themed shooter and the influence of the larger forces that helped to create it? As Kellner reminds his readers, the new "modes of information *and* entertainment that permeate work, education, play, social interaction, politics and culture" are born of a process that "has produced the most extensive concentration and conglomeration of these industries in history, as well as an astonishing development and expansion of technologies and media products" (Kellner 2003: 13). Here, concentration and proliferation are key notions. While there may be competition, or at least the appearance of choice, the concentration of ownership and power within media industries has expanded greatly. As Kellner's earlier study of the Persian Gulf War demonstrates, when an industry like television news becomes not only connected to but also reliant on state and military power structures for access and content, the result is often favourable to the state and military (Kellner 1992).

More concretely, the military-themed shooter game came to resemble the increasing number of military representations in Hollywood's output and on television. The desire for immediacy and authenticity encourages, as Bolter and Grusin (2000) argue, the gravitation toward screened reality following the logics of remediation characteristic of contemporary culture.[2] The emerging videogame industry was influenced, aesthetically and discursively, by the "small" screen of television (both historical drama and journalism) as much as the "large" screen of Hollywood. Producers and fans tended, especially early in its development, to base notions of realism and authenticity on formal and aesthetic principles largely derived from representations of warfare seen on TV or in film (combat sequences from blockbuster films being especially influential). In terms of narrative structure, characterization and ideology, military-themed videogames borrowed heavily from their filmic counterparts. Also notable was the stylistic and discursive influence of television, in particular the war imagery (some provided to the networks by the Pentagon itself) associated with war reporting.

By 2000, war as subject matter was much more prominent within North American culture; it further expanded after the events of September 11, 2001, and the military quagmires in which the U.S. and its allies were participants. In this era of endless media reproductions, remediations, and interactions, citizen-consumers were important participants. As Der Derian (2001) wrote:

> We were entering a digitally enhanced *virtual immersion*, in which instant scandals, catastrophic events, impending weather disasters, "wag-the-dog" foreign policy, constructive simulations, live-feed wars, and quick-in, quick-out interventions into stillborn or moribund states are all available, not just primetime, real time, but 24/7, on the TV, PC, and PDA. (209)

After the events of September 11, 2001, immersion was increasingly achieved in virtual battlefields and imagined theatres of war.

A few central questions arise. Who creates, controls, or otherwise influences these imagined environments? To whom is access given? And what are they allowed or not allowed to do within these spaces? On a simple level, the virtual worlds of interactive entertainment are interesting for the time that can potentially be devoted to them. For the single-player portion of a military-themed shooter it could take, on average, ten to twenty hours to complete missions in the overarching storyline. Networked or online multiplayer portions of a game can be experienced for hours at a time, and the amount of time a player spends overall with the multiplayer portions of popular titles (where they might interact with ten to sixty other players) is sometimes staggering.[3] These virtual battlefields are not the only spaces available to players; entertainment industries increasingly provide access to a variety of related social spaces and (sub)cultural formations (Jenkins 2006b). From the early use of online chat and forums to community-based wiki and machinima projects, the interactive aspects of modern videogames make them highly social in nature. Since the average videogame player tends to be oriented toward technology and online-computer interactions (fans of first-person shooters and military-themed shooters in particular tend to identify themselves as "hardcore" technologists), community-formation around these types of entertainment products is particularly robust. But as Jenkins also reminds us (2006a), these new cultural spaces forming around modern entertainment also tend to be commercialized spaces, primarily controlled by commercial interests.

For the genre of the military-themed shooter, given its proximity to state/military power, the question of influence is crucial. Given the immersive nature of the medium, and the fact that the genre is often held up for its realism and fidelity in (re)creating historical, contemporary and even hypothetical conflicts, an analysis of its dominant forms can reveal the ways a culture of militarism is perpetuated.

This brings us back to 1999 and the Emotion Engine. The generation of synthetic emotion and immersion in new cultural landscapes was the broad promise of the expanding "tech" world, helping to fuel the phenomenal growth of a financial bubble that burst only a few months later. The allure of fluid identities roaming vast virtual frontiers was both frightening and exhilarating. The videogame could be seen as paradigmatic of the era since it had reached a level of formal and technical refinement that allowed for such immersive experiences on a grand, mass-produced scale. Describing the medium as "liquid architecture," journalist and writer Stephen Poole argues that when playing "the videogame player is absorbed by the system (2000: 236)." "For the duration of the game," Poole states, the player "lives among signs (another way of describing the dissolution of self-consciousness in the videogame experience)" (197).

The fluidity of identity and the fact that virtual experiences were increasingly accepted as valid raises important questions about their representational and interactive strategies. The portrayal of war and violence more generally, including tendencies toward glorification and aestheticization, the portrayal and definition of patriotism, and questions about the accuracy of historical recreations of U.S. and world history become paramount. The close and circular relationships between the military's use of computer simulations and the commercial products of the videogame industry are especially problematic given the assumption made by many young players about the medium: that it is a cutting-edge learning or educational tool at the same time that it is a modern, cutting-edge form of mass entertainment. Both may be true on their own but when it comes to warfare, such assumptions can be dangerous. Videogames are born of the same cultural processes which Der Derian (2001) identifies with the ability to make war "virtuous" (virtual and infused with virtue). Indeed, these forces seem capable of completely overwhelming alternative and often more truthful representations of warfare and contemporary world politics. We cannot discount the resources and influence of the state/military nexus in maintaining these virtuous representations and spaces, nor the uncanny ways that war itself seems to be a self-perpetuating social force. Hallin (1997) makes the compelling case that war itself is a richly symbolic cultural system that allows ordinary citizens to participate "in history" and that encourages other social institutions and commercial interests to mobilize symbolic meanings that support and reinforce that same system.

In a book depicting the corrupting and perverting effects of war, war correspondent Chris Hedges admits that his book is a futile attempt to counter the seductive, all-pervasive and self-perpetuating nature of war, and tries to come to terms with his own culpability in perpetuating its noble image:

I learned early on that war forms its own culture. The rush of battle is a potent and often lethal addiction, for war is a drug, one I ingested for many years. It is peddled by mythmakers—historians, war correspondents, filmmakers, novelists, and the state—all of whom endow it with qualities it does possess: excitement, exoticism, power, chances to rise above our small stations in life, and a bizarre and fantastic universe that has a grotesque and dark beauty. It dominates culture, distorts memory, corrupts language, and infects everything around it, even humor.... The enduring attraction of war is this: even with its destruction and carnage it can give us what we long for in life. It can give us purpose, meaning, and reason for living.... It gives us resolve, a cause. It allows us to be noble. (Hedges 2002: 3)

Playing War: From Board Games to Interactive Entertainment

In addition to these general benefits, there are others of which we are less sure. One of these addresses a worry of the military historian that has existed for some time, but which has seemed particularly acute since the coming of the Vietnam War, that has been a general turning-away not only from war, but from an interest in any things military or security-related by many people. We feel that the interest that hobby wargames has engendered has helped to counteract this trend, a trend which might have very dangerous and grave results. (Glick and Charters 1983: 580)

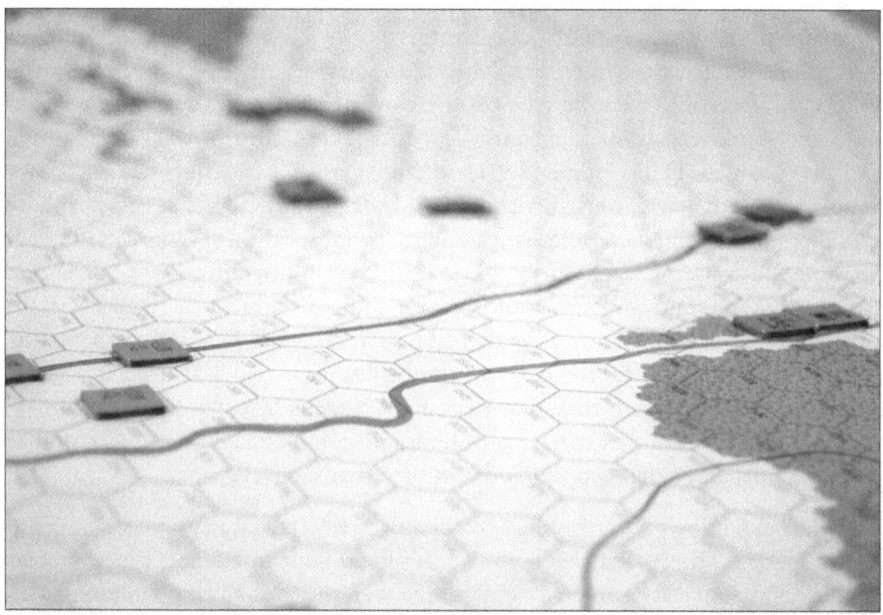

Fig. 1 Detail of a game of Firefight: Modern U.S. and Soviet Small Unit Tactics *(1976) showing "hex" map and cardboard counters.*

Glick and Charters are not referring to videogames; the "hobby wargames" they describe were war boardgames, sometimes known as "hex and counter" war games. Commercial hex wargaming began in the 1950s and gained in popularity until the 1990s, when this style of game increasingly moved to the personal computer. Over the years, hundreds of games have been produced commercially, making room for an active community of players who would regularly meet at conferences, contribute new battle scenarios and tweak rule sets, as well as publish their own games. For the most dedicated fans, these games were as much simulations as games (Dunnigan 1992: 163) since they allowed players to re-create infamous battles and more fully explore aspects of military history.

As military analysts and historians, Glick and Charters argue that hex wargames, especially the most advanced, realistic versions available commercially, could offer students of military history another method to study particular battles or military campaigns that was more detailed and accurate than histories written in "the conventional narrative style" (Glick and Charters,1983: 568). The hex wargame industry, especially in that period, was a segment of popular culture where war was a primary subject of interest and taken seriously as both entertainment and a learning tool. Glick and Charters follow in the tradition of looking at the meaning of games or toys and the influence these cultural artifacts might have on public attitudes toward war. Brown (1990), for instance, argues that toy soldiers contributed to the imperialistic and militaristic ambitions of England in the period preceding the First World War. Machin and Van Leeuwen (2009) discuss ways that contemporary war toys allow children to enact dominant discourses and values surrounding war, especially as they relate to or may be reflected in current events. Looking at the board game more generally, Adams and Edmonds (1977) consider its development in America not only as a reflection of certain symbolic meanings but as a vehicle for transmitting dominant social values. Reflecting the belief that the educational process is not limited to traditional leaning institutions, they see board games as examples of "deliberate, systematic, and sustained effort[s] to transmit and evoke knowledge, attitudes, values, skills, and sensibilities" (359). The hex game represented, for the period before the widespread adoption of the personal computer, an appropriate medium for such purposes.

Military wargaming (sometimes referred to by the original German term, *Kriegspiel*) has been used for military instruction and training since its development by early 19th-century Prussian military officers. Hobby or amateur wargaming has existed alongside its military counterpart almost from the beginning of the 20th century. H.G. Wells was an early proponent of miniature wargaming using model soldiers, reference charts, rulers, and even realistic terrain, and he along with other amateurs and hobbyists helped to formalize rules and to popularize and commercialize the hobby (Wells 1913). The painting and collecting of miniature soldiers and equipment was key for many early hobbyists, and is still a popular and lucrative pastime. Starting in the late 1950s, the hex wargames focused on wargaming itself, replacing the toy-like model soldiers for printed, cardboard counters.

At the height of their pop-ularity, hex wargames approached a degree of sophistication, abstraction and detail that enhanced their use as a simulation and educational tool. The U.S. military became involved in the commercial hex wargame industry through relationships with certain publishers and game designers, encouraging the circulation of individuals between commercial and Pentagon projects. *Mech War 77: Tactical Armoured Combat in the 1970s* (1975) and *Firefight: Modern U.S. and Soviet Small Unit Tactics* (1976) are two examples. *Firefight* was partially funded by the U.S. Army as a tactical training tool for future NATO/Warsaw-Pact combat at the unit level. *Mech War 77*, which simulated mechanized combat between the U.S. and Soviet Union in West Germany, was introduced into the curriculum of the Army War College in the late 1970s (Macedonia 2002). These games provide players with detailed discussions of doctrine and tactics of each nation simulated in the game, and provide a highly abstracted but interactive forum in which terrain, ballistics, weapons, and even troop morale can be simulated in a variety of scenarios. Rather than simulating past wars, many of the games from this period simulate future/hypothetical combat, scenarios usually related to the shifting conditions of the Cold War. James F. Dunnigan was the lead designer on both games and the company he helped establish, Simulations Publications Inc. (SPI), was instrumental in defining and

Fig. 2 Image of the box contents for Firefight *(1976), including rules of play, reference data and charts, maps and tray for counters.*

popularizing the genre of hex wargames. A central figure for the wargaming community, Dunnigan dedicated a book and monthly journals to game design, military history and analysis. He wrote books about military history and, like many other gamers associated with SPI, became a regular "military expert" for Gulf War coverage in the early 1990s.

The hex wargame reproduces historical battles from different eras, with the modern period (Second World War to the present) being especially popular. Complex and detailed, they provide players with access to extensive data pertaining to warfare of the period, including force capabilities, doctrine, the effects of topography and tactics. The rules and scenarios for these games span ten to twenty pages and the various magazines and journals devoted to the hobby often publish analysis and related historical information. While not emotionally jingoistic (the games adopt a serious but neutral tone), the games tend to reproduce dominant military discourse surrounding specific conflicts and the (unquestioned) need for military solutions to geopolitical problems. This is readily apparent if we examine a few of the games that took conflict in the Middle East for their subject matter. Published over the course of two decades, they either simulate a future conflict or recreate the Persian Gulf War of 1991. *Oil War: American Intervention in the Persian Gulf* (1975) covers a hypothetical attempt by the U.S. and its allies to take control of oil-producing states in the region. The scenario, which rather crudely gathers Iran, Iraq, Saudi Arabia, Kuwait, Qatar and Bahrain together under the moniker "Arab," simulates the military strengths of the various combatants in the region so that players can "game" a number of possible scenarios. The initial edition of *Gulf Strike: Land, Air and Sea Combat in the Persian Gulf* was released in 1983, with a scenario update published in 1988 and an expansion module entitled *Desert Shield* released in 1990 as the Persian Gulf War was unfolding.[4] *Arabian Nightmare: The Kuwait War* (1990) was published in the November issue of *Strategy and Tactics*, after Iraq's invasion of Kuwait but before the attacks by the U.S.-led coalition. The political complexities surrounding the region are better reflected in the rules and accompanying articles (especially when compared to the earlier *Oil War*) but the focus is still combat. *A Line in the Sand* (1991) is not a traditional "hex" game, but a complex board game that simulates combat, politics and diplomacy. Finally, *Back to Iraq* (1993) provides a variety of scenarios, including the involvement of France and the U.K., and renewed hostilities between Iran and Iraq. The focus is still conflict between Western allies and the oil-producing states.

What is most interesting and consistent among these games is how faithfully they reproduce dominant justifications and discourses surrounding war, specifically in relation to Western "interests" in the region. *A Line in the Sand* reinforces some of the most contentious truisms of the period, including the argument that Iraqi aggression was completely unprovoked or that Iraq intended to invade Saudi Arabia. Despite the abundance of historical information, simplistic explanations, assumptions or justifications are ever-present. Pointing out that the game's realism stems from the fact that the main designer was a U.S. Navy Intelligence analyst, a reviewer of *Back to Iraq* remarks: "After playing it just one time I asked myself, 'Could the leaders of Iran and/or Iraq really be dumb enough to wade into a new war against the Western powers?'" (Irby 1994: 14). Typically, there is little awareness in these games of the destabilizing role that Western powers have played in the region or the controversy, prior to the Persian Gulf War, over U.S. diplomatic statements to the Iraqi government that the U.S. would not intervene in Iraq's conflict with Kuwait over issues of financial warfare, oil production quotas, debt and drilling in disputed border regions (Frank 1992). Instead, war is reduced to reference charts and abstract rules with just enough information to allow for simplistic interpretations of the realities of global politics.

Most interesting, but perhaps not surprising, is that the region's oil reserves are treated not as national resources of the respective countries involved, but as the de facto preserve of Western powers. In the introduction to *Desert Shield* (the 1990 expansion for *Gulf Strike*), the designers explain the game's evolution against the backdrop of current events:

> Since the original printing of *Gulf Strike* in 1983, events in the Persian Gulf have once again heated up. In 1988 [the year of release for the first update] it was the last convulsions of the Iran-Iraq war that brought the US and their Western Allies into a confrontational naval escort that guaranteed access to the region's oil. In 1990, it is the grandiose desires of a cunning butcher that have caused this expansion module, as the world's oil access is once again threatened. (*Desert Shield* Rules Book 1990: 2)

While wrapping Western actions in an air of humanitarian concern, Dunnigan himself, in one of the accompanying articles for *Arabian Nightmare*, argues that the justification for intervening in the Persian Gulf is the moral duty to protect other countries from the effects of fluctuations in oil prices:

> With the price of oil nearly doubling again because of Iraq's invasion, citizens of industrialized nations will suffer, but inhabitants of Third World nations will die by the millions. Many people in the West, and especially the media, are ignorant of these effects. (Dunnigan 1990: 8)

While these games reflect the dominant discourse surrounding military conflict and U.S./Western hegemony, they offer to players a unique perspective from which to understand and interact with warfare. These hex wargames can provide detailed (though abstracted) knowledge of battles, logistics, tactical implications of terrain, etc. For players, the ability to compete and simultaneously to interact with history or current events, re-enact tactics and strategy or develop their own, or simply watch as a famous battle unfolds on a kitchen table, adds dimension to military history. The fact that the industry published historical analysis of games and military history and that the U.S. military was involved in the commercial aspects of the industry no doubt contributed to the belief that these games were "serious" simulations.⁵

The complexity of these games was a double-edged sword. While it added to the allure and pleasure for some people, the steep learning curve limited the potential audience. A single game might take hours or days to complete, some players becoming so detailed in their pursuit of realism that "troop panic" and wind direction were incorporated into the ever-expanding reference charts and rule books. The development of the personal computer market opened the hex wargame to new audiences who knew them as "strategy" or "real-time strategy" games, and who might have formerly found reading, interpreting and applying the rules to be extremely tedious. While the boardgame version of the hex wargame is still popular among dedicated fans, it has largely been supplanted by its computer-based counterparts. Even with the expanding popularity of PCs, the hex/strategy style of game had limited popularity, as the complexity and abstraction of the "hex" games cannot provide the spectacle and kinaesthetic sensations of individual combat, especially as represented in post-Second World War television and film. Consequently, it was the military-themed shooter, a very different style of game that would more closely resemble the combat genre of film, that emerged in the mid-to-late 1990s and overshadowed other genres. It flourished within a North American media context that was once again captivated by nostalgia for the Second World War and then overcome by the political and ideological tensions following 9/11.

This period, very different from the one Glick and Charters had in mind, saw the release of a number of high-profile, popular representations of war, including *The Thin Red Line* (1998), *Saving Private Ryan* (1998), *U-571* (2000), *Enemy at the Gates* (2001), *Pearl Harbor* (2001), *Black Hawk Down* (2001), *We Were Soldiers* (2002), *Windtalkers* (2002) and the TV series, *Band of Brothers* (2001). The films were notable not only for their favourable portrayals of the military and its involvement in past conflict, but also because their sudden popularity marked a sharp contrast with the relative absence of war films after the Persian Gulf War (cf. Lacy 2003; Pollard 2002; Wetta and Novelli 2003; Young 2003). Describing them as a new form of moral rearmament, Tom Doherty observed that: "All of the war-minded films embrace a set of suddenly au courant values—a respect for public servants in uniform, a sympathy for military codes of conduct, and a celebration of the virtues forged in the crucible of combat" (2002: 4). The films reflect a patriotic nostalgia attributed, in part, to directors and producers who, as part of the "boomer" generation, grew up surrounded by the mythical status of the Second World War (Bondar 2001; Moses 2002).

The military-themed games of this period evolved in a milieu of excessive patriotism and increasing cooperation between the military and media industries. The Pentagon became much more directly involved in the videogame industry. The military commissioned training simulators that were commercially released and provided assistance to developers, but also created its own online military-themed shooter franchise. Whether in the form of a film or videogame, the representations of war from this period tended to gloss over political and ideological questions and reduce war to an individual's heroic exploits on a seemingly realistic-looking but immersive and entirely aestheticized battlefield.

The Military-Themed Shooter: The Combat Genre Film Made "Real"

> No one can identify with a B-52 and, as Michael Sherry pointed out long ago, we rarely witness bombing raids from below. Ground combat proves much more satisfying. The camera always faces out against the enemy, or inward at the grievous wounds enemy fire causes. The individual soldier fighting for his life becomes the victim of war; those he kills, since they are so evidently bent on his destruction, the perpetrators of violence. His innocence is ours. (Young 2003: 254-55)

Unlike hex wargames, the military-themed shooter game provides the visceral and kinaesthetic pleasures of combat for players. To be more specific, these games provide access to a highly sanitized and aestheticized experience of combat. The designers of these games strive for realism (predominantly defined in terms of photorealism), but combat is designed to be fun for players. Multi-player modes of play more closely resemble an elaborate form of tag than combat and single-player modes, even when they strive for realism or historical authenticity; they have to make many sacrifices in order to ensure the players' experience of combat is an entertaining one.

A sort of hyperrealism dominates the genre. Weapons and equipment are modelled in intricate detail and the authenticity and atmosphere of landscapes are highly valued. Civilians are almost completely absent in these games and while gore is sometimes exaggerated, the general tendency is for the effects of violence to be hidden (Kingsepp 2003). Narrative is almost always present in single-player aspects of these games and developers often borrow heavily from the generic stories and characters seen in Hollywood and on television. In many ways, the military-themed shooter is an extension of the combat film which evolved in Hollywood throughout the postwar period (cf. Basinger 2003). In fact, since narrative is generally confined to the beginning and end of missions and the focus is squarely on combat, it might be more correct to say that the military-themed shooter is simply the expanded and interactive version of a combat film's battlefield scenes.

This is true even when we look back to precursors to the genre. The shooting games that were popular in the 1980s included remakes of films like *Rambo* and *Platoon*. Although the technology of the time only allowed for a top-down or side view of the action, with scrolling or stationary backgrounds, the games managed to offer the remediated pleasures of the filmic original, albeit in a highly simplified form. Developments in the early 1990s, notably the use of the CD-ROM and 3D graphical rendering, allowed for three-dimensional perspectives and expanded narratives, largely restricted to pre-rendered cut-scenes between the actual missions themselves. By the end of the decade, designers of military-themed shooters were openly and enthusiastically looking to recreate the atmosphere and combat of Hollywood blockbusters. The highly stylized opening of *Saving Private Ryan* (1998) was particularly influential. The first mission of *Medal of Honor: Frontline*, released in 2002, so closely resembled that battle scene that players would often refer to it as the "Saving Private Ryan" level.

To characterize military-themed shooters as entirely derivative of the Hollywood combat film would be unfair, however. The genre evolved greatly, developing compelling variations on gameplay and focusing on different historical and contemporary conflicts. Some games might allow the player to adopt the persona of a single character as he (there are few playable female characters in the genre) progresses through a tour of duty or a specific campaign. In other games, sometimes referred to as squad-based shooters, the player can shift between individual members of a squad or play as squad leader and issue commands to others within the group. In team-based, multi-player games, the player may be able to choose between different classes of soldier (infantry, sniper, medic, etc.) which allows for both specialization and teamwork. Since weapons are often modelled with astonishing levels of detail, including sound and performance (especially when utilizing controllers capable of force feedback), a player can *feel* the difference between weapons. This can affect gameplay as some titles incorporate the time it takes to reload different weapons into account and may even allow for a weapon to become jammed. And although it is often the object of ridicule by fans and critics, artificial intelligence has advanced so that both enemy and friendly non-playable characters can act and react with increasing levels of believability.

Fans are being provided with an expanding number of titles offering various styles of gameplay as well as choice of historical conflict. The Second World War is by far the most represented. The mythical status of the conflict and its clear distinctions between good and evil make it popular among fans and publishers looking to stay clear of controversy. Unlike the First World War, which was characterized by rather crude weaponry and trench warfare, the weapons and type of warfare characteristic of the Second World War are better suited to the tastes of modern audiences. The voluminous history of the conflict provides ample archival and human resources for developers to draw upon during the design stages. Since they know the audience is likely to be well-versed in the popularized history of the conflict, it is not uncommon for developers to put substantial resources into historical research when recreating a particular campaign or even the exploits of a particular regiment. Consequently, many of the most popular videogame franchises are set within this conflict. The *Brothers in Arms* series and the long-running *Medal of Honor* series have been extremely successful, as have the *Call of Duty* and the *Battlefield* franchises, though both have recently made the shift away from the Second World War to contemporary, modern warfare.

If the Second World War is over-represented, the opposite is the case for Vietnam. Major franchises tend to stay clear of the conflict, and games that take Vietnam as subject matter and setting tend to be low budget affairs directed at a narrow audience. Still, despite its marginal status, or perhaps because of it, the subgenre of Vietnam games often takes more risks in terms of the representation of violence (the psychological effects are a more prominent theme), as well as in the design of gameplay and story. *Shellshock: Nam '67* (2004), controversial for featuring prostitution and drugs (the player could collect battlefield "souvenirs" and intelligence which could be converted to in-game currency to purchase items or services), did not shy away from controversial aspects of the conflict. Whether it critiqued or revelled in the violence and controversy is another question. After the completion of the game, players could enter a cheat code, widely available online or in the official guide to the game, to enter "psychedelic" mode, in which the player progresses through the same missions but sees the realistic colour palette reduced to pinks, purples, yellows and orange hues (sometimes referred to as "LSD" mode).

The Vietnamese landscape and jungle warfare that became a hallmark of the conflict presents interesting possibilities for players and developers. *Vietcong: Purple Haze* (2004) attempted to recreate the experience of moving with a squad with a Vietnamese guide through the jungles. The slow pace and sounds of the environment, mixed with the heightened awareness brought on by expectation of imminent combat, gave some indication of what jungle warfare must have been like. The story echoes the period's rifts and controversies. *Men of Valor* (2004), one of the first games to feature an African-American as the main, playable character, explores some of the racial components of the conflict and the period. Most interesting perhaps is the way that the music of the period is handled. Popular music of the era, especially iconic songs associated with the civil rights and anti-war protests, make regular appearances in these games. Used in cut-scenes and trailers, these songs often float over stylized montages of combat and explosions or accompany the player, alongside his compatriots, as they move into the jungle during the opening stage of a mission. The music associated with war protests by one generation might be slowly converted in the minds of some younger gamers into anthems accompanying jungle combat in Vietnam.

As mentioned previously, the First World War is rarely seen in the military-themed shooter genre, likely because the equipment, weapons and combat of that period do not match well with modern interests and because the conflict is slowly fading from popular memory. When the conflict does appear, it is usually in sci-fi-based shooters, like *Darkest of Days* (2009), or alternate histories such as the first-person shooter *Iron Storm* (2002). Other conflicts, like the U.S. Civil War, are rarely seen. *The History Channel: Civil War—A Nation Divided* (2006) and its sequel, *The History Channel: Civil War—Secret Missions* (2008), are recent exceptions. Both games carefully navigate through the North-South divide and the fact that both are co-produced by The History Channel contributes to their rather unwieldy titles. As would be expected, the developers took many liberties with the conflict, most notably in the case of weapons and tactics, so that it feels more like 20th-century combat wrapped in a 19th-century veneer.

Contemporary warfare forms the basis for another large segment of games in the genre. These include the relatively few games that take the Persian Gulf War or the Iraq War as settings or, the greater majority which use hypothetical conflicts, often in actual locations but set vaguely in the present or very near future. *Conflict: Desert Storm* (2002) allows players to choose to play as U.S. or British special forces during the Persian Gulf War. Its sequel, *Conflict: Desert Storm II – Back to Baghdad* (2003) was also set during the Persian Gulf War, despite being released during the early stages of the Iraq War. The subtitle "Back to Baghdad" was added for the North American release of the game. *Army of Two* (2008), a highly stylized and wide-ranging game set in Somalia, Afghanistan, Iraq, China and the U.S., is one of the few games to approach the subject of hired mercenaries and military contractors. Somalia is featured in *Delta Force: Black Hawk Down* (2003) and its many sequels, all of which followed the success of the film *Black Hawk Down*. Most games use fictionalized or hypothetical events set in real locations, usually in the near future. Actual combat between nations, their proxies, or anti-terrorism, or some combination of these, comprise the dominant subject matter. Despite their hypothetical nature, and not unlike the contemporary espionage or special-ops novel, realism is important when it comes to weapons, vehicles, tactics, setting and enemies, including suitable racial characteristics, dress and music. While weaponry is a fetishized aspect of the genre as a whole, the ability to see and use cutting-edge equipment and weaponry (even some in the development stage) is an especially prominent feature of these games.

The U.S. Army routinely hosts members of development teams for brief introductions to tactics and the use of weapons, with the goal of ensuring that their modelling and representation will be as accurate as possible. Future soldier-weapon systems become prominent features in these games, and are central to some of the most popular franchises. The Land Warrior system then being developed by the Army was featured in NovaLogic's *Delta Force: Land Warrior* (2000). NovaLogic's subsidiary, NovaLogic Systems, had been contracted to provide a computer game to the Army so that soldiers could become acquainted with new technologies being developed, including a computer screen built into the helmet, a GPS device, and specialized radio communications. The resulting game was "spun off" as a commercial title. Likewise, the popular *Ghost Recon* series, created by a developer

Fig. 3 Depiction of the use of the Future Force Warrior system by the Ghost Recon *series.*

from an idea by Tom Clancy, has incorporated Future Force soldier systems into many later games in the series. Developed in ten-year cycles by the U.S. Army's Natick Soldier Center, these systems, like the Land Warrior system, are meant to develop and incorporate new technologies into the uniform and equipment of the infantry soldier. The Future Force Warrior system was central to *Ghost Recon: Advanced Warfighter* (2006) and *Ghost Recon: Advanced Warfighter 2* (2007). It features see-through computer displays built into the helmet, video cameras mounted on helmets and weapons, and various communications devices giving the player the ability to control equipment such as unmanned aerial vehicles. The next generation of the Future Force system is being used in the next game in the series, *Ghost Recon: Future Soldier*, slated for release in 2011.

It is not surprising that the U.S. military has become so involved in the genre. Within these games combat is rendered as a fun but challenging spectacle; more importantly, they provide a highly controlled virtual space in which individuals can encounter a wide variety of military equipment, training, concepts and terminology, as well as rich symbolism and military traditions. But beyond the confines of the games themselves lie the vast cultural and commercial connections that comprise the videogame industry and its fans. The videogame, as part of the larger "technology boom," has for years been regarded by marketers as a cutting-edge way to reach children and teenage demographics. Within the North American videogame industry in particular, the military-themed shooter and the first-person shooter genre more generally occupy very high-profile positions. These games tend to receive the most attention and praise by critics and industry publications, despite the fact that sales figures for the broad genre of "shooters" is about the same as the other major genres.[6] The genre caters to young, male demographics and those who would self-identify as hardcore or "true" gamers: long-time players who consider themselves to be extremely tech-savvy and knowledgeable about the medium. Since the early 1990s, when the first FPSs began to emerge on the PC and, shortly thereafter on networked PCs and home consoles, modern shooters have driven technical innovations and the move to ever-more-powerful hardware in the industry. Seen in its entirety, the genre of the military-themed shooter attracts desirable demographics, including those considered trend-setters, and allows the military to associate its brand with a forward-looking industry. Given the close relationship between the military and its industrial contractors, both within the videogame industry and in related industries, it is not difficult to understand why the U.S. military would become so directly involved.

America's Army attracted a great deal of media attention when it was first released as a free online PC game in 2002. It was originally conceived by the Army's Office of Economic and Manpower Analysis after recruiting quotas were not filled in the late 1990s. Created by the U.S. Army and a Naval postgraduate research institute, it was subsequently turned into a licensed franchise. According to the Army Colonel responsible for the original concept, the videogame was meant to address the "reduced opportunities for vicarious insights into military service" brought about by force reductions and the end of the draft:

> Hence, whereas in the past a young American could gain insights into military service by listening to the recollections or the advice of an older brother, an uncle, a father, or perhaps a neighbor, today opportunities for such insights are relatively scarce. (Wardynski 2004: 6)

America's Army was thus tied directly to U.S. Army recruiting programs, where player performance and other user statistics could be collected, and players had to graduate from basic training before being allowed to advance in the game. The game created an online presence, tapping in to the fans' tendencies to form "clans" and gather online in forums. Serving U.S. soldiers playing the game would be identifiable to other players, creating a virtual space for soldier-citizen interactions. As a recruiting and quasi-training tool, the *America's Army* franchise turned out be a very successful public relations move and an important "in" with crucial segments of the videogame market.

America's Army was not the U.S. Army's only foray into the videogame market, nor was it the only branch of the military to take such steps. The Army helped fund the Institute for Creative Technologies at the University of Southern California with the goal of gathering together researchers in artificial intelligence and computer graphics along with personnel from Hollywood and the videogame industry. One of their projects, *Full Spectrum Warrior*, was released for Microsoft's

Xbox console in 2004. The commercial release, based on a training tool developed for the Army (the Army version was available in commercial release by using a widely available "cheat code"), was a hybrid strategy/shooter simulating the use of two squads in urban terrain. In similar fashion, the U.S. Marines commissioned a training simulation game which formed the basis for *Close Combat: First to Fight*, released in 2005 but set in Beirut in 2006. Not to be outdone, the U.S. Navy has cooperated with developers for the popular *SOCOM: U.S. Navy SEALs* franchise since the release of the first title in 2002.

Across the military-themed shooter genre, the influence of Hollywood can be seen in the forms of characterization, notably the use of the "diverse-but-unified" group of soldiers which, according to Basinger, became established as a formulaic element of the combat film as early as the Second World War (2003: 46-54). With games that have a direct relationship with the U.S. military, this formula takes a very literal form. In the Hollywood combat genre film, the "diverse group" is a commonly used narrative device which ensures that a diverse audience can find a favorite character-type with whom to identify. The device is common in military-themed shooters and used with little modification. Predictably, games that are set in the Second World War borrow heavily from the films set during the same conflict. Although fewer in number, the same can be said of those games using Vietnam as their setting. When it comes to games where the U.S. military is involved, this narrative device takes on very intriguing characteristics. In *Full Spectrum Warrior*, the personalities given to in-game soldier-characters closely resemble the Army's intended demographics and are communicated through familiar cinematic devices in the game's opening cutscenes. The fact that the game was originally designed as a training tool for the U.S. Army and the Army version is available on the same disc adds to the sense of authenticity, bringing the world of soldiers to the experience of playing the game. For *Close Combat: First to Fight*, marketing materials stressed that the game was made with the help of Marines "fresh from combat" in the Middle East and that the in-game characters were based on actual, active-duty Marines. This means (if the marketing materials are taken more or less as fact by players) that the randomly-assigned characters which make up the player's fire team might actually include the avatars of real U.S. soldiers.

These games' virtual immersion fulfills the U.S. military's need to furnish "vicarious insights" for domestic populations. This function is further enhanced when this immersion takes place alongside serving combat soldiers. Whether these virtual insights are based on reality, propaganda or the remediated reflections from film or television is less important than the belief that these games provide proximity to the military itself.

Fig. 4 Collage of screenshots from the opening sequence of Full Spectrum Warrior *showing the adaptation of the "diverse group" from the Second World War combat genre film.*

Conclusion: The Virtual Experience of U.S. Empire

In her discussion of the resurgent combat film, Marilyn Young identifies the point of view of the soldier as a central characteristic, not only of the genre, but of its potential influence on audiences: "The tight focus on the situation of the combat soldier is inherently dramatic," she says, "and by screening out everything save the immediate context in which he fights, recent war movies, wherever they are set, serve as all-purpose propaganda instruments" (Young 2003: 255). In these dominant media representations of war, war is reduced to the battlefield, and as Young points out, such a narrow point of view, especially when it appears to merge cameras and guns, is inherently propagandistic since it tends to force identification in equally narrow ways.

With the advent of the military-themed shooter, this process is sometimes realized quite literally, as players can occupy the position and determine the actions of a central protagonist while fighting alongside simulated and sometimes real soldiers. What results is a virtual, heavily remediated experience of technologized war. It is a space that one can inhabit but which—symbolically, narratively, discursively, and even experientially—represents a highly controlled and carefully scripted form of spectacle. In this technologized space, WikiLeaks, anti-war protests and competing discourses pertaining to war are rarely allowed entrance.[7] The legacy of Vietnam, the status of the U.S. as a neo-imperial hegemon, civilians, civilian casualties and even death are abstracted or effaced entirely and replaced with an "authentic" experience of war that is clean and exhilarating.

This experience extends beyond the immediate perceptual confines of the games. Enveloped in the history, symbolism, tactics and doctrine of the military, players are simultaneously immersed in the larger culture of the military itself, especially as this relates to other media and the activities of fan communities. While not completely ubiquitous, the U.S. military has maintained a heavy presence in a significant entertainment industry, and in doing so has created an effective virtual culture which can stand in for reality. While maintaining contact with critical demographics, they feed off the influence and popularity of both the industry and the medium. To rephrase this in terms of modern marketing, the military gets to interject its brand image into the lives of its audience in order to create a virtual space where individuals can interact with the brand on an emotional and highly symbolic level. Given the prominent place of the military-themed shooter within the North American videogame industry, this presence potentially extends well beyond the dedicated base of hardcore fans to casual gamers and even those who simply come into contact with the industry's marketing and well-oiled hype machine.

The effectiveness of these games is perhaps best thought of not in terms of how they might radically change opinion or individual behaviour, but in terms of how they reinforce dominant imagery and discourses surrounding war, especially for youthful domestic audiences who have never personally experienced war and rarely see its direct effects. Although there is an abundance of killing in these games, death is largely absent. Civilians are rarely seen, the bodies of dead enemies disappear from view after a few seconds, and when killed the player simply restarts the game. This merges beautifully with the dominant image of war as seen in Hollywood film or on cable or network television news. War, at least for North American audiences, can be spectacular, clean, heroic and even fun.

The degree to which this ideology is made true is perhaps reflected in how uninformed the average U.S. citizen is with regard to the realities and effects of war. Despite the interconnected array of communications and information technology available to the average consumer, and the utter dependence of the modern consumer lifestyle on cheap and increasingly militarized access to petroleum, the level of ignorance about what is undertaken in the world in order to maintain the American Dream is staggering.[8] This ignorance is evident when trying to determine and comprehend a simple fact: the number of Iraqi civilians that have been killed since the U.S. and U.K.-led invasion in 2003. One group, Iraq Body Count, which calculates casualties by confirming and cross-referencing international media reports, put the figure somewhere between 89,369 and 97,568 as of October, 2008.[9] In a cluster sample survey published in the British medical journal, *The Lancet*, it was estimated that through September 2004 more than

100,000 "excess deaths" (defined as fatalities above the pre-invasion civilian death rate) occurred due to the invasion (Roberts et al. 2004). Another study, organized by the Johns Hopkins University and Al Mustansiriya University, estimated that as of 2006, 654,965 excess deaths had occurred since the invasion (Burnham et al. 2006). Yet another, released in September 2007 by the British polling firm Opinion Research, put the number at a staggering 1,220,580.[10] In a 2007 U.S. poll, when asked to estimate the number of Iraqi casualties, the median answer given by respondents was 9,890 (Associated Press 2007). Alas, such figures do not prove much, nor can they be used as evidence of the effectiveness of the military-themed shooter game. The general effectiveness of the military-industrial-entertainment-complex and any outgrowth of its activities, such as the military-themed shooter, can perhaps be comprehended in the gulf between numbers like 9890 and 1.2 million. Or, perhaps it resides in the uncomfortable realization that with all the technology available to us, we have no idea how many have been killed in one of the first conflicts of the 21st century.

Viewed in its larger historical context, the military-themed shooter will likely come to be seen as a complex and multifaceted form of cultural expression that is the logical result of the internal forces of a global superpower. Its technological foundations were laid during the Cold War and Space Race, when the U.S. was at its height militarily, industrially and financially. Interestingly, it reached an incredibly high degree of aesthetic and technical development during a period when the U.S. entered into two costly and highly dubious wars, when its industrial base had already been weakened, and with an economic and financial system that was about to implode. It is tempting to see these developments as the product of a military empire in decline and the increasing need to convince as much of its citizenry as possible that its goals remain just and noble while ensuring that the costs and effects of war are obscured from view.

It seems that with detailed knowledge of the battlefield comes much ignorance about war. Such is life inside (and next to) the empire.

Notes

1. While that is a much more accurate term, I am still partial to that used by U.S. Senator William Proxmire in 1970: "the military-industrial-bureaucratic-trade-association-labor-union-intellectual-technical-academic-service-club-political complex" (Proxmire 1970: 8-9).

2. In fact, in the era of convergence, the interactive nature of the videogame medium is perfectly suited to the industrial practices of modern media conglomerates and their propensity to leverage intellectual content across media holdings and in different media. As Paul Ward (2002) has noted, fans of a modern franchise like *Toy Story* can interact with the story, characters, and larger animated world in film, videogame, or toy form. For Ward, videogames are perfect vehicles for fans to explore the larger "universe" of the modern entertainment franchise.

3. For *SOCOM II: U.S. Navy SEALs*, a popular title for the PlayStation 2, it was revealed in March 2004 that the average *SOCOM II* player spent 4.2 hours a day with online games and that in the first 100 days of *SOCOM II*'s release, players logged 31.5 million hours playing the game online. At the time, numbers like these were often featured in press releases as evidence of how the videogame industry was overtaking rival media industries (IGN 2004).

4. Significantly, the U.S. military would utilize Gulf Strike when it wanted an off-the-shelf wargame to test scenarios while Iraq's invasion of Kuwait was unfolding (Dunnigan 1992: 256-64).

5. There was some awareness of the negative implications of this as well. Fans debated both the ethics of using current events as subject matter and the ethics of working with government or the military. The debate can be found across various issues of *Strategy and Tactics* in 1974. *Moves* magazine published a very interesting essay by a fan on these issues (especially as th pertained to SPI), see Hoffman (1975).

6. In my experience, this fact is very surprising to many university students, including fans of the genre and those who might admit to knowing relatively little about the industry. But data produced by the Entertainment Software Association (www.theesa.com) in the U.S. and Canada for their yearly "Essential Facts on the Computer and Video Game Industry" (general data but useful in this measure), has shown that the broad category of "shooters" consistently accounts for about 10 per cent of the market over the last number of years. When asked what they think the percentage of sales is, some students provide answers as high as 70 or 80 per cent.

7. The lone exception might be the artist Joseph DeLappe and his "Dead in Iraq" project. DeLappe, using his screen name "dead-in-iraq," enters an online match of America's Army and manually types the name, age, service branch and date of death of each service person who has died in Iraq into the text dialog screen meant for communication between players. Despite verbal abuse by other players and being kicked off of servers, DeLappe vows to complete the project by typing in the names of all service personnel killed in Iraq.

8. Since this essay focuses on the U.S. military, my comments here are restricted to U.S. citizens. In reality, however, the forces that I am describing apply equally to Canada and Western nations more generally. When one looks at recent history, it is Western nations (and English-speaking, Christian democracies in particular) that have formed some of the most dominant militaristic and imperialistic institutions dominating the globe.

9. The Iraq Body Count website is available at: http://www.iraqbodycount.org/.

10. A press release on the study, as well as tables and data, is available at: http://www.opinion.co.uk/Newsroom_details.aspx?NewsId=78.

References

Adams, David Wallace and Victor Edmunds. Making Your Move: The Educational Significance of the American Board Game, 1832 to 1904. *History of Education Quarterly*. 17(4): 359-83.

Anderson, Robin. 2003. That's Militainment: The Pentagon's Media-Friendly "Reality" War. *Extra!* (Fairness and Accuracy in Reporting). May/June. http://www.fair.org/extra/0305/militainment.html.

Associated Press. 2007. Americans Unaware of Iraqi Death Toll. 24 February. http://www.msnbc.msn.com/id/17310383.

Basinger, Jeanine. 2003. *The World War II Combat Film: Anatomy of a Genre*. Middletown, CT: Wesleyan University Press.

Bayer, Martin. 2003. Playing War in Computer Games: Images, Myths, and Reality. In *War and Virtual War: The Challenge to Communities*, edited by R.W. Westphal, Jr., 71-86. Oxford: Inter-Disciplinary Press.

Bolter, Jay David and Richard Grusin. 2000. *Remediation: Understanding New Media*. Cambridge, MA: MIT Press.

Bondar, John. 2001. Saving Private Ryan and Postwar Memory in America. *American Historical Review* 106(3): 805-17.

Brown, Kenneth D. 1990. Modelling for War? Toy Soldiers in Late Victorian and Edwardian Britain. *Journal of Social History* 24(2): 237-54.

Burnham, Gilbert, Shannon Doocy, Elizabeth Dzeng, Riyadh Lafta and Les Roberts. 2006. The Human Cost of the War in Iraq: A Mortality Study, 2002-2006. Bloomberg School of Public Health, Johns Hopkins University and School of Medicine, Al Mustansiriya University. http://mit.edu/humancostiraq/reports/human-cost-war-101106.pdf.

De Landa, Manuel. 1991. *War in the Age of Intelligent Machines*. New York: Zone.

Der Derian, James. 2001. *Virtuous War: Mapping the Military-Industrial-Media-Entertainment Network*. Boulder, CO: Westview Press.

Desert Shield. 1990. Rules Book. Baltimore, MD: Victory Games Inc.

Doherty, Tom. 2002. The New War Movies as Moral Rearmament: *Black Hawk Down* and *We Were Soldiers*. *Cineaste* 27(3): 4-8.

Dunnigan, James F. 1990. Why Fight over the Persian Gulf? *Strategy and Tactics* 139(November): 8.

———. 1992. *The Complete Wargames Handbook*. New York: Quill/William Morrow.

Dyer-Witheford, Nick and Greig de Peuter. 2009. *Games of Empire: Global Capitalism and Video Games*. Minneapolis, MN: University of Minnesota Press.

Frank, Andre Gunder. 1992. A Third-World War: A Political Economy of the Persian Gulf War and the New World Order. In *Triumph of the Image: The Media's War in the Persian Gulf—A Global Perspective*, edited by Hamid Mowlana, George Gerbner and Herbert I. Schiller, 3-21. San Francisco: Westview Press.

Glick, Stephen P. and L. Ian Charters. 1983. War, Games, and Military History. *Journal of Contemporary History* 18(4): 567-82.

Hallin, Daniel C. 1997. The Media and War. In *International Media Research*, edited by John Corner, Philip Schlesinger and Roger Silverston, 206–31. New York: Routledge.

Hedges, Chris. 2002. *War Is a Force that Gives Us Meaning*. New York: Anchor Books.

Hoffman, Carl. 1975. A Blatantly Subjective Evaluation of the Brilliant Egotist, Simulation Publications, Inc. *Moves* 22(August-September): 23-26.

Hooks, Gregory. 1990. The Rise of the Pentagon and U.S. State Building: The Defense Program as Industrial Policy. *The American Journal of Sociology* 96(2): 358-404.

Irby, Kirk. 1994. Back to Iraq. *Fire and Movement* 95(July): 14-19.

IGN. 2004. SOCOM TV: Large Online PS2 Community Threatens Primetime TV Shows. IGN Online. 4 March 2004. http://ps2.ign.com/articles/496/496618p1.html.

Jenkins, Henry. 2006a. *Convergence Culture: Where Old and New Media Collide.* New York: New York University Press.

———. 2006b. *Fans, Bloggers, and Gamers: Exploring Participatory Culture.* New York: New York University Press.

Kellner, Douglas. 1992. *The Persian Gulf TV War.* Boulder: Westview Press.

———. 2003. *Media Spectacle.* New York: Routledge.

Kingsepp, Eva. 2003. Apocalypse the Spielberg Way: Representations of Death and Ethics in *Saving Private Ryan, Band of Brothers* and the Videogame *Medal of Honor: Frontline.* In *Level Up,* edited by Marinka Copier and Joost Raessens. CD-ROM. Utrecht: Utrecht University.

Lacy, Mark J. 2003. War, Cinema, and Moral Anxiety. *Alternatives* 28(5): 611-36.

Leonard, David. 2004. Unsettling the Military Entertainment Complex: Video Games and a Pedagogy of Peace. *Studies in Media and Information Literacy Education* 4(4). http://utpjournals.metapress.com/content/4lu7213r34740854/.

Lenoir, Tim. 2000. All But War is Simulation: The Military-Entertainment Complex. *Configurations* 8(3): 289-335.

Leslie, Paul, ed. 1997. *The Gulf War as Popular Entertainment: An Analysis of the Military-Industrial Media Complex.* Lewiston, NY: Edwin Mellen.

Macedonia, Michael. 2002. Games, Simulation, and Military Education. Forum Futures 2002. EDUCAUSE, Forum for the Future of Higher Education. http://net.educause.edu/ir/library/pdf/ffp0206s.pdf.

Machin, David and Theo Van Leeuwen. 2009. Toys as Discourse: Children's War Toys and the War on Terror. *Critical Discourse Studies* 6(1): 51-63.

Moses, Michael Valdez. 2002. Virtual Warriors: Nostalgia, the Battlefield, and Boomer Cinema. *Reason* 32(8): 54-60.

Pollard, Tom. 2002. The Hollywood War Machine. *New Political Science* 24(1): 121-39.

Poole, Steven. 2000. *Trigger Happy: The Inner Life of Video Games.* London: Fourth Estate.

Proxmire, William. 1970. *Report from Wasteland: America's Military-Industrial Complex.* New York: Praeger.

Robb, David L. 2004. *Operation Hollywood: How the Pentagon Shapes and Censors the Movies.* New York: Prometheus Books.

Roberts, Les, Riyadh Lafta, Richard Garfield, Jamal Khudhairi and Gilbert Burnham. 2004. Mortality Before and After the 2003 Invasion of Iraq: Cluster Sample Survey. *The Lancet* (Online), 29 October. http://image.thelancet.com/extras/04art10342web.pdf.

Suid, Lawrence. 2002. *Guts and Glory: The Making of the American Military Image in Film,* revised ed. Lexington, KY: University of Kentucky.

Virilio, Paul. 1989. *War and Cinema: The Logistics of Perception.* Trans. Patrick Camiller. London: Verso.

Ward, Paul. 2002. Videogames as Remediated Animation. In *ScreenPlay: Cinema/Videogames/Interfaces,* edited by Geoff King and Tanya Krzywinska. London: Wallflower Press.

Wardynski, Casey. 2004. Informing Popular Culture: The America's Army Game Concept. In *America's Army PC Game: Vision and Realization*, edited by Margaret Davis. U.S. Army, MOVES Institute, Yerba Buena Art Center 6-7. http://www.movesinstitute.org/~zyda/pubs/YerbaBuenaAABooklet2004.pdf.

Wells, H. G. 1913. *Little Wars: A Game for Boys from Twelve Years of Age to One Hundred and Fifty and for That More Intelligent Sort of Girls Who Like Boys' Games and Books*. Boston: Small, Maynard and Company.

Wetta, Frank J. and Martin A. Novelli. 2003. Now a Major Motion Picture: War Films and Hollywood's New Patriotism. *Journal of Military History* 67(3): 861-82.

Young, Marilyn B. 2003. In the Combat Zone. *Radical History Review* 85(Winter): 253-64.

Ian Roderick

Mil-bot Fetishism: The Pataphysics of Military Robots

ABSTRACT

This paper begins by identifying a tendency in the mass media to represent military robotics in a manner that endows the devices with a degree of automation and agency that is actually beyond the technology. Military robot fetishism is not simply based upon an irrational or mistaken belief about the real capacities of the robots but, instead, their fetish value stems from their positive valuation according to a code of functionality (Baudrillard) that rests upon the risk-transfer labour of the robot. Acting as (Western) soldier surrogates, the promise of the military robot is one of casualty reduction but asymmetrically so. This fetishism arises, as Mulvey proposes, out of the difficulty of representing military reality—namely that waging war has not become a scientifically guided rational-antiseptic enterprise but continues to be a gruesome and violent activity. The fetishization of military robots can be attributed to the need to ameliorate a reality that is politically difficult for western governments and their militaries. In this context, military robotics becomes a science of imaginary technical solutions to the problem of war legitimation. The promotion of military robot fetishism in the mass media means that the military robot as fetish comes to circulate within both martial and civilian lifeworlds, re-legitimizing warfare and affording further militarization of civic life.

RÉSUMÉ

Le fétichisme « mil-bot » : pataphysique des robots militaires

Cet article commence par définir la tendance des mass médias à représenter les robots militaires de manière à conférer à ces engins un degré d'automation et d'agir qui est en réalité au-delà de la technologie. Le fétichisme des robots militaires ne se fonde pas seulement sur une croyance irrationnelle ou erronée au sujet des capacités réelles de ces robots : leur valeur en tant que fétiche provient de la valeur positive qu'on leur accorde en fonction d'un code de fonctionnalité (Baudrillard) qui repose sur le fait que les risques sont transférés au travail du robot. Agissant en tant que substituts des soldats (occidentaux), les robots militaires garantissent une réduction des pertes, mais de manière asymétrique. Ce fétichisme provient, selon Mulroney, de la difficulté de se représenter la réalité – à savoir que la guerre n'est pas devenue une entreprise rationnelle et aseptisée, mais qu'elle est toujours une activité horrible et violente. On peut attribuer la fétichisation des robots militaires au besoin d'améliorer une réalité politique difficile pour les gouvernements occidentaux et leurs militaires. De cette manière, la robotique militaire devient une science de solutions techniques imaginatives au problème de la légitimation de la guerre. La promotion du fétichisme des robots militaires dans les mass médias signifie que le robot militaire en tant que fétiche en arrive à circuler à la fois dans les univers militaires et civils, redonnant une légitimité à la guerre et permettant de pousser plus loin la militarisation de la vie civile.

¤

Our major role is to sanitize the battlefield....
Predator operator quoted in Singer (2009a: 34)

To read the newspaper or follow popular science and technology, it would seem that Unmanned Ground Vehicles (UGVs) have really taken off. The January 2006 issue of *Popular Science* promises readers an inside look at "Tomorrow's Robot Army." Under the sub-heading "Steps to Lethality," it is enthusiastically announced that "We could be at the dawn of a golden age of military UGVs" (Lerner 2006: 45). To be sure, military applications of robotic technologies have been rapidly expanding in the 21st century. For example, a small number of Talon robots were initially deployed in 2000 for Explosive Ordnance Disposal (EOD) work in Bosnia. Today the U.S. Department of Defense has procured more than three thousand of the robots for use in Iraq and Afghanistan as both EOD and reconnaissance equipment (Bray 2009). Likewise, Peter Singer observes that when U.S. forces first invaded Iraq, there were no robots on the ground, by 2004 there were 150 ground robots in use and "by the end of 2008, there were about 12,000 robots of nearly two dozen varieties operating on the ground in Iraq. As one retired Army officer put it, the 'Army of the Grand Robotic' is taking shape" (Singer 2009b). Fuelled in part by "the IED crisis," the robotics industry has been stoked by large amounts of development funding coming from Defense Advanced Research Projects Agency (DARPA) and expanding procurement contracts.[1] The U.S. is not alone in the development of military robotics—according to Singer there are forty-three countries with active military robotics programs—but it is the biggest player (2009b).

As Singer notes, ground robots take a variety of forms, from a robotic arm mounted upon armoured Buffalo EOD vehicles to the more familiar PackBots and Talons. Of course, "weaponized" robots are now also in development. South Korea has stationed robotic machine gun emplacements, developed by Samsung Techwin, on its DMZ, but these have more in common with industrial robots than those more familiar mobile devices. Foster-Miller has adapted its Talon robot to produce Special Weapons Observation Reconnaissance Detection Systems (SWORDS)[2] and has since introduced Modular Advanced Armed Robotic System (MAARS), tele-operated tracked robots that can be mounted with a rifle, light machine gun, grenade or incendiary rocket launcher. While the Samsung's SGR-1 Security Guard Robot does operate with considerable autonomy (equipped with surveillance, tracking, firing and voice-recognition systems, it has an automatic mode that will allow it to "decide" to fire upon its acquired target), most devices including SWORDS are tele-operator controlled. What is interesting is the degree to which autonomy is imputed to these tele-operated robots despite the fact that they are in essence sophisticated remote control devices.[3]

Underlying these representations of military robots as autonomous agents is a kind of techno-fetishism. However, military robot fetishism is not simply based upon an irrational or mistaken belief about the real capacities of the robots; instead, their fetish value stems from their positive valuation according to a code of functionality that rests upon the risk-transfer labour of the robot. At the same time, the values imputed to the mil-bot fetish are understood as representing multiple constituencies and more specifically draw upon the public's historically recent veneration of the soldier's life in order to rearticulate differing civil and martial systems of value into a hegemonic ordering. In this way, military robotics becomes a science of imaginary technical solutions to the problem of war legitimation. Thus, the promotion of military robot fetishism in the mass media means that the military robot as fetish comes to circulate within both martial and civilian life worlds, re-legitimizing warfare and affording further the militarization of civic life.

Documenting Robot Love

In addition to numerous newspaper reports and features (cf. Roderick 2010), military robots have been showcased for the public through a variety of forms of what can be termed "nonfiction entertainment" (cf. Fürsich 2003). By nonfiction entertainment, I am referring to the content of science and technology popularizers such as *Popular Mechanics* and *Popular Science*, as well as the televisual programming content produced for specialty cable channels such as those owned by Discovery Communications Inc. and A&E Networks. Fürsich characterizes nonfiction entertainment as a genre of media content that is "situated between traditional journalistic or public service values and commercial interests" and that tends to be largely driven by readily available content that is characteristically promotional in intent (2003: 132). For example, the home-DVD *Popular Mechanics: The New Technologies of War* incorporates a Future Combat Systems promotional video produced by Boeing and SAIC, the lead contractors for the recently cancelled program. The result is that nonfiction entertainment is typically "non-critical, non-political, combined with a focus upon celebratory worldwide understanding" (132). Consequently, nonfiction entertainment productions, whether in magazine or televisual form, are easily stove-piped with the promotional aims of those who have commercial interests in whatever the particular production is to profile. To put it bluntly, such content can be understood as infomercials that, rather than selling directly to the potential purchaser, draw upon existing public interest so as to promote public support for often already existing vendor-purchaser relationships and the use of public monies in the acquisition of the military commodities being showcased.

Not surprisingly, then, nonfiction entertainment treatments of military robotics tend to bring forth the same talking points that are continually reiterated by military and contractor spokespersons. The robots are invariably venerated for their ability to "go in harm's way" and "save lives." What is particularly striking about the way military robots are represented here is that they are consistently introduced as not only life-saving but also an autonomous if not anthropomorphized technology. Almost invariably, the verbal and visual text introduces the robot as some sort of independently operating device.

Though the robots are obviously inanimate, tele-operated objects, the language and video editing used to introduce the robots to the viewers frequently represents the robotic device in question as an actor in its own right. Typically, the robot is initially presented to the viewer moving across a landscape and described by the narrator as or in comparison to a human soldier. Thus in *Robo-Warriors* (A&E Home Video 2007), the History Channel video opens as follows:

Narrator: "In the war on terrorism, meet America's newest and deadliest soldier."

Narrator: "A three-foot-tall, robotic sharp-shooter, named SWORDS"

[video of robot moving and firing with no sign of controller]

Narrator: "Armed with a machine gun and precision aiming platform, its aim is so accurate and so lethal, that SWORDS virtually never misses its target."

It is only after about a minute into the video that it is revealed that the robot is not operating autonomously:

Narrator: "SWORDS is operated by soldiers safely out of harm's way [shot of soldier-operator at a controller] who control its movements, choose its targets, and fire its weapons all from a laptop computer. With its night and thermal vision, and seven camera capacity, SWORDS can locate and destroy an enemy up to a mile away."

Similarly, in the "Smart Weapons" (2006) episode of *FutureWeapons*, the portion of the program dedicated to the SWORDS robot again opens with footage of a robot that seems to function autonomously.

> Host: "Imagine a soldier that never has to eat or sleep. Who never experiences fear. And never complains."
>
> [Cuts back and forth between medium distant full shots of host and close up partial shots of different parts of the moving SWORDS Talon robot]
>
> Host: "Who is three feet tall, has four eyes, and can see in the dark."
>
> [Cuts between POV shot of robot and back to medium close-up of host]
>
> Host: "And, who is so attached to his weapon that it takes a screwdriver and pair of pliers to take it from him."
>
> [Cuts between close-up of host and SWORDS robot fitted with a light machine gun being discharged.]

Not until just past one minute into the narrative is the viewer told: "This smart, wheeled assassin is controlled by a soldier calling the shots from a safe distance from the enemy," and the device is revealed to be operating tele-remotely through the visual representation of the soldier-operator. Indeed, this manner of introducing the robot has become such a convention that in the Oscar winning film *The Hurt Locker* (Bigelow 2008), which is fundamentally about an EOD technician's "addiction" to going into harm's way, the opening scene also commences with a PackBot seemingly racing independently into a suspected IED site as it is being evacuated.

This animism of the military robots is further accomplished by the practice of representing them as objects of affection. For example, in the "Future Combat" episode of *FutureWeapons* the host kneels down beside a Future Combat Systems SUGV robot:

> [robot "head" is swivelling and then rises as host talks]
>
> Host: "This cute little guy right here is SUG-V—Small Unmanned Ground Vehicle. It's a man portable robot that goes and does reconnaissance missions. You can send him into harm's way and keep your soldiers safe."
>
> [host pats robot on "head"]
>
> Host: "Good job."

Another example of this appears in the *Popular Mechanics* magazine feature "America's Robot Army":

> The MULE is toying with my emotions. After running through its full range of articulated positions—a hilarious diagnostic dance routine that

has it pivoting, rising and tipping its wheels off the road—the object is now ramming a car. The sedan offers little resistance, sliding across the asphalt. Like proud owners watching their pit bull tear through a chew toy, the small crowd of defense contractors and engineers are chuckling. (Sofge 2008: 63)

The comparison to a dog is not uncommon and certainly works to remind the reader of the familiar adage about the dog's special relationship to "man." Robots are often treated by their operators in the field as familiar objects of affection and this is demonstrated in the practice of naming robots. EOD teams, for example, are often quoted providing pet names for their assigned robots and manufacturers such as iRobot have made great mileage out of this practice in their publicity. Thus in *Robo-Warriors* (History Channel 2007), a clip shows a soldier explaining that they have named their 'bots Stimpy and Ren ("Ren is on standby in the truck right now") and that Stimpy is "probably the most valuable asset we have to the team." Treatments such as these contribute to the image of the robot as reliable helpmate that can only be of benefit to soldiers in the field.

As these examples suggest, the robots are frequently presented in an animistic fashion or as artificially intelligent devices capable of fulfilling tasks independent of the actual controller. While this is most common when introducing the device, it is also not uncommon to further animate the robot when detailing its capacities. Accordingly, even after revealing the SWORDS robot to be tele-operated, the *Robo-Warriors* video continues to represent the robot as if it were an autonomous technology: "With its night and thermal vision and seven camera capacity, SWORDS can locate and destroy an enemy up to a mile away." Clearly, it would actually be the soldier-operator that would "locate and destroy an enemy" using the technical features of the SWORDS robot.[4] And while it may be tempting to dismiss this predilection for representing the robots as autonomous devices as a symptom of the over-valuation of the robot based upon a misunderstanding of the robot's real capacities, I would like to propose a somewhat different interpretation.

Fetishism and Social Value

The convention of having the robot roll out before the viewer and then revealing what is actually "making it go" is obviously done for effect. Presenting the robot in this fashion certainly has a greater impact than simply commencing with a shot that includes both robot and operator. Clearly what is happening is that the robot is being offered up to the viewer as a marvellous object, indeed as a techno-fetish. It initially seems to behave as if it possesses a life of its own, but its animation is not the result of spirits but rather of technology. It is precisely this obsession with (re)presenting the robot as an autonomous technology that contributes to its positive valuation as a technical solution to a "needed" functionality.

Characterizing military robotic devices as fetish objects is not without its problems. Fetishism as a concept enters into social theory in the proto-anthropological accounts of "savage" peoples and their supposed practices of worshiping objects. Both Freud and Marx inherit this conception of fetishism, attributing to it a misunderstanding of the nature of the object's significance and the misattribution of qualities properly associated with human subjects to objects instead. In being used to pass judgment on a perceived over-valuation of an object as indicative of a false consciousness of the real conditions of the world, fetishism would seem to be of limited usefulness in thinking through the actual processes of valuation that endow the object with its special significance.

In his critique of Marxian political economy, Baudrillard observes that the "term 'fetishism' almost has taken on a life of its own. Instead of functioning as a metalanguage for the magical thinking of others, it turns against those who use it and surreptitiously exposes their own magical thinking" (1981: 90). For Baurdrillard, calling upon fetishism to describe human relations with objects is a kind of fetish itself: "it is the conceptual fetish of vulgar social thought" (88). Turning to the "great fetish metaphor" is dangerous he argues because it forestalls analysis by allowing one to substitute rigorous thought with a kind of magical thinking about the thinking of others. As such, the metaphor of fetishism depends upon and simultaneously shores up a rationalistic metaphysics. In being able to reveal irrational thought and erroneous judgment of others, one can readily dispatch any doubt that one's own thought is anything but both rational and sound. Baudrillard then warns us that invoking fetishism "is dangerous not only because it short-circuits analysis, but because since the 18th century it has conducted the whole repertoire of occidental Christian and humanist ideology" (88).

At the same time, this does not preclude using the concept of fetishism to think critically about the magical thinking of others (cf. Roderick 2010). Hornborg, for example, draws from Latour's call for a symmetrical anthropology to propose an "anthropology that does not merely represent an urban, 'modern' perspective on the 'pre-moderns' in the margins, but that is equally capable of subjecting modern life itself to cultural analysis" (Hornborg 2006: 22). For Hornborg, fetishism is not simply a false understanding of subject-object relations but rather constitutes a strategy for knowing the world. Hornborg points to a more positive or productive understanding of the process of fetishism. Similarly, Dant understands the fetish object to be a site of mediated social value so that its perceived special qualities are emergent through a process whereby "[o]bjects are noticed, are given attention, are drawn into relevance and constituted as meaningful through social interaction" (Dant 1999: 121). The fetish object is not simply a negation of a repressed or misunderstood reality, nor is it simply "reflecting back the ideas and beliefs of its worshippers, it is transforming them or, in the language of actor-network theory, 'translating' them" (44). The fetish is more than a sign—like any medium, the materiality of the fetish does not simply "carry" the sign or significance of its value but rather imbeds itself in its "message," (re)articulating it so as to privilege a particular trajectory out of many possibilities (Akrich and Latour 1992: 259). Therefore, the fetish has inter-subjective consequences for the fetishists.

Despite his forewarning of the fetishism of fetishism, Baudrillard opens the door to a more productive or "positive" conception of fetishism. He revisits the etymology of fetish and draws on an earlier meaning that precedes its more familiar usage as a sign of misattribution or misunderstanding:

> Today it refers to a force, a supernatural property of the object and hence to a similar magical potential in the subject.... But originally it signified exactly the opposite: a *fabrication*, an artifact, a labor of appearances and signs. (1981: 91)

Baudrillard then argues that "[i]f fetishism exists it is thus not a fetishism of the signified ... it is a *fetishism of the signifier*" (1996: 93). The fetish value of the object stems not from obfuscated social labour but rather from the very social labour invested in fetishizing the object itself. It is precisely the role the fetish plays as a sign or "mediator of social value" (Dant 1999: 41) that begins to explain the fascination the fetish holds for the fetishist. Fetishism can be understood as "a sign of cultural labor" (Baudrillard 1981: 91) rather than as a mistaken belief in the order of things, which can lend itself to the production of a metalanguage for thinking critically about magical thinking and the social values of others. My intention is not to simply adopt a celebratory stance toward fetishism but rather to re-appropriate the term so as to engage critically with the magical thinking that gives the military robot its fetish status. We may at some level all be fetishists, but what we choose to fetishize is telling.

For an object to acquire the status of fetish, it must be transformed into a sign of cultural value and this transformation is accomplished through its appropriation into social relations. If we accept Baudrillard's thesis that *both* human need and object use are socially constituted, then the fetish object derives its status not through any intrinsic property but rather through the significance granted to its perceived or attributed capabilities (1981: 63-87). And just as needs are socially derived, the functionality of the object is not so much an intrinsic property as what ties the object to a system of needs and practices which arise in relation to those defined needs. According to Baudrillard:

> "functionality" in no way qualifies what is adapted to a goal, merely what is adapted to an order or system: functionality is the ability to become integrated into an overall scheme. An object's functionality is the ability to become a combining element, an adjustable item, within a universal system of signs. (1996: 67)

It is the degree to which the robot cannot only offer a "needed" functionality but exceed it—offer it in excess—that gives it its value and thus allows it to gain the status of fetish. Therefore, in order for the object to be venerated, "it must be valued according to a code of functionality which orders both human subjects and material objects" (Dant 1999: 49). The mil-bot fetish ties its fetishists to what I shall develop as a scheme of risk-transfer militarism.

Following Dant, the concept of fetishism is extended to become an analytic tool that examines how the social value of some objects is overdetermined "through ritualistic practices that celebrate or revere the object, a class of objects, items from a 'known' producer or even the brand name of a range of products" (1999: 56). One could argue that the convention of animating and then revealing the "true nature" of the robots serves as a ritual of organizing, investing with significance, endowing with values and capacities, incorporating into social action and relations and, ultimately, revering the military robot. Furthermore, the use of provided footage, corporate spokespersons and military experts contribute to a consistent and coherent tone of reverence toward military robots as a class of objects, specifically robots manufactured by contractors such as Foster-Miller and iRobot, whose prestige is enhanced by a public brand awareness of their wares. The point is not whether the autonomous representations are true or false but rather that the military-robot fetish takes on a special status through multiple positive valuations which ultimately overdetermine the value of the robot as something that has the capacity to do special "needed" things.

While the fetish value of the military robots is realized in part through their animistic representation, fetish value is further accomplished through the reverence toward their "needed functionality" as a life saving technology that is able to keep soldiers out of harm's way by taking on the risks those soldiers would otherwise face. In *Robo-Warriors*, Vice Admiral Joe Dyer (Ret.), President of Government and Industrial Robots Division at iRobot declares: "In the old days, a very, very courageous person would put on a bomb suit and walk out and with great focus and great courage deal with a bomb that might go off at any second. Today, you send the robot" (History Channel 2007). This sentiment is echoed by Major General Rob Scales (Ret.) who appears in *Robo-Warriors* as a military expert: "It's the Pentagon's dream that one day these futuristic machines will be able to perform functions that are dangerous for men and women in uniform. It would be useful if we had a surrogate, a machine to do that." And again, the same theme is repeated by military research scientist Chuck Shoemaker of the Army Research Lab, Development and Engineering Command: "The potential to have robot vehicles go out ahead in harm's way is one of the things that certainly keeps us excited about pushing the technology every day." It is the cumulative effect of reverently over-coding the robot with valued forms of functionality in these practices that endows them with fetish value.

The understanding of the military robot as a proxy for the human soldier is taken to its logical extremes in the "Future Warrior" episode of *Future Weapons* (Discovery 2008):

> Host: "But is it pushing it a bit to start thinking of the SMSS as a robotic member of the squad?"
>
> Lockheed Martin contractor: "The SMSS should be treated as another soldier. Basically, you should give it orders, tell it what you want it to do, and let it go do it. And like the soldier, it will either complete the mission or if it gets confused, doesn't understand, find something that wasn't expected, turn around essentially and ask you for further instructions just like a soldier would.
>
> Host: "And if the SMSS is really expected to step up on the frontline, then it seems only fair to give it a gun."

The SMSS or MULE robot is equal to the obedient soldier and in an appeal to fairness the host proposes that it too should be entitled to bear arms. Is the SMSS soldier-like or is the soldier robot-like?

Dant asserts that the fetishization of an object is accomplished by "[e]xpressing desire for and approval of the object and what it can do, celebrating the object, revering it, setting it apart, displaying it, extolling and exalting its properties, eulogizing it, enthusiastic use of it," and clearly, nonfiction entertainment treatments of military robots follow the recipe to the letter. In their enthusiastic, uncritical, sycophantic and willing boostering of the arms industry, the producers of such media content consistently engage unerringly in the discursive action crucial to the production of fetish value.

The Robot Fetish as Heteroglossic Object

If mil-bot fetishism depends upon the cumulative, enthusiastic and worshipful treatment of these technical objects—to the degree that the robots are broadly adored—they must then be able to accommodate internal differentiations. Fetish objects, no matter how privately worshipped, are always social. If fetish objects are overdetermined as Dant proposes, it is in part because they are materializations of social heteroglossia. Bakthin uses the term heteroglossia to connote the internal diversity of any national language, and within the seemingly coherent, rule-bound, whole of a given language one will find a multitude of subjected forms. "Closely connected with the problem of polyglossia and inseparable from it is the problem of heteroglossia *within* a language, that is, the problem of internal differentiation, the stratification characteristic of any national language" (Bakhtin 1981: 67). Likewise, if the reverence of the fetish object is arrived at through its status as a mediator of social value then it too must be internally stratified in terms of being able to accept the adoration of multiple constituencies. At the risk of literalizing Bakhtin we can borrow his account of the internal and surrounding heteroglossia of the "object":

> Along with the internal contradictions inside the object itself, the prose writer witnesses as well the unfolding of social heterglossia *surrounding* the object, the Tower-of-Babel mixing of languages that goes on around any object; the dialectics of the object are interwoven with the social dialogue surrounding it. (1981: 278)

In this respect, fetish objects with broad appeal must internalize competing and contradictory attributions of fetish value. Rather than assuming that military techno-fetishism is founded upon top-down monovalent codings, it is far more fruitful, though infinitely more complicated, to acknowledge the multi-voicedness of technical objects. As Thibault suggests:

> Bakhtin's concept [of heteroglossia] provides us with a way of breaking with the presumed intersubjective unity of the knowing subject and the object of knowledge, [for example, language.] Bakhtin's concept shows us that there is no necessary and unified point of reference for social meaning making practices, just as there is no given, determinate worldview that is simply mirrored or reflected in, say, language. (Thibault 1991: 104)

In other words, mil-bot fetishism cannot be reduced to a single unifying set of values.

Drawing from Feenberg, Pretorius's account of military technology is suggestive of a more heteroglossic understanding of the techno-fetishism of military artifacts (Pretorius 2008; cf. Feenberg 1999). In seeking to champion a social constructivist approach to technology[5], Pretorius argues that the social significance of military technologies is not simply disseminated in a top-down fashion:

> To argue that efficiency and rational control are the sum total of meaning embodied by these technologies privileges the role that dominant technological actors play in technological design and negates the role of ordinary people and their life-world experience of these technologies. (2008: 302)

Pretorius seeks to remind us of the polysemy of military artifacts and that the meanings of technological artifacts are accomplished through reference to material life-world experiences:

> These life-world experiences would include those of the soldiers who operate military technologies, the enemy who are targeted by them, the civilians who are killed in their line of fire, the international "human shields" that brace a conflict situation to impose a form of restraint on their deployment, those who feel liberated from political oppression as a result

of their use, the diverse, transnational lobby groups that protest against their use, and the scores of people who become aware of their existence and application through the mass media or by word of mouth. (Pretorious 2008: 302)

I do not propose to provide an exhaustive inventory of the different kinds of meanings that the military robot may bear, nor do I believe that the nonfiction entertainment texts that I am referring to in this paper are sufficiently dialogical to include oppositional meanings. Pretorius's argument, however, points to the fact that the military robot as fetish must circulate in different life-worlds, different realms of experience and therefore the common sense by which reality is perceived and judgments made. The fetish value of the robot stems from its ability to circulate and bear meaning in both martial and civilian life-worlds.

For Schutz and Luckman, the life-world entails "not only the 'nature' experienced by me but also the social (and therefore the cultural) world in which I find myself; the life-world is not created out of merely the material objects and events which I encounter in my environment" (1973: 5). The life-world as the "province of reality which the wide-awake and normal adult simply takes for granted in the attitude of common sense" (3) is something akin to what Bourdieu calls practical sense, that which facilitates the making of choices without recourse to conscious calculation: "social necessity turned into nature" (Bourdieu 1990: 69). Therefore, we need to acknowledge that on one hand, mil-bot fetishism is not reducible to the values of the militaries and their contractors and that on the other hand, as the mil-bot fetish circulates through both civil and martial life-worlds, it re-articulates the differing systems of interpretation into a hegemonic ordering of social values.

Pataphysical Solutions to War Legitimization

Understanding the appeal of the life-saving mil-bot for the civilian requires that it be contextualized in terms of both a changed public attitude towards the soldier and an expectation on the part of the public that warfare can be efficiently conducted with a minimum of civilian casualties. Firstly, soldiering today is seen as more of a profession or at least a skilled occupation than as the last resort against unemployment or simply as cannon fodder (Shaw 2002: 357; 2005).[6] Secondly, publics have come to expect that wars can be fought with precision and that only enemy combatants will be killed when necessary. Western governments understand full well that to neglect either expectation will carry serious political consequences.

Shaw argues that in response to the political risks of waging war, Western states[7] have sought to re-legitimize warfare by seeking to fight wars in a manner intended to limit the risks faced by Western military forces (2002; 2005). As Maj. General Scales (Ret.) puts it in *Robo-Warriors* (2007):

> The object of the American style of warfare is to fight our wars at minimum cost to human life. So anything we can do to reduce that cost by putting machines in front of men [laugh] replacing men with machines of course, is something this nation has been trying to do for many years.

The "survivability" of Western troops has therefore increasingly become a fundamental scientific and political problem for Western states as they seek to conduct warfare while minimizing the domestic political risks of waging war. This is most apparent in weaponry that is engineered to maximize "lethality" and in protective equipment and medical care designed to maximize survivability. The result is a gross asymmetry of casualties between Western and non-western military forces in military conflicts. Appropriately, Shaw terms this new Western way of war "risk-transfer warfare."

Risk-transfer warfare is accomplished by the refinement of "military power, at three main levels: strategy, weaponry and media management. The combination of these elements enables the West to fight wars at little human cost to itself" (Shaw 2002: 349). Shaw argues that risk-transfer warfare is in fact a further refined form of militarism that carries few political consequences. Mil-bot fetishism fits perfectly within this refinement of military power and militarism since the robots are made to operate on all three levels: they are integrated into a strategy of conducting warfare at a distance; they allow soldiers to fight tele-remotely; and as fetish objects, they lend themselves perfectly to the delivery of a message that all is being done to reduce casualties. Military robot fetishism then arises, as Mulvey proposes, out of the difficulty of representing reality—namely that waging war has not become a scientifically guided rational-antiseptic enterprise but continues to be a gruesome and violent activity (1993: 5). In the context of risk-transfer militarism, the military robot functions therefore as a pataphysical or imaginary technical solution to the political problem of war legitimization.

The concept of 'pataphysics is derived from the work of Alfred Jarry and my appropriation of the term here is admittedly not entirely faithful to Jarry's project. As Doctor Faustroll, Jarry defines 'pataphysics as:

> *the science of that which is superinduced upon metaphysics, whether within or beyond the latter's limitations, extending as far beyond metaphysics* ... the science of imaginary solutions, which symbolically attributes to their lineaments the properties of objects described by their virtuality. (1996: 21)

'Pataphysics is proposed as a transgressive practice of examining the laws which seek to preside over exceptions and further co-opting science in the name of poetics; however, my borrowing of pataphysics is intended to point to the excess that is crucial to the "functioning" of mil-bot fetishism.

Christian Bök helps us understand Jarry's superinduction when he proposes that "[r]ather than build operative devices for harnessing thought ... the 'pataphysician must instead build excessive devices for unleashing thought" (2002: 29). The mil-bot fetish is, I would argue, an excessive device, but given its hegemonic supra-function, one for harnessing rather than unleashing thought. By referring to the representations of the science of military robots as pataphysical thinking (rather than simply magical), my intent is to call attention to the imaginative work being done in the development of the mil-bot fetish. My use of the term pataphysics is therefore to convey the idea that in partnership, military administrators, scientists and contractors are engaging in their own pataphysics by presenting the mil-bot as an imaginary technical solution to the problem of casuality reduction which in turn is a solution to the problem of the re-legitimization of warfare. Mil-bot fetishism is not simply a false metaphysics that produces a (mis)truth about the "real" nature of the military robot; instead, it foregrounds the imaginative contemplation/evaluation of the capacities and capabilities of the robots as technical objects, which in turn brings them to life.

At the root of mil-bot fetishism is the construction of a pataphysical solution to the problem of war legitimacy. The nonfiction entertainment features that endow military robots with fetish value must be understood as part of the media management component of risk-transfer militarism. They send the mil-bot fetish into the civilian life-world as part of strategy for colonizing and ultimately militarizing everyday life by making it amenable to the needs of risk-transfer militarism.

In Western states today, war is experienced very differently than from past wars of attrition that fed upon total mobilization and mass call-ups. For the general public with little first hand knowledge, warfare is something experienced and enters into knowledge largely through mediated forms. As Compton observes:

> The experience of warfare is, for a majority of Western citizens, limited to spectacle. Western liberal democracies require the support of public opinion to wage war. The bulk of the population is mobilized, not as soldiers and producers of war armaments, but as "spectators of war," who are sold on the rightness of battle in the name of sacred universal values. (2005: 46)

Seeing the mil-bot fetish come to life plays out like a micro-spectacle that dramatizes a conception of war that imagines the mil-bot to be a scientifically guided rational-antiseptic enterprise. Everyone (the Department of Defense, the contractors, the producers, the host and, of course, the audience) understands that the devices are not able to function autonomously but for one spectacular moment, they seem to come to life, able to solve the problem of how to protect Western soldiers and fight wars with precision. When Compton writes that the "news spectacle dramatizes a political world beyond the everyday experiences of people while simultaneously offering explanations, admonitions and reassurances for social problems" (2005: 41), it is not difficult to extend this to nonfiction entertainment. In presenting the mil-bot fetish as an imaginary technical solution to the problem of casualty aversion and the brutal realities of war, nonfiction entertainment becomes "constitutive of the process by which cognitive maps are constructed and used by individuals and social groups" (Compton 2005: 42). Such entertainment sends the mil-bot fetish into the civilian life-world and thus constructs a set of spectacular mediated experiences that have the potential to restructure the civilian life-world, paving the way for its further militarization by remapping realms of experience and "adjusting" the common sense by which reality is to be perceived and judgments made.

Conclusion

I have sought to demonstrate how nonfiction entertainment engages in military techno-fetishism by producing the kinds of ritualistic practices that revere the military artifact and invest it with social value. In the case of military robots, this value, I argue, is not simply based upon an irrational or mistaken belief about the real capacities of the robots but rather on their ability to be over-coded with a "needed" functionality. The repeated act of extolling the robots' ability to "go in harm's way" and "save lives" over-determines their social value, giving them the status of fetish object. As such, the mil-bot literally seems to take on a life of its own in nonfiction entertainment.

Not only are the robots venerated as life-saving technologies, they are consistently introduced as autonomous if not anthropomorphized technology. However, this predilection for representing the robots as autonomous devices is not simply a symptom of over-valuation based upon a misunderstanding of the robots' real capacities. Instead, the convention of animating and then revealing the tele-operational nature of the robots serves as a ritual for organizing, investing with significance, endowing with values, incorporating into social action and relations and, ultimately, revering the mil-bot fetish.

At the root of this mil-bot fetishism is the construction of a pataphysical solution to the problem of war legitimization. At the same time however, I do not want to suggest that the meaningfulness of the mil-bot fetish is determined in a top-down manner. Mil-bot fetishism ties the military robot to a system of needs and practices which arise in relation to those defined needs. This means that while mil-bot fetishism is not reducible to the values of the militaries and their contractors, the mil-bot fetish circulates through both civil and martial life-world and has the potential to re-articulate those differing systems of interpretation into a hegemonic ordering of social values. Accordingly, mil-bot fetishism is intended to be experienced as micro-spectacles that seek to remap the realms of civilian experience and public common-sense so as to encourage perceptions and judgments which favour risk-transfer militarism. It works to bind public sentiments regarding casualty avoidance with practices of warfare that will not only assure far greater mortality for non-Western soldiers, but will also assure, indirectly, the deaths of civilians since as Shaw points out, in risk-transfer warfare:

> The care taken for civilians is not only *less* than the care taken for American soldiers, it is *undermined* by a policy adopted to keep the latter safe. Risk to civilians is reduced not as far as practically possible, but as far as judged necessary to avoid adverse global media coverage. *Civilians' risks are proportional not to the risks to soldiers ... but to the political risks of adverse media coverage.* (2002: 355)

Celebrating the robot as a life-saving device does not affirm the value of human life but in fact allows Western states the opportunity to sidestep that fundamental principle.

Notes

1. According to a 2006 *Boston Globe* article, what began "as a 12-person office to develop quick strategies for combating homemade bombs in Iraq – has quietly expanded into a $3 billion-per-year arm of the Pentagon, with more than 300 employees and thousands of contract workers, according to Pentagon data" (Bender 2006).

2. By 1982 the U.S. Army's Missile Command (MICOM) had already begun to sponsor research into the development of mobile robotic platforms that would allow a soldier-operator to remotely fire anti-armour weapons. Grumman actually introduced a tele-operated weaponized robotic platform similar to SWORDS called the Robotic Ranger in 1985 (Geisenheyner 1989; Everett and Gage 1996), but it was never adopted and presumably the project was cancelled. Since the deployment of the initial three SWORDS robots, which to date have reportedly not been used in combat, Foster-Miller has developed its successor, the MAARS robot. To date, only one has been shipped in 2008 under contract to the U.S. military's Explosive Ordnance Disposal/Low-Intensity Conflict (EOD/LIC) Program in Iraq (Foster-Miller 2008).

3. While addressing the interrelationship between the development of control systems, automated technologies and military artifacts is germane to the broader understanding of the import being granted to robotics by defence strategists and planners, the focus of this article is how public support for their procurement is being promoted through what is often termed "militainment." Elsewhere I have addressed these broader themes in terms of automation, artificial intelligence, control and training systems (Roderick 2007, 2008, 2009). For a discussion of the historical specificity of this interest in automation, see Roderick (2010: 8-9)

4. Indeed, as I will address below, representatives from Foster-Miller and the U.S. military are in fact often at pains to remind the viewers and presumably the producers that when it comes to weaponized robots, it is always a human that makes the decision to fire.

5. Though for the purposes of this paper I am primarily focusing upon the sign value of the object, I am not actually proposing a social constructivist approach to technology. Nonetheless, Pretorius's argument is helpful in alerting us to the fact that the significance and social value of a military artifact is not predetermined.

6. Indeed the Canadian Armed Forces has published a leadership manual entitled *Profession of Arms* in Canada which sets out to codify the values, ethos, and role of the military in civil society.

7. I use the deficient term Western to connote the small number of world states such as Canada, the United States, the United Kingdom, Germany, Italy, Australia, Japan, etc., which are tied together through relatively stable and enduring political, military and economic relationships.

References

Akrich, Madeline and Bruno Latour. 1992. A Summary of a Convenient Vocabulary for the Semiotics of Human and Nonhuman Assemblies. In *Shaping Technology/Building Society*, edited by W. Bijker and J. Laws, 259-64. Cambridge, MA: MIT Press.

Bakhtin, Mikhail M. 1981. *The Dialogic Imagination: Four Essays*, edited by Michael Holquist. Trans. Caryl Emerson and Michael Holquist. Austin, TX: University of Texas Press.

Baudrillard, Jean. 1981 [1972]. *For a Critique of the Political Economy of the Sign*. Trans. C. Levin. St. Louis, MO: Telos Press.

———. 1996 [1968]. *The System of Objects*. Trans. James Benedict. New York: Verso.

Bender, Brian. 2006. Panel on Iraq Bombings Grows to $3b Effort. *The Boston Globe*, 25 June. http://www.boston.com/news/world/middleeast/articles/2006/06/25/panel_on_iraq_bombings_grows_to_3b_effort/.

Bigelow, Kathryn (dir.). 2008. *The Hurt Locker* (film). Voltage Pictures (prod.).

Bök, Christian. 2002. *'Pataphysics: The Poetics of an Imaginary Science*. Evnaston, IL: Northwestern University Press.

Bourdieu, Pierre. 1990. *The Logic of Practice*. Trans. Richard Nice. Stanford, CA: Stanford University Press.

Bray, Hiawatha. 2009. Battlefield Robot Had Security Hole: Insurgents Could Steal Video Before Local Firm Made Fix, *The Boston Globe*. 19 December. http://www.boston.com/business/technology/articles/2009/12/19/battlefield_robot_had_security_hole/. Accessed 30 December 2009.

Compton, James R. 2005. Shocked and Awed: The Convergence of Military and Media Discourse. In *Global Politics in the Information Age*, edited by Peter Wilkin and Mark Lacy, 39-62. Manchester: Manchester University Press.

Dant, Tim. 1999 *Material Culture in the Social World: Values, Activities, Lifestyles*. Philadelphia, PA: Open University Press.

Discovery Communications Inc. 2006. Smart Weapons, *FutureWeapons*, Season 1, Episode 5. First aired 17 May.

———. 2007. Future Combat, *FutureWeapons*, Season 2, Episode 12. First aired 2 April.

———. 2008. Future Warrior, *FutureWeapons*, Season 3, Episode 6. First aired 5 May.

Everett, H.R. Bart and Douglas W. Gage 1996. A Third Generation Security Robot, *SPIE Mobile Robot and Automated Vehicle Control Systems*, Boston MA, 20-21 November, 290. http://www.spawar.navy.mil/robots/land/robart/spie96.html. Accessed 30 December 2009.

Feenberg, Andrew. 1999. *Questioning Technology*. New York: Routledge.

Foster-Miller. 2008. First MAARS Robot Shipped to U.S. Military, Press Release, 4 June. http://www.foster-miller.qinetq-na.com/pressreleases/first_maars_robot_shipped.htm. Accessed 30 December 2009.

Fürsich, Elfiede. 2003. Between Credibility and Commodification: Nonfiction Entertainment as a Global Media Genre. *International Journal of Cultural Studies*, 6(2): 131-52.

Geisenheyner, Stefan.1989. Do Military Robots Have a Future in Land Warfare? http://www.thefreelibrary.com/Do+military+robots+have+a+future+in+land+warfare%3f-a08536675. Accessed 28 July 2010.

History Channel. 2007. *Robo-Warriors*. A & E Home Video.

Hornborg, Alf. 2006. Animism, Fetishism, and Objectivism as Strategies for Knowing (or not Knowing) the World. *Ethnos* 71(1): 21-32.

Jarry, Alfred. 1996. *Exploits and Opinions of Dr. Faustroll, Pataphysician*. Trans. Simon Watson Taylor. London: Exact Change.

Koch Vision. 2007. *Popular Mechanics: The New Technology of War*.

Lerner, Preston. 2006. Robots Go to War. *Popular Science* 286(1): 42-46; 96.

Mulvey, Laura. 1993. Some Thoughts on Theories of Fetishism in the Context of Contemporary Culture *October* 65(Summer): 3-20.

Pretorius, Julien. 2008. The Technological Culture of War. *Bulletin of Science, Technology, and Society* 28(4): 299-305.

Roderick, Ian. 2007. (Out of) Control Demons: Software Agents, Complexity Theory and the Revolution in Military Affairs. *Theory & Event* 10(2).

———. 2008. Putting the Posthuman in the Loop: Future Combat Systems and Post-Disciplinary Training. *Journal for Cultural Research* 12(4): 301-16.

———. 2009. Bare Life of the Virtuous Shadow Warrior: The Use of Silhouette in Military Training Advertisements. *Continuum: Journal of Media and Cultural Studies* 23(1): 77-91.

———. 2010. Considering the Fetish Value of EOD Robots: How Robots Save Lives and Sell War. *International Journal of Cultural Studies* 13(3): 1-19.

Schutz, Alfred and Thomas Luckman. 1973. *The Structures of the Life-World*. Trans. Richard M. Zaner and H. Tristam Engelhardt, Jr. Evanston, IL: Northwestern University Press.

Shaw, Martin. 2002. Risk-Transfer Militarism, Small Massacres, and the Historic Legitimacy of War. *International Relations* 16(3): 343-60.

———. 2005. *The New Western Way of War: Risk Transfer War and its Crisis in Iraq*. Malden, MA: Polity Press.

Singer, Peter W. 2009a. *Wired for War: The Robotics Revolution and Conflict in the Twenty-first Century*. New York: Penguin Press.

———. 2009b. Military Robots and the Laws of War. *The New Atlantis* 23(Winter): 25-45. http://www.thenewatlantis.com/publications/military-robots-and-the-laws-of-war. Accessed 30 December 2009.

Sofge, Erik. 2008. Ultimate Fighting Machines: First-Gen Armed Robots are Tough, Smart and Packing Plenty of Heat. Welcome to the Age of the Real Killer Apps. *Popular Mechanics* 185(3): 58-63.

Thibault, Paul. 1991. *Social Semiotics as Praxis: Text, Social Meaning Making, and Nabakov's Ada*. Minneapolis: University of Minnesota Press.

Mary Sterpka King

Preparing the Instantaneous Battlespace: A Cultural Examination of Network-Centric Warfare

ABSTRACT

The aftermath of the Cold War signalled a revision in the global position of the United States and a new emphasis on the country's status as a military superpower. Liberated from the stand-off between rivals that existed with the Soviet Union, the United States military has been able to greatly expand its scope of operational theories and aspire toward global dominance, using such programs as the Air Force's Global Reach, Global Strike, The Navy's Aegis Program and the Department of Defense, Joint Vision 20/20 Full Spectrum Dominance. Each of these examples suggests the expansion of the battlefield to well beyond what had been understood as the limits of military ambition. By exploiting the strategic capabilities of information based technologies, military thinking has been reoriented in a number of fundamental ways, all of which are associated with the doctrinal conceptualization of the Revolution in Military Affairs and the development of Network-Centric Warfare. Despite a change in presidential administrations, the tendency to globalize the battlespace prevails.

RÉSUMÉ

Préparer instantanément l'espace de guerre : examen culturel de la guerre en réseau

La période suivant la fin de la Guerre froide a suscité une révision du positionnement mondial des États-Unis et a placé l'accent sur le statut de superpuissance militaire du pays. Sorties de l'impasse qu'était la confrontation avec l'Union soviétique, les forces armées américaines ont pu étendre largement l'envergure de leurs théories opérationnelles et aspirer à la domination mondiale, au moyen de programmes tels que les Global Reach et Global Strike de l'Air Force, le système Aegis de la Navy et le « Spectre de la domination totale » du programme Joint Vision 2020 du Ministère de la Défense. Chacun de ces exemples suggère l'expansion du champ de bataille bien au-delà de ce que l'on tenait autrefois pour les limites de l'ambition militaire. En exploitant les capacités stratégiques des technologies de l'information, la pensée militaire s'est réorientée vers un certain nombre de fondamentaux, tous associés à la conceptualisation doctrinale de la révolution dans les Affaires militaires et le développement d'un réseau guerrier centralisé. Malgré le changement d'administration présidentielle, la tendance à la mondialisation du champ de bataille se maintient.

¤

Network-Centric Warfare (NCW) is a military doctrine developed by the United States Department of Defense and designed to mobilize information into a competitive fighting advantage through the networking of operations and forces. NCW is an attempt to adapt to the rapid changes associated with information systems and the globalization of the economy, against the operational challenges of all-volunteer forces. Globalization and technological transformation have led to a greater need for interoperability on the part of military. The idea of networking is comprehensive throughout the planning and implementation of the doctrine. Melding human action and military capability, NCW signifies the integration of human systems and technical capacity into a networked, joint command structure. This total integration of forces has been theorized to encompass an expanded theatre of operations designed for globally scaled missions in order to achieve global dominance, both militarily and through the use of information systems. The transition is associated with new partnerships with other military and with the private sector. The paradigm relies on contract arrangements to carry out the majority of operations, including the management of troops, design of weapons systems, formulation of strategy and procurement of supplies and support arrangements. Network-Centric warfare represents the most seismic change to the U.S. military since the Department of Defense was established in 1947.

The evolution of Network-Centric warfare emerged from the confluence of three historical trajectories: the rapid technological change associated with the globalization of communications and technology, which has led to a greater emphasis on networking; the rise of militarism as an ideology following the Cold War, which reorganized the military along the lines of joint operations with tightened control at the top; and, finally, the increasing privatization of government functions. The paradigmatic foundation of NCW borrows from corporate economic restructuring as a model, particularly the managerial theory of "just-in-time" (JIT), production designed for rationalizing systems and increasing communication through networks of labour, technologies and transport. In military terms, and using an integrative approach, JIT networking seeks to produce responsive firepower and massed effects in real-time operation. The concept of massed effects borrows from the language of complexity theory to suggest that effects will be overwhelming and multiply in a self-organizing fashion.

The concept of interoperability comes into play as a means for achieving total informational awareness through the integration of military systems and manpower into the global command structure. The paradigm, in some sense, presents a double-edged paradox in that the magnification capabilities of NCW global risk scenarios produce a quest for an unachievable level of perceptual awareness. Nonetheless, the impetus behind this organizational logic requires the creation of a total global security environment. Toward this end, the goal of NCW is to establish a "predictive culture" throughout all service branches, agencies, organizations and personnel and among allies and private contractors. The human and technological elements of NCW are merged into a networked membrane outfitted with acute sensory capabilities. The key for NCW operators is to maintain an integrated network that enables precise and instantaneous reaction. NCW assumes a level of sensitivity resting within each weapon system, information system and human actor. Within this calculation, there is a collapsing of geographic distance. The instantaneous response expected from network-centric operations requires total knowledge not only to defeat an "unprepared adversary, but also to the defeat of a world as a field" (Virilio 1986: 133). Underlying this is an ecology of responsiveness emulating the command-driven logic of an integrated computer network.

The research informing this paper is derived from a range of intersecting literature that links the role of technological transformation with economic restructuring and the rise of various networked social formations (Castells 1996; DeLanda 1991; Harvey 2006; Hirst and Zietlin 1989; Wallerstein 2009). The research also incorporates defence literature, including formative work (Arquilla and Ronfeldt 1996, 1998; Cebrowski and Gartska 1998; Shultz 1991; VanCreveld 1991) and a wealth of recent military literature on technological and economic transformation (Berkowitz 2003; Cares 2006; Mitchell 2009; Safranski 2008). In addition, the article incorporates an emerging body of cultural theory focused on new forms of conflict (Armitage 2006; Berkowitz 2003; Blackmore 2005; Singer 2003; Turse 2008; Virilio 1986, 1991, 2009). Such literature is enhanced by a small body of anthropological research dedicated to examining military transformation in the current era (Grey 1997; Keenan 2009; Gutmann and Lutz 2010). The majority of anthropological material, however, is focused on the use of ethnographic knowledge in intelligence operations (Gonzalez 2009; Miyoshi 2007). This paper attempts to examine wholesale conceptual changes in the military from a cultural, as well as anthropological, perspective. It is part of a larger, ongoing ethnographic study on the social effects of military privatization. The work is intended to render a more contextualized picture of the economic and technical transitions associated with the rise of networked forms of warfare, and to supply a historical context for envisioning the virtual simulation of battle in the context of the globalization of warfare.

This article first examines the conceptual history of the Network-Centric Warfare paradigm and identifies the communicative features that have informed its evolution. It also interrogates NCW as a general framework concerned with the nature of conflict, conceived as global in scope and reliant upon simulated information. Second, it will identify the discursive features of NCW based on the conceptualization of global threats in terms of intrinsic qualities (stereotypical signatures of cultural difference, i.e., radical Islam). The discursive features include the development of an aesthetic of soldiering suitable for establishing conditions favourable to U.S. interests. These conditions are predicated on the continuous assessment of threats and instantaneous global response.

Finally, changes in military strategy associated with network-centrism are predicated on the concept of the network as a weapon, with all of the assumed cultural, geographic and temporal features built into the operation of the system. Therefore, the paper poses questions related to the transformation of military strategy and the potential dislocations between the ideals of the Network-Centric paradigm and the reality of an evolving doctrine of warfare that has no identifiable cultural, geographic or temporal boundaries.

Historical Background

The term Network-Centric Warfare is usually credited to Vice Admiral Cebrowski and John J. Garstka in their 1998 article entitled "Network-Centric Warfare: Its Origin and Future." Preceding this publication, Admiral William A. Owens produced an article for the Institute of National Security Studies, entitled "The Emerging System of Systems," which described a constellation of firepower combined with manpower to produce "dominant battle-space knowledge" including the use of sensors, precision weapons and command and control systems with "enhanced situational awareness, rapid target assessment and distributed weapons management" (Owens 1996). Owens's paper became one of the conceptual templates for the Joint Vision 2010 plan issued by the Joint Chiefs of Staff, introducing concepts such as, "Dominant Maneuver," "Precision Engagement," "Focused Logistics" and "Full Spectrum Dominance." The article aimed to theorize a range of missions, from peacekeeping to full-scale warfare that uses technology to achieve massed effects through information superiority" (Mitchell 2006: 5). A number of publications underscored the growing interest in information regarding conflict scenarios, including "The Rise of Netwar" by Arquilla and Ronfeldt (1998); "Understanding Information Warfare" by Alberts et al. (2001); and "Power to the Edge: Command and Control in the Information Age" by Alberts and Hayes (2003). The foundational ideas, however, have been mostly attributed to the writings of Vice Admiral Arthur Cebrowski and John Gartska.

The emergence of Network-Centric Warfare corresponded with the broader transformations attributed to the globalization of economy and culture, popularized by the work of futurist critics Alvin and Heidi Toffler, who coined the phrase "The way we make wealth is the way we make war" (1993). Such transformations have also been theorized in terms of "Postmodern War" (Grey 1997). Changes in military doctrine have been predicated on the accelerated role of communication technologies in military planning and the "co-evolution of economics, information technology and business processes and organizations" (Kellner 2003: 3). Manuel Castells conceptualizes these changes in terms of the "network society," emphasizing the broader social and economic transformations brought about by communication technologies and the connection between technological changes in the military and business (1996). NCW borrows from the fields of organizational behaviour, economics, anthropology, biology and sociology, and makes use of the popular understanding of chaos and complexity theory. The conceptual ideas of NCW are often encapsulated in the language of management studies, and use social networking as a framework to better understand the effects of technology, strategy, organization, performance and personnel effectiveness in combat (Edison 2006). NCW signifies a reconceptualization of the concept of warfare associated with technological change and the cultural traits necessary for the mastery of the military environment through coordinated information, training and weapons systems.

The early stages of NCW emerged from U.S. Department of Defense planning after the Second World War, derived from new computational capabilities of computer networks coupled with the development of advanced weapons and detection systems (Mitchell 2006; Castells 1996: DeLanda 1991). This transformation involved political, economic and cultural changes associated with globalization, and the spectacular technological development of the postwar period. Many changes were instigated within the military, including developments with imaging, the Internet, microprocessing and complex systems research. These innovations were accomplished through government, military and university research partnerships (Castells 1996; DeLanda 1991).

The Second World War saw the rapid technological development of imaging, radar, communications and targeting weapons systems. The U.S. strategy during the Cold War focused on containment; conflicts were usually carried out through proxy rather than direct opposition. Massive retaliation was almost unthinkable under the threat of mutually assured destruction; granted, the military has to develop flexible responses involving diplomacy and the use of surveillance and information systems to achieve defence objectives. The Cold War witnessed a period of deepening technological development, against the incipient realization of the coming nature of conflicts that foreshadowed the fall of the Soviet Union.

During the Vietnam War, the United States military faced a number of operational and manpower challenges. The Vietnam War was fought with a demoralized, draftee army. Given the unpopularity of the war, it was unlikely that the decade-long conflict would have continued without a conscripted military (Bradford and Brown 2008). The Vietnam War also combined unclear military objectives, vacillating between low intensity skirmishes to large-scale aerial and ground bombardment. After the engagement in Vietnam, strategic planners began reformulating objectives for military engagement with a focus on technological capabilities and an all-volunteer force.

When the Vietnam War ended, the U.S. was left with a smaller force based on voluntary service, and a reduced defence budget. The abolishment of military conscription represented a preliminary step toward greater reliance on contract arrangements and the privatization of military service. This normalization of conflict was consistent with other late-capitalist reorganizations, such as the reconceptualization of the soldier's body and its performance in terms of labour expectations. Like similar flexible labour regimes, the emphasis switched from a dedicated workforce to one of increasing adaptability and greater force delivery (Hirst and Zeitlin 1989). The military's version of economic rationalization became synonymous with the new military criterion of synchronization.

Throughout the 1970s and 80s, the U.S. Navy and Air Force developed informational warfare strategies with an increasing focus on both deterrent and low-intensity conflict. Much of the emphasis remained an outgrowth from the heyday of Soviet/U.S. posturing. This tendency formed the paradigmatic foundation for thinking about conflict following the collapse of the Berlin Wall. Yet the rapid advancement of technical means also enlarged spheres of interest through the use of optical tools, including the Star Wars Strategic Defense Initiative, computer-directed command-and-control systems, precision-guided munitions and stealth and satellite imaging. These played a role in the development of the NCW concept. The increased influence of operational theories of warfare also grew out of the attempt to learn from the Vietnam conflict, which was seen as a failure of coordination among service branches and called for the implementation of unified operational objectives (Thom 2000).

When the Cold War came to an end, the situation created a large void in the security environment. Global threats became less predictable, more variable and empowered in new ways. Moreover, the conventional responses to conflict were at their weakest. As former Soviet countries demobilized, a large influx of decommissioned soldiers entered the global labour pool. At the same time, a flood of cheap weapons were discharged from the former communist nations. The end of the Cold War re-instigated regional and civil conflicts that had previously been contained (Singer 2003). Postcolonial states dependent on patronage during the height of U.S./Soviet tensions began dissolving as a result of internal political pressures.

Since the end of the Cold War, the incidence of civil war has increased spectacularly, while global growth in the number of conflict zones has doubled (Kaldor 1999; Singer 2003; van Creveldt 1991). At the same time, the aftermath of the Cold War signalled a revision in the global position of the United States, placing a new emphasis on the country's status as the remaining military superpower. No longer constrained by the stalemate between rivals that existed with the Soviet Union, the U.S. military was able to expand its scope of operational theories and aspire toward global regimes of dominance, using programs such as the Air Force's Global Reach, Global Strike, the Navy's Aegis Program and the Department of Defense Joint Vision 20/20 Full Spectrum Dominance.

This reorientation reflected the expansion of the battlefield to beyond what had been understood as the limits of military ambition (Mitchell 2006). By exploiting the strategic capabilities of information-based technologies, military thinking was reoriented in relation to the doctrinal conceptualization of both the Revolution in Military Affairs (RMA) and the development of Network-Centric Warfare. The technological features of weapons programs and the increasingly global reach of such technologies underscores the ability to render, geo-strategically, an enlargement of military awareness, planning and intervention strategies on a global scale. It has also enabled the U.S. to engage other militaries in order to leverage its own security needs through joint planning, training, missions and the sharing of technology.

Revolution in Military Affairs

The Revolution in Military Affairs is a futuristic theory about the coming nature of warfare derived from technical and organizational recommendations for the restructuring of U.S. forces and their allies. The RMA theory rests on transformations in communications, information and space technologies. Often referred to as "The transformation," it involves a move toward total systems integration and is accompanied by other totalizing efforts such as the Office of Total Information Awareness and Total Situational Awareness programs.

The earliest RMA research was done by Marshal Nikolai Ogarkov and his colleagues for the Soviet Armed Forces during the 1970s and 80s (Metz and Kievit 1995). U.S. interest in the topic was initiated by Andrew Marshall, head of the internal Pentagon think tank The Office of Net Assessment (Trilling 2002). Support for the doctrine grew within political circles associated with the 1992 Defense Planning Guidance Initiative and the 1997 Project for a New American Century, involving former Vice President Dick Cheney, Paul Wolfowitz and Donald Rumsfeld, as well as a core group of pro-defence conservatives (Trilling

2002). The idea was disseminated to other nations also exploring the RMA's transformative effects on organization and technology. Canadian interest in the RMA began in the late 1990s, fuelled in part by an eagerness to maximize the nation's military capabilities. Commitment to the RMA, however, was also stimulated by a desire to avoid the geopolitical marginalization associated with non-adoption of the doctrine (Sloan 2002).

In the U.S., the RMA was greatly facilitated by the passage of the U.S. *Goldwater Nichols Act* in 1986, which initiated a sweeping transformation of the U.S. military. The Act entailed a streamlining of the military chain-of-command, consolidating control with the President and the Secretary of Defense. The *Goldwater-Nichols Act* initiated changes with both the chain-of-command and the interaction of the services, unifying these services under a Unified Combatant Command. The Commander-in-Chief of the Army underwent a name change to Combatant Commander (CCDR), enacted in 2002 by Rumsfelt, who reasoned that the title "Commander-in-Chief" should be reserved solely for the U.S. president. Under the new organization, CCDR designations were transformed to emphasize joint commands, missions and training. New personnel requirements for officers mandated joint duty and joint professional development instruction, while completion of joint ventures became a requirement for eligibility for promotion. Moreover, the overall orientation of the branches shifted from mission-driven commands to those focused on a geographic region within a global theatre of operations (Lederman 1999).

The new commands, finalized by 2007, have been broken into their regional responsibilities and functional duties, designated into ten geographic areas: U.S. Africa Command, U.S. Central Command, U.S. European Command, U.S. Pacific Command, U.S. Northern Command and U.S. Southern Command. The four functional duty commands include: U.S. Joint Forces Command, U.S. Special Operations Command, U.S. Strategic Command and U.S. Transportation Command. Each command is led by a four-star general or admiral chosen by the Secretary of Defense and the President, and confirmed by Congress. Strategic partnership in NORTHCOM includes Canada and Mexico, while USSOUTHCOM is building partnership capacity with Countries in the Caribbean, as well as in Central and South America. Thus, the development of partnerships corresponds to strategic interests in the geographically designated region.

The reorganized chain-of-command runs from the President to Secretary of Defense to the combatant commanders of the Unified Combatant Commands. Under the *Goldwater-Nichols Act*, the Service Chiefs have been delegated a secondary role in the conduct of war, and their duties have been relegated to organizing, training and equipping soldiers. Service chiefs no longer exercise operational control over their forces. Of all the service branches, the Army has undergone disproportionate effects from the reorganization, losing its traditional control over the Central Asian, European and Southern theatres. In addition, the RMA represented a de-emphasis on provisioning for regular soldiers and a reallocation of resources to joint commands and special operations (Lederman 1986).

Validation for the RMA was fuelled in part by what was regarded as the dramatic asymmetrical victory by the U.S. in the 1991 Gulf War. U.S. dominance was evident in the use of satellite technologies, precision-guided weapons and communications systems. The swift success in the first Gulf War provided confirmation of the RMA's success, allowing U.S. commander Army General Norman Schwarzkopf to exercise full control over all service branches without having to consult with their respective commanders. The media coverage also made him a television star (Bourne 1999; Khalilzad, White and Marshall 1999).

The 1986 *Goldwater-Nichols Act* allowed for shared resources, eliminating some of the competition between branches for resources and equipment. It had a disciplining effect on the individual services by removing a good portion of operational authority over the respective branches. It also decreased disagreement within the command structure and created the context for service branches to share smart weapons, stealth and drone technologies, while increasing the move toward the interoperability of communications between services, thus stimulating the development of a joint doctrine. Without the restructuring in the Act, the integration of branches and restructuring and implementation of doctrinal changes would not have transpired. The *Goldwater-Nichols Act* was the most important step for realizing the goals of the RMA and for the implementation of Network-Centric Warfare.

The effect of changes to overall structure cannot be overstated. If the traditional organization of the military is pyramidal (i.e., hierarchical), then the new shape might be characterized as a standing arrow. The *Goldwater-Nichols Act* transferred an unprecedented amount of control to the Chairman of the Joint Chiefs of Staff, who holds almost as much authority as the Secretary of Defense. As the Secretary determines the appointment of the Joint Chiefs, this reinforces the tendency to appoint commanders of similar mind, thereby increasing the tendency of the two positions to ideologically converge and decreasing the diversity of opinions available. In turn, this further solidifies presidential authority over military matters, and reinforces authority at the top by creating a command structure that mirrors the doctrinal position of the President.

The self-reinforcing tendency is further solidified by consolidating the middle and upper command into a joint structure answerable immediately to the Secretary of Defense. Troops are broken into a two-class system made up of regulars, who disproportionately inhabit the bottom, and elite forces who are granted a great

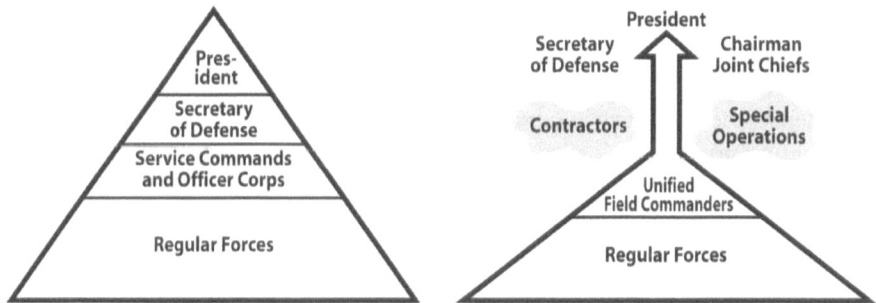

Fig. 1
Integrated Command Chain Specified by the Goldwate- Nichols Department of Defense Reorganization Act *of 1986.*

deal of operational and tactical autonomy. The *Act* set the stage for the private sector's greater involvement in warfare. Elite forces are now able to blend together in a grey universe of special operations, soldiers for hire, clandestine operatives and contract companies that characterize the field of conflict.

The *Goldwate-Nichols Act* has spelled the end of the public monopoly on the military with a shift toward private militarism (2003: 8). A wide spectrum of military and security functions that used to be exclusively under the public domain are now open to contractors. This has increased new supplies and demands in the global military market, many of which have been filled by for-profit military companies. This shift was facilitated by the philosophy of privatization dominating government discourse in the latter half of 20th century. Moreover, the failure of command economies in the former Soviet Union tended to further validate market driven approaches (Castells 1996; Harvey 2005; Singer 2003). By the 1990s, whenever governments on the left and right of the political spectrum addressed budget issues, they tended to fall back on the private sector. During the Clinton presidency, *The National Performance Review* stipulated the privatization of previously untouched areas of government, such as schools and prisons (Singer 2003). Privatization has since become the guiding principle of leading global financial institutions, such as the World Bank, the International Monetary Fund and the World Trade Organization. While the RMA was responsible for the move toward restructuring the military, it was the accelerated political drive toward privatization that provided the foremost catalyst for the growth of the global, for-profit defence industry.

Total System Integration

Network-Centric Warfare is predicated on the centrality of networks as a way of conceptualizing the organizational challenges of new technologies. It relies on joint operations between services, contractors and partnerships with other militaries. The doctrine is articulated in the strong managerial language of just-in-time production. Simulations also play a critical role in how sensors, technologies and individual soldiers are reconceptualized as interchangeable parts of a system of systems. The new doctrine dramatizes the move from strategic warfare based on standing armies to a brand of pre-emptive warfare based on developing an informational ecology throughout the military. The goal is to establish a "predictive culture" (Phister, Busch and Plonisch 1996; Virilio 2009) able to penetrate all service branches, agencies, contractors, organizations and personnel in a process enabling instantaneous and precise reaction.

The culture of predictive surveillance differs from the concept of "comprehensive insurance" that dominated the intelligence-gathering of the last century and was focused on amassing information for national defence. The ambition of predictive surveillance is to secure supremacy on all fronts, from the globalization of geopolitical relations to the militarization of circumterrestrial space. "Defenfscive" and "Offencive" lose their meaning in the face of a genuine world security force made up of transnational, networked military partnerships organized around deterrence, or what Paul Virilio terms the "pure offensive" of global power (Virilio and Lotringer 1983: 41-47). While NCW supporters may refer to the transformation in the military as revolutionary, the concept of total deterrence has a politically reactionary quality that aims to logistically extend geo-presence into resource-rich networks using information as a panoptical weapon.

Like the distributed functions of a computer network, the objective is to attain "massed effects" from an economy of force by instantaneously moving technology and manpower where they are needed (Murdock 2002). The doctrinal precedents follow a progressive logic. NCW is to be achieved through a team effort aimed at the integration and synchronization of capabilities in the different service branches, based on the observation that a networked force improves information sharing, which in turn allows for the collaboration necessary to enhance the quality of information and achieve a shared situational awareness. Increased situational awareness enables the synchronization of capabilities, meant to increase the effectiveness of operations (Cebrowski and Gartska 1998).

The premise underlying the NCW concept is that military operations will increasingly capitalize on the advantages of information technology. Assuming that transformations in the economy and business are the actual driving forces in a new era of war, the military must shift from stationary operations to networked operations. This shift entails envisioning the military as part of a continuously adapting ecosystem. The model self-consciously mimics

> the dynamics of growth and competition that have emerged in the modern economy. The new dynamics of competition are based on increasing returns on investment, competition within and between ecosystems, and

competition based on time. Information technology (IT) is central to each of these. (Cebrowski and Garska 1998: 3)

The NCW model displays much of the promotional language common in business marketing, with its emphasis on competition, capitalization and the rationalization of personnel.

NCW employs the language of "just-in-time" corporate restructuring when referencing "Network-Centric Retailing" (Cebrowski and Garska 1998: 3). The model uses Walmart as an example of an outperforming company able to achieve competitiveness by shifting to Network-Centric operations. Walmart is credited with translating information superiority into a competitive advantage by establishing an operational architecture of sensors, scanners and a transaction grid exhibiting a high level of awareness "within its retail ecosystem" of ninety million transactions per week (4). This information is shared with suppliers in real-time to control their production and distribution and to manage supply chains. Cebrowski and Gartska note that when Walmart sells a lightbulb, a signal goes to General Electric telling them to make a new one. This degree of synchronization is purported to meet seasonal needs and market preferences in real-time. The Walmart model of synchronization operates to create local awareness within each store day by day, letting neighbourhood stores identify new opportunities, re-price items based on competition, or prominently display items with higher volume to increase sales (1998).

The NCW appropriation of just-in-time management language paints a compelling picture of synchronicity. It moves from viewing partners as independent to conceiving of them as part of the military's own continuously adapting ecosystem, able to increase speed and profits from the automated command and control systems implemented on a transactional grid. NCW entails a major conceptual leap from seeing other militaries as competitors to envisioning them as an extension of U.S. force projection. Theoretically, the shift to NCW involves a transition away from drawn-out conflicts to faster, effective war fighting characterized by the speed of command and synchronization. Running throughout the paradigm is the metaphor of the computer with its push-button execution of command. The level of control attributed to NCW allows them to "lock out" enemy strategy and "lock in" success, permitting forces to develop the "speed of command." The wording implies disseminating the orders from above almost immediately to the units and individuals on the battlefront, while reducing the friction derived from a commander's lack of access to direct knowledge of battlefield. In principle, NCW enables forces to organize from the bottom up, mirroring the self-synchronizing capability present in both computers and ecosystems to "meet the commander's intent" (Cebrowski and Garska 1998: 3)

At the heart of the change are the technologies, referred to as "force multipliers" (1998). The change involves a move away from slow, heavy, dedicated equipment to light, rapid, flexible and smart weapons systems that can be networked into the larger system and thereby increase their effects. Weapons like exoskeletons, computerized helmets and eyepieces have been designed to augment a soldier's capabilities (Jordan 2007; Shachtman 2009). Such weapons share similarities with the smart technologies designed for the consumer market to facilitate networking and technology integration. However, military technologies differ in that the self-organizing capabilities have been enhanced for automated response. Technologies have been designed to be autonomous, such as unmanned aerial vehicles for strategic intelligence, reconnaissance and reaction. The arsenal includes weaponized imagery technologies augmented by satellite and aircraft surveillance, synthetic aperture radar, electro-optical cameras and infrared and other sensors. Video teleconferencing has augmented the development of a Common Operating Picture. Technologies in development include minesweepers, smart bombs, predator drones, nano-robotics and microscopic weapons with viral engines—all of which enhance the overall predictive culture of networked operations (Kellner 2007). Scale is a factor in the miniaturization of weapons that are light and transportable and have flexible uses. Another class of weapons merit descriptives such as "intelligent" and "brilliant," underscoring their ability to think for themselves. These carry built-in communication relays to add to the overall networking capabilities.

The technologies are networked in such a way as to become smaller or larger depending on the military objectives. Virilio calls this altered experience the "logistics of perception" based on the use of optical substitution in battle. The disruption of time and space is a dimension of postmodern warfare, evident not only in the televised spectacle that simultaneously brings images closer even as they are sanitized of conflict, but also in the disappearance of the topographical features of war (Virilio and Lotringer 1983: 49). Conflict, in this sense, becomes a war of images, an infowar in which the disparity between the image of battle and actual battle falls subject to the enhancements and distortions of sensory disturbance. Accordingly, perceptual substitution reduces sight to the function of "a sighting device," a form of vision without looking that "registers the waning of reality" (Armitage 2000).

Synthetic Architecture

The disciplinary circuits of control within a network emanate from both its decentralized structure and its unseen surveillance capabilities (Foucault 1985; Galloway and Thacker 2007). The dispersed nature of networks allow for a hyper vigilance, deploying decentralization as a means to re-centralize control. The impulse corresponds to Hardt and Negri's idea of biopower, harnessing the non-human aspects of networks (emergent systems, atoms, rhizomes and swarm dynamics) for the purpose of linking biology with the informatics of

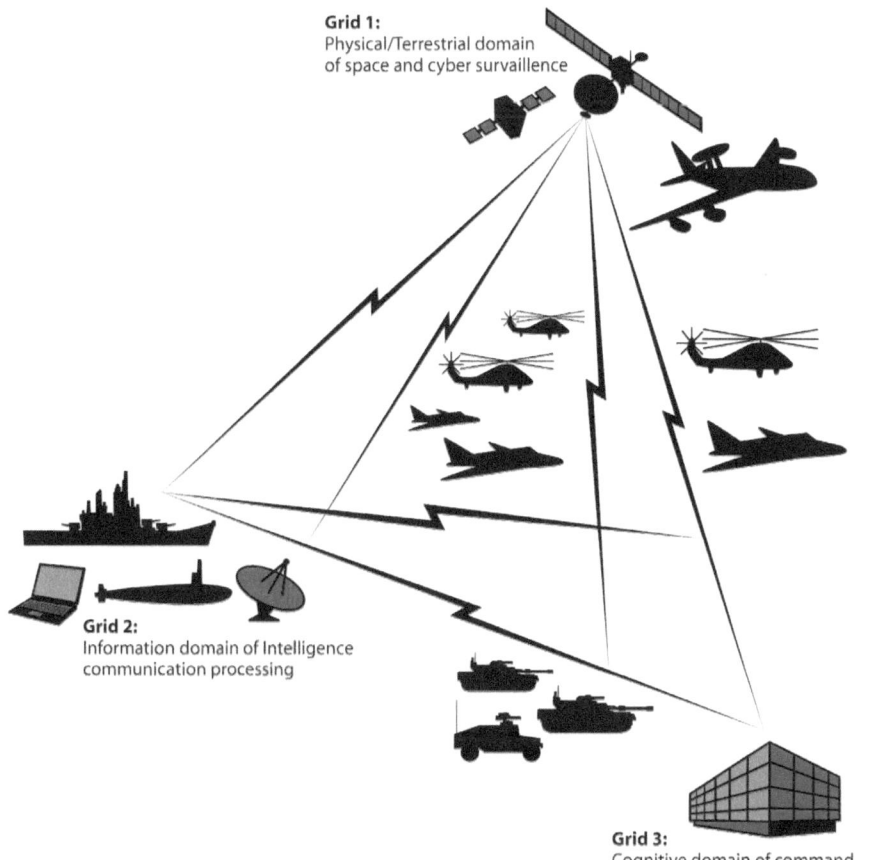

Fig. 2
The three domains of the network-centric battlespace.

control (2001). According to Gilles Deleuze, the signature of a control society is its dispersal and self-organizing capacity, its ability to transmute, mold and constantly change from one instant to the next (2002). Theoretically, this level of adaptability allows for the continuous monitoring and control of an environment remotely.

The doctrine of network-centrism starts with three premises of how the environment is sensed. The battlespace environment is sensed in terms of the physical domain, where events occur and are perceived by individuals and sensors. The data from the physical domain is then transfered to the information domain. Once received and processed, that information becomes part of the cognitive domain, where it is analyzed and acted upon. The three domains replicate the "observe, orient, decide, act loop" feedback cycle first identified by Colonel John Boyd of the U.S. Air Force (Luddy 2005).

An underlying assumption guiding the conceptualization of a networked military is that the modern environment is too complex to be understood by any one individual, organization or service branch. Information technologies permit the rapid sharing of data, to such an extent that "edge entities," those at the frontlines, should be able to pull information from repositories rather than relying on centralized headquarters to anticipate information needs and to "push" data to them (Alberts and Hayes 2003). The premise underlying NCW is that the more information that is available, the better. Edge entities have the most direct access to battle knowledge. Thus, the idea is to empower the edges by shortening the links of data transferred directly to the command, where the decision-making actually occurs. In this conceptualization, "edges" are assumed to be small units on the frontline, representing the individual, highly trained special operations soldiers in direct contact with the enemy. The impulse remains to brake the interceding links between command and the edges, so as to allow the command post to have direct contact with the most expert soldiers.

Cebrowski and Gartska argue that as a first step toward accomplishing this networked ecology, the network environment should be conceived of as a grid referencing the Global Information Grid (GIG). The authors recognize the advantages of a robust network topology on the battlefield, advocating the empowerment of the edges as an effective response to the kind of strategic environments present in the network age, including asymmetrical and urban warfare scenarios. Network-centrism is the cornerstone of the new Office of Force Transformation as mandated by the Secretary of Defense (Luddy 2005). The GIG serves as the intelligence backbone of the Department of Defense, as well as an evolving perceptual system, enhancing the visualization process through sensors, registers and data-absorption tools to produce an emergent picture of the global conflict environment.

The Global Information Grid serves as the technical framework to facilitate network-centric operations. It is an all-encompassing system governing all communication aspects of the Department of Defense. Advanced weapons, sensors and command and control systems are linked to the grid, actualizing the "system of systems" that is integral to the military's massive integration effort originally specified by Albert and Hayes (2001). The grid architecture comprises a range of information acquisition tools including sensors, radar, radio frequency, infrared receptors, low light and optical devices, acoustical detectors and human operators. Another level of the grid incorporates communication satellites, data transmission, microwave relays and computers and command centres. The information grid transmits all of the sensory information, intelligence and orders in real-time, efficiently connecting logistics to control operations. The transaction grid utilizes the sensor and information grids to guide weapons to targets. Other weapons are considered "brilliant" since they contain auxiliary sensors able to attack autonomously by responding to self-initiated data streams (Murdock 2002).

More than a decade ago, the Pentagon began referencing the technical framework to facilitate Network-Centric operations through the Department of Defense Architecture Framework (DoDAF). The framework is the master platform for organizing both the system architecture and the enterprise architecture into an integrated network. It acts as a mechanism for visualizing and understanding the complexity of the NCW paradigm using graphics and textual references, and sets the protocols for interaction with the Global Information Grid. It also identifies the goals for interoperability. It is the interface for both military personnel and corporate contractors (Singer 2003). The system uses the acronyms of military-speak combined with the marketing language of global business.

The DoDAF evolved from two directives: the Command, Control, Communications, Computers, Intelligence, Surveillance and Reconnaissance (C4ISR) and Technical Architecture Framework (TAFIM) programs. These two programs were initiated by the 1996 U.S. *Clinger-Cohen Act*, designed to improve the government's management of information resources. The DoDAF went into operation in 2003 as a visualization device for providing a common operating picture that integrates information across the spectrum of missions, organizations, joint operations and multinational arrangements. It sets the rules and relationships and identifies a set of products for enhancing the entire system. The architecture includes families of systems, systems of systems and NCW systems. The framework acts as a shared interactive repository organized into Levels of Information System Interoperability.

The larger DoDAF framework is articulated in terms of products. The inventory offers a set of products used by defence customers and military and business personnel. These are all integrated into an architectural system containing portals and links meant to aid in visualizing the operational environment and complexity of human and technological relationships that make interoperability possible. The DoDAF framework is meant to interact with other systems, including the NATO Architecture Framework, the U.K. Ministry of Defense Architecture and the multinational IDEAS group comprised of Australia, Canada, the U.K. and the U.S. The DoDAF virtualizes the shared operating picture and demonstrates the available work products. A number of militaries have been developing NCW protocols, such as Australia and Sweden (Luddy 2005), but other countries have experienced difficulty overcoming the costs associated with the technology and installation. Countries unable to implement their own NCW technical architecture have opted for niche roles or secondary positions in the service of the overall Network-centric operations (Luddy 2005: 17; Mitchell 2009).

Countries wanting to participate in joint operations need to upgrade their capabilities in order to interface with the DoDAF architecture. The Canadian military exercises its coalition task force responsibilities in conjunction with NORTHCOM, the U.S. Departments of Homeland Security and Homeland Defense. This involves increasing integration within the country's own military, government and civil agencies, including Canada Command. For the most part, the Canadian military has been able to integrate its capabilities effectively with the U.S. Joint Command structure, although challenges have arisen with communications and the willingness of the U.S. Command to share information freely.

It has been noted that Canadian officers benefit from the training and expertise obtained on joint missions (Mitchell 2009). For many nations, however, this task has been difficult. To be considered for joint operations, an individual country must demonstrate its interoperability capabilities. Performance is evaluated in a simulated operational environment that provides the context from which to assess the DoDAF/C4ISR solutions. Countries must improve their command to meet the specifications of conventional and irregular warfare, demonstrate real-time voice and text translation and implement multinational joint staff coordination and information sharing. Countries must also demonstrate planning for psychological operations, computer network operations and electronic recovery missions. Each partner is expected to comply with the functional interoperability of forces, by integrating its communication and weapons systems while utilizing C4ISR military and business tools. Countries wishing to engage in joint operations must maintain integration with both the relevant business and military partnerships (Frank 2009).

In 2005, the U.S. *National Defense Authorization Act* set up the Business Transformation Agency (BTA), responsible for the enterprise architecture of the DoDAF. The *Act* gave to the business community the authority to determine priorities in the development and installation of the architecture for the DoDAF. The main focal areas for the BTA include investment management and the alignment of services, systems and solutions in support of the objectives of interoperable business solutions for the DoDAF. Two principle areas of enhancement include visualization enhancements and end-to-end enhancements that improve the business flows of the network architecture. The BTA has been granted authorization to define the business capabilities needed to achieve the priorities and to define the combinations of enterprise systems and initiatives needed to realize defence capabilities.

The development of the DoDAF exemplifies a significant shift in the values and priorities governing military planning. Private companies have been given a leading role in developing the architecture that defence capabilities depend on. The rationalization of defence functions has led to a dependence on the

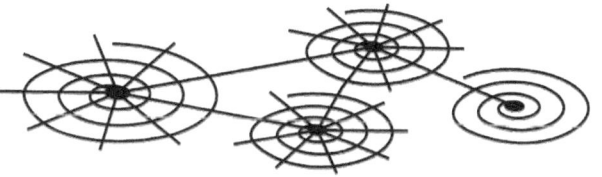

Fig. 3
Sampling of network
mapping based on social
connectivity.

- **Visualization** *involves auto-identification, matching social network links with categoric signatures of identification.*
- **Recursive functions** *amplify and multiply risks to include connections circumstantially attached through association.*
- **Feedback Loops** *reinforce the identification of risks through iteration of network tracking.*

private sector to stay abreast of cutting-edge technical development. Though the military has been unable to compete for personnel with the private sector, the underlying philosophy of NCW nevertheless depends on the operational concept of "information dominance" (Singer 2003: 64). The Department of Defense relies on private contracts for the training of personnel, troubleshooting and repair of equipment, and programming of military matters. Often the companies that engineer high-tech weapons are the only ones who can maintain them. As the U.S. military becomes more reliant on the profit-seeking sectors to achieve its objectives, such companies will become more integral to determining the conflict spectrum, from designing the weapons to providing technical support advice in the field. This is leading to a greater civilianization of warfare, which stands in marked contrast to the traditional form of warfare as violence between powerful states for political purposes (Singer 2003: 64; von Clausewitz 1997).

The synthetic battlespace precludes civilian involvement in the representation of threats. The use of simulation by the military is not new; war games have been employed since the Second World War. However, recently developed simulation capabilities have included a level of automation and integration that permits almost immediate results, as the technology doing the simulating necessitates less human input (Krebs 2002). In the virtual simulation of warfare there is a higher propensity for false proof, however, because the representation of threats remains formulated from a synthetic automation of data that cycles through a feedback loop that rests on itself for verification.

Many network mapping simulations operate in a radial fashion, emanating from a central point to encompass an increasing number of connections through snowball sampling. Studies in complexity modelling demonstrate that a characteristic feature of a network is its ability to expand continuously, incorporating wider areas into its conceptual framework. This is particularly true of social network modelling, where the mapping of connections eventually achieves a level of density that approximates the "six degrees of separation" problem, in which everyone is connected to everyone else on the planet by six or fewer acquaintances (Milgram 1967; Newman 2003; Watts 1999). In network modelling, threats lose much of their specificity as they are scripted together into a universal risk schematic. Individuals are networked together through their associative connections on a network grid, whether or not those connections exist in the real world. Amounting to a "guilty by virtual association" approach, the model may be less effective in identifying terrorists than in expanding the categories of definitions that qualify as pre-terrorist, since the sensory capability of computer-automated networking leads to a level of hyper-vigilance that exponentially widens what gets included as "threatening."

These new dangers are identified as unconventional threats, while the protagonists are drawn from the low-intensity spectrum of warfare (van Creveldt 1991). In the absence of clear enemy definitions, fighting becomes focused on possible threats. These are portrayed as multiplying and driven by different logics other than statecraft; for instance, criminal behaviour and drug conflicts in Colombia, or the control over the diamond and coltan mines in the Congo. The largest force propelling such conflicts is money. The protagonists have also changed to include terrorists, forced child recruits,and soldierless forces such as pirates and looters. Key to the conceptualization of risk is the process of visualization. The visualization determines the threats and what kinds of actions and manpower are needed for intervention. At the far end of the risk scenario, the shaping of threats has broadened to include a number of unconventional actors, such as nongovernmental activists rechristened as "militant activists," or civilians abducted from conflict regions who are re-termed enemy combatants (Arquilla and Ronfeldt 1996, 1997). In many cases, the visualization of such groups bears the stereotypical signature of cultural difference (i.e., tribal, radical, militant). Such identifications contain sweeping categorical assumptions about the intent and nature of the threats posed.

The globalization of conflict has meant that supposed terrorists operate within the multicultural environments of countries like the United States and Canada. In the case of the 2001 attack on the World Trade Center, the hijackers dressed in Western clothes and were virtually indistinguishable from the millions of Muslims living in the country. Tracking the full range of networking tools may thus be ineffective in preventing future attacks (Downey and Murdock 2003).

The aim of developing techniques for classifying and managing groups sorted by levels of danger replaces individual suspicion with categorical suspicion. The presumption of guilt implied in such a task implicates whole groups of people, while the burden remains on the individual to demonstrate their innocence against a field of presumed guilt. The networked systems of surveillance now under development obtain information from every available source. Such a level of acquisitiveness dismantles the protective shield between the military and the civil domain traditionally relied upon to uphold civil liberties, and protects against unwarranted search, seizure and detention. The entire project elevates defence objectives across the whole of civilian life and marks the shift toward a fully globalized militarized culture (Downey and Murdock 2003: 79).

Conclusion

The road from prediction to pre-emption is a short one. One of the greatest ironies of the Network-Centric paradigm is that the concept has been formulated at a time when the United States has reached the apex of military might. The U.S. is the undisputed leader in defence spending and advanced weapons development. The country's technical superiority has inspired a philosophy of insecurity that permeates the whole of military culture and that theorized a spectrum of conflict out of a multitude of small threats that, when combined in a synthetic architecture, amount to a cumulative threat portrayed as omnipresent and ongoing.

The history of postwar technology has included the development of perceptual technologies from motion detectors to satellite monitoring systems, which have in turn enabled a global perspective to emerge. This picture has been realized through the optical and sensing capabilities of networked systems. The transition entails the emergence of a world-view, both through the data and sensing streams, but also a world-view as in a conceptual template for thinking about military strategy. In the completion of NCW capabilities, complex registers have been combined with the architecture of networked systems to produce a universally coherent image of danger in a globalized world. Through its technical and strategic dominance, the United States has been able to convince its allies to adopt and implement the NCW vision as a new cooperative strategy of planetary warfare.

The NCW paradigm is heavily reliant on simulation technologies involving the projection of risks and the automated reaction to those risks. The intelligence and implementation functions have been built into the synthetic architecture of the GIG and the DoDAF network, a military network engineered as a co-project between the Department of Defense and private contractors. In another sense, the concept of Network-Centric Warfare is a simulation in itself; a conceptual product concerned with the virtual rendition of threats, predictions and the art of soldiering. The architecture is not independent of physical reality but rather interacts with the spatial and temporal frameworks of lived life. The objects and data received through the medium of the sensors produce an emergent picture, while the registering and representation of that reality is relegated to an integrated machine. Thus, the task of the DoDAF is not to represent real dangers, but to collapse the distinction between the real and the copy (Baudrillard 1981). The simulative framework of the NCW is associated with non-places; that is, the normalized experience of virtual space without attachment to definitive time or place (Auge 1995). In this representation, there is a mismatch between the construction of problems and their solution.

The discourse of threat inherent to NCW is virtualized apart from the intrinsic or extrinsic dangers that may exist. Threat becomes the guiding force behind the logic of automated command. The detection of threats is obtained through all of the sensory relays within the networked conflict spectrum. The automation compresses the steps between retrieving information, discerning threat and eliminating threat. The idea depends on the synchronization of all forces and capabilities into a common operating picture. Synchronization purportedly "enables the kill chain" (Phister, Busch and Plonische 1996). Yet while information superiority may translate into a faster reaction, such responsiveness does not always translate into a desired outcome (Luddy 2005). Automated information loops have led to an increase in civilian deaths and incidences of firing on allies (Drew 2009; King 2008; Thompson 2008). This problem is exacerbated by the failure of allies of even the most technologically advanced countries to keep up with the technical requirements of NCW. Thus, the goal of global integration is undercut by the inability to reliably communicate with other militaries.

The assumption underlying my focus on information in the NCW paradigm is that advances in technology will supply more information to operators at various levels in the "sensor to shooter chain," leading to the elimination of uncertainty (Bolia, Vidulich and Nelson 2006). This understanding suggests that uncertainty is an obstacle that can be overcome by adding more information. Still, no amount of data can compensate for poor intelligence, nor can it alter uncertainty. War is all about the nature of chance. Chance multiplies the uncertainty of all circumstances and interferes with the course of events (von Clausewitz in Bolia, Vidulich and Nelson 2006: 4). Contemporary studies of complexity regard uncertainty as an inherent property of the physical world. Thus, more information does not equal less uncertainty but tends to multiply the opportunities for error.

Since the early days of air power, military leaders have promoted one version or another of "massed effects" intended to strike an enemy's position and lead to a swift, bloodless victory (Douhet in Barnett 1999: 36-39). The concept of massed effects is similar to the historical doctrines of the *blitzkrieg*, cluster bombing and today's "shock-and-awe" strategy. The reference to massed effects represents a resurrection of counterinsurgency doctrine, with its proposition about warfare as a long, open-ended affair. In this sense, massed effects find new life in Cebrowski and Gartska's "lock out" strategy (1998). The core of the idea, however, remains predicated on the notion that "punishment equals control" (Barnett 1999: 36-39). According to Barnett, the collateral damage from such operations remains very high and comes seriously close to the definition of war crimes. The greater technological capability of information-age weaponry increases the potential for civilian casualties. Massed effects become a way to deliver an enormous amount of irreversible damage and increase the potential of escalating conflict. The NCW ideal of information dominance is too complicated to control from a remote position. As such, "massed effects" is merely an antiseptic term for weapons of mass destruction (36-39).

In a technical paper for the Air Force Research Laboratory entitled "Unintended Consequences of the Network-Centric Decision Making Model," Bolia, Vidulich and Nelson argue that the automation of the command chain has the potential for accidental consequences (2006). The issue stems from the need to avert the problems associated with information overload, resulting in the automation of much of the processing that might otherwise be relegated to human actors. Automation may vary from simple calculation, tracking entities and data fusion, to more involved, automated decision support relying on a spectrum of fully autonomous combat vehicles and weapons systems.

Decision-making in the military functions as a chain. Traditional military theory distinguishes between three levels of war decision-making: strategic, operational and tactical. Authority is conferred on the basis of rank and varies according to expertise. Consequences from decisions thus differ in magnitude based on that authority. One of the problems of NCW is that it makes quality information available on all levels of the command chain. Decision-making authority is decreased to lower levels, which theoretically expedites the execution of time-sensitive targeting. This is a concept referred to in network-centric parlance as "power to the edge" (Alberts and Hayes 2003: 1).

A fundamental challenge to NCW decision making is this devaluation of the command chain (Bolia, Vidulich and Nelson 2006). This may not mean much from a civilian standpoint, yet the hierarchy of the command chain is what discourages decision-making at inappropriate levels. Changes in the decision-making chain generate uncertainty as to the rules of engagement during war. The situation allows commanders to retain their authority while distributing accountability. In the event of a poor or illegal operation, there is an increased tendency to pass responsibility on to the lowest levels.

Without clear rules of engagement, two predictable outcomes result. First, there is an increase in civilian casualties, stemming from confusion about what counts as a legitimate target. Second, problems with accountability are exacerbated by a command structure in which decentralized units are granted a wide amount of autonomy and informational decisions are devolved to lower levels. Ultimate authority is concentrated at the top of the command chain, which is nonetheless insulated from the consequences. The basic structure multiplies the potential for so-called "isolated incidents"—unintended casualties resulting from misinformation or an improper response to information. Thus, the standing arrow configuration of Network-Centric operations allows lower-level soldiers to hazard the brunt of responsibility. The situation is complicated by the presence of contractors who, by their designation as civilian support, are exempt from prosecution. Ceding control of the automation of warfare to the private sector increases the risks of unintended consequences.

The wholesale adoption of the Network-Centric paradigm is largely an outcome of the move away from state-centric warfare and toward pre-emptive war with a heavy reliance on simulated information. Yet the distinction between the real and unreal is misleading in this sense, since all effects of warfare are devastatingly material. Network-centric warfare ultimately ends in human-centric casualties (Barnett 1999; Bolia, Vidulich and Nelson 2006). The doctrine provides insulation from the immediate results of automation, though it does not resolve mounting questions about its limitations.

Note

Many thanks to Manuel King for considerable help with the illustrations for this article, to Brian Murphy for excellent consultation, to the reviewer for insightful comments, and to the editors for their patience and assistance.

References

Alberts Donald and Richard Hayes. 2003. *Power to the Edge: Command and Control in the Information Age*. Santa Monica Command and Control Research Program.

Alberts, Gartska, Richard E. Hayes and David Signori. 2001. *Understanding Information Warfare*. http://www.dodccrp.org/html4/books_downloads.html. Accessed 29 March 2007.

Armitage, John. 2000. Beyond Postmodernism? Paul Virilio's Hypermodern Cultural Theory. *CTheory* Nov. 15. http://www.ctheory.net/articles.aspx?id=133. Accessed 13 February 2010.

———. 2006. The Elite War on Utopia. *TOPIA* 15: 69-90.

Arquilla, J. and Ronfeldt. 1996. *The Advent of Netwar*. Santa Monica: RAND MR-789-OSD

Arquilla, John and David Ronfeldt, eds. 1997. *In Athena's Camp*. Santa Monica: RAND.

Arquilla, John, David Ronfeldt and Graham and Mellisa Fuller. 1998. *The Zapatista Social Netwar in Mexico*. RAND Abstracts Document No: MR-994-A.

Auge, Marc. 1995. *Non-Place: Introduction to an Anthropology of Supermodernity*. New York: Verso.

Barnett, Thomas. 1999. *The Seven Deadly Sins of Network-Centric Warfare*. U.S. Naval Institute. http://thomaspmbarnett.com/published/7d.htm. Accessed 13 May 2006.

Baudrillard, Jean. 1981. *Simulacra and Simulation*. Trans. Shelia Glaser. Ann Arbor: University of Michigan Press.

Berkowitz, Bruce. 2003. *The New Face of War*. New York: Simon and Schuster.

Bolia, Robert, Michael Vidulich and Todd Nelson. 2006. Unintended Consequences of the Network-centric Decision-making Model: Considering the Human Operator. Paper of the Airforce Research Laboratory. Wright-Patterson Airforce Base, OK. http://docs.google.com/viewer?a=v&q=cache:ER6aHwKt_ZUJ:www.dodccrp.org/events/2006_CCRTS/html/papers/054.pdf+Bolia,+Vidulich+and+Nelson,+2006&hl=en&gl=us&sig=AHIEtbSl8MtdHW0TkQ2NFEKA7fu9yVhBDg. Accessed 28 June 2008.

Bourne, Christopher. 1999. Unintended Consequences of the *Goldwater-Nichols Act. JFQ* (Spring 1998): 99-108.

Blackmore, Tim. 2005. *War X*. Toronto: University of Toronto Press.

Bradford, Zeb and Frederic Brown. 2008. America's Army: A Model for Interagency Effectiveness. Westport, CT: Praeger Security International.

Business Transformation Agency of the Department of Defense. http://www.bta.mil/products/BEA/html_files/dodaf.html

Cares, Jeffrey. 2006. *Distributed Networked Operations: The Foundations of Network-Centric Warfare.* New York: Universe.

Castells, Manuel. 1996. *The Rise of the Network Society.* New York: Blackwell.

Cebrowski, Arthur and John Gartska. 1998. *Network-Centric Warfare Its Origin and Future*. In Naval Institute Proceedings. http://all.net/books/iw/iwarstuff/www.usni.org/Proceedings/Articles98/PROcebrowski.htm. Accessed 7 August 2003.

Coalition Warrior Interoperability Demonstration (WID) 2009. Defense Information Systems Agency Office of Procurement Directorate, Location DITCO-NCR Solicitation Number: CWID2009 (revised) Primary Point of Contact: Edward Shannon Frank, Contract Specialist. https://www.fbo.gov/indexs=opportunity&mode=form&tab=core&id=9ad750134a13843b77bcdfc27ebb3e0d&_cview=0&cck=1&au=&ck=. Accessed 20 September 2009.

De Landa, Manuel. 1991. *War in the Age of Intelligent Machines*. New York: Zone Books.

Downey, John and Graham Murdock. 2003. The Globalization of Guerrilla Warfare. In *War and the Media*, edited by Daya Kishan Thussu and Des Freeman, 70-86. London: Sage.

Drew, Christopher. 2009. Human Rights Group Says 29 Civilians Killed by Israeli Air Attacks in Gaza. *New York Times,* 30 June, A14.

Deleuze, Gilles. 2002. Postscript on Control Societies. In *CTRL Space: Rhetorics of Surveillance from Bentham to Big Brother,* edited by Thomas Levin, Ursula Frohne and Peter Weibel, 318-21. Cambridge, MA: MIT Press.

Edison, Thomas. 2006. Social Networking Analysis: One of the First Steps in Net-Centric Operations. *Defense Acquisition Review Journal.* http://www.dau.mil/search/gsaresults.aspx?k=+pubs||arq||2005arq||2005arq-40||Edison.pdf. Accessed 14 December 2007.

Foucault, Michel. 1985. *Discipline and Punish: The Birth of the Prison.* New York: Vintage.

Frank, Edward Shannon. 2009. Coalition Warrior Interoperability Demonstration, (CWID). Solicitation # CWID2009. Defense Information Systems Agency Office of Procurement Directorate DITO-NCR. http://www.fbo.gov/index?tab=core&=opportunity&mode=form&id=gad750134. Accessed 2 May 2009.

Galloway, Alexander and Eugene Thacker. 2007. *Exploit*. Minneapolis: University of Minnesota Press.

Gonzalez, Roberto, 2009. *American Counterinsurgency: Human Science and the Human Terrain.* Chicago, IL: Prickly Paradigm Press.

Gray, Christopher. 1997. *Postmodern War*. New York: Guilford Press.

Grey, Christopher Hables. 1997. *Postmodern War: The New Politics of Conflct*. New York: Guilford Press.

Gutmann, Matthew and Catherine Lutz. 2010. *Breaking Ranks: Iraq Veterans Speak Out against the War.* Berkeley, CA: University of California Press.

Hardt, Michael and Antonio Negri. 2001. *Empire*. Cambridge, MA: Harvard University Press.

Harvey, David. 2005. *A Brief History of Neoliberalism*. New York: Oxford University Press.

Hirst, Paul and Jonathan Zeitlin. 1989. *Reversing Industrial Decline, Industrial Structure and Policy in Britain and Her Competitors*. Oxford: Berg Publishers.

Jordan, Kenneth. 2007. The Consolidation of Networks for Outsourcing. Case Studies in National Security Transformation Paper #12 prepared for the Center for Teaching and National Security Policy.

Kellner, Mark. 2007. Networking the Air Force Defense News. http://integrator.hanscom.af.mil/2007/May/05242007. Accessed 3 December 2009.

Khalilzad, Zalmay, John White and Andrew Marshall. 1999. *Strategic Appraisal: The Changing Role of Information in Warfare*. Santa Monica, CA: Rand Corporation.

Kaldor, Mary. 1999. *New and Old Wars: Organized Violence in a Global Era*. Cambridge, MA: Polity Press.

Keenan, Jeremy. 2009. *The Dark Sahara: America's War on Terror in Africa*. New York: Pluto Press.

Kellner, Douglas. 2003. *The Politics and Costs of Postmodern War in the Age of Bush II*. http://www.gseis.ucla.edu/faculty/kellner/essays/politicscostspostmodernwar.pdf. Accessed 8 August 2009.

King, Laura. 2008. Coalition Friendly Fire Kills Nine Afghan Soldiers. *LA Times*, 23, October. http://articles.latimes.com/2008/oct/23/world/fg-afghan23. Accessed 20 September 2009.

Krebs, Valdis. 2002. Mapping Networks of Terrorist Cells. *Connections* 24(3): 43-52.

Lederman, Gordon. 1999. *Reorganizing the Joint Chiefs of Staff:* The Goldwater-Nichols Act *of 1986*. http://books.google.com/books?id=ANmsazlpQ10C&pg+ PR10&lpg=P R10&dq=reorganizing+the+joint+chiefs+of+staff+gordon+lederman&source=bl&ots =8fdnRh UqVt&sig=Ej054ecKoQIWzwNsA-dM8cqboFA&hl=en&ei=iCR7Spv7MY j8MfOV5PoC&sa= X&oi=book_result&ct=result&resnum=1#v=onepage&q=&f=false. Accessed 2 July 2009.

Luddy, John. 2005. The Challenge and Promise of Network-Centric Warfare. *Lexington Institute*. http://www.lexingtoninstitute.org/docs. Accessed 5 April 2006.

Metz and Kievit. 1995. *Strategy and the Revolution in Military Affairs: From Theory to Policy*. http://www.au.af.mil/au/awc/awcgate/ssi/stratrma/pdf. Accessed 31 July 2007.

Milgram, Stanley. 1967. The Small World Problem. *Psychology Today* 2:60-67.

Mitchell, Paul. 2006. *Freedom and Control in Military Networks*. Singapore: Institute of Strategic Studies.

——. 2009. *Network-Centric and Coalition Operations: The New Military Operating System*. London: Routledge.

Miyoshi, Jager. 2007. *On the Uses of Cultural Knowledge*. Strategic Studies Institute, U.S. Army War College. http://www.StrategicStudiesInstitute.army.mil/. Accessed 3 December 2009.

Murdock, Paul. 2002. Principles of War on the Network-Centric Battlefield: Mass and Economy of Force. *Parameters* 32: 86-95.

Newman, Mark. 2003. The Structure and Function of Complex Networks. *SIAM Review* 45(2003): 167-256.

Owens, Admiral William A. 1996. The Emerging System of Systems. *Strategic Forum* 63. Institute for National Strategic Studies.

Phister, Paul, Timothy Busch and Igor Plonisch. 1996. *Joint Synthetic Battlespace: Cornerstone for Predictive Battlespace Awareness.* Air Force Research Laboratory Information Directorate. Rome, NY. http://www.dodccrp.org/events/8th_ICCRTS/pdf/005.pdf. Accessed 19 June 2008.

Safranski, Mark. 2008. *The John Boyd Roundtable: Debating Science, Strategy, and War.* Ann Arbor: Nimble Books.

Shachtman, Noah, 2009. The Army's New Land Warrior Gear: Why Soldiers Don't Like It. *Popular Mechanics.* http://www.popularmechanics.com/technology/military/4215715. Accessed 11 April, 2010.

Singer, Peter W. 2003. *Corporate Warriors.* New York: Cornell University Press.

Shultz, R. 1991. The Low Intensity Conflict Environment of the 1990s. *The Annals of the American Academy of Political and Social Science* 517:120-34.

Sloan, Elinor. 2002. *The Revolution in Military Affairs.* Montreal: McGill-Queen's University Press.

Thom, William. 2000. Africa's Security Issues through 2010. *Military Review (Dept. of the Army Professional Bulletin* 100-99-5/6 80(4). http://www.cgsc.army.mil/milrey/English/JulAug00/thom.htm. Accessed 19 August 2009.

Thompson, Mark. 2008. Afghan Civilian Deaths: A Rising Toll. *Times Online,* 4 September. http://www.time.com/time/magazine/article/0,9171,1838778,00.html. Accessed 20 September 2009.

Toffler, Alvin and Heidi. 1993. *War and Anti-War.* Boston: Little and Brown.

Trilling, Roger. 2002. Why the War Works. *Village Voice,* 13-19 November. www.villagevoice.com/issues/0246/trilling.php. Accessed 4 January 2003.

Turse, Nick. 2008. *The Complex.* New York: Metropolitan Books.

Van Creveld, M. 1991. *The Transformation of War.* New York: Free Press.

Virilio, Paul. 1986. *Speed and Politics,* translated by Mark Polizzotti. New York: Semiotext(e).

———. 1988. *The Vision Machine.* Bloomington and London: Indiana University Press.

———. 1991. *The Aesthetics of Disappearance.* New York: Semiotext(e).

———. 2000. *The Information Bomb.* New York: Semiotext(e).

———. 2008. *Negative Horizon: An Essay in Dromoscopy,* translated by Michael Degener. New York: Continuum Books.

———. 2009. War and Cinema: *The Logistics of Perception.* New York: Verso.

Virilio, Paul and Sylvere Lotringer. 1983. *Pure War.* Trans. Mark Polizzotti. New York: Semiotext.

von Clausewitz, Carl. 1997. *On War.* Hertfordshire, U.K.: Wordsworth Classics.

Wallerstein, I. 2009. *The United States Confronts the World.* New York: Paradigm.

Watts, Duncan. 1999. Networks, Dynamics and the Small World Phenomenon. *AJS* 105(2): 493-527.

Gary Genosko

The Terrorist Entrepreneur

ABSTRACT

This paper theorizes by means of classical and contemporary social and political theory the figure of the terrorist entrepreneur. The figure is extracted from *The 9/11 Commission Report*—loosened from the person of Khalid Sheik Mohammed, coordinator of the attacks on the World Trade Centre, shown to express violations of category differences between East and West introduced by Max Weber and still in circulation today. Drawing upon contemporary Italian political theory of semiocapitalism and the strange fauna of political and rhetorical entrepreneurialism found in the works of Maurizio Lazzarato and Paolo Virno, the contemporary features of the terrorist entrepreneur are described.

RÉSUMÉ

L'entrepreneur terroriste

Cet exposé théorise au moyen de théorie sociale et politique classique et contemporaine la figure de l'entrepreneur terroriste. La figure est trouvé dans *la Rapport de la Commission Americain de 9/11* et est détachée de la personne de Khalid Sheik Mohammed, coordonnateur des attaques sur le World Trade Center à New York. La figure est remettre en cause en termes de la façon dont il exprime des violations des différences de catégorie entre l'est et l'ouest présentés par Max Weber et toujours dans la circulation aujourd'hui. Utilisant la théorie politique italienne contemporaine de semiocapital et les explications de la faune étrange de l'entrepreneurialisme politique et rhétorique dans les écrits de Maurizio Lazzarato et Paolo Virno, les dispositifs contemporains de l'entrepreneur de terroriste sont presentés.

¤

An entrepreneur is someone who manages to combine given elements in a new way, like a wordsmith.

—Paolo Virno (2006: 43)

This paper mobilizes a number of figures of the entrepreneur that have run through classical and contemporary sociological thought, from Max Weber's "capitalist entrepreneur" and Howard Becker's "moral entrepreneur" (1963), through Maurizio Lazzarato"s (2007) recent analyses of "political entrepreneurs," including Berlusconi and Benetton and Paolo Virno's version of the recombinant rhetorician (2006), all the way to Richard Florida's recasting of artists and new media workers as "model entrepreneurs" of the creative class (2004). In so doing, I contextualize the emergence of an extreme figure of our time: the terrorist entrepreneur.

My analysis of the figure of the terrorist entrepreneur begins with *The 9/11 Commission Report: Final Report of the National Commission on Terrorist Attacks Upon the United States* (Kean 2004). In the *Commission Report*, the figure is linked with a specific person, Khalid Sheik Mohammed (KSM), sometimes referred to as the "mastermind" of the "planes operation." The process of extraction consists of loosening the figure from the person himself. Contra Foucault, I seek neither to query the discursive production of the figure and its reproduction in the *Commission Report*, nor to embed the figure in the *Commission Report*'s reception. Rather, I begin by posing a series of questions inspired by classical Weberian sociological theory to address how Weberian distinctions between East and West are rehearsed and subsequently transgressed in the *Commission Report*'s examination of the events leading up to September 11, 2001, especially as they concern fundamental differences of culture, accounting and religiosity. However, I am not content to leave it at that. The second phase of theorizing the terrorist entrepreneur requires re-embedding the extracted figure in contemporary socio-political theory that addresses the character of semiocapitalism. What interests me in this somewhat sprawling literature is the key place occupied by new entrepreneurs. Again, I will take care not to permit this figure to settle on the empirical examples that inspired Lazzarato (2007), Franco "Bifo" Berardi (2009) and others to theorize semiocapitalism, such as Silvio Berlusconi, the Benetton Group, and the drug companies. In addition, I introduce Paolo Virno's reflections on the ancient figure of the rhetor, sophistry and Wittgensteinian language games in order to reveal the general attributes of the new entrepreneur without reductively conflating these attributes with "terrorism," or conflating "terrorism" with a Schumpeterian-type entrepreneurialism.

In the second phase of the paper, the passage from capitalist to terrorist and the foray into post-Fordist semiocapitalism requires the interrogation of a cast of strange new entrepreneurial figures, together with further theorization of key aspects of semiocapital: general intellect and the partial immateriality of labour in relation to its process and products. These new entrepreneurial types are subjectivities generated under the conditions of semiocapitalism.

Classical Weberian Questions

The figure of the terrorist entrepreneur emerges through a close examination of key passages of *The 9/11 Commission Report*. Read against the grain, these passages offer a qualified valorization of al-Qaeda leaders and field commanders, specifically KSM.

By drawing on Weber's *The Protestant Ethic and the Spirit of Capitalism* and his "Prefatory Remarks to *Collected Essays in the Sociology of Religion*" (2002a, 2002b), we can gain specific insight into one crucial yet neglected element of the events of September 11, 2001. Weber is a good first guide to one of the most troubling figures in *The 9/11 Commission Report*: the terrorist entrepreneur. The figure emerges as a result of the violation of a longstanding conceptual distinction found in Weber between *oikos* and economy (1968).

Weber helps us read the *9/11 Commission Report* not by providing answers, but by providing a conceptual-critical orientation for good questions, the sorts of questions that—according to journalist Benjamin DeMott—encourage readers of the *Report* not to "join the ranks of the blameless" (2004). Such questions provide insight into the report's self-deconstruction of the terrorist entrepreneur figure by recuperating an ecumenical coupling of religion and capitalism.

How does Weber's "capitalistic entrepreneur" character serve as a touchpoint for a reading of the "terrorist entrepreneur" figure in the *Commission Report*? What do these two figures have in common? Weber admits that all sorts of "unrestrained" and unethical capitalistic adventurers and daredevils hell-bent on making money—not to mention "undisciplined" labourers, pirates and cheats—have contributed to the development of capitalism, but argues that what may be universal is not necessarily for that reason bound to the spirit of capitalism (2002a: 361). At first glance, terrorists do appear to belong to this degraded group. But the *Commission Report* gives us more to consider on this question, especially the troubling fifth chapter, "Al-Qaeda Aims at the American Homeland," which begins with a section titled "Terrorist Entrepreneurs." This text is the empirical origin of the figure. What is at stake in this conjoining of terrorist and entrepreneur is the degree to which the terrorist initiative is valorized by its link to the spirit of entrepreneurialism. It is not a question of whether or not a valorization takes place, but of its method and degree.

On one hand, the *Commission Report* simply reproduces the standard distinction, already available in Weber, between West and East, between transparency and opacity, between business and household. For example, in referring to voluntary charitable giving (*zakat*) in Saudi Arabia, the *Report* states that "the Western notion of the separation of civic and religious duty does not exist in Islamic countries" (2004: 372). For the *Commission Report*, the problem is the absence of any "oversight mechanism," that is, the lack of any guarantors of transparency supervising donations and charities. This problem extends into the Saudi government, which collects *zakat* in the manner of a "payroll witholding tax." The *Commission Report* concludes that "social and religious traditions complicate adjustment to modern economic activity" (2004: 374). By accepting the figure of the terrorist entrepreneur, however, the *Commission Report* suggests that the differences between West and East are not so great or, at the very least, that monetary flows inevitably involve a certain degree of opacity. Weber's treatment of the distinctions between *oikos* and place of business provides a ready context for this crossover. The lack of separation between household and workplace was exemplified, he thought, by "the oriental bazaar and [by] the *ergasteria* [workshops] of other cultural regions" (Weber 2002a: 362). Another middle-ground example Weber cites is the *kasbah*. Today, we might hazard that despite the protestations of the *Commission* the networks of *hawala*, a system of value-transfer on which al-Qaeda relied, function as complicating, globalized forms of community bookkeeping that involve both personal interests (charitable giving) and business interests (2004: 171; 499, n. 124). The Commissioners never cite the Western versions of these middle grounds found in contemporary capitalism.

Weber describes the ethical foundation of the capitalist entrepreneur as a calling toward which one is obliged. As Weber explains, labour is the ascetic technique of worldly Protestantism, producing uncertain signifiers of salvation in God's service. The question of calling is an issue for every "new style" entrepreneur (Weber 2002b: 26). We can even find it in the *Commission Report*, although perhaps it is just another dangerous slip—not a return to a language of crusade against the East, but a calculated, Weberian insight. In 1988, Osama bin Laden and Ayman al Zawahiri declared in writing and in news conferences a global *fatwa* on the United States, without possessing the religious. authority to do so. As Muslims, bin Laden and al Zawahiri were apparently compelled to issue the *fatwa*, and those called upon wereare compelled to exercise a "duty" to fulfill it. The *Report* understands it this way: "bin Laden saw himself as *called* 'to follow in the footsteps of the Messenger and to communicate his message to all nationals'" (2004: 48, emphasis added). It is history in reverse: if, for Weber, the calling outstrips its religious roots, giving way to "pure utilitarianism," this effort to generalize the impulse beyond Christian ascetic technique finds similar expression in the Muslim re-faithing of the calling (2002b: 122). The *Report* captures this re-faithing, characterizing bin Laden and al Zawahiri as terrorist businessmen who take up "religious enthusiasm" when it suits their interests. It is best to put this matter paradoxically, using Weber's terms: these two key figures want to be—and *must* be—entrepreneurs (2002b: 120).

The study of bin Laden presented by the *Commission Report* is a portrait of a "terrorist financier," an intelligence label used by the Counterterrorist Centre used circa 1997 (2004: 342). This 1997 investigation—itself an update from 1995—was, unfortunately, the last national terror estimate completed before the events of September, 11, 2001. Needless to say, the *Commission Report*'s characterization of bin Laden demands some scrutiny. Earlier, the *Report* states that "by 1997, officers in the bin Laden unit [of the CIA] recognized that [he] was more than just a financier" (2004: 109). He was, no doubt, an "extremist financier," known to have funded Egyptian and Yemeni terrorists in the early 1990s (109). Nothing was done to "attack" his money, however, despite the National Security Advisor's apparent interest in terrorist finances and the Saudi government's detaining of "an important al-Qaeda financial official, Mandani al Tayyib" without allowing the U.S. access to him (122).

Much rumour and guesswork had surrounded the sources of bin Laden's funds, although by 1998 intelligence knew that he was *not* using his personal inheritance to finance al-Qaeda (Kean 2004: 122). Whether this contradicted his characterization as financier is not a moot point, as it partially absolves him from household-boundedness. His situation was able to "evolve," as Weber would have it, and to take multiple economic orientations beyond mere "want satisfaction" (1968 I: 381). The revelation that bin Laden did not use his personal fortune to finance the events of September 11, 2001 is perhaps decisive in dispelling any lingering thoughts that his economic interests were merely the sort of "house-dependent wealth-utilization" considered typical of the East. This also interrupts Bryan Turner's attempt to drive a wedge between Weber's emphasis on warriors as the social carriers of Islam—a "major flaw"—and proponents of prophetic religion, and his emphasis on bureaucrats and "financiers" who prefer religious skepticism and abhor notions such as "automatic salvation" from an honourable death (1974: 95-6).[1] What I am describing concerns a scattering of categories in which adventurous financiers embrace warrior tastes for prophecy while simultaneously employing sober bureaucratic savvy and scientific training toward the staging of terror operations.

The figural construction of al-Qaeda through its finances reaches a significant plateau in the fifth chapter of the *Commission Report*, where a new vocabulary emerges in the discussion of threats to the "American homeland." What is new is the use of the term "terrorist entrepreneurs" to describe al-Qaeda's "enterprising and strong-willed field commanders," such as KSM, who was the manager of the 9/11 attacks and is "the model of the terrorist entrepreneur" (2004: 145). KSM is thus not *a* figure, but *the* figure against which all others are measured, rendering him eerily original. Clearly, intelligence was deeper and more up-to-date on KSM, who was captured in 2003, than on bin Laden, a discrepancy that contributed to the construction of several profiles. The *Report* admits that the published depiction was based on KSM's self-characterization as an "entrepreneur seeking venture capital and people," with al-Qaeda "underwriting" him like a rogue insurance company (2004: 154). I am less concerned with the CEO-fetish at work here than with the careful representation of a fiercely "independent" and "autonomous" freelancer. KSM was an idea man endowed with many of the attributes of the capitalist entrepreneur outlined by Weber: rationality, sobriety, technical competence in calculation. He was, in short, a "capable coordinator," a fact confirmed by peer review (2004: 150). In the choice of "entrepreneur," however, there is a troubling ambivalence, owing to the validation of the balance between initiative and risk and the dimension of personal responsibility the word evokes. Surely the valorization of the entrepreneurial self in an age of neoliberalism is nothing less than a validation of the effort to achieve autonomy based on self-belief, no matter how fantastical, determined, committed or tied to explicit goal setting: what some postmodern management theorists characterize as "infantile managerial technologies of the self" (Ericsson 2003). In the past, this self-development was chalked up to the "narcissistic personalities" of modern bureaucracies' managerial class (Lasch 1979). Today, "creatives" in a seemingly boundless "cultural" industry are "paradigms of entrepreneurial selfhood" (Ross 2008: 32).

The terrorist entrepreneur, unlike his latter day capitalist colleague, *does* need a "religious." foundation of asceticism, and al-Qaeda—like any capitalist organization—contained specialized, trained officials (Weber 2002a: 358). In Weber's eyes, this would have made al-Qaeda both modern and quasi-Occidental. Indeed, the capitalist entrepreneur is at once a very old and very pervasive figure, its types and numbers concentrated in, but by no means limited to, the West. That KSM, an American-trained engineer, ran a "rational industrial organization" is not doubted by the authors of the *Commission Report*, and the Commission's readiness to label him an entrepreneur is not astonishing, although it is unsettling. In calling terrorism a "career"—which is better than a mere "job"—the *Commission Report* lurches perilously close to praising the terrorists' Western know-how (2004: 153).

Readers of Weber with an interest in the applicability of *The Protestant Ethic* to Islam have noted a significant overlap between economic ethics and the Islamic faith: "direct responsibility to God, honesty in dealing, hard work, frugality, a methodical ordering of time in daily life, rational calculation, etc., are all strongly pronounced in Islamic faith" (Alatas 1991: 254). For my purposes, this list also includes the calling and asceticism. Of course, there is no uniformity across schools of Muslim thought, and non-religious factors highly determine the degree of capitalist spirit at play in a given place. Several commentators have examined this problematic quite thoroughly, by exploring, for example, the link between acquisitive desire and pilgrimage, the influence of institutions of religious education in rural versus urban settings, and the responses to colonialism in varying degrees of Islamicization around the Muslim world (Geertz 1991: 271).

There is an "ascetic motive" (Weber 2002b: 120; 2004: 184) in the lifeworld of the terrorist entrepreneur, which is constructed obliquely in the *Commission Report* through references to "mountainous redoubts" like Tora Bora, and expressions of wonderment at 21st-century cave dwellers. Caves, box cutters, bad teeth and modest training methods all imply a certain kind of asceticism, and U.S. military leaders have insisted that good ordnance was wasted by "firing expensive

Tomahawk missiles merely at 'jungle gym' terrorist training infrastructure" (Kean 2004: 351). The entire "planes operations," it is estimated, cost no more than $400-500,000; the hijackers even wired "excess funds" back to Al-Qaeda by in the days before the attack, a good instance of administrative "diligence" (Kean 2004: 172, 252; Weber 2002b: 12).

What comes as a complete surprise to the Commission is that al-Qaeda, despite—or rather, by dint of—this worldly asceticism, was more global than the U.S. (and "us"): in 1998, al-Qaeda was described as a "loose transnational network" and a "global network" (2004: 98, 118). Al-Qaeda combined a renunciation that reaches toward death in the duty to pursue *jihad* with a surpassing of the limits of the *oikos*, escaping along the vector of entrepreneurialism into a world that was remodelled, to paraphrase Weber, by a radical, renunciatory asceticism, a "fatalism" imbued with spiritual *and* material weight (Kean 2004: 161).

What are we to make of the terrorist entrepreneur? This term, deployed by the authors of the *Commission Report* without any real critical reflexivity, readily deconstructs itself. Surely, the Commissioners simply put one and one together: KSM's self-characterization as an entrepreneur and his astute management of a terrorist organization allow the term to pass. What needs to be investigated is how semiocapital constructs an entrepreneurial subjectivity by means of social subjection; evidently the attributes of cognitive labour, which were possessed in abundance by KSM, satisfied the Commissioners.

First, however, we must explore the sociological sense of the term, as it corresponds to Howard S. Becker's classic coinage "moral entrepreneur" (1963). It is familiar and similar, and yet equally strange. The entrepreneur has an "absolute ethic" and enlists professional assistance to get the job done. As Becker explains, the entrepreneur engages in a "moral enterprise" (1963: 145). If the mission is accomplished, the entrepreneur very often finds herself out of a job; in the case of 9/11, many involved in the operation were killed or captured. Organization-building and the creation and enforcement of new rules dissipate in the event of success or failure—or, this is what we are led to believe as al-Qaeda enters new phases and takes on other shapes. In a way, this is the terrible destiny of the terrorist entrepreneur figure, a destiny that was already hinted at in the early 20th century when Thorstein Veblen used "undertaker" as a synonym for "entrepreneur" in describing the character of businessmen (Veblen 1978: 41).

By deploying the term "terrorist entrepreneur," the *Commission Report* authors reveal a belief in the constantly diversifying entrepreneurial spiritus. Certainly their description of the recruitment of Western-educated "free labour" for the planes operation mirrors Weber's understanding of capitalist organization (2002b: 362; Kean 2004: 237). Nonetheless, naysayers such as R. T. Naylor think that the *Report*'s characterization of al-Qaeda as a coherent, hierarchical and transnational organization is misguided and misleading (2002: 289-90). According to Naylor, former associates of underworld economic organizations from the American Mafia through the Medellin cartel to al-Qaeda, often consciously attempt to render their testimonies through a corporate organigramme. Thus far I have used Weber's descriptions of the spirit of capitalism to understand the representation of the terrorist entrepreneur figure as a force that marks a dangerous limit in *The 9/11 Commission Report*, rather than to dispute the veracity and accuracy of the figuration. At this point I turn to some more recent thinking about entrepreneurs via Paolo Virno and Maurizio Lazzarato.

Phase Two: Strange New Entrepreneurs in the Era of Semiocapitalism

The concept of semiocapitalism aims, first and foremost, at vanquishing false antinomies and updating stale distinctions like the structuralist opposition between the signifier and the real and the Marxist division between desire and the economic infrastructure. Specifically, the concept endeavours to capture the complex relations *between* the semiotic and material strata, insofar as informational commodities are created by info- or digital labourers, whose work is described as the immaterial labour of the cognitariat or the semiotic production of knowledge workers. Immaterial labour is a rich semiotic concept that refers to both products and labour processes. A product such as information has a corporeal manifestation in an autonomous object, no matter how abstract this may seem, and affective production that takes place in the service sector often has both manual and intellectual aspects (Hardt 2006: 48-49). In short, the semiotic subtlety of immateriality lies in the complementary statements that immaterial products are not entirely immaterial and immaterial labour is not entirely cognitive.

The neologism semiocapitalism combines general semiotics with a contempor-ary and potentially final formula of capitalism. It also participates in a periodization of sorts, as the concept references the flexibilies of post-Fordism, evoking mobile, productive spaces such as the factory and the minimal state, the rise of precarious labour, the externalization of labour onto communities of consumers and users, and the financialization of the economy. Most importantly, the term denotes a fundamental shift that has occurred in post-Fordist production. Consider the implications of Berardi's remark: "The rise of post-Fordist modes of production, which I will call semiocapitalism, takes the mind, language and creativity as its primary tools for the production of value" (2009: 21). In other words, the production of value in post-Fordist capitalism occurs through the appropriation of general human semio-communicative capacities—what Marx calls "general intellect"— in a manner that is lightly, if at all, mediated by things or product-objects. General intellect is often referred to a "general knowing." For example, Virno explains that "we live in a time, the post-Fordist era, in which human nature has become an economic stake. Every aspect of human nature ... constitutes raw material for production" (2006: 24). Human semiosis and subjectivity are directly and immediately productive of value through their combination in semio-commodities. Nevertheless, the extent to which semiocapitalism involves mediation remains a key point for consideration; some commentators, such as Akseli Virtanen, have insisted that it takes place "without the necessity of mediation or a corporeal form" (2004: 226). Virno was one of the first to advance the view that all the traits of general intellect—including "formal and informal knowledge, imagination, ethical tendencies, mentalities, and 'language games'—function themselves as productive 'machines' in contemporary labour and do not need to take on a mechanical body or an electronic soul" (2001: 1). Semiocapitalism seemingly takes us far beyond simplified industrial labour, the work day and the factory model, to an era in which complex tasks are undertaken at any time and in any place by cognitive labourers—designers, philosophers, engineers, computer scientists—yoked to increasingly mobile, extensive electronic networks of exploitation, and by those (KSM included) who appropriate their cognitive surplus value. Every life-skill and experience can be appropriated by capitalism as a direct engine of production. Lest we forget, these life-skills and experiences can also be cooperatively reappropriated for the destruction of capitalism by immaterial labour, or, as I am suggesting here, harnessed by self-identified terrorist entrepreneurs striving to devastate the "West" (Raunig 2010: 25-26).

In *Multitude*, Virno considers the relation between innovation and entrepreneurialism. Like Becker, Virno puts a strict limit on entrepreneurial innovation; although he sees creativity as inherent to human nature, he specifies that innovation is intermittent (Virno 2008: 69-70). By interpreting jokes as projective diagrams of innovative actions, and by employing ideas such as economist Joseph Schumpeter's notion that the entrepreneur resignifies existing polysemic resources (Schumpeter 1934: 132-33), Virno uncovers a new entrepreneurial figure. This entrepreneur is eccentric, resourceful, timely and capable of suddenly transforming common situations—that is, she possesses the ability to move from the regularity of old rules to the creative exceptionality of new rules and back again. According to Virno, this movement is undertaken intermittently: we are all entrepreneurs, we only occasionally activate this capacity.

For Virno, as for Schumpeter, the entrepreneurial function is not capitalistic—indeed, he finds the connection "sickening and odious" when used apologetically (Virno 2008: 146). In this light, the entrepreneur is not a CEO. Rather, this figure swerves, treading a new path by behaving differently: existing materials are used uniquely. For Virno, this material innovation is akin to using a clause in a way that runs counter to facts and generates ambiguity. A phrase such as "to wish me the enemy to capture," for example, allows a number of interpretations, while the reversal of an if-then clause's implicative force, in which the consequent becomes the antecedent, scrambles the typical logical order. According to Virno, the linguistic art of novel combinations "forges a new way of taking action" (147).

The wordsmith and the terrorist share this capacity for combinatory innovation and the exploitation of others' resources.

The Weberian notion that the terrorist entrepreneur blurs the line between household and business, crossing back and forth from one to the other and making use of resources to realize specific operations, dovetails constructively with Virno's appreciation of the art of combination, which renders the line between grammatical figure and empirical regularity ambiguous. Importantly, Virno refuses to conflate the entrepreneur with the capitalist, or with any particular profession whatsoever—except, perhaps, with the sophist. Instead, he associates entrepreneurialism with the flash of wit and with unusual insight. Perhaps this is KSM's genius: to have fashioned himself into the model of a terrorist entrepreneur, and to have done so in a way that made it through to the *Final Report*—a very successful self-entrepreneurial event in its own right.

"Capitalism," Félix Guattari states, "seizes individuals from the inside" (1996: 220). This formidable production of subjectivity has led Lazzarato to reject the description of contemporary capitalism as a mode of production, and to accept capitalism's characterization as a "machine of subjectivation" which the process of immaterial labour brings to a pinnacle:

> On the one hand, the individual brings the subjectivation process to its pinnacle, because in all these activities [of self-entrepreneurship] s/he involves the "immaterial" and "cognitive" resources of her/his "self;" while on the other s/he inclines toward identification, subjectivation and exploitation, given that s/he is both her/his own master and slave, a capitalist and a proletarian, the subject of enunciation and the subject of the statement. (Lazzarato 2006: 3)

The cognitarian and semiocapitalist are the same self-valorizing entrepreneur. Cognitive entrepreneurialism was rife during the dot-com bubble, and businesses created though the investment of intellectual assets—like new search algorithms and plans for the next web—formed alliances with investment brokers and speculators. This is the context in which KSM's self-valorization of terror management as entrepreneurialism may be understood: it is one of the strangest and most troubling offspring of semiocapital. Yet it is not so strange that it could not be included in the *Commission Report*. Its strangeness was familiar enough, even if it had not been widely named: KSM was obeying himself—the self-entrepreneur—as a subject of enunciation, but only insofar as this accorded with semiocapital's constitution of subjectivity as subject of the statement. The new terrorist entrepreneur is a slave to himself, but also a master—an operative and coordinator, but also a manager (Deleuze and Guattari 1987: 130-31).

Virno alerts us to the sophistry involved in attributing a constancy to entrepreneurial innovation. One finds such sophistry in the promotional thought of Richard

Florida, who attaches creativity to a diverse "class" of actors—that is, to highly educated professionals in the guise of entrepreneurial labourers, who "*create meaningful new forms*" (Florida 2004: 34). For Florida, creativity is innate, while in Virno's Marxian language it is part of species-being (*Gattungswesen*) but must be spurred by open, urban culture in a vaguely historical trajectory—a "rise" or even "loss of position" here and there—after which it seems to self-perpetuate (2004: 4). Although Virno and Florida both link human nature and creativity, the former's focus on language and the latter's interest in economic geography result in fundamentally different understandings of the entrepreneurial function: for Virno, it is an intermittently deployed logico-linguistic resource that is transferable to political praxis, though not necessarily under capitalism. For Florida, meanwhile, entrepreneurialism is constant enough to be indexed statistically in its ongoing capitalistic dynamism; as such, creativity is the ultimate alibi for capitalism and its newest forms of exploitation.

Another figure looms large on the semiocapitalist stage: Silvio Berlusconi. If Richard Florida is an intellectual entrepreneur performing a slick act with creativity, then Berlusconi is a political entrepreneur in whom the roles of producer of surplus-value, media boss and politician "reciprocally presuppose one another" (Lazzarato 2007: 87-88). The erasure of the distinction between the economic and the political gives rise, Lazzarato argues, to a new capitalist figure who does not merely "manipulate" the media but controls the decoded flows of labour, consumption, communication and desire. Where flows conjoin, profit is made by the figure who can both relay and intensify flows, modulating their speeds and decelerations.

Lazzarato finds the Benetton Group a perfect example to begin with, as this multinational excels at producing surplus-value at the conjunctions of flows, which are the points at which production is visible; one cannot speak of a Benetton labour force or factory. Lazzarato describes Benetton's strangeness in terms of its capacity to "federate" extant, autonomous nodes of production in a fluid network form, suggesting that the company's

> extraction of surplus-value is no longer the result of the direct exploitation of labour; on the contrary, exploitation is organized by the small and medium-sized units of production, or self-exploitation is self-organized by "enterprise individuals," called "autonomous labour" in Italy. (2007: 87)

The flows that the Benetton Group fixates on are financial circuits (investment capital) and high-tech communicational networks, in which productive marketing flows construct consumers. These networks trump the flows of labour and distribution, undertaken by means of franchises. What makes the Benetton Group a perfect example of political entrepreneurialism is the dovetailing of two productions: as goods become significational, publicity tends to collapse onto the production of consumer subjectivity. Lazzarato identifies the immaterial production of subjectivity as the fundamental political and economic technique of affective labour. In other words, surplus-value and social subjectivity are co-produced and exploited by political entrepreneurs. Of course, the production of subjectivity is not fully controllable, and remains available for resistant or aberrant recodings. Often, however, these recodings are just the work of creatives, who have themselves been subjectified into self-entrepreneurial positions.

When this kind of enterprise occurs at the state level, as Lazzarato finds with Mediaset, Berlusconi's vulgar communicational empire of television, football and game shows, communications and politics enter into a non-hierarchical relation of mutual presupposition. Whether Berlusconi makes meaning is an open question, as his penchant for constitutive definitions and idiocy makes him—as Berardi likes to remark—part Humpty Dumpty and part Ubu Roi (2011). While the communicational matrix and post-Fordist society may be mutually supporting, they are not fully integrated. Not yet, at least.

Conclusion

The *Commission Report*, read first through a Weberian filter, shows how the blurring of the distinction between business and household in the absence of administrative oversight, coupled with the union of civic and religious duty, creates a fertile ground for the wily terrorist entrepreneur. Free to creatively conjoin resource-flows, using specialized personnel, venture capital and logistics—not to mention American education and fantasies of destruction—the fiercely independent terrorist entrepreneur innovatively assembled autonomous networks for a time-bound operation, achieving the global spectacularization of mass devastation. Like any good semiocapitalist, the terrorist entrepreneur did not invest in fixed capital, but hijacked it, sloughing off other productive functions onto the bodies of labourers—the ones with the box cutters—on tight budgets. Axiomatically uniting "Eastern" and "Western" abstract quantities by introducing charity into capitalist flows, by cynically and conveniently circulating "religious" practices, by displaying a cosmopolitan facility of movement between American universities and Al-Qaeda training camps, and by transmitting household and financial money flows across electronic transfer points, the terrorist entrepreneur forces us to recognize that global Empire realizes capitalist axiomatics. Ultimately, the actions of the terrorist entrepreneur push the figure toward the limit it wants to displace, while simultaneously reconstituting a new relative limit, as it mixes Islamic social codes with capitalist decoding their alleged anathema. The innovations of the terrorist entrepreneur are not in the service of capitalism, but they feed off of capital's restless flows, becoming part of them and exploiting their tendencies.

Read through Virno and Lazzarato, the political entrepreneur contributes to this capitalist axiomatic by assembling autonomous resource-flows—some material and others immaterial, like imagination—and extracting surplus-value from the points of their conjunction. Capitalism wants to work directly on decoded flows, that is, on networks without regulatory reference points. The capitalist axiomatic is immanent to decoded flows, but may lose what flexibility it has if coding operations are introduced in specific domains. The state may become more isomorphic with the capitalist axiomatic under the direction of a political entrepreneur like Berlusconi, but Lazzarato insists it is more likely that such an impetus will come from the expansion and maturation of the surveillance state through post-disciplinary experiments of informatic control.

There is another route, however, to this same concluding suggestion. The terrorist entrepreneur *qua* neuro-worker has helped to create this high-tech, networked form, and has remained plugged into it, animated by ideological fictions but fixated on managing the transfers of signs and money and, when necessary, on hijacking fixed capital—airplanes—for a new arrangement of given elements. General intellect is not objectified into machinery by the terrorist entrepreneur; that is, in post-Fordism, a rupture has been introduced into the relationship between general intellect and fixed capital. Hijacking contributes to the growing insignificance of fixed capital by entering into the breach of the *without*—firms without factories—and participating in in the rolling dematerialization and centrifugalization of production.² Further, to borrow an idea from Schumpeter, "creative destruction" is essential to capitalism's evolution (1942: 83). It occurs from within, as old economic structures are destroyed by new ones—technologies, goods, markets, modes of production, transportation—and everything about human life becomes raw material for production. This process is spurred by the terrorist entrepreneur through new, spectacular combinations of attack, with the caveat that it leaves no easy exit from the world thus engendered. And this is why the terrorist entrepreneur, like the moral entrepreneur, is always prepared for any end to an operation, whatever profits and losses it brings, no matter what the damage.

Notes

An earlier version of this paper was given under the title of "Bad Accounting: Weber After 9/11," at the conference The Spirit of Capitalism, 1905-2005: Max Weber Today, University of British Columbia, Vancouver, 2004. I am grateful for the kind invitation of Tom Kemple. I would also like to thank Samir Gandesha for reminding me of the significance of Weber's *Protestant Ethic* for understanding the financial spirit of terrorism. In addition, I have profited from many conversations with Franco Berardi about semiocapitalism. Finally, I would like to acknowledge the assistance of Barbara Godard. Her invitation to deliver the paper "What is Semiocapitalism?" at the Toronto Semiotic Circle meeting at Victoria College in early 2010 was supported by a generous and rigorous discussion of concepts that considerably advanced my thinking.

1. Weber's brief discussion of Islam emphasizes the divergence between its "martial promises" and Puritan asceticism (1968 II: 32-27). However, Weber then swerves so as to admit, beyond the effects of its ordinances regarding avoidances (i.e., gambling), that one can locate asceticism within a military caste grounded on "rigid discipline" and

"martial order." This is the context for understanding terrorism as martial, entrepreneurial and thus religious asceticism. Turner's charge against Weber on this point—"Whatever Islam may have been, it was not a warrior religion" (not to mention his hedging on this point)—also rightly accuses Weber of placing too much emphasis on "values of the desert" (Turner 1974: 98, 143-44, 141). Weber himself suggests that choice of the warrior as social carrier does not cancel out the possibility of asceticism. The alternative source, for Turner, was the merchant, whose role Weber underplayed. Here, I am claiming in contemporary terms that one finds ample asceticism *pace* Turner: business activity as a calling (142). For Turner, however, the parallels between the Protestant ethic and Islam are "superficial and derivative" (147). The conditions in which an asceticism adequate to a modern, reformed Islam might emerge are beyond the European borrowings described by Turner (148ff).

2. In the process of dematerialization, not everything disappears. Industrial labour does not disappear, but is relocated to locations where wages are low and regulations are lax. Certain segments of cognitive capitalism follow along and are "externalized" for the same reasons. Geographic marginalization of the moment of hard materialization accompanies the deferral and provides automated support for the processes of recombination, so that program languages, data formats and the rest cohere and combine into a legible frame for an info-commodity. Mobile devices (giving the illusion of independence and self-enterprise) and techno-financial routines (illusorily autonomous but beholden to shareholder value) impose a rigorous fluidity and demand constant innovation and collabouration. For Berardi, the "soul of semiocapitalism" is non-material content—semiocommodities in their semio-digital ecologies—and how they may, in some cases, wend their way not back into but *through* other distributed nodes of informatized networks, as fixed capital. Coordinated hijacking, unlike sabotage, bastardizes the arrangements of fixed capital that are already mutating (see also Marazzi 2010: 57-59).

References

Alatas, Syed Hussein. 1991. The Weber Thesis and South East Asia. In *Max Weber: Critical Assessments* 1(2), edited by Peter Hamilton, 244-58. London: Routledge.

Becker, Howard S. 1963. *Outsiders: Studies in the Sociology of Deviance*. New York: Free Press.

Berardi, Franco "Bifo." 2009. *The Soul at Work: From Alienation to Autonomy*. Trans. F. Cadel and G. Mecchia. Los Angeles: Semiotext(e).

———. 2011. *After the Future*, edited and introduced by Gary Genosko and Nick Thoburn. Oakland, CA: AK Press.

Deleuze, Gilles and Félix Guattari. 1987. *A Thousand Plateaus*. Trans. B. Massumi. Minneapolis, MN: University of Minnesota Press.

DeMott, Benjamin. 2004. Whitewash as Public Service. *Harper's*, October 2004.

Ericsson, Daniel. 2003. *Technologies of the Entrepreneurial Self*, Växjö University, Sweden. CMS 3 Proceedings. http://www.mngt.waikato.ac.nz/research/ejrot/cmsconference/20030proceedings/criticalrealist/ericsson.pdf.

Florida, Richard. 2004. *Cities and Creative Class*. New York and London: Taylor and Francis.

Geertz, Clifford. 1991. Religious Belief and Economic Behavior in a Central Javanese Town: Some Preliminary Considerations. In *Max Weber: Critical Assessments* 1(2): 259-87. London: Routledge.

Guattari, Félix. 1996. Capital as the Integral of Power Formations. In *Soft Subversions*.

Trans. C. Wolfe and S. Cohen, 202-24. New York: Semiotext(e).

Hardt, Michael. 2006. Production and Distribution of the Common. In *Being An Artist in Post-Fordist Times*, edited by P. Gielen and P. De Bruyne, 45-53. Rotterdam: NAI.

Kean, Thomas H. 2004. *The 9/11 Commission Report: Final Report of the National Commission on Terrorist Attacks Upon the United States*. Authorized Edition. New York: W. W. Norton.

Lasch, Christopher. 1979. *The Culture of Narcissism: American Life in An Age of Diminishing Expectations*. New York: W. W. Norton.

Lazzarato, Maurizio. 2006. The Machine. Trans. Mary O'Neill. European Institute for Progressive Cultural Politics. http://www.eipcp.net/transversal/1106/lazzarato/en.

———. 2007. Strategies of the Political Entrepreneur. Trans. Timothy S. Murphy. *Substance* 36(1): 87-97.

Marazzi, Christian. 2010. *The Violence of Financial Capitalism*. Trans. K. Lebedeva. Los Angeles: Semiotext(e).

Naylor, R. T. 2002. *Wages of Crime: Black Markets, Illegal Finance, and the Underworld Economy*. Montreal and Kingston: McGill-Queen's University Press.

Raunig, Gerald. 2010. *A Thousand Machines*. Trans. Aileen Derieg. Los Angeles: Semiotext(e).

Ross, Andrew. 2008. The New Geography of Work. *Theory, Culture and Society* 25(7-8): 31-49.

Schumpeter, Joseph A. 1934. *The Theory of Economic Development. An Inquiry into Profits, Credit, Interest, and the Business Cycle*. Cambridge, MA: Harvard University Press.

———. 1942. *Capitalism, Socialism, and Democracy*. New York: Harper and Brothers.

Turner, Bryan S. 1974. *Weber and Islam: A Critical Study*. London: Routledge and Kegan Paul.

———. 1981. *For Weber: Essays on the Sociology of Fate*. Boston: Routledge and Kegan Paul.

Veblen, Thorstein. 1978. *The Theory of Business Enterprise*. New Brunswick, NJ: Transaction Books.

Virno, Paolo. 2001. *General Intellect*. Trans. A. Bove. http://generation-online.org/p/fpvirno10.htm.

———. 2006. The Dismeasure of Art: An Interview with Paolo Virno. In *Being An Artist in Post-Fordist Times*, edited by P. Gielen and P. De Bruyne, 17-44. Rotterdam: NAI.

———. 2008. *Multitude: Between Innovation and Negation*. Trans I. Bertoletti, J. Cascaito and A. Casson. New York: Semiotext(e).

Virtanen, Akseli. 2004. General Economy: The Entrance of the Multitude into Production. *ephemera* 4(3): 209-32.

Weber, Max. 1968. *Economy and Society*. Vols 1, 2 and 3, edited by G. Roth and C. Wittich. New York: Bedminster Press.

———. 2002a. *The Protestant Ethic and the Spirit of Capitalism and Other Writings*, translated and edited by P. Baehr and G. C. Wells. New York: Penguin.

———. 2002b. Appendix II: Prefatory Remarks to *Collected Essays in the Sociology of Religion*. In *The Protestant Ethic and the Spirit of Capitalism and Other Writings*, 356-72. New York: Penguin.

James Compton

Fear and Spectacle on the Planet of Slums

ABSTRACT

This paper seeks to better understand the structure of feeling in Western liberal democracies following the spectacular terrorist attacks of September 11, 2001. Numerous commentators have made the case that the post-9/11 era is marked by a new form of political domination—one distinguished by fear. It's argued that an "emerging spectacle of terrorism" has displaced older forms of fascist and consumer spectacles. Here, fear is viewed as a key "organizing principle" in a symbolic universe in which an abundance of the Real displaces simulacrum. Instead of the spectacular organization of the polity through consumerism, social domination is secured through the spectacle of terror and fear. This paper challenges this argument, and with it the suggestion that political communication be understood as post-representative. Following Raymond Williams, the paper investigates the production of global affect by asking what is dominant, what is residual and what is emergent about the spectacle of fear? In doing so it argues that the spectacle of commodity production remains firmly integrated with the state and the regime of capitalist globalization and renewed forms of primitive accumulation. Victims of spectacular forms of "accumulation by dispossession" in Western societies and the global South are now visible to each other, exposing the fearful terrain of the global affect of the Real.

RÉSUMÉ

Peur et spectacle sur la planète des bidonvilles

Cet article vise à mieux comprendre la structure du sentiment né dans les démocraties libérales occidentales à la suite des spectaculaires attaques terroristes du 11 septembre. De nombreux commentateurs ont admis que l'ère post-11 septembre se distingue par une nouvelle forme de domination culturelle – celle de la peur. On avance que « le spectacle émergent du terrorisme » a remplacé les anciennes formes de spectacles fascistes et consuméristes. Ici, la peur est considérée comme un « principe organisateur » clé, dans un univers symbolique dans lequel l'abondance du réel remplace le simulacre. Au lieu de l'organisation spectaculaire du politique à travers le consumérisme, la domination sociale est assurée par le spectacle de la terreur et de la peur. Cet article contredit cet argument, en suggérant que la communication politique peut se comprendre comme étant post-représentative. À la suite de Raymond Williams, cet article interroge la production d'une incidence mondiale en recherchant ce qui est dominant, ce qui est résiduel, et ce qui est émergent dans ce spectacle de la peur. Ce faisant, il avance que le spectacle de la production de biens de consommation reste fermement intégré dans l'État et le régime de la mondialisation capitaliste et un renouvellement des formes de l'accumulation primitive. Les victimes de formes spectaculaires « d'accumulation par dépossession » dans les sociétés occidentales et dans les pays du Sud sont à présents apparentes les unes aux autres, laissant voir le redoutable terrain de l'incidence mondiale sur le Réel.

¤

> All historical knowledge can be represented in the image of balanced scales, one tray of which is weighted with what has been and the other with knowledge of what is present. Whereas on the first the facts assembled can never be too humble or too numerous, on the second there can be only a few heavy, massive weights.
> Walter Benjamin (1999: 468)

This paper seeks to better understand the "structure of feeling" in Western liberal democracies following the spectacular terrorist attacks of September 11, 2001. In doing so, I hope to move beyond some of the now familiar tropes of 9/11 in an attempt to think through the possibilities of global democracy.

Numerous commentators have made the case that the post-9/11 era is marked by a new form of political domination—one distinguished by fear. Since September 11, 2001, Ulrich Beck has added "the risk of transnational terrorist networks" to his list of three constitutive layers of the modern risk society—the first being "ecological crises," followed by "global economic crises" (Beck 2005: 6). Carl Boggs and Tom Pollard have noted the extent to which a "legitimate public fear of real-life terrorism enables the media to sensationalize one of the greatest symbols of modern barbarism through visual constructions of savage Others" (Boggs and Pollard 2006: 349). Indeed, Hollywood's production of spectacular images of terrorism has been cited as an integral part of hegemonic discourse, alongside nationalism and consumerism, in the ongoing struggle to maintain public support for American imperialism amid the chaos of foreign wars and economic instability (Boggs 2005; Forsyth 2004). Henry Giroux (2006), among others, argues that an "emerging spectacle of terrorism" has displaced older forms of fascist and consumer spectacles. Here, fear is viewed as a key "organizing principle" in a society in which an abundance of the Real displaces simulacrum. In this, the spectacular events of 9/11 are held up as a crucial historical moment.

In what follows, I proceed with a historical-material analysis that remains sensitive to both historical continuities and contingencies, while seeking to locate fear and spectacle within a broader social totality. In doing so, I am careful to heed Richard Sennett's advice to avoid "the chrysalis theory of human history" (Sennett 1978: 23). One type of society or political system does not suddenly end only to begin anew the following day. Do the spectacular events of September 11 mark an epochal break in the regime of spectacular domination, from a spectacle of consumption to one of fear? Or are we experiencing a mixture of old and new forms of spectacular culture, from consumer spectacles to government propaganda and jihadist videos?

Raymond Williams encourages scholars to map out the "structures of feeling" unique to a society: "specifically affective elements of consciousness and relationships: not feeling against thought, but thought as felt and feeling as thought" (Williams 1977: 132). Following Williams, I suggest we understand the production of global affect by asking what is dominant, what is residual and what is emergent about the spectacle of fear. In doing so, I argue that the spectacle of commodity production remains firmly integrated with the state and the regime of capitalist globalization. This dominant fact notwithstanding, the renewed prominence of forms of primitive accumulation, or "accumulation by dispossession"—from military adventures to the enclosures of shanty towns— may hold the clue to what Williams calls the "pre-emergence" of culture: the "active and pressing but not yet fully articulated" aspects of culture (Williams 1977: 126). Victims of spectacular forms of "accumulation by dispossession" in Western societies and the global south are now visible to each other, exposing the fearful terrain of the global affect of the Real.

Spectacular Representation and Fear

Before we map the dominant, residual and emergent aspects of fear in Western society, we need to further explore debates over the relationship between fear and spectacle. According to Giroux, "unlike Guy Debord's society of the spectacle," which is governed by the image commodity, "the spectacle of terrorism affirms" a politics of war and death "over the aesthetics of commodification" (Giroux 2006: 49). Of crucial importance, says Giroux, is that citizenship, already weakened by decades of neoliberal emphasis on individual greed and self-interest, has further collapsed: the consumer citizen, now gripped by a visceral sense of fear, substitutes a "compassion for the Other with a fear for oneself" (49).

Instead of the spectacular organization of the polity through consumerism, social domination is secured through the spectacle of terror and fear; in place of the spectacle's "false unity of appearances" (Debord 1994), "politics reveals itself through the raw display of power and brutal force" (Giroux 2006: 48). We have, it would seem, re-entered the Hobbesian world of state-induced fear, though without what Hobbes considered to be its societal benefits.

Today, this critique has an enormous popular valence on the left. In its more populist form, reproduced most prominently at anti-war rallies, the critique relies on a set of tropes: principally that the Bush regime engaged in a neo-fascist imperial gambit. Domestic surveillance and intimidation attached to a Manichean patriotism—"you're either with us or with the terrorists"—moved well beyond the Dixie Chicks to threaten the entire world. Shock-and-awe, Abu Ghraib and Guantanamo Bay form the triptych of the regime's brand of fearful imperial domination.

In this new regime, the production, distribution and consumption of media are central. As Giroux correctly observes, the global diffusion of information and communication technologies has contributed to the proliferation of images, from the collapse of the World Trade Centre towers to "gruesome beheadings" and the impromptu lynching of former dictators (Giroux 2006: 50). In observing these phenomena, Giroux expands his argument to suggest that the proliferation of new imaged-based media technologies has "created new opportunities for performance, presentation, advertising, propaganda, and for political work of all kinds" (72). These technologies, he says, cannot be thought of as a mere extension of capitalist production, but instead "constitute a new stage in global capitalist development and must be grasped as structural phenomena that reconstitute the very terrain of the political" (72). These new technologies enable the flow of global capital while simultaneously providing opportunities for resistance.

With this theoretical move, Giroux has aligned himself with an influential strain of scholarship, most prominently associated with Michael Hardt and Antonio Negri (2000, 2004), that views production in the services, leisure and media industries as constitutive of "social production—not only the production of material goods but also the production of communications, relationships, and forms of life" (2004: xv). Hardt and Negri argue that "immaterial labour" is at the heart of global post-Fordist production; crucial to the flexibility of the system is the production of "ideas, images, affects, and relationships," or "bio-political production" (xvi).

It is this move to the production of affect that is said to transform spectacular relations. Affect is positioned as a key modality of information-based, networked communication; it is involved in the simultaneous production of new forms of societal control and potential avenues of flight. Nicholas Thoburn argues that under conditions of bio-political production, subjectivity is multifarious and open to production at the level of the everyday, i.e., at the bio-political level (Thoburn 2007). No longer is individual subjectivity given solely by membership in large institutional formations, such as the family, citizenship or the industrial workplace. Political communication, Thoburn argues, is less concerned with addressing communities through representation or signification of ideology; instead, in image-based capitalist cultures, the production of affect acts directly on the body; it is "pre-subjective" (85). The "system works not at the level of meaning or signifying content but by the modulation of nervous, pre-subjective response" (85). Citing work by Brian Massumi (2005), Thoburn suggests that the Bush regime's response to 9/11, including the use of colour-coded terror alerts, should be understood in this manner. Following Scott Lash (2007), and contrary to Boggs and Pollard (2006) and Forsyth (2004), power should be understood as post-hegemonic.

This paper challenges the suggestion that political communication should be understood as post-representative. Along with Beverley Best I take the position "that from the point of view of an expanded historical field, affect and mediation are not oppositional or antagonistic" (Best 2009: 24). As Ernesto Laclau has argued, politics is impossible without some form of articulation (Laclau 2004: 26).

Giroux correctly points out that the production of affect is not limited to the state. In this trans-national public sphere, stateless groups now have the ability to speak back. Indeed, I would argue that forms of viral video are an important element in the current production of global affect. Giroux is correct to say that "images of fear, shock and hate are now global" (Giroux 2006: 53) and, we might add, ready for download. The spectacle of fear is a global commodity.

There is indeed much truth in Giroux's analysis, particularly the insistence on the dialectical role of new media. These truths notwithstanding, I argue that we should not mistake the part for the whole. Our historical narrative cannot begin with the "post-9/11 World." It is precisely the insistence that history begins anew that is the problem. Indeed, the very incantation of the phrase "post-9/11" has all too often been used to hypostatize terror. In doing so, a complex social process is frozen. Reactionary forces on the right have taken advantage of this move. The phrase "They hate us because of our freedoms" resonates in a context that is at once ahistorical and occidental. It is a Westernized view of history that reifies the global Other.

To focus exclusively on the objects of spectacular phenomena is to miss the broader context in which the spectacle of fear is produced. It is not enough to examine the performance of the politics of fear; one must also understand the politics of the performance of fear. That is to say, we need to better understand the social relations that both produce and are produced by the spectacle. We need to gauge the extent to which social relations are mediated through the modalities of capitalist society—a society of commodity production, distribution and consumption. Has spectacular consumer society been surpassed or subsumed by a society of fear? Or, do important aspects of the society of spectacle remain, such as spectacular representations of power? Is the spectacular production of fear a new phenomenon? Or, is fear constitutive of modernity? Answers to these questions will influence democratic responses to a society of fear and impact assessments of potential success.

The Dominant—Commodity Circulation

In *The Society of the Spectacle*, Debord (1994) distinguishes between two forms of spectacular relations in late modern societies: diffuse and concentrated. In Europe and North America, where commodity relations are firmly entrenched, we find the diffuse spectacle. The concentrated spectacle, on the other hand, is epitomized by Stalinism and its valorization of state bureaucracy and organizational efficiencies. Under purely concentrated spectacular relations, there is but one image commodity signified through a cult of personality. In *Comments on the Society of the Spectacle*, Debord (2002) abandons the distinction and argues that the two forms have fused into an integrated spectacle.

Let us begin by examining these two integrated spectacular forms by asking: what is the present state of the commodity? When Debord began his *Society of the Spectacle* with a détournement of the first lines of Marx's *Capital*, he wrote: "the whole life of those societies in which modern conditions of production prevail presents itself as an immense accumulation of *spectacles*. All that once was directly lived has become mere representation" (Debord 1994: 12). Debord's argument updates Marx's concept of commodity fetishism, a process in which commodities take on a central role in the mediation of social relations. In the market, commodities have exchange-value in relation to each other or in relation to money, which represents them abstractly; their value is misrecognized. Value *is* based on human labour (abstract labour) but it appears to be based on the inherent qualities of the commodity being exchanged. Value is, therefore, perceived in a phantasmagoric form as a relation between things instead of a relation between people. The world of real social relations (wage labour, relations of production and gender, race and class divisions) becomes occluded in the fantastic realm of commodities, which in turn alienates individuals from their real social existences (Marx 1976). Under the generalized conditions of the society of the spectacle, the commodity form has become pure image, an arbitrary image that can be used, discarded and reused countless times under varying circumstances while connoting disparate meanings.

The circulation of the commodity form—its production, distribution and consumption—has not decreased; instead, it prevails globally. The financialization of the global economy has, if anything, increased its speed, intensity and global scope. Indeed, as Edward Comor argues, capitalist consumption remains "a central mediator of virtually all human relations" including economic and political globalization (Comor 2008: 2). What underlines this process of mediation is "the fact that capitalist production requires workers to sell their labour *as a commodity*—a requirement stemming from the crucial role labour plays in capital's drive to accumulate more capital" (9). This "compulsion" remains dominant, as is the need for the state to ensure that affordable transactions between capital and labour are possible. What has changed are the policies used to achieve the goal. Neoliberal deregulation and privatization have shifted the responsibility of maintaining a healthy and capable workforce to the market. Zygmunt Bauman states that the responsibility to "recommoditize" labour "is left to the worries of individual men and women" who must use their own private resources to upgrade themselves for the flexible requirements of capital (Bauman 2007: 9-10). Without the Fordist promise of job security, the flexible just-in-time and until-further-notice labour contracts of post-Fordism—or "liquid modernity," as Bauman prefers—create enormous insecurity and anxiety (Bauman 2000: 147; Sennett 2006: 52). Moreover, in a society of consumers, "no one can become a subject without first turning into a commodity," notwithstanding clashing characterizations of subjects as cultural dupes or heroic consumers (Bauman 2007: 12). Consumer culture remains the privileged site of identity formation, and image management remains the first principle of agency in a society of consumers. As Jackson Lears (1983) and later Don Slater (1997) argued, the presentation of a "pleasant social self" in everyday life and in the workplace is a central aspect of modernity; the exchange-value of presentation can, and often does, trump the use-value of a person's skills and ability. This objective relation remains with us whether looking for a job, wooing votes or collecting "friends" for our Facebook page. Furthermore, the aestheticized violence in jihadist videos helps close the sale with its intended audience and also strikes fear.

Consumer society promotes dissatisfaction. The failure of commodities to fulfill their promise is a core contradiction and structural necessity, as is the promise (hope) that the next purchase just might work this time. In addition, disaffection "saps confidence and deepens the sentiment of insecurity, becoming itself a source of the ambient fear it promises to cure or disperse—the fear that saturates liquid modern life and the principal cause of the liquid modern variety of unhappiness" (Bauman 2007: 46).

Consumption, argues Comor, is "globalization's (and capitalism's) most compelling idea" (Comor 2008: 12), but it requires assistance to achieve its hegemonic status. Globalization has been driven by capital's need for spatio-temporal expansion, and from the beginning has required enforcement by state authority through legal implementation of contractual property relations or military might. The end game remains the establishment of "a private space of contractual material relations of production and exchange" (Rosenberg 2005: 42).Unlike social theorists such as Anthony Giddens (1990), Justin Rosenberg refutes the claim that information and communication technologies have contributed to a fundamentally new kind of society. Rosenberg points out that what Marx identified as the "universalizing tendency of capital" contained within it a tendency toward geographical expansion and the constant redevelopment and deployment of technology (Rosenberg 2005: 21). The so-called period of globalization during the 1990s reveals "the organic tendencies of the old" regime "now reasserting themselves, in a new situation, and on an historically unprecedented scale" (52).

Indeed, David Harvey argues that capital accumulation, beginning with the original primitive accumulation, has always required "a fund of assets outside of itself … to confront and circumvent pressures of overaccumulation" (Harvey 2003: 143). Capitalism, from the beginning, was other-directed and continues today to take the form of "accumulation by dispossession" (144). This drive has taken various forms over the years: the enclosure of the commons through the privatization and commodification of land; colonialism; and the privatization of formerly public assets, such as utilities, broadcasting and healthcare. More recently, accumulation by dispossession occurred in the spectacular 2007 collapse of the sub-prime mortgage industries caused by essentially legalized ponzi schemes.

From the broader historical perspective outlined above, the invasion of Iraq and the so-called War on Terror should not be seen in isolation as mercurial acts of neoconservative hubris. Nor does it signal a break with a regime of societal reproduction through consumption and accumulation by dispossession. As Iain Boal, et al. of Retort (Retort 2005) have argued, it was part of a succession of imperial post-Second-World-War military interventions—think Korea, Vietnam, Chile, Lebanon, Nicaragua, Panama—which together marked war as a permanent aspect of late capitalist modernity. During times of so-called peace, similar objectives of enclosure and dispossession are enforced through the policies of the Washington Consensus, such as liberalization of trade and enforced privatization. Shock-and-awe is but one tactical form of the spectacle's integration with capital's global policeman: the American state-military complex. For Retort, the anti-war chant of "No blood for oil" distracts from the broader imperative of the present conjuncture's form of primitive accumulation.

The election of Barack Obama, despite the hope for change he signified, has not heralded substantive material change in the War on Terror. Guantanamo Bay is scheduled to close, but the CIA continues to have the authority to carry out renditions of prisoners to foreign countries. Obama was awarded the Nobel Peace Prize, but the Nobel laureate's acceptance speech served to justify NATO's 30,000-soldier troop surge in Afghanistan announced only a week earlier. As predicted by Tariq Ali, Obama's administration, a full year into its term, has the characteristics of "imperialism with a human face" (O'Keefe 2009). Obama provides the image of hope and change and a benign neoliberal regime.

Here we see what Retort believe are "the contradictions of military neoliberalism under conditions of spectacle" (Retort 2005: 15). The imperial project and global commodity circulation cannot be sustained over time without the maintenance of "patterns of belief and desire, levels of confidence, degrees of identification with the good life of the commodity" (26). The state requires image management; it requires spectacle. "This world of images had long been a structural necessity of a capitalism oriented toward the overproduction of commodities, and therefore the constant manufacture of desire for them; but the by the late 20th century it had given rise to a specific polity" (21). Global capitalism requires the "free" flow of capital and commodities enforced through dispossession of others and the spectacular control of images; the rub is that the state is now vulnerable to spectacular attack. It is at the level of the image that the state is now vulnerable. According to Arjun Appadurai:

> States find themselves pressed to stay "open" by the forces of media, technology and travel which had fueled consumerism throughout the world and have increased the craving, even in the non-Western world, for new commodities and spectacles. On the other hand, these cravings can become caught up in new technologies, mediascapes, and eventually, ideoscapes, such as democracy in China, that the state cannot tolerate as threats to its own control over ideas of nationhood and peoplehood. (Appadurai 1990: 14)

These contradictions emerge, says Appadurai, because "the United States is no longer the puppeteer of a world system of images, but is only one node of a complex transnational construction of imaginary landscapes" (4). The fear and jingoism reproduced by the American military-entertainment complex (Boggs and Pollard 2006; Compton 2006) is shadowed by fundamentalist spectacles of violence and the imagined communities they seek to reproduce.

The Residual—Fear and Modernity

That fear is a key structuring affect of political order has been recognized from the time Machiavelli counselled the Prince that it is better to be feared than loved, and Hobbes argued that fear could provide a "negative moral foundation" for society. It does not originate in the post-9/11 political environment. There is a long and bloody record of political elites using fear to govern. More recently, during the mid-20th century, the spectacle of a possible nuclear holocaust weighed heavily on the public mind of British and American citizens, and supported attempts to pacify the citizenry. Models of personal and collective agency were rehearsed through air-raid drills in public schools, where students were taught to duck under their desks (Bourke 2005: 260-261). To this horror we may add the fear of a world-wide communist conspiracy promoted by U.S. Senator Joseph McCarthy in the 1950s.

Fear, argues David Altheide, is "socially constructed and managed by political actors to promote their own goals" (2006: 18). Indeed, the active social construction of fear is pervasive; its "ur" form is the crime story, a cornerstone of the journalistic craft which routinely constructs normative boundaries of deviance (Altheide 2006: 80; Ericson, et al. 1987). News coverage of international terror simply reproduces the trope. "The scenario of 'out of control' evil calls forth a heroic retort as a kind of narrative response in the mediated drama" (Altheide 2006: 65). The fabulist construction of heroine Private Jessica Lynch is perhaps the most obvious example (Compton 2006). Moreover, Altheide argues that these narratives became fused with the institution of consumption itself, "as government and business propaganda emphasized common themes of spending/buying to help the country get back on track" (Altheide 2006: 95).

The integration of commercial and state interests with fear is longstanding. The pervasive poverty of 19th-century Britain and America buttressed a fear of destitution that was encouraged by public authorities. Joanna Bourke informs us that "providers of public assistance were determined to retain (indeed, even boost) this element of fear. After all, they reasoned, public assistance should not be made *too* easy in case people jettisoned all economic anxieties, thus damaging the economy" (Bourke 2005: 27). The pervasiveness of fear and its commodification encouraged a profitable death industry. Grave robbing—a relatively common occurrence in the early 19th century—was outlawed in Britain in 1832; nevertheless, laws passed by parliament under the Anatomy Act normalized the use of bodies for the purpose of dissection by anatomists. Bodies of people who died as paupers could be appropriated for the purposes of dissection if unclaimed after forty-eight hours. The popular press fanned anxiety through the publication of lurid stories about dissections, while a "link between fear and corporate profit was forged, with the increase in the sale of Industrial Assurance" to provide funds for a decent funeral (Bourke 2005: 29-30). Fear, it turns out, is good for business.

According to Andrew Tudor, "fearfulness in varying degrees is part of the very fabric of everyday social relations.... Fearfulness appears to have become a way of life in modern society" (Tudor 2003: 238). It is mediated through a "complex of physical, psychological, social and cultural relations" (239). Marshall Berman (1988) argues persuasively that capitalist modernity breeds uncertainty, change and anxiety. Creative destruction—capitalism's need to smash what it creates—makes permanent change imperative. And this constant change and innovation cannot be cut off from the rest of everyday life; the pressure to revolutionize production spills over and affects social and cultural life. Georg Simmel noted in 1903 that individuals protected themselves from the "shock of the new" by creating "a protective organ" which took the principal intellectual form of "rationally calculated egoism" (Simmel 1971[1903]: 327). In the modern city, where day-to-day relationships were mediated by market transactions, the

> money economy and the domination of the intellect stand in the closest relationship to one another. They have in common a purely matter-of-fact

attitude in the treatment of persons and things in which a formal justice is often combined with an unrelenting hardness. (326-27)

Simmel had identified a link between fear and rationality that was constitutive of the everyday social relations found in modernity. Coping with the "shock of the new"—the constant effrontery of strangers—necessitated strategies for keeping emotions at a distance.

According to Walter Benjamin, the conscious response to the "shock of the new" was the principle method of protecting a fragile individual psyche from the trauma imposed by the technologically altered modern world (Benjamin 1999: 447; Koepnick 1999: 147). In order to fend off constant bodily stimuli, the modern individual required strategies of perception. The stand-offish aesthetic play of the *flâneur*, detailed by Benjamin, maintained his separateness from the crowd. The *flâneur* turned "reality into a phantasmagoria" (Buck-Morss 1992: 24). The tragedy, argued Benjamin, is that these perceptual and aesthetic strategies of modern survival anaesthetized individuals. Susan Buck-Morss argues that drug use is, in this sense, constitutive of modernity. The use of opium, cocaine and "ether frolics" are modern phenomena. But the political significance is cognitive. "The experience of intoxication is not limited to drug-induced, biochemical transformations. Beginning in the 19th century, a narcotic was made out of reality itself" (22). The privatized fantasies of bourgeois consumers merged with the changing public spaces of the Paris arcades and the phantasmagorias of consumer displays (22). In this sense, fear, a bodily response induced by the shock of modern life, was managed cognitively; it was mediated through the commodity relations of consumer culture.

The need to manage the "shock of the new" has not receded. Networked capitalism's drive for spatio-temporal control has contributed to immense "social acceleration" and subsequent

> alienation from space and time, from the objective world, the social world, and the self, since the appropriation of novel places, objects, persons as well as experiences, and subsequent familiarization with them, requires time no longer available to individuals in a high-speed society. (Rosa 2005: 457-58)

In this sense, the use of mobile and digital social networking technologies and the inter-subjective relations produced through them must be assessed in the broader context of networked global consumer culture (Comor 2008). Moreover, as Bauman argues, networked consumer culture makes social disconnection as easy as social connection; it is the ability to disconnect from the unwanted and discard the Other, more than the ability to create social bonds, that is the essential charm of digital networks—its "safety device" (Bauman 2007: 107).

The Emergent—Fear of a Slum Planet

The imperial adventures of the United States along withand its "coalition of the willing" in Iraq were justified by conjuring fears of Weapons of Mass Destruction (WMDs) and the imagined whiff of nuclear mushroom clouds. These were top-down fabrications designed to scare populations into supporting a controversial and deadly political agenda. But while the "reckless militancy" of an "American empire of fear" has rightly angered critics such as Benjamin Barber (2003: 15), it does not by itself capture the pervasive nature of political fear in modern societies.

To grasp this fear means moving beyond viewing political fear in isolation as a weapon deployed by elites to secure domination, despite political propaganda's continued existence. As Corey Robin observes, "political fear reflects the interests and reasoned judgments of the fearful about what is good for them, and responds to real dangers in the world" (Robin 2004: 162). The perception and appreciation of fear is embedded in a complex matrix of modern social relations. For Hasana Sharp, following Spinoza, the apperception of this social complex is reason itself: "reason is the apprehension of our existence as pervasively affective, and determined by our 'being inside' a complex constellation of other beings" (Sharp 2005: 607). What then are some of the components of this complex constellation?

Mike Davis (2006) has used the term "planet of slums" to describe the impoverished billions currently being thrown by enclosure and industrialization into the shanty towns of Cairo, Rio de Janeiro and Mumbai without medical care, clean water or the stability of their traditional agrarian communities. The material gulf between this planet of slums and our own planet of malls is enormous. And yet they are increasingly interconnected via the global diffusion of information and communication technologies, and the deteritorialized flows of "money, commodities, and persons" that are made visible through the representations of "the mediascapes and ideoscapes of the modern world" (Appadurai 1990: 12).

Globe-spanning communication technologies have expanded opportunities for atomized members of the slum and mall planets to be made visible to each other. John Thompson (2004) has documented how newspapers, followed by radio and television, helped to construct a "mediated visibility" in which the few (political elites) are made visible to the many (citizens). New digital media technologies expand this modern dynamic of information leakage. Examples include jihadist propaganda videos, Abu Ghraib photos and the hanging of former Iraqi dictator Saddam Hussein. What may be characterized as emergent is how information flow is "also an explicit strategy of individuals who know very well that mediated visibility can be a weapon in the struggles they wage in their day-to-day lives" (31).

The heightened global awareness supported by new digital technologies is often referenced optimistically. Libertarian and liberal writers celebrate how markets reveal the "wisdom of crowds" (Surowiecki 2005; Sunstein 2006), while some theorists of spectacle (Giroux 2006; Stallabrass 2006) argue that the use of new media technologies to create alternative and independent media sites is a dialectical response to the lack of democracy in corporate media, an attempt to construct a space for collective dialogue and participation. According to Julian Stallabrass:

> Spectacle too has its own dialectic: of internal globalization of the social, and the globalization of communication and with it consciousness—specifically with the increasing realization of poverty and injustice on a global scale, which is as much a feature of radical Islam as of the anti-capitalist movement. (2006: 104)

However, this global awareness has the potential to be as reactionary as it is progressive. The speed with which global capital, information and media flow stands in contradiction to the slow-time required for democracy (Rosa 2005). This dynamic casts doubt on the good intentions of globalized social movements. "Tactically, political time clashes with media time. Rapidly co-ordinated, high profile protests at transnational summit meetings are subsumed by the real time logics of global news coverage" (Hope 2006: 22). Jodi Dean characterizes the networked communication environment as a "fantasy of abundance" that "both expresses and conceals the shift from message to contribution" in which the exchange value of circulating digital contributions trumps the use value of particular and sometimes incompatible messages (Dean 2005: 59). The particularity of material experience is erased through a circulation of the "fantasy of global unity" (68-69).

When large sections of North America, Europe and the Asia-Pacific region are acutely aware of their extraordinary wealth relative to the rest of the world, there are rich possibilities for a politics of fear, based on anxieties about dispossession and revenge at the hands of the slum-dwellers lurking outside the mall (Dyer 2008). The increased visibility between the mall and slum planets has created opportunities for them to affect each other. As Sharp points out, the 2004 Madrid train bombings sparked worldwide rail alerts (Sharp 2005: 597). But the affective relations of the planet of slums and the planet of malls is not restricted to moments of acute and appalling violence; it can be experienced at the level of the everyday, particularly in a culture characterized by generalized and free-floating anxiety.

Numerous commentators have drawn attention to the fact that the middle class of wealthy Western nations have not faired well under neoliberal globalization (Krugman 2006; Steingart 2006a). Comparative living standards have fallen and an already weak union movement has diminished in size, accounting for only 8 per cent of private sector workers in the United States. In fact, the union membership rate has slipped by more than 75 per cent from its peak in the mid 1940s (Steingart 2006b). The precariousness of American labour and the documented abuse of workers is a central component of what Corey Robin calls "fear, American style" (Robin 2004: 227-48). In such a labour climate, American workers are increasingly hard-pressed to display solidarity with their opposites in the planet of slums, let alone support a radical redistribution of global product and wealth. Bauman notes that "by 1870 income per head in industrialized Europe was eleven times higher than in the poorest countries of the world. In the course of the next century or so the factor grew five-fold, reaching fifty by 1995" (Bauman 2000: 140). By 2004, one-third of the world's population accounted for 3.2 per cent global consumption (Comor 2008: 6).

The situation has worsened. The 2007 global recession sparked by unregulated capital financialization and the collapse of sub-prime mortgage markets (themselves supported by the rising debt loads of middle- and working-class citizens trying to sustain the spectacle of consumption that their declining real incomes could no longer support) is now visible to all. These developments should be viewed in relation to two other impending long-term crises: a global food crisis and climate change. From this holistic perspective, we can see the tension between the material interests of the planet of malls and planet of slums.

The spectacular 2008 food riots in Egypt, Haiti and Ethiopia are dialectically related to worker protests and street violence in European cities in early 2009. Add to this the knowledge that Western governments and corporations are buying up arable land in Africa to secure their own food supplies, while government-subsidized biofuel production has been blamed by the World Bank for driving up the price of food by 75 per cent between 2005 and 2008, and you have a volatile social cocktail (Borger 2008; Chakrabortty 2008). Mark Featherstone states the problem concisely:

> What is clear about the network society is that even the rich cannot rest easy in their luxury because they know that the misery of absolute poverty could fall upon them in the wake of some new normal crisis of capitalism. (Featherstone 2008: 194)

Fear of terror, fear of WMDs, fear of migrants and fear of cheap foreign labour are all, in a way, variants on this theme.

Building on Mike Davis's work, Slavoj Žižek has suggested that the possibilities for 21st-century radical politics depends on whether movements of slum dwellers emerge as the "counter class" to the first-world's "symbolic class" of managers, information and cultural workers, or whether alliances between sections of these groups are possible (Žižek 2007: 58). David Harvey makes a similar point when he argues that the traditional Left in Western societies has focused too much on workers' struggles to improve their conditions of reproduction. He suggests these efforts should "be seen in a dialectical relation with the struggles against accumulation by dispossession" (Harvey 2003: 176). Bridges need to be built between these groups. For the latter possibility to be realized, democratic activists in the developed nations need to come to terms with the fearful terrain of the global affect of the Real.

Concluding Thoughts on Fear and Global Democracy

Recent scholarship has tried to establish an analytical framework with which to understand the potential for a democratic transnational public sphere. As we have seen, scholars have noted how new information and communication technologies, including satellites and the Internet, have unleashed an unprecedented exchange of information. We must strive to use these opportunities to find commonalities while remaining sensitive to how "real-time news and online media have the potential to unleash disorder and chaos, as much as the rational critical scrutiny expected of the ideal fourth estate" (McNair 2005: 173). Work by Nancy Fraser (2007) has endeavored to advance Habermas's (1989) theorization of a national public sphere by arguing that a critical theory of transnational public opinion must "account for the legitimacy and political efficacy of public opinion" (Fraser 2007: 24). The first step, Fraser argues, is to interrogate the conditions of "participatory parity" among transnational actors; the second is to examine the "translation and capacity conditions of existing publicity" (24). Here, work on the transcultural political economy of global communication (Chakravartty and Zhao 2008) is valuable.

If we are to "think past terror"—borrowing Susan Buck-Morss's useful phrase— we must understand the global social field of discursive production (Buck-Morss 2003). Buck-Morss correctly observes that "democracy on a global scale" requires the production of solidarity across and beyond particular social fields, bounded as they are by history, language, geography and ethnicity, and yet linked by the global diffusion of information networks (4). But this task will not be easy; more communication does not necessarily result in understanding and harmony. The global field of discursive production may reveal a surplus of real material inequalities between global haves and have-nots that reinforces the fear of the Other.

Note

The author would like to thank reviewers of the manuscript for their thoughtful suggestions. He also wishes to thank Beverley Best, Edward Comor, Nick Dyer-Witheford and Sharon Sliwinski. The paper has benefited enormously from their collegial comments and intellectual rigour.

References

Altheide, David. 2006. *Terrorism and the Politics of Fear*. Lanham, U.K.: Rowan and Littlefield.

Appadurai, Arjun. 1990. Disjuncture and Global Difference in the Global Cultural

Economy. *Public Culture* 2(2): 1-24.

Barber, Benjamin. 2003. *Fear's Empire*. New York: Norton.

Bauman, Zygmunt. 2000. *Liquid Modernity*. Cambridge, U.K.: Polity.

———. 2007. *Consuming Life*. Cambridge, U.K.: Polity.

Beck, Ulrich. 2005. The Silence of Words and the Political Dynamics in the World Risk Society. In *Planetary Politics: Human Rights, Terror, and Global Society*, edited by Stephen Eric Bonner, 3-20. Lanham, U.K.: Rowman and Littlefield.

Benjamin, Walter. 1999. *The Arcades Project*. Trans. by Howard Eiland and Kevin McLaughlin. Cambridge and London: Belknap Press.

Berman, Marshall. 1988. *All That is Solid Melts into Air: The Experience of Modernity*. New York: Penguin.

Best, Beverley. 2009. Fredric Jameson et la Dialectique de l'Affect. *Cahiers de Recherche Sociologique* 47:23-45.

Boggs, Carl. 2005. The New Militarism: Imperial Overreach. In *Planetary Politics: Human Rights, Terror, and Global Society*, edited by Stephen Bonner, 71-86. Lanham, U.K.: Rowman and Littlefield.

Boggs, Carl and Tom Pollard. 2006. Hollywood and the Spectacle of Terrorism. *New Political Science* 28(3): 335-51.

Borger, Julian. 2008. Rich Countries Launch Great Land Grab to Safeguard Food Supply. *Guardian*, 22 November. http://www.guardian.co.uk/environment/2008/nov/22/food-biofuels-land-grab. Accessed 23 November 2008.

Bourke, Joanna. 2005. *Fear: A Cultural History*. Emeryville, CA: Shoemaker and Hoard.

Buck-Morss, Susan. 1992. Aesthetics and Anaesthetics: Walter Benjamin's Artwork Essay Reconsidered. *October* 62: 3-41.

———. 2003. *Thinking Past Terror: Islamism and Critical Theory on the Left*. London: Verso.

Chakrabortty, Aditya. 2008. Secret Report: Biofuel Caused Food Crisis. *Guardian*, 4 July. http://www.guardian.co.uk/environment/2008/jul/03/biofuels.renewableenergy. Accessed 4 July 2008.

Comor, Edward. 2008. *Consumption and the Globalization Project: International Hegemony and the Annihilation of Time*. New York: Palgrave MacMillan.

Compton, James R. 2006. Shocked and Awed: The Convergence of Military and Media Discourse. In *Global Politics in the Information Age*, edited by Peter Wilkin and Mark Lacy, 39-62. Manchester, U.K.: Manchester University Press.

Chakravartty, Paula and Yuezhi Zhao. 2008. *Global Communications: Towards a Transcultural Political Economy*. Lanham, U.K.: Rowan and Littlefield.

Davis, Mike. 2006. *Planet of the Slums*. London and New York: Verso.

Dean, Jodi. 2005. Communicative Capitalism: Circulation and the Foreclosure of Politics. *Cultural Politics* 1(1): 51-74.

Debord, Guy. 1994. *The Society of the Spectacle*. New York: Zone Books.

———. 2002. *Comments on the Society of the Spectacle*. London: Verso.

Dyer, Gwynne. 2008. *The Climate Wars*. Toronto: Random House.

Ericson, Robert V., Patricia M. Baranek and Janet B. L. Chan. 1987. *Visualizing Deviance: A Study of News Organization*. Toronto: University of Toronto Press.

Featherstone, Mark. 2008. The State of the Network: Radical Anxiety, Real Paranoia and Quantum Culture. *Journal for Cultural Research* 12(2): 181-203.

Fraser, Nancy. 2007. Transnationalizing the Public Sphere: On the Legitimacy and Efficacy of Public Opinion in a Post-Westphalian World. *Theory, Culture and Society* 24(4): 7-30.

Forsyth, Scott. 2004. Hollywood Reloaded: The Film as Imperial Commodity. In *Socialist Register 2005: The Empire Reloaded*, edited by Leo Panitch and Colin Leys, 108-23. London: Merlin Press.

Giddens, Anthony. 1990. *The Consequences of Modernity*. Palo Alto, CA: Stanford University Press.

Giroux, Henry. 2006. *Beyond the Spectacle of Terrorism: Global Uncertainty and the Challenge of the New Media*. Boulder, CO, and London: Paradigm Publishers.

Habermas, Jürgen. 1989. *The Structural Transformation of the Public Sphere: An Inquiry into a Category of Bourgeois Society*. Trans. Thomas Burger. Cambridge, MA: MIT Press.

Hardt, Michael and Antonio Negri. 2000. *Empire*. Cambridge, MA: Harvard University Press.

———. 2004. *Multitude: War and Democracy in the Age of Empire*. New York: Penguin.

Harvey, David. 2003. *The New Imperialism*. Oxford: Oxford University Press.

Hope, Wayne. 2006. Global Capitalism, Temporality, and Oppositional Public Spheres. Paper presented to the International Association of Media Communication Conference (IAMCR), July, in Cairo, Egypt at the American University.

Koepnick, Lutz. 1999. *Walter Benjamin and the Aesthetics of Power*. Lincoln, NB: University of Nebraska.

Krugman, Paul. 2006. The Great Wealth Transfer. *Rolling Stone*, 30 November. http://www.rollingstone.com/politics/story/12699486/paul_krugman_on_the_great_wealth_transfer. Accessed 5 September 2007.

Laclau, Ernesto. 2004. Can Immanence Explain Social Struggles? In *Empire's New Clothes: Reading Hardt and Negri*, edited by Paul A. Passavant and Jodi Dean, 21-30. New York: Routledge.

Lash, Scott. 2007. Power after Hegemony: Cultural Studies in Mutation? *Theory, Culture and Society* 24(3): 55-78.

Lears, T. J. Jackson. 1983. From Salvation to Self-Realization: Advertising and the Therapeutic Roots of the Consumer Culture, 1880–1930. In *The Culture of Consumption*, edited by Richard W. Fox and T. J. Jackson Lears. New York: Pantheon.

Marx, Karl. 1976. *Capital, Vol. 1.*, Trans. Ben Fowkes., London: Penguin Books.

Massumi, Brian. 2005. Fear (the Spectrum Said). *Positions* 13(1): 31-48.

McNair, Brian. 2005. The Global Public Sphere: Fourth Estate or World Information Disorder? In *Global Politics in the Information Age*, edited by Mark Lacy and Peter Wilkin, 171-85. Manchester, U.K.: Manchester University Press.

O'Keefe, Derrick. 2009. Tariq Ali on Obama: Imperialism with a Human Face.

Rabble.ca. 16 February. http://www.rabble.ca/print/news/interview-tariq. Accessed 18 January 2010.

Retort. 2005. *Afflicted Powers: Capital and Spectacle in a New Age of War*. London and New York: Verso.

Robin, Corey. 2004. *Fear: The History of Political Idea*. Oxford and New York: Oxford University Press.

Rosa, Hartmut. 2005. The Speed of Global Flows and the Pace of Democratic Politics. *New Political Science* 27(4): 445-59.

Rosenberg, Justin. 2005. Globalization Theory: A Post Mortem. *International Politics* 42:2-74.

Sennett, Richard. 1978. *The Fall of Public Man: On the Social Psychology of Capitalism*. New York: Vintage.

———. 2006. *The Culture of the New Capitalism*. New Haven, CT: Yale.

Simmel, Georg. 1971[1903]. The Metropolis and Mental Life. In *On Individuality and Social Forms: Selected Writings*, edited by Donald N. Levine, 325-39. Chicago: University of Chicago Press.

Sharp, Hasana. 2005. Why Spinoza Today? Or, "A Strategy of Anti-Fear." *Rethinking Marxism* 17(4): 591-608.

Slater, Don. 1997. *Consumer Culture and Modernity*. Cambridge, U.K.: Polity.

Stallabrass, Julian. 2006. Spectacle and Terror. *New Left Review* 37:87-106.

Steingart, Gabor. 2006a. A Superpower in Decline: America's Middle Class Has Become Globalization's Loser. *Spiegel Online*, 24 October. http://www.spiegel.de/international/0,1518,439766,00.html. Accessed 9 September 2007.

Steingart, Gabor. 2006b. A Casualty of Globalization: Death of the Unions. *Spiegel Online*, 27 October. http://www.spiegel.de/international/0,1518,445043,00.html. Accessed 9 September 2007.

Sunstein, Cass R. 2006. *Infotopia: How Many Minds Produce Knowledge*. Oxford: Oxford University Press.

Surowiecki, John. 2005. *The Wisdom of Crowds*. New York: Anchor Books.

Thoburn, Nicholas. 2007. Patterns of Production: Cultural Studies after Hegemony. *Theory, Culture and Society* 24(3): 79-94.

Thompson, John B. 2004. The New Visibility. *Theory, Culture and Society* 22(6): 31-51.

Tudor, Andrew. 2003. A (Macro) Sociology of Fear? *The Sociological Review* 51(2): 238-56.

Williams, Raymond. 1977. *Marxism and Literature*. Oxford and New York: Oxford University Press.

Žižek, Slavo. 2007. Multitude, Surplus, and Envy. *Rethinking Marxism* 19(1): 46-58.

OFFERING

Christopher Dornan

Unknown Soldiers: On the Comparative Absence of the Military from Canadian Entertainment Film and Television

Is there a G8 nation that does not, as a matter of course, mine its military as a subject for popular fiction in film and television?

As the world knows, the United States certainly does. The list of movies and TV programs America has made about the Second Iraq War alone is already as long as your arm, from the hastily made TV movie *Saving Jessica Lynch*, to the Steven Bochco series *Over There*, from *Stop-Loss* to *Generation Kill* to *The Hurt Locker*, winner of the 2010 Academy Award for Best Picture.

From their most ancient military engagements to their most recent, almost all G8 nations grapple with the memory of their soldiers in armed conflict: their triumphant victories, their tragic losses, the cost of their profession to themselves and to others. The British do it, the French do it, the Italians do it, even the Japanese do it.

Some of these popular entertainments valorize the military. Some are scathing critiques. Some attempt to document the horror and futility of war. Some try to show how honour and courage is still possible even in the face of sheer terror. Others hope for no more than to illustrate what war does to people, even to those who aren't combatants.

All of them, in one way or another, are attempts to reproduce the experience of war, and thus to make an audience that has never been in combat feel what it is like. If only in that regard, they are all doomed to failure, because it cannot be done. The HBO series *Band of Brothers* is as good a depiction of war on the screen as has ever been achieved. As skilfully as the jeopardy might be rendered, it is still after all only jeopardy for the characters on the screen. And thank god for that.

Any entertainment that truly reproduced what war and combat feel like would be unwatchable. It would be unthinkable.

But all of these entertainments are necessary. They are means by which a society confronts its military actions, for good and for ill. The same United States that made John Wayne's Vietnam war movie *The Green Berets* also made *Johny Got His Gun*, *Apocalypse Now* and *The Phil Silvers (Sgt. Bilko) Show*. Whether they are jingoistic screeds, baleful laments or absurdist comedies, they are invitations to a culture to consider an aspect of itself, and one every bit as important as the other staples of prime-time entertainment: the police, the judiciary, the intelligence apparatus or the health care system.

And why not? As narrative material, the combat services are every bit as laced with jeopardy as any cop show, any lawyer show, or any hospital melodrama—only more so. It would be odd, would it not, if a nation quite pointedly ignored its military past and present when it got around to making dramatic entertainment?

Alone among the G8 nations, Canada apparently has no great appetite for making war movies. It is not a country with much of an appetite for making war either, so perhaps that explains it. Canada goes to war, yes, but only when we believe the cause is right, and the proof of that lies in the fact that we chose to do so when we were not pressured to do so (Korea and Afghanistan) and refused to do so when we were pressured (Vietnam and Iraq II). So perhaps we are not so troubled about our armed forces that we have to make movies about them.

Still, it is an odd absence in the cultural imaginary. The raid on Dieppe was a crucial and tragic episode in the country's history, and yet it took us more than fifty years, from 1942 until 1993, to make a CBC TV movie about it. It took us ninety-one years to make a movie about Passchendaele.

So why do we not pay more dramatic attention to our military? Or, rather, why do we in the main surrender our popular depictions of the military to the news and documentary media? Documentary accounts and news reports are both welcome and essential, but the latter are often formulaic. Whether CBC, CTV or Global, the national news devotes the same rote sixty seconds to showing an honour guard offloading a coffin at the airstrip in Trenton. That media attention is necessary, but it is not sufficient. People who die on behalf of others deserve more than just dutiful notation of their death. There are some truths that are best plumbed through fiction, through drama, through art.

One might argue that there isn't much of a Canadian film or television industry in the first place, so why complain that the military does not feature on Canadian screens? But the premise is not true, and has not been true for quite some time. The Canadian independent production industry is comparatively robust. It makes *Flashpoint* and *Intelligence* and *The Border*, and any number of one-hour dramas.[1]

One might argue that programs featuring military conflict are too expensive for our domestic film and TV industry to undertake. But again that is not true. Yes, reproducing the grand sweep of battlefield war—Waterloo, Pearl Harbour, Stalingrad—requires a cast of thousands, a special effects team and a gargantuan budget. But it is not necessary to restage the failed Commonwealth defence of Hong Kong in order to capture crucial elements of war with dramatic realism. What one needs instead is talent.

Plus, (thankfully) Canada has had precious few such set battles on its own soil. Between them, the encounter between opposing forces on the Plains of Abraham in 1759 and the final charge at Batoche 126 years later lasted less than the average running time of a feature film.

Flashpoint, Intelligence and *The Border* are high-production-value programs full of people carrying guns and shooting at one another. And there is an episode of *DaVinci's Inquest* that takes place start to finish in a back alley in Vancouver. The production costs of making a one-off TV movie set entirely in a First World War trench would be exactly the same.

No, it is not the production costs that prevent Canadians from making movies and TV programs about their military. It is a deep cultural ambivalence. To celebrate our military triumphs is to applaud how our people killed other people, and we are not terribly comfortable with that. To rehearse our failures, meanwhile, is to remind ourselves that one of our soldiers beat a Somalian teenager to death in 1993, so shameful an episode that the elite Airborne regiment was disbanded in its wake. And no one is going to bankroll a movie about that.

Even our vaunted peacekeeping efforts are not without their unspeakable tragedies, when we could not keep the peace. Is there a thinking Canadian who does not know the story of Romeo Dallaire and the horror in Rwanda? It is to our credit and General (now Senator) Dallaire's that the film *Shake Hands With The Devil* was made. Canada is one of the few countries that makes movies about other people's wars. We bear our responsibility and we bare our shame.

That is why dramatizations of war and combat are so essential. News reports from the front are necessary, but partial at best and untrustworthy at worst. We need more than bulletins and dutiful footage of flag-draped caskets being loaded onto transports at Kandahar airfield. This is a country that has to airlift its military personnel into harm's way. If we kill other people and if our people are killed, honour demands that we confront and consider why and how.

The most recent, extended and prominent—if that is the word for a series that precious few people saw—dramatic depiction of Canadian troops in a combat theatre was *ZOS: Zone of Separation*. Produced by Whizbang Films, a partnership of actor/writer Paul Gross and producer Frank Siracusa, *ZOS* was an eight-part series about Canadian troops attempting to enforce a peace in the town of Jadac, set in a fictionalized Bosnia. The series was created by Malcolm MacRury, one of the writers of the HBO series *Deadwood*, and directed by Mario Azzopardi, a stalwart of the Canadian independent production industry from its earliest days (he directed twenty-three episodes of the Toronto-shot CBS series *Night Heat* in the 1980s), one of whose specialties is shooting the pilot episodes of potential series, thereby establishing their look and tone.

A dark—and at times darkly funny—treatment, *ZOS* was a complex narrative charting not only the efforts of a unit of Canadian peacekeepers new to Jadac to maintain a ceasefire between Muslim and Christian militias, but the work of a detachment of four UN military observers—unarmed troops—headed by a Canadian, the lone woman in the group, Captain Sean Kovacs. Deftly shot and directed, crisply written, and with a cast that included international stars Colm Meany and Lolita Davidovitch, the series had both style and high production values, and its launch was accompanied by a sophisticated website that included an interactive web game in which players had to negotiate their way out of Jadac.[2]

Although the series was faulted by Forces veterans for rudimentary errors (actors not knowing how to stand properly at attention, how to salute, how to wear their berets, etc.),[3] it was nonetheless highly praised by those who appreciated its narrative strengths.[4] Although the ultimate aim was clearly to tell a compelling story, the series was at the same time an exploration of the ways in which blood hatreds fuel themselves, of the horrific absurdities of war (and civil war in particular) of the dangers and follies of trying to "keep the peace" and of the motives of those who insert themselves into others' conflicts and the price of doing so.

And the series quite deliberately foregrounded its "Canadian-ness" rather than attempting to pass itself off as a generic production for the international market. As the series opens, the contingent of UN peacekeepers is pulling out, and the Canadian, UN Military Observer Captain Kovacs, is awaiting their replacements, fellow Canadians. "Knowing my luck," she says ruefully, "they'll be Albertans."

Later in the series, a Muslim strongman attempts to ingratiate himself with some of the Canadian troops by offering to buy them a beer. "Sure," says one of the soldiers. "I'll have a Blue." The Bosnian furrows his brow. "Who drinks blue beer?"

As good as *ZOS* was, it aired in Canada in January and February 2009 on the subscription channels Movie Central and The Movie Network, and never aired again or anywhere else. It picked up a paltry two awards at the 2009 Geminis in minor categories. More than a year-and-half later, it has yet to be released to DVD. Although it has an international agent, it has garnered no international sales—and why would it? Who would want to tune in to a series showing Canadian soldiers struggling to negotiate a political minefield in a tinderbox of a country?

Not even Canadians, apparently. A shame. It is our loss. We tried to make an honest dramatic interrogation of why we send soldiers into harm's way in other countries' conflicts, but it sank like a pebble in a well. The absence to be interrogated is not Canada's failure to make such programs; it is apparently Canadians' absence of interest in them.

Notes

1. See, for example, Corus Entertainment's account of its 2010 production for Movie Central: www.corusent.com/home/CorusentFiles/files/.../MadeWithPay2010.pdf.

2. www.zostv.com.

3. See http://forums.army.ca/forums/index.php?topic=82136.0.

4. See http://www.imdb.com/title/tt0995027/usercomments and http://complicationsensue.blogspot.com/2009/01/zos-zone-of-separation.html.

OFFERING

Jim Daems

"i wish war wud fuck off": bill bissett's Critique of the Military-Cultural Complex

This paper examines the critique of our increasingly militarized culture in the work of the Canadian poet/artist bill bissett. Throughout his artistic career, bissett has been critically attuned to the infiltration of militarization in Canadian culture—from his early anti-Vietnam work to the present day conflicts in Iraq and Afghanistan, along with Canadian corporate complicity in these military theatres. In an interview published in *Issue*, for example, bissett states:

> we're constantly being told everything is temporary. We don't get the chance to find out for ourselves, we're just constantly told that.... I guess it's all based on the war machinery. Most cultures that exist on the planet today are based on war economies. (nd: 29)

bissett's insight highlights "the simultaneously material and discursive nature of military dominance" (Lutz 2002: 725). The focus here will primarily be on one poem and two collages that span approximately thirty years of bissett's work. I will argue that bissett is, in Paul Virilio's term, a "pitiful" artist. In *Art and Fear*, Virilio contrast the "pitiless" work of art with the "pitiful" work of art. For Virilio, avant-garde "modern art, from German Expressionism and Dada to Italian Futurism, French Surrealism and American Abstract Expressionism ... developed first a reaction to alienation and second a taste for anti-human cruelty" (Armitage 2006: 2). In part, as the avant-garde's artistic practices were appropriated by popular culture—i.e., the shock strategy now so familiar in advertising and, increasingly, in the mass media—what was initially a reaction to the banality and violence of the world, in an attempt to recuperate modern alienation by reinvigorating life through art, progressed at a remove from life. In effect, art developed as an attack on life commensurate with an unethical aesthetic of disappearance evident in corporate, scientific and military interests. While Virilio can be critiqued for his apparent reliance on a social death instinct, as well as for taking some of the more violent pronouncements of Dada and Surrealist manifestos too literally, his concept of the pitiful artist is important.

Virilio argues:

> If so-called old-master art remained *demonstrative* right up until the nineteenth century with Impressionism, the art of the twentieth century became *monstrative* in the sense that it is contemporary with the *shattering effect* of mass societies, subject as they are to the conditioning of opinion and MASS MEDIA propaganda—and this, with the same *mounting extremism* evident in terrorism or total war. (2006: 19)

The pitiless artist mercilessly assaults the viewer. In his most recent book, *sublingual*, bissett, carrying over a familiar concern from his earlier work, recognizes the "awkward trewths" poets must tell in the face of "th horror uv unpunishd unilateral war / fare th terror uv th / imperialist state" (2008: 79). Yet, bissett does not respond to this with "mounting extremism." He remains acutely attuned to humanity, and follows the prescription that John Armitage finds in Virilio's book: "Given that aesthetics and ethics are ailing, Virilio advises that artists show mercy on both" (2006: 5). Armitage continues:

> He [Virilio] argues that instead of producing a merciless art of presentation, with its live TV images of genuine torment and aggression, its wretchedness, self-destruction, disfigurement, extinction, and abhorrence, contemporary artists should reclaim the evacuated space of the art of representation, the space of symbolic yet crucially sympathetic images of violence.... Taking the poetic truth of brutal reality out of the loop, today's lethal presentational art of scientific voyeurism is powerless to express the actual extent of human cruelty. (2006: 4)

bissett's work reclaims this space and represents "the poetic truth of brutal reality" and "the actual extent of human cruelty." His is an empathetic, pitiful art.

To understand the extent of bissett's critique, we must first consider his use of language. Even a cursory reading of bissett's poetry alerts us to his resistance to the control imposed upon our interpersonal communication and thought by the established rules of spelling, syntax and grammar: "bissett's rejection of traditional literary values and systems can be read as a rejection of certain modes of western thought.... In effect, each time bissett writes, he is making a socio-political statement by rejecting a certain value structure" (Jirgens 1992: 76). The mass media's complicity with the militarization of our culture works to normalize its presence in order to attain "a unilateral purity, whereby decisions already taken are presented for passive admiration" (Debord 2002: 6), resulting in a subsequent "disappearance of our former vocabulary" (31). bissett's consistent concern is to revitalize our language—and the stress here is on *our* language in a radically egalitarian sense. For bissett, the big, master narratives occupy—in an almost militaristic way—our minds. In a sense, these master narratives think our thoughts for us. As bissett states on the jacket of *narrativ enigma / rumours uv hurricane*:

th frigilitee n inkompleysyun uv all narrativs reelee storeez uv kours can b kondensd an ar 2 b mor portabul mor undrstandabul n in sew dewing lose much uv theyr effikasee n reel accuracy ar oftn platforms uv propaganda n spin mostlee n what we settul 4 in ordr 2 xperiens stabilitee evn sum uv th time if thr is anee kompleysyun that dynamic map cartographee is with our makrs. (2004)

"[W]e're constantly being told everything is temporary," thereby making us more willing to accept these narratives—the discursive aspect of militarization and its material consequences—"2 xperiens stabilitee."

For me, one of the strangest examples of this is the opening of *The 9/11 Commission Report*:

> Tuesday, September 11, 2001, dawned temperate and nearly cloudless in the eastern United States. Millions of men and women readied themselves for work. Some made their way to the Twin Towers, the signature structures of the World Trade Center complex in New York City. Others went to Arlington, Virginia, to the Pentagon. Across the Potomac River, the United States Congress was back in session. At the other end of Pennsylvania Avenue, people began to line up for a White House tour. In Sarasota, Florida, President George W. Bush went for an early morning run. For those heading to an airport, weather conditions could not have been better for a safe and pleasant journey. Among the travelers were Mohamed Atta and Abdul Aziz al Omari, who arrived at the airport in Portland, Maine. (Kean 2004: 1)

This oddly novelistic opening is banal. It approaches Bulwer-Lytton's much parodied, "It was a dark and stormy night ...." Yet it does reveal how, following 9/11, "Conceptions of security in particular have been increasingly militarized, coming to depend on military needs and perspectives for their definitions" (Stabile and Rentschler 2005: viii). We abrogate our social responsibilities in exchange for a debased experience of stability based on ready-made thoughts and phrases. bissett, however, consistently undercuts ready-made phrases, often by taking them literally as in "watching broadcast nus:" "i see th salmon talks will / resume on monday / well thank god at least th / salmon ar talking" (1999: 5). The poem ironically highlights human failings. bissett's use of anecdotes also challenge our society's reliance on the ready-made phrase. The dead language of power and the military diction sweeps aside human suffering as mere "collateral damage."

In "deehydraysyun citee," for example, three first-person anecdotes are juxtaposed with insights regarding the ruling elite. Art, in this case, not only acts as a key form of social respiration; it also rehydrates our social structures which are gradually being stifled by what Virilio calls "endo-colonization:" "The war-machine tends toward societal nondevelopment.... On one hand it's a matter of not depleting resources, on the other of not developing civilian society because it hinders the development of military society, the means of waging war" (Virilio and Lotringer 2008: 68). The underdevelopment of the civilian economy is also evident in the debasement of language and art. In addition, the headnote quotation for "deehydraysyun citee"—"...waiting 4 a rebirth uv / faith n wundr... Edith Sitwell"—is commensurate with Virilio's pitiful artist, as "we should not forget for a moment that the words PITY and PIETY are consubstantial" (2006: 21).

As in so much of bissett's poetry, "deehydraysyun citee" begins with an anecdote. In effect, this compositional technique is commensurate with the way that bissett works with images in collage:

> stuk in the freezing sleep klinik not at all heetid save a
> buck biggr margin worth mor thn treeting othr peopul
> well (2008: 78)

The poem immediately establishes "th forces uv oppressyun" which are defined by their willingness to treat human beings as a means to an end—in this case, the profit margin. This is a world devoid of empathy, deliberately neglecting to extend help and respect to the "othr." In effect, the western world is stuck on the buck, exacerbating the underdeveloped nature of the civilian economy, an internalized barrier that prevents full, empathetic recognition of the other. The pitiful speaker in "deehydraysyun citee" is constituted by his empathetic eye. Apparently driven by "thees terribul timez" to find some redress at the sleep clinic, the speaker of "deehydraysyun citee" immediately connects the situation and setting—the microcosm of the clinic–to a much wider context:

> ... why isnt president
> bush being tried 4 war crimes pre emptiv invading uv
> anothr countree irak killing n killing n 4 ovr 5 yeers is
> killing thousands uv innosent peopul 4 oil 4 rhetorik 4
> self aggrandizement 4 wepon sales (2008: 78)

The speaker's concerns here link the profit driven clinic with the war economy—the "othr" being carried over into "anothr"—highlighting the same means driven relationship. In addition, treating people poorly in order to "save a / buck" demonstrates the same mindset required for weapons production, war and the self-aggrandizement of the ruling elite represented by George W. Bush. There is more profit in killing "innosent peopul theyr skins blown off / theyr bodeez vapour bombs clustr bombs" (2008: 78) than in taking care of them—of the Other. This is the "greed uv th elite," and the possibility that "we can b rich 2" if we accept this as a way to treat others pitilessly, without empathy or love (79). In effect, the opening anecdote prompts this question: how can the ruling elite itself sleep at night when it is responsible for this carnage and dehumanization of the other?

The poem represents a world in which people are either a means to profit and self-aggrandizement or an obstacle to these goals, in which case they are blown away. Hence, the second first person anecdote:

> xcellent frend n me crossing street car drivr honks agressiv
> lee at pedestrian pushing sumwun in a wheel chair peopul
> may think ths is ok now leedrs make fals promises n pushing
> evreewun out uv th way n kill maybe world leedrs have al
> wayze dun ths th nus is out (78)

The contrast here between "pushing sumwun in a wheel chair" and "pushing / evreewun out uv th way" critically highlights, again, the means-to-an-end rationale of our society. The pedestrian respects the other, while the driver, aggressively honking the horn, has already bought into the lack of empathy and humanity evident in both the operation of the sleep clinic and the ruling elite. The driver believes the promise of riches and status because, in contrast to the speaker, he sees through the eyes pitilessly constituted by the elite. The driver demonstrates the end result: "if they cud make us as brutal as them / we cud nevr criticize th rulrs," thinking that "ths is ok" (79). The speaker, on the other hand, stresses free will and responsibility: we become this way only "if we want / 2 b." We do not have to accept the offers and promises of the ruling elite in order to be "on the rite side." "Rite" itself alludes to "right-wing" (conservative, republican) and "rite" as in ceremony or ritual: the spectacle of the "deth industree." The notion of pushing, too, is significant for another reason. The speaker consistently, and critically, plays with the word "arms"–arms that push a wheelchair and arms as weapons. The second stanza, for example, reads:

> th insayshabul murdrous greed wepons uv mass destruksyun
> ther werent anee sew leev get out regime change remembr
> that wun sew split it is a pandoras box leedrs are oftn gang
> strs manicuring finessing arms sales evreewun sells 2
> evreewun (78)

Arms, as in weapons ("th / biggest deth industree"), and arms as in a means to push people out of the way. But, in a more positive sense, arms push a wheelchair, and arms can embrace the other—"hug n love / sumwun" (79). Note also that the elite manicure and finesse people in order to attempt to make "us as brutal as them." The very explicit binary of this line again highlights a significant concern of bissett's—the harm of patriarchal binary thought as he balances the clause on that central "brutal" equivalence. The word "insayshabul" also plays with the notion of unspeakable brutality and critically contrasts with how we address each other—"how dew we help / talk abt it."

> We come, then, to the third anecdote of the poem:
> drink sevn glasses uv watr a day manee poets tho not enuff
> tell awkward trewths whos listning 2 change killing thousands
> uv iraki peopul who nevr had wepons uv mass destruksyun
> 2 dfend themselves is ok n is not yet impeechabul getting yr
> cock suckd in th oval office is impeechabul n kills nowun
> watching th deths uv innosent peopul theyr skins blown off
> theyr bodeez vapour bombs clustr bombs whatevr kills (78)

How are we to read this stanza? The speaker asserts that "manee poets tho not enuff / tell awkward trewths." But this assertion follows an apparent untruth–"drink sevn glasses uv watr a day." In a sense, the preceding statement regarding drinking water is "awkward." But is it necessarily "wrong," particularly when juxtaposed to actions that are, ethically, wrong? Is this the speaker's point—that we selectively recognize "wrongs"? In other words, the poet's innocuous error is meant to force us to confront the behaviour of George W. Bush and Bill Clinton—actions which have far greater consequences, but ones which many, such as the car driver honking the horn, do not recognize as wrong.

But, then, how does this rumination on the binary of right and wrong relate to the following images of death? Note the key line break—"nowun / watching th deths uv innocent peopul." No one watching—at least in an empathetic, pitiful way. At best, the problem is one of apathy. We are constantly confronted by selective images of death and suffering by the mass media. Yet, as Susan Sontag states, if we do pay attention to these images, they "should not distract you from asking what pictures, whose cruelties, whose deaths are *not* being shown" (2003: 14). bissett is pitifully aware of this, and the lines recall the brutal equivalence of making us like them, both the perpetrators and the media. Claiming that suffering (much greater, but from the same causes as that of the speaker at the sleep clinic and the wheelchair incident) is "right" is absurd. The speaker is critically juxtaposing "awkward trewths"—glasses of water and murder. This is further balanced by the comparison-contrast of "killing thousands / uv iraki peopul" with "getting / yr cock suckd." The pitiful artist sets the poetic truth of brutal reality before us. In our media saturated world, killing garners less attention than Clinton's sexual encounter with Monica Lewinski. Indeed, the line break also suggests the sex act coinciding with violent images on television. This is the imperialist self of "dont want to suck anee empire" (bissett 2004: 130) and the horrible image of "old mens cocks" and "sheets uv blood around th / phallus" (bissett 2005: 56). bissett remains empathetic to both the death and suffering of war and the domestic consequences of militarization that provide not only weapons but also an acquiescent population. The perversity of this, suggested in the poem, would come back to haunt the U.S. with the "war porn" of the Abu Ghraib photographs:

a parody of the war itself, pornography becoming the ultimate form of the abjection of war which is unable to be simply war, to be simply about killing, and instead turns itself into a grotesque infantile reality-show, in a desperate simulacrum of power. (Baudrillard 2005b: 206)

The statement "whos counting" (echoed in "whos world" and "whos listning") is also important: do we quibble over seven or eight glasses of water per day when we only know that "thousands" have died in Iraq, and that we will probably never know the exact number? "nowun / is rite now in our world." Again, a play on words–"rite" as in the judgement of right and wrong, or "right" as in "right in the head"? In the same way that it is important to us that we take in enough liquids in a day—that we count the glasses of water we drink—we also need to keep an account of the killing. By denying the aesthetics of disappearance in taking account of the slaughter of war, bissett's art is pitifully rehydrating society. bissett's awareness of this is evident in the many poems and collages that explicitly address war and our complicity in an increasingly militaristic society.

In both form and content, bissett's *song uv soul* collage from *medicine my mouth's on fire* engages with our "war economy." The collage is composed of photographs cut out of mass publications, two pieces of text and paintings by bissett. Like the anecdotes in "deehydraysyun citee," the diversity of the source material and its composition in the collage both critically reveal our complicity in "th murdr show" that our culture has become (bissett 1972b: np).

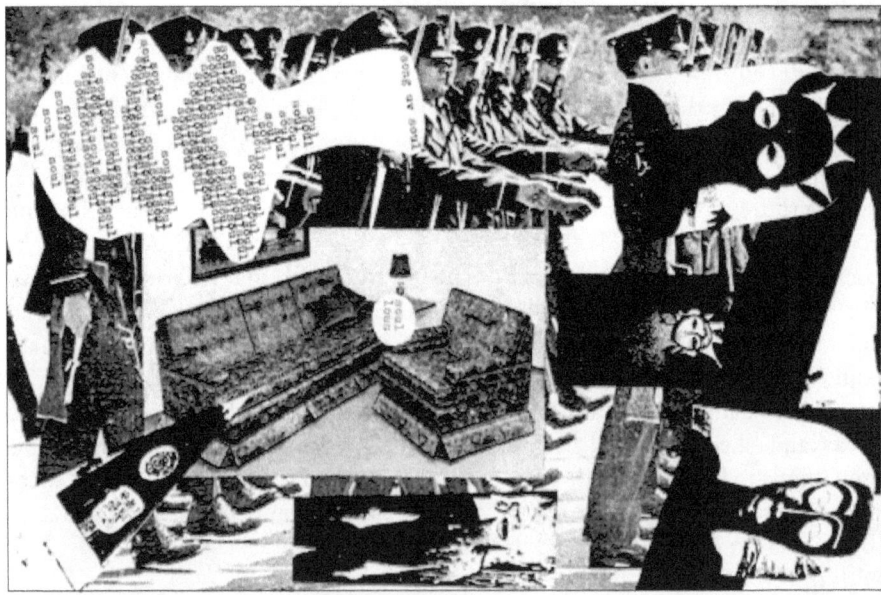

Fig. 1 song uv soul *(1974), courtesy of bill bissett.*

To state the obvious, bissett's *song uv soul* collage clearly lacks a traditional sense of artistic unity–one which is arrived at by leading the eye to the primary subject, relegating the rest of the composition to a purely supporting role (the background). This is most evident by considering the largest component of the collage: the marching troops. This image comprises, perhaps determines, the entire collage. Parts of it move in and out of the composition, statically mimicking the motion of the march—appearing and disappearing between and under the other elements that it is brought into critical juxtaposition with—creating a static film. What is most striking about troops on parade here is the orderliness, the uniformity, the non-descript faces and the angularity that the photograph establishes within the composition. The angularity culminates in the bayonet ends, themselves motioning back to an earlier form of warfare (also evoked by the dress uniforms and the mass formations which, like bayonets, are no longer part of war). The marching troops establish a unified, albeit externally motivated, mechanistic rhythm of movement and intention. Their presence throughout the collage signals an obvious criticism of the "war machinery." But it is the nature of the composition itself to fragment that unity.

The mass-produced photograph of, essentially, mass-produced soldiers finds its correlative in the mass-produced photograph of mass-produced furniture. The juxtaposition of these elements alerts us to a connection between the troops and the furniture—sofa, chair, end-table with lamp and decorative print. As Jean Baudrillard argues in *The System of Objects:*

> pieces of furniture confront one another, jostle one another, and implicate one another in a unity that is not so much spatial as moral in character. They are arranged about an axis which ensures a regular chronology of actions; thanks to this permanent symbolization, the family is always present to itself. (2005a: 13)

Baudrillard adds that, "the primary function of furniture and objects ... is to personify human relationships, to fill the space that they share between them, and to be inhabited by a soul" (14). Baudrillard's insight that the arrangement of furniture is ethical, rather than spatial, relates well to the composition of *song uv soul*, as, in effect rearranging our spaces implies a rearrangement of our ethics. bissett is alerting us to the ethical relationship between the "war machinery" of our society and our everyday lives in our homes. The photograph of the furniture—possibly from a newspaper advertisement, a catalogue or an interior decorating magazine—invites us into a private, domestic setting minus the inhabitants. As an advertising technique, we are to imaginatively locate ourselves, as potential consumers, in this arrangement—picture it as ours. But, projecting ourselves into this domestic arrangement is an act of alienation, and the alienation of human relationships personified by the furniture is made evident by bissett's inclusion of text in the furniture photograph—"soul / luos," a soulless interior.

Also significant in Baudrillard's reading of the system of objects is the "axis which ensures a regular chronology of actions" implied within the arrangement of furniture. The juxtaposition of the troops and the furniture suggests a unity of such a chronology. But it is not the clock that rules the chronology of our interiors; it is the march. bissett alerts us to this fact by having the metronome overlay the legs of the troops and the domestic interior. Hence, the connotations of intimacy and family conveyed by the furniture are disrupted by the sharp intrusion of the decorated metronome—and the shape of the metronome echoes the bayonets. In addition, the metronome signifies a mechanically imposed rhythm, as opposed to the beat of the heart or the rhythm of breathing which are the purely human measures that are absent within the furniture arrangement. The beat of the metronome also echoes the steady, rhythmic beats of the uniform steps of the march so as to highlight the critical significance of the juxtaposition of these three elements in the collage.

In essence, then, part of the comforting, intimate setting of our homes is predicated upon the "war machinery" symbolized here by the marching soldiers in the *song uv soul* collage. bissett may also be suggesting that our household interiors are as uniform as these troops in terms of both appearance and intention—it is all a mechanical march. Baudrillard's comments can further this reading. If we see our furniture arrangements as confrontational in the way that Baudrillard does, then the same aggression predominates in human relationships, such as those in "deehydraysyun citee."The collage suggests this.The metronome, the sofa, the end-table and the soldiers' feet all share the same sharp diagonal angle, and that angle confronts and jostles the chair. Marching and furniture arrangement suggestively share the same discipline. Just as military drill is a means of mass-production, our domestic uniformity is a means to mass-producing "individuals," a sign of endo-colonization. We become the spectacle which, "as the concrete inversion of life, is the autonomous movement of the non-living" (Debord 1977: thesis 3).

There is one more important element within the furniture photograph: the print on the wall. Within our mass-produced society, art has often become subservient to the needs of the military and the economy. It is no longer respiratory or rehydrating. The print—seemingly a conventional idyllic landscape thrown in with the furniture purchase—is cut off. In itself, it is not a significant part of the furniture arrangement (any sort of decorative print will do). But its decorativeness ironically links the domestic to the troops, as the straight lines of the print's frame are commensurate with the orderliness of the drill formation. The print, too, is ironically prophetic of the opening paragraphs of the *9/11 Commission Report*. The *song uv soul*, however, importantly overlays both the print and the troops, countering their orderly, straight lines. The rhythm of *song uv soul*, for example, is not that of the metronome or the march. Both of those, as noted above, are mechanically imposed. The form of the poem is also not pre-imposed on the poet's imagination.

bissett also incorporates reproductions of his paintings into the collage along with two poems. There are four figures, traditionally defined, three of these are portraits and one is a three-quarter-length figure. bissett is not ascribing primacy to his own, individually creative works because these are photocopied reproductions. In this way they come into contact with other mass-produced representations and the traditional distinction between life and art is challenged. In other words, bissett's concern here is with the composition first and foremost (even though it tends to subordinate his paintings in this case). Thomas Crow argues that "collage disrupts the false harmonies of oil paintings by reproducing the disposability of the late-capitalist commodity. The principle of collage construction itself collapses the distinction between high and low by transforming the totalizing creative practices of traditional painting into a fragmented consumption of

Fig. 2 redecorate now *(1972), courtesy of bill bissett.*

already existing manufactured images" (Antliff and Leighton 2001: 196). Crow's statement may overly fetishize this fragmentation. In reading bissett's collages, we cannot fetishize individual parts. bissett wants us to recognize the human relationships which the commodified fragment tends to represent in our daily lives. By recognizing the human relations within capitalism and how these have come to be defined increasingly by military interests, the significance of things may reveal not only the whole (or its absence), but also the soul. What may be most revealing in this regard is the half of a capital A—language and communication, *song uv soul*. "A" is the beginning, the alpha and omega of human society that the spectacle has hijacked: "*Separation* is the alpha and omega of the spectacle" (Debord 1977: thesis 63). Importantly, A is also the first letter of *art* and its promise of social regeneration, rehydration and respiration. The importance of the interior in *song uv soul* is clear if we consider it in light of another bissett collage, *redecorate now* (1972).

redecorate now prompts us to break free of the confinement and limitations imposed upon us by our interiors—ideological confines evident in the *song uv soul* collage, for example. Emphasis is on the word "now" in the title. It is an ethical imperative. As in *song uv soul*, our interiors are as much physical as psychic spaces, and their arrangement, as Baudrillard points out, implies an ethic. In *redecorate now*, a board is stapled to another ground—over either the frame of the canvas stretcher or to the canvas inside the frame of the stretchers. In relation to the title of the piece, this suggests something in need of renovation—in terms of an interior, a hole in a wall or a broken window that is nailed over awaiting repair. But, against the "high" art remnants of the portrait in the collage, bissett carries through his critique of artistic tradition. Hence, the ethical imperative includes a renovation of our entire culture by juxtaposing painting, in terms of visual art, with the more apparently mundane act of painting one's interior. We might suggest, then, that the idyllic, mass-produced landscape in the *song uv soul* collage (like the narrative opening of the *9/11 Commission Report*) similarly covers a hole in our culture. In effect, *redecorate now* is insisting that we must take as much care in redecorating our interiors, and even our public spaces, as we must "now" take in the care of our souls through art: "its alrite we pay for bridges / why not art if we dont pay for n protect art weul have more wars fr / sur its wun or th othr" (bissett 1985: 94). We have choices beyond those offered by the text of the catalogue page included in the collage—"REDECORATE NOW. Mix or match these top-quality fixtures to suit your décor needs," and the colour chart. These are limited, mass-produced options, and we need to think beyond the limitations of pre-packaging and ready-made directives, just as we need to think beyond ready-made phrases.

Over this, bissett pastes a photograph of a woman in a supermarket with another photograph of an artillery piece, with "Made in Canada" on it. The woman's arm, reaching out for apples, now seems to be holding the artillery piece cushioned against her hip, highlighting the choices of our society and economy—food or weapons. The image is curiously both iconic and prophetic—evoking film stills of Faye Dunaway's role in *Bonnie and Clyde* (1967) and the famous photograph of the kidnapped Patty Hearst as a member of the Symbianese Liberation Army (1974). We could read this as an aggressive image: for example, is the woman taking on the role of these women attacking the status quo? In that sense, the image could challenge bourgeois gender expectations of the domesticated female, while ironically revealing a militarized domesticity. Or, is the woman going to blow a hole in culture and fulfil the Italian Futurist dream? Is she defending her right to food? Either way, the image aggressively points to the phallocentric nature of war while making its ethical appeal. The choice is ultimately ours—consent to militarization in our society or take back civilian space.

redecorate now powerfully critiques the war economy's profits from arms sales while people starve in a way similar to "deth industree" of "deehydraysyun citee"; indeed, most of the Western world's weapons end up being used in starving, poverty-stricken Third World countries. We cannot be proud of the "Made in Canada" sticker on the weapon. The faded nature of the photograph also contrasts sharply with the sensual colours of Renoir's Impressionist portrait. Our drab lives, souls and culture may need colour, redecoration, but not at the expense of other people. The artist clearly rejects the "high" art image as complicit with the worst of our culture and deconstructs its status by surrounding it with a drab brown and positioning it upside down. But the image is tantalizingly deceptive. It is still very much like a Renoir—the colour and the way it is applied to the collage. Yet it is an erasure. bissett is ironically erasing conventional social norms and ways of looking at things, as *redecorate now* is something one hears and sees at places like IKEA and The Home Depot. The statement on the catalogue page, "FULL HOME INSTALLATION INSTRUCTIONS INCLUDED WITH EVERY ITEM ON THIS PAGE" now includes the artillery piece. Mix and match it with your bathroom décor. It is clearly part of our civilization, and bissett pastes a definition of "civilization" across the descriptions of medicine cabinets: "As used in the context of this volume, it refers to urbanization and the complexity of culture resulting from or influenced by urbanized communities." Civilization comprises more than bathroom fixtures, weapons and "urbanized communities." We can only limit our understanding of "civilization" in such a simplistic way at our own peril:

> At the dawn of industrial modernity, Baudelaire declared, "*I am the wound and the knife*." How can we fail to see that, in the wake of the hecatomb of the Great War, when Braque and Otto Dix found themselves on opposite sides of the trenches in the mud of the Somme, modern art for its part forgot the wound and concentrated on the knife—the bayonet. (Virilio 2006: 16)

bissett has not forgotten the wound and, therefore, remains a pitiful artist confronting the militarization of our society.

Note

I would like to thank bill bissett for his permission to reproduce the images included in this essay.

References

Antliff, Mark and Patricia Leighton. 2001. *Cubism and Culture*. London: Thames and Hudson.

Armitage, John. 2006. Art and Fear: An Introduction. In *Art and Fear*, by Paul Virilio, 1-13. London: Continuum.

Baudrillard, Jean. 2005a. *System of Objects*. Trans. James Benedict. London: Verso.

———. 2005b. *The Conspiracy of Art: Manifestos, Interviews, Essays*. Trans. Ames Hodges. Los Angeles, CA: Semiotext(e).

bissett, bill. n.d. bill bissett interview: (seagull on yonge street). In *Issue*, 29-31. Vancouver Art Gallery library file.

———. 1972a. *words in th fire*. Vancouver, BC: blewointment.

———. 1972b. *redecorate now*, collage.

———. 1974. *medicine my mouth's on fire*. Toronto: Oberon Press.

———. 1985. *canada gees mate for life*. Vancouver, BC: Talonbooks.

———. 1999. *scars on th seehors*. Vancouve, BC r: Talonbooks.

———. 2004. *narrativ enigma / rumours uv hurricane*. Vancouver, BC: Talonbooks.

———. 2005. *northern wild roses / deth interrupts th dansing*. Vancouver, BC: Talonbooks.

———. 2008. *sublingual*. Vancouver, BC: Talonbooks.

Debord, Guy. 1977. *Society of the Spectacle*. Detroit, MI: Black and Red.

———. 2002. *Comments on the Society of the Spectacle*. Trans. Malcolm Imrie. London: Verso.

Jirgens, Karl. 1992. *bill bissett and his Works*. Toronto: ECW Press.

Kean, Thomas H. 2004. *9/11 Commission Report: Final Report of the National Commission on Terrorist Attacks upon the United States*. New York: Norton.

Lutz, Catherine. 2002. Making War at Home in the United States: Militarization and the Current Crisis. *American Anthropologist* 104(3): 723-35.

Sontag, Susan. 2003. *Regarding the Pain of Others*. New York: Picador.

Stabile, Carol A. and Carrie Rentschler. 2005. States of Insecurity and the Gendered Politics of Fear. *NWSA Journal* 17(3): vii-xxv.

Virilio, Paul. 2006. *Art and Fear*. Trans. Julie Rose. London: Continuum.

Virilio, Paul and Sylvère Lotringer. 2008. *Pure War: Twenty-Five Years Later*. Trans. Mark Polizzotti. Los Angeles, CA: Semiotext(e).

OFFERING

Darin Barney

Miserable Priests and Ordinary Cowards: On Being a Professor

"Who would want to begin?"
Jacques Rancière, *The Ignorant Schoolmaster* (1991: 17)

Where I work, strong emphasis is placed on graduate education. As in many graduate programs, students are required to complete a seminar in which they are introduced to various aspects of the profession, to the language of advanced study and scholarly research, and to our discipline. The hope is to begin the process of their habituation to the institutional and cultural norms of academic life. A couple of years ago, it was my turn to run this seminar, and in what I now concede was a moment of gratuitous cruelty, I elected to begin by assigning several texts that cast critical light on the contemporary university, texts that attempted to measure the distance between certain historical but persistent ideals concerning the role, orientation, ethos and practice of the university and the material reality of what it has become under the auspices of neoliberal, technological capitalism. And so the students were treated to sobering accounts of the eclipse of priority on teaching by something that gets called research, the decline of the useless arts and humanities in relation to the useful arts and techno-sciences, the precariousness of contingent academic labour vis-à-vis the tenured professoriate, the erosion of the university's independence of inquiry via a gradual assimilation of the priorities of the state and corporate capital and the collapse of collegial governance at the hand of executive administration. And they learned of the manner in which all of this has been accompanied by insidious discourses of excellence, accountability, leadership, partnership, renewal and innovation.

The effect of these texts was catastrophic, as the optimism, energy and purpose with which intelligent students customarily commit themselves to graduate education was systematically crushed in the first fortnight by a self-satisfied ass who had the audacity to make such a gambit from the extremely privileged and secure position of being a Canada Research Chair and tenured professor at McGill University. What was I thinking? Demystification? Reflexivity and self-examination aimed at generating critical consciousness? The actual outcome was paralysis: this was professionalization as demoralization. I had wounded them and, when they asked me why, I did not have a satisfactory answer. I think I do now: I did it because I felt guilty, and I wanted them to share the burden of my complicity. Of course, they also asked me many good questions about the state of the university and the academy: is the university really such a *terrible* place (no); isn't this just a conservative, romantic, nostalgic lament dressed up in critical clothing (partly); haven't many of the reforms to traditional university faculties, disciplines, curricula and practices been good from the perspective of justice and equality (yes); aren't there significant sites at the university that escape or exceed the hegemonic logic of neoliberalism (yes, there are); isn't the university still one of the few institutional settings where something like independent and critical thought, even radicalism, has a viable place (yes, it's true).? But none of them ever once looked me in the eye and asked me the questions I dreaded: Where were *you*? What did you *do*? How did things get this way? Is it because you, *professor*, allowed this to happen? Is it because you did *nothing*?

And, so, an apology is in order.

Assuming diagnoses of the contemporary decline of the liberal, humanistic, critical, relatively autonomous university are accurate, what would it take to rescue the institution from its final instrumentalization under the auspices of technological neoliberalism, and to instead orient it toward what Ian Angus, in his recent and insightful book *Love the Questions: University Education as Enlightenment*, identifies as its rightful role as a place for "reflection with public significance situated at the contested sites of network society"? (2009: 132). Angus closes the book by suggesting that hope for realizing this possibility lies in "a widespread reflection and debate about the role of higher education in society," in which a population that values "free thought" and "democratic participation"—a population made up of citizens, parents who worry about their children's futures, young adults who "crave ideas" and "older people" who want to "understand their lives"—will come to see that "a university devoted to the humanistic ideal is a part of that project" (133).

I would like to explore an alternative possibility: halting the slide of the university into ultimate instrumentalization and re-orienting it toward what Professor Angus calls "the humanistic ideal" demands not just public reflection and debate, but political intervention, specifically an intervention that would take the form of active resistance, led not by a public of citizens but by university professors. In what follows, I will try to measure the remoteness of this possibility.

Politics exposes power and joins questions about what is just and good to political judgement and action. To *politicize* is to expose the characteristics of power in a manner that demands response, to open matters of justice and the good to judgement by and among a plurality of people, and to act on the judgements that arise from that exposure. For the most part, we live under conditions in which exposure of the sources and character of power and inequality fail to move us, in which fundamental questions about justice and the good go unasked by most people, most of the time, and in which the risk of political action is one that few people are prepared to take. Contrary to our fondest democratic imaginings, politics is not what defines a citizen in her daily practice; it is, instead, a burden that most citizens would rather avoid. In many ways, this is what contemporary citizenship is: a license to abstain from the burdens of political judgement and action.

Under these conditions, engagement in political judgement and action is not normal. Instead, politics is a pathological event that a reasonable person would normally avoid if she had the choice. Politics *happens* to us, it is not something we normally *choose* to do. Politics—responding to the exposure of power, joining questions about justice and the good to judgement and action—is exceptional, disruptive, antagonistic, risky and dangerous. Politics is like a sore that erupts on the smooth skin of democracy. Following Jacques Rancière, we might say that politics tends to arise only in response to a fundamental wrong, a wrong that takes the form of a structuring exclusion or silencing, a basic miscount that produces an antagonism between the whole and the "part of those who have no part" (1999: 11). Such wrongs typically materialize in the structure of publicity itself, at the border between those who are counted as part of the public and those who are not. We might say that politics arises to refuse or contest the social, conventional and material inequalities that are institutionalized over and against the incontestable equality that is otherwise basic to our humanity. It is for this reason that politics is always threatening. Politics is not the realization of our innermost essence, and it is not necessarily joyful, festive or fun; it is work, onerous, dangerous work, work we would rather not have to do, but that we must do because we are moved by a wrong that is intolerable. This is how politics happens.

And this is one of the reasons politics does not tend to happen to professors in the context of the university: we do not experience what goes on at the university as a fundamental and structuring wrong by which we are excluded, brutalized or discounted. In relation to the university, professors are not "those who have no part" and we are not, for the most part, silenced. Professors like me take part—we play a part, have a part, participate—in the university every day. We teach and decide and consent, whether expressly or tacitly. And we speak and write, often critically, as I am doing now. Politics does not happen to professors at universities because we do not experience the university as the site of a material wrong, even if we disagree with how the place is run from time to time. This is not always the case: sometimes the university is the site of a wrong done to individuals—people who are denied the part that is due to them on unjust grounds such as race, ideology, gender or sexuality—and, in these cases, other individuals often become politicized, and take the risk of standing up with, or on behalf of, those who have been wronged, to demand that they be counted.[1] But such moments are exceptional—their exceptionality is what qualifies them as political. Normally, there is no *collective* experience of the university as the site of a fundamental wrong that might move professors *collectively* to take the risk of a political intervention.[2] The university is *defined* by the structural *inclusion* of professors. Professors *count*. And so politics does not tend to happen to them, at least not there.

Another way to put this is to say that professors are not moved to intervene politically in the future of the university because the university as it exists is something they deeply *enjoy*, in the manner of Slavoj Žižek's rendering of Lacan's *jouissance*, or enjoyment. In her book on Žižek, Jodi Dean describes *jouissance* as "an excessive pleasure and pain, that something extra that twists pleasure into a fascinating and unbearable intensity..... Enjoyment is that 'something extra' for the sake of which we do what might otherwise seem irrational, counter-productive, or even wrong" (Dean 2006: 4). The university is the structure of the professor's enjoyment. It is not just that we like the university more or less as it is and enjoy the material benefits, privileges, security and status that come with being a part of it. It is also that we enjoy the suffering or pain that we endure in order to be part of university. There is nothing that academics enjoy more than their suffering: careerist students who can't read and can't write and can't think; colleagues who are lazy and insufferable; granting agencies that are biased against our work; incompetent, corrupt, bean-counting administrators; governments run by philistines. We enjoy them all. We could not live without them. Our suffering is what distinguishes us. And, in rare moments, our enjoyment of the pleasures and pain of the university converge: we get on airplanes and stay in hotels and stand in front of audiences and say clever things about how the university makes us suffer and then go back home and submit articles based on what we have said and add lines to our CVs and get raises for doing it.

Where, in the midst of all this, is there a wrong fundamental enough to motivate professors to act politically and risk undermining the structure of their own enjoyment? Even existential commitment to the "humanistic ideal" will not suffice, especially since we can enjoy even that, and enjoy its demise perfectly well by running around the country talking about it while *doing* nothing. There is even the possibility that those of us who fantasize about the salvation of the university might enjoy our ongoing failure to achieve it. As Dean puts it:

> the very failure to satisfy desire can become itself a source of enjoyment. The circular movement of drive is enjoyable; enjoyment, in other words, is the pleasure provided by the painful experience of repeatedly missing one's goal.... The nugget of enjoyment is not what one is trying to reach but cannot, it is that little extra that adheres to the process of trying. (2006: 6)

At this point, our enjoyment derives not from the achievement of our end—a university in which the humanistic tradition is recovered—but rather from an investment in the very means by which the achievement of that end is perpetually deferred: the university as it is. As Dean writes: "enjoyment results when focus shifts from the end to the means, when processes and procedures themselves provide libidinal satisfaction" (7). This is the very formula for the peculiar and somewhat pathetic sort of conservatism that most professors, especially we critical ones, inhabit.

Recovering the possibility of the humanistic university requires something of professors that we are not normally situated or inclined to provide: a political intervention that would disrupt our own enjoyment of the university as it is. Politics of this sort is not something a reasonable person would normally choose to do. It is something that happens to a person, and a person has to have courage in order to be taken by politics when it does happen.

In his attempt to characterize the 20th century, Alain Badiou describes it as a "call to courage" that was haunted by fear, a fear that continues to stand in the way of most of us becoming political subjects. According to Badiou:

> what immobilizes the individual, what leads to his powerlessness, is fear. Not so much the fear of repression and pain, but the fear of no longer being the little something one is, of no longer having the little one has…. We like our life to be orderly so as to avoid insecurity. And the subjective guardian of this orderliness is fear. (2007: 124)

The name Badiou gives to the subjectivity of fear is "ordinary cowardice," a conservative, middle-class obsession with personal security defined by the reliability of our conventional identities, relationships, responsibilities and rewards—what he describes as "the routines of place and time"—however diluted these might be. Security is what the middle classes can count on, and very few of us, even those who count themselves as progressive, political or leftist, would actually be willing to wager it against the uncertainties of meaningful material change.

According to Badiou, "one of the fundamental questions is that of knowing how not to be a coward" (124). Courage is the opposite of cowardice. Part of courage is tenacity—holding on—in the face of an impossible situation occasioned by a wrong that cannot be tolerated. I have suggested that professors do not normally experience the university as the site of a wrong that would move them to hold on to justice despite its apparent impossibility. However, our experience of the university does promote ordinary cowardice, whereby we cling fearfully to the security of established regimes and their little comforts. It thus becomes clear that the possibility of politics demands a type of courage that is more than just holding on. It demands something truly *extra*ordinary. It demands letting go.

As Badiou writes:

> in the end, in order to cease being a coward one must fully consent to

becoming. The crucial idea is this: *the reverse of cowardice is not will, but abandonment to what happens*. What tears one away from the ordinary rule, from 'sedentary, static, orderly life' is a particular kind of unconditional abandonment to the event. (125)

To let go is to allow ourselves to be moved into uncharted and unpredictable territory. Becoming political is not about being a hero. Politics is not something that we will ourselves into but, rather, something to which we abandon ourselves. The joining of judgement and action in political commitment arises, Badiou writes, "not from a lucid decision, but from a special form of passivity, from a total abandonment to what [is] taking place" (125-26). We *let* ourselves become political by letting go of the security of what already is, in the face of our fear of the incalculable future into which events might lead us. Acts of resistance require this sort of passivity, this giving oneself over to the uncertainty of an untold future. The various discourses of risk by which we are surrounded in popular culture make us reluctant to let ourselves go in this way. And so we find ourselves susceptible to the appeal of what Badiou calls the "miserable priests": those pragmatic calculators who weigh the potential costs of resistance or action against its uncertain benefits, and determine that the risks are too great to bear next to the certainty of an anemic, but at least stable, present. "At the century's end," Badiou writes, "the priest is everywhere" (145).

Politics requires the extraordinary courage to let go, a type of courage that is rare in technological and democratic societies, perhaps because the security offered by life in the republic of choice is so satisfying for so many of us. It is especially satisfying for those of us who are professors, even those of us who make our bread by biting the hand that feeds us. We might recall here Max Horkheimer's 1934 observation that "a revolutionary career does not lead to banquets and honourary titles, interesting research and professional wages. It leads to misery, disgrace, ingratitude, prison and the unknown, illuminated only by an almost superhuman belief" (qtd. in Leslie 1999: 119). It bears mentioning that, in 1969, these sentences were reprinted on leaflets circulated in Frankfurt to protest Horkheimer's and Adorno's conservative response to the student movement. I am not sure I can think of many colleagues, including those who are very critical of the university, who would be prepared to let go of being a professor. I am not sure I am; in fact, I am pretty sure I am not. My point here is not to moralize, but rather to apologize: I am guilty. Professors, I am trying to say, are structurally discouraged.

What to do in this situation is not clear. It does seem that the professor's customary response to her own discouragement will not suffice, at least not if the issue at hand is the necessity of a political intervention in the ultimate instrumentalization of the university. The professor's customary response to discouragement is to retreat into the consolation of thought. It is, to use Angus's terms, a retreat into enlightenment. In the note on enlightenment appended to his text, Angus refers to Kant's famous borrowing from Horace to declare the motto of enlightenment, *"Sapere aude!* (Have courage to use your own reason!)" (qtd. in Angus 2009: 140). Angus goes on to say that, for Kant, "Enlightenment is the public effect of critique and rests upon the prior courage of the one who dares to think for him or herself" (140). However, when it comes to professors at least, the coupling of courage and thinking misreckons it. For a professor, it takes no courage to "think for him or herself": that is what a professor enjoys most, and it is what a professor gets paid for. Enlightenment, for the professor, is a refuge from that which would really call upon her courage: political action that would have her relinquish the security of her own native domain. Thought, even critical thought, is the professor's alibi for action not taken. Kant's formula of enlightenment thus corresponds perfectly to the Lacanian concept of the fetishistic disavowal, which Žižek identifies as the signature operation of contemporary ideology: *"je sais bien, mais quand même"* (I know very well, but all the same… (2007: 79). I *know* very well, but all the same I act as if I do not know, or I do not act at all. I know very well what is happening at and to the university, but all the same, *I am a professor*. In this respect, it is interesting that Kant's rendering of the motto of the Enlightenment as "Have courage to use your own reason!" stops exactly short of the next, arguably more important word in the passage he quotes from Horace: *"Incipe"*(Ferry 1956: 7). Begin.

Notes

This offering is based on remarks made at an event celebrating the publication of Ian Angus's *Love The Questions: University Education as Enlightenment* (Arbeiter Ring, 2009), held at the Institute for the Humanities, Simon Fraser University, Vancouver, BC, March 19, 2010.

1. It bears mentioning that Ian Angus exemplified this sort of individual bravery in his protest against his university's violation of the academic freedom of David Noble. For details on the case, see the material gathered at the link to "The University" on Angus's Web site at http://www.ianangus.ca/.

2. The obvious exception might be faculty strikes, though these are increasingly rare and, in any case, their status as political interventions is inconsistent and ambiguous.

References

Angus, Ian. 2009. *Love the Questions: University Education as Enlightenment*. Winnipeg, MB: Arbeiter Ring.

Badiou, Alain. 2007. *The Century*. Cambridge, U.K.: Polity.

Dean, Jodi. 2006. *Žižek's Politics*. New York: Routledge.

Ferry, David, ed. 1956. *The Epistles of Horace*, Book I. Cambridge, U.K.: Cambridge University Press.

Leslie, Esther. 1999. Introduction to the Adorno/Marcise Correspondence on the German Student Movement. *New Left Review* 233 (Jan-Feb): 119.

Rancière, Jacques. 1991. *The Ignorant Schoolmaster: Five Lessons in Intellectual Emancipation*. Trans. Kristin Ross. Palo Alto, CA: Stanford University Press.

Žižek, Slavoj. 2007. *How to Read Lacan*. New York: W. W. Norton.

FORUM

Jill Didur and Susan Gingell

Editors, Author Meets Critics Forum

Responses to

Emberley, Julia. 2007. *Defamiliarizing the Aboriginal: Cultural Practices and Decolonization in Canada.* Toronto: University of Toronto Press.

This past February (2010), as athletes from different parts of the world were being welcomed as visitors (at least by representatives of VANOC) to the site of the Vancouver Winter Olympics, the media paid much attention to the Games taking place on Lil'wat, Musqueam, Squamish and Tsleil-Waututh First Nations' territory. An article posted during the run-up to the games on the website for the Aboriginal Pavilion notes, the four host First Nations were recognized as Official Partners in the 2010 Winter Games, and the Olympic Organizing Committee was collaborating with Aboriginal leaders in those communities "to ensure that the Nations' traditions and protocols [were] recognized and respected in the planning and hosting of the Games" (Aboriginal 2008). Simultaneously, across the country in Quebec on the Kahnawà:ke Mohawk reserve, the media focused on another story, one that also concerned First Nations' territory and traditions but, in this case, people were not being welcomed—they were being sent eviction notices. As reported in the mainstream Canadian media as well as *The Eastern Door,* a weekly newspaper in the Kahnawà:ke community, 26 non-Native partners of Mohawk residents were sent such notices by the Mohawk Council of Kahnawà:ke (MCK) on February 1, 2010 and given a 10-day deadline to comply. Joe Delaronde, a spokesman for the MCK was widely quoted in the national media as explaining: "Every single person in this community knows (from a band rule adopted in 1981) that ... we have the right to determine who lives here. I don't know why people think it has anything to do with racism ... our laws say (non-natives) don't have the right to live here" (Brennan 2010).

Early on, the MCK threatened to publish the names of the 26 people who were sent the notices if they did not comply with the order to leave. To date, however, names have not been published. While many initial reports on the controversy suggested that the whole community was fully behind the MCK's move to issue eviction notices, subsequent coverage indicated that the Council's action was taken after receiving approximately one hundred complaints about non-Natives living on the reserve and that significant dissent has been registered in the pages of *The Eastern Door*. Most notable is an open letter from the Quebec Native Women's Association (QNW), whose president Ellen Gabriel wrote:

> QNW is troubled with the decision taken by the Mohawk Council of Kahnawà:ke (MCK) to evict non-native residents from the community of Kahnawà:ke, a decision which ruptures the family unit and the community as a whole. It is imperative that clarification be made regarding Mohawk customs as a huge misconception has been conveyed by the MCK that misrepresents all Mohawk people to the public. (QNW 2010)

What interests us about this controversy is how the statement by the QNW hinges on what counts as a traditional way of understanding kinship and family in Mohawk culture, a complex matter that can be better opened up and examined through the theoretical, historical and cultural research and analysis presented in Julia Emberley's *Defamiliarizing the Aboriginal: Cultural Practices and Decolonization in Canada*, a book that is the focus of this cluster of "Author Meets Critics" review essays. As Emberley writes in the preface to her book, "[w]hether as ideology, discourse, or signifying system, 'the family' figured as an Enlightenment metaphor for power" (2007: xvi). She also notes that "[b]y the end of the nineteenth century, the distinction between family and empire would completely implode—family ideology would become civilizational ideology, and visa [*sic*] versa, the one the microcosm of the other" (xvi). Emberley's study is particularly timely and relevant to ongoing efforts to find a resolution to the current controversy in the Kahnawà:ke Mohawk reserve, a community with a growing population (currently close to 8000) and a long history of resisting colonial assaults on its territory, culture and sovereignty. The MCK reminds its critics and the media that the reserve is comprised of a mere 13,000 acres, and is located on the edge of a major urban centre (Montreal), perhaps resulting in a higher than average incidence of non-Native members living on the reserve.

Additionally, with the passing of Bill C-31 in 1985, many previously deregistered women re-registered as status Indians and put more pressure on band councils to accommodate their desire for residency. However, as Emberley points out:

> [s]ince the Indian Act required reserve residency as a precondition for voting on the band council decisions, women who were excluded from residency were also excluded from the decision-making process that determined who would and would not get housing. Within this woman/governance/space matrix, indigenous women continued to experience discrimination and oppression. (64)

Required by the British Columbia Court of Appeal to promote greater gender equality in Indian registration among Aboriginal women and their children, the Canadian Government has proposed new amendments to the Indian Act, but as another QNW open letter observes, no

> new resources would be allocated to Band Councils to provide for new registrants, even though according to INAC itself, at least 45,000 individuals could gain Indian Status! As with Bill C31 in 1985, in the absence of guarantees of additional funds for these purposes, many reserve communities will resist the increased membership that will occur as a result. (QNW 2010)

Defamiliarizing the Aboriginal includes a close reading of the section titled "Women's Perspectives" in the *Report of the Royal Commission on Aboriginal Peoples* (*RRCAP*). Emberley discusses what she calls a

> biohistory of state policies and government interventions [in Canada] that set out to impose a hierarchical gender division of governance, on lands, territories, and housing ownership, accomplished first by legislating a racial and then a bureaucratized or *institutionalized* identity of the Indian. (Emberley 2007: 61)

This biohistory continues to be relevant in the various responses different parties have made to the eviction notice controversy in Kahnawà:ke. A significant part of Emberley's argument about why contemporary critiques of the patriarchal and colonial history of the family have failed to decolonize issues around Indian status even after the enactment of Bill C-31 is that sexual difference and gender relations in the family continue to be naturalized. So, for example, when the QNW argues in its open letter in opposition to the actions taken by the MCK that "traditional Mohawk customs dictates [sic] that a man who marries a Mohawk woman can and should reside in the woman's community" and that "[a]ccording to Mohawk customs, women are the titleholders of the land," (QNW 2010a) Emberley's work suggests that the QNW's response, like some of the findings she analyzes on gender discrimination in the *RRCAP*, naturalize sexual difference in ways that unwittingly rehearse colonial knowledge claims. "Inadvertently" Emberley points out with regards to similar conclusions in the *RRCAP*,

> this unacknowledged notion of "sexual difference," which is as much culturally and historically constructed and specific as patriarchy, reinscribes a fundamental aspect of the patriarchal and racial colonial logic that led to and perpetuated the oppression of First Nations women in the first place. Within this framework, matrilineal relations—in opposition to the colonial patriarchal/racial lines of descent imposed through government policy—are regarded as "natural" and, therefore, as a "natural basis" for furthering indigenous nationalism. (Emberley 2007: 65-66)

The open letter by the QNW repeatedly refers to the MCK eviction notices as violating "traditional Mohawk customs" by disregarding women as "the titleholders of the land." While the emphasis on pre-colonial "tradition" and "custom" could be understood as socially constructed, it also risks being read as a more "natural" form of practice for Mohawks. Furthermore, here as well as in Emberley's examination of efforts by First Nations women to achieve gender equity in all decision-making bodies in Native communities, QNW and other parties who oppose the actions of the MCK leave the idea of "the family" (something that Emberley describes as "the site of [Native women's] most intense and unrelenting oppression in the forms of sexual abuse and domestic violence") largely unexamined and thus naturalized as well (Emberley 2007: 67).

Though the mainstream Canadian press has largely responded to the eviction controversy as simply a form of "reverse racism" (see for example the *Maclean's* article "Whitey, go home") debate within Kahnawà:ke has been more nuanced (Patriquin 2010a). For example, while a Facebook page set up by local resident Jeremiah Johnson called "Non-natives out of Kahnawake?" has mainly produced a set of polarized comments, Johnson himself is quoted in a March article in *The Eastern Door* as speaking out against the MCK threat to make public names of those sent eviction notices (Bonspiel 2010). Similarly, even as the article notes that Johnson himself "has spoken out against non-natives living in the community on the Facebook group he created," he also suggested that more community consultation is needed to resolve the situation (Bonspiel 2010: 4). "There's a legal form for non-member residency," Johnson states, "[and] [i]f there was a non-native living here and the community was alright with it, I'd be okay with it. They're not just open and shut cases" (qtd. in Bonspiel 2010). Like the QNW response to the eviction notices, the code of membership referenced as the grounds for issuing the eviction notices by the MCK is also somewhat caught up in the biohistory of empire. Here, the heteronormative profile of the colonial family has also been partially assimilated and naturalized in the community's conceptions of family, resulting in the privileging of married couples with children. "It's important to note that there are hundreds of non-natives living here, not just these 26," observes Stephen Bonspiel, editor of *The Eastern Door*, and vocal critic of the eviction notice, in an interview with *Maclean's* magazine in February:

> Some have been adopted in and have little or no Mohawk blood, but they have become a part of the community. Others married into the community, have children and/or great grandchildren and they will not be targeted, according to the MCK, because they can no longer procreate. I'm not even making that part up. A number of chiefs have said that. (Patriquin 2010)

Marriage versus cohabitation, and procreation versus hegemonically transgressive sexual relations seem to be other naturalized notions of identity that have found their way into the management of the band's residency code. "From the filiative symbolics of blood relations to the political affiliative kinships of 'women' and 'men,' 'lesbians' and 'gays,' 'First Nations' and 'non-First Nations,'" writes Emberley, "emerges a tapestry of interwoven allegiances, truths, histories, and loves than cannot be easily pulled apart" (2007: 259).

We cite this ongoing controversy as evidence of the relevance and currency of the ideas Julia Emberley explores in *Defamiliarizing the Aboriginal*. For these and other reasons discussed in invited responses to the book, by Terry Goldie, Deanna Reder and Jennifer Andrews, Susan Gingell and I chose it for the Author Meets Critics forum we organized and hosted for the annual meeting of the Canadian Association for Commonwealth Literature and Language Studies (CACLALS) at Carleton University in May of 2009. Since 2005, Susan and I have coordinated and chaired three different sessions focusing on recent book publications of our members' work meant to stimulate a sense of intellectual community-building in the area of postcolonial and Indigenous studies. Following a pattern established with these first two events, we have here compiled a revised (and in this case substantially expanded) version of the book review previously published in *Chimo* (CACLALS's news journal) in advance of the event at the conference, and then requested the "Critics" along with the "Author" to prepare a written version of their 15-minute presentations at that event. The results of that discussion can be perused in the material that follows. Publishing this cluster of material as a kind of collaborative extended review essay will, we hope, continue to stimulate engagement with Emberley's book at the moment when its insights seem highly relevant to the Canadian cultural context.

Jill Didur, Concordia University, Montreal, May 2010

References

Aboriginal Pavilion. 2008. *In their Words: Tewanee Joseph*. 25 February 2008, http://www.fourhostfirstnations.com/in-their-words-tewanee-joseph/. Accessed 4 May 2010.

Bonspiel, Steve. 2010. Mohawk Council Chief Regrets Eviction Letters. *The Eastern Door* 19(11), 26 March, 1, 4. http://kahnawake.com/answersback/wp-content/uploads/EasternDoorMarch262010.pdf. Accessed 4 May 2010.

Brennen, Richard. 2010. Evicting 26 Non-Natives Splits Reserve. *thestar.com*, 21 February. http://www.thestar.com/news/canada/article/768952--evicting-26-non-natives-splits-reserve. Accessed 4 May 2010.

Emberley, Julia V. 2007. *Defamiliarizing the Aboriginal: Cultural Practices and Decolonization in Canada*. Toronto: University of Toronto Press.

Patriquin, Martin. 2010a. Inside the Kahnawake evictions. *Macleans.ca*, 10 February. http://www2.macleans.ca/2010/02/10/inside-the-kahnawake-evictions/. Accessed 5 May 2010.

———. 2010b. Whitey, Go Home. *Macleans.ca*, 2 May. http://www2.macleans.ca/2010/05/02/whitey-go-home/. Accessed 4 May 2010.

Quebec Native Women Inc. 2010a. Re: Evictions of Non-Native Residents, Open Letter. 8 February. http://www.faq-qnw.org/documents/LetterMCKeviction KahnawakeFEB2010.pdf. Accessed 4 May 2010.

———. 2010. Open Letter, Re Bill C-3- An Act to Promote Gender Equality in Indian Registration by Responding to the Court of Appeal for British Columbia Decision in McIvor v. Canada (Registrar of Indian and Northern Affairs)—Amendments to the Indian Act. 12 March. http://www.faq-qnw.org/documents/BillC-3March2010-EN.pdf. Accessed 4 May 2010.

Susan Gingell

Suffering the Imposition of the European Bourgeois Family on Aboriginal Peoples in Canada and the Routes to Healing

When I began drafting this response to Julia Emberley's *Defamiliarizing the Aboriginal: Cultural Practices and Decolonization in Canada*, my sense of the book's importance was tied principally to its unearthing of the roots of violence against Aboriginal women and children exemplified by three related horrific phenomena: the serial butchery that Robert "Willie" Pickton engaged in on his Vancouver-area pig farm; the multiple murders John Martin Crawford committed in the 1990s at various sites in Alberta and Saskatchewan; and the devastation of Aboriginal families across generations that was wrought by those agents of Church and State responsible for the residential school experience in Canada. As I wrote, however, a number of related stories that were circulating in Aboriginal and women's activist circles in Saskatchewan and in local and national news media made starkly clear that in no sense is such violence relegated to the past by the convictions of Pickton and Martin, the apology to residential school survivors, and the increasingly troubled attempts to launch Canada's own Truth and Reconciliation Commission.

The first story reached me late the afternoon of January 8, 2009, in an email to members of Iskwewuk E-wichiwitochik/Women Walking Together, a Saskatoon- and now internet-based activist group with a dual mandate: to support the families and friends of those Aboriginal women in Saskatchewan who, according to the Native Women's Association of Canada Sisters in Spirit researchers, are among the 582 Indigenous women whom their database now lists as disappeared or murdered (Sisters 2010: 9) and to engage in public education activities around the issue. The email that arrived January 8 bore a depressingly familiar message: yet another Aboriginal woman had gone missing in Saskatchewan, this time in the Choiceland area.[1] A second email arrived later that day from another member of Iskwewuk, whose own aunt had disappeared in 2007, and, despite repeated determined searches, remained unfound. This message reported that the body of the woman publically reported missing earlier that day had been discovered. Cause of death was yet to be determined. These communications were taking place against the background of the Saskatoon trial of Brian Roger Casement for the murder of Victoria Jane Nashacappo, 21, who went missing September 25, 2002. The *Saskatoon StarPhoenix* ran reports on the trial from January 5 to January 22, 2009 announcing on the latter date Casement's conviction the previous day for first-degree murder (Adam 2009: A3).

On February 26, the Saskatoon paper headlined "Kids in Crisis" as a result of the Saskatchewan Children's Advocate, Marvin Bernstein, having sent to the Saskatchewan legislature his report entitled "Breach of Trust: An Investigation into Foster Home Overcrowding in the Saskatoon Service Centre." The title page of the report carries the warning: "This report contains strong language and explicit content. It is not suitable for children" (Bernstein 2009: 4). Multiple accounts of gut-wrenching child-on-child and foster parent-on-child violence contained in this report underlie some Ministry of Social Services case workers' reported fears that they are "removing children from unsafe homes, only to place them in unsafe overcrowded foster homes" (qtd. in Bernstein 2009: 33). Of course, not all the children in foster care are maltreated and not all in care in Saskatchewan are of Aboriginal descent, but many are. The Saskatoon *StarPhoenix* quotes Felix Thomas, Chief of the Saskatoon Tribal Council, as saying in response to Bernstein's report, "These report findings confirm the suspicions that our children are not better served, but in fact are in greater jeopardy, when placed into the care of the minister" (Kids in Crisis 2009: A7).

I have tried to recreate something of the context of living in this persistent storm front of events to make clear one of the reasons for making Emberley's book the subject of the Author Meets Critic Forum at the 2009 conference of the Canadian Association of Commonwealth Literature and Language Studies (CACLALS) and its more extended discussion in this published forum. My intent is also to explain both the sense of urgency about the situation that *Defamiliarizing the Aboriginal* addresses and my conviction that its main findings need to be made available in a more broadly accessible form than the scholarly book. Emberley's is in the main an elaborated Foucauldian genealogical project that examines both (a) the writing of European men's putative origins in the always illusory Primordial Father of Freudian theory, and (b) the colonial state's installing of the European bourgeois family as the ideal form of social governance in the allegedly private sphere.

Defamiliarizing the Aboriginal makes two major contributions. The first is to demonstrate in concrete and engaging detail how, to the gross and too frequently fatal detriment of Aboriginal women and children, ideologies of race, class and gender operated in the micrological political arena of the family in concert with the instituting and maintenance of racist, patriarchal political governance in the macrological public sphere. The second is to demonstrate how Aboriginal artists are intervening in the Canadian imaginary by abrogating and appropriating the semiotic apparatuses through which colonialism produced the figure of the Aboriginal that has proved so lethal to First Nations, Inuit and Metis peoples.

The grounding of Emberley's work in European philosophy, sociology and political and literary theory, while producing a sophisticated account of her subject for academics—and I do not for a minute wish to depreciate the value of this achievement—inevitably leads her to use a vocabulary and a writing style that would surely be alienating to the majority of those women whose lives are addressed in the book. Even the unfolding of Emberley's argument is in at least one key dimension problematically structured. Readers uninitiated into psychoanalytic theory will in all likelihood remain puzzled after reading about the reference in chapter one's main title: "An Origin Story of No Origins: Biopolitics and Race in the Geographies of the Maternal Body." Such readers have to wait for an explanation until they encounter chapter two's discussion of secular European Enlightenment stories that initiated the concept of the virtuous savage as the infantile but paradoxically noble roots of European masculinity. This representation, Emberley makes clear, resulted in the dehistoricizing of the figure of the Aboriginal, "rendering the myth of Europe's infancy rootless ... and le[aving] the European imaginary with an origin story of no origins" (2007: 77). Moreover, Emberley argues, the myth of the vanishing savage engendered a heightened anxiety for Europeans who understood their own origins to be in Aboriginal Man.

Taking a materialist approach to the body and embodied power, Emberley uses a performative method of analysis that she identifies as an "analytics of dis/memberment" (2007: 3). In the context of bringing together examples from various media of the ways in which the discourses of the family have been written on and through the bodies of Aboriginal people in Canada, Emberley makes visible a number of concealed connections. Among them are those between the allegedly separate public and private spheres and the coincident work of both repressive and ideological state apparatuses and of cultural production to advance settler interests and destroy Indigenous kinship relations and the social formations those relations worked to constitute. Emberley's method of arriving at what Gerald Vizenor would call a post-Indian state equally entails the unmaking or disassembling of the allegedly fixed and immutable truths of the two figures key to her analysis, Aboriginal Man and Bourgeois Woman. The performative quality of her analysis takes its most creative and overtly feminist form in what Emberley calls the "biotextual reassemblage" (2007: 91) of chapter three. Arguing that the wounded, dismembered and disabled body requires different representational practices than those employed by medicine, law, industrial capitalism and education to discipline the Aboriginal body, she devises a transactional strategy that brings various materials into contact with one another so as to "disrupt their apparent regimes of knowing and seeing" (93). She confronts the spectre of the Primordial Father in one of its most potent foundational texts, Freud's *Totem and Taboo*, by dismembering it in order to patch strategically selected passages, reproduced in italic rather than cited with page numbers according to academic protocol, into her rebellious daughter's deconstruction of the family romance.

Defamiliarizing the Aboriginal provides a compelling account of the link between the imposition of the European bourgeois family on Indigenous people in Canada and violence against Aboriginal women and children. Emberley makes the link by duly attending to the Indian Act and its amendments and other institutional means, most notably the residential school system and forced conversion to Christianity that in their overlapping ways sought to destroy and replace Indigenous kinship relations. However, as a work of cultural criticism, her book focuses most extensively on representational practices. Mindful of not adding the epistemological violence of a mono-disciplinary approach to the various forms of physical, spiritual, psychological and cultural violence that Aboriginal women and children experienced in colonial times and continue to endure in the neocolonial Canadian state, Emberley draws on a broad range of visual and print textual materials. These include: the murals of the British Columbia legislative building's lower rotunda; family portraits and their inscriptions from the digital archive of British Columbia's Royal Museum; the Mary T.S. Schäffer collection in Banff's Whyte Museum; films such as Robert Flaherty's *Nanook of the North*; an advertisement (following Anne McClintock) for Pears' soap; and fiction such as Pat Barker's *Regeneration* trilogy. Over and against such colonizing representations, Emberley sets the life writing of Yvonne Johnson and Rudy Wiebe's *Stolen Life: The Journey of a Cree Woman*, Jane Ash Poitras's mixed media work *Transparent Parents Singing Hearts*, Nadia Myre's beading over of the Indian Act, and Tomson Highway's *Kiss of the Fur Queen*. The latter is also counter-discursively positioned in relation to a television melodrama, *Where the Spirit Lives*, scripted by Keith Ross Leckie, which Emberley maintains reveals the impact of residential school violence in the 1930s in part by also demonizing the lesbian teacher in the movie. Emberley thus shows herself alert to the problematic ideological operations in work which advocates justice for Aboriginal peoples but remains blind to oppressions of another sort.

The book's rich account of colonizing and decolonizing cultural practices is inherently political, but an overtly activist vision informs Emberley's urging that affiliative political kinships be forged to participate in the kind of transnational "domestic politics" to which M. Jacqui Alexander and Chandra Talpade Mohanty in *Feminist Genealogies, Colonial Legacies, Democratic Futures* have called their fellow feminists. Emberley's own concern is specifically to counter not just the already existing results of what she calls "colonial domicide," but also "some of the more dangerous and virulent revivals of 'the family' in fundamentalist contexts, including, of course, Canada and the United States" (2007: 237). The "family" that fundamentalists seek to revivify Emberley understands as "nothing short of a myth used to naturalize heterosexual reproductive relations" (2007: 47) and as the site of what she points out is a mode of colonization rarely attended to in postcolonial studies.

That at least one other major anti-racist, anti-imperialist feminist materialist scholar in Canada has since the publication of *Defamiliarizing the Aboriginal* made both the Canadian government's imposition of the European bourgeois family and its particularly deleterious effect on Aboriginal females the focus of her attention suggests just how valuable a line of inquiry Emberley initiated. Historian Sarah Carter's 2008 book, *The Importance of Being Monogamous: Marriage and Nation Building in Western Canada to 1915*, argues that the Canadian state's late 19th- and early 20th-century efforts to impose monogamy on First Nations peoples and Mormons was a key part of establishing the hegemony of white masculinity in the Canadian West and making this form of masculinity the foundation for the nation. Enacting this plan entailed various forms of coercion to get Mormons to abandon polygamy and Aboriginal peoples to give up the polygamous relationships, serial unions and occasional same-sex partnerships that had been their traditional forms of socio-sexual relations before contact. Carter shows that women in particular benefited from the greater flexibility of non-monogamous relationships because such relationships enhanced women's power in their interactions with men. This latter point was precisely the one that Canadian proponents of monogamy and opponents of divorce anxious about the looser American law on this matter seized on to argue for their positions. By contrast, an enforced lifelong heterosexual union set up avowedly to exclude all other sexual partners worked to establish the husband as incontrovertible head of the household and the wife as submissive subordinate. Moreover monogamous marriage was continuous with and mutually reinforcing of patriarchal power in the public sphere. Thus Emberley's and Carter's books in tandem provide an even more compelling argument that the family was a key site for colonizing and maintaining white patriarchal hegemony than either book makes on its own.

Hope that the dire situation to which both Emberley's and Carter's books speak can in fact be ameliorated lies not only in the politically fired artistry of Aboriginal cultural workers that *Defamiliarizing the Aboriginal* documents, but also in the kind of elective political kinship groups that Emberley envisions as desirably supplanting the European bourgeois family and sees as requisite for transnational political work. Exemplars of such groups are the Saskatoon-based Iskwewuk E-wichiwitochik; the organizing committee of the 2008 Regina conference "Missing Women: Decolonization, Third Wave Feminisms, and Indigenous People of Canada and Mexico"; and the Congress Committee to End Indifference to the Disappearance of Aboriginal Women Now (CCEI-DAWN). The latter group was founded at the instigation of Queen's University professor Jacqueline Davies and OISE graduate student June Starkey after the partly CACLALS-sponsored showing, at the 2007 Congress of the Social Sciences and Humanities, of *Finding Dawn*, Christine Welsh's (2006) film about the disappearances and murders of over five hundred Aboriginal women in Canada in the previous thirty years. Furthermore, in addressing Emberley's book in its Author Meets Critic forum at the 2009 Congress, CACLALS continued its tradition of paying sustained attention to the decolonizing work so necessary to the achieving of just relations between Aboriginal peoples and the newcomers in Canada.

Note

1. Though I did not learn of the result of the search for this missing sister until January 2010, I discovered when researching for the revised version of the original *Chimo* review that the body of Ella Arleen Brown was found January 8, 2009, in a field outside Choiceland, just northeast of Prince Albert, Saskatchewan. The CBC Saskatchewan story of that day about the successful search for Brown reported that she was dressed only in a sweater, pants and toque despite the -25 degree Celsius temperature exacerbated by wind-chill (Searchers 2009). An autopsy was to be conducted, though the RCMP did not suspect foul play according to a report of January 8, 2009, in the *Nipawin Journal* (Search Finds 2009). To the best of my knowledge, the results of the autopsy were not reported in the media; however, if we were to pursue the question what could have possessed a woman to go out into such cold so under-dressed, one trail may lead back to the operations of the colonial and neocolonial Canadian state.

References

Adam, Betty-Ann. 2009. Casement Guilty of First Degree Murder. *Saskatoon StarPhoenix*, 22 January, A3. http://www.thestarphoenix.com. Accessed 24 January 2010.

Bernstein, Marvin. 2009. Breach of Trust: An Investigation into Foster Home Overcrowding in the Saskatoon Service Centre. Saskatchewan Children's Advocate's Office. 25 February. http://www.saskcao.ca/documents/FHOC_Report_022509.pdf. Accessed 26 January 2009.

Carter, Sarah. 2008. *The Importance of Being Monogamous: Marriage and Nation Building in Western Canada to 1915*. Edmonton: University of Alberta Press.

Kids in Crisis. 2009. *Saskatoon StarPhoenix*, 26 February, A1, A7.

Search Finds Body of Missing Woman Near Choiceland. 2009. *Nipawin Journal*. 8 January. http://www.nipawinjournal.com. Accessed 24 January 2010.

Searchers Find Missing Woman Dead after Two Days in Sask. Cold. 2009. CBC Saskatchewan. 8 January. http://www.cbc.ca/sask. Accessed 24 January 2010.

Sisters in Spirit 2010 Research Findings. 2010. http://www.nwac-hq.org/en/documents/2010_NWAC_SIS_Report_EN_Lite.pdf. Accessed 7 May 2010.

Welsh, Christine, dir. 2006. *Finding Dawn*. National Film Board of Canada. http://www.onf-nfb.gc.ca/eng/collection/film/?id=52581.

Terry Goldie

Familiarizing Flaherty and Freud: A Response to Julia Emberley's *Defamiliarizing the Aboriginal: Cultural Practices and Decolonization in Canada*

I presume you might have noticed the genders of the authors of the commentaries assembled here. I am not quite the dead white male but certainly an older white male. Thus I am in at least some ways the symbol of the target of Julia's book.

I also was on the supervisory committee for the dissertations of both Julia Emberley and Jill Didur. Perhaps this also makes me a potential academic patriarch. In reference to Freud, Julia says, "But why, I ask, must we fear the authority of our intellectual fathers?"(Emberley 2007: 94). I presume I should take that to heart.

Of course over the years I have had various fleeting moments of contact with Julia. She was one of the organizers of a conference called Global Queeries, where I gave a paper on "Gay India." I made many people there angry by referring to my knowledge of India as that of a white tourist and then offering observations about Indian male-male sex practices. As my friend Rinaldo Walcott asked, "Have you no instinct for self-preservation?" The same could be said here, as I might be seen to be reintroducing the decidedly unwanted "Law of the Father."

But if that is my role, so be it. I would first, however, like to assert this patriarch's opinion of Julia's work. She is certainly one of our best scholars. There are very few Canadian academics who come anywhere near her achievements in analyzing colonial and postcolonial tensions. Among other contributions that are, if not unique, certainly rare, is her ability to focus attention on Canada in analyses with an ardent awareness of transnational possibilities. As well, she keeps an eye on not just gender but also sexuality, most impressively in her book *The Cultural Politics of Fur* (1997) and now again in *Defamiliarizing the Aboriginal*.

Well, I suppose that is the end of the warm fuzzies. One of my PhD students told me last week that she is always afraid to come to my office. I remarked that I always thought of myself as warm and cuddly, albeit cuddly metaphorically. She said at best she would call me "bluntly critical."

To be "bluntly critical" about *Defamiliarizing the Aboriginal* might seem a mistake. The book is often brilliant, usually radiant. Every page stimulates thought. The insights are incessant. I was especially impressed by the chapters on Barker's *Regeneration* (1991) and on *Stolen Life* (1998), by Rudy Wiebe and Yvonne Johnson, which thoughtfully engage the complexity of the concepts implied by the title. The title has a particular theoretical bounce, which suits Julia's methodology. The book is highly dependent on Foucault and somewhat on other theorists such as Derrida. Like many of the best Canadian books on colonial issues, Julia finds French theorists a significant resource but casts very few glances at Canadian scholars, including those who have worked directly on this material, perhaps because they are often not as theoretically implosive. I found the language at times intimidating. I am sure Julia feels it is justified by the theoretical import but I am not convinced it always is: sometimes I found it stood in the way of an excellent piece of analysis.[1] Just as one example, Emberley says that "the exclusion of First Nations women from public arenas of political decision-making and newly formed political institutions" was justified by the "bio-politics of control over the so-called species body" (54). Is that really the most direct way of making her point?

But that first word, *defamiliarizing*, is an example of something that works very well, although in ways that Julia does not highlight. I should note my spellchecker doesn't like the word and the *OED* online doesn't include it. But the *OED* deigns to include a different form, "defamiliarization." Its Russian form, *ostranenie*, was brought into critical language by the Russian formalist, Viktor Shklovsky. He saw defamiliarization, that is, taking the ordinary and adding aesthetic qualities that make the ordinary seem extraordinary, as one of the primary tasks of art.

Julia makes no reference to Shklovsky or even to *ostranenie* but rather just leaves the pun for her readers to dissect. For most of us, *familiar* is that easy word used by Julia in her preface: "Most of us are familiar with the figure of the wild man…" (xv); but she goes on to situate it rather more specifically:

> The ideology of individualism perpetuated by the rise of the bourgeois family in the nineteenth century and its authoritative father figure created this singular focus on his significant Other. This text, however, places the figure of primitive man in relation to the bourgeois woman, and takes the position that both these figures were integral to an imperialist configuration in which racial and sexual difference, and colonization, were irreducible and entirely interrelated forms of power and domination. (xv)

Thus the "familiar" is of the family, its earlier meaning. The book is defamiliarizing both in the sense of estranging the familiar representation of the Aboriginal family through holding it up to the lens, and also in the sense of convincing us of the necessity that the Aboriginal woman remove herself from the ideal of the colonized family.

But if I can take one more step backwards through etymology, the Latin root of the term *familiar* is in *familia*, the household, and *famulus*, the servant. This etymology certainly situates the term in a way that suits Julia's argument because the domestic is defined through the dominated, but it also suggests the extent that this word goes beyond what she calls the bourgeois family. The *familia* is an understanding of any potential domestic unit. It becomes an elastic universal, as the term might be *famulus* to any *familia*. One of the successes of the more sensitive recent studies of sexuality, both historical and transnational, is to show that the family seems to be key to most relationships but that there might be no limit to the forms that the family can take. [2]

This has been the character of narratives of the family. Two of the focuses of Julia's book are *Nanook of the North* and Freud. She sees the narrative of the film and Freud's theories as reflecting an imperialist and colonizing view of the bourgeois family. Thus both are familiar in both senses of the word.

I wonder why Julia did not pay more attention to the extensive scholarship on *Nanook of the North*. The film has become the classic case—often represented as the origin—for the way the ethnographic documentary familiarizes and defamiliarizes. Part of the process is simply mechanical: Flaherty's cameras could not have shown such scenes had he tried simply to capture reality. Part of the problem is a sense of the public: I have no idea why Flaherty called the hero Nanook but it seems likely that he felt the man's proper name, Allakariallak, was too difficult for the audience. Another part is the typical problem of an ethnography that wishes to emphasize tradition. Flaherty wanted to represent something akin to pre-contact life and so Allakariallak was told to use traditional tools although he normally used a rifle.

Julia says, for example, that "The connotations of sexual excess are compounded by shots of Nanook eating raw food with relish" (86). Perhaps. But, like the pear eating scene in the classic film *Tom Jones* (Richardson 1963)—a major moment in my adolescence—is this not an assumption of Flaherty's intention or even a rather Freudian assumption of what eating raw food looks like? Julia believes this is the message of the film: "it is in the failure of Nanook and his virtual family to *realize* itself (i.e., become the reality that is the proper civilized family) that the civilized, bourgeois, heterosexual family is affirmed" (86). Perhaps. My reading of the film, however, is that this is but one example of the film's constant balance between the familiar and the "defamiliar": this is a family just like yours, except they eat raw meat. Some of the differences are very large: this is a family just like yours, although instead of having groceries delivered, they are always on the cusp of starvation. Some other examples are small and titillating, such as the *National Geographic* topless scene: this is a family just like yours but with a different view of privacy.

Julia's comment on Freud as an intellectual father arises in a consideration of Freud's *Totem and Taboo*. She says:

> I am purposefully transgressing the rules of scholarly decorum here by citing bits and pieces of Freud's text (in italics) and weaving those fragments into my own text in a way that disintegrates and distorts the original. This sacrilegious act goes to the heart of an academic taboo. (94)

Julia then offers an extensive rhetorical justification that incorporates a quotation from Freud about "primitive and conservative academics" that she of course uses against him. She asks the question, "Why do we treat the original text like a taboo fetish, as if it contained the spirit of our ancestors?"(94). But I wonder if removing parenthetical references erases the taboo fetish or rather re-emphasizes it. With page numbers, the reader might go back to the original and grapple directly with Freud the writer of a book. In Julia's version the most analogous of methods is the way believers quote the words of Muhammed or Christ, without reference except that it comes from the ultimate source.

Of course, Julia does not see Freud as the source of all wisdom but rather as a source of oppression. She states:

> the science of psychoanalysis was one method of sacrificing the history of a people to a conservative and imperial knowledge and, in so doing, committing a form of epistemic genocide in which real indigenous societies are completely eradicated and denied historical and ontological autonomy. Rather, indigenous societies become a reductive non-embodiment of a non-European Other in which to locate the traumatic effect of the violence of the European bourgeois state. (108)

Steven Marcus made the wonderful comment that "It's impossible to make a statement about Freud being right or wrong since he is always both" (Marcus 1972: xli). Agreed, Freud is no doubt not all that right and even more wrong in *Totem and Taboo*. Part of his problem was that his primary source for ethnographic material was James Frazer, an armchair ethnographer who was often too sweeping in his assumptions. But what was Freud doing in *Totem and Taboo*? Julia's answer to that rhetorical question is another: "Why is Freud so concerned to fix the meaning of Aboriginal Man at this time? I think the answer lies in his fear of communism as a possible site for the dissolution of the bourgeois family, a political structure of power that he was obviously heavily invested in"(Emberley 2007: 98).

This seems to suggest that Freud was some kind of booster for the bourgeois family. Of course, the average bourgeois family at the time did not see it that way and most still do not. They rather see him as destroying the bourgeois family, or at least providing a series of worms that constantly eat away at it. It is possible that imposing the bourgeois family is Freud's unintended agenda but I suspect his assertion of the family has much broader implications. Thus, Freud believed that all of human history showed the importance of reproduction and kinship. As one part of this belief, homosexuality must be a pathology, although he believed it should not be criminalized or even a cause for discrimination. He saw all societies as handling such pathologies differently but ultimately the problem of dealing with same-sex desire is universal because it is a concern of reproduction and kinship, which are also universal.

Freud's reactions in *Totem and Taboo* are shaped by his bourgeois Viennese Jewish experience. Thus he refers to "savages who, according to our standard, are ... very immoral" (Freud 1913: 103). This is not a comment on some universal truth but rather on "our" limited standards. It is not a justification for any policy, much less imperialism. Instead, it is his lead-in to the question of why incest taboos are universal even in a culture that might seem, to "us," very immoral. His answer, of course, is that incest taboos are innately human. Thus all human structures, whether bourgeois Viennese Jewish or savage, must include, in some form, an incest taboo.

I have a similar reaction to Julia's view of the Oedipus complex: "the oedipal myth attempts to secure a history of continuity for the bourgeois nuclear family by recreating its origins in the Primitive Family…" (Emberley 2007: 100). Is this a history or rather once again the universal? It is not that the primitive leads to the present, but that the primitive is in this sense the same as the universal.

So what does this discussion tell us about the Indian problem? Well, the first thing "us" needs to realize is that the so-called Indian problem is, as Lenore Keeshig-Tobias said many years ago, not an "Indian problem" at all but a white problem (2005). However, the pain of this white problem is felt by whites only in the form of white guilt—not a very large pain. On the other hand, this white problem causes a myriad of pains to First Nations. As a white, non-activist outsider, someone from the ivory tower, I would say that one of the worst of these pains is teen suicide. As I was driving down the highway to Newfoundland just before the 2009 Congress of the Social Sciences and Humanities conference at which the Author Meets Critic event on Julia's book took place, there was yet another piece on the CBC about a teenage Native boy who killed himself. The speaker was a First Nations social worker who called on the Canadian state to do something, although she offered no specific idea of what that should be, except perhaps more therapists and counsellors. In her despair she referred to her confusion that the young man had such a stable family, a stay-at-home mother and a father who was active in band affairs. She wondered how this could happen in such a family. Julia twice refers to teen suicide in her book. She asserts that it is one of the products of colonialism. Given that all aspects of First Nations' life are in a large part the product of colonialism, her assertion is no doubt true. But what to do?

Before I heard that radio program I had just been the external examiner for a dissertation by Molly Blyth on contemporary Indigenous literature. Her title, taken from Gerald Vizenor (1999), was "Tricky Stories are the Cure." The problem with the rhetorical flourish, of course, is that it often asserts more than the rhetorician believes. I doubt that either Vizenor or Blyth believes that tricky stories will cure. I doubt that Julia has any delusion that "defamiliarizing the aboriginal" is the cure. This important book might be the beginnings of a cure for the white problem, but it will do little to heal the pain that the white problem produces. The social worker has found that the family—the bourgeois family?—has not cured the pain either.

It is fitting that this conference saw the launch of Jo-Ann Episkenew's *Taking Back Our Spirits: Indigenous Literature, Public Policy, and Healing* (2009). To the extent that literature can ever hope to heal such widespread damage not just to individuals but to many Aboriginal cultures, Episkinew offers some possibilities. *Defamiliarizing the Aboriginal* is in a different tradition: colonial critique, a description of the poisons that have created the disease. It asserts a very deep recognition of the fact that all First Nations people recognize and a few whites have been able to assert, encapsulated in the title of a book by Claude Denis, *We Are Not You* (1997). This also offers no cure but it provides a base on which any cure must be built.

Notes

1. I should note here that this criticism is the same as I received for my book *Fear and Temptation*, in 1989. I mention this partly to admit to being a bit of a pot calling the kettle black but also to assert that I am not in any sense anti-theoretical.

2. A few examples are Bernstein and Reimann (2001), Lehr (1999) and Sullivan (1999).

References

Barker, Pat. 1991. *Regeneration.* New York: Plume.

Bernstein, Mary and Renate Reimann, eds. 2001. *Queer Families, Queer Politics.* New York: Columbia University Press.

Blyth, Molly. 2009. Tricky Stories are the Cure. PhD diss. Trent University.

Denis, Claude. 1997. *We Are Not You: First Nations and Canadian Modernity.* Peterborough: Broadview.

Emberley, Julia. 1997. *The Cultural Politics of Fur.* Ithaca: Cornell University Press.

Episkenew, Jo-Ann. 2009. *Taking Back Our Spirits: Indigenous Literature, Public Policy, and Healing.* Winnipeg: University of Manitoba Press.

Flaherty, Robert J, dir. 1921. *Nanook of the North.* Rèvillons Frères.

Freud, Sigmund. 1913. *Totem and Taboo: Resemblances between the Psychic Lives of Savages and Neurotics.* Trans. A. A. Brill. New York: Moffatt, Yard.

Goldie, Terry. 1989. *Fear and Temptation: The Image of the Indigene in Canadian, Australian and New Zealand Literatures.* Montreal: McGill-Queen's University Press.

Keeshig-Tobias, Lenore. 2005. After Oka—How Has Canada Changed? *An Anthology of Canadian Native Literature in English*, edited by Daniel David Moses and Terry Goldie, 3rd ed., 257-58. Toronto: Oxford University Press.

Lehr, Valerie. 1999. *Queer family Values: Debunking the Myth of the Nuclear Family.* Philadelphia: Temple University Press.

Marcus, Steven. 1972. Introduction. *Three Essays on the Theory of Sexuality*, by Sigmund Freud. Trans. James Strachey. New York: Basic.

Richardson, Tony, dir. 1963. *Tom Jones.* United Artists.

Sullivan, T. Richard. 1999. *Queer Families, Common Agendas: Gay People, Lesbians and Family Values.* New York: Harrington Park.

Vizenor, Gerald and A. Robert Lee. 1999. *Postindian Conversations.* Lincoln: University of Nebraska Press.

Wiebe, Rudy and Yvonne Johnson. 1998. *A Stolen Life: The Journey of a Cree Woman.* Toronto: Knopf.

Deanna Reder

What's Not in the Room?: A Response to Julia Emberley's *Defamiliarizing the Aboriginal*

Of central concern to Julia Emberley's *Defamiliarizing the Aboriginal* is the "irreducible wounded body" (2007: 93), more specifically the broken bodies of Indigenous women and children who have suffered under colonial violence. Emberley proposes that the root cause of this violence is the western-European equation of the Aboriginal man as "bourgeois man's 'Other'," (7), and it was the subsequent imposition of the white bourgeois family, complete with its patriarchal rule, racial supremacy and colonial governance that disrupted pre-existing Aboriginal kinship structures.

The key thesis of Emberley's work is that Aboriginality is a concept in the western-European imagination that is deployed through the mechanisms of the Canadian government and cultural production, with a particular focus on the family unit. Colonial logic warrants that if the imagined Aboriginal is savage and threatening, then the imposition of bourgeois family ideals is the most effective strategy to undercut Indigenous kinship networks and render Indigenous people compliant and weakened, thereby undermining their collective or community identities and nullifying their claims to land.

Emberley proposes a method to "address" (a term meant to be more comprehensive than *analyze*) the irreducible wounded body (93). Early on in chapter three she introduces a method she calls *biotextual reassemblage*, "a different organization of knowledge" (93). She pulls together a wide variety of topics and sites of study to produce "the juxtaposition of disparate elements, a montage effect of readings, materials, arguments and poetics that permits a diffuse look at the technologies and techniques deployed in the service of colonial governance and its educational, juridical and medical institutions" (93). Consequently, *Defamiliarizing the Aboriginal* as montage brings together not only commonly studied factors usually considered when examining colonization, factors "such as economic expansion, territorial annexation, the exploitation of natural resources, and the abuse of individual and collective rights [but also] the everyday living practices of the family" (23). Using her method of montage, Emberley interrogates the categories of the Savage and the Civilized by examining works by Freud and Marx alongside films about Tarzan and *Nanook of the North*;[1] she scrutinizes the racist, colonial state narrative in the murals of the British Columbia provincial legislature as well as in the family portraits in that province's archives; she studies domestic violence not only in RCMP records about the disappearance (and suspected murders) of an Inuit mother and child in the 1940s but also the limits of and potential for healing in the auto/biography of abuse victim and convicted murderer, Yvonne Johnson.

It seems appropriate, then, to adopt Emberley's method in order to discuss *Defamiliarizing the Aboriginal*. I consider her text as a physical space, specifically a contemporary middle-class living room[2] full of disparate objects in order to convey how generative her approach is (albeit sometimes confusing and anti-intuitive) as well as to suggest gaps in her analysis and thus prompt a reconsideration of her conclusions.

Given the premise that Emberley's text can be imagined as a living room, we can imagine on the feature wall a fireplace, fuelled by gas, ignited by the flick of a switch. There are the typical furnishings and knick-knacks that do not seem ill-placed unless more closely inspected. For example, as you enter, some of the first objects noticed are the somewhat charming picture frames perched on the mantle of the fireplace—with images first of a woman with a baby and second of a mother and child. But these are not family photographs of people with names and histories. If you peer closely at the photos you will see that both are of Indigenous people and that they have been damaged through scratches inscribed upon them: the first is titled "Indian Woman with Papoose" and the second bears the title "The Indian Madonna," even though the woman with the relaxed and sunny smile bears little resemblance to the icon in European paintings.[3]

Sitting next to these frames on the mantle are three books by the same author, Pat Barker's *Regeneration* trilogy, the first in the series with its Booker Prize nominee sticker prominently displayed.[4] Another pile of books sits next to it. If you don't look carefully you will miss that under copies of work by Freud and Derrida is a lesser known book, *Stolen Life: The Journey of a Cree Woman*—co-authored by Rudy Wiebe, Yvonne Johnson and a third author—"the *spirit* of the text and of the law" (Emberley 2007: 225).[5] Moving the other books aside, you are able to see the photo on the front cover that sits jarringly—violently juxtaposed beside the sanguine Indian family portraits. The image is of little Yvonne Johnson—as she describes herself—"smiling so desperately, with my arms wrapped tight around my chest, holding myself together…" (qtd. in Emberley 2007: 218). Beside her, somewhat resembling their great-great-grandfather Big Bear, is her handsome but doomed brother Earl "wearing a white T-shirt with a dark horizontal band

[that] looks like a wide rope cinched tight around his [neck ... I mean] chest" (qtd. In Emberley 2007: 218).⁶

In the middle of the living room is a coffee table and sitting upon it is a comic book opened up to reveal a brawny, muscular Johnny Weissmüller look-a-like, Tarzan with a sultry, underdressed Jane in his arms, swinging through the trees as he gives out his customary call. Beside it is a coffee table book of images from the Mansell Collection, published by Time Inc. Unfortunately this book is secured shut by a tiny but formidable lock that can only be opened by a call to the publishers.⁷

Also in the room is a small side table, and sitting upon it is a small skeleton displayed upon a board. A small engraved label explains that it is the remains of a child of indeterminate gender.⁸ Sitting next to it is a carving of a two-spirit figure from an undetermined Indigenous nation.⁹

Of course this living room has a couch, and on it is the famous filmmaker, Robert Flaherty, apparently unconcerned that his two common-law wives (the very two who play the wives of Nanook in Flaherty's pseudo-documentary), are absent.¹⁰ The only evidence of them is on the sixty-inch flat screen TV, which is playing the same loop over and over again: the beginning section of *Nanook of the North* when "the Great Hunter" disembarks from his kayak holding a small child, followed by another woman emerging from the kayak with a puppy in her arms, and then an RCMP officer holding a gramophone.¹¹ The television is on mute.¹² Underneath the flickering lights of the TV is Robert Flaherty lying on the couch in his underwear and wife-beater T-shirt, telling his problems to Sigmund Freud, who is sitting by the fire in a Lazy Boy.

Freud is, in fact, not listening to Flaherty but rather staring into the fire, reenacting the well-known scene in philosophy when Descartes famously played with a ball of wax until he concluded "cogito ergo sum—I think, therefore I am." Freud, however, does not have a ball of wax but instead is playing with a bar of Pears' soap, slowly forming the conclusion: "I am not primitive—like **them**—and yet I am."¹³

To complete the scene, among the family photographs carefully modelled after white bourgeois ideals, the books and the skeleton, the flickering film, Flaherty on the couch, and Freud by the fireplace on the Lazy Boy, is a large, oval, deep red carpet that might very well be ... it is hard to tell ... a giant pool of blood.

I reimagine Emberley's scholarship in this way in order to emphasize it as provocative, ambitious and comprehensive. And as much as I am convinced by her central argument that "the technologies of representation, including film, photography, and print culture, disseminated images that contributed ... to the imposition of the bourgeois European and patriarchal family on indigenous societies" (Emberley 2007: 3), I wonder how the discussion might be extended with the inclusion of a few more objects in the imaginary living room.

I draw on the work of historian Carol Williams, who, like Emberley, completed research at the British Columbia provincial archives. Her 2003 monograph, *Framing the West*, looks at race, gender and photography in the Pacific Northwest. Imagine if on the mantle next to the photograph of the Indian Madonna were the family portraits that urban wage-earning Salish people living in villages near Nanaimo on Vancouver Island began to commission in unprecedented numbers in the 1890s (Williams 2003: 141). Williams describes these portraits "as motivated by personal choice rather than bureaucratic or political scrutiny" (41). Not simply in service to state motivations of assimilation, some of these images were used for specifically Salish purposes, Williams argues. She writes that "[a]pparently commercial portrait photographs ... gradually replaced the customary goat-hair effigies (*hwisi*), or rag figures [in ceremonies], which symbolically represented a deceased ancestor" (152). Furthermore, argues Williams, Coast and Straight Salish people "incorporated nineteenth-century portraiture to honor the past accomplishments of a departed ancestor" (153).

These adaptations do not necessarily contradict Emberley's analysis of family portraits, which draws upon a "dialectical materialist approach ... to understand how images become *representative* in colonial history ... [asking what] it is that they represent or are made to represent" (Emberley 2007: 158); perhaps, however, more than one reading of the Indigenous family portraits is necessary. Certainly there is much to ponder in Emberley's conclusions that Indigenous family portraits, following the conventions of the genre, conform to "colonial governing practices and relations of patriarchal power" (161). However, it is likely that Salish people in the 19th-century, who sought out family photographs for their own purposes, would see the activity differently.

Now I would like to pause to insist that I am not suggesting too-easy categories of "subjugated" versus "resistant." I am not suggesting that because these people had agency they were using modern technology subversively. This interpretation, to my mind, reinscribes the imperialist narrative that translates all Indigenous action as reaction and ascribes to the colonial power the impetus for all movement. Certainly, I think Salish people used technology in ways that made sense to them, but their use had less to do with having an eye on the oppressive powers about them and with being subversive, and more to do with the creative adaptation of technology to express themselves within Salish culture.

For example, in the early 1900s Annie Charles, from Beecher Bay on Vancouver Island, had embedded into her own portrait the image of an unidentified woman as if it were hanging like a jeweled pendant on a choker ribbon around her neck. I am not concerned with how she was responding to or trying to subvert the mechanisms of church and state, but I am taken by how she was using newly accessible technology to express Salish ideas or understandings, in this case, according to Williams, "commemorat[ing] a female relation" (2003: 148).

Another example of interpretations of photography based on indigenous concepts is the work of Tsimshian art historian Mique'l Askren. Her Alaska community of Metlakatla has typically been portrayed by Christian missionaries as an example of successful assimilation, and the body of work by Tsimshian photographer Benjamin Alfred Haldane (1874-1941) has been considered evidence of this success. Askren, in her Master's thesis, re-examines this archive to argue that contrary to the conventional interpretation of Haldane's photography as that by a westernized Christian, his photographs document the prevailing existence and value of "Tsimshian traditions that were thought to be replaced by Euro-American ways of living"(Askren 2007: np).

This focus on Indigenous interpretations of media is what Seneca scholar Michelle Raheja calls "visual sovereignty." In her article "Reading Nanook's Smile: Visual Sovereignty, Indigenous Revisions of Ethnography, and *Atanarjuat*," she writes:

> Under visual sovereignty, filmmakers can deploy individual and community assertions of what sovereignty and self-representation mean and, through new media technologies frame more imaginative renderings of Native American intellectual and cultural paradigms, such as the presentation of the spiritual and dream world, than are often possible in official political contexts. (Raheja 2007: 1165)

Like Emberley, Raheja also discusses the arguments of film critic Fatimah Romy, who declared *Nanook of the North* to be "cinematic taxidermy" (qtd. in Raheja 2007: 1161). However, using the concept of visual sovereignty, Raheja hesitates to "disregard the complicated collaborative nature of the film's production" (1161). She cites as points to consider: (a) the daily influence that the Inuit production crew had on the shooting of the film; (b) its inspiring influence on Inuit artist Peter Pitseolak to take up a successful career as a photographer, and (c) the contemporary and enduring feeling of "great pride in the strength and dignity of [Inuit] ancestors" (Raheja 2007: 1162) who had worked on the film.

Raheja concludes that these benefits "demonstrate how visual sovereignty ... reframe[s] a narrative that privileges indigenous participation and perhaps points to sites of indigenous knowledge production in a film otherwise understood as a purely Western product..."(1162). This is a different approach than Emberley's stated evaluation that representational violence has "bound and reduced the complexity of indigenous lived experiences to a fixed set of images, a panoramic phantasmania of *aboriginality* whose ghostly presence would haunt the apparent immortalizing technologies of re-production" (Emberley 2007: 12). If Raheja is writing for an Indigenous audience, exploring the possibilities of Indigenous interpretations, Emberley draws on the language of postcolonial theorists to limit these interpretations. The trope of "haunting" represents, say Cynthia Sugars and Gerry Turcotte:

> the "spectral" legacies of imperialism and globalization ... [that appear] in the form of unresolved memory traces and occluded histories resulting from the experience of colonial oppression, diasporic migration, or national consolidation ... readily figured in form of ghosts or monsters that "haunt" the nation/subject from without and within. (2009: vii)

In this schema there is no Indigenous presence; instead there is Emberley's definition of *Aboriginality*, to which she argues, Indigenous life experience is reduced: "both a semiotics of subjugation and a mode of colonial representational violence in which the subject is made to vanish from historical veracity and reappear as a simulacrum" (Emberley 2007: 12).

Anishinaabe theorist Gerald Vizenor (1998) reworks Jean Beaudrillard's ideas about simulation to discuss something very similar to Emberley's understanding of *Aboriginality* as she defines it. For Vizenor, the *Indian* is a colonial invention, a simulation that has taken on a life of its own to become a free-floating signifier that celebrates "the absence of people, not their presence" (Samson 2000: 287). In other words, the stereotype of the Indian, without tribal affiliation, dressed in traditional garb that belongs to neither a particular historical nor a contemporary context, reinforces the idea that Indigenous people do not exist and that their claims to land or rights are irrelevant. However, according to Amy J. Elias, Vizenor proposes a "second kind of simulation, one with potentially positive consequences" (Elias 2000: 88). In *Manifest Manners* (1994), Vizenor writes about a Yana man who purportedly was captured by California police and heralded as the last member of a California tribe. In 1911 Ishi, who spoke no English, was captured and housed in a museum, the subject of public curiosity and research. In the museum he demonstrated how his tribe had used certain material items, and he worked with a linguist to record his language until his death by tuberculosis in 1916.

According to Vizenor, Ishi became the embodiment of the Vanishing Indian, de-contextualized and de-historicized as a simulation. His name in the Yana language even means "man" because Ishi never revealed what he was called by his people. But Vizenor also argues that Ishi's "stories were his survivance" (1994: 134) because "the power of the spoken word goes with the stories of the survivors, and becomes the literature of survivance" (135). Even if the man known as Ishi had stories that were untold and unheard, he emerges from them and not from the imagination of the colonizer, regardless of how he is read by his audience or even how he performs.

This variation of the idea of simulation differs from Emberley's *Aboriginality* because Vizenor accepts the existence of Indigenous stories that pre-exist the colonial narrative as well as the existence of *survivance*, the term coined by Vizenor to mean "more than survival, more than endurance or mere response, the stories of survivance are an active presence (Vizenor 1998: 15). Emberley, on the other hand, does not accommodate the existence of survivance in her critique. For example, Emberley discusses a description in Leslie Feinberg's *Transgender Warriors* of the author having an epiphany when coming across a figure of a "two-spirit" in a museum. Feinberg writes: "What stunned me was that such ancient and diverse cultures allowed people to choose more sex/gender paths, and this diversity of human expression was honored as sacred" (Feinberg 1993: 23). Emberley disapproves of this reading, arguing that Feinberg is simply copying yet another moment of "discovery" of the Aboriginal. Emberley explains:

> The narrative of discovery tends to position indigenous societies within a culturally relativist context, in this case, of sexual identities, and, furthermore, relegates indigenous people to a mythic past from which they have never advanced. While a plurality of sexual identities apparently valorizes "inclusivity," in the context of decolonization they more often than not signal a process of *assimilation*, the mimetic production of simulated figures of oppression and liberation that disavow the discontinuous realities of imperialism in the lives of indigenous people. (2007: 241)

While it is true that Feinberg is drawing upon a familiar narrative of discovery and exoticization, it is notable that Feinberg considers Indigenous ideas of gender and sexuality to be relevant. While it would be incorrect to state that historically all Indigenous communities in the Americas had and have identical sexual and gender categories, it is true that many did and still do have three or four genders and that people in these categories were and are respected. These histories and stories have been valuable enough to contemporary queer Indigenous people that in 1990 in Winnipeg, at the third annual intertribal Native American/First Nations gay and lesbian conference, the term *two-spirit* was adopted as an alternative to *gay* and the now reviled *berdache*. This plurality of sexual identities does not disavow the existence of imperialism in the lives of Indigenous people, but rather celebrates the survival of our people and our stories and the existence, the presence, of our people and our stories today.

What are missing in the imaginary living room are the stories of Indigenous people, not only to be heard but to be used as interpretive devices. It is time that we draw upon Indigenous perspectives in our analysis. For example, there is a long-standing European sign system that interprets the representation of a woman and youngster as Madonna with the Christ child. At what point will we open up our imaginations to shift our focus from European narratives to ones from Native America? Could not the scene of mother and child evoke thoughts of First Woman? How would it shift our analysis if we thought of domestic abuse through the stories of Rolling Head or Sedna the Sea Witch?

To Emberley's credit, her juxtaposition of diverse elements, her *biotextual reassemblage*, is bravely innovative and critically generative. To relate more colloquially to my description of her text as a physical space, I would acknowledge that "there's a lot going on in that room." Even so, that living room is haunted by Indigenous absence. What is needed is a space that is not thought of as haunted but rather one where the existence of the spiritual alongside physical dimensions can do the work of reclamation using our epistemologies as sources—to build a place in which Indigenous history, interpretation, academic voices and perspectives can be present.

Notes

1. Nanook of the North, a film made in 1922 by Robert Flaherty, is credited as the first documentary, though Emberley shows it is really a quasi-documentary.

2. I choose the living room as it is typically the most public space within the privacy of the home, a space of both formality and intimacy.

3. See Chapter Five: "The Family in the Age of Mechanical Reproduction" and more specifically the photographs on pages 172 and 174 taken by travelogue writer Mary T. S. Schäffer in 1907 and 1908.

4. Emberley analyzes these texts in Chapter Four: "Post/Colonial Masculinities: The Primitive Duality of 'ma, ma, man' in Pat Barker's *Regeneration* Trilogy."

5. Emberley argues that Yvonne Johnson, rather than being co-author to her auto/biography, is in fact "a phantom storyteller" with a tenuous relationship to language and literature; first, Johnson was born with a cleft lip that made it difficult for her to speak as a young child, making her even more voiceless and vulnerable to sexual abuse; second, because she is an Indigenous woman raised in poverty and violence, a victim of incest and a criminal convicted of murder. The only coherent narrative we can derive of her life is the one fashioned by her co-author, Wiebe, to weave a "textual resolution to colonial violence" (Emberley 2007: 225).

6. Just as Yvonne Johnson's ancestor, Big Bear, was hanged in prison, her big brother Earl was found hanged in his prison cell at age eighteen.

7. In Chapter Three, "Originary Violence and the Spectre of the Primordial Father: A Biotextual Reassemblage," Emberley notes that "you cannot go and leisurely browse through" (132) over a million images and illustrations that comprise the Mansell collection, which was purchased by Time Inc. in 1997. Instead, a proposal for research on one image or a topic must be provided to the Time Life Syndicate and "they will research it for you" (132).

8. In Chapter Six, "Inuit Mother Disappeared: The Police in the Archive. 1940-1949," Emberley discusses a tragic case of the suspicious death of an Inuit woman married to a French-Canadian trapper; when police began to investigate the death, they found the corpse of one child of indeterminate gender and the stories of at least one other child whose death was never formally reported.

9 . This figure is meant to represent the one Leslie Feinberg talks about in her book *Transgender Warriors* (1993) that Emberley discusses in Chapter 8: Genealogies of Difference: Revamping the Empire? or, Queering Kinship in a Transnational Decolonial Frame."

10 . While in standard biographies of Robert Flaherty, his wife of 37 years, Frances Hubbard, is occasionally mentioned, the fact that he had affairs with at least one of the actresses that played wives of Nanook is rarely discussed. Emberley's source cites that he had affairs with both (86).

11 . In fact, in the film, Nanook emerges from a kayak with a young child, followed by a woman with a young baby and followed by another young woman with a puppy. Emberley reads this as a 20th-century origin story in which "the Kayak 'gives birth' to the Aboriginal family ... momentarily render[ing] invisible how ethnographic documentary uses filmic technology to construct its image of an Eskimo Way of Life" (75). In another scene in the film, Nanook meets the only white man in the film at the trading post and is enthralled when the shopkeeper shows Nanook and his family the gramophone. My amendment of this fact, by including an "RCMP officer holding a gramophone" is meant to hint at the implicit presence of the RCMP, who represent the state bearing gifts of technology. The Canadian state will within a generation of the production of this film assign numbers to all Inuit as a bureaucratic attempt to track people, eventually moving them off the land and into town settlements.

12 . While Nanook of the North is a silent film, I suggest the TV is on mute because, as Emberley suggests, the film says less about Inuit life than "the Euro-American middle-class family and its sense of itself as socially normal" (79).

13 . The Pears' soap refers to Anne McClintock's reading in *Imperial Leather* (1995) of soap ads as commodity racism, the mechanism that combines the racist belief in European superiority and the expansion of Imperial commerce to the colonies, reinforcing the binary of clean and White with dirty and dark. Emberley uses McClintock's ideas as an example of "the image/text/commodity matrix" (124), "arenas of contestation, commodification, and technologies of exclusion for the purposes of attempting to secure the hegemonic disposition to rule for the once British, and now American, bourgeoisie" (133).

References

Askren, Mique'l. 2007. From Negative to Positive: B.A. Haldane, Nineteenth-Century Tsimshian photographer. MA Thesis. University of British Columbia.

Elias, Amy J. 2000. Holding Word Mongers on a Lunge Line: the Postmodernist Writings of Gerald Vizenor and Ishmael Reed. In *Loosening the Seams: Interpretations of Gerald Vizenor*, edited by Robert A. Lee, 85-108. Bowling Green, OH: Bowling Green University Press.

Emberley, Julia V. 2007. *Defamiliarizing the Aboriginal: Cultural Practices and Decolonization in Canada*. Toronto: University of Toronto Press.

Feinberg, Leslie. 1993. *Stone Butch Blues*. Milford, CT: Firebrand Books.

———. 1997. *Transgender Warriors: Making History From Joan of Arc to Dennis Rodman*. Boston, MA: Beacon Press.

Lee, A. Robert, ed. 2000. *Loosening the Seams: Interpretations of Gerald Vizenor*. Bowling Green, OH: Bowling Green University Press.

McClintock, Anne. 1995. *Imperial Leather: Race, Gender, and Sexuality in the Colonial Contest*. New York: Routledge.

Raheja, Michelle H. 2007. Nanook's Smile: Visual Sovereignty, Indigenous Revisions of Ethnography, and *Atanarjuat [The Fast Runner]*. *American Quarterly* 59(4): 1159-85.

Samson, Colin. 2000. Overturning the Burdens of the *Real:* Nationalism and the Social Sciences in Gerald Vizenor's Recent Words. In *Loosening the Seams: Interpretations of Gerald Vizenor*, edited by Robert A. Lee, 279-93. Bowling Green, OH: Bowling Green University Press.

Sugars, Cynthia and Gerry Turcotte, eds. 2009. *Unsettled Remains: Canadian Literature and the Postcolonial Gothic.* Waterloo, ON: Wilfrid Laurier University Press.

Vizenor, Gerald. 1994. *Manifest Manners: Narratives of Postindian Survivance.* Lincoln: University of Nebraska Press.

———. 1998. *Fugitive Poses: American Indian Scenes of Absence and Presence.* Lincoln: University of Nebraska Press.

Williams, Carol. 2003. *Framing the West: Race, Gender, and the Photographic Frontier in the Pacific Northwest.* New York: Oxford University Press.

Jennifer Andrews

Re-reading Photographs through the Lens of *Defamiliarizing the Aboriginal*

I have admired Julia Emberley's work since reading her first book, *Thresholds of Difference* (1993), when I was a graduate student and thus eagerly anticipated the release of her new monograph, *Defamiliarizing the Aboriginal*. Julia's exploration of what I would call "big ideas"—those large theoretical questions that intimidate many of us—means that her books have always been for me a source of inspiration. She possesses a fearless intellect that combines political urgency and acute perception with the desire to make her readers think differently and precipitate change. Having just completed my own manuscript on contemporary Native North American women's poetry, I was ready to be re-energized by Julia's most recent exploration of how Native peoples are portrayed by non-Natives and construct themselves in opposition to white Western psychoanalytic and politically-inflected family structures.

Defamiliarizing the Aboriginal, as Susan Gingell notes in her (2009) review of Emberley's book, is a powerful and compelling text, though as Susan rightly argues the book's choice of discourse likely will alienate those who are not thoroughly versed in literary, psychoanalytic and political theory. Moreover, there are moments when the expansive scope of the book threatens to overwhelm readers with its complex dance through analyses of Freud, Engels and the novels of Pat Barker. The multiple foci of Emberley's analysis have shaped her understanding of the primordial father, a spectral figure that, in turn, fundamentally impacts upon conceptions of Aboriginal "otherness." Given the book's explicitly nation-bound subtitle, *Cultural Practices and Decolonization in Canada*, I recurrently wondered while reading it: where are the close readings of Canadian texts? There are some terrifically engaging and occasionally unexpected examples of Canadian works provided, mostly in the latter half of *Defamiliarizing the Aboriginal*, that illustrate both the predominance of the primordial father and subversion of that concept. Emberley references a range of media from photographic archives and RCMP records to Indigenous women's autobiographies and plastic arts (in particular film and beading) in her book. But the discussions of these are, in most cases, all too brief. Moreover, though the book includes a plethora of plates in Chapter Five, which deal with archival photographs, I wanted to see more; for instance, a plate sampling Nadia Myre's beaded work *Indian Acts* would have been superb. I have undertaken the time-consuming task of negotiating image rights and plate costs and have written extensively about Native people and photography; the reality is that presses don't like to pay for plates—they are work-intensive for authors and presses alike. Moreover, permissions can be difficult and costly to get. But as someone who favours the inclusion of close readings to ground theory and to illustrate its pragmatic value, as I read this book, I kept thinking of texts from my own research that would, if put into conversation with Julia's book, compliment and complicate her argument.

For the remainder of this paper, I want to offer a very brief look at how two Native Canadian women poets use photography in a way that intersects with, and further illuminates, Emberley's discussions in *Defamiliarizing the Aboriginal*. The first is Marilyn Dumont (1996), a Cree/Metis writer, activist and film-maker, who includes a photo of her mother and herself as child at the beginning of her first book, *A Really Good Brown Girl* (Fig. 1). This collection of poems published in 1996 received a great deal of attention in part because of Dumont's poignant and politically-charged depictions of race and gender discrimination by whites and Natives alike. Dumont's poems recall the hardships of being dark skinned and having to live a "dual life" in which "I had white friends and I had Indian friends and the two never mixed and that was normal" (Dumont 1996: 15). The photograph, which appears on the left hand side across from the title page attests to the complexities of that liminal stance. Labeled "Photo of author with her mother, Calgary, c. 1962" (2), the image is juxtaposed with the book's title, a loaded phrase that Dumont's poetic "I" uses at the end of a poem called "Memoirs of A Really Good Brown Girl," to mock an English professor's attempt to alter her speech patterns.

Fig. 1
Portrait of Marilyn Dumont with her mother. Calgary, ca. 1962.

Dumont's choice of photograph and title page become ironically layered symbols of the historical challenges faced by the "really good brown girl" on the streets of Calgary with her mother circa 1962, whose ghostly white face and hands and large body protectively shield the young child from harm (2). Notably it is Dumont who looks right at the camera while her mother turns her gaze away by looking into the distance, creating a palpable tension between bodily presence and emotional absence within the photo itself. In a recent interview, Dumont explained that the picture was acquired from a city street photographer who peddled the shots he took of strangers: "I think the picture really illustrated for me, more just in the physical relationship, how large my mother looked and how small I looked. It gave the sense that she was there protecting me and how innocent I look and how vulnerable to shame we are as children" (Andrews 2004: 148). For Dumont, the photograph also reveals her childhood naïveté about her brown skin, and specifically the fact that racism is not merely an individual problem but rather "the majority of it is just to do with the world we live in" (148), though as a child she tended to internalize and blame herself for feeling different. Indeed, in the image Dumont's legs dissolve into the white background suggesting that she too appears—and sees herself—as ghostly by virtue of her dark skin.

In *A Really Good Brown Girl*, the photograph that opens the collection becomes a tangible trace of memories that is only fleshed out when put into poetic form; Dumont's mother died around the time the book was published and thus the picture and text become an active tribute to her presence—despite her physical absence. The title Dumont gives to the image becomes a way of talking to her mother's ghost, while acknowledging the inadequacy of such a dialogue. Her text also raises fundamental questions about how one defines or identifies a ghost, by suggesting that skin colour and gender are an integral part of the politics of ghosting, a point that is especially significant when coupled with a poem Dumont has written about her father titled "ghosted" which appears in her second collection, *green girl dreams mountains*. Here the speaker laments the figurative consumption of her father by colonial stereotypes of white maleness as Dumont portrays the complexity of her family dynamics and the structures and institutions that led to her mother's and her own experiences of physical and emotional violence.

Located near the conclusion of a section aptly called "Homeground," in which poems such as "not Dick & Jane" emphasize the bleakness of the speaker's childhood in an ironic fashion by invoking the 1950s white brother and sister duo used in easy readers, "ghosted" tells the story of "a father who hid in a manly bottle, and / a mother who kept one eye on him / and the other on her suitcase" (Dumont 2001: 28). The poem itself begins with the image of a "liquor-grin" that turns the speaker's father into a caricature on "the skid row streets" he frequents when away from his manual labour job and out for a night of fun (33). The narrator then describes the father's elaborate preparations for these weekend adventures and his wife's ambivalence about his binge drinking, which she understands is a reaction to his frustrations at "the whiteman who is always boss / at his own cheap labour / at the money that never goes far enough" (33). Dumont's speaker is especially attentive to the ways in which self-perception and visibility are altered once the father figure leaves the private domain of the household. Whatever self-love is suggested by the father's act of crouching "over the washbasin" and leaning into "a small mirror / as one would into a kiss" (33) to ensure the perfect shave and a handsome profile is undercut by the reality of his daily life which is one of second-class citizenry. Moreover, the speaker makes it very clear that the visibility of the father within the household—even as an irritant to his wife—is trumped by the racism and resulting invisibility that he faces on the job, which he tries to forget with alcohol. This paradox of (in)visibility has a devastating result as the speaker's father is "taken again / ghosted away / from the one who is my father / into a stranger, into an Indian / staggering down the street (34). By describing the shift from familiar family figure to Native stranger and ghost, the poetic "I" makes plain how the father's increased visibility on the street erases her own private vision of him, sober, "as the one who is my father" (34); thus perception and point of view become critical factors in determining who is visible and whether that visibility is indeed beneficial to the individual and his or her community. But the speaker's own invisibility, her lack of visual presence in the text, and her paradoxical control of the written words on the page make her far more powerful than her father, exposing the dangers of presuming that to be seen is to be heard. Instead, her poem demonstrates that visibility needs to be used strategically, rather than destructively as is the case with her father, who has become consumed by an image over which he has no control.

By placing the picture of her mother at the beginning of *A Really Good Brown Girl*, Dumont challenges the "spectral violence" that Emberley notes is integral to culturally hegemonic models of the Aboriginal family (Emberley 2007: 12) and displaces the primordial father; instead, she insists upon the primacy of her mother. By placing the photograph of her mother at the beginning of a poetry collection about her own identity, Dumont interrogates the naturalization of the family unit and the colonial web of power that has traditionally determined how the family should appear. Of course, some elements of Dumont's photo confirm the continued hegemony of colonial practices and modes of representation. The portrait accords with European bourgeois notions of what constitutes family rather than acknowledging Native kinship relations. Moreover, Dumont and her mother are clothed in what one could call "colonial garb" (164) to the extent that they are wearing suitably lady-like and city-appropriate attire according to white North American post-Second World War standards of middle-class propriety, including the stark white-toned scarf that further illuminates the contrast between Dumont's skin and hair colour and the lightness and brightness of the photo's cityscape backdrop. And Dumont's collection itself offers poetic reminders of her mother's insistence that her daughter behave appropriately; in "Squaw Poems," for example, Dumont's speaker recalls her mother's damnation of "another Indian woman" with the words, "black squaw," and takes that as "the measure of what I should never be," aspiring instead to be "so god-damned respectable that white people would feel slovenly in my presence" (Dumont 2001: 18). But Dumont also refashions the static nature of this image of colonization, and her legacy of shame, with the title of her collection, *A Really Good Brown Girl*, and the subversive quality of her own self-presentation in visual and verbal terms. As Dumont recalls, her desire to claim and retain the moniker of "a really good brown girl," recounted in the poem "Memoirs of a Really Good Brown Girl," becomes a challenge to the violent imposition of colonizing measures on Aboriginal women and children—from her brother's white fiancée's attempts to physically scrub away Dumont's brown-ness so she can be a idealized version of a flower girl, to an English professor's asking when he read the title, "you mean really well, don't you?" to which Dumont's speaker emphatically replies, "No, I mean really good" (Dumont 1996: 15).

For Cree poet Louise Halfe, kinship relations are central to her understanding of self. Halfe initially published her second collection, *Blue Marrow* (1998), with a mainstream Canadian press, McClelland and Stewart, which used on the book's cover a formal portrait of her great-grandparents, framed in a oval border, thus paradoxically duplicating historical models of representational violence done to the Aboriginal family. And this travesty occurred despite the contents of the collection which itself explores and critiques that violence while also paying homage to generations of Halfe's female kin who have shaped her life. In the McClelland and Stewart edition, there are three prominent images: the black-and-white formal oval-shaped portrait of Halfe's great great-grandparents which appears on the cover of the collection, a casual unlabelled shot of family members, including Halfe herself as a small child, placed nine pages into the text, and finally, a small author's photo on the back cover of the book, which shows Halfe gazing sideways. However, when the press decided not to produce another print run, Coteau Books, a small press located in Halfe's home province of Saskatchewan that had published her first collection, agreed to release a second, slightly altered edition of *Blue Marrow* (2004a). One of the most notable changes to this edition is in the choice and form of the photographs that Halfe includes; as Halfe explains in the "Acknowledgements" to the new edition, "I was given an opportunity to revisit the text in a new way, and I am deeply appreciative of the vision that resulted from this" (Halfe 2004a: 101). The Coteau cover image splices a photograph of "the author's grandmothers," her father's mother and three sisters, with an image of the Northern Lights (iv), a choice that seems especially appropriate for a poet whose translated Cree name is Sky Dancer (see Fig. 2). And the oval-shaped formal

shot of Halfe's great-great-grandparents now appears inside the book, between the acknowledgements and the first page of the text, visually representing the focus of the collection: "a Cree woman's" search for "a past that is both personal and communal, remembered and imagined" through the "stories her foremothers whisper, shout, and sing as their voices roll across the prairie" (Cook 2000: 85). Thus, her great-great-grandmother's stereotypical visage of stoic silence is framed by Halfe's dedication to her mother and grandmother on one side, and a prayer to the "Voice Dancer," the "Guardian of Dreams and Visions" on the other (Halfe 2004a: 1), the latter of which was absent from the earlier edition of *Blue Marrow*.

Halfe's direct invocation of the Cree Spirits on the first page of *Blue Marrow* is followed by a fragmented version of the well-known Christian hymn, *Glory Be to the Father*, which is also a new addition to the collection. In this case, however, the standard references to the Father, the Son and the Holy Spirit are replaced by the Cree words for "Mother Earth," "the Grandmother Keeper of the Sacred Legends," and "Dream Spirit," as outlined in the book's Cree-English glossary (2004a: 107-108). Halfe reconfigures the Christian conversion tactics imposed on the Cree, in which the female power of Spirits (at least as depicted in *Blue Marrow*) was displaced by a singular male god. She brings renewed life to her great-grandparents' portrait by situating it between her textual efforts to embrace her Cree language and spiritual belief system and her visual invocation of her grandmothers on the front cover. Moreover, Halfe notes that the front cover also challenges white western notions of family with a patriarch at the helm, explaining that "it's [a picture of] my father's mother and her three sisters so automatically they became my grandmothers. They're not my great aunts as [the] mainstream would perceive [them]. They're my grandmothers" (Andrews 2004: 3). And she continues this effort to reclaim her ghostly female ancestors' stories and her role as a living descendent by including a different author photo on the back page of the text, a shot of Halfe smiling and gazing directly into the camera.

While the biographical note with the author photo is more detailed in the second edition of Halfe's *Blue Marrow*, the other images within the collection remain unlabelled, a deliberate and ironically-charged choice, which as the poet explains in a recent interview, reflects the fact that "[t]hey [non-Native settlers and officials] wanted us nameless" (Andrews 2004: 3). Her frustration with this historical tendency to not identify Native peoples by name leads Halfe to ask, "Why should I provide names when there is a litany of names that you guys figured out?" (3). Halfe expresses her anger at the imposition of colonial names on her family tree in *Blue Marrow* by refusing to identify her ancestors in her own text, an ironic gesture that focuses attention on the unsaid dimensions of her female Cree ancestors' lives, which she reimagines throughout the collection. The absence of identifying names and dates on the photographs in the latest edition of *Blue Marrow* reminds readers that it is a collection that in many respects continues to privilege those familiar with the Cree language, tribal traditions and history. For instance, Halfe's use of the image of her grandmothers that is digitally juxtaposed with the beauty of the Northern lights may be, for many readers, merely aesthetically pleasing, creating a sense of the power that these women possess even in death, as the women hover like ghosts in the sky above the nighttime horizon. But as Linda Jaine and Louise Halfe explain in "Traditional Cree Philosophy: Death, Bereavement and Healing," the Cree believe that "the Northern Lights occur when the Spirits [of the dead] are dancing" (Halfe and Jaine 1989: 11); hence, Halfe's coupling of these two images takes on an added, culturally specific reference for those who are "in the know" by reminding those readers of the significant roles that these women ghosts continue to play in the lives of their female Cree descendents.

Certainly, *Defamiliarizing the Aboriginal* provides a sophisticated critical framework for reading the photographs I've mentioned here, in this way contributing to an understanding of the colonial violence done to Aboriginal people by obscuring Native kinship relations with the figures of the European bourgeois family. Such alternative identifications and constructions of familial relations enact the ideas that are outlined in Emberley's book but they also add to and complicate the textual examples she provides. By drawing links to contemporary Native and Canadian texts here, I want to draw readers' attention to the applicability of theory, its pragmatic and indeed, its potential social, cultural and political value when put into conversation with Aboriginal texts that are themselves focused on reconfiguring the colonized family, or recognizing pre-colonial Native family structures as primary. But I also wish to highlight the differences between and among Native texts—the individual cultural differences with which each female poet addresses her own understanding of family through language and image. Dumont and Halfe explore what Emma LaRocque has called "the art of reinvention" (LaRocque 2006: 15) for their own purposes and thus, invariably stretch and rework the boundaries of theory to articulate their distinct selves.

References

Andrews, Jennifer. 2004. "Among the Word Animals": A Conversation with Marilyn Dumont. *Studies in Canadian Literature* 29(1): 146-60.

———. Forthcoming. *In the Belly of a Laughing God: Reading Humour and Irony in Native North American Women's Poetry*. Toronto: University of Toronto Press.

Cook, Méira. 2000. Bone Memory: Transcribing Voice in Louise Bernice Halfe's *Blue Marrow*. *Canadian Literature* 166:85-110.

Dumont, Marilyn. 1996. *A Really Good Brown Girl*. London: Brick.

———. 2001. "ghosted." *green girl dreams mountains*, 33-34. Lantzville, BC: Oolichan:

Emberley, Julia V. 1993. *Thresholds of Difference: Feminist Critique, Native Women's Writings, Postcolonial Theory*. Toronto: University of Toronto Press.

———. 2007. *Defamiliarizing the Aboriginal: Cultural Practices and Decolonization in Canada.* Toronto: University of Toronto Press.

Gingell, Susan. 2009. Review of *Defamiliarizing the Aboriginal. Chimo* 57: 17-21.

Halfe, Louise. 1998. *Blue Marrow.* Toronto: McClelland and Stewart.

———. 2004a. *Blue Marrow* revised ed. Regina: Coteau Books.

———. 2004b. Interview by Jennifer Andrews. Unpublished tape transcription: 1-15.

Halfe, Louise and Linda Jaine. 1989. Traditional Cree Philosophy: Death, Bereavement, and Healing. *Saskatchewan Indian* March: 11.

LaRocque, Emma. 2006. Opening Address. *Studies in Canadian Literature* 31(1): 11-18.

Julia Emberley

When Author Meets Critic ...
The Worlding of Epistemologies

When Susan Gingell and Jill Didur initially contacted me about presenting my book for the "Author Meets Critic" event during the Canadian Association of Commonwealth Language and Literature conference at the 2009 Congress, I was, of course, delighted and honoured. Each of the responses by the brilliant and creative critics, Jennifer Andrews, Terry Goldie and Deanna Reder, addressed an aspect of epistemological inquiry; they also raised questions about how to inquire into the very meaning of what constitutes epistemology or epistemologies. Ironically, this was the place of departure for my book, *Defamiliarizing the Aboriginal*, to the extent that I originally wanted to move away from the stranglehold of the scientific episteme and focus, instead, on modes of textuality and their representational effects as constituting alternative knowledges. In other words, I wanted to shift the epistemic centre from "knowledge" in its narrowly defined scientific sense to a broader understanding that could encompass the visual, textual and plastic arts, and, in so doing escape the hard core knowledge industries of the information manufactory. The more elastic forces of creativity represent for me neglected sites of knowing. The critical responses to my book have provided me with an opportunity to re-enter the fold of epistemology and to consider the ways my work questions the construction of scientific epistemologies, especially those related to Freud and the psychoanalytical paradigm and Marxist and Marxist-feminist discourses on the family. Moreover, it is essential, I think, to combine this critical perspective with the affirmative recognition that Indigenous epistemologies are already in circulation, especially in forms of storytelling, some of which I examined in my earlier book *The Cultural Politics of Fur* (1997), where I looked at what I called the "storytelling technologies" by Inuit storytellers used to comprehend animal/human relations. In *Defamiliarizing the Aboriginal*, I continued this work by examining some of the Indigenous artistic and literary practices based in Indigenous storytelling epistemologies. The problematic I initiated in these previous works, I would now characterize as a turn toward the *worlding of epistemologies*.

First on the agenda is the question of language and theoretical speculation. I am, as it were, a self-professed theory nerd. But my attachments to theory are far more playful and genuine when is comes to exploring the limits of language—the limits of what language can express—and also the limits of Western epistemological frameworks. I explore further the limit of the Western episteme in a forthcoming essay, by examining Lewis Henry Morgan's 19th-century account of the Iroquois "Laws of Hospitality" and Jacques Derrida's deconstructive foray into "cosmopolitan hospitality."[1]

This investigation of hospitality and the domestic archive in Morgan is in no way intended to demonstrate the possibility of any influence on Derrida of Morgan's work; rather, bringing Morgan and Derrida into conversation is, I think somewhat significant, even provocative, in terms of thinking about an ethics of hospitality today, especially in non-European territories. I am concerned to trace different lines of knowledge transfer, in order to disclose "cosmopolitan hospitality" as an already existing concept and not, as is generally thought, a strictly European enlightenment conception. Ironically, it would appear to have its roots *ab origine*—stemming from the aboriginality of ethnographic construction. Nevertheless, Doris Pilkington's storytelling memoir engages in an Indigenous ethics of cosmopolitan hospitality by extending an invitation to the reader to hear her story. Her work shifts the epistemic centre from its European conception and returns the notion of cosmopolitan hospitality to its Indigenous epistemological context in which the notion of hospitality is situated in the material protocols and kinship affiliations of the home, family and territory.

I find that the further I test the limits of theoretical texts, the more I am permitted entry into the subtext of aboriginal subjugation as the dialectic outcome of European imperial conquest. What can one do with such texts but push their meaning into sense, into the sensory experience of what it is they lose in their self-regulatory and paranoid attempts to keep *Ab Origine* on the other side of the door? It would seem necessary to find another exit strategy. Thus language lies at the limits of multiple inquiries into epistemologies.

Are there different epistemologies? Can the differences between frameworks of knowing be reconciled as the current neoliberal cultural logic of redress would argue for? Can one find in Freud and same-sex families, as Terry Goldie would have it, a text and mode of existence that is equally familiar and defamiliarizing, both universal and particular? Goldie notes in "Critic meets Author" that "The *familia* is an understanding of any potential domestic unit. It becomes an elastic universal, as the term might be *famulus* to any *familia*. One of the successes of the more sensitive recent studies of sexuality, both historical and transnational, is to show that the family seems to be key to most relationships but that there might be no limit to the forms the family can take." While I appreciate the strategic logic at play in Goldie's emphasis on the heterogeneity of the familial apparatus, it still needs to be said that there *are* limits to the form the family can take both legally and socially. While the human(e) potential for a seemingly infinite variety of family forms might be desirable, the family is a social and cultural form and therefore subject to any given society's legitimating and disciplinary practices. But the "family" is also, and I think that here Goldie and I agree, a potential site of resistance. That is why the right to a family has been and continues to be fought for. Even Marx, and especially Engels, in *The Communist Manifesto*, recognized that the exploitation of labour both in the factory and in the home made the experience of familial love a near impossibility, as do social forms of violence such as homophobia, racism and sexism. I remain adamant that the imperial and colonial forces that destroyed Indigenous kinship relations by attempting to supplant them with the alienating form of the European bourgeois family was a major factor in the history of Canadian cultural genocide. What would it take to recognize that Indigenous kinship modes of affiliation are incommensurable with European models of "the family" but not critically unobtainable on the basis of a combined Indigenous epistemological and cultural materialist approach? One first has to re-read Marx and Engels through the pores of feminism, critical race and queer theory, and then one has to combine such a reading with Indigenous knowledges of kinship as a political and social matrix of culturally constructed relations. This is a material and epistemological possibility.

Goldie's debate with me over Freud is similarly troubled by the relationship between history and "the universal." Of my critique of Freud's use of the so-called Primitive Family to situate the significance of the European Bourgeois Family, Goldie asks, "Is this a history or rather once again the universal? It is not that the primitive leads to the present, but that the primitive is in this sense the same as the universal." Why do I feel like I have taken a step back into the *unworlded* sphere of liberal humanism? A place where the mythic has been transformed into the universal? Can't something be universal, such as kinship relations, and also subject to historical and geopolitical forces? Why either/or? Is Goldie in danger of conflating philosophical truth with historical truth? Yes, I think so.

Goldie's critique unravels the crux of the problem that the worlding of epistemologies poses. What, in other words, is to be done with the *inassimilable* that Indigenous kinship relations unfold? Goldie argues for an approach that reconciles such differences in reading Freud's use of the Primitive Family as an instance of his (that is Freud's) capacity to recognize its universality. But the recognition of the Primitive Family as part of a universal family comes at a price—the disavowal of the history of imperialism and the colonial restructuring of Indigenous kinship societies. At the centre of colonial restructuring was the destruction of a kinship political-*oeconomy*. The term "oeconomy" refers to the economy of the household. Through government policies and legislation such as the *Indian Act*, women's and children's bodies were targeted. In addition to the violence created by such legislative documents, I include other modes of representation such as Robert Flaherty's filmic representation of the Inuit family in *Nanook of the North* (1976) and Freud's use of ethnography in *Totem and Taboo* (1913) to shore up his theory of oedipalization. I constructed an *assemblage* of theoretical, visual and legislative materials in chapter three of my book to demonstrate the pervasiveness of an imperial idea and how various modes of representation, including the legislative, the visual and the theoretical were all part of a complex network of the colonial episteme, and importantly, at times constituted a form of *representational violence*. Not only is it vital to recognize the forms that colonial violence can take, it is equally important to subject the use of violence, in all its representational and other material forms, to a process of Indigenization.

One of the major effects of the hegemonic shift that occurred with the postcolonization of an Indigenous kinship political-oeconomy was the realization of patriarchal nationalism. Such is the context, I believe, in which to comprehend the drawing of Indigenous men into complicity with the patriarchal family of bourgeois civilization. In exchange for the social power they would accrue in supporting this move, they were offered "subjecthood" within the newly emerging postcolonial nation that was Canada. The cultural logic of reconciliation comes at a price and that "price" is patriarchal state membership. Such are the contradictions of the "inclusionary" politics of neoliberalism.

Instead of a cultural logic of political redress that acknowledges "differences" only to try to absorb them into the philosophical regime of universals-without-history, I would suggest an approach that seeks to trace the incommensurabilities that lie at the edge of "worlds," where an inquiry into epistemologies means amassing the discourses of knowledge within an historical context and with reference to its specific contingencies. Aboriginality was one of the key contingencies of European discourses of civilization during its "enlightenment" period. What is becoming evident through the production of Indigenous epistemologies and ontologies is that *Aboriginality* was civilized man's transcendental dream of a vast, unending and unlimited plenitude of existence—like something you might find in the Arctic, in the final footsteps of Dr. Frankenstein, or in Flaherty's homosocial bond with his imaginary simulacrum, Nanook.

What we need to do is *dis-locate* (rather than re-locate) *the episteme*, to suggest, for example, as I think Deanna Reder does in "Critic meets Author," that this so-called Other is not in some distant Neverland but right smack in the middle of your living room. Bringing it "home" is what it's all about. And, not surprisingly, this "home" is uncannily familiar as Jennifer Andrews demonstrates in her interviews with Indigenous poets, Marilyn Dumont and Louise Halfe, in which she discusses the importance of photographic images of family life. These images come to represent a medium through which to unravel several stories and layers of kinship—those between people and those between images and texts. Reder seeks to shift the epistemic centre from "a long standing European sign system" to one that draws on the language and ideas of Indigenous knowledges. She inquires:

> At what point will we open up our imaginations to shift our focus from European narratives to ones from Native America? Could not the scene of mother and child evoke thoughts of First Woman? How would it shift our analysis if we thought of domestic abuse through the stories of Rolling Head or Sedna the Sea Witch?

I think what she proposes is part of an exciting new direction in Indigenous studies. One place to pursue such a new critical direction lies in the material worlding of epistemologies so that we can recognize within everyday sites of knowledge production traces of material evidence that can be picked up and interrogated for what they can tell us about other ways of seeing and knowing. This might mean taking the risk of dipping my hand into that bloody pool in Deanna's construction of a living room (i.e., a room that also "lives") and pulling out Sedna's fingerless body, not in order to rescue her but to hear her story—and, importantly, to respond.

Note

1. See my forthcoming article "Epistemic Encounters: Indigenous Cosmopolitan Hospitality, Marxist Anthropology, Deconstruction and Doris Pilkington's *Rabbit-Proof Fence*," in *English Studies in Canada*, Spring 2010.

References

Department of Indian and Northern Affairs Canada. 1981. *Indian Acts and Amendments, 1868-1950*, 2nd ed. Ottawa.

Emberley, Julia V. 1977. *The Cultural Politics of Fur*. Montreal: McGill-Queen's University Press.

———. 2007. *Defamiliarizing the Aboriginal: Cultural Practices and Decolonization in Canada*. Toronto: University of Toronto Press.

Flaherty, Robert J., dir. 1976. *Nanook of the North*. (1922). Home Vision Video.

Freud, Sigmund. 1913. *Totem and Taboo: Resemblances between the Psychic Lives of Savages and Neurotics*. Trans. A. A. Brill. New York: Vintage.

Marx, Karl and Friedrich Engels. 2004. *The Communist Manifesto* (1888). Edited and translated by L. M. Findlay. Peterborough, ON: Broadview Press.

Pilkington, Doris. 1996. *Follow the Rabbit-Proof Fence*. Brisbane, AU: University of Queensland Press.

REVIEW ESSAY

Len Findlay

Barbara Godard—Navigating Literary and Cultural Traffic

Review Essay of

Barbara Godard. 2008. *Canadian Literature at the Crossroads of Language and Culture*, edited by Smaro Kamboureli. Edmonton: NeWest Press.

Literary studies have flourished as an important component of several interrelated forms of cultural sovereignty (and cultural cringing) in Canada. Too often, however, this flourishing has occurred via the self-insulation and overzealous guardianship of the "purely" literary against the claims of language (what literature is made of) and culture (the primary frame within which literature can both assert its distinctiveness and increase its reach and resonance beyond the page or stage). For anyone hoping that academics will dare to forsake the safe scholarly or institutional path for a crossroads where traffic is still significantly unregulated despite the surveillance devices and social forces of several sorts committed to policing curiosity and expression, take heart. Accidents both good and bad will continue to happen at the convergence of linguistic and cultural thoroughfares, and Barbara Godard was a good accident waiting to happen in such sites. Again and again she stopped the academic and literary traffic, causing delays and detours in the daily professorial or scholar-mendicant commute and demanding that order and efficiency disclose their sources and beneficiaries. She was a senior scholar with a fierce allegiance to traditional forms of humanities homework, but she was equally committed to cultural jamming, political protest, unsettler culture and the irreducible indeterminacies that put all forms of authority recurrently at risk. In short, she was an example to us all.

This much awaited collection brings together nine of Barbara Godard's essays written over the course of almost twenty years. The essays have been well selected and chronologically arranged (with two astutely disruptive exceptions) to demonstrate Professor Godard's remarkable intellectual range, remorseless intelligence and unflinchingly political engagement with the ideals and actualities of literary, cultural and social institutions. These essays are preceded by an extended "conversation" between the collection's editor, Smaro Kamboureli, and Godard during which a series of well chosen questions and shrewd elaborations elicit some remarkable insights into Canadian academic and cultural history. These exchanges are a must-read for anyone interested in how Canada acquired a sense of itself, its literatures and its cultural and political distinctiveness from the 1960s through the 1980s. Evidently at ease with her interlocutor, and drawing on her remarkable memory and critical sense of her own social formation (and deformation), Godard reveals how her student activism at high school—especially its anti-nuclear, internationalist and anti-imperialist expressions—prepared her to see (and increasingly name for what it was) the male colonial humanities club of her undergraduate years at the University of Toronto. There she looked in vain for Canadian writers and women writers on the curriculum, only to find that such interests were privately pursued by a few faculty in an almost clandestine way. Ontario in the 1960s seemed to lag behind Quebec in its radical and nationalist impulses, and Godard, with the active encouragement of Malcolm Ross who edited the New Canadian Library series, realized that U of T was no place for an emergent comparativist, feminist theorist who "In an era of liberation struggles, saw ... parallels between Africa and Canada's situation as a political colony of England, an economic colony of the US, and a colonialist power in relations with Quebec and aboriginal peoples" (20).

Her move to graduate studies at l'Université de Montréal brought Godard into contact with visiting Marxist theorist Lucien Goldmann and with a leading comparativist and proponent of the sociology of literature from l'Université de Bordeaux, Robert Escarpit, under whose supervision she would complete her doctoral dissertation. An immediate beneficiary of exposure to another mother country in another language and with quite different intellectual traditions, Godard moved from Quebec to Paris and Bordeaux. In Paris in 1968 she took a course from Roland Barthes just as he was "taking the deconstructive turn" (23). With Goldmann and Barthes she was able to read her quasi-revolutionary present through the historical and fictional mediations of 1789 and 1848. In addition, she taught in the same department as Hélène Cixous at l'Université de Paris VIII, Vincennes, where the curriculum was as hotly debated as was the role of the student movement in refashioning French universities by renegotiating relations among students, intellectuals and workers. Heady stuff!

As many feminist scholars have shown—though to uneven effect—resistance and revolution are habitually gendered masculine. The girls can have the occasional walk-on—or more frequently, lie-down—role, but, really, social transformation is a job for the lads. However, her early and abiding interest in women writers in Quebec, and her encounters with Cixous and Christine Brooke-Rose in Paris, positioned Godard well to identify and contest patriarchal and paternalistic views wherever she encountered them and to help deconstruct the academic apparatus of injustice. In the 1960s and early 1970s, arguably more than ever before, change was being conceived and pursued along the channels (or "intersexions") of race and gender as well as class, and Godard embraced that reorientation. She returned to Canada with an extraordinary set of competencies and interests that would be eagerly snapped up by any university worth its salt ... or so one might have thought. Student unrest and the assertiveness of youth more generally in Canada had induced profound cultural changes well assessed by Bryan Palmer (2009) in his recent book on the 1960s, but Godard nonetheless found "there were no jobs" except on a limited contract basis at York. Then as now, cultural work, especially activist, unsubduably smart work, was deliberately under-resourced in the hope it would go away or eke out a muted and precarious existence on the margins of academe and in the gutters of urban Canada. It took close to seven years for Godard to achieve a tenure-track appointment at York, even while she was developing crucial literary and cultural networks with a virtual "Who's Who" of Canadian writers, artists and critics, refusing distinctions between cultural production and critique while honing her skills as editor, bibliographer, translator and collaborator (with Frank Davey at Coach House Press, for instance). Her membership in an earlier generation of the academic prekariat brought home to her with lasting force the fact that language and culture are always comparative, "always positioned in relation to another temporal moment or geopolitical space and so considered not in terms of identity but of relationality within vectors of power" (26-27). That is why so much of her teaching and writing insists on identifying the institutional conditions under which it is produced. For anyone anxious about the compromises that attend the institutionalizing and nationalizing of cultural studies, and that should include all readers of *TOPIA*, Godard shows what it takes to make a career out of skepticism, candour and transdisciplinary creativity and critique.

Godard's influence as a teacher and mentor has been remarkable. Indeed, a sense of what she was sharing with her students helps one to understand a large swath of theoretically inflected literary and cultural scholarship in Canada over the past two decades. Very directly connected to her pedagogy, her essays are amazingly well informed, a display of intellectual currency without compromise or trendiness. More often prismatic than diaphanous, and occasionally outright runic, her writing offers intriguing connections to a broad range of texts, issues and topics, one of the most important of which is feminism in several tongues and registers: English, French, Aboriginal, Afro-Caribbean. And here I have to say that one of the key principles in my own teaching and writing—namely, that gender is *never* irrelevant to the interpretation of any cultural text or practice—owes much to Godard's example. Especially impressive was her ability to combine selfless building with unsparing analysis, nourishing *Fireweed* and *Tessera* and a clutch of new and progressive Canadian learned societies while effectively challenging academic and other masculinities and sexualities in more conservative settings and trying to educate more established colleagues while at times enduring some very fierce and personally targeted attacks.

The effort to replace or interrupt master discourses like "Freudianism, Marxism, and structuralism" (90) would have been unthinkable and unachievable without the theoretical and practical work of feminists. However, as Godard herself has regularly demonstrated, gender guarantees nothing; recognition of gender's constructed and contingent nature is not the termination of struggle but one of its most important yet everchanging sites. And so Godard's connections to and promotion of Quebec theorists/writers like Nicole Brossard, Madeleine Ouellette-Michalska and Louky Bersianik extended her sense of sisterhood-in-struggle while requiring her to relive the realities of two solitudes within the fraught radical/liberal mutualities of a proto-feminist nation. Godard's 1990 essay on "Critical Discourse in/on Quebec" (83-107) charts uncomfortably the looping of this strain of Quebec feminism through the American academy before it could be fully welcomed by feminists in English Canada. Telling such a story can lose you personal friends and allies as well as readers, especially in smugly or defensively unilingual circles, but Godard was up to that task. She took up the challenge again nine years later in another magisterial essay reprinted in *Canadian Literature at the Crossroads of Language and Culture*, "A Literature in the Making: Rewriting and the Dynamism of the Cultural Field," where she tracks and analyzes the reception of Quebec women's literary work by scholars in the US and in English Canada via the "aesthetic and social discourses of literary criticism"(273). This transnational triangulation allows her to expose an American need for successful women authors and a related American need to feminize the whole of Canada. Meanwhile, English Canada is seen to be obsessed academically with the deconstruction of individual texts and journalistically with author-centred global marketing and aesthetic "greatness." What is missing in all of this, according to Godard, is "the social labour through which certain positions are produced as aesthetic subject (*auctor*) while others are reduced to the position of marginalized other." Appealing to the authority of Bourdieu as already a more formidable force (with the at least equally influential Jacques Dubois) in Quebec than elsewhere in Canada, Godard proceeds to affirm that "Modalities of cultural practice can be defined only as a system of differential positions taken in relation to other possible *prises de position* within a political economy of the sign. Conflicts between different positions create the particular structure of a field through a dialectic of distinction between restricted and general fields of production" (275). Godard marks incidents of "slippage" between institution and field which allow literary criticism to act as "the ideologeme 'autonomy' in a compensatory discourse of the Quebec field of production that affirms its specificity in a dialectical relation with an other," the dominant Paris-Montreal axis "in which the colonial power retains its prestige if not all its power," (277) while the feminizing of the Quebec and Canadian nations continues from several sources and in multiple styles of co-optation and (re)containment.

Perhaps the most enduringly suggestive work gathered here concerns translation. *Tessera's* 1989 issue on "Translating Women" is seen rightly by Godard as a "distinctive contribution of a 'Canadian school of translation theory'" (43), and she built on that work in many of her subsequent writings. Her approach locates language within the institutions and fields of exchange in a broad but internally differentiated and dynamic system *and* in relation to that system's inevitable excesses and exteriors. For Godard, the instability of the Canadian literary system makes translation imperative and hence, endlessly fraught, haunted by "the nostalgia for purity" (116). Whether in the Canadian state's Official Languages Act (1969) and the grants-in-aid program that followed in 1972, or in Quebec's structuralist and nationalist traditions, aporias remain and miscues express and sometimes aggravate the incommensurabilities and asymmetries they aim to alleviate. Meanwhile, an Aboriginal dissenter from white feminisms like Lee Maracle employs a revisionist historiography to effect the "dis/placement of bilingualism, the heteroglossia of the translation effect" (147). Godard had a remarkable ability to read all sorts of literary, political and cultural texts as productive but coerced and coercing renditions of each other, so that translation in both the narrowest and in the most inclusive senses "does not transform meaning so much as it *invents* meanings as a function of the ideological conflicts *within* the translating culture" (278). This claim may seem a mite deterministic or reductive, but Godard pushes back against her own certitude whenever she suspects a glibness in her analysis or ignorance in her encounter with new work or a culture relatively unfamiliar to her. The final essay in this collection, "Relational Logics: Of Linguistic and Other Transactions in the Americas" (2005), was published in Brazil. Its opening is a brilliant rehearsal of key themes and dynamics in the construction and devouring of the Americas in the name of modernity and in the furtherance of genocide and greed and of the attendant Eurocentrism of a residual comparative literature combined with the resistance offered by an emergent comparative cultural studies. Like a Canadian Galleano, she engages once again with "symbolic goods and the materiality of expressive forms," including visual art and film, as she offers a richly suggestive, magically allusive account of the forces at work in the formation (and deformation) of "a new hemispheric imaginary" (318). Godard convenes langscape and landscape, borderline, Babel and anthropophagy in a stunning "interanimation of peripheries" (357), mostly Canadian and Brazilian. The notion of crossroads does not have the dynamic multidimensionality to capture what is accomplished in this essay. Indeed, I cannot think of anyone else capable of writing such a piece, and I recommend it and its companions as a source of tutelage, provocation and inspiration.

References

Palmer. Bryan D. 2009. *Canada's 1960s: The Ironies of Identity in a Rebellious Era.* Toronto: University of Toronto Press.

REVIEW ESSAY

Nic Veroli

Dada's Last Dada and the Communism to Come

Review Essay of

Badiou, Alain. 2009. *Second Manifeste pour la Philosophie*. Paris: Éditions Fayard.

Badiou, Alain. 2009. *L'hypthese Communiste*. Fécamp, France: Nouvelles Éditions Lignes.

Condrescu, Andrei. 2009. *The Posthuman Dada Guide: Lenin and Tzara Play Chess*. Princeton, NJ: Princeton University Press.

Negri, Antonio. 2009. *The Porcelain Workshop: For a New Grammar of Politics*. New York: Semiotexte.

Therborn, Göran. 2009. *From Marxism to Post-Marxism?* London: Verso.

We are faced today with an unprecedented historico-institutional constellation. Marxism has reached its termination as a political-theoretical sequence and capitalo-parliamentary democracy has become nearly hegemonic while social inequality is once again reaching the heights of ignominy, thereby undermining the democratic legitimacy of the neoliberal state. Even more daunting is the increasingly collapsed border between the neoliberal state and its totalitarian *doppelganger*. On one hand, then, there is a crisis of historical proportions of whatever can still be called "The Left." On the other, there is a meltdown of whatever might have at one point been called "liberal democracy." How can a democracy be constructed that guarantees social equality so as to make substantive its promise of political equality? Only a strong answer to this question can be the basis of a renewed critical political praxis, and perhaps, even, of *any* political praxis. That such an answer has not yet been invented cannot be an argument against the investigation that the question prescribes. Indeed, the ecological crisis, which seems only to worsen as global inequalities become more widespread, makes the construction of such an answer the more urgent.

If to think about politics today means to think within the horizon posed by this question, then Andrei Codrescu's *The Posthuman Dada Guide: Tzara and Lenin Play Chess* is a monument to failure. Codrescu's explicit intention is to defend the relevance of Dadaism, what he views as the 20th-century's most radical artistic avant-garde at the dawn of the "posthuman" age. What can an artistic movement invented in the cafés of war-torn Europe in the late teens of the 20th century teach 21st-century cyborgs, with their cell phones, iPods and virtual bodies? "This is a guide for instructing posthumans in living a Dada life" (1). It is an interesting, though paradoxical proposition since Dadaism was defined at its inception by a rejection of European civilization in the wake of absurd massacres of the First World War. Dada is thus first and foremost a critical gesture. "The first Dadas lived in cities that contained the means for a thorough critique of the world" (3). The question that seems to be hinted at here is thus: What might a radical critical aesthetics look like in the early 21st century? What might the history of Dadaism have to contribute to such an aesthetics? In what way might it be deemed Dadaist?

But the book itself turns out to be a simple apology for advertising and an argument for the further integration of art into the corporate economy. Thus, to the question of the relationship between the social and the political in the 21st century, Codrescu's answer is simply: more of the same. Since artists are for him "entrepreneurs of the imagination" (62), just as U.S. capitalists, the only thing that makes sense is an alliance—a merger even—between the historical avant-garde and the corporate executive. Never mind that this corporate structure is responsible for the fleecing of 90 per cent of the world's population, or that it is leaving tens of millions jobless and homeless in its quest for profits or invents ever-more efficient and affordable means of mass social control (from student debt to psycho-pharmaceuticals to internet filters and telephone network databases…). Codrescu is blind to all of this, absorbed as he is by the drama of the Cold War. Just as with U.S. neoconservatives, there is only one political gesture he understands: that which distinguishes between friend and enemy. But whereas the neocons have moved on from "Communism" to "Islamo-fascism" over the last few decades, Codrescu has only one dada: Lenin. It thus turns out that the actual question around which the book is organized is: "Who won the game? After the collapse of Soviet-style communism in 1991, it looked as though Dada had. But if it had, why do the non-soviet posthumans of late capitalism feel such despair? Could it be that late-capitalism posthumans have arrived at the Leninist future without communism? And if they have, is the game still going on, and does Dada still have work to do?" (12)

Codrescu answers these questions with a resounding "yes indeed!" As surprising as that might seem, the current tendency of capitalism to reduce everyone to a robot is in fact the fault of Lenin. And thus, the only solution is more Dadaist irreverence, like the kind that Codrescu distributes on a regular basis as a commentator on

National Public Radio. Luckily for him, he is just shocking enough to titillate the delicate sensibilities of NPR's white middle-class liberal audience, without ever stepping over the line into what would be *offensive*. But since when has the avant-garde been inoffensive (i.e., acceptable to the status quo)? Codrescu accomplishes the amazing interpretative feat of making what was the most virulent aesthetic critique of so-called "civilization" in the 20th century into one of its greatest pillars in the 21st century. The only real question there is about Codrescu's book is why Princeton University Press, a reputable publishing house, which regularly releases works of impeccable scholarship and remarkable insight, would back it. To this question, I have no answer.

There are some thinkers, however, who are trying to confront the pressing questions of our nascent century seriously and constructively. In recent publications, Göran Therborn, Antonio Negri and Alain Badiou stake out their own positions in a dialogue about the reconstruction of radical emancipatory, equalitarian politics. A former Althusserian Marxist, Therborn today represents the pole of social democracy on the defensive worldwide. For him to be "on The Left" means to be strongly committed to some version of the welfare state accompanied by a parliamentary political system. This view is the official program of most centre-left parties around the world, such as the NDP in Canada, the Democratic Party in the U.S. and the Socialist Party in France. The fundamental proposition of such a position is that so long as the state apparatus is properly managed in order to insure the more or less equitable redistribution of wealth, justice has been achieved in the form of economic equality. It is noteworthy that while Therborn's discussion in *From Marxism to Postmarxism?* is premised on this view, he never articulates it clearly, wedded as he is to an understanding of social scientific objectivity that precludes any critical consideration of his own perspective.

This view also remains hegemonic on the left, despite the spectacular collapse, from the end of the 1980s onward, of the political forces that had sustained the project. Therborn notes this collapse and gives two basic explanations for it: On one hand there has been the global reduction of the historical subject of Marxist politics, the industrial proletariat, which "declined from 19 to 17 per cent [between 1965 and 1990], and among the 'industrial countries' from 37 to 26 per cent" (18). On the other hand, and perhaps more importantly, Therborn laments the failure of social democratic governments to properly manage worldwide inflationary tendencies and rising unemployment during the 1970s, which provided the opportunity for the return of classical economic liberalism under the name of "neoliberalism" (114). Nowhere does Therborn reflect on this failure seriously—probably because of the positivistic prejudice I noted above—and one suspects that the sheer admission of it is difficult for him, as it seems practically tantamount to giving up on the project of human emancipation. But this is precisely where a critical and explicit consideration of what it might mean to "be on The Left" would help get around that implicit but paralyzing sense of doom.

There are reasons for social democracy's historic failure and for its contemporary failure of nerves, and they cannot be reduced to monetarist causes like inflation. The political project of social democracy failed for three basic reasons. It failed first because capital reneged on the historical compromise of the post-1945 world once it became clear that the Cold War was just play-acting (Wallerstein 1995). Secondly, it became clear to the technocratic elite during the 1970s that the high levels of redistribution of wealth necessitated by welfare state policies hindered capital accumulation and investment levels, which ultimately led to the curbing of social spending (Harvey 1991, 2007). Thirdly, and perhaps most crucially, social democracy failed because the project itself was contested from below by those to whom the wealth was being redistributed. For committed intellectuals and activists like Therborn, the project of social democracy is a prison whose bars are made of memories. Social democratic politicians may still win elections once in a while but they no longer can achieve much of what they promise, and in any case, no longer promise much of anything. Therborn's book, while it provides a broad and generous survey of various quantifiably identifiable "Left" movements and theoretical traditions across the world, fails to answer its own question: what happens after social democracy?

Since the publication in 1985 of two short books in French, Alain Badiou's *Peut-on penser la politique?* (1985) and Félix Guattari and Toni Negri's *Communists Like Us* (1990), some intellectuals have begun asking themselves how to rethink the relationship between Marxism and communism. Does the collapse of Marxist politics mean that communist desires are now invalid? What happens to the moral commitment to universal equality after the decline of its main theoretico-political embodiment in the 20th century? For more than twenty years, both Badiou and Negri in Europe, along with some North American intellectuals, have been trying to construct theoretical frameworks that can address these questions squarely.[1] Today, these efforts are yielding both theoretical and practical fruits.

There are two prongs to this project. First, there is the historical effort to understand what happened to Marxism and how to relate to it now. This question is particularly tricky because Marxism is, among other things, a very compelling philosophy of history. Even if one rejects any philosophy of history, breaking with it means developing an alternative conception of history and of one's relationship to the past. For Badiou the termination of a political sequence does not necessarily mean its implicit condemnation since he refuses the Hegelian assumption that history is a totality that progresses from particularity to absolute universality. In other words, Badiou agrees with Heidegger and Foucault that there is no such thing as progress, though he refuses both the ethnic substantialism of the former and the nominalism of the latter. Instead Badiou argues that universal truths permeate the historical flux at certain moments in time or in Events. The political sequence that gave birth to Marxism, began, according to Badiou, with the French Revolution and exhausted itself in the global upsurge of 1968. For

Badiou, though the sequence has come to an end, the "communist hypothesis" has not. His most recent works, a collection entitled *L'hypothèse communiste* and a short book, *Second Manifeste pour la Philosophie*, are an attempt at interpreting the meaning of the "failure" (*l'échec*) of the modern political sequence, and part of his effort to give a metaphysical justification for a politics based on a positive idea of justice. Both books represent a systematic attempt at resurrecting a living communist project. But, while the first is an outstanding work of historico-philosophical interpretation, and the second an overview of an impressive metaphysical construction, there is something deeply absent from them both: a concrete, material reality that grounds the philosophical speculation. There is no doubt that Badiou is a compelling analyst of the history of social movements and revolutions, who is capable of looking at them from the perspective of these events' explicit commitment to communism while remaining deeply critical of their shortcomings, but this cannot hide a deficit in his understanding of the present and of emerging political forces.

The contemporary content of the communist hypothesis remains utterly obscure for Badiou. Aside, paradoxically, from its abstract Marxist-Leninist formulation as the withering away of the state, private property and social classes, Badiou can only say that communism must practise a politics "at-a-distance-from-the-state" (2009b: 202), what some of us have been calling a *politics without the state* (George and Mudede 2002). This shortcoming is, it seems to me, the result of the metaphysical grounding of politics which Badiou operates in *Being and Event* (2005), and more recently in the *Second Manifeste pour la Philosophie*. This grounding is entirely retrospective: "The Event," in fact, has always already happened, and the only question is one of "fidelity" to its truths. The very structure of the thought seems to preclude a substantive reference to the present. Even more problematic is the fact that Badiou's categories are so general that they either seem to undermine the communist project or to let it slip through. The second problem is exemplified by Badiou's treatment of "truth bodies" in the *Second Manifeste*. A truth body is essentially an entity composed of those who adhere to the trace left behind by an Event, for our purposes those who believe in "the idea of communism." It is different from other bodies, not only because its claims are universal (this is its "truth"), but also in that from its parts (i.e., those whose actions compose it) are subtracted the usual material interests of bodies. Those who are its parts are so even if it requires them to abandon their biological needs or economic interest (2009c: 30-31). But if communism is not in the actual material interest of generic humanity as Marx argued it was, then communism can only be an empty chimera, even if it is "the truth."

Antonio Negri's work is, in a way, the negative image of Badiou's work. Where Badiou is single-mindedly retrospective, Negri theorizes the consistency of the present (through notions such as "Imperial sovereignty," the "postmodern caesura" and "biopower") and the historically emergent categories of a new communism ("biopolitics" and the "common"). Where Badiou seems to abandon himself to an astounding voluntarism, Negri develops an analysis of new forms of communist subjectivity ("constituent power," "exodus," "multitude" and "immaterial labor").

Negri's newest book, *The Porcelain Workshop*, is subtitled "For a New Grammar of Politics." In it he attempts to link all of these concepts—which are essentially the product of the last thirty years of his reflection (and of his collaboration with Michael Hardt)—into one systematic whole. Negri takes up the problem of the rupture between the classical sequence of revolutionary politics and the present moment, but he thinks it from the standpoint of three related transitions in the warp and woof of the present. First, from the perspective of political economy, he conceives of the development of the welfare state as the reaction of capital to the insurgency of labour from 1917 to 1968. Second, from the perspective of the political theory of sovereignty, Negri argues that the political power of the state is transformed, in this very development, from a transcendent power in the 19th and early 20th centuries to an immanent network that controls society's activities in depth, delineating the transition from classical liberal sovereignty to "biopolitical sovereignty."[2] Thirdly, from a geopolitical perspective, Negri argues the transition from modernity to postmodernity can be thought under the syntagma of "globalization" as the crisis of national sovereignty. This crisis is manifest in the increasing insignificance of national boundaries in economic and social processes, and by the irreducibility of differences in the global populations (i.e., "the multitude") that are becoming an object of control by global financial and political organizations (19-23).

From here Negri continues the work of developing the concept of a "common." The notion of "common," that which is shared by all—from air and water to language and information—is the basis for thinking through the development of an alternative to both the private property that characterizes capitalist states and the public property of socialism. Neither privatization nor nationalization, argues Negri, is a real political or economic solution to any of the problems—ecological or social—facing the global multitude today. Only the extension of the common, that is to say the maximal pushing back of the frontiers of both state and market can deal with these challenges (61-76).

Negri's position provides the theoretical and programmatic basis for that famed "third way" that is neither capitalism nor socialism (Negri and Scelsi 2008), so frequently promised over the last twenty years, and which has only resulted in Clintonism and Blairism so far. That the influence of his thought has already been acknowledged by some political leaders is one thing (Chavez and Harnecker 2005). But the fact that it can actually power a legislative and activist agenda worldwide, one that does not require its own party is entirely different and, so far as I can tell, something genuinely unique in recent leftist theoretical work.

But while Negri's thought is compelling in all the ways that Badiou's seems limited, it is precisely where Badiou is at his best—in his thinking about time and history—that Negri is at his weakest. For instance, there is no substantive rethinking in Negri of the Hegelian legacy of Marxism or of the theory of a world-historical subject. That Negri now calls this subject "the multitude" instead of "proletariat," invoking the ideas of Deleuze and Spinoza (Negri & Scelsi 2008; Negri 2000, 2004) is not terribly compelling since this multitude still seems to function just as if it were a Hegelian Collective subject. If it did not, then why would its strivings so strikingly resemble those of Hegel's World Spirit? This sort of metaphysical fudging—essentially pointing to a subject, but without the support of a theory of subjectivation—is easy to forget when one is in the throws of political action or involved in the minutiae of strategic analysis, but it comes back to haunt Negri's position with a vengeance when the historical situation changes. It then becomes clear, as happened after Western state apparatuses whipped up a storm of fear in their populations in the Fall of 2001, in such a situation the cavalier attitude toward metaphysics and the theory of the subject of Negri were no longer adequate to the situation, and that is precisely when Badiou's project gained in momentum and popularity.

What the 20th century teaches us, if anything, is that social equality by itself, without political equality, leads to dictatorship and the rule of bureaucratic elites, what went under the name of State Socialism in the Soviet block prior to its dissolution in the 1980s. But what the twenty years since have made clear is that political equality without social equality leads just as surely to dictatorship and to the indefinite extension of the state of exception. While they diverge in significant ways, the ideas of both Negri and Badiou are complementary and need to be somehow reconciled in order to produce a philosophico-political framework that is both morally suasive and politically efficacious. Only on such a basis will we be poised to answer the question of the 21st century, namely that of the articulation of social and political equality.

Notes

1. Notably, this review was unable to discuss the work of the American intellectuals who have been travelling this path, but the main ones should at least be mentioned: Hakim Bey, Murray Bookchin, John Zerzan. It is interesting to note that whereas the Europeans identify themselves as "communists," the Americans overwhelmingly prefer to talk about "anarchism," even if many of them come out of the same tradition (Marxism) and set of problems.

2. On the classical liberal state, see Balakrishnan (2000: 87-100) and on the transition to biopolitical sovereignty, see Foucault (1990: 133-60).

References

Badiou, Alain. 1985. *Peut-on penser la politique?* Paris: Editions Seuil.

———. 2005. *Being and Event*. Trs. Oliver Feltham. New York: Continuum.

———. 2009b. *L'hypthese Communiste*. Fécamp, France: Nouvelles Editions Lignes.

———. 2009c. *Second Manifeste pour la Philosophie*. Paris: Éditions Fayard.

Balakrishnan, Gopal. 2000. *The Enemy: An Intellectual Portrait of Carl Schmitt*. New York: Verso.

Chavez, Hugo and Martha Harnecker. 2005. *Understanding the Venezuelan Revolution*. Trs. Chesa Boudin. New York: Monthly Review Press.

Foucault, Michel. 1990. *The History of Sexuality*, v.1. New York: Vintage.

George, Diana and Charles Mudede, eds. 2002. *Politics without the State*. Seattle: Seattle Research Institute.

Guattari, Félix and Toni Negri. 1990. *Communists Like Us*. Trans. Michael Ryan. New York: Semiotext.

Harvey, David. 1991. *The Postmodern Condition*. Hoboken, NJ: Wiley-Blackwell.

———. 2007. *A Brief History of Neoliberalism*. New York: Oxford University Press.

Negri, Antonio and Raf Valvola Scelsi. 2008. *Goodbye Mr. Socialism*. New York: Seven Stories Press.

Wallerstein, Immanuel. 1995. *After Liberalism*. New York: New Press.

REVIEWS

Shaobo Xie

Writing "in Terms of a Different Durée": A Review of *Jameson on Jameson*

Review of

Jameson, Fredric. 2007. *Jameson on Jameson: Conversations on Cultural Marxism*, edited by Ian Buchanan. Durham, NC: Duke University Press.

Fredric Jameson is one of the vanishing breed of encyclopedic-minded intellectuals whose writings vary enormously in topics, ranging from theories of history, hermeneutics, literary criticism, cultural politics to science fiction, film, music and architecture. As the most innovative American literary theorist and one of the most prominent Marxist cultural critics writing today, Jameson relentlessly resists the "pull of the practical-empirical and the logic of the market" (Jameson 2007: 238) not only by way of always historicizing, always translating among different aspects of social life, but by way of writing in a style that is itself resistance to reification or commodification. As such Jameson may be at times "difficult" to read and his gigantically comprehensive corpus of work demands of his readers patience and tenacity if they intend to have a productive encounter with it. The recently published *Jameson on Jameson: Conversations on Cultural Marxism* edited by Ian Buchanan is good news to those who need an "easy" access or an enabling introduction to Jameson's encyclopedic writings. This timely, useful, enriching volume consists of ten interviews between Jameson and other critics conducted during two decades. It covers a large variety of issues such as postmodernism, modernism, logic of capital, commodification, representation, allegory, narrative, totality, Utopia, spatialization and world literature. Its interview format of communication allows the interviewee to articulate his ideas and positions in a delightful conversational style, except that it stands unrivalled to books of its kind in scope, lucidity and depth. It also allows readers space for grappling with the same issues and concepts through different angles and in different contexts, granting them a heightened sense of kinship or consistency between the interviewee's earlier positions and later ones. Most importantly, the interviewers' critical insight, intellectual acumen and tactful posing of questions offer Jameson enabling contexts and points of entry for discussing dense concepts and complex issues with a rare clarity and an uncompromising profundity.

One of the provocatively enlightening moments of the volume is when Jameson cautions his interviewers not to think of him as a "Western Marxist" in the general sense of the term, for he is "more of an economic fundamentalist" with a persistent "insistence on the omnipresence of class struggle, and on the dynamics of capital itself," whereas Western Marxism oftentimes risks "slipping into purely cultural critique or this or that psychoanalytic worldview" (203, 204). Here one finds the key, I should say, not only to perceiving the unfailing consistency of Jameson's answers to various questions posed by his interviewers, but to understanding him "inside out" as a Marxist thinker and critic. Throughout the interviews, Jameson draws attention to the economic logic or mode of production as the key factor of social life and historical change. His conception of three phases of modern consciousness or representation is coterminous with his conception of three phases of capitalism, the former being regarded as the latter's correlative. In other words, the economic logic is the "organizing dynamic" (187), and all socio-cultural changes need to be traced back to it. Jameson's signature as a Marxist critic consists in his insistence that to each of the three stages of capitalism, namely the phase of national capitalism, the monopoly or imperialist stage of capitalism, and the moment of transnational or global capitalism, "corresponded a certain set of cultural forms and forms of consciousness" (77), hence the coeval movements of realism, modernism and postmodernism. What connects the domain of political economy and that of cultural production is the thought of totality and its representation. In the period of realism when social life was organized by the logic of national capital, people believed that they knew "what a nation-state was, what a collectivity was, who the enemy was, who was on top and underneath in social classes," and therefore "the issue of representation of a social totality was a problem that could be solved" (141). In the modernist period, under the reign of capitalist imperialism, metropolitan society "extends beyond its national borders and the inside now includes parts of the outside like the colonies" (141). That is, the totality of social life was no longer visible and its representation became a disconcerting crisis. If the high modernists were still at pains to represent the unrepresentable in the spirit of doing the impossible, then representation is totally given up in the age of postmodernism, when global capitalism breaks down the orders of nation-states and the entire globe is interconnectively decentred and "no longer has centers of power" (142). The postmodern world propelled by digital technology and transnational capital changes kaleidoscopically and the totality of society is "out of sight for good" (142).

Another great pleasure of the volume is Jameson's majestically formulated distinction between difference and differentiation, which is matched only by his theorizing of the separation in *A Singular Modernity* (2002). The postmodern age is defined by standardization and collectivization generated by digitalized capitalism. When responding to the question whether the world is dominated by the logic of difference or the logic of sameness, Jameson remarks, "it makes me wonder how many illusions are present in the appeal to difference, even if the logic of the system is differentiation, when by producing difference, it is producing a new form of standardization" (117). Here differentiation is standardization renamed and the post-Fordist economic system has now become a machine for such differentiation (116). It is in this sense that Jameson posits differentiation in contradistinction to difference. There is no real cultural difference while the logic of commodity has colonized nature and the human psyche; nor is there any "lonely rebel" (115) resisting the system of capital when "everyone in one way or another is caught in [the] force field of late capitalism" (187). There is no genuine alternative to the ongoing system if it is not a fundamental change of the late capitalist economic logic. Jameson rehearses the position in different interviews that, despite local, ethnic, cultural, aesthetic differences pertaining to different social groups and geographical spaces, and despite various Nietzschean projects committed to rehabilitating and celebrating difference, the world is increasingly standardized and collectivized by the desire of capital or the logic of commodity. Commodification, the desire for profit, consumerism, schizophrenic temporality, the split subject, the inflation of culture, pastiche, the eclipse of historicity, and the loss of critical distance, all these are the defining features of societies penetrated or dominated by the economic logic of global capitalism. In the entire empire of global capital, differentiation is being deployed as a primary strategy of conquering difference or times and spaces of otherness. As such, differentiation amounts to "a new way of seeing identity as difference" (117), a way of reinforcing or universalizing the logic of commodity via admitting defused or depoliticized difference or resistance.

The greatest reward of the interview book to admirers of Jameson is, I venture to say, his explication and practice of the dialectic. One has to agree with the claim made by Ian Buchanan in his foreword to the volume that "it is the development of dialectical criticism that stands as Jameson's supreme achievement" (x). In Jameson's estimate, the dialectic speaks of three emphases or three jobs. It emphasizes the logic of situation, the necessity of ceaselessly undermining established historical narratives, and most important of all, contradictions. In other words, the dialectic derives knowledge of things from their concrete, historically specific situations instead of individual consciousness or subjective intention; it constantly questions and exposes theories or narratives as no longer adequate or relevant when displaced into new historical moments; it is always at pains to detect and uncover contradictions in everything, be it a system, an institution, a social formation, or a theoretical formulation. Obviously, Jameson regards the ability or necessity to detect contradictions as the key step of the dialectic, for one is always already "dialectical whether one knows it or not" if one "insists on" contradictions (194).

It is his explication and application of the dialectic as such that leads to his belief in social transformation. He sees capitalism as perpetually contradictory as Marx did, as a permanent crisis, and in his view the contradictory system of capitalism unravels what it builds (164). Its constantly innovated or revolutionized technology and methods of production as well as its rapidly augmented wealth are always accompanied by "structural unemployment, increasing poverty, environmental disaster" (164). Jameson reveals himself as a politically committed thinker when he sees "the dialect in a utopian way as a thought mode of the future" (194). His description of the dialectic points to a future-oriented, change-oriented mode of thinking, an open-ended process of thinking toward a utopian future through constantly negating and negotiating with a certain undesired present. That is why the dialectic "has never been fully realized" (194). It is here that Jameson distinguishes between Marxian contradiction and Nietzschean difference, for while the former results in social transformation the latter as an "eternal return," a permanent struggle, "never leads anywhere" (147).

Jameson on Jameson: Conversations on Cultural Marxism is a must for all those who are interested in Marxist analysis of culture and society, or have a passion for dialectical thinking, and for imagining toward alternatives to capitalism. If I were to find fault with the book, however, I would say that its subtitle may provoke some doubt. As already mentioned, Jameson claims to be "more of an economic fundamentalist" whose key emphases are class struggle and the dynamics of capital whereas, in general, Western Marxism, which is somewhat synonymous with cultural Marxism in Jameson's definition, exclusively focuses on cultural critique. In this sense, "cultural Marxism" does not seem to be the accurate name for Jameson's Marxist system of thought. Another problem I have with the volume concerns a perceived moment of inconsistency or exaggeration in Jameson himself. On one hand, he asserts that the postmodern globe "no longer has centers of power" (142); on the other, he keeps talking about the gap between centre and periphery, or between metropolitan centre and third-world periphery. What is at stake here is the relationship between centre and power. According to dictionary definitions, "centre" signifies an organizing or structuring principle, universal norm or a source of authority, influence, decision or action. A centre of any kind, be it located in a college English class, in a discursive space, in a nation-state, or in the empire of global capitalism, always carries a certain kind of power. Therefore the centre versus the periphery is the centre of power versus the periphery dominated. It goes without saying that the world today remains largely dominated by the Western centres of power, or, to borrow terms from Stuart Hall, global capital is still "centered in the West, and it always speaks English" (179). Just as real difference, the difference that poses resistance to the system of global capital, is more of a desire for difference than difference itself, so a world with no centres of power is something yet to be achieved.

Jameson can be read as either inconsistent or exaggerative when he says that the world no longer has centres of power while at the same insisting on the distinction between the metropolitan centre and the third-world periphery. In spite of this inconsistency or exaggeration, however, a world without centres of power, an internationally democratized world, is an important part of Jameson's Marxist utopian agenda. His innovative Marxism includes rewriting the Marxian class struggle in terms of the Colonizer/Colonized confrontation. His utopian vision of the future is a world without any form of oppression and exploitation. He took it upon himself to introduce Marxism to his fellow countrymen when it was largely shunned or distorted in the U.S. and for a few decades he has been consistently pursuing the Marxist problematic—class struggle, the logic of capital, ideology, representation and commodification, the problematic that is not popular despite its urgency in the day of corporatized university and commodified culture. In this sense, Jameson is one of those who have the rare "courage," to borrow terms from Alain Badiou, to think and write "in terms of a different *durée* to that imposed by the law of the world" (41). This "virtue of courage" is exactly what threads through all his responses to his respective interviewers collected in this volume.

References

Badiou, Alain. 2008. The Communist Hypothesis. *New Left Review* 49(January-February 2008): 29-42.

Hall, Stuart. 1997. The Local and the Global. In *Dangerous Liaisons: Gender, Nation, and Postcolonial Perspectives*, edited by Anne McClintock, Aamir Mufti and Ella Shohat, 173-87. Minneapolis: University of Minnesota Press.

Jameson, Fredric. 2002. *A Singular Modernity: Essay on the Ontology of the Present*. London: Verso.

Jameson, Fredric. 2007. *Jameson on Jameson: Conversations on Cultural Marxism*, edited by Ian Buchanan. Durham, NC: Duke University Press.

Julia Aoki

Cities in Motion

A Review of

Boutros, Alexandra and Will Straw, eds. 2010. *Circulation and the City: Essays on Urban Culture*. Montreal: McGill-Queen's University Press.

Alexandra Boutros and Will Straw's *Circulation and the City: Essays on Urban Culture* is one outcome of the Culture of Cities Project, a Toronto-based collaborative initiative that has brought together scholars from the social sciences, humanities and fine arts to study urban cultures, with a focus on Montreal, Dublin, Toronto and Berlin. This, the Culture of Cities Project's most recent published work, offers analyses of movements—of bodies, things, ideas, expressions—in, through and beyond city limits that constitute urban spaces. The anthology is organized thematically in three sections, which address: (1) the imperceptible or seemingly unstable and ephemeral deployments of language, wireless technology and urban planning prescriptions that comprise the city even as their cultural movements and uses exceed it; (2) the punctuated vectors of movement that compose multiple and overlapping temporalities in the city, such as the erasures effected through the detention or deportation of members of diasporic communities, localized inscriptions of global religious practices, temporary performance spaces enabled by the infrastructure of mass transportation and the coordination of multiple rhythms that enable urban space; and (3) temporally and spatially situated structures of circulation that influence the distinctive character of a city, such as those that circumscribe the movements of the commodity object, the urban dweller and discourses of urban renewal and planning.

It is a necessarily incomplete project, but through the assemblage of case studies of various dynamic urban movements, a common strategy attuned to the material contours of urban rhythms comes into view that presupposes the process of transmission as a cultural act. The circulations of people, literature, technology and religion, among others, are processes of meaning-making that at once act upon the material conditions that make them possible and are acted upon by the "interpretive communities, institutional structures, and social codes and practices that govern vectors of mobility" (11). This is not to say that these essays are subsumed by this strategy; it is less a fully formed methodology than an interpretive approach that demonstrates a commitment to the temporal and spatial distinctiveness of their objects of study.

The conceptual cornerstone of this collection is "circulation," a term with increased currency in the social sciences, and which can in part be attributed to the work of anthropologists Benjamin Lee and Edward LiPuma. For these authors, the circulation of cultural forms exists within a self-reflexive structure of reciprocal social action; that is, cultural forms are propelled by the presupposed existence of interpretive communities, which in turn, through discursively mediated practice, perform the boundaries of cultures of circulation. As such, the innumerable forces of movement that seemingly threaten to dissolve, in the fashion of postmodern fragments and fluidities, a singular structure such as the city, are in fact "reciprocal performative acts of promising and agreeing [that] create a quasi-objective social totality that then governs their actions" (Lee and LiPuma 2002: 193). LiPuma and Lee's "cultures of circulation" offer insight into the intention behind *Circulation and the City* to engage with the contours of material cultural expression, which move through and act upon the city with varying and overlapping tempos, yet are constitutive of a conceptual whole.

Entered through the rhythms and movements of specific material forms, the external contours of less tangible cultural practices, and the situated contexts of circulation, the individual essays complicate rationalizing discourses that diminish city spaces to their fixed and immediate attributes. Instead, rigorously dynamic and textured case studies detail materially embedded cultures of circulation, ranging from the variable forms of speech that promote and inhibit spatially contingent social movement, to individuals and communities whose temporalities and mobilities are made volatile by their state-designated status, to the typologies of urban dwellers who inform our understandings of space even as they consistently elude us. The essays in *Circulation and the City* remind us that our urban environments are not containers for accumulating objects and people; they are spaces of layering, intersecting and punctuated rhythms and movements of everyday life.

References

Lee, Benjamin and Edward LiPuma. 2002. Cultures of Circulation: The Imaginations of Modernity. *Public Culture* 14(1): 191-213.

Angela Joosse

Unfurling the Visual

Review of

Elavia, Firoza, ed. 2008. *Cinematic Folds: The Furling and Unfurling of Images.* Toronto: Pleasure Dome.

The range of artworks examined in the sixteen essays of *Cinematic Folds* includes new media pieces, performances, experimental films, horror movies, works by video artists, as well as experimental drawings. What unites these essays is not a focus on a specific medium or genre, but rather the fact that they all contend with cinematic events. Many of the essays also engage with the philosophy of Gilles Deleuze, following through with the implications of his thought in relation to the cinema. Throughout the volume, writing styles range from theoretical analysis to more experimental writing, yet all the essays contain detailed and visceral descriptions of the cinematic works through which their theorizations unfold. The majority of essays in the anthology are new, but reprinted contributions by scholars such as George Toles, Erin Manning, Anna Powell and Steven Eastwood serve to effectively fill out the book's exploration of the many facets of the cinematic. Sequences of film stills, drawings and photographs are also intermeshed with the texts. These images, curated by Linda Feesey, perpetually bring the reader back to the affective impact of images, contribute to filling out the central themes of the book, and also attend to the irreducible gap between word and image.

What is proposed, in bringing this apparently eclectic collection of images and essays together under the rubric of the "cinematic," is a particular approach to theorizing cinematic works. Firoza Elavia's introduction to the volume serves to map out the philosophical implications of thinking in terms of the cinematic. Here she conceptualizes the cinematic "as the movement within and also beyond film frames; it is the asynchronous movement of the mind between world and image" (9). The cinematic, conceptualized as movement, emphasises the experience of cinematic works as temporal proceedings. Thus, rather than "objects" of study drawn out along medium specific or disciplinary lines, the reader of this anthology encounters Deleuze-inflected "events," "multiplicities" and "becomings." The question becomes one of how the cinematic might be considered as "real experience," in its own right, and not strictly as a veil or sign that points to something else. Elavia accordingly shifts the question of what *is* an image, to the question "what can the image do?" (11) Some of the general themes of the anthology as a whole begin to emerge most clearly when consideration is given to this question of what the cinematic image can do.

Many of the essays in the anthology draw out the way that cinematic artworks can blur the bounds between "subject" and "object," emphasising the resonance between the body of the viewer and the artwork. For example, Shannon Bell writes about the way the "noise music and rhythmic/antirhythmic flashing and stopping visuals" of Istvan Kantor's work "sets off the central nervous systems into matching rhythmic convulsions" (109). And in her description of performance pieces by Survival Research Laboratories, Elavia articulates the "sympathetic attunement" that occurs between the cells of the body and the high powered noise frequencies of SRL's performances (131). Throughout the anthology, many of the essays highlight the way that such experiences' attunement are enabled through cinematic experiences that engage with bodily sensation and emotion; this is characterized in Ils Huygens' essay on the "affective regime of fear" in a selection of recent Japanese horror films (53). Moreover, the way that vision integrates with embodied experience is also addressed in a number of the contributions to the anthology. fsIn her essay on electronic colour, Carolyn Lee Kane concurrently draws out the idea of "haptic visuality," or the way that vision can function like touch (199). And Anna Powell, through her examination of certain highly sensuous films by Stan Brakhage, Tony Conrad and Carolee Schneemann, shows how the eyes are not necessarily relegated to the distancing function of the "gaze," but can act as "a conduit between inside and out both organic and anorganic" (234).

A number of the essays in *Cinematic Folds* also draw attention to the way the cinematic image can overwhelm the senses to the effect of breaking down rigid ideas and distinct identities. For example, Jon Davies highlights the import of sensory overload in Ryan Trecartin's *A Family Finds Entertainment*, when he writes, "The bright colours and loud noises, the entire aesthetic, signifies impatience, immediacy, pure *id*, a world where anything is possible because nothing has become grown-up, static and formalized" (106). The realm of subjectivity becomes the particular focus of this creative/ destructive force in several essays in the volume. Carlos Kase examines the role of the camera as a provocative and anxiety inducing agent, showing how certain films by Andy Warhol, Shirley Clarke and Yoko Ono work through highly charged cinematic situations to loosen raw human emotion and dismantle performed subjectivities in front of the camera. Louis Kaplan's essay on "killer artists" opens up a critique of the "myth of authenticity" performed by Expressionist artists (49). Kaplan locates this critique in two films that depict artists who go so far as to incorporate murder into their creative practices. What is at stake here at the intersection between violence and creativity is the fold between art and life. As Elavia states in her essay on "molecular becomings," "Art, rather than being a representation *of*, or *about*, or even a representational system of the semantic order is, in fact, a construction of the real that is yet to come, that constructs a new type of reality" (132).

Furthermore, the alteration of time and shifts in perception that can occur through cinematic works, also emerge as a key themes in a number of essays in the volume. These essays show that one of the things the cinematic image can do is generate new modes of perception. For example, George Toles scrutinizes the presence of the "time close-up" in Martin Arnold's films; through repetition and delay time is altered and the some of the invisible moments of the cinema become perceptible. Erin Manning shows how Etienne-Jules Marey's cinematic experiments, though aimed at drawing out the imperceptible, proceed to create new techniques for perception. Manning states that, "Time collapses into an intensity of process and what we feel is not the object of the experience, but the flow of experience itself" (165). And within his essay, Troy Rhoades unpacks video artist Woody Vasulka's concept of the "time/energy object" to carve out a nuanced understanding of the connection between the digital and the virtual, the moving electronic signal and the visual video image.

The diverse scope of *Cinematic Folds* offers descriptions of both inventive new works, as well as influential past artworks. The collective impact of the anthology also asserts an innovative approach to conceptualizing such works through the philosophical lens of the cinematic. Generally, the introductory context given by Elavia combined with the focus of many of the essays and images, distinguish cinematic experience from established media theories of representation, medium specificity and the gaze. Thus, this anthology will be of significant interest to students and scholars interested in exploring ideas of expanded cinema, the connection between cinema and affect, and the event nature of cinematic experience. Though Elavia also distances the philosophical approach of the volume from questions of ontology and from phenomenology, no rigorous critique of these other areas of philosophy is formed throughout the anthology. The most nuanced philosophical thinking contributed in *Cinematic Folds* surrounds exploring the implications of complex ideas put forward by Deleuze and Guattari, such as becomings, multiplicities, rhizomatics, the virtual and the body without organs in relation to cinema.

Barbara Fister

The Digital Book—Still Pending

Review of

Gary Hall. 2008. *Digitize This Book! The Politics of New Media, or Why We Need Open Access Now.* Minneapolis: University of Minnesota Press.

Many arguments for open access are based on a simple pragmatic argument: the goals of scholars and their publishers are at odds when access to research results is hindered by high prices. By making research available for free through the web, scholars can share their work; it won't only be available to the few who have access to a large, well-funded research library. Gary Hall, a professor of media and performing arts at Coventry University in the U.K., goes beyond that simple economic argument (which is sufficiently complex in practice to keep its proponents busy making the case in its most pragmatic terms) and analyzes how academic publishing in general and publishing in the field of cultural studies in particular operate in ways that often undermine both the theory and practice of the discipline.

Combining theory (including deconstruction as well as the work of new media theorists) with practice (the author is the founder of the open access journal *Culture Machine* and of CSeARCH, a cultural studies open access archive), Hall probes what it is we're doing when we conduct scholarship, unpacks the contradictions inherent in our publishing traditions, and proposes a role for open access in both reinventing cultural studies and in creating a new university. In short, Hall makes a strong argument for open access, but it is one that is more theoretically sophisticated and more intellectually challenging than most.

In analyzing the arguments advanced for open access, he makes the case that they often fail to demand real change, that they simply exchange one set of neoliberal values for another, continuing to support the capitalist goals of a "knowledge economy" by offering to disseminate the products of "knowledge workers" more efficiently, thus leading to greater productivity and progress without examining the underlying structures that support the creation and dissemination of work. For example, Hall interrogates the arguments Stevan Harnad makes for creating open access through self-archiving of materials that have been through the traditional channels, relying on the endorsement of traditional publishing practices and simply transferring the product of those practices online with all their vested authority intact.

Hall sees in digitization the potential to fundamentally re-examine the ethics of scholarly communication and its often unarticulated adherence to traditional institutional authority. He wants to see cultural studies embrace new modes of communication, asking whether the discipline's attention to social movements and political discourse can't be extended and embodied in developing alternative institutions and practices for their work. Open access could do more than transform the economics of scholarly publication; it could offer ways to reinvent and embody the work itself. "If our understanding and analysis of new media is to be effective," he argues, "we need to be able to 'do' *both* theory and practice, while simultaneously challenging any simple differentiation between them" (34-35). He carries out this argument by offering four sets of "metadata"—chapters inserted throughout the book in which he explores the underlying systems and protocols that go into discussions of new media. Above all, he resists easy answers, believing that the future shape of scholarship and new media must remain undefined. In his final Metadata, he argues that "it is the structurally open and undecidable nature of the situation ... that gives it ethical and political force" (215). In other words, the future of open access is best left open.

It's ironic that *Digitize This Book!* is not, itself, an open access document. It has been published through the traditional channels, vetted by a university press that has allowed it to be partially browseable through Google Book Search, a commercial venture designed to broaden the contours of Google's searchable universe by including non-Web material and (if the settlement of a class action lawsuit with authors and publishers goes forward) to enter the digital publishing market as a new and most likely monopolistic mega-distributor of electronic book content. The imperative statement of the title is curiously denied by the book itself. Perhaps it's a postmodernist prank. Or perhaps it's just demonstrating that something we arguably need remains constrained by the rules of old media.

Cris Costa

There Is More Than One Way to Rethink Poetics

Review of

Maria Damon and Ira Livingston, eds. 2009. *Poetry and Cultural Studies: A Reader.* Urbana: University of Illinois Press.

As a result of its critical discussions, appeals, assertions, questions and problematics, *Poetry and Cultural Studies: A Reader*, edited by Maria Damon and Ira Livingston, effectively frames and reframes cultural poetics while interrogating, circumscribing and mapping the fields of poetics and cultural studies. In the process, the collection also challenges the fundamental concepts that have defined poetry and cultural studies.

Joseph Harrington's essay, "Poetry and the Public: The Social Form of Modern U.S. Poetics," contains the following insight: "As access to official culture, such as grant funding and university professorships, declines, and as a grassroots poetry culture continues to thrive, one wonders if poetry studies and its object of study aren't going in opposite directions" (280). This question, in all of its various forms, arises time and again throughout the anthology. Nonetheless, as one follows the book's threads, one begins to realize how inefficient our conception of "grassroots poetry" is. This is not an anthology that propagates populist poetry for the sake of empowering people and living up to romantic ideals—for example, the fantasy of returning the power of language to a populace that may or may not want it (but was it ever taken away? Do we really believe that people are poetically illiterate?). This anthology also does not suggest that academics should dumb-down their teaching of poetry to allow for greater accessibility. Instead, *Poetry and Cultural Studies* places many dearly-held ideas and structural designs, including empowerment, disempowerment, modes of pedagogy, approaches, purpose and material, into crisisl. And while the editors note that "no anthology can be completely comprehensive or fully representative" (15), further stating that "each reader will likely be struck by glaring omissions from her or his own canon of poetics as cultural critique" (16), I would hasten to add that there is much more that this anthology includes than excludes.

Indeed, the anthology addresses the materiality of poetry, poetics and politics—that is, the manifestations of the material (acting social subjects, capital, criticism, canonization, institutionalized practice, etc.)—through the production of poetry, and the manifestation of poetry as a consequence of the material. And yet, even as I note the presence of such worthwhile discussions within the collection, I must also note that in the assertion that such discussions provide a definitive topic that ties *Poetry and Cultural Studies* together as a volume, my own intent falls short. Thus, I must swivel the language and change my thesis, or, as Bernstein writes in "A Blow Is Like an Instrument," "make up [my] own rules," then break them (366).

The anthology is about examining the relationship between international marginalized cultures and the marginalized communities at our doorstep that produce and/or play with poetry as a result of sociopolitical conditions. The social subject implicated may (or may not) produce national poetry, revolutionary poetry, pop-cultural poetry, "bad" poetry, populist poetry, worker's poetry, love poetry, collective poetry, poetry-workshop poetry and even "song" poetry. As a result of this dynamic, a host of parallel and interconnected questions emerge. How is the poetic language of the subjects (the subjected) who feature in W. E. B. Du Bois's "Of the Sorrow Songs" similar or different to the music produced by contemporary rappers, as investigated by Robin D. G. Kelley in "Kicking Reality, Kicking Ballistics: Gangsta Rap and Postindustrial Los Angeles"? What are the connections between Rimbaud's adolescent poetry of affect, as discussed in Kristin Ross's "Rimbaud and the Transformation of Social Space," and the poetry of the inner-city, female, youths discussed in Damon's "Tell Them about Us: Some Poems from Southie"? How do these same youths fall under the middle-class, patriarchal, white-capitalist gaze that Maya Angelou's performance at the Clinton inauguration endured? Why do we expect worker-poets, in all countries, to function and write like folk-poets? Must populist poetry be "anti-literary"? How do Kantian ethics regarding "taste" and "sensitivity" still affect our reading of different genres of poetic works? Why don't Bedouin women show emotion, proclaiming their disinterest of love and men, and why do they then secretly and shamefully listen to love poetry? What's genocide got to do, with it?

A prime reason for the differences between these articulations of the trouble with poetry in the public sphere has to do with the fact that the notion of the 'public' is always already gendered and racialized. So the ideology making it difficult for a poet to speak with anything other than a private voice will bear unevenly, sometimes contradictorily, on women and men, nonwhites and whites" (Zofia Burr, "Of Poetry and Power: Maya Angelou": 433).

Again, my supposition regarding the supposed focus of this volume proves insufficient. While the relationship between socio-political forces and the social subject provides the pivot for many works in *Poetry and Cultural Studies*, such discourse rarely leaves room for discussions of form, and one might just as readily assert that the anthology *is really* about the cultural poetics of form: form as a linguistic structure, as tactile presentation, as a method of sonic delivery or address, and as a feature or outgrowth of socio-political conditions. Thus, considered as an anthology on form and, of course, aesthetics, the collected works in *Poetry and Cultural Studies* explore everything from the vocal to the textual to the architectural and the classical lyric to postmodern language poetry to *tibishi* (poetry graffiti). In fact, the anthology itself has a formal mandate. Its thirty-four essays are divided into six subsections: Precursors, Ethnography, Mass Culture/Cultural Politics, National (De)Formations, Subject (De)Formations and Reinventing Tradition. In these categories, contemporary, institutionalized poetry and criticism (particularly modernist forms) are juxtaposed with the poetry, presentation and reception of marginalized ethnic groups in North America and internationally.

In this respect, the anthology creates a line of flight distinct from the academy to communities. Damon and Livingston thus propose, through the compilation of these texts, a new approach to the idea of the avant-garde. In fact, the anthology might even suggest that we find a new term for it (Miguel Algarin's "Nyorican Language," the last essay in the collection, documents the development of new language in a time of Puerto Rican social revolution). On the other hand, "Poetry and Cultural Studies" the anthology might suggest a different kind of action, for "it is not language, but people, who make revolutions" (Kamau Brathwaite, "History of the Voice, 1979-1981": 419). Yet, a social revolution is not what the collected texts, as a whole, propose—and especially not a social revolution fuelled by poets running through the streets clutching their manuscripts and reciting on podiums—but a revolution in our discourse, a revolution in the academy and education at large, and a revolution in our thinking.

Despite the fact that the anthology largely focuses on American texts/topics, rather than "North American" ones (e.g., Canadian content falls short), it raises discussions, issues and questions that transcend borders. While it does not, and cannot (as an already 450-page text), represent every possible group or approach to the study of poetry and culture—for example, queer poetics, First Nations and a host of feminisms are lacking—it provides a new frame of analysis to approach these literatures. I perceive this text as a staple in the instruction of poetics and culture. It is analytical, critical, motivated and readable. Its multi-platformed discussions respond to each other, allowing for the beginning of a working knowledge of the field (for students) and a reframing of the field (for advanced scholars). As a whole, the anthology suggests a move away from specialization—increasingly mandated by funding institutions complying to neoliberal pressures—toward a richer, more diverse knowledge of poetics and its relationship to other forms of cultural production.

Notes on Contributors

MARY ALEMANY-GALWAY obtained a PhD from Warwick University. She has written *A Postmodern Cinema: The Voice of the Other in Canadian Film* (2002, Scarecrow Press), as well as various articles on Canadian and New Zealand film. She co-edited *Peter Greenaway's Postmodern/Poststructuralist Cinema* (Scarecrow Press, 2001). Presently, she teaches Media Studies at Massey University in New Zealand.

STUART ALLAN is Professor of Journalism in The Media School, Bournemouth University, U.K.

KARI ANDÉN-PAPADOPOULOS is Associate Professor in the Department of Journalism, Media and Communication, Stockholm University, Sweden.

JENNIFER ANDREWS is a professor in the Department of English at University of New Brunswick and co-editor of *Studies in Canadian Literature*. She is the co-author of *Border Crossings: Thomas King's Cultural Inversions* and author of the forthcoming book, *In the Belly of a Laughing God: Humour and Irony in Native Women's Poetry* (University of Toronto Press).

JULIA AOKI is a PhD candidate at Simon Fraser University's School of Communication. In her work as volunteer coordinator for the Powell Street Festival, Julia developed an interest in the impact of spatial organization and regulation, collective spatial practices and historical narratives on the construction of social identities. She has explored these issues academically through her MA work on historical narratives in Oppenheimer Park, Vancouver, and creatively through the Toronto-based LOT Group's project on mid-century bungalows in Willowdale.

NEIL BALAN teaches at the University of Saskatchewan. A PhD candidate in the Graduate Program in Humanities, York University, he is completing a dissertation on the relationship between counterinsurgency warfare and biopolitics.

DARIN BARNEY is Canada Research Chair in Technology and Citizenship, and Associate Professor of Communication Studies at McGill University, where he directs the graduate programs in Communication Studies. He is President of the Canadian Communication Association, and the author of several books and articles on technology and politics.

Jody Berland is Professor in the Department of Humanities, York University, Toronto. She is author of *North of Empire: Essays on the Cultural Technologies of Space* (Duke University Press 2009), awarded the Canadian Communication Association G.G. Robinson Book Prize for 2009, and editor of *TOPIA: Canadian Journal of Cultural Studies*. She has published widely on spatial and environmental themes in cultural studies.

BILL BURNS's work about animals and civil society has been shown and published widely. His recent shows include the Institute of Contemporary Arts in London; the KW Institute for Contemporary Art in Berlin; the Wellcome Trust in London; Kunsthallen Nikolaj in Copenhagen and the Museum of Modern Art in New York. He has published numerous books and essays including *When Pain Strikes*, a scholarly anthology (1999); *Bird Radio* (2007) and *The Guide to the Flora and Fauna Information Station: 0.800.0FAUNA0FLORA* (2008).

SUSAN CAHILL is a PhD Candidate and Teaching Fellow in the Department of Art at Queen's University, Kingston. Susan's academic interests include museum and visual studies, cultural theory and conflict history. Her dissertation examines the intersections of dominant national/ist narratives with visual culture and conflict history in Canada and Australia between 2001 and 2010. She is a co-founder and co-editor of the new online journal *Shift: Queen's Graduate Journal of Visual and Material Culture*. Susan received a SSHRC Michael Smith Foreign Study Supplement to conduct archival research at the Australian War Memorial in Canberra and was hosted by the Australian National University in the fall of 2009 in conjunction with this award.

JAMES R. COMPTON is Associate Professor in the Faculty of Information and Media Studies at the University of Western Ontario. He is author of *The Integrated News Spectacle: A Political Economy of Cultural Performance* (Peter Lang, 2004) and co-editor of *Converging Media, Diverging Politics: A Political Economy of News Media in the United States and Canada* (Lexington Books, 2005). He is a former reporter/editor with the Canadian Press/Broadcast News wire service.

DAVID A. CLEARWATER received his PhD from McGill University and teaches in the Department of New Media at the University of Lethbridge.

CRIS COSTA works in Vancouver. She holds an MA in English from Simon Fraser University. Her research areas include contemporary and experimental literature, CanLit, and cultural theory. She is a member of the Kootenay School of Writing. She writes poetry and prose.

JIM DAEMS teaches in the English Department at the University of the Fraser Valley. He is the author of *Seventeenth-Century Literature and Culture* (Continuum, 2006) and articles on John Milton, Harry Potter and gender issues.

JILL DIDUR teaches postcolonial literature and theory in the English Department at Concordia University, Montreal. She is author of *Unsettling Partition: Literature, Gender, Memory* (University of Toronto Press, 2006). Her current research considers the discursive and material relationships between the plant collecting practices and memoirs of colonial botanists and horticulturalists in South Asia, contemporary postcolonial writing about the Himalayas and alpine and rock gardening culture globally.

CHRISTOPHER DORNAN is the director of the Arthur Kroeger College of Public Affairs at Carleton University, and an associate professor in the School of Journalism and Communication.

JULIA EMBERLEY is Professor of English at the University of Western Ontario. She teaches cultural politics and indigenous decolonization. Recent articles appear in *West Coast Line*, *Australian Humanities Review*, *Jeunesse: Young Peoples, Texts, Cultures*, *Journal of Postcolonial Writing* and *English Studies in Canada*.

LEN FINDLAY is an award-winning teacher, Professor of English and Director of the Humanities Research Unit at the University of Saskatchewan. A Fellow of the Royal Society of Canada, he was the Northrop Frye Professor of Literary Theory at the University of Toronto for 2000-2001. Widely published in 19th-century comparative studies, literary theory and the nature and role of universities and the humanities in Canada, his more recent work includes a co-edited collection, *Pursuing Academic Freedom: "Free and Fearless"?* (Purich Press).

BARBARA FISTER, a librarian at Gustavus Adolphus College in Minnesota, publishes widely on the future of libraries and publishing, critical information literacy, and on popular reading practices.

BLAKE FITZPATRICK is Professor and Graduate Program Director, Documentary Media (MFA) Program, School of Image Arts, at Ryerson University. He is an active photographer, curator and writer. His research interests include the photographic representation of the nuclear era, the Cold War and contemporary responses to militarism. He has exhibited his visual work in solo and group exhibitions in Canada and the United States and his most recent curatorial initiative was the exhibition, *War at a Distance* (co-curated with Karyn Sandlos and Roger I. Simon).

HOWARD FREMETH is a PhD candidate in Communications at Carleton University. His dissertation examines the political economy of the memorialization of Canadian military history.

GARY GENOSKO is Canada Research Chair in Technoculture at Lakehead University. His most recent books are *Félix Guattari: A Critical Introduction* (Pluto, 2009) and, with Scott Thompson, *Punched Drunk: Alcohol, Surveillance and the LCBO, 1927-75* (Fernwood, 2009). He has recently completed work on two new books: *Franco Berardi, After the Future*, co-edited and introduced with Nick Thoburn, and *Remodeling Communication: From WWII to the WWW*.

SUSAN GINGELL teaches and researches decolonizing and transnational literatures at the University of Saskatchewan. Her current research on the textualizing of the oral in the Canadian context includes studies of Indigenous writings of the oral.

TERRY GOLDIE is author of *queersexlife: Autobiographical Notes on Sexuality, Gender and Identity* (Arsenal Pulp, 2008), *Pink Snow: Homotextual Possibilities in Canadian Fiction* (Broadview, 2003) and *Fear and Temptation: The Image of the Indigene in Canadian, Australian and New Zealand Literatures* (McGill-Queen's, 1989). He is editor of *In a Queer Country: Gay and Lesbian Studies in the Canadian Context* (Arsenal Pulp, 2001) and co-editor, with Daniel David Moses, of *An Anthology of Canadian Native Literature in English* (Oxford, 2005). His next project is tentatively titled: *The Man Who Invented Gender: John Money*.

ANGELA JOOSSE is a PhD candidate in Joint Program in Communication and Culture at York and Ryerson Universities. Her graduate work examines the intersection of film, philosophy and visual art. Joosse also makes experimental film, video and installation pieces, a number of which have received national and international exhibitions. She is a member of two collectives in Toronto: the Loop collective of media artists, and LOT: Experiments in Urban Research.

MARKUS KIENSCHERF is a PhD Candidate in Sociology at the Graduate School of North American Studies, Free University Berlin. His research is focused on governmental responses to changes in and the increasing blurring of domestic and international security. Markus also worked as a project manager for a sustainable transport consultancy in the Netherlands and the United Kingdom.

MARC LAFLEUR is currently completing his PhD in Anthropology at York University in Toronto. His dissertation investigates the intersection of affect, sovereignty and spectacle in American nuclear heritage and display. He is also in the initial stages of a new project on veterans and depleted uranium.

ULE LINKE is professor of anthropology at Rochester Institute of Technology, Rochester, NY. Her principal areas of interest include the political anthropology of the body, racial formations, regimes of exclusion, violence and genocide, the politics of memory and suffering and human rights. Linke's major publications include *Blood and Nation: The European Aesthetics of Race* (University of Pennsylvania Press, 1999), *German Bodies: Race and Representation After Hitler* (Routledge, 1999) and, as co-editor, *Cultures of Fear: A Critical Reader* (Pluto Press, 2009). Recent essays include Contact Zones: Rethinking the Sensual Life of the State (*Anthropological Theory*, 2006), and Gendering Europe, Europeanizing Gender in *Handbook of Modern European History* (Oxford University Press, 2010).

A. L. MCCREADY is a doctoral candidate in English and Cultural Studies at McMaster University, Hamilton. The relationships between militarization, neoliberal globalization, and Canadian national identity form the crux of the dissertation, which McCready pursues from an anti-imperialist, anti-racist feminist theoretical perspective.

CAROLE R. MCKENNA received her PhD in Justice Studies and Social Inquiry from Arizona State University, Tempe. Previously she was a Visiting Asst. Professor in the Sociology Department at Montana State University and an Associate Faculty of Justice at Arizona State University. Her research and publications include topics such as torture and international relations with Canada, culture and the socialization process, domestic violence, justice theory, family, marriage, and militarism.Her recent book is titled, *Militarism: The Power Arrangements between Soldiers, Wives, and the Military-Industrial-Service-Complex* (2009). Currently, she is teaching sociology at Ferris State University in Big Rapids, Michigan.

DEANNA REDER is an assistant professor in First Nations Studies and English at Simon Fraser University. She is the co-editor, with Linda M. Morra at Bishop's University, of *Troubling Tricksters: Revisioning Critical Conversations* (2010). She recently has been named series editor for the Indigenous Studies Series at Wilfrid Laurier University Press.

ERIN RILEY is a photographer based in Toronto where she has worked as an editorial photographer with her work appearing in many national newspapers and magazines. She is a recent graduate of the MFA in Documentary Media program at Ryerson University. With her roots in the documentary tradition, it is the storytelling aspect of photography that is the driving force in her work. She continues to further her interest in achieving a balance between documentary and art.

IAN RODERICK is an assistant professor in Communication Studies at Wilfrid Laurier University. His research interests include cultural studies of technology, visual communication and technology, and social semiotics. His recent publications address such topics as contemporary martial discourse, embedded training systems, software agents, and post-disciplinary regimes of control.

MARY STERPKA KING received a PhD in cultural anthropology from the University of Massachusetts, Amherst with a concentration in globalization and networks and is now teaching at Northeastern University, Boston.

NIC VEROLI is a political philosopher and writer, currently residing near Woodstock, NY.

SHAOBO XIE is an Associate Professor in the Department of English at University of Calgary. He is Review Editor of *ARIEL*. He has published on literary theory, postcolonial studies, cultural studies, globalization, comparative literature, translation, and Chinese modernity.

BC STUDIES
The British Columbian Quarterly

University of British Columbia
Buchanan E162 - 1866 Main Mall
Vancouver, BC, Canada V6T 1Z1
T: 604-822-3727
E: info@bcstudies.com
www.bcstudies.com

A journal of informed writing on British Columbia's cultural, political, and economic life, past and present.

BC Studies Book Reviews now online at
www.bcstudies.com/reviews

In recognition of the value of open, web-based access to intellectual content, we have posted some of our material online. Upcoming and recently published book reviews and review essays will be freely accessible at www.bcstudies.com/reviews. Visit the "Book Reviews" tab on our website for upcoming reviews, and individual issue pages for those recently published.

Contributions appearing in our Case Comments section of the journal are also available: www.bcstudies.com/casecomments. Check out www.bcstudies.com/audio for select mp3 audio articles which are available to stream or download free of charge.

ANNUAL SUBSCRIPTION

CANADA
(PLUS TAX)

Individual
$65.00 CAD

Institution
$110.00 CAD

Students
$45.00 CAD

INTERNATIONAL
(INCLUDES POSTAGE)

Individual
$77.00 USD

Institution
$122.00 USD

Students
$57.00 USD

UPCOMING THEME ISSUE

Okanagan (2011) - Publication of this issue will coincide with the international conference hosted by The University of British Columbia Okanagan in association with *BC Studies* on:

Sustainability and Change:
Studies in BC's Past, Present & Future Communities
May 5 to 7, 2011

B.C. Studies Program Committee at UBCO is still accepting proposals (panels and sessions, papers, posters) for this event. For more information, please visit www.bcstudies.com or email bcstudies2011@gmail.com.

RECENT THEME ISSUES

The British Columbia Court of Appeal, 1910-2010 no. 162, $15.00
Guest Editors - John McLaren, Hamar Foster, Wes Pue

The Court is a central institution in the history, constitution, and public life of the province and the centenary provides an opportunity for critically engaged scholarly assessments of its role and that of the judiciary overall. This issue discusses the many themes in British Columbia Studies (colonialism, aboriginality, labour, race, immigration, gender, environment, etc.) that have been refracted through the Courts' lenses.

Middle Fraser no. 160, $15.00
Guest Editor - Cole Harris

This issue focuses on land and livelihoods along the middle reaches of the Fraser River, British Columbia's most defining river, which Simon Fraser descended in 1808 and miners converged upon fifty years later. The articles focus on commemorating the Middle Fraser - large pit-house villages, placer mining, and grassland ranching - rather than the events that opened it to the outside world.

To order, please contact us at info@bcstudies.com *or* 604-822-3727

www.bcstudies.com

boundary 2

an international journal of literature and culture

Paul A. Bové, editor

boundary 2 approaches problems in the areas of literature and culture from a number of politically, historically, and theoretically informed perspectives. boundary 2 remains committed to understanding the present and approaching the study of national and international culture and politics through literature and the human sciences.

Recent special issues

"American Poetry After 1975" (36:3)
Charles Bernstein, special issue editor

"The Sixties and the World Event" (36:1)
Christopher Connery and Hortense J. Spillers, special issue editors

---

Subscribe today to receive *boundary 2* (three issues per year).

Online access, RSS feeds, and table-of-contents alerts are included with a print subscription.

Individuals: $33
Students: $20 (photocopy of valid student ID required)
Additional postage fees apply for international subscribers.

To order, please visit
dukeupress.edu/boundary2

Published on behalf of the Association for Canadian Studies in the United States

American Review of
Canadian Studies
Editor: **John Purdy**, *Western Washington University, USA*

American Review of Canadian Studies (*ARCS*) is a refereed, multidisciplinary, quarterly journal. Published since 1971 by the *Association for Canadian Studies in the United States* (*ACSUS*), it examines Canada and the Canadian point of view from an American perspective. Its articles - both interdisciplinary and disciplinary - explore Canada's arts, cultures, economics, politics, history, and society, recognizing Canada's distinctive position in the world.

NEW! *ARCS* **Digital Archive Now Available**
Visit the *ARCS* journal homepage to view the complete digitized archive of *ARCS* issues, as well as to register for table of content alerts or view subscription information:

www.tandf.co.uk/journals/rarc

TOPIA: Canadian Journal of Cultural Studies

Call for Papers

Guest Editor: Nandi Bhatia
Department of English
University of Western Ontario, London, Canada

Bollywood and the South Asian Diaspora

TOPIA 26, Fall 2011

This special issue of *TOPIA* seeks essays that attempt to expand and deepen our understanding of the fraught relationship between Bollywood, global cinemas and the South Asian diaspora. Existing scholarship on Bollywood presents it as a complex terrain for the production of multiple and intersecting narratives about "homelands" and imagined communities of diaspora across transnational sites. Because the escalating global circulation and consumption of Bollywood demands further thinking of this relationship, both in terms of the contentions that mark the framing of "Bollywood" in the diaspora as well as the myriad possibilities it provides, this special issue solicits papers on the following (but not limited to) suggested topics that will enable further conversations and dialogue.

- Representing narratives of migrancy, home, relocation, and displacement
- Representing gender, class and caste, and communal and nationalist politics in South Asia, in the diaspora
- Bollywood and diasporic aesthetics
- Industrial, aesthetic, capitalistic and political contexts for Bollywood film
- Audiences, communities, fans, cults: cultures of reception and consumption
- Melodrama, dance, music: traditions of performance
- Literary adaptations, Bollywood style

Please submit all proposals and manuscripts to TOPIA editorial office 240 Vanier College, York University. **Deadline: February 1, 2011**

For general inquiries, contact the guest editor:
Dr Nandi Bhatia
Department of English
University of Western Ontario,
Nbhatia2@uwo.ca

Public Culture

To read a sample issue online, visit
publicculture.dukejournals.org.

Join the discussion.

For more than twenty years *Public Culture* has mapped the capital, human, and media flows drawing cities, peoples, and states into transnational relationships and political economies.

A subscription includes online access to all current and back issues of the journal, including

"The Public Life of History" (#54)
Bain Attwood, Dipesh Chakrabarty, and Claudio Lomnitz,
special issue editors

"Cultures of Democracy" (#51)
Dilip Parameshwar Gaonkar,
special issue editor

Subscribe today to *Public Culture*
(three issues each year).
Online access, RSS feeds, and table-of-contents alerting are included with a print subscription.

Individuals, $37
Students, $25 (photocopy of valid student ID required)
Additional postage fees apply for international subscribers.

To place your order, please visit
dukeupress.edu/publicculture.

New from JODY BERLAND

"A major contribution by one of the contemporary world's most original and influential thinkers working on the intersection of communication with cultural studies."—MEAGHAN MORRIS

North of Empire
Essays on the Cultural Technologies of Space
JODY BERLAND
408 pages, 33 illustrations, paper, $24.95

www.dukeupress.edu

DUKE UNIVERSITY PRESS

Material Culture Review
Revue de la culture matérielle

A venue for refereed articles and research reports encompassing a range of approaches to interpreting culture through an analysis of people's relationships to their material world. Critical reviews of books, exhibitions, and historic sites, artifact studies and reports on collections encourage the use of material evidence in understanding historical change and continuity. Manuscripts are accepted in both English and French. *MCR* is published twice annually.

Material Culture Review
Revue de la culture matérielle
Cape Breton University
P.O. Box 5300
Sydney, Nova Scotia B1P 6L2
Canada

ISSN: 1718-1259
http://culture.cbu.ca
mcr_rcm@cbu.ca

TOPIA
CANADIAN JOURNAL OF CULTURAL STUDIES

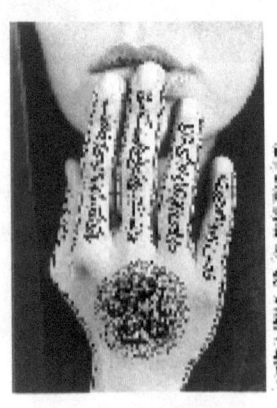

2010 Subscriptions

Institutional $ 90 Individual $ 45 Student $ 25

For subscribers outside Canada,
the rates are payable in U.S. funds

Name _____

Affiliation _____

Address _____

City _____ Prov./State _____

Telephone _____ Email _____

☐ Enclose payment of $ _____
  Make cheques payable to Wilfrid Laurier University Press
☐ Charge credit card in the amount of _____

Visa or Mastercard number _____

Signature _____ Expiry _____

"One of the truly valuable and
exciting new journals in the field
of cultural studies..."
— Lawrence Grossberg,
University of North Carolina

Send form and payment to:
Wilfrid Laurier University Press
75 University Avenue West
Waterloo, ON N2L 3C5
Fax: 519.725.1399
Tel: 519.884.0710 ext. 6124
E-mail: press@wlu.ca

www.ingramcontent.com/pod-product-compliance
Lightning Source LLC
Chambersburg PA
CBHW022006300426
44117CB00005B/57